Financial Analysis Techniques

$$\text{Return on Average Total Assets} = \frac{\text{net income}}{\text{average total assets}}$$

$$\text{Times Interest Earned} = \frac{\text{operating income}}{\text{interest charges}}$$

$$\text{Operating Ratio} = \frac{\text{cost of goods sold} + \text{operating expenses}}{\text{net sales}}$$

$$\text{Current (or Working Capital) Ratio} = \frac{\text{current assets}}{\text{current liabilities}}$$

$$\text{Quick (Acid) Ratio} = \frac{\text{quick assets}}{\text{current liabilities}}$$

$$\text{Inventory Turnover} = \frac{\text{cost of goods sold}}{\text{average inventory (at cost)}}$$

$$\text{Accounts Receivable Turnover} = \frac{\text{net sales}}{\text{average accounts receivable}}$$

$$\text{Debt Ratio} = \frac{\text{total debt}}{\text{total assets}}$$

$$\text{Equity Ratio} = \frac{\text{total owner's equity}}{\text{total assets}}$$

$$\text{Debt-to-Equity Ratio} = \frac{\text{total debt}}{\text{total owner's equity}}$$

Pricing

Selling Price
= cost + markup
= cost × (100% + markup rate based on cost)
= cost ÷ (100% − markup rate based on selling price)

Conversion of Markup Rates to Another Base

$$\text{Markup Rate on Cost} = \frac{\text{markup rate on selling price}}{100\% - \text{markup rate on selling price}}$$

$$\text{Markup Rate on Selling Price} = \frac{\text{markup rate on cost}}{100\% + \text{markup rate on cost}}$$

Markdown = original selling price − reduced selling price

$$\text{Markdown Rate} = \frac{\text{markdown}}{\text{original selling price}}$$

Taxes

Property Tax = assessed value × tax rate

Sales Tax = sales price × tax rate

Insurance

$$\text{Life Insurance Premium} = \text{rate per } \$1000 \times \frac{\text{face amount of policy}}{\$1000}$$

Michelle Hugunin

Michelle Hugunin

Operational Mathematics for Business

Second Edition

R. C. PIERCE, JR.

University of Houston

W. J. TEBEAUX

Southwestern Bell

Wadsworth Publishing Company

Belmont, California

A Division of Wadsworth, Inc.

Mathematics Editor: Peter Fairchild
Signing Representative: Ragu Raghaven

Printed in the United States of America

1 2 3 4 5 6 7 8 9 10—87 86 85 84 83

ISBN 0-534-01235-3

Library of Congress Cataloging in Publication Data

Pierce, R. C.
  Operational mathematics for business.

  Includes index.
  1. Business mathematics. I. Tebeaux, W. J.
II. Title.
HF5691.P556   1982   513'.93   82-10977
ISBN 0-534-01235-3

Second Edition Preface

In 1981 President Ronald Reagan signed the Economic Recovery Tax Act of 1981. The act had significant impact on both business and consumers. This second edition is our effort to address some of the changes wrought by the Tax Act of 1981. We also took the opportunity to enhance the first edition based on suggestions from some of our many users. Briefly stated, the major changes in the second edition are as follows:

1. *Chapter Tests.* We added a comprehensive test at the end of each chapter. This test will allow the student to test his or her knowledge of the material when the problems are presented out of context.

2. *Additional Problems.* We have expanded many problem sets in order to allow greater flexibility in teaching material. Of course, the *solutions* to odd-numbered problems remain as a learning aid. The review exercises contain odd-numbered *answers only*. Problems have also been added to the cumulative reviews for each part.

3. *Negotiable Order of Withdrawal.* The chapter on banking (Chapter 3) has been expanded to reflect some of the new money management devices available to consumers—negotiable order of withdrawal (NOW) accounts.

4. *Cost Recovery.* The Tax Act of 1981 caused significant changes in the process of depreciation. Chapter 9 presents the Accelerated Cost Recovery System (ACRS) created by the tax act; and it relates depreciation and cost recovery for that period when both apply.

5. *Present (and Future) Value of Annuities.* The discussion of amortization (Chapter 14) has been expanded to include the present value of an annuity and the future value of an annuity. Also, we have included new tables relating to annuities.

6. *Securities Purchases.* Chapter 15 (Stocks and Bonds) has been expanded to include the actual mechanics of the transfer of ownership in securities.

7. *Taxes.* Chapter 17 (Taxes) has been expanded to include the fundamentals of income tax. Obviously, income tax is a dynamic field. As such, no text could remain current for long. For this reason, we attempted to provide information on the fundamental process without detailed use of Internal Revenue Service forms. The tax tables are included to familiarize the student with what lies ahead.

8. *Graphing.* The discussion of graphing (Chapter 19) has been expanded to include graphing an equation and circle graphs.

9. *Statistics.* The discussion of statistics (Chapter 20) has been expanded to include measures of variation and the normal distribution in order to give a more complete analysis of data.

10. *Glossary.* The glossary has been greatly expanded. The additional terms will assist the student in completing the first question of each Chapter test. The expanded glossary also enhances the book's value as reference material.

11. *Other Changes.* There are other minor changes made to enhance the "teachability" of the text.

We received many suggestions and comments from users (both students and teachers) of the first edition of *Operational Mathematics for Business*. We are very grateful for these comments and solicit your comments on the second edition. We would also like to express our appreciation to our excellent editors at Wadsworth Publishing Company—Mr. Richard Jones and Mr. Peter Fairchild, and to the following reviewers, whose input was so helpful:

Curtis Askim, Santa Rosa Junior College
Anthony Brunswick, Delaware Technical and Community College
Daniel Fendel, San Francisco State University
Jim Hale, Vance-Granville Community College
Jerry Jones, Aiken Technical College
Ray MacTague, Moorpark College
Cada Parrish, Longwood College
Gary Phillips, Oakton Community College
Thomas Rossi, Broome Community College
David Strong, Prince George's Community College
Richard Tinney, Tidewater Community College
Ron Waite, Blue Mountain Community College
Tom Williams, Seward County Community College

R. C. Pierce, Jr.
William Jene Tebeaux

First Edition Preface

Operational Mathematics for Business is the result of our efforts to provide students with a vehicle for enhancing their mathematical skills and increasing their understanding of many concepts they will encounter in a business career. This text is intended for use in a one-semester course in business mathematics. Although the material exceeds the amount normally covered in a single semester, it is our intention to provide some flexibility in choice of topics and depth of coverage.

The text is divided into five parts. **Part One** provides a complete review of mathematical skills from operations with fractions to solving equations. **Part Two** discusses procedures normally encountered in business, beginning with acquisition of merchandise (purchasing) through measuring the success of the business (via financial statements). **Part Three** presents the mathematical aspects of financial management progressing from simple interest through amortization and sinking funds to corporate financing. **Part Four** discusses topics of benefit to the individual both as a business manager and as a consumer. **Part Five** shows how graphing and statistics are used in decision making and gives an introduction to the metric system.

Several instructional features are used throughout the text to increase its effectiveness as an instructional tool.

1. Each of the five parts begins with an overview that serves to orient the reader to the structure and content of the ensuing chapters. Each part concludes with a cumulative set of review problems designed to reinforce the student's overall comprehension of the concepts presented in that part.

2. Each chapter is preorganized in an introduction. This introduction presents the general learning objectives desired and their relevance to business operations in order to capitalize on the student's pragmatic motivation for learning the material. The chapters are subdivided into sections focusing on one major concept. Each section is accompanied by a set of problems that begin with routine drill exercises and progressively increase in difficulty. Each chapter concludes with a comprehensive set of review problems.

3. The text has numerous examples written in a straightforward format: each example first states the problem, then presents a detailed solution. Examples are presented for every concept discussed.

4. The marginal notation of key factors and formulas provides for ready reference and quick location of items within a chapter.

5. Answers to selected problems are normally given to allow students to verify the accuracy of their work. If the student's answer does not agree with that given in the text, the answer is of little benefit in helping the student determine his mistake. Hence, we have included *worked-out solutions* deriving the answers to odd-numbered problems in each section.

6. A glossary of major mathematical and business terms is included.

7. A list of key formulas used in the major concepts requiring mathematical computations is included. This list provides a ready reference for use during the course and a future business career.

Most of us really do not know what a book is like until it has been used in class and we get feedback on how it works. That is why later editions of texts are generally better learning and teaching tools than are earlier editions.

A first edition can never be a third edition. But it can come close if we get—and respond to—enough advance help from experienced teachers. The following reviewers have made an invaluable contribution to the reliability and teachability of this text:

William Babcock, Motlow State Community College

Barry J. Bomboy, J. Sargeant Reynolds Community College

Mary B. Fuller, St. Louis Community College at Forest Park

Bernard Karne, Laney College

John Kroencke, Victor Valley College

Gwendolyn Loftis, Oscar Rose Junior College

Frank Martin, Chattanooga State Technical Community College

Frank O. McDaniels, Delaware County Community College

Alta Givens Mears, Oscar Rose Community College

Jerry W. Miller, College of DuPage

Gena Ousley, Chaffey College

S. Rondfong, Youngstown State University

Helen Schoon, Madison Area Technical College

William Scott, Ocean County College

We would also like to thank the *Wall Street Journal*; Frank D. Kleinworth III of Tools, Inc.; and Sidney Dean of South Main Bank for their contributions to the text. Our very special thanks go to Linda B. Pierce; Wesley J. Knebel, CLU of Connecticut Mutual Life Insurance Company, and Bob Hataway of State Farm Insurance Company for their technical assistance in manuscript content. The manuscript would not have been possible without the expert typing of Jan Want. Last, but certainly not least, our deepest appreciation to Richard Jones, Mathematics Editor, Wadsworth Publishing Company, for his continuing support during the manuscript preparation.

R. C. Pierce, Jr.
William Jene Tebeaux

Contents

Second Edition Preface   xi

First Edition Preface   xiii

P A R T   O N E   **Basic Mathematics for Now and Later**   **1**

Overview   1

Chapter 1   **Fractions**   **3**

Introduction   3

1.1   Meaning of Fractions: Equivalent Fractions   3

1.2   Addition and Subtraction of Fractions   11

1.3   Multiplication and Division of Fractions   15

1.4   Mixed Numbers: Order of Operations   21

Review Exercises   25

Chapter Test   26

Chapter 2   **Decimals**   **28**

Introduction   28

2.1   Place-Value Notation; Addition and Subtraction   28

2.2   Multiplication of Decimals   33

2.3   Division of Decimals   35

Review Exercises   40

Chapter Test   41

Chapter 3 **Banking Transactions**   **43**

Introduction   43

3.1   The Checking Account   44

3.2   The Bank Statement   48

3.3   Bank Reconciliation (Balancing the Checkbook)   50

3.4   Negotiable Order of Withdrawal (NOW) Accounts   60

Review Exercises   64

Chapter Test   70

Chapter 4 **Percent**   **72**

Introduction   72

4.1   Percents and Fractions   72

4.2   Percents and Decimals   75

4.3   Operations with Percents, Decimals, and Fractions; Aliquot Parts   78

4.4   Applications of Percents   81

Review Exercises   87

Chapter Test   87

Chapter 5 **Percent**   **89**

Introduction   89

5.1   Defining an Equation   89

5.2   Solving an Equation Containing One Unknown   91

5.3   Solving Word Problems   95

Review Exercises   100

Chapter Test   101

Cumulative Review Exercises / PART ONE   102

P A R T   T W O **Mathematics for Business**   *105*

Overview   105

Chapter 6 **Purchasing**   **107**

Introduction   107

6.1   The Invoice and List Price   108

6.2   Trade Discounts   112

6.3   Cash Discounts   117

Review Exercises   122

Chapter Test   123

Chapter 7	**Pricing: Markup and Markdown**	**125**
	Introduction	125
	7.1　Markup	126
	7.2　Pricing	130
	7.3　Markdown	138
	Review Exercises	141
	Chapter Test	142
Chapter 8	**Inventory and Overhead**	**143**
	Introduction	143
	8.1　Inventory Valuation	145
	8.2　Estimating Inventory Values	151
	8.3　Other Inventory Items	160
	8.4　Overhead	166
	Review Exercises	170
	Chapter Test	171
Chapter 9	**Depreciation (Cost Recovery)**	**173**
	Introduction	173
	9.1　Straight-Line Depreciation Method	175
	9.2　Units-of-Production Depreciation Method	181
	9.3　Sum-of-the-Years-Digits Depreciation Method	185
	9.4　Declining-Balance Depreciation Method	190
	9.5　Accelerated Cost Recovery System (ACRS)	194
	Review Exercises	203
	Chapter Test	204
Chapter 10	**Financial Statements and Distribution of Profits**	**206**
	Introduction	206
	10.1　The Balance Sheet (or Statement of Financial Position)	207
	10.2　The Income Statement	216
	10.3　Other Financial Analysis Techniques	222
	10.4　Distribution of Profits	233
	Review Exercises	238
	Chapter Test	239
Cumulative Review Exercises / PART TWO		241
PART THREE	**Mathematics of Money**	**245**
	Overview	245

Chapter 11   Simple Interest   **247**

Introduction   247

11.1   Making a Loan   247

11.2   Simple Interest   249

11.3   Future Value; Present Value   254

11.4   Calendar Dates   259

Review Exercises   265

Chapter Test   265

Chapter 12   Simple (Bank) Discount   **267**

Introduction   267

12.1   Bank Discount; Factoring   267

12.2   Discounting Interest-Bearing Notes   273

12.3   Effective Rate of Interest   278

Review Exercises   282

Chapter Test   283

Chapter 13   Compound Interest   **284**

Introduction   284

13.1   Future Value at Compound Interest   285

13.2   Present Value at Compound Interest   297

13.3   Effective Rate of Interest   302

Review Exercises   306

Chapter Test   307

Chapter 14   Amortizing a Debt   **308**

Introduction   308

14.1   Repaying a Debt—Interest in Dollar Values   309

14.2   Amortizing a Debt—S% per Year Add-on   317

14.3   Amortizing a Debt—S% Compound Interest per Year   320

14.4   Sinking Fund   330

14.5   Other Applications of Annuities   334

Review Exercises   339

Chapter Test   340

Chapter 15   Stocks and Bonds   **342**

Introduction   342

15.1   Bonds   342

15.2   Investing in Bonds   345

15.3   Stocks   356

15.4 Investing in Stocks 359

15.5 Stocks vs. Bonds—Summary 366

Review Exercises 366

Chapter Test 367

Cumulative Review Exercises / PART THREE 369

P A R T   F O U R *Mathematics in Everyday Living* 371

Overview 371

Chapter 16 **Ways and Adjustments** **373**

Introduction 373

16.1 Salaries 373

16.2 Hourly Wages 377

16.3 Piece Rate 382

16.4 Commissions 385

16.5 Adjustments to Wages 388

Review Exercises 394

Chapter Test 395

Chapter 17 **Taxes** **397**

Introduction 397

17.1 Sales Tax 398

17.2 Property Tax 402

17.3 Federal Income Tax 406

Review Exercises 413

Chapter Test 414

Chapter 18 **Insurance** **416**

Introduction 416

18.1 Fire Insurance 417

18.2 Motor Vehicle Insurance 423

18.3 Life Insurance 428

Review Exercises 444

Chapter Test 445

Cumulative Review Exercises / PART FOUR 447

P A R T   F I V E *Mathematics for Presentation and Analysis of Information* 451

Overview 451

Chapter 19   **Graphs**   **453**

   Introduction   453

   19.1 Line Graphs   453

   19.2 Bar Graphs and Pictograms   465

   19.3 Circle Graphs   472

   Review Exercises   477

   Chapter Test   477

Chapter 20   **Statistics**   **479**

   Introduction   479

   20.1 Data and Their Organization   480

   20.2 Mean   484

   20.3 Median   488

   20.4 Mode   491

   20.5 Standard Deviation and Normal Distribution   494

   Review Exercises   498

   Chapter Test   499

Chapter 21   **Metric System**   **501**

   Introduction   501

   21.1 Measures of Length   502

   21.2 Measures of Weight   506

   21.3 Measures of Volume and Temperature   509

   Review Exercises   513

   Chapter Test   513

Cumulative Review Exercises / PART FIVE   514

Glossary   **517**

Tables   **527**

Solutions to Odd-Numbered Exercises   **595**

Index   **636**

Part One

Basic Mathematics for Now and Later

O V E R V I E W

math in business

Business is a "quantitative" field of endeavor; one must work with quantities (or amounts) of many things. It might be amounts of money, inventory, sales, interest, discount, tax, and so on. The amounts are always represented by numbers. In order to "do business," a solid foundation in working with numbers is essential. Once you can work with numbers individually (i.e., do accurate computation), the next step is to work with relations between different sets of numbers. Both aspects of quantitative operations are contained in this part of the text. Applications to business are included in the development.

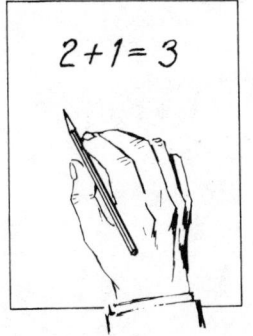

Computation

The numbers most commonly used in business are fractions, decimals, and percents. Basic operations involving these quantities are presented in Chapters 1, 2, and 4. The presentation is what might be termed a "classical" approach. Explanations are based on the assumption that the reader is going to work the problems "by hand" using paper and pencil. Hence, some attempt is made to explain the "why" as well as the "how" of computation.

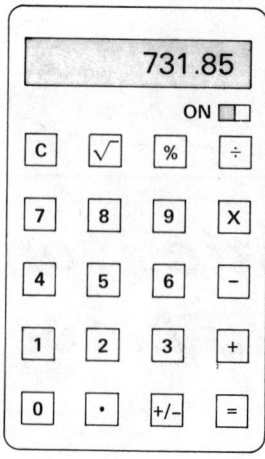

Computation—Alternative Approach

If a hand-held or other calculator is to be used to work the problem, the reader might want to omit sections explaining details of computation. Such sections are those on addition, subtraction, multiplication, and division of decimals. However, mathematical procedures such as the order of operations must be understood. Incorrect mathematical procedures, even if computationally correct, will give the wrong answer. The comprehensive test at the end of Part I might be helpful in determining how much time should be spent in this area.

CHAPTER 1

Fractions

INTRODUCTION

One frequently needs to work with a *portion* of a whole quantity. An item might be on sale for less than the regular price or an investor might want to place part of his money in stock and another part in bonds. These problems require working with a portion of a whole quantity, that is, a fraction of the regular price of the item or a fraction of the total amount of money the investor has.

1.1 Meaning of Fractions: Equivalent Fractions

It is important to understand exactly what a fraction is.

Definition

what a fraction is

A *fraction* is a number expressed in the form $\dfrac{a}{b}$, where a and b are whole numbers and b is not zero.

Some familiar fractions are $\dfrac{1}{2}$ and $\dfrac{1}{4}$. Notice in the definition that we have used letters to represent numbers. Letters used to represent numbers are called *literal numbers*.

literal numbers

By letting a letter (such as a) stand for all whole numbers, we can communicate that all whole numbers are being considered without having to write them all. (Of course, we could not write them all in any case, because there are infinitely many.) Any letter of the alphabet may be used as a literal number, that is, to represent a number (or numbers).

Fractions as a Portion of the Whole

Fractions may represent a portion of a whole quantity. The quantity might be a birthday cake to be divided among children at a party, an estate to be divided among the surviving heirs, or some other (more abstract) quantity. Whatever the whole, it may be represented pictorially by a (rectangular) box.

Suppose that a cake is to be cut into six pieces (of equal size). The cake might be cut as shown in Fig. 1.1. Each portion of the cake represents one-sixth of the whole; that is, each portion is $\frac{1}{6}$.

Figure 1.1

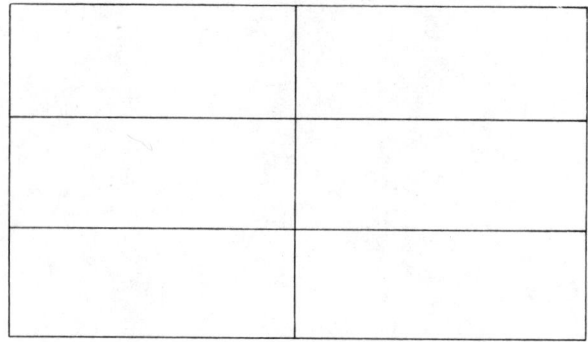

If one person gets two portions, the amount he receives is $\frac{2}{6}$ (read two-sixths) of the whole. The portion $\frac{2}{6}$ may be shown pictorially by the shaded area as in Fig. 1.2.

Figure 1.2

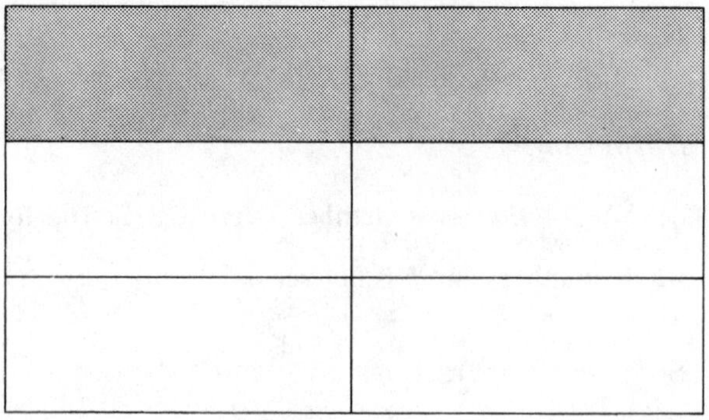

Definition

denominator   **The lower (or bottom) number of a fraction is called the *denominator*. The denominator indicates the number of equal portions into which the whole is divided.**

numerator   **The upper (or top) number of a fraction is called the *numerator*. The numerator indicates the number of portions with which we are working.**

the terms of a
fraction

In general, the numerator and denominator are called the *terms* of a fraction.

The terms of the fraction $\frac{3}{4}$ are 3 and 4. The number 4 is called the denominator. The number 3 is called the numerator. The fraction $\frac{3}{4}$ indicates that the whole was divided into 4 equal portions and we are working with 3 of them.

Occasionally, you may see a *slash* (/) used to separate the terms of a fraction (or as a fraction bar). Strictly speaking, this is not correct. The fraction bar is, by definition, a *horizontal* line segment. However, the (/) is often used for convenience.

Example 1

Make a pictorial representation and identify the numerator and denominator of the following fractions.

a. $\frac{1}{2}$ *b.* $\frac{3}{4}$ *c.* $\frac{2}{5}$

SOLUTION

	Fraction	Pictorial Representation	Numerator	Denominator
a.	$\frac{1}{2}$		1	2
b.	$\frac{3}{4}$		3	4
c.	$\frac{2}{5}$		2	5

Commonly, fractions are given names based on the relative sizes of their numerators and denominators.

Definition

proper fraction

A *proper fraction* is one in which the *numerator is smaller than the denominator*, assuming a positive value for the numerator and denominator.

The fractions $\frac{1}{2}, \frac{3}{4}$, and $\frac{1}{6}$ are examples of proper fractions.

Definition

improper fraction

An *improper fraction* is one in which the *numerator is larger than the denominator*; that is, the fraction represents more than one whole quantity.

The fractions $\frac{3}{2}, \frac{5}{4}$, and $\frac{11}{3}$ are examples of improper fractions.

Equivalent Fractions

By using fractions, it is possible to represent the same amount (or portion of a whole quantity) in different terms, that is, by using *different* numerators and *denominators*. For example, $\frac{2}{6}$ of a cake is the same amount as $\frac{1}{3}$ of a cake. Pictorially, $\frac{2}{6}$ means ⬚ and $\frac{1}{3}$ ⬚

Since both $\frac{2}{6}$ and $\frac{1}{3}$ represent the same portion of the whole, they are called *equivalent fractions*.

Definition

equivalent fractions

Fractions are called *equivalent* if they represent the same portion of the whole (i.e., the same amount) even though they contain different terms. That is, $\frac{a}{b}$ is equivalent to $\frac{c}{d}$ if $\frac{a}{b} = \frac{c}{d}$, where b and d are not zero.

The ability to determine fractions that are equivalent to a given fraction is one of the keys to successfully working with fractions. Therefore, we need a method of finding equivalent fractions.

larger and smaller terms

Fractions that are equivalent to a given fraction may be determined through multiplication or division of the terms by nonzero whole numbers other than 1. If multiplication is used, the equivalent fraction(s) is said to be in *larger* (or *higher*) terms. If division is used, the equivalent fraction(s) is said to be in *smaller* (or *lower*) terms. Each case will be considered.

Example 2   Determine three fractions (in larger terms) that are equivalent to $\frac{1}{3}$.

SOLUTION   We may choose any nonzero whole number to be multiplied times the numerator and denominator of the given fraction $\left(\frac{1}{3}\right)$. Suppose that we choose 2, 3, and 9. Then

$$\frac{1 \times 2}{3 \times 2} = \frac{2}{6}; \text{ that is, } \frac{1}{3} \text{ is equivalent to } \frac{2}{6}$$

$$\frac{1 \times 3}{3 \times 3} = \frac{3}{9}; \text{ that is, } \frac{1}{3} \text{ is equivalent to } \frac{3}{9}$$

$$\frac{1 \times 9}{3 \times 9} = \frac{9}{27}; \text{ that is, } \frac{1}{3} \text{ is equivalent to } \frac{9}{27}$$

Each of the fractions $\frac{2}{6}, \frac{3}{9}$, and $\frac{9}{27}$ is in larger terms than $\frac{1}{3}$; they contain larger numbers.

This process should not seem unreasonable. For instance, if we double the denominator (i.e., multiply by 2), we are doubling the number of parts into which the whole is divided. However, at the same time, we are also doubling the numerator, the number of parts with which we are working. The result is simply to represent the original portion (or amount) with larger terms.

Conversely, equivalent fractions can be produced by division. The determination of fractions that are equivalent to a given fraction can be done by dividing the terms of the fraction by a nonzero whole number other than 1. In this case, the equivalent fraction will be in *lower* terms than the (original) given fraction.

Example 3   Determine three fractions in lower terms that are equivalent to $\dfrac{40}{100}$.

SOLUTION   We may choose any nonzero whole number that will divide evenly into both the numerator and denominator. We choose 2, 5, and 10. Then

$$\frac{40 \div 2}{100 \div 2} = \frac{20}{50}; \text{ that is, } \frac{40}{100} \text{ is equivalent to } \frac{20}{50}$$

$$\frac{40 \div 5}{100 \div 5} = \frac{8}{20}; \text{ that is, } \frac{40}{100} \text{ is equivalent to } \frac{8}{20}$$

$$\frac{40 \div 10}{100 \div 10} = \frac{4}{10}; \text{ that is, } \frac{40}{100} \text{ is equivalent to } \frac{4}{10}$$

Each of the fractions $\dfrac{20}{50}, \dfrac{8}{20},$ and $\dfrac{4}{10}$ is in *lower terms* than $\dfrac{40}{100}$; they contain smaller numbers.

Division of the terms of a fraction by the same nonzero whole number is also called *reducing* the given fraction. The resulting equivalent fraction is **reduced form**   a *reduced form* of the given fraction.

Definition

If both the numerator and denominator of a given fraction are divided by the *largest* nonzero whole number *that will go evenly into both*, the resulting
reducing to lowest   **fraction is said to be *reduced to its lowest terms.***
terms

Twenty is the largest number that will go evenly into the terms of $\dfrac{40}{100}$.

Therefore, $\dfrac{40}{100}$ reduced to its lowest terms is $\dfrac{40 \div 20}{100 \div 20} = \dfrac{2}{5}$.

Example 4 Reduce each of the following to its lowest terms.

$a.$ $\dfrac{30}{100}$ $b.$ $\dfrac{15}{20}$ $c.$ $\dfrac{13}{39}$

SOLUTION

$a.$ $\dfrac{30 \div 10}{100 \div 10} = \dfrac{3}{10}$; that is, $\dfrac{30}{100}$ reduced to lowest terms is $\dfrac{3}{10}$.

$b.$ $\dfrac{15 \div 5}{20 \div 5} = \dfrac{3}{4}$; that is, $\dfrac{15}{20}$ reduced to lowest terms is $\dfrac{3}{4}$.

$c.$ $\dfrac{13 \div 13}{39 \div 13} = \dfrac{1}{3}$; that is, $\dfrac{13}{39}$ reduced to lowest terms is $\dfrac{1}{3}$.

How is the largest number (that will divide evenly into the terms of the fraction) determined? One might proceed by trial and error, that is, by trying larger and larger numbers until the largest is found. However, a more organized way can be developed.

Prime Numbers

In arithmetic, you might have studied prime numbers.

Definition

prime numbers

Prime numbers **are counting numbers (***other than 1***) that** *cannot* **be divided evenly except by 1 and the number itself.**

Examples of prime numbers are 2, 3, 5, 7, 11, 13, 17, 19, and 23. Each can be divided *only* by 1 and by itself. Numbers such as 4, 6, 8, 9, 10, and 12 are *not prime* numbers. They are called **composite** numbers. For example, 4 can be divided evenly by 2; 6 can be divided evenly by 2 and 3; 8 can be divided evenly by 2 and 4; and so on.

fundamental theorem

Fundamental Theorem—Prime Numbers

Any number that is not a prime number can be expressed as a product of prime numbers.

reducing fractions using primes

By expressing the terms of a given fraction as the products of prime numbers, one can more easily reduce the fraction to its lowest terms.

For example, $\dfrac{30}{100} = \dfrac{2 \times 3 \times 5}{2 \times 2 \times 5 \times 5}$. Since 2 is a factor of both terms, it may be divided into the terms; the result will be $\dfrac{1 \times 3 \times 5}{1 \times 2 \times 5 \times 5}$. If 5 is divided into the terms, the result will be $\dfrac{1 \times 3 \times 1}{1 \times 2 \times 5 \times 1}$. Now, there are *no factors common to the terms* (except 1), so no more division can be done. Therefore, $\dfrac{30}{100} = \dfrac{1 \times 3 \times 1}{1 \times 2 \times 5 \times 1} = \dfrac{3}{10}$ in lowest terms.

Example 5 Reduce the following fractions to lowest terms.

  a. $\dfrac{12}{28}$ **b.** $\dfrac{30}{84}$ **c.** $\dfrac{6}{18}$

SOLUTION

  a. $\dfrac{12}{28} = \dfrac{2 \times 2 \times 3}{2 \times 2 \times 7} = \dfrac{1 \times 1 \times 3}{1 \times 1 \times 7} = \dfrac{3}{7}$. (The terms are divided by 2 twice.)

  b. $\dfrac{30}{84} = \dfrac{2 \times 3 \times 5}{2 \times 2 \times 3 \times 7} = \dfrac{1 \times 1 \times 5}{1 \times 2 \times 1 \times 7} = \dfrac{5}{14}$. (The terms are divided by 2 and 3.)

  c. $\dfrac{6}{18} = \dfrac{2 \times 3}{2 \times 3 \times 3} = \dfrac{1 \times 1}{1 \times 1 \times 3} = \dfrac{1}{3}$. (The terms are divided by 2 and 3.)

Checking for Equivalence

Determination of equivalent fractions can be done by multiplication and division. However, suppose that *two fractions are given* and you want to know *if they are equivalent*. For example, is $\dfrac{6}{14}$ equivalent to $\dfrac{39}{91}$? This could be determined by reducing both to lowest terms and comparing the resulting fractions. However, there is a quicker way.

equivalent fractions
cross products

Two fractions are *equivalent* provided that their cross products are equal. The *cross products* are found by multiplying each fraction's numerator by the other fraction's denominator. Fraction $\dfrac{a}{b}$ is equivalent to fraction $\dfrac{c}{d}$ if $ad = bc$.

That is, $\dfrac{a}{b} = \dfrac{c}{d}$ if $ad = bc$.

If $\dfrac{6}{14}$ is equivalent to $\dfrac{39}{91}$ $\left(\text{i.e., } \dfrac{6}{14} = \dfrac{39}{91}\right)$, then the cross products $\left(\dfrac{6}{14} \times \dfrac{39}{91}\right)$ are equal. Since $(6)(91) = 546$ and $(14)(39) = 546$ (i.e., $546 = 546$), the given fractions are equivalent.

Example 6   Determine if the following pairs of fractions are equivalent.

a. $\dfrac{1}{3}, \dfrac{2}{6}$ *b.* $\dfrac{6}{15}, \dfrac{14}{35}$ *c.* $\dfrac{2}{4}, \dfrac{4}{6}$

SOLUTION   *a.* $\dfrac{1}{3} \times \dfrac{2}{6}$. The cross products are equal (i.e., $6 = 6$); hence, $\dfrac{1}{3} = \dfrac{2}{6}$.

b. $\dfrac{6}{15} \times \dfrac{14}{35}$. The cross products are equal (i.e., $210 = 210$); hence, $\dfrac{6}{15} = \dfrac{14}{35}$.

c. $\dfrac{2}{4} \times \dfrac{4}{6}$. The cross products are *not* equal (i.e., $12 \neq 16$); hence, $\dfrac{2}{4}$ and $\dfrac{4}{6}$ are *not* equivalent.

Exercises 1.1

1. Express $\dfrac{1}{2}$ in higher terms with a denominator of 12.

2. Express $\dfrac{3}{4}$ in higher terms with a denominator of 40.

3. Express $\dfrac{8}{10}$ in higher terms with a numerator of 40.

4. Express $\dfrac{3}{7}$ in higher terms with a numerator of 21.

5. Express $\dfrac{9}{10}$ in higher terms with a denominator of 100.

6. Express $\dfrac{1}{7}$ in higher terms with a numerator of 100.

7. Express $\dfrac{8}{10}$ in lower terms with a denominator of 5.

8. Express $\dfrac{30}{60}$ in lower terms with a numerator of 10.

9. Express $\dfrac{75}{100}$ in lower terms with a denominator of 20.

10. Express $\dfrac{16}{80}$ in lower terms with a denominator of 40.

■ Reduce each of the following to lowest terms.

11. $\dfrac{10}{12}$ **12.** $\dfrac{98}{100}$ **13.** $\dfrac{20}{35}$ **14.** $\dfrac{70}{60}$

■ Are the following pairs of fractions equivalent?

15. $\dfrac{1}{10}$ and $\dfrac{5}{50}$ **16.** $\dfrac{2}{7}$ and $\dfrac{3}{8}$ **17.** $\dfrac{9}{10}$ and $\dfrac{8}{9}$ **18.** $\dfrac{11}{121}$ and $\dfrac{2}{22}$

19. Is $\dfrac{1}{2}$ mile equivalent to $\dfrac{5}{10}$ mile?

20. Is $\dfrac{1}{4}$ of a dollar equivalent to $\dfrac{25}{100}$ of a dollar?

21. Suppose that you are offered a $\dfrac{3}{21}$ share or a $\dfrac{4}{28}$ share of a business for $10,000. Which should you take?

22. If you *add* the same nonzero number to the numerator and denominator of a fraction, will you get an equivalent fraction?

1.2 *Addition and Subtraction of Fractions*

meaning of addition

Addition is an operation of combining *like things* to get a sum or total. The requirement of *like things* cannot be emphasized too strongly. You might have heard someone (naively) say that *one plus one equals two*, as if no other result were possible. This is *not necessarily* true. Certainly, one book plus one book *is* two books, but is *one dollar* plus *one pencil* equal to two of something?

Implicit in the statement $1 + 1 = 2$ is that each 1 represents the *same thing*. *Unlike things cannot be added.* The requirement of like things (before addition can be done) is crucial.

The situation is similar for subtraction. One may *subtract* 2 books *from* 5 books, leaving 3 books. However, it is *not possible* to subtract 2 *books* from 5 *pencils*.

The same principle (of having like things) certainly applies to addition and subtraction of fractions. For fractions to be "alike," they must not only represent the same things, they *must have like* (also called *common*) *denominators*. In the following discussion, it will be assumed that the fractions are of like things so that we may concentrate on the importance of their denominators.

Addition of Fractions

Addition: like denominators

To add fractions *having common denominators*, add the numerators of the fractions and put their sum (or total) over the common denominator.

That is,

$$\frac{a}{b} + \frac{c}{b} = \frac{a+c}{b}, \qquad b \text{ not zero}$$

Example 1 Add the following fractions.

a. $\frac{1}{5} + \frac{3}{5}$ **b.** $\frac{3}{10} + \frac{4}{10}$

SOLUTION   **a.** $\frac{1}{5} + \frac{3}{5} = \frac{1+3}{5}$ or $\frac{4}{5}$

b. $\frac{3}{10} + \frac{4}{10} = \frac{3+4}{10}$ or $\frac{7}{10}$

The rule for adding fractions can be generalized. To add *more* than two fractions (having common denominators), simply add *all* the numerators and put the sum over the common denominator.

Example 2 Add $\frac{1}{13} + \frac{7}{13} + \frac{3}{13}$.

SOLUTION $\frac{1}{13} + \frac{7}{13} + \frac{3}{13} = \frac{1+7+3}{13} = \frac{11}{13}$

When addition (or any operation with fractions) is completed, it is customary to reduce the answer to lowest terms (if it is not already in lowest terms). A reduced answer $\left(\text{such as } \frac{1}{2}\right)$ is often easier to understand than an equivalent answer $\left(\text{such as } \frac{49}{98}\right)$.

Example 3 Add $\frac{1}{6} + \frac{2}{6} + \frac{1}{6}$. Reduce the sum to lowest terms.

SOLUTION $\frac{1}{6} + \frac{2}{6} + \frac{1}{6} = \frac{1+2+1}{6} = \frac{4}{6}$. Reducing, $\frac{4 \div 2}{6 \div 2} = \frac{2}{3}$. Therefore, $\frac{1}{6} + \frac{2}{6} + \frac{1}{6} = \frac{2}{3}$.

Subtraction of Fractions

Subtraction: like denominators

To subtract fractions (having *common denominators*), subtract their numerators and put the difference over their common denominator. That is,

$$\frac{a}{b} - \frac{c}{b} = \frac{a-c}{b}, \, b \text{ not zero.}$$

Example 4   Find $\dfrac{5}{7} - \dfrac{2}{7}$.

SOLUTION $\dfrac{5}{7} - \dfrac{2}{7} = \dfrac{5-2}{7} = \dfrac{3}{7}$

The rules for addition and subtraction should be intuitively appealing. If the denominators are alike, the fractions are "alike," in that they represent equal size portions of the whole. The numerators indicate the number of portions with which you are working. Hence, we find the sum or difference of the number of portions (that are alike) by adding or subtracting the numerators.

Suppose that the fractions to be added or subtracted *do not* have common denominators. What can be done? For example, suppose that Kay has $\dfrac{1}{2}$ yard and $\dfrac{1}{3}$ yard of cloth. How much cloth does she have? She *cannot* add $\dfrac{1}{2} + \dfrac{1}{3}$ in their present terms. They *do not have common denominators.*

However, Kay does have some total amount of cloth. To find the total, she has two options.

How do you add or subtract when the denominators are different?

Options for Adding or Subtracting Fractions with Unlike Denominators

Option 1. Express all the fractions in equivalent forms that *do have common denominators*, then add or subtract as before.

Option 2. Use the following rule:

$$\frac{a}{b} \pm \frac{c}{d} = \frac{ad \pm cb}{bd}$$

In either case, reduce the answer to lowest terms.

If Kay chooses option 1, she may express *both* fractions with common denominators of 12. Then

$$\frac{1}{2} + \frac{1}{3} = \frac{6}{12} + \frac{4}{12} = \frac{6+4}{12} = \frac{10}{12} = \frac{5}{6} \text{ yard}$$

If Kay chooses option 2, then

$$\frac{1}{2} + \frac{1}{3} = \frac{(3 \times 1) + (2 \times 1)}{(2)(3)} = \frac{3+2}{6} = \frac{5}{6} \text{ yard}$$

Either way, the sum is the same. If more than two fractions are to be added or subtracted, this method is applied to two at a time.

All that is required to add or subtract fractions, by option 1, is that they have *common denominators*. Kay could have used a number *smaller* or *larger* than 12. The smallest possible denominator is called the *least* (or *lowest*) *common denominator* (denoted LCD). The LCD is desirable because it allows us to work with smaller numbers and it makes the answer easier to reduce. However, the LCD is *not required*, just a common denominator.

In option 2, a common denominator is determined automatically.

Example 5   Perform the indicated operations. Use both options 1 and 2.

$$a. \ \frac{1}{3} + \frac{2}{5} \qquad b. \ \frac{7}{8} - \frac{1}{3}$$

SOLUTION $a. \ \dfrac{1}{3} + \dfrac{2}{5}$

Option 1. Express both fractions with the same denominator. If 30 is chosen, then

$$\frac{1}{3} + \frac{2}{5} = \frac{1 \times 10}{3 \times 10} + \frac{2 \times 6}{5 \times 6} = \frac{10}{30} + \frac{12}{30} = \frac{10 + 12}{30} = \frac{22}{30} = \frac{11}{15}$$

Option 2

$$\frac{1}{3} + \frac{2}{5} = \frac{(5 \times 1) + (2 \times 3)}{(3)(5)} = \frac{5 + 6}{15} = \frac{11}{15}$$

$b. \ \dfrac{7}{8} - \dfrac{1}{3}$

Option 1. Express both fractions with the same denominator. If 24 is chosen, then

$$\frac{7}{8} - \frac{1}{3} = \frac{7 \times 3}{8 \times 3} - \frac{1 \times 8}{3 \times 8} = \frac{21}{24} - \frac{8}{24} = \frac{21 - 8}{24} = \frac{13}{24}$$

Option 2

$$\frac{7}{8} - \frac{1}{3} = \frac{(7 \times 3) - (1 \times 8)}{(8)(3)} = \frac{21 - 8}{24} = \frac{13}{24}$$

Both options for adding and subtracting fractions with unlike denominators are commonly used. The reader should be familiar with both.

Example 6   In a recent storm, John's house sustained some roof damage. He needs $\frac{2}{3}$ of a square of shingles to repair the garage and $\frac{1}{4}$ of a square to repair the roof over the living room. How many squares of shingles are needed?

SOLUTION $\dfrac{2}{3} + \dfrac{1}{4} = \dfrac{(4 \times 2) + (3 \times 1)}{3 \times 4} = \dfrac{8 + 3}{12} = \dfrac{11}{12}$ of a square of shingles.

Exercises 1.2

■ Perform the indicated operations and reduce the answer to lowest terms.

1. $\dfrac{1}{8} + \dfrac{4}{8}$ **2.** $\dfrac{7}{100} + \dfrac{9}{100}$ **3.** $\dfrac{1}{12} + \dfrac{4}{12} + \dfrac{1}{12}$

4. $\dfrac{1}{15} + \dfrac{11}{15} + \dfrac{3}{15}$ **5.** $\dfrac{7}{8} - \dfrac{3}{8}$ **6.** $\dfrac{98}{100} - \dfrac{38}{100}$

7. $\dfrac{5}{13} - \dfrac{4}{13}$ **8.** $\dfrac{13}{17} - \dfrac{6}{17}$ **9.** $\dfrac{1}{3} + \dfrac{1}{4}$

10. $\dfrac{2}{7} + \dfrac{1}{3}$ **11.** $\dfrac{3}{11} + \dfrac{1}{2}$ **12.** $\dfrac{1}{10} + \dfrac{6}{100}$

13. $\dfrac{9}{10} - \dfrac{1}{2}$ **14.** $\dfrac{13}{14} - \dfrac{2}{7}$ **15.** $\dfrac{2}{3} - \dfrac{1}{6}$

16. $\dfrac{98}{100} - \dfrac{1}{10}$

17. Bill did $\dfrac{1}{2}$ of a job yesterday and $\dfrac{2}{5}$ of the job today. How much of the job has he done?

18. Richard bought $\dfrac{1}{2}$ cord of wood. If he already had $\dfrac{3}{5}$ of a cord, how much does he have altogether?

19. Nellie invests $\dfrac{2}{100}$ of her salary in stock and $\dfrac{1}{25}$ in bonds and makes no other investments. What fraction of her salary is invested?

20. $\dfrac{1}{8} + \dfrac{1}{2} + \dfrac{1}{4}$

1.3 Multiplication and Division of Fractions

Suppose that you want to purchase an item normally selling for $4.00 that is on sale for $\dfrac{1}{2}$ price. How much will you pay? Of course, the answer is $2.00. But how do you compute $\dfrac{1}{2}$ of $4.00?

In mathematical statements such as $\dfrac{1}{2}$ of 4, the word "of" usually means "to multiply." That is, $\dfrac{1}{2}$ of 4 means $\dfrac{1}{2} \times 4$.

**whole number times
a fraction**

Multiplication of a Whole Number and a Fraction

Step 1. Write the whole number (in fractional form) by putting the number over 1. For example, write 4 as $\frac{4}{1}$.

Step 2. Multiply the numerators of the fraction and the whole number (in fractional form) to get the numerator of the product. Multiply the denominators together to get the denominator of the product. That is,

$$a \times \frac{c}{d} = \frac{a}{1} \times \frac{c}{d} = \frac{a \times c}{1 \times d} \quad \text{or} \quad \frac{ac}{d}, \qquad d \text{ not zero}$$

Reduce the product to lowest terms.

Hence, $\frac{1}{2} \times 4 = \frac{1}{2} \times \frac{4}{1} = \frac{1 \times 4}{2 \times 1} = \frac{4}{2} = 2.$

Example 1   Multiply $7 \times \frac{2}{3}$.

SOLUTION $7 \times \frac{2}{3} = \frac{7}{1} \times \frac{2}{3} = \frac{7 \times 2}{1 \times 3} = \frac{14}{3}$

**new symbols for
multiplication**

There are several commonly used symbols that indicate multiplication. Consider the problem of 3 times 4. Then

$$3 \times 4 = 12$$
$$3 \cdot 4 = 12$$
$$(3)(4) = 12$$
$$3(4) = 12$$

The "$\times$" is used in arithmetic but it can be confusing in algebra. The "$\cdot$" is nice in algebra, but it can be confusing in arithmetic. Parentheses are frequently used in both algebra and arithmetic. Parentheses can be placed around both factors or just one of them. All notations are commonly used. Note that if a number and a letter (or two letters) are adjacent with no symbols, *multiplication is understood*. For example, $3X$ is understood to mean $(3)(X)$, and XY is understood to mean $(X)(Y)$.

Example 2   Find $(10)\left(\frac{2}{100}\right)$. Reduce the product to lowest terms.

SOLUTION $(10)\left(\dfrac{2}{100}\right) = \left(\dfrac{10}{1}\right)\left(\dfrac{2}{100}\right) = \dfrac{20}{100} = \dfrac{2}{10} = \dfrac{1}{5}$

How would two (or more) fractions be multiplied together? Consider $\dfrac{1}{2} \times 4$ again. We could express 4 as some fraction, say $\dfrac{12}{3}$ ($=4$). So an equivalent problem would be $\dfrac{1}{2} \times \dfrac{12}{3}$. We know that the answer should still be 2. What process must be done in order that $\dfrac{1}{2} \times \dfrac{12}{3}$ will equal 2?

multiplication of
fractions

> **Multiplication of Fractions**
>
> **Step 1.** *Multiply the numerators* of the fractions together. The number you get is the *numerator* of their product.
>
> **Step 2.** *Multiply the denominators* of the fractions together. The number you get is the *denominator* of their product.
>
> That is, $\dfrac{a}{b} \times \dfrac{c}{d} = \dfrac{a \times c}{b \times d}$. Reduce the product to lowest terms.

Therefore, $\dfrac{1}{2} \times \dfrac{12}{3} = \dfrac{1 \times 12}{2 \times 3} = \dfrac{12}{6} = 2$, just as it should be.

Note: You might want to reduce the fraction first, this will allow you to multiply smaller numbers.

Example 3   Multiply $\dfrac{2}{3} \cdot \dfrac{5}{8}$.

SOLUTION $\dfrac{2}{3} \cdot \dfrac{5}{8} = \dfrac{2 \cdot 5}{3 \cdot 8} = \dfrac{10}{24} = \dfrac{5}{12}$

Example 4   Multiply $(3)\left(\dfrac{1}{4}\right)\left(\dfrac{2}{9}\right)$.

SOLUTION $3 \times \dfrac{1}{4} \times \dfrac{2}{9} = \dfrac{3 \times 1 \times 2}{1 \times 4 \times 9} = \dfrac{6}{36} = \dfrac{1}{6}$

Example 5   A suit that usually sells for \$123.00 is on sale for $\frac{1}{3}$ off the regular price. Find the amount saved.

SOLUTION   One-third of the regular price is

$$\frac{1}{3} \times \$123.00 = \frac{\$123}{3} = \$41.00$$

The amount saved is \$41.

Division of Fractions

It has been noted that a fraction may represent a division problem. For example, the fraction $\frac{1}{2}$ may be interpreted as one quantity divided into two parts (i.e., $1 \div 2$). Suppose that three quantities are to be divided into five equal parts; then each portion is $\frac{3}{5}$, or $3 \div 5$. If a fraction is interpreted as a division problem, the *denominator* is the *divisor*; that is, the *denominator is divided into the numerator*.

Interpretation of a fraction as division necessitates the exclusion of

division by zero is undefined

zero (0) from the denominator. For example, $\frac{6}{2} = 3$ because $3 \times 2 = 6$. However, $\frac{6}{0} = ?$ That is, what number multiplied by zero yields 6? Of course, there is no such number. Therefore, *division by zero is undefined*.

Before dividing fractions, let us review division of whole numbers. Suppose that you have $6 \div 2$. Then

$$6 \div 2 = \frac{6}{2} \qquad \text{by the divisional interpretation of a fraction}$$

$$= \frac{6 \times 1}{1 \times 2}$$

$$= \frac{6}{1} \times \frac{1}{2} \qquad \text{by the definition of multiplication of a whole number and a fraction; } or$$

$$= 6 \times \frac{1}{2}$$

Therefore, $6 \div 2 = 6 \times \frac{1}{2}$. In other words, dividing 6 by 2 is the same as multiplying 6 times $\frac{1}{2}$. The numbers 2 and $\frac{1}{2}$ are called *reciprocals* or *multiplicative inverses* (of each other).

reciprocals, multiplicative inverses, inverted fractions

Definition

Two numbers whose product is one (1) are called *reciprocals* or *multiplicative inverses*.

Since $2 \times \frac{1}{2} = 1$, $\frac{1}{2}$ and 2 are reciprocals. Similarly, $\frac{3}{4}$ and $\frac{4}{3}$ are reciprocals, since $\frac{3}{4} \times \frac{4}{3} = \frac{12}{12} = 1$. The *reciprocals* of fractions are sometimes called *inverted fractions*.

To solve the problem $6 \div 2$, we may convert the problem to $6 \times \frac{1}{2}$ and get the quotient of 3. To divide by any nonzero number, we need only *multiply by its reciprocal (multiplicative inverse* or *inverted form)*.

dividing by a fraction

Division by a Fraction

To divide by a fraction, replace the fraction by its reciprocal and multiply. That is,

$$\frac{a}{b} \div \frac{c}{d} \text{ is equal to } \frac{a}{b} \times \frac{d}{c}$$

change to reciprocal
and multiply

Example 6   Compute $8 \div \frac{3}{2}$.

SOLUTION   Convert $8 \div \frac{3}{2}$ to a multiplication problem using the reciprocal of the divisor. That is,

$$8 \div \frac{3}{2} = 8 \times \frac{2}{3}$$

$$= \frac{16}{3}$$

Hence, $8 \div \frac{3}{2} = \frac{16}{3}$.

It might seem peculiar to change a division problem to multiplication by the reciprocal. However, the procedure is easily performed and we can rely on our knowledge of multiplication.

Example 7   Find $\dfrac{7}{8} \div \dfrac{4}{5}$.

SOLUTION $\dfrac{7}{8} \div \dfrac{4}{5} = \dfrac{7}{8} \times \dfrac{5}{4}$

$= \dfrac{7 \times 5}{8 \times 4}$

$= \dfrac{35}{32}$

Note: Any time you divide by a fraction, use the reciprocal and multiply. It does not matter what the first number is. The first number may be a whole number or another fraction.

Example 8   Find $2 \times \dfrac{1}{3} \times \dfrac{4}{5} \div \dfrac{5}{2}$.

SOLUTION $\dfrac{2}{1} \times \dfrac{1}{3} \times \dfrac{4}{5} \div \dfrac{5}{2} = \dfrac{2}{1} \times \dfrac{1}{3} \times \dfrac{4}{5} \times \dfrac{2}{5} = \dfrac{2 \times 1 \times 4 \times 2}{1 \times 3 \times 5 \times 5}$

$= \dfrac{16}{75}$

Example 9   The Footloose Shoelace Company wants to cut 375 yards of string into $\dfrac{3}{4}$-yard-long shoelaces. How many laces will result?

SOLUTION $375 \div \dfrac{3}{4} = 375 \times \dfrac{4}{3} = 500.$

There will be 500 laces each $\dfrac{3}{4}$ yard long.

Exercises 1.3

■ Perform the indicated operations and reduce the answer to lowest terms.

1. $\dfrac{2}{3} \times \dfrac{5}{4}$ **2.** $\left(\dfrac{5}{8}\right)\left(\dfrac{2}{7}\right)$ **3.** $\left(\dfrac{1}{2}\right)\left(\dfrac{1}{2}\right)$ **4.** $\dfrac{3}{7} \times \dfrac{7}{3}$ **5.** $\dfrac{2}{5} \times \dfrac{5}{2}$

6. $\dfrac{5}{7} \times \dfrac{14}{10}$ **7.** $\dfrac{5}{9} \times \dfrac{2}{10}$ **8.** $128 \times \dfrac{1}{2}$ **9.** $60 \times \dfrac{2}{3}$ **10.** $\left(75\right)\left(\dfrac{3}{5}\right)$

11. $6 \div \dfrac{1}{2}$ **12.** $8 \div \dfrac{3}{4}$ **13.** $\dfrac{5}{8} \div \dfrac{2}{3}$ **14.** $\dfrac{9}{10} \div \dfrac{1}{5}$ **15.** $\dfrac{3}{5} \div \dfrac{3}{5}$

16. $\dfrac{4}{7} \div \dfrac{4}{7}$ **17.** $\dfrac{5}{8} \div \dfrac{8}{5}$

18. What is $\dfrac{2}{3}$ of $60?

19. An item that usually sells for $240 is on sale for $\dfrac{1}{4}$ off. How much can be saved by purchasing the item on sale?

20. Three-fourths of a cake is to be divided into six equal parts. Each piece is what fraction of the whole cake?

21. John's insurance pays $\dfrac{4}{5}$ of his medical expenses. During a recent illness John incurred medical expenses totaling $375. How much did the insurance company pay?

22. A company budgets $\dfrac{2}{5}$ of its income for salaries and the president of the company receives $\dfrac{1}{8}$ of the salary budget. What fraction of the company's income goes to its president?

23. How much will you pay for an $837 item on sale at $\dfrac{2}{3}$ off?

24. Juan pays $\dfrac{3}{8}$ of his salary of $1275 per month in income tax. How much tax does he pay each year?

25. One-third of an estate is divided equally among four heirs. What fraction is received by each heir?

26. What is $\dfrac{7}{8}$ divided by $\dfrac{3}{4}$?

27. If you invested $4000 last year and this year you invested $\dfrac{3}{5}$ as much as last year, how much did you invest this year?

28. If you paid $\dfrac{8}{10}$ of the usual $90 price for a new coat, how much did you pay?

1.4 *Mixed Numbers: Order of Operations*

Thus far, we have treated the basic operations (of addition, subtraction, multiplication, and division) individually. Frequently, problems are encountered that involve two or more different operations, such as $3 + 2(5) - 8 \div 2$. In this case, all four operations are to be performed in the same problem. Does it matter in what order the operations are performed? The answer is a definite *yes*! Some operations must be done before others. The order of operations is as follows:

when to do what

Order of Operations

Step 1. Parentheses—Do any operations within (or inside) parentheses first.

Step 2. Multiplication and division (in order of occurrence from left to right).

Step 3. Addition and subtraction (in order of occurrence from left to right).

Example 1

Compute $3 + 2 \times 5 - 8 \div 2$.

SOLUTION

Step 1 is not performed, since the problem contains *no* parentheses.

Step 2.	$3 + 10 - 8 \div 2$	multiplication
	$3 + 10 - 4$	division
Step 3.	$13 - 4$	addition
	9	subtraction

Therefore, $3 + 2 \times 5 - 8 \div 2 = 9$.

Mixed Numbers

It was noted previously that *improper* fractions represent more than one whole quantity. For example, $\dfrac{3}{2}$ means , that is, $\dfrac{2}{2} + \dfrac{1}{2}$. However, $\dfrac{2}{2} = 1$, so $\dfrac{3}{2} = \dfrac{2}{2} + \dfrac{1}{2} = 1 + \dfrac{1}{2}$. The sum of $1 + \dfrac{1}{2}$ is frequently written as $1\frac{1}{2}$ for brevity, leaving the plus (+) *understood*. Such numbers are called mixed numbers.

mixed numbers

Definition

A *mixed number* is one that contains a whole number and a fraction, with the plus (+) understood.

The number $2\frac{1}{3}$ means $2 + \dfrac{1}{3}$. A mixed number can always be changed to an improper fraction. By definition $2 + \dfrac{1}{3} = \dfrac{6}{3} + \dfrac{1}{3} = \dfrac{7}{3}$. However, the following procedure is used for convenience.

Converting a Mixed Number to a Fraction

converting a mixed
number to a fraction

To convert a mixed number to a fraction, multiply the denominator of the fraction by the whole number and add the result to the numerator of the fraction.

Put the result over the denominator of the fraction.

Example 2   Change $3\frac{1}{5}$ to a fraction.

SOLUTION

$$3\frac{1}{5} = \frac{(5 \times 3) + 1}{5} = \frac{15 + 1}{5} = \frac{16}{5} \quad \text{or} \quad 3 + \frac{1}{5} = \frac{15}{5} + \frac{1}{15} = \frac{16}{5}.$$

Example 3   Change $7\frac{2}{3}$ to a fraction.

SOLUTION

$$7\frac{2}{3} = \frac{(3 \times 7) + 2}{3} = \frac{21 + 2}{3} = \frac{23}{3} \quad \text{or} \quad 7 + \frac{2}{3} = \frac{21}{3} + \frac{2}{3} = \frac{23}{3}.$$

Remember the order of operations: multiplication precedes addition.

Conversely, an improper fraction may be changed to a mixed number. To do so, the divisional interpretation of a fraction is required.

Changing a Fraction to a Mixed Number

changing a fraction
to a mixed number

An improper fraction may be changed to a mixed number by dividing the denominator into the numerator to get a (whole-number) quotient and a remainder. The (whole-number) *quotient* **is the whole-number part of the mixed number.**

Put the *remainder over* the *denominator* (or divisor) to get the fractional part of the mixed number.

Example 4   Express $\frac{40}{13}$ as a mixed number.

SOLUTION   Compute $40 \div 13$; $13\overline{)40}$. The whole number is 3; the fraction is $\frac{1}{13}$.
$$\begin{array}{r} 3 \\ 13\overline{)40} \\ -39 \\ \hline 1 \end{array}$$

Therefore, the mixed number is $3\frac{1}{13}$.

Improper fractions are frequently changed to mixed numbers *for ease of interpretation*. For example, $7\frac{1}{2}$ is more easily understood than is $\frac{30}{4}$ or $\frac{15}{2}$.

Mixed Operations

If a problem contains several operations and several different kinds of numbers, change all the numbers to the same type and follow the order of operations.

Example 5

Compute $3 \times \frac{1}{2} + \left(\frac{2}{3} \times \frac{1}{5}\right) - \frac{1}{4} \div \frac{1}{5}$.

SOLUTION

Following the order of operations,

Step 1. $3 \times \frac{1}{2} + \left(\frac{2}{3} \times \frac{1}{5}\right) - \frac{1}{4} \div \frac{1}{5}$ inside parentheses

Step 2. $3 \times \frac{1}{2} + \frac{2}{15} - \frac{1}{4} \div \frac{1}{5}$ multiplication

           $\frac{3}{2} + \frac{2}{15} - \frac{1}{4} \div \frac{1}{5}$ division

Step 3. $\frac{3}{2} + \frac{2}{15} - \frac{5}{4}$ addition

           $\frac{49}{30} - \frac{5}{4} = \frac{98}{60} - \frac{75}{60} = \frac{23}{60}$ subtraction

Therefore,

$$3 \times \frac{1}{2} + \left(\frac{2}{3} \times \frac{1}{5}\right) - \frac{1}{4} \div \frac{1}{5} = \frac{23}{60}$$

Exercises 1.4

■ Convert the following improper fractions to mixed numbers.

1. $\frac{12}{10}$ **2.** $\frac{22}{7}$ **3.** $\frac{13}{2}$ **4.** $\frac{14}{5}$ **5.** $\frac{28}{6}$ **6.** $\frac{30}{4}$

■ Change the following mixed numbers to fractions.

7. $1\frac{1}{2}$ **8.** $2\frac{2}{3}$ **9.** $2\frac{1}{5}$ **10.** $4\frac{1}{7}$ **11.** $5\frac{2}{3}$ **12.** $6\frac{1}{8}$

■ Perform the indicated operations.

13. $\dfrac{1}{2} + \dfrac{1}{3} - \dfrac{2}{4} + \left(\dfrac{1}{2} \times \dfrac{1}{3}\right)$

14. $\left(\dfrac{1}{3} - \dfrac{1}{7}\right) + \dfrac{3}{21}$

15. $\dfrac{2}{3} + \dfrac{5}{6} - \dfrac{1}{3} \times \dfrac{3}{2}$

16. $\dfrac{1}{2} + \dfrac{1}{3} \div \dfrac{2}{6}$

17. $\dfrac{4}{7} \div \dfrac{3}{2} + 1\dfrac{3}{21}$

18. $\left(1\dfrac{1}{4}\right)\left(2\dfrac{1}{5}\right) - \dfrac{6}{10} + \dfrac{1}{5}$

19. One room needs $5\frac{1}{4}$ yards of carpet, another needs $1\frac{2}{3}$ yards, and another needs $10\frac{1}{5}$ yards. How much carpet is needed?

20. Three bottles hold $\frac{4}{5}$ quart, $\frac{1}{2}$ quart, and 2 quarts. How much do they hold altogether?

21. A stock selling previously for $6\frac{3}{8}$ is down $\frac{7}{8}$. What is the current price?

22. This year's profit of Delta Corporation is down $1\frac{1}{3}$ million from last year's record profit of $6\frac{1}{4}$ million. What is this year's profit?

23. The prime interest rate of $9\frac{3}{4}$ percent is raised $\frac{1}{2}$ percent. What is the new rate?

24. A stock selling for $5\frac{3}{8}$ goes up by $4\frac{1}{2}$. What is the new price?

Review Exercises / Chapter 1

1. Express $\dfrac{2}{13}$ in larger terms with a denominator of 52.

2. Reduce $\dfrac{6}{34}$ to lowest terms.

3. Are $\dfrac{2}{7}$ and $\dfrac{6}{21}$ equivalent fractions?

■ Perform the indicated operations and reduce the answer to lowest terms.

4. $\dfrac{1}{9} + \dfrac{3}{9}$

5. $\dfrac{1}{4} + \dfrac{2}{4} + \dfrac{1}{4}$

6. $\dfrac{20}{25} - \dfrac{10}{25}$

7. $\dfrac{2}{3} + \dfrac{5}{6}$

8. $\dfrac{1}{15} + \dfrac{2}{5}$

9. $\dfrac{5}{6} - \dfrac{2}{5}$

10. $\left(\dfrac{5}{8}\right)\left(\dfrac{4}{7}\right)$

11. $\dfrac{5}{7} \div \dfrac{10}{21}$

12. $\dfrac{3}{4} \div \dfrac{3}{4}$

13. $2\frac{1}{2} + 4\frac{1}{3}$

14. $\dfrac{3}{4} - \left(\dfrac{1}{4}\right)\left(2\right)$

15. $\dfrac{7}{8} - \dfrac{1}{16} + \dfrac{1}{4} \times \dfrac{1}{4}$

16. Anita jogged $1\frac{1}{2}$ miles and rode her bicycle $2\frac{8}{10}$ miles. How far did she travel?

17. James inherited $\frac{1}{4}$ of a \$10,000 estate. How much did he receive?

18. What is the sale price of a \$99 item selling for $\frac{1}{3}$ off?

19. One-half of a cake is divided into three equal parts. Each piece is what fraction of the whole?

20. If you do $\frac{1}{3}$ of a job before noon and $\frac{1}{4}$ of the job after noon, how much is left to do tomorrow?

21. A business is owned by three partners. If one partner owns $\frac{3}{8}$ of the business and another partner owns $\frac{1}{4}$, how much does the third partner own?

22. Marie kept a record of how she spent her workday as part of a time-management study. She spent $2\frac{1}{4}$ hours typing, $\frac{1}{2}$ hour filing, $1\frac{1}{4}$ hours in a meeting, $1\frac{3}{4}$ hours preparing a report, and $\frac{3}{4}$ hour interviewing a prospective employee. How much time did she spend working?

23. Thomas worked the following number of hours each day last week: $8\frac{1}{4}$, $7\frac{1}{2}$, $7\frac{3}{4}$, $8\frac{1}{2}$, $6\frac{3}{4}$, and $3\frac{1}{2}$. If 40 hours is considered a regular workweek, how much overtime did he work?

24. Zeke paid only $\frac{4}{9}$ of the regular \$81 price for his new radio. How much did he pay?

25. Vivian bought 16 shares of stock selling for \$$4\frac{1}{8}$ per share. How much did she pay?

26. How much would 28 shares of stock selling for \$$10\frac{3}{8}$ per share cost if you had to pay an additional \$25.50 in taxes and fees?

27. If you worked 20 hours for \$$5\frac{1}{4}$ per hour, how much would you earn?

28. Wanda took $1\frac{3}{5}$ hours getting to work and $1\frac{5}{8}$ hours coming home. How much time did she spend traveling?

Chapter Test / Chapter 1

1. Define the following terms. (*Hint:* Use the glossary at the end of the book.)

    a. fraction   *b.* literal number   *c.* numerator   *d.* denominator

    e. prime number   *f.* reciprocal   *g.* terms   *h.* portion

    i. mixed number   *j.* equivalent

2. Compute each of the following:

  a. $\dfrac{1}{2} + \dfrac{2}{5} \times \dfrac{5}{6} - \dfrac{3}{4} \div 3$

  b. $\left(\dfrac{1}{2} + \dfrac{2}{3}\right) \times \dfrac{5}{6} - \dfrac{3}{4} \div 3$

  c. $\left(\dfrac{1}{2} + \dfrac{2}{3}\right) \times \left(\dfrac{5}{6} - \dfrac{3}{4}\right) \div 3$

  d. $\dfrac{1}{2} + \dfrac{2}{3} \times \left(\dfrac{5}{6} - \dfrac{3}{4}\right) \div 3$

  e. $\dfrac{1}{2} + \dfrac{2}{3} \times \dfrac{5}{6} - \left(\dfrac{3}{4} \div 3\right)$

  f. $\left(\dfrac{1}{2} + \dfrac{2}{3} \times \dfrac{5}{6}\right) - \left(\dfrac{3}{4} \div 3\right)$

3. J. F. Breaux purchased $78\frac{4}{5}$ acres of land. He later sold $21\frac{1}{4}$ acres. How many acres does he have left?

4. A company has 360 employees. If $\frac{2}{5}$ are females, how many female employees are there?

5. In a class of 34 students, 4 failed the final exam. What fraction of the class passed the final exam?

6. Landcorp purchased a 520 acre tract. One-fourth of the tract will be used for streets. The remaining part will be divided into 780 lots. What will be the size of each lot?

7. Are the fractions $\frac{15}{27}$ and $\frac{16}{28}$ equivalent?

8. Are the fractions $\frac{15}{27}$ and $\frac{10}{18}$ equivalent?

9. Classify each of the following as a *proper* or *improper* fraction.

    a. $\frac{5}{4}$ *b.* $\frac{4}{5}$ *c.* $\frac{5}{6}$ *d.* $\frac{3}{3}$ *e.* $\frac{7}{8}$ *f.* $\frac{5}{1}$

10. Express each of the following as the product of prime numbers.

    a. 10   *b.* 60   *c.* 39   *d.* 23   *e.* 144

11. A stock selling for $11\frac{3}{4}$ went up by $2\frac{1}{8}$. What is the new price?

12. Give the multiplicative inverse of each of the following:

    a. $\frac{1}{3}$ *b.* $\frac{7}{8}$ *c.* $\frac{5}{2}$ *d.* 4   *e.* $\frac{3}{3}$ *f.* $\frac{2}{5}$

13. Zeta, Inc., wants to use $\frac{1}{4}$ of the company's profit to purchase new equipment. Two-thirds of the portion allocated for new equipment will be used to purchase a new truck.

    a. What fraction of the company's profit will be spent on the truck?

    b. If the company's profit is $42,000, how much is available to spend on the truck?

14. If you pay $\frac{4}{5}$ of the regular $280 price of a new suit, how much do you pay?

CHAPTER 2

Decimals

INTRODUCTION

Decimal numbers (called simply *decimals*) are probably the most commonly used numbers. For example, a problem being computed with the aid of a calculator is always worked (and the answer given) in decimals. Sometimes, decimals are called *decimal fractions*, because they are useful in representing quantities that contain fractional amounts. In fact, any number that you will use in this book, whether it is a whole number, fraction, mixed number, or percent, can be expressed as a decimal.

In this chapter we will discuss the meaning of decimals, operations with decimals, and some common applications of decimals.

2.1 Place-Value Notation; Addition and Subtraction

Numbers such as 2.38, 17.923, and 1.25 are *decimal numbers* or *decimal fractions*. For brevity, they may simply be called *decimals*. Their most distinguishing feature is the period (.) called the *decimal point*. The individual

digits   numbers that make up the decimal are called *digits*.

Each digit in a decimal has a special meaning based on its place or position (relative to the decimal point). This can be shown as follows:

place value

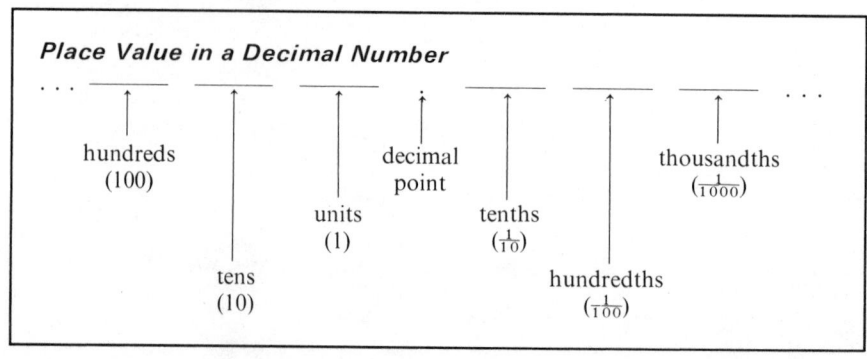

Place Value in a Decimal Number

hundreds (100)   tens (10)   units (1)   decimal point   tenths ($\frac{1}{10}$)   hundredths ($\frac{1}{100}$)   thousandths ($\frac{1}{1000}$)

The digit immediately to the *left* of the decimal point is called the ones or *units* digit. It indicates the number of units contained in the number. The digit to the left of the units digit is called the *tens* digit. It indicates the number of tens contained in the number, and so on.

The digit immediately to the *right* of the decimal point is called the *tenths* digit. It tells the number of $\frac{1}{10}$'s contained in the number. The digit to the right of the tenths digit indicates the number of $\frac{1}{100}$'s, and so on.

Addition of Decimals

Remember that addition is an operation of combining "like" quantities to find the total. In fractions, this means that the quantities must have common denominators. This information is also useful in discussing addition of decimals, because some of the digits represent fractions.

addition process

> ### Addition of Decimals
> **Step 1.** Place the decimal numbers to be added one beneath the other with the *decimal points in a column*.
> **Step 2.** Add the digits that represent the same thing. Start by adding the digits in the column on the right and proceed to the left. If the sum in any column is ten or more, record the rightmost digit in that column and "carry" the left digit to the next column to the left. Continue the add-and-carry process until reaching the leftmost column of the problem.

The following examples illustrate the process.

Example 1   Add 17.23, 0.5, and 42.0.

SOLUTION   **Step 1.** First, place the numbers beneath each other, keeping the decimal points in a column.

Step 2. By adding, we have

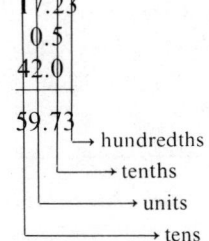

By placing the decimal points in a column, you are *automatically* adding "like" quantities, that is, tens to tens, units to units, tenths to tenths, hundredths to hundredths, and so on.

calculator

When addition of decimals is done with the aid of a calculator, we simply "punch in" the decimal point at the appropriate place. The appropriate sum and "carried" amounts are done automatically.

Example 2   Add 29.7, 85.6, and 0.72.

SOLUTION

```
    12 ←——— "carried"
    29.7
    85.6
     0.72
   ——————
   116.02
```

Example 3   Cary went to the store and purchased items costing $0.38, $1.29, $0.78, $2.06, with $0.23 tax. How much did she pay?

SOLUTION   The total cost of the purchase is

```
    $0.38
     1.29
     0.78
     2.06
     0.23
    ——————
    $4.74
```

Subtraction of Decimals

To discuss subtraction, it is convenient to name the quantities involved.

minuend,
subtrahend,
difference

The number being "*subtracted from*" is called the *minuend*. The number being *subtracted* is called the *subtrahend*. The answer is called the *difference*.

```
  7    minuend
 −2    subtrahend
 ——
  5    difference
```

As with addition, only "like" things can be subtracted. Eight books *minus* three books equals five books. However, eight books minus three tables does not equal five (of anything). "Unlike" quantities *cannot* be subtracted.

subtraction process

Subtraction of Decimals

Step 1. Put the subtrahend *beneath* the minuend with the decimal points in a column.

Step 2. Subtract the lower digits from the corresponding upper digits. If the lower digit is larger than the upper digit, "borrow" ten from the column immediately to the left.

Since the decimal points are in a column, you will always be subtracting "like" things: tens from tens, units from units, tenths from tenths, and so on.

Example 4   Subtract 2.34 from 18.47.

SOLUTION   *Step 1.* Write the numbers beneath each other with the number being subtracted (the subtrahend) on bottom. Subtract the lower digits from the upper digits.

$$
\begin{array}{r}
18.47 \\
-\ \ 2.34 \\
\hline
16.13
\end{array}
$$

Step 2   16.13   is the difference

Notice that 4 hundredths were subtracted from 7 hundredths, 3 tenths from 4 tenths, 2 units from 8 units, and 0 tens from 1 ten.

Example 5   If 35.7 is the minuend and 12.9 is the subtrahend, find the difference.

SOLUTION   The problem is

$$
\begin{array}{r}
35.7 \\
-12.9 \\
\hline
\end{array}
$$

To subtract 9 tenths from 7 tenths, we must borrow 1 unit $\left(=\dfrac{10}{10}\right)$ from the column to the left. Hence,

$$
\begin{array}{r}
35.7 \\
-12.9 \\
\hline
22.8
\end{array}
$$

Exercises 2.1

■ Add the following.

1. 14.2, 13.7, 21.8   **2.** 12.1, 1.03, 22.0   **3.** 27.1, 18.62, 9

4. 231.6, 1.025, 7.1   **5.** 42.1, 30.01, 6.029, 341.2   **6.** 75, 0.50, 7.5

■ Subtract the following.

7. 98.6 − 42.3   **8.** 76.49 − 3.28   **9.** 275.4 − 74.5

10. Minuend = 137.648, subtrahend = 26.13, difference = _____?

11. Minuend = 2.649, subtrahend = 0.723, difference = _____?

12. Subtrahend = 1.246, minuend = 42.1, difference = _____?

13. Subtrahend = 234.1, minuend = 600, difference = _____?

14. Jan's grocery receipt is as follows:

0.81	GR
1.17	GR
0.63	GR
0.89	GR
0.89	GR
1.39	PR
1.39	MT
1.59	MT
2.87	MT
0.75	MT

How much does she owe?

15. If Kay has $5.38 and Jay has $4.72, what is the difference of the amounts they have?

16. Bill's tax deductions are as follows:

medical expense	$623.52
interest paid	$271.60
state tax	$421.32
contribution to charity	$ 79.48

What is his total deduction?

17. A TV set that sells for $399 is on sale for $82.67 off. What is the sale price?

18. Carolyn's temperature was 101.4 degrees. After taking medicine, it went down 2.8 degrees. Find her temperature.

19. If you write checks for $123, $7.36, $2.47, and $12.14, what is the total?

20. A company's profit decreased from $1,328,275.63 to $938,635.94. What is the difference?

21. The stock of ABC Company selling for $42.50 per share went up $2.50 on Monday, $3.25 on Tuesday, then went down $1.75 on Wednesday and $4.12 on Thursday. What was its price after Thursday?

2.2 Multiplication of Decimals

multiplication
process

> **Process of Multiplication of Decimals**
>
> **Step 1.** Multiply the two numbers as if they were whole numbers (i.e., ignore the decimal points).
>
> **Step 2.** Place the decimal point in the product such that there are the same number of digits to the right of the decimal as there are in all factors.

Example 1 Find $(23.1)(1.7)$.

SOLUTION

$$
\begin{array}{r}
2\,3.1 \\
\times\ 1.7 \\
\hline
1\,6\,1\,7 \\
2\,3\,1 \\
\hline
3\,9.2\,7 \\
\end{array}
$$

Step 1. Ignore the decimal points and work as if the problem were $(231)(17)$.

Step 2. Now, since there is a total of two digits to the right of the decimals in the factors, there should be two digits to the right of the decimal point in the product.

Unlike addition, the decimal points need *not* be in the same column. Place the factors so that the rightmost digit of one factor is directly beneath the rightmost digit of the other factor.

Example 2 Find the product of 12.03 and 127.1.

SOLUTION Multiply, ignoring the decimal points.

$$
\begin{array}{r}
1\,2.0\,3 \\
1\,2\,7.1 \\
\hline
1\,2\,0\,3 \\
8\,4\,2\,1 \\
2\,4\,0\,6 \\
1\,2\,0\,3 \\
\hline
1\,5\,2\,9.0\,1\,3 \\
\end{array}
$$

Since there are a total of three digits to the right of the decimal points, there should be three digits to the right of the decimal point in the product.

The product of $(12.03)(127.1) = 1529.013$.

If three or more factors are to be multiplied, multiply *any* two first. This product is then multiplied by one of the remaining factors. Continue until all numbers have been multiplied together.

Example 3   Compute $(13.1)(7.4)(2.03)$.

SOLUTION   Multiply any two factors, for example 13.1 and 7.4. Then multiply this product by the remaining factor of 2.03.

$$
\begin{array}{r}
1\,3.1 \\
\times\,7.4 \\
\hline
5\,2\,4 \\
9\,1\,7 \\
\hline
9\,6.9\,4 \\
\times\,2.0\,3 \\
\hline
2\,9\,0\,8\,2 \\
0\,0\,0\,0 \\
1\,9\,3\,8\,8 \\
\hline
1\,9\,6.7\,8\,8\,2
\end{array}
$$

Example 4   W. J. decided to carpet his living room. It will require 24 square yards of carpet. If the carpet costs $9.95 per square yard, how much will it cost?

SOLUTION   The cost of the carpet is 24 square yards $\times$ $9.95.

$$
\begin{array}{r}
9.9\,5 \\
2\,4 \\
\hline
3\,9\,8\,0 \\
1\,9\,9\,0 \\
\hline
2\,3\,8.8\,0
\end{array}
$$

The carpet will cost $238.80.

Exercises 2.2

■ Compute the following.

1. 6.38×1.22 **2.** 72.35×2.1 **3.** 132.7×2.64

4. 1.003×4 **5.** $(721)(3.31)$ **6.** $(4.1)(0.32)(2.05)$

7. $(0.001)(0.1)$ **8.** $(2.4)(0.24)(0.024)$

9. Richard purchased 6 items costing $2.25 each. What is the total cost?

10. Jeff has $2.76. Craig has 2.5 times as much. How much does Craig have?

11. Junior bought 4 sheets of plywood at $9.98 per sheet and 6.5 pounds of nails for $0.49 per pound. How much was his purchase?

12. If material costs $4.98 per yard, how much do 3.25 yards cost?

13. How much would 120 ball-point pens cost if they were $0.18 each?

14. Ellis copied 428 pages at a cost of $0.11 each. How much did he spend?

15. Find the product of 0.0341 and 2.015.

16. What is the cost of 9.6 feet of pipe selling for $1.10 per foot?

17. If the purchase in problem 16 requires $0.52 sales tax, what is the total price?

18. Compute: (100) (0.001) (1000) (0.01) (10).

19. Find the price of 2.403 acres of land selling for $6999.95 per acre.

20. Find the cost of 4.3 pounds of hamburger selling for $1.70 per pound.

2.3 *Division of Decimals*

dividend

divisor, quotient

remainder

To discuss division it is helpful to name the numbers involved. The number *being divided* is called the *dividend*. The number you are dividing into the dividend is called the *divisor*. The answer is called the *quotient*. If the divisor does not go into the dividend evenly (a whole number of times), the number remaining is called the *remainder*.

There are several symbols used to indicate division. Suppose that we want to divide 8 by 2. We may write $8 \div 2$ (read eight divided by two). $\frac{8}{2}$ (read eight over two), or $2\overline{)8}$ (read two into eight). The symbol $(\overline{)}\,)$ is sometimes called the *long-division symbol*.

division symbols

The fraction notation and "$\div$" are used to indicate that division is to be done. But the long-division symbol $(\overline{)}\,)$ is the one used during the actual computation with decimals.

division process

The Process of Division

Step 1. Write the problem with the $\overline{)}$ symbol. Put the *divisor on the left* (outside) of the symbol and the *dividend underneath*.

Step 2. If there is a decimal point in the divisor, move it to the right side (end) of the divisor. Move the decimal in the dividend the same number of places to the right. (Sometimes you may need to attach some zeros to the dividend to facilitate moving the decimal.)

Step 3. Place the decimal point in the quotient *directly above* the decimal point in the dividend.

Step 4. Proceed with division as if you were using whole numbers.

Example 1   Find $26.84 \div 1.2$.

SOLUTION   To solve $26.84 \div 1.2$, move the decimal point one place to the right in both the divisor and dividend. This gives $268.4 \div 12$.

$$
\begin{array}{r}
22.3 \\
12\overline{)268.4} \\
-24 \\
\hline
28 \\
-24 \\
\hline
44 \\
-36 \\
\hline
8
\end{array}
$$

how to end a division problem

Since there are no more digits in the dividend to bring down, a decision must be made. We have three options.

Option 1. Since there is no number to bring down, we may stop and leave the 8 at the bottom of the problem. Then we say we have a remainder of 8.

Option 2. Put the remainder of 8 over the divisor of 12 (getting the fraction $\frac{8}{12}$) and put the fraction behind the quotient, giving a mixed number answer:

$$
\begin{array}{r}
22.3 \, \frac{8}{12} \\
12\overline{)268.4}
\end{array}
\qquad \text{or} \qquad 22.3\tfrac{2}{3}
$$

Option 3. Attach some zeros to the dividend and keep dividing until you get some desired number of decimal places in the quotient.

$$
\begin{array}{r}
22.366 \ldots \\
12\overline{)268.4000} \\
24 \\
\hline
28 \\
24 \\
\hline
44 \\
36 \\
\hline
80 \\
72 \\
\hline
80 \\
72 \\
\hline
80
\end{array}
$$

Note: If we keep dividing, sooner or later the quotient will begin to repeat. In this case, we will now get 6's forever.

Which option is chosen depends on the nature of the problem being solved.

To determine if the quotient is correct, we may want to check a division problem.

Checking Division

To check division, multiply the quotient by the divisor and add the remainder to their product. The result will be equal to the dividend if the problem is solved correctly.

Suppose that we have a dividend of 13 and a divisor of 3. The quotient is 4 with a remainder of 1. That is,

$$
\begin{array}{r}
4 \\
3\overline{)13} \\
-12 \\
\hline
1
\end{array}
$$

This can be checked by multiplying the quotient (4) by the divisor (3) and adding the remainder (1): $3 \times 4 + 1 = 12 + 1 = 13$. Since the dividend is 13, the quotient (and remainder) are correct.

Example 2   If 18.4 is the divisor and 723 is the dividend, find the quotient and remainder.

SOLUTION   *Step 1.* Since 18.4 is the divisor and 723 is the dividend, the problem may be written as follows: $18.4\overline{)723}$.

Step 2. Move the decimal point to the right (end) of the divisor. Move the decimal in the dividend the same number of places (a zero must be attached to the divisor). Now the problem is $184\overline{)7230}$.

Note: The decimal was moved to make the problem easier; that is, we are now dividing by a whole number, not a decimal. Moving the decimal in *both* does not change the answer; we just multiplied both the divisor and dividend by 10.

Step 3. By dividing, we have

$$
\begin{array}{r}
39 \\
184\overline{)7230} \\
-552 \\
\hline
1710 \\
-1656 \\
\hline
54
\end{array}
$$

The quotient is 39 with a remainder of 54.

To check, compute $(39)(184) + 54 = 7230$. Since the dividend is also 7230, the answer is correct.

Converting a Fraction to a Decimal

It was noted in Chapter 1 that a fraction may be interpreted as a division problem. In this case, the *denominator is the divisor; the numerator is the dividend.*

Example 3   Express $\dfrac{27}{5}$ as a decimal.

SOLUTION   Divide the numerator (27) by the denominator (5).

$$
\begin{array}{r}
5.4 \\
5\overline{\smash{)}27.0} \\
-25 \\
\hline
20 \\
20 \\
\hline
0
\end{array}
$$

Hence, $\dfrac{27}{5} = 5.4$.

In division, it must be clear which number is the divisor and which is the dividend. If they are reversed, the answer will be different. For example, $27 \div 6$ is not the same as $6 \div 27$.

Converting a Decimal to a Fraction

We may convert 5.4 to a fraction by multiplying by $\dfrac{10}{10}$ ($=1$). That is, $5.4\left(\dfrac{10}{10}\right) = \dfrac{54}{10} = \dfrac{27}{5}$. In general, we may convert a decimal to a fraction by multiplying by $\dfrac{10}{10}, \dfrac{100}{100}, \dfrac{1000}{1000}, \ldots$, whichever is necessary to move the decimal to the right of the last digit.

Example 4   *a.* Convert 0.5 to a fraction.
  b. Convert 0.37 to a fraction.

SOLUTION   *a.* $0.5\left(\dfrac{10}{10}\right) = \dfrac{5}{10} = \dfrac{1}{2}$

  b. $0.37\left(\dfrac{100}{100}\right) = \dfrac{37}{100}$

Rounding Off

Suppose that you are working a problem in which the answer is in dollars and cents. Dollars and cents are always expressed as decimals with two digits to the right of the decimal point, such as $5.28. What can be done with expressions such as $5.2734 or $4.5782? They are *rounded off* to two decimal places. The following rule is used in this text.

rounding off a decimal

> **Rule for Rounding Off**
>
> **Step 1.** Determine the number of decimal places (to the right of the decimal point) that you want in the answer.
> **Step 2.** Examine the digit in the next decimal place to the right.
> **Step 3.** If the next digit is 5 or more, add *one* to the digit in the decimal place to which you are rounding and delete all the digits to its right. If the next digit to the right is 4 or less, delete all the digits to the right.

The quantity $5.2734 rounds off to $5.27 (since the digit to the right of 7 is less than 5). The quantity $4.5782 rounds off to $4.58 (since the digit to the right of 7 is 5 or more; in particular, it is 8).

After the rounding off, the new number is an *approximation*. That is, the rounded-off number is not equal to the original. But remember: an approximate answer may be accurate enough in certain situations. You may round off to as many decimal places of accuracy as is appropriate for the particular problem under consideration. However, when working with large numbers, rounding off can result in considerable error.

Exercises 2.3

■ Find the quotient and remainder.

1. $28 \div 5$ **2.** $42.7 \div 3.1$ **3.** $\dfrac{138.2}{12.1}$ **4.** $1.9\overline{)83.246}$

■ Express the quotient as a mixed number.

5. $17.16 \div 3.1$ **6.** $128.49 \div 2.3$

■ Express the quotient as a three-place decimal.

7. $37.2 \div 12.5$ **8.** $271.63 \div 1.7$

■ Express the following fractions as decimals.

9. $\dfrac{3}{8}$ **10.** $\dfrac{3}{40}$ **11.** $\dfrac{6}{50}$ **12.** $\dfrac{9}{15}$

■ Round off each number.

13. 1.784 to two decimal places.   **14.** 27.658 to two decimal places.

15. 1.786 to two decimal places.   **16.** 29.6531 to three decimal places.

17. Four people are to get equal shares of $9634.16. How much does each receive?

18. If 4.5 yards of cloth costs $26.55, what is the price per yard?

19. You drive 294.1 miles and use 16.4 gallons of gasoline. Find the miles-per-gallon figure.

20. If you purchase 450 items for $1425.50, what is the cost per item?

21. Convert each of the following to fractions.

    a. 0.28   *b.* 0.06   *c.* 0.024   *d.* 1.2

Review Exercises / Chapter 2

1. Sue wrote checks for $1.38, $125.52, $20.90, $100, and $19.46. Find the sum.

2. Last year Bill earned $14,628.72. This year his income was $1235.41 less. What is this year's income?

3. Minuend = 0.078, subtrahend = 0.00325, difference = ?.

4. Find the product of 1.32, 0.21, and 2.1.

5. Find the quotient and remainder of 20.9 ÷ 5.2.

6. Express $\dfrac{5}{16}$ as a decimal.

7. Round off $238.4621 to two decimal places.

8. Round off $47.2184 to two decimal places.

9. Divide 7.346 by 14.2 and round the quotient to three decimal places.

10. Marie bought items costing $0.25, $1.39, and $2.43, with a tax of $0.26. Find the total.

11. An item that sells for $399.95 is on sale for $72.35 off. What is the sale price?

12. If you purchase four items for $1.49 each, what is the amount of your purchase?

13. Otto worked 30.5 hours at $5.82 per hour. How much did he earn?

14. If you pay $3.06 for 2.55 pounds of hamburger meat, what is the price per pound?

15. Tony rented a car for 23 cents per mile and drove the car for 164.7 miles. How much did he pay?

16. Find the quotient if 0.07812 is divided by 0.024.

Chapter Test / Chapter 2

1. Define the following terms:

    a. digit   **b.** minuend   **c.** subtrahend

    d. difference   **e.** product   **f.** factors

    g. dividend   **h.** divisor   **i.** quotient

2. Compute each of the following:

a.	**b.**	**c.**
314.6	51623	1.0236
2.635	48791	0.0714
1251.04	20100	2.0023
76.8	52700	13.3999
+ 9.347	+36984	+ 0.8787

d.	**e.**	**f.**
12.90876	0.793462	12.3
− 7.98739	−0.007999	− 0.98765

g.	**h.**	**i.**
3.0594	0.9743	984.62
× .0651	× .0051	×897.5

    j. $7.0468 \div 1.3756$ **k.** $847.345 \div 21.9847$ **l.** $.0378 \div 127.462$

3. Find the price of 132.76 feet of rope selling for 6.35 cents per foot.

4. Round off 21.982714 to the nearest

    a. thousandth   **b.** hundredth   **c.** tenth;   **d.** unit.

5. Express $\frac{9}{5}$ as a decimal.

6. In the number 2,384,782.6593, what is

    a. the tens digit?

    b. the units digit?

    c. the tenths digit?

    d. the thousandths digit?

    e. the millions digit?

7. Where is the decimal point in the number 635?

8. Express each of the following as a fraction.

    a. 0.80   **b.** 2.3   **c.** 0.05

    d. 131   **e.** 0.623   **f.** 2.03

9. If you purchase 6 items costing $1.24 each, what is the amount of your purchase?

10. What is the net price of a $628.42 item on sale for $131.67 off?

11. If you drive 180.5 kilometers and use 35.1 liters of gasoline, find the kilometers per liter.

12. Express the quotient of 23.46 ÷ 2.12 as

    a. a quotient and remainder.

    b. a mixed number.

    c. a 2-place decimal. (*Hint:* Compute to 3 decimal places and round off to 2 decimal places.)

CHAPTER 3

Banking Transactions

INTRODUCTION

Man's first attempts at commerce were in the form of *barter*, the physical trading of goods between two individuals each having what the other wanted. However, it was not always easy to find someone wishing to trade six pigs and a dozen chickens for your cow—not to mention the inconvenience of carrying the cow around while looking. There must be a better way! Man then came upon the idea of establishing a monetary system in which items could be purchased with units of money having a known value, such as gold coins. This helped, but there was still the problem of carrying quantities of money for large purchases. There was also the danger of loss or theft when carrying money. Then man progressed one step further and began using a *checking account*. With such an arrangement, money could be exchanged conveniently through a third party.

The basic principle behind the checking account is simple. Mr. Dough carries his money to a third party (the bank) and leaves it for safekeeping. When Mr. Dough wishes to buy something from Mr. Ray, he gives Mr. Ray a piece of paper representing the desired amount of money. Mr. Ray then takes the paper to the third party (the bank) and receives his money. Such an arrangement has some obvious advantages. First, it is convenient. There is no need to carry sums of money and risk loss or theft. Second, the piece of paper and its travels through the bank provide an excellent record of payment of transactions.

Figure 3.1 shows the steps just described in terms of today's banking process. In step 1 Mr. Dough deposits money in his checking account in the South Main Bank. Mr. Dough can then give a check to Mr. Ray to pay for goods or services (step 2). Mr. Ray will deposit the check in his own bank account in the Second National Bank (step 3). The Second National Bank forwards the check to the Federal Reserve clearinghouse (step 4), which in turn forwards the check to Mr. Dough's bank (step 5). The money from Mr. Dough's account is transferred back to Mr. Ray's account through the Federal Reserve system.

Figure 3.1

the checking process

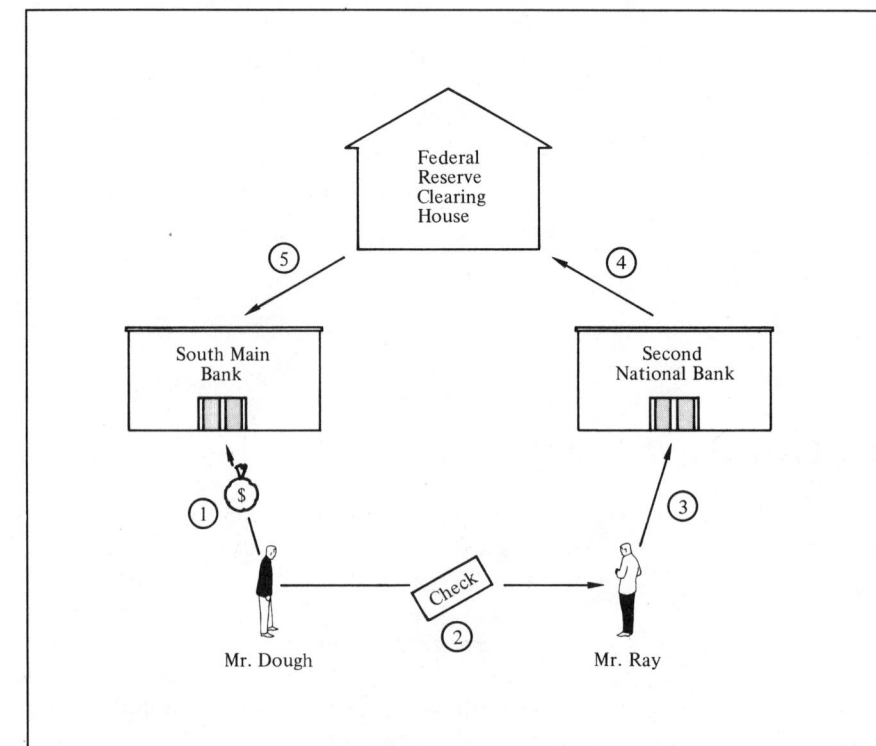

In this chapter, we will discuss some of the records necessary in checking accounts. We will also discuss *negotiable order of withdrawal* (*NOW*) accounts. NOW accounts are essentially checking accounts on which the bank pays interest between the time money is deposited and the time the "check" or order of withdrawal is paid. Most of the discussion will involve the check (or NOW order) register, the account statements, and how to reconcile these records.

3.1 *The Checking Account*

The first step in the check procedure is establishing a checking account. This is done by simply choosing a bank and making arrangements for the bank to pay your money as directed by your written checks. These arrangements consist primarily of depositing money in the bank, completing a *signature card* (Figure 3.2), and obtaining checks. The signature card authorizes the bank to pay money from your account for checks signed by persons whose signatures appear on the signature card.

Figure 3.2
Signature Card

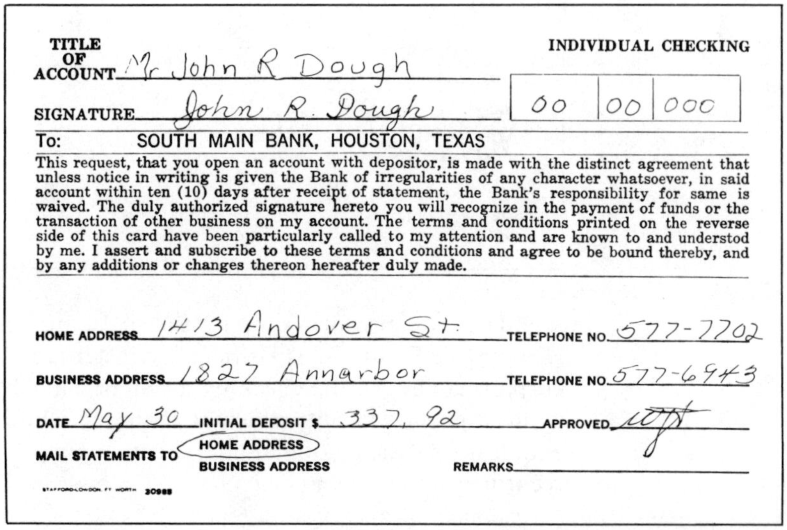
TITLE OF ACCOUNT Mr John R Dough

INDIVIDUAL CHECKING

SIGNATURE John R. Dough | 00 | 00 | 000

To: SOUTH MAIN BANK, HOUSTON, TEXAS

This request, that you open an account with depositor, is made with the distinct agreement that unless notice in writing is given the Bank of irregularities of any character whatsoever, in said account within ten (10) days after receipt of statement, the Bank's responsibility for same is waived. The duly authorized signature hereto you will recognize in the payment of funds or the transaction of other business on my account. The terms and conditions printed on the reverse side of this card have been particularly called to my attention and are known to and understod by me. I assert and subscribe to these terms and conditions and agree to be bound thereby, and by any additions or changes thereon hereafter duly made.

HOME ADDRESS 1413 Andover St TELEPHONE NO. 577-7702

BUSINESS ADDRESS 1827 Annarbor TELEPHONE NO. 577-6943

DATE May 30 INITIAL DEPOSIT $ 337.92 APPROVED

MAIL STATEMENTS TO HOME ADDRESS / BUSINESS ADDRESS REMARKS

Money can now be withdrawn from the bank by a *check* (Figure 3.3). The check contains all necessary information about how much to pay (both in numbers and written form to ensure transfer of only the amount intended) and whom to pay ("Pay to the order of"). The computerized numbers at the bottom of the check identify the bank and account to aid the Federal Reserve clearinghouse in processing the check.

Figure 3.3
Check

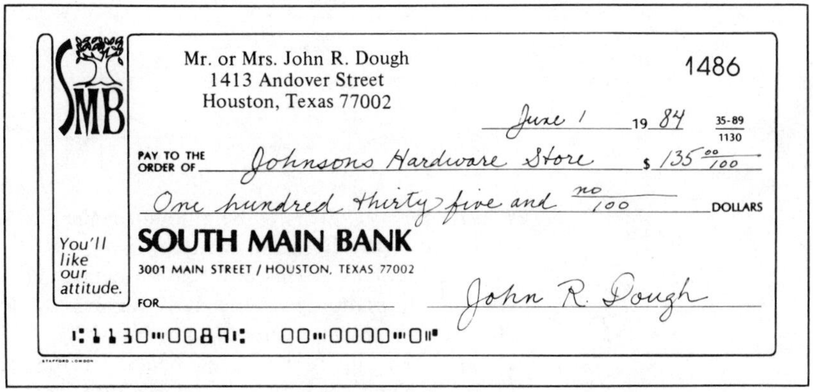
SMB

Mr. or Mrs. John R. Dough
1413 Andover Street
Houston, Texas 77002

1486

June 1 19 84 35-89/1130

PAY TO THE ORDER OF Johnsons Hardware Store $ 135 00/100

One hundred thirty-five and no/100 DOLLARS

SOUTH MAIN BANK
3001 MAIN STREET / HOUSTON, TEXAS 77002

You'll like our attitude.

FOR John R. Dough

⑆1130⑈0089⑆ 00⑈0000⑈0⑈

Future deposits to the checking account should be accompanied by a *deposit slip* (Figure 3.4). The deposit slip contains all information pertinent to the account and the amount deposited. It helps ensure that the deposit is made to the proper account.

Figure 3.4
Deposit Slip

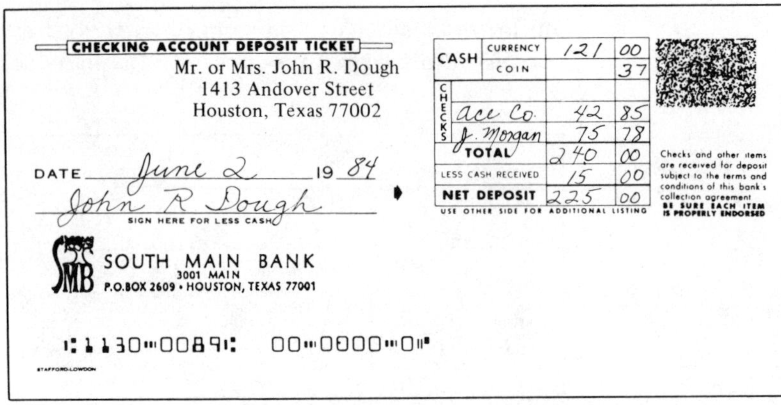

CHECKING ACCOUNT DEPOSIT TICKET
Mr. or Mrs. John R. Dough
1413 Andover Street
Houston, Texas 77002

DATE June 2 19 84
John R Dough
SIGN HERE FOR LESS CASH

SOUTH MAIN BANK
3001 MAIN
P.O.BOX 2609 • HOUSTON, TEXAS 77001

CASH	CURRENCY	121	00
	COIN		37
CHECKS	Ace Co.	42	85
	J. Morgan	75	78
TOTAL		240	00
LESS CASH RECEIVED		15	00
NET DEPOSIT		225	00

USE OTHER SIDE FOR ADDITIONAL LISTING

Checks and other items are received for deposit subject to the terms and conditions of this bank's collection agreement. BE SURE EACH ITEM IS PROPERLY ENDORSED

⑆1130⑈0089⑆ 00⑈0000⑈0⑈

The major record kept by the checking account holder is the *check register* (see Figure 3.5). The check register records all checks given and the current balance in the checking account. This information is vital because a check given without sufficient money in the bank could result in legal action against the account holder. From Figure 3.5 you will see how correctly recording all checks and deposits enables Mr. Dough to know the status (or *balance*) of his account.

Figure 3.5
Check Register

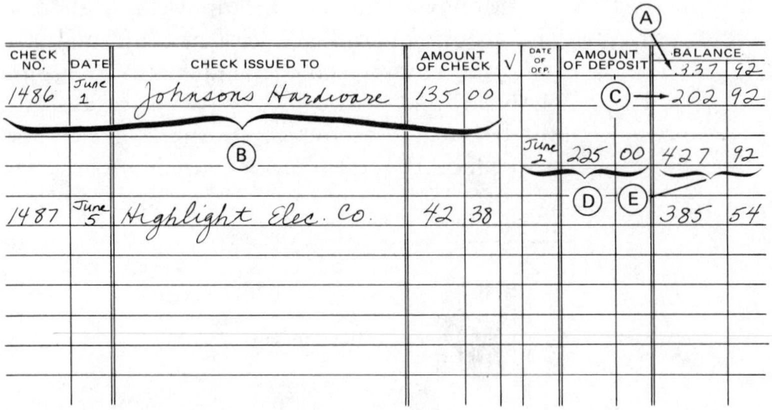

CHECK NO.	DATE	CHECK ISSUED TO	AMOUNT OF CHECK	√	DATE OF DEP.	AMOUNT OF DEPOSIT	BALANCE
							337.92
1486	June 1	Johnsons Hardware	135.00				202.92
					June 2	225.00	427.92
1487	June 5	Highlight Elec. Co.	42.38				385.54

A. *Balance forward*—This is the amount in the checking account *before* the check to Johnson's Hardware was written.

B. *Check information*—This information details the check written. Notice that the entered information gives the check number (1486), the date (June 1), the payee (Johnson's Hardware), and the amount of the check ($135.00).

C. *Balance*—This figure is the new balance in the account. If we take the amount in the checking account *before* check 1486 was given and subtract the amount of check 1486, we have the new balance (or *balance forward*) in the account. Or,

	Balance before check 1486 (i.e., A)	$337.92
less	Amount of check 1486 (i.e., B)	− $135.00
equals	New balance forward (i.e., C)	= $202.92

D. *Deposit*—This information gives the date of the deposit (June 2) and the amount of the deposit ($225.00).

E. *Balance*—Since Mr. Dough put money *into* his account, we would expect the new balance to increase above the old balance. And, of course, it will increase by the amount of the deposit. Hence, the balance forward is the balance prior to the deposit (item C) *plus* the amount of the deposit (item D). Or,

	Balance before deposit (i.e., C)	$202.92
plus	Amount of deposit (i.e., D)	+ $225.00
equals	New balance forward (i.e., E)	= $427.92

Exercises 3.1

■ Use the check register below and record the bank transactions for Rameriez Cleaners in problems 1–6.

Check No.	Date	Check Issued to	Amount of Check	√	Date of Dep.	Amount of Dep.	Balance
3226	6/27	Jones Co.	227 32				2897 42

1. Mr. Rameriez paid Ace Cleaning Supply Company $384.29 with check 3227 on June 29.

2. Check 3228 was given to Mac's Garage for $92.89 for repairs on the delivery truck on July 2.

3. Mr. Rameriez deposited $127.42 on July 3.

4. Check 3229 was written to Building Maintenance Company for $235.00 on July 5.

5. On July 7 check 3230 was written for an incorrect amount. That check was destroyed and check 3231 was written to Reliable Utility Company for the correct amount of $138.62.

6. Mr. Rameriez deposited $326.52 on July 9.

3.2 *The Bank Statement*

bank statement

We have discussed the major record that a checking account holder must keep in order to determine the balance in his account. This record is the check register. However, the bank also keeps a record of transactions. Once a month the bank will send a copy of its records to the account holder in the form of a *bank statement*. This bank statement gives a complete summary of all transactions as recorded by the bank for the checking account during the past month. Figure 3.6 shows and describes a typical bank statement.

Figure 3.6

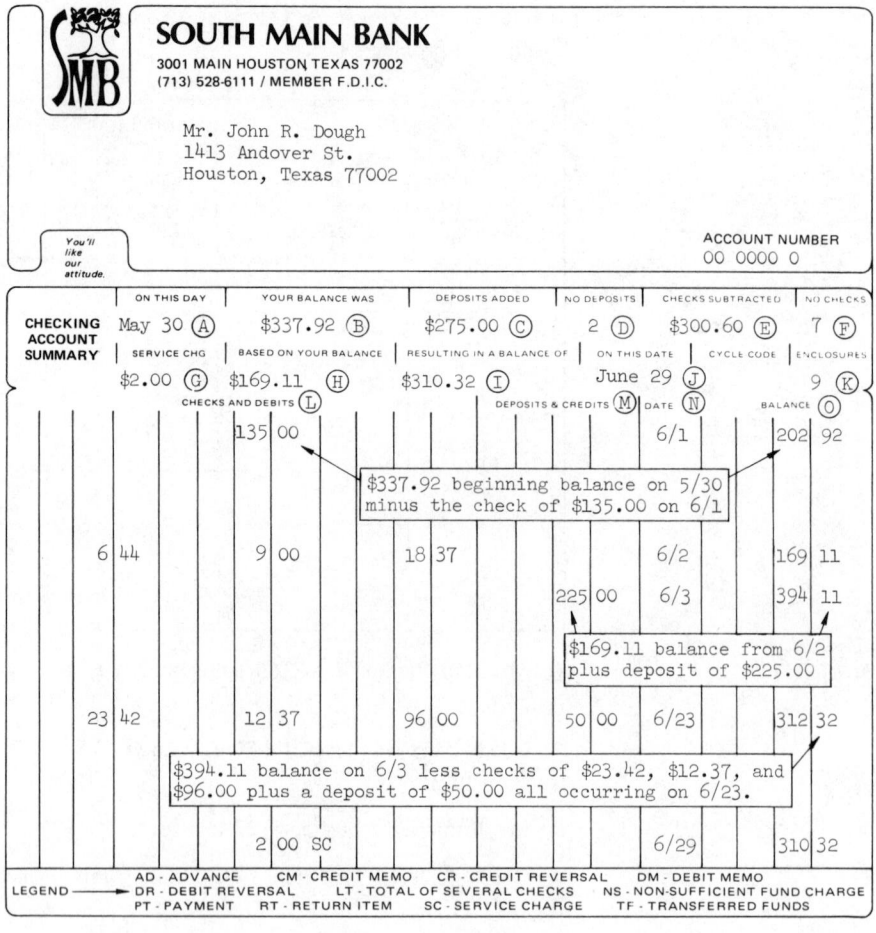

A.   This date is the first day included in the month of the current statement. It will also coincide with the last date (item J) of the previous month's bank statement.

(*art continues on p. 49*)

B. This is the amount of money in the account as of the date in item A. It is also the same amount as shown in item I of the previous month's bank statement.

C. This dollar amount is the sum of all deposits made to the account in the current month. It includes both automatic deposits and deposits made by Mr. Dough.

D. This is the *number* of deposits added to the account in the month.

E. This dollar amount is the sum of all checks paid by the bank during the month. It also includes automatic payments.

F. This is the number of checks and automatic payments made for the account during the month.

G. This dollar amount is the service charge that the bank charges the account holder for processing the deposits and checks.

H. This dollar amount is the balance in the checking account during the month upon which the service charge is calculated.

I. This dollar amount is the balance in the account at the end of the month after all deposits, checks, and service fees for the month have been recorded.

J. This date is the final date of the current bank statement. Any checks or deposits after that date will appear on the next bank statement.

K. This figure is the total number of transaction records processed for the month. It includes deposit slips and checks. These items are returned to the account holder for income tax purposes and proof that the money was paid as the checks directed.

The next items of the bank statement give detailed transactions that resulted in items A through K.

L. These are the checks and "debits" (subtractions) from the account by specific check amount and date (item N).

M. These are the deposits and "credits" (additions) to the account by specific amount and dates (item N).

N. The calendar date the transaction in items L and M was processed by the bank is shown here.

O. This dollar amount is the balance in the checking account at the end of the day following all transactions made (items L and M).

There are some special transactions that can affect the checking account balance without any recurring actions on the part of the account holder. Consider the following example.

Example 1   Suppose that Mr. Dough wants to buy a new car. He can make arrangements for a loan through the bank handling his personal checking account. He may have his monthly payment on the car loan automatically transferred from his account to the bank. Such a *bank draft* procedure could be made with parties outside the bank also. Mr. Dough must remember to record the draft in his check register, however. Otherwise, his account balance will be in error.

Of course, there are two types of transactions that will affect the checking account:

1. Money coming into the account (*automatic deposits*).
2. Money going out of the account (*automatic drafts*).

Automatic deposits could include items such as deposit of Social Security checks by the U.S. government, and deposits of payroll checks from an employer. Automatic drafts could include repayment of installment-type loans (car payments, house payments, etc.) and deposits to a savings account. These transactions will be recorded by the bank on the bank statement but must be recorded by the account holder in his records.

3.3 *Bank Reconciliation (Balancing the Checkbook)*

From our discussion in Section 3.2, you may have noticed an important point in record keeping which is worthy of further discussion. Transactions occur in both the bank's and the account holder's records of which the other is unaware. For example, automatic deposits and drafts occur in the bank records and the account holder is unaware of these transactions *unless* a specific notation is made in the account holder's record. Also, checks have been issued by the account holder that have not "cleared" the bank. To truly reflect the account balance, the bank records must be adjusted for these checks. Our last step in ensuring that all banking transactions have been accurately completed is the matching of the bank statement and the check register to verify that both records show the same dollar balance. This process is known as *bank reconciliation* (or "balancing the checkbook").

balancing the checkbook

Before attempting a bank reconciliation, however, the following steps should be taken on the checkbook records:

1. All checks should be accounted for to ensure that no check was given and not recorded in the check register.
2. All checks returned by the bank should be compared with the check register to verify that the amount of the check given was correctly recorded. While verifying the amount of the checks returned, note which checks have been processed by entering a check mark ($\sqrt{}$) in the check mark column of the check register (see Figure 3.5). Designating checks in this manner facilitates determining which checks have not been received by the bank (a necessary process in balancing the checkbook).
3. All necessary subtractions and additions should be verified to eliminate arithmetical errors.

We can now reconcile the bank statement and the check records.

The procedure for bringing both the check records and the bank records to a *correct balance involves adjusting each record* for those items not yet recorded in that record. The resulting balances for both records should be equal. Figure 3.7 outlines the proper bank reconciliation procedure. This process is used primarily in reconciling business records which involve numerous, complex transactions. We will also discuss the common procedures for personal checking accounts. The principles are the same, but the process is somewhat simpler.

The following examples illustrate adjustments necessary to properly reconcile bank records.

Figure 3.7

Bank Reconciliation Procedure	
Bank Record (Statement)	Checkbook Records (Stubs or Register)
1. Balance shown on bank statement plus 2. Deposits made by the account holder but not recorded by bank minus 3. Checks given by account holder but not yet processed by the bank	1. Balance shown on records plus 2. Automatic deposits received by bank minus 3. Automatic withdrawals, service charges, checks given to the account holder by a person with insufficient funds, etc.
= Bank Statement Balance	= Checkbook Balance

If all transactions are correctly recorded and accounted for, these two balances will be equal.

Note: The adjustments made to the checkbook records are those transactions directly involving the bank, of which the account holder is not aware. Conversely, the adjustments made to the bank records are those transactions directly involving the account holder, of which the bank is not aware. In reconciling records it often helps to determine who was aware of the transaction (bank or account holder) and adjust the other record accordingly.

Example 1   Dr. C. Ching just received his bank statement. His bank statement showed a balance of $1862.21 and his check register shows a balance of $2539.06. Dr. Ching had $387.42 in checks outstanding and had made a deposit of $864.27 that had not been recorded on the bank statement. He has not recorded his monthly automatic draft of $200.00 for medical insurance in his check register. What is Dr. Ching's current checking account balance?

SOLUTION We can arrive at the proper balance by taking the balance from each set of records and adjusting for transactions not noted in that record.

Item	Bank Balance	Checkbook Balance
1. The outstanding checks of $387.42 were recorded in the checkbook but have not cleared the bank. That amount must be deducted from the bank records.	$1862.21 − 387.42	$2539.06
2. The $864.27 deposit has not yet been recorded by the bank, so the bank balance must be increased by that amount.	+ 864.27	
3. The $200 automatic draft has been recorded in the bank's records but not the check records; that amount must be deducted from the check records.		− 200.00
Total (or balance)	$2339.06	$2339.06

Example 2 The Craig Motor Company received its June bank statement, which showed a balance of $10,379.02. At the time Mr. Craig received the bank statement, his check stub balance was $9135.66. In analyzing both records, Mr. Craig found the following:

1. There were three checks totaling $631.46 that Mr. Craig had written which the bank had not processed.
2. The bank had collected a note in the amount of $2030.00 for Craig Motors. The note was owed to Craig Motors but Mr. Craig had arranged for payment directly to the bank.
3. The bank charged Craig Motors $13.50 for the current month's service charge.
4. A check given to Craig Motors by W. W. Wilcox in the amount of $50.00 has been returned for insufficient funds (i.e., Mr. Wilcox did not have enough money in his account to redeem the check).
5. Mr. Craig recorded check number 1998 incorrectly in his records. The check was given for $897.00 and recorded in the stubs as $870.00.
6. Mr. Craig has authorized quarterly payment of his business insurance by bank draft. He had failed to record the $183.00 payment in his records.
7. Mr. Craig has deposited a check for $1144.60 which does not appear on the bank statement.

What is the correct checking account balance for Craig Motor Co. in June?

SOLUTION   We will begin by taking the balances from both of the records (checkbook and bank statement) and adjust each, *keeping in mind that adjustments should be made to the record not affected by the transaction.*

		Balance	
Item		*Bank*	*Checkbook*
		$10,379.02	$9,135.66
1. Outstanding checks in the amount of $631.46 not processed by the bank must be deducted from the bank record.		− 631.46	
2. Since Mr. Craig was unaware that the note for $2030 had been paid, his records must be increased by this amount.			+2,030.00
3. Mr. Craig was not aware of the $13.50 bank service charge, so he must subtract this amount from the checkbook balance.			− 13.50
4. The $50.00 check by Mr. Wilcox has been given by Mr. Craig to the bank as a deposit. He was not aware that Mr. Wilcox had insufficient funds to cover the check; his deposits are thus $50.00 less than he thought.			− 50.00
5. Check number 1998 was recorded for $870.00 and the actual amount was $897.00 or $27.00 more than Mr. Craig's records show. Therefore, his records must be decreased by $27.00.			− 27.00
6. The $183.00 payment by the bank is one that Mr. Craig was not aware of; hence his records should be decreased by that amount.			− 183.00
7. The $1144.60 deposit has not been processed by the bank; hence that amount should be added to the bank statement balance.		+ 1,144.60	
Total (new balance)		$10,892.16	$10,892.16

After proper adjustments, both the checkbook records and the bank statement records have the same total. This indicates that the records balance and the amount in the checking account is $10,892.16.

The procedure for balancing the personal checking account is basically the same. The steps are usually outlined on the back of the bank statement (see Figure 3.8).

The following example shows how to balance the bank statement as generally outlined on the statement.

Figure 3.8

TO BALANCE YOUR STATEMENT

	OUTSTANDING CHECKS		
DATE	CHECK	AMOUNT	
	TOTAL		

1. Compare and mark off endorsed checks, charges and deposits against your checkbook listing.

2. List in your checkbook, all items which appear on this statement but have not been listed in your checkbook. Example: Signature Credit Advances, Automatic Payments, and Check Printing Costs.

3. After completion of the above:

    A.   Enter your Statement Balance   _____

    B.   Add: Amounts Deposited since Date of Statement   _____

    C.   TOTAL: (Add A and B)   _____

    D.   SUBTRACT: Outstanding Check Total   _____

            Balance   _____

Please examine this statement upon receipt and if no error is reported within fourteen (14) days, the account will be considered correct. All items are credited subject to final payment.

Example 3

Ms. Richard's check register currently shows a balance of $187.22. She receives her bank statement, which shows a balance of $329.46. The bank statement reflects a $7.50 charge for printing checks that Ms. Richard had not recorded. Ms. Richard has made a deposit of $275.00 which is not included on this statement. All outstanding checks are shown. Can you help Ms. Richard balance her checkbook?

SOLUTION

We can obtain a balance from the bank statement as follows:

1. Compare and mark off endorsed checks, charges and deposits against your checkbook listing.

2. List in your checkbook, all items which appear on this statement but have not been listed in your checkbook. Example: Signature Credit Advances, Automatic Payments, and Check Printing Costs.

3. After completion of the above:

    A.   Enter your Statement Balance $329.46

    B.   Add: Amounts Deposited since Date of Statement   275.00

    C.   TOTAL: (Add A and B)   604.46

    D.   SUBTRACT: Outstanding Check Total   424.74

            Balance   179.72

OUTSTANDING CHECKS			
DATE	CHECK	AMOUNT	
3/9	1872	78	60
3/9	1873	9	89
3/10	1876	22	39
3/12	1878	110	00
3/15	1879	53	22
3/15	1880	150	64
	TOTAL	424	74

Ms. Richard's checkbook balances. After completing the bank statement balance ($179.72), Ms. Richard must subtract $7.50 from her check register to reflect the cost of printing checks. When she does, the bank balance and the check register balance will both equal $179.72.

As a final step in balancing your checkbook, you should mark the last entry in the check register, i.e., identify the last entry in the check register where the records balance. If the check register and the bank statement do not agree, you must verify your register entries for arithmetic errors. Your mark at the last entry of balance will tell you exactly how far back you must go in checking for errors.

At the beginning of this section, we discussed three steps which should be taken on the check records prior to beginning the bank reconciliation procedure. If done properly, these steps will ensure a true balance after the checkbook register and the bank statement are correctly adjusted for outstanding checks, special transactions, and so on. However, if the two adjusted records do not balance, there is a simple step we can take to help identify the error. If the error has been caused by a *transposition* (i.e., changing the order of the numbers, such as $139.00 recorded as $193.00) or a *slide* (i.e., a misplaced decimal, such as $13.90 recorded as $1.39), the difference between the adjusted check register balance and the adjusted bank statement balance will be evenly divisible by 9.

Example 4

Gary is attempting to balance his checkbook. After properly adjusting both the check register and the bank statement balances, he still has a discrepancy between the two records. Since he did not verify the amount of the checks actually processed by the bank against the amount of the checks recorded in the check register, he did not notice that check number 1362 was written for $164.00 and was recorded as $146.00. Does he have a quick indicator of where his problem is?

SOLUTION

Yes. We know that all necessary adjustments have been correctly made to the records and that they would balance except for check 1362. The discrepancy between the two records is the difference between what was paid by the bank ($164.00) and what was recorded in the check register ($146.00) or $18.00. The difference is evenly divisible by 9 (i.e., $18.00 ÷ 9 = 2), hence Gary suspects a transposition or slide error. He must verify the actual checks against the check register to determine which error is involved.

Note: You may wish to verify that this procedure works on slides, keeping in mind that the difference will be evenly divisible by 9 (but not necessarily a whole number).

Exercises 3.3

■ Reconcile the following bank records using the given information.

1. The check register balance is $527.32 and the bank statement balance is $686.54. Three checks totaling $384.22 and a deposit of $225.00 are outstanding.

Check Register

Check No.	Date	Check Issued to	Amount of Check		√	Date of Dep.	Amount of Deposit		Balance	
									1388	90
1042	6/12	Hanover Co.	42	60	√				1346	30
1043	6/13	Wells Adv.	21	88						
						6/14	375	00		
1044	6/16	Morris Supply	44	11						
1045	6/18	Ace Chemical	73	42						
						6/20	1037	64		
1046	6/21	Tebco Inc.	200	00						
1047	6/21	National Sales	63	75						
1048	6/22	Hart Insurance	247	12						
1049	6/23	Mercantile Nat'l	245	72						
1050	6/24	Mitchell & Garcia	64	94						
1051	6/25	Nat'l Mortgage	365	50						
1052	6/28	Star Leasing	380	27						
1053	6/29	Liberty Gazette	22	00						
						6/30	1000	01		
1054	7/2	Mitcher Co.	18	38						
1055	7/5	Allen & Allen	67	53						
1056	7/6	Reliable Elec. Co.	77	45						
1057	7/9	L. K. Adams	38	00						
1058	7/10	Norton & Evans	46	40						
						7/11	125	00		
1059	7/12	Consumer Gas Co.	34	94						
1060	7/16	Armstrong Elem. Sch.	15	00						
1061	7/17	Pierce Tire Co.	227	00						
1062	7/19	Anderson Plumbers	103	20						
						7/20	250	00		
1063	7/22	Bug Away Exterminator	47	50						
1064	7/22	AAA Service	103	27						

Bank Statement

Checks and Debits				Deposits and Credits		Date	Balance	
						6/16	1346	30
21	88			375	00	6/19		
44	11	73	42	1037	64	6/21		
63	75	200	00			6/23		
64	94	245	72			6/26		
380	27	365	50	1000	01	7/1		
22	00	247	12			7/5		
18	38					7/8		
67	53	77	45			7/9		
				125	00	7/12		
38	00	34	94			7/14		
46	40					7/16		
15	00					7/17		

2. The bank statement balance is $892.29 and the check register balance is $618.02. Four checks totaling $286.52 are outstanding. There is a bank service charge of $12.25 for printing checks.

3. The check register balance is $204.76 and the bank statement balance is $483.65. Outstanding checks total $409.88 and deposits since the bank statement were $330.99. There was also an automatic deposit of $200.00.

4. The bank statement balance is $2294.36 and the check stub balance is $2136.12. Outstanding checks totaled $842.99 and outstanding deposits were $602.25. A check that was deposited (for $82.50) has been returned for insufficient funds.

5. The bank received automatic deposits totaling $235.00 and automatic drafts totaling $185.00. The check register balance was $848.05 and the bank statement balance was $987.80. Outstanding checks totaled $89.75 and there were no deposits.

6. The bank statement balance was $1847.23 and the check register balance was $1268.87. Outstanding checks were $82.29, $146.50, $328.22, and $184.72. New check charges were $15.00. A previously deposited check for $148.37 has been returned.

7. A check register and bank statement are given on pages 56 and 57. Find the final balance of each and reconcile the records to a true balance.

8. The check register and bank statement for Design Interiors are shown. Compute the balances and reconcile the records. Make any necessary adjusting entries.

Check Register

Check No.	Date	Check Issued to	Amount of Check	√	Date of Dep.	Amount of Deposit	Balance
							982 23
227	8/4	Betters Carpets	384 20	√			598 03
228	8/5	VOID					
229	8/5	Custom Cabinets	89 62				
230	8/6	E. Elston	122 50				
					8/7	847 50	
231	8/7	Wallpapers Inc.	289 47				
232	8/8	Kover-all Paints	74 23				
233	8/9	Elec. Co.	224 36				
234	8/10	City Water	42 20				
235	8/10	Cogs Gas Co.	84 35				
					8/11	226 45	
236	8/12	Lamps Aline	129 63				
237	8/12	Edison Fabrics	307 90				
238	8/13	Natural Plants Inc.	84 16				
					8/16	404 00	
239	8/18	Universal Bank	372 50				
					8/19	807 25	
240	8/20	Mercantile Supply	49 50				
241	8/23	A-1 Electric	134 75				
242	8/25	Yellow Pages Ads	219 50				
					8/27	300 00	
243	8/29	Allied Automotive	92 27				

Check Register—*continued*

Check No.	Date	Check Issued to	Amount of Check	√	Date of Dep.	Amount of Deposit	Balance
244	9/1	Copy Cat	61 97				
245	9/3	Anderson & Anderson	98 25				
246	9/6	Tel. Co.	103 47				
247	9/8	Murry's Supply	184 68				
248	9/10	Daily Eagle	78 95				
					9/12	389 50	
249	9/12	Spearman Bros.	146 32				

Bank Statement

Checks and Debits			Deposits and Credits	Date	Balance
122 50			847 50	8/7	1323 03
89 62				8/8	
289 47	74 23			8/9	
224 36	84 35			8/11	
42 20			226 45	8/12	
129 63	307 90			8/14	
125 00 RT			404 00	8/17	
372 50	15 00 SC		807 25	8/20	
49 50	134 75			8/25	
			300 00	8/27	
92 27				9/3	
98 25				9/6	
184 68				9/9	

RT = returned check for insufficient funds
SC = bank service charge

9. Evelyn's bank statement shows a balance of $136.22. That statement does not reflect a deposit of $327.65 and outstanding checks of $354.28. Assuming there are no bank transactions of which Evelyn is unaware, what should her check register balance be?

10. Albert's last bank statement had a balance of $247.29, which did not include his last two deposits (totaling $527.50). He has $489.52 in checks outstanding and a current check register balance of $295.77. The bank statement reflects a $3.00 service charge and $7.50 charged for new checks. Is Albert's check register correct? If not, what would you suspect?

11. The check register showed a balance of $513.82 and the bank statement had a balance of $401.76. There were outstanding deposits of $100.50 and $210.25, and outstanding checks of $184.17, $23.95, $47.62, and $81.20. The service charge totaled $3.25, a previously deposited check for $125.00 had been returned for insufficient funds, and a $10.00 charge had been made by the bank to correct a deposit error. What was the account balance?

12. The bank statement balance was $80.97 and the check register balance was $417.92. Outstanding checks were $19.92, $106.34, $44.99, $137.62, and $88.65. Miscellaneous charges included a returned check ($89.00), an automatic payment ($147.35), the service charge ($4.50), and check-printing costs ($6.00). Outstanding deposits totaled $487.62. What is the correct balance?

3.4 *Negotiable Order of Withdrawal (NOW) Accounts*

Banks have historically been the financial institutions that have provided checking account services. Recall our discussion of the checking process in Section 3.1. Money is deposited by an individual into a checking account. The money stays in the bank until a check is given and is processed through the Federal Reserve System. The length of time between the deposit and the actual payment of the money can be significant. During that time, the bank has use of the money and it does not have to pay interest to the account holder. Other financial institutions, primarily savings and loan associations, have long been aware of this "cash flow" situation. Personnel in that industry felt they could gain access to much more money if they could pay interest on money in the account (as a savings account) yet still allow the convenience of checking arrangements (as a checking account). To provide such an arrangement, negotiable order of withdrawal (NOW) accounts were formed. NOW accounts are similar to checking accounts, but they have two important differences:

1. Interest is paid on the money deposited in the NOW account.
2. A NOW account is not technically a demand account (legally, payments from the account may be delayed for 30–90 days; however, this restriction is usually not enforced).

The basic processes of a NOW account are similar to those of a checking account. Deposits are made to the account (using deposit slips). When the account holder chooses to use the money, he gives a withdrawal order that looks like a check. The withdrawal order is "cleared" through the Federal Reserve System like a check.

Other minor differences between checking accounts and NOW accounts should be mentioned. With a checking account, you receive your canceled (paid) checks with your bank statement. NOW accounts usually provide a detailed account statement (identifying order number and amount paid) but don't return the actual withdrawal orders. Most withdrawal orders are printed with two parts so that you "write" a copy of the order for your records at the same time that you write the order itself. Restrictions usually apply to NOW accounts. These restrictions may vary substantially depending on the financial institution providing the account service. The minimum initial deposit required may vary from as little as $200 to as much as $3000; in addition, you must maintain a minimum balance (again the amount varies) at all times or pay a monthly service charge.

Many NOW accounts offer greater flexibility in how money may be withdrawn than do checking accounts. Automatic deposits and drafts are available just as with checking accounts; however, many NOW accounts also offer telephone transaction capability. You simply call the financial institution and, by giving proper identification codes, verbally authorize payments.

Record keeping for a NOW account is just like record keeping for checks. There is an "order register" for recording withdrawal orders given, posting deposits, and bringing the balance forward. A NOW account is reconciled in the same manner as a bank statement for a checking account. When the NOW account statement arrives, orders that have been paid are compared with the order register to determine the amount of orders outstanding. Automatic deposits and payments must be added or subtracted as appropriate if they have not been recorded in the order register. However, the NOW account statement will contain the *interest* earned on the NOW account for that month. This interest must be added to the balance in the order register to reconcile the account correctly.

Example 1   Fred Green has a NOW account at Universal Savings and Loan. His November statement balance was $835.12 and his order register showed a balance of $507.35. The following orders were outstanding: no. 1309, $107.16; no. 1313, $16.48; no. 1315, $28.67; no. 1316, $187.85; and no. 1317, $84.22. The account statement showed interest of $2.17 earned for the month, and it also reflected two telephone authorizations (totaling $98.78) that Fred had not recorded in his order register. What is the true balance in Fred's account?

SOLUTION   We reconcile these records by making appropriate changes to the record not involved in the actual transaction.

	Order Register	Account Statement
Record balance	$507.35	$835.12
Less: Outstanding orders		
1309		− 107.16
1313		− 16.48
1315		− 28.67
1316		− 187.85
1317		− 84.22
Telephone transactions	− 98.78	
Plus: Interest on account	+ 2.17	
Balance	$410.74	$410.74

The true balance in the account is $410.74.

Exercises 3.4

1. The balance in a NOW account statement is $412.36 and the order register balance is $202.29. Since the balance in the account dropped below the minimum amount required, there was a $4.00 service charge. Interest earned for the month was $1.09 and there are orders totaling $212.98 outstanding. Reconcile the account to a true balance.

2. M. Charles has a balance of $1837.42 in his order of withdrawal register. His statement from Deep Water Savings and Loan shows a balance of $1652.56 and $2.38 in interest earned for the month. His minimum balance in the account during the month exceeded the $1000 minimum required by Deep Water; therefore, there were no service charges on the account. Withdrawal orders outstanding total $489.46 and deposits mailed since the account statement total $587.32. Two telephone transactions were authorized by Mr. Charles during the month; one for $133.48, which had been recorded, and one for $89.38, which Mr. Charles forgot. Reconcile the account.

3. R. Liebscher maintains a NOW account at the Right Bank of Commerce. The bank requires that a minimum balance of $1500 be kept in the account at all times or a service charge of $4.50 per month is made. In addition, the bank charges a fee of $0.10 per withdrawal order processed. Mr. Liebscher's July statement showed a balance of $2204.36, with $8.28 in interest earned, and that 21 withdrawal orders were processed. His account balance did not drop below $1500. Withdrawal orders outstanding total $843.76 and a deposit of $500 has been mailed since the date of the statement.
     a. What is the true balance of the account?
     b. What should Mr. Liebscher's register show before reconciling, assuming no errors have been made?

4. Reconcile a NOW account given the following information
     a. Statement balance $1838.88

b. Service charge $3.00
c. Interest earned $4.89
d. Deposits made since the date of the statement (1) $304.25
                                                       (2) $100.00
e. Telephone payment not recorded $29.90
f. Withdrawal order register balance $1877.06
g. Outstanding withdrawal orders   (1) $124.28
                                                       (2) $13.47
                                                       (3) $91.89
                                                       (4) $122.81
                                                       (5) $41.63

5. Mary Ellen is trying to reconcile her NOW account statement. The balance shown on her statement is $1134.34 with interest of $3.95 earned for the month. She has automatic payments made for her rent ($225.00) and her car ($178.44); she hasn't recorded either in her register. Outstanding withdrawal orders total $493.27 and deposits added but not processed total $645.28. She telephoned a payment authorization for $39.85 but recorded it in her register as $38.95. Her register balance now shows $1686.74. What is the true balance in the account?

6. The balance on a NOW account statement is $976.42 and the balance on the order register is $837.61. There were orders totaling $167.38 outstanding and a telephone payment (of $19.85) not recorded by the account holder. There was also interest earned of $3.78 and a charge of $12.50 for new orders. What is the account balance?

7. L. Ludwig has a balance of $1371.49 in her NOW order register. Her monthly statement shows a balance of $1395.34, and $4.81 in interest earned. There were no service charges on the account, outstanding orders totaled $219.04, and a deposit of $200.00 had been mailed since the account statement was prepared. Reconcile the account.

8. Mr. Fritch's savings and loan association requires a minimum balance of $1000 in the account at all times; otherwise, a service charge of $5.00 is made for the month. The savings and loan also charges $0.10 per order processed. Mr. Fritch's September statement shows a balance of $1108.73 (although at one time during the month the balance was $901.18). Interest earned for the month was $5.81 and 27 orders were processed by the savings and loan association. Mr. Fritch's order register shows a balance of $1078.56 and there are orders totaling $317.06 outstanding. Mr. Fritch also made a deposit of $285.00 on the day he received his statement. What is the account balance?

9. Reconcile a NOW account given the following information:
  a. Statement balance $1104.36
  b. Interest earned $2.96
  c. Service charges $3.00
  d. Telephone payment not recorded $96.38
  e. Withdrawal order register balance $1307.90
  f. Deposits made since the date of the statement (1) $311.00
                                                        (2) $196.04

g. Outstanding withdrawal orders

(1) $11.37
(2) $146.33
(3) $99.06
(4) $143.16

10. Robert Wilson is trying to reconcile his NOW account balance. The balance shown on his statement is $1437.42; and in his register, the balance is $1546.69. Interest earned for the month was $6.03 and automatic payments of $136.00 and $95.00 were made but not recorded. Outstanding orders totaled $291.63 and deposits added but not processed amounted to $174.13. He telephoned a payment authorization of $126.42 but recorded it in his register as $124.62. What is the true balance in Robert's account?

Review Exercises / Chapter 3

■ Mr. John Dough received the following bank statement and canceled (or paid) checks for last month's activity in his checking account. His check register is also shown. Reconcile the two records to determine the balance in his account using Figure 3.9.

Figure 3.9
Check Register

CHECK NO.	DATE	CHECK ISSUED TO	AMOUNT OF CHECK		√	DATE OF DEP.	AMOUNT OF DEPOSIT		BALANCE	
									351	05
103	6/19	Discount Barn	137	12					213	93
104	6/20	Hi-Top Cleaners	12	27	√				201	66
105	6/25	Rx Drug Store	28	46	√				173	20
106	6/29	Rogers Brothers	46	00					127	20
107	6/30	Chic Shop	58	17					69	03
						7/1	804	32	873	35
108	7/2	Mid Continent Mortgage Co.	268	40					604	95
109	7/3	Elec Co	38	27					566	68
110	7/5	Food Mart	120	00					446	68
111	7/8	Telephone Co	14	68					432	00
112	7/10	Minit Mart	64	82					367	18
						7/12	120	00	487	18
113	7/18	Gas Co	29	56					457	62
114	7/20	Handy Man	48	54					409	08
115	7/22	Nolans	23	99					385	09
116	7/25	Fashion Plate	89	47					295	62
117	7/28	Interior Designs	76	38					219	24
						7/29	250	00	469	24
118	8/1	Mid. Cont. Mortgage	268	40					200	84
119	8/3	Elec Co.	47	95					152	89
120	8/4	Food Midgit	136	12					16	77
						8/5	465	00	481	77
121	8/5	Telephone Co.	22	12					459	65

REMEMBER TO RECORD AUTOMATIC PAYMENTS / DEPOSITS ON DATE AUTHORIZED.

[*Canceled (or paid) checks are shown on pages 65–69.*]

SOUTH MAIN BANK

3001 MAIN HOUSTON TEXAS 77002
(713) 528-6111 / MEMBER F.D.I.C.

Mr. John R. Dough
1413 Andover St.
Houston, Texas 77002

You'll like our attitude.

ACCOUNT NUMBER
00 0000 0

CHECKING ACCOUNT SUMMARY	ON THIS DAY	YOUR BALANCE WAS	DEPOSITS ADDED	NO DEPOSITS	CHECKS SUBTRACTED	NO CHECKS
	June 30	$310.32	$1,174.32	3	$1,123.90	13
	SERVICE CHG	BASED ON YOUR BALANCE	RESULTING IN A BALANCE OF	ON THIS DATE	CYCLE CODE	ENCLOSURES
	$3.00	$110.74	$357.74	July 29		16

CHECKS AND DEBITS					DEPOSITS & CREDITS	DATE	BALANCE
		58 17			804 32	7/1	1 056 47
		268 40				7/2	788 07
		137 12				7/3	650 95
	14 68	120 00				7/7	516 27
		38 27				7/8	478 00
		64 82				7/11	413 18
					120 00	7/12	533 18
		154 50 PT				7/15	378 68
	48 54	29 56				7/21	300 58
	89 47	76 38		23 99		7/28	110 74
					250 00	7/29	360 74
	46 00	3 00 SC				7/29	311 74

LEGEND

AD - ADVANCE	CM - CREDIT MEMO	CR - CREDIT REVERSAL	DM - DEBIT MEMO
DR - DEBIT REVERSAL	LT - TOTAL OF SEVERAL CHECKS		NS - NON SUFFICIENT FUND CHARGE
PT - PAYMENT	RT - RETURN ITEM	SC - SERVICE CHARGE	TF - TRANSFERRED FUNDS

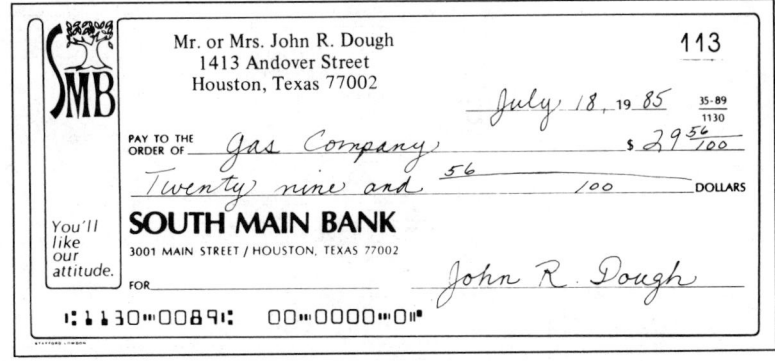

Mr. or Mrs. John R. Dough
1413 Andover Street
Houston, Texas 77002

113

July 18, 19 85   35-89
                   1130

PAY TO THE ORDER OF Gas Company $ 29 56/100

Twenty nine and 56/100 DOLLARS

You'll like our attitude.

SOUTH MAIN BANK
3001 MAIN STREET / HOUSTON, TEXAS 77002

John R. Dough

FOR

⑆1130⑆0089⑆   00⑆0000⑆0⑆

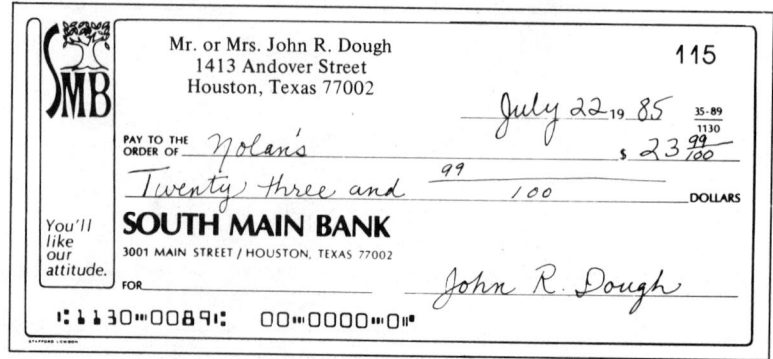

Mr. or Mrs. John R. Dough
1413 Andover Street
Houston, Texas 77002

106

SMB

June 29, 19 85   35-89 / 1130

PAY TO THE ORDER OF   Rogers Brothers $ 46 00/100

Forty, six and   no   100   DOLLARS

You'll like our attitude.

SOUTH MAIN BANK

3001 MAIN STREET / HOUSTON, TEXAS 77002

FOR _____   John R. Dough

⑈1130⑈0089⑈   00⑈0000⑈0⑈

☰ **CHECKING ACCOUNT DEPOSIT TICKET** ☰

Mr. or Mrs. John R. Dough
1413 Andover Street
Houston, Texas 77002

CASH	CURRENCY	15	00
	COIN	5	00
CHECKS	Adams Co	100	00

DATE _____ 7/12 _____ 19 85

John R. Dough
SIGN HERE FOR LESS CASH

TOTAL	120	00
LESS CASH RECEIVED		
NET DEPOSIT	120	00
USE OTHER SIDE FOR ADDITIONAL LISTING

Checks and other items are received for deposit subject to the terms and conditions of this bank's collection agreement. **BE SURE EACH ITEM IS PROPERLY ENDORSED**

SMB   SOUTH MAIN BANK
3001 MAIN
P.O.BOX 2609 • HOUSTON, TEXAS 77002

⑈1130⑈0089⑈   00⑈0000⑈0⑈

Mr. or Mrs. John R. Dough
1413 Andover Street
Houston, Texas 77002

107

SMB

June 30, 1985   35-89 / 1130

PAY TO THE ORDER OF   Chic Shop $ 58 17/100

Fifty eight and   17   100   DOLLARS

You'll like our attitude.

SOUTH MAIN BANK
3001 MAIN STREET / HOUSTON, TEXAS 77002

FOR _____   John R. Dough

⑈1130⑈0089⑈   00⑈0000⑈0⑈

Mr. or Mrs. John R. Dough
1413 Andover Street
Houston, Texas 77002

115

SMB

July 22, 19 85   35-89 / 1130

PAY TO THE ORDER OF   Nolan's $ 23 99/100

Twenty three and   99   100   DOLLARS

You'll like our attitude.

SOUTH MAIN BANK
3001 MAIN STREET / HOUSTON, TEXAS 77002

FOR _____   John R. Dough

⑈1130⑈0089⑈   00⑈0000⑈0⑈

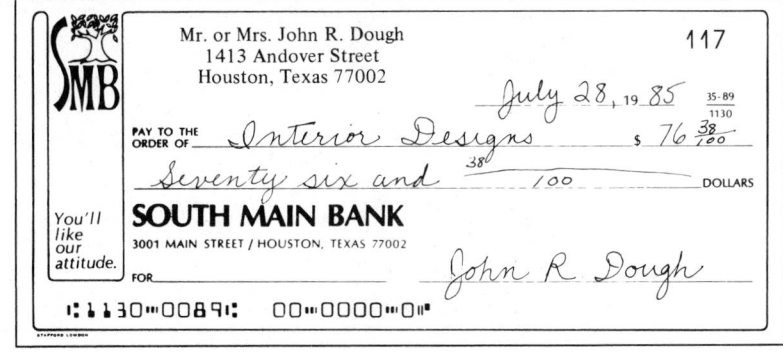

Check 116

Mr. or Mrs. John R. Dough
1413 Andover Street
Houston, Texas 77002

116

July 25, 19 85   35-89 / 1130

PAY TO THE ORDER OF _Fashion Plate_ $ 89 47/100

Eighty nine and 47/100   DOLLARS

You'll like our attitude.

SOUTH MAIN BANK
3001 MAIN STREET / HOUSTON, TEXAS 77002

FOR ___   John R. Dough

⑆1130⑈0089⑆ 00⑈0000⑈0⑊

Deposit Ticket

☰ CHECKING ACCOUNT DEPOSIT TICKET ☰
Mr. or Mrs. John R. Dough
1413 Andover Street
Houston, Texas 77002

CASH	CURRENCY		
	COIN		
CHECKS	Tebco	804	32
TOTAL			
LESS CASH RECEIVED			
NET DEPOSIT		804	32

USE OTHER SIDE FOR ADDITIONAL LISTING

DATE July 1 19 85

SIGN HERE FOR LESS CASH

Checks and other items are received for deposit subject to the terms and conditions of this bank's collection agreement. **BE SURE EACH ITEM IS PROPERLY ENDORSED**

SOUTH MAIN BANK
3001 MAIN
P.O.BOX 2609 • HOUSTON, TEXAS 77002

⑆1130⑈0089⑆ 00⑈0000⑈0⑊

Check 108

Mr. or Mrs. John R. Dough
1413 Andover Street
Houston, Texas 77002

108

July 2, 19 85   35-89 / 1130

PAY TO THE ORDER OF _Mid Continent Mortgage Co_ $ 268 40/100

Two hundred sixty eight and 40/100   DOLLARS

You'll like our attitude.

SOUTH MAIN BANK
3001 MAIN STREET / HOUSTON, TEXAS 77002

FOR ___   John R. Dough

⑆1130⑈0089⑆ 00⑈0000⑈0⑊

Check 117

Mr. or Mrs. John R. Dough
1413 Andover Street
Houston, Texas 77002

117

July 28, 19 85   35-89 / 1130

PAY TO THE ORDER OF _Interior Designs_ $ 76 38/100

Seventy six and 38/100   DOLLARS

You'll like our attitude.

SOUTH MAIN BANK
3001 MAIN STREET / HOUSTON, TEXAS 77002

FOR ___   John R. Dough

⑆1130⑈0089⑆ 00⑈0000⑈0⑊

SOUTH MAIN BANK		Date: 07-15-85	Account Number: 00-0000-0
HOUSTON, TEXAS			
WE CHARGE YOUR ACCOUNT FOR ITEMS LISTED AS FOLLOWS:			AMOUNT
Installment Loan #34125 due monthly on the 15th per your instructions.			$154. 50
		TOTAL ➤	$154. 50

Made By:	Name: Mr. John R. Dough
Approved:	Address: 1413 Andover St.
	City: Houston, Texas 77002

⑆1130⑉0089⑆

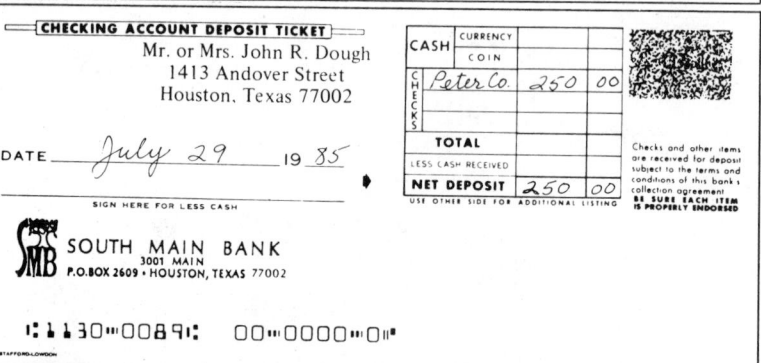

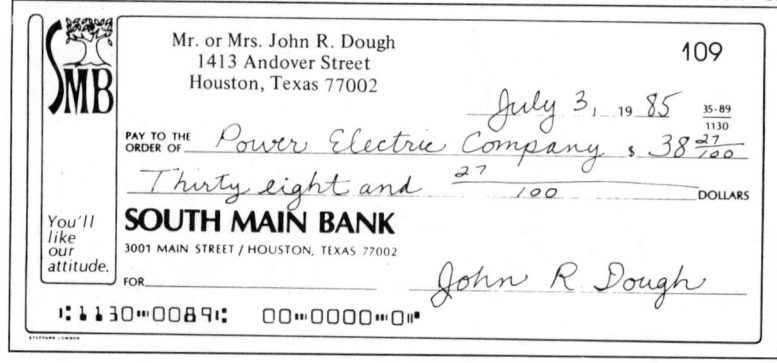

S M B

Mr. or Mrs. John R. Dough
1413 Andover Street
Houston, Texas 77002

111

July 8, 19 85   35-89 / 1130

PAY TO THE ORDER OF _Telephone Company_ $ 14 68/100

Fourteen and 68/100   DOLLARS

You'll like our attitude.

SOUTH MAIN BANK
3001 MAIN STREET / HOUSTON, TEXAS 77002

FOR _____   John R. Dough

⑈1130⑈0089⑈   00⑈0000⑈0⑈

S M B

Mr. or Mrs. John R. Dough
1413 Andover Street
Houston, Texas 77002

112

July 10, 19 85   35-89 / 1130

PAY TO THE ORDER OF _Mini Mart_ $ 64 82/100

Sixty four and 82/100   DOLLARS

You'll like our attitude.

SOUTH MAIN BANK
3001 MAIN STREET / HOUSTON, TEXAS 77002

FOR _____   John R. Dough

⑈1130⑈0089⑈   00⑈0000⑈0⑈

S M B

Mr. or Mrs. John R. Dough
1413 Andover Street
Houston, Texas 77002

114

July 20, 19 85   35-89 / 1130

PAY TO THE ORDER OF _Handy Man_ $ 48 54/100

Forty eight and 54/100   DOLLARS

You'll like our attitude.

SOUTH MAIN BANK
3001 MAIN STREET / HOUSTON, TEXAS 77002

FOR _____   John R. Dough

⑈1130⑈0089⑈   00⑈0000⑈0⑈

S M B

Mr. or Mrs. John R. Dough
1413 Andover Street
Houston, Texas 77002

103

June 19, 19 85   35-89 / 1130

PAY TO THE ORDER OF _Discount Barn_ $ 137 12/100

One hundred thirty seven and 12/100   DOLLARS

You'll like our attitude.

SOUTH MAIN BANK
3001 MAIN STREET / HOUSTON, TEXAS 77002

FOR _____   John R. Dough

⑈1130⑈0089⑈   00⑈0000⑈0⑈

TO BALANCE YOUR STATEMENT

	OUTSTANDING CHECKS		
DATE	CHECK	AMOUNT	
	TOTAL		

1. Compare and mark off endorsed checks, charges and deposits against your checkbook listing.

2. List in your checkbook, all items which appear on this statement but have not been listed in your checkbook. Example: Signature Credit Advances, Automatic Payments, and Check Printing Costs.

3. After completion of the above:

   A.   Enter your Statement Balance   _____

   B.   Add: Amounts Deposited since Date of Statement   _____

   C.   TOTAL: (Add A and B)   _____

   D.   SUBTRACT: Outstanding Check Total   _____

   Balance   _____

Please examine this statement upon receipt and if no error is reported within fourteen (14) days, the account will be considered correct. All items are credited subject to final payment.

Chapter Test / *Chapter 3*

1. Define the following terms

    a. check   *b*. (account) balance

    c. check register   *d*. bank statement

    e. NOW account   *f*. bank reconciliation

2. The check register balance is $437.85 and the bank statement balance is $320.01. There are 6 checks (totaling $212.86) and a deposit of $330.70 not yet processed by the bank. What is the reconciled balance?

3. The bank statement shows a balance of $1137.82 and the check register balance is $1514.83. A review of the records showed that deposits of $2137.02 and checks totaling $1864.28 had not been processed. An automatic payment of $250.50 and an automatic deposit of $148.00 had been processed but not recorded. The bank's service charge for the month was $1.77. What is the reconciled balance?

4. Judith's check register shows a balance of $306.42. The check register does not reflect an automatic payment from the account for $89.95 and a bank service charge of $2.00. A check-printing charge of $8.50 has not been recorded. Assuming that no errors have been made, what should be the balance shown on Judith's bank statement?

5. Armando received a bank statement showing a balance of $417.64. After the statement had been mailed, Armando made a deposit of $375.00. Outstanding checks total $386.66. There was no monthly service charge, but Armando had failed to record an automatic payment of $233.00. Assuming no other errors or activity of which Armando is unaware, what should be the balance in his check register?

6. Kevin has a NOW account at the Great Universal Savings and Loan. His account statement for this month shows a balance of $1836.52. Interest paid for the month was $4.63. Not shown on the statement are deposits of $414.89 and outstanding orders of withdrawal totaling $638.11. There was no service charge on the account. Kevin's order register shows a balance of $1608.67. Do the records agree? What is the reconciled balance?

7. The statement balance in a NOW account shows $2847.41. Outstanding orders totaling $1138.49 and a deposit of $407.52 have not been recorded. Also, an automatic deposit of $104.64 and the cost of new withdrawal orders ($8.75) have not been recorded in the register. Interest paid for the month is $6.04. If the register balance is $2014.51, do the records agree? What is the reconciled balance?

8. L. Riddell has just received her NOW account statement. It shows a balance of $836.56, which includes $1.63 paid in interest. Service charges on the account were $5.00. Ms. Riddell's register showed a balance of $777.31. Outstanding checks totaled $137.62. There was also a check previously deposited by Ms. Riddell in the amount of $75.00 that has been returned because of insufficient funds. What is the reconciled balance?

9. The balance on the bank statement is $609.46 and the balance in the check register is $470.09. The following checks are outstanding: no. 629, $84.36; no. 631, $17.40; no. 638, $47.65; no. 639, $77.06; and no. 640, $36.40. Check no. 625 in the amount of $22.75 was recorded in the check register as $27.25. The bank's service charge was $3.00 and a deposit of $125.00 has not been processed by the bank. Reconcile the true balance.

10. Roberta M. received her NOW account statement, which showed a balance of $477.65. Her lowest balance dropped below the required minimum; therefore, she had to pay a service charge of $5.00. The interest earned on the account was $1.07 and checks outstanding totaled $264.33. Deposits not shown totaled $375.00 and a telephoned payment request for $37.50 had not been recorded by Roberta. Reconcile the records assuming the register balance was $629.75.

CHAPTER 4

Percent

INTRODUCTION

The word "percent" is derived from the Latin "per centum," which literally means "by the hundred." This division into 100 parts is well suited to business applications, for two reasons: first, division by 100 can be readily accomplished merely by moving the decimal point; and second, our money system is based on the dollar, which is composed of 100 cents. Consequently, percents are frequently encountered in our everyday world. Discounts on sale items and interest rates on loans and investments are expressed in percent. To understand such business transactions, you must know the meaning of percents and how to use them.

4.1 Percents and Fractions

Since percent literally means "by the 100," it is no surprise that percent is a fraction with a denominator of 100.

Definition

What is percent? **Percent** is a fraction having a denominator of 100:

$$x \text{ percent} = \frac{x}{100}$$

For example, 2 percent means $\frac{2}{100}$, 5.5 percent means $\frac{5.5}{100}$, and so on.

The use of percent is so common that one would expect to find a "shorthand notation" for percent that is easy to write and universally the percent symbol understood. Such a shorthand notation (or symbol) does exist. The percent symbol is "%." It is obtained from the 100 denominator by slanting the "1" and placing it between the two "0's." The percent symbol is placed on the right-hand side of the numerator and replaces the denominator of 100. Sometimes the left-hand zero and the slanted "one" are connected in the percent symbol, giving "%." This change is simply a matter of style. The symbols "%" and "%" mean the same thing.

---

fraction to percent | **Changing a Fraction to a Percent**

To change a fraction (with a denominator of 100) to a percent, change the 100 to % and place it to the right of the numerator.

Note: The percent % is used *in place of* the 100.

Example 1 | Change the following fractions to percents.

a. $\dfrac{5}{100}$ b. $\dfrac{2.3}{100}$ c. $\dfrac{253}{100}$

SOLUTION | a. $\dfrac{5}{100} = 5\%$ b. $\dfrac{2.3}{100} = 2.3\%$ c. $\dfrac{253}{100} = 253\%$

How could we change a fraction *that does not have a denominator of 100* to percent? Fractions *not having a denominator of 100* may be converted to an equivalent form having a denominator of 100. For example, $\dfrac{4}{25}$ can be converted to $\dfrac{16}{100}$, which is 16%.

Example 2 | Express each of the following fractions as a percent.

a. $\dfrac{5}{100}$ b. $\dfrac{3}{20}$ c. $\dfrac{7}{50}$

SOLUTION | a. By definition, $\dfrac{5}{100} = 5\%$.

b. $\dfrac{3}{20} = \dfrac{3 \times 5}{20 \times 5} = \dfrac{15}{100} = 15\%$

c. $\dfrac{7}{50} = \dfrac{7 \times 2}{50 \times 2} = \dfrac{14}{100} = 14\%$

Some fractions, such as $\frac{1}{8}$, cannot be easily changed to a denominator of 100. In this case we will change the fraction to a decimal $\left(\frac{1}{8} = 0.125\right)$, then change the decimal to a percent, as will be shown in Section 4.2.

Sometimes it is desirable to change percents to fractions. To do this, reverse the process used in Example 1.

percent to fraction

Changing a Percent to a Fraction

To change a percent to a fraction, change the % to 100 and place it as the denominator of a fraction whose numerator is the given percent.

Example 3   Change the following percents to fractions (reduce to lowest terms).

a. 6%   *b.* 7.5%

SOLUTION   *a.* $6\% = \frac{6}{100} = \frac{3}{50}$

b. $7.5\% = \frac{7.5}{100} = \frac{75}{1000} = \frac{3}{40}$

Exercises 4.1

■ Change the following fractions to percents.

1. $\frac{7}{100}$ **2.** $\frac{2}{100}$ **3.** $\frac{14}{100}$ **4.** $\frac{4}{25}$ **5.** $\frac{3}{50}$ **6.** $\frac{3}{10}$ **7.** $\frac{3}{2}$ **8.** $\frac{14}{25}$

9. $\frac{1}{4}$ **10.** $\frac{6}{20}$

■ Change the following percents to fractions. Reduce the fraction to lowest terms.

11. 12%   **12.** 50%   **13.** 32%   **14.** 17%   **15.** 5.5%   **16.** $7\frac{3}{4}\%$

17. $5\frac{1}{4}\%$ **18.** 6.28%

19. If Mac inherits $1000 of a $5000 estate, what percent did he receive?

20. If 100 of 500 people like Tasty Toothpaste, what percent like it?

21. An item that costs $100 sells for $125. The cost is what percent of the selling price?

22. What does 1000% equal?

4.2 *Percents and Decimals*

As you know, decimals are frequently used in business, as are percents and fractions. Therefore, it may be useful to convert percents to decimals, and vice versa.

Decimals are changed to percent by moving the decimal point and attaching the % symbol.

decimal to percent

Changing a Decimal to a Percent

To change a decimal to a percent, move the decimal point two places *to the right* and attach the percent symbol (on the right side of the resulting number).

For example, 2.856 is 285.6%. The foregoing rule is a shortcut for the following process.

$$2.856 = 2.856 \times 1$$

But $1 = \dfrac{100}{100}$, so

$$= 2.856 \times \frac{100}{100}$$

By using the definition of multiplication of fractions, we get

$$= \frac{285.6}{100}$$

which is

$$= 285.6\%$$

Since the detailed change from a decimal to a percent is rather long and involved, the shortcut is a useful, laborsaving device.

Example 1

Change 0.034, 2.713, and 37 to percents.

SOLUTION

In each case, move the decimal point two places to the right and attach the "%" symbol.

$$0.034 = 3.4\% \qquad 2.713 = 271.3\% \qquad \text{and } 37 = 3700\%$$

Note that it is sometimes necessary to attach extra zeros (on the right side of the number) to facilitate the conversion to percent. For instance, $2.3 = 230\%$. This is similar to the conversion of 37 to 3700% in Example 1.

Now consider the conversion of a percent to a decimal. Suppose that an item is on sale for 25% off of the regular price. To compute the amount of savings, the percent of discount is multiplied times the regular selling price. However, to do this, the percent should be changed to a decimal.

percent to decimal   **Changing a Percent to a Decimal**

To change a percent to a decimal, move the decimal two places to the left and remove the percent symbol.

That is, $35.5\% = 0.355$ in decimals. Again, this can be done in detail as follows:

$$35.5\% = \frac{35.5}{100} \qquad \text{Now, divide 35.5 by 100, and get}$$

$$= 0.355$$

Example 2   Change the following percents to decimals.

    a. 60% ***b.*** 8% ***c.*** 2.3% ***d.*** $5\frac{1}{2}\%$

SOLUTION
    a. $60\% = 0.60$ or 0.6
    b. $8\% = 0.08$. In order to move the decimal point two places to the left, a zero must be included as a placeholder.
    c. $2.3\% = 0.023$
    d. $5\frac{1}{2}\% = 0.05\frac{1}{2}$

Remember, the rules are shortcuts. If you forget which way to move the decimal, just "unscramble" the % symbol and put back the denominator of 100. Then convert the problem by the longer procedure.

Fractions Again

You saw in Section 4.1 that fractions could be expressed as percents by expressing them in an equivalent form having a denominator of 100. However, fractions such as 1/8 cannot be conveniently expressed with a denominator of 100. Hence, another method was promised.

At this point, we know how to change a fraction to a decimal and how to change a decimal to percent. By combining this knowledge, we can convert *any* fraction to a percent, as follows:

fraction to percent
$$\text{change fraction} \xrightarrow{\text{to}} \text{decimal} \xrightarrow{\text{to}} \text{percent}$$

This process is long but effective. For example,

$$\frac{1}{8} \quad \rightarrow \quad 0.125 \quad \rightarrow \quad 12.5\%$$
$$\text{fraction} \quad \text{decimal} \quad \text{percent}$$

The following example illustrates this process.

Example 3   Convert the following fractions to percents.

   a. $\dfrac{1}{4}$ *b.* $\dfrac{3}{8}$ *c.* $\dfrac{2}{5}$

SOLUTION   *a.* $\dfrac{1}{4} = 1 \div 4 = 0.25 = 25\%$

              b. $\dfrac{3}{8} = 3 \div 8 = 0.375 = 37.5\%$

              c. $\dfrac{2}{5} = 2 \div 5 = 0.4 = 40\%$

   To convert a fraction (that is, a nonterminating decimal) such as $\frac{1}{3}$ to a percent requires three steps.

Step 1. Divide the numerator by the denominator until you have *two digits to the right* of the decimal point in the quotient.

Step 2. Express the quotient as a mixed number. That is,

$$\frac{1}{3} = 3\overline{\smash{)}\begin{array}{r} 0.33 \\ 1.00 \\ -9 \\ \hline 10 \\ -9 \\ \hline 1 \end{array}} \quad \text{or} \quad 0.33\tfrac{1}{3}$$

Step 3. The mixed number ($0.33\frac{1}{3}$) can be expressed as a percent by deleting the decimal point and attaching the % symbol. Hence, $\frac{1}{3} = 0.33\frac{1}{3} = 33\frac{1}{3}\%$.

Example 4   Express $\frac{1}{7}$ as a percent.

SOLUTION   **Step 1.** $\begin{array}{r} 0.14 \\ 7\overline{\smash{)}1.00} \\ -7 \\ \hline 30 \\ 28 \\ \hline 2 \end{array}$

Step 2. $0.14\frac{2}{7}$

Step 3. $14\frac{2}{7}\%$

Exercises 4.2

■ Convert the following decimals to percents.

1. 0.25   **2.** 0.07   **3.** 4.81   **4.** 2.6   **5.** 0.023   **6.** 54

■ Convert the following percents to decimals.

7. 50%   **8.** 27%   **9.** 6%   **10.** 5.25%   **11.** 0.3%   **12.** 26.1%

■ Convert the following fractions to percents.

13. $\dfrac{1}{8}$ **14.** $\dfrac{3}{8}$ **15.** $\dfrac{1}{3}$ **16.** $\dfrac{4}{5}$ **17.** $\dfrac{1}{40}$ **18.** $\dfrac{7}{12}$

19. An item is on sale at 40% off. What fraction of the price is saved?

20. Ellen got $\dfrac{1}{8}$ of her allowance. What percent did she receive?

4.3 Operations with Percents, Decimals, and Fractions; Aliquot Parts

We now have three ways to express numbers. They may be expressed as fractions, decimals, or percents. For example, the number 0.35 may be written as 0.35, $\dfrac{35}{100}$, or 35%. In many problems, two (or more) different types of numbers may be found. In such problems convert all the numbers to the same type before doing any computation. Whether you convert all the numbers to decimals, all to percent, or all to fractions will depend on the particular problem being solved.

Example 1   Compute $2\% + \dfrac{4}{25} + 0.36$ by changing them

a. all to decimals   **b.** all to fractions   **c.** all to percents

SOLUTION

a. By changing all the numbers to decimals, we have $0.02 + 0.16 + 0.36 = 0.54$.

b. By changing all the numbers to fractions we have

$$\frac{2}{100} + \frac{4}{25} + \frac{36}{100} = \frac{2}{100} + \frac{16}{100} + \frac{36}{100}$$

$$= \frac{54}{100} \text{ or } \frac{27}{50}$$

c. By changing all the numbers to percents, we have $2\% + 16\% + 36\% = 54\%$.

Remember, to solve a problem involving different operations, the order of operations given in Chapter 1 must be observed.

Example 2   Compute $\dfrac{4}{10} + (2\%)(48)$ using decimals.

SOLUTION   Just change all numbers to decimals, then perform the operations. Remember, multiplication is done before addition.

$$0.4 + (0.02)(48) = 0.4 + 0.96 = 1.36$$

The conversion of a number from one form to another is not much fun (to say the least). Since a few fractions occur frequently in everyday problems, tables are available that give the equivalent fraction, decimal, and percent forms. Such tables are called *tables of aliquot parts.*

Definition

aliquot parts   **All *aliquot parts* of a number divide evenly (i.e., with no remainder) into that number.**

For example, the number $\dfrac{1}{3}$ is an aliquot part of 1 because $1 \div \dfrac{1}{3} = 3$ (a whole number). The number 0.5 is an aliquot part of 1, since $1 \div 0.5 = 2$ (i.e., 0.5 divides 1 evenly).

In business, knowing the commonly used aliquot parts of 1 can simplify many computations. Table 4.1 gives the most common aliquot parts of one in three equivalent forms.

TABLE 4.1   **Aliquot Parts and Equivalent Forms**

Aliquot Part	*Decimal Equivalent*	*Percent Equivalent*
$\dfrac{1}{2}$	0.5	50%
$\dfrac{1}{3}$	$0.33\frac{1}{3}$	$33\frac{1}{3}\%$
$\dfrac{1}{4}$	0.25	25%
$\dfrac{1}{5}$	0.20	20%
$\dfrac{1}{6}$	$0.16\frac{2}{3}$	$16\frac{2}{3}\%$
$\dfrac{1}{7}$	$0.14\frac{2}{7}$	$14\frac{2}{7}\%$
$\dfrac{1}{8}$	0.125	12.5%

(continues over)

TABLE 4.1
(*continued*)

Aliquot Part	Decimal Equivalent	Percent Equivalent
$\dfrac{1}{9}$	$0.11\frac{1}{9}$	$11\frac{1}{9}\%$
$\dfrac{1}{10}$	0.10	10%
$\dfrac{1}{11}$	$0.09\frac{1}{11}$	$9\frac{1}{11}\%$
$\dfrac{1}{12}$	$0.08\frac{1}{3}$	$8\frac{1}{3}\%$
$\dfrac{1}{20}$	0.05	5%
$\dfrac{1}{25}$	0.04	4%
$\dfrac{1}{50}$	0.02	2%
$\dfrac{1}{100}$	0.01	1%

The following example shows how aliquot parts may be used to simplify computation.

Example 3   A shipment of 1200 items contains $8\frac{1}{3}\%$ defective items. How many defective items are in the shipment?

SOLUTION   You would like to compute

$$8\tfrac{1}{3}\% \times 1200$$

From Table 4.1, we find that $8\frac{1}{3}\% = \dfrac{1}{12}$. By using $\dfrac{1}{12}$ instead of $8\frac{1}{3}\%$, we have $\dfrac{1}{12} \times 1200 = 100$ defective items.

If you know (or have available) a table of aliquot parts, numbers that would be difficult to handle in computation may be replaced by an equivalent (but simpler) form of the number. It may save a long, tedious conversion and simplify computations.

Exercises 4.3

■ Perform the indicated operations using decimals.

1. $\dfrac{1}{2} + 0.33 + 2\%$ *2.* $0.75 + \dfrac{1}{5} - 1\%$ *3.* $\dfrac{1}{20} + 0.68 + \dfrac{1}{4}$

4. $\dfrac{1}{4} - 0.08$ **5.** $\dfrac{3}{5} + 0.02 - 3\%$ **6.** $\dfrac{1}{25} + 0.6 + 8.5\%$

■ Perform the indicated operations using fractions.

7. $33\frac{1}{3}\% + 0.50$ **8.** $53\% - 0.23$ **9.** $0.08\frac{1}{3} + 0.16\frac{2}{3}$

10. $3 \times 14\frac{2}{7}\%$ **11.** $\dfrac{4}{10} + (0.05)(100)$ **12.** $0.125 + 25\% - 0.075$

■ Use aliquot parts to solve the following.

13. Compute $11\frac{1}{9}\%$ of 198.   **14.** Compute $9\frac{1}{11}\%$ of 121.

15. Compute 4% of 250.   **16.** Compute $0.33\frac{1}{3}$ of \$120.

17. Compute $0.16\frac{2}{3}$ of 600.   **18.** Compute $14\frac{2}{7}\%$ of 210.

■ Complete the following table.

	Aliquot Parts	*Decimal Equivalent*	*Percent Equivalent*
19.	$\dfrac{1}{15}$	_____	_____
20.	$\dfrac{1}{16}$	_____	_____
21.	$\dfrac{1}{40}$	_____	_____

22. In a shipment of 1100 items, $9\frac{1}{11}\%$ are defective. How many items are defective?

23. Thelma inherited $16\frac{2}{3}\%$ of \$600,000. How much did she receive?

24. The Leaky Ship Co. reports that its sales are down 12.5% from last year's record \$18,000,000. How much have sales decreased?

25. Viola received an $8\frac{1}{3}\%$ discount on a \$600 purchase. How much was the discount?

26. If 100 out of 900 employees are absent from work, what percent is absent?

4.4 *Applications of Percents*

In the previous sections we considered the meaning of percents and their use in arithmetic computation. Now, let us consider how percents are used in everyday situations.

Suppose an item that regularly sells for \$60 is on sale at 10% off its regular price. How many dollars can you save by purchasing the item while it is on sale?

To determine the amount (or portion of the selling price) that can be saved, three quantities must be considered:

1. The regular selling price (or *base* amount) of $60.
2. The percent (or *rate*) saved of 10%.
3. The amount (or *portion*) saved. (?)

The mathematical relationship among the quantities base, rate, and portion may be expressed in the form of an equation.

$p = rb$

> **Formula 4.1**—Base, Rate, and Portion Relationship
>
> The portion is equal to the rate times the base:
>
> portion = rate × base
>
> This may be expressed in literal numbers as
>
> $$p = rb$$
>
> where p = portion
> r = percent (rate)
> b = base

Note: The term percentage is commonly used for portion. However, the percentage (portion) might be confused with the percent (rate). Therefore, percentage will be used infrequently.

Now we can use Formula 4.1 to complete the introductory example.

Example 1   An item regularly selling for $60 is on sale at 10% off. What portion of the selling price can be saved by purchasing the item while it is on sale?

SOLUTION   The portion (saved) $p = rb$, where $r = 10\%$ and the base = $60. Therefore,

$$p = (10\%)(\$60)$$

$$= (0.10)(\$60)$$

$$= \$6.00$$

Six dollars can be saved by purchasing the item on sale.

Example 2   A suit that normally sells for $167.50 is on sale at 20% off. How much will be saved by purchasing the suit while it is on sale?

SOLUTION $p = (20\%)(\$167.50)$

$$= (0.20)(\$167.50)$$

$$= \$33.50$$

You will save $33.50.

Finding a portion by multiplication of the rate and base is probably the most common application of the relationship $p = rb$. However, since the formula is also an equation, if we are given any two of the three quantities involved, the third quantity can be determined.

Finding the Base

Suppose that the portion and the percent (rate) are given. How could the base be found? We may restate Formula 4.1 (i.e., solve for the base) as follows:

$b = p/r$

Formula 4.2

To find the base when a percent and portion are known, divide the portion by the rate:

$$\text{base} = \frac{\text{portion}}{\text{rate}}$$

Symbolically,

$$b = \frac{p}{r} \quad \text{or} \quad b = p \div r$$

where b = base
p = portion
r = rate or percent

Example 3

The rate is 12% and the portion is 120. Find the base.

SOLUTION

By the formula $b = p \div r$, we have

$$b = 120 \div 12\%$$
$$= 120 \div 0.12$$
$$= 1000$$

Example 4

You can save $15 by purchasing a chair on sale at 25% off. What was the original price of the chair?

SOLUTION

The percentage is $15 and the rate is 25%. Therefore, the original price (the base) is

$$b = \$15 \div 25\%$$
$$= \$15 \div 0.25$$
$$= \$60$$

Finding the Rate

If the portion and the base are known, the rate may be calculated by solving Formula 4.1 for the rate.

$r = p/b$

Formula 4.3

If the portion and base are known, the rate can be found by dividing the portion by the base:

$$\text{rate} = \frac{\text{portion}}{\text{base}}$$

Symbolically,

$$r = \frac{p}{b} \quad \text{or} \quad r = p \div b$$

where r = rate or percent
p = portion
b = base

When finding the rate, always use the portion as the numerator (or dividend). The base is always the denominator (or divisor).

Example 5   The portion is 40 and the base is 160. Find the rate.

SOLUTION   Since $r = p \div b$, we have

$$r = 40 \div 160$$
$$= 0.25$$
$$= 25\%$$

Note: The rate is a percent number. Therefore, the decimal value of r must be converted to a percent after the division is completed.

Example 6   A table that usually sells for $350 is on sale for $100 off the regular price. What is the percent (rate) of the discount?

SOLUTION   Since $r = p \div b$,

$$r = \$100 \div \$350$$
$$= 0.2857$$
$$= 28.57\%$$

The table is on sale for 28.57% off the regular price.

Percent Increase and Percent Decrease

The percent increase or decrease is the difference in two numbers divided by one of the numbers.

Suppose that the number of employees absent from work rose from 55 last week to 70 this week. The difference in the number of absent employees is 15. To determine the percent (or rate) of increase, divide the difference (15) by the base from the earlier time period (55) and express the quotient as a percent. Hence, the percent increase in employee absenteeism is

$$r = \frac{15}{55} = 0.27\tfrac{15}{55} \quad \text{or} \quad 27\tfrac{3}{11}\%$$

Percent increase (or decrease) is an application of the formula $r = \dfrac{p}{b}$, where p is the difference in the two numbers being compared and b is the base (usually for the earlier time period.)

Example 7   After receiving some adverse publicity, sales of a product decreased from 200 to 80 items per day. Find the percent decrease in sales.

SOLUTION   Percent decrease $r = \dfrac{\text{difference}}{\text{base}}$

$$= \frac{200 - 80}{200}$$

$$= \frac{120}{200}$$

$$= 0.60 \quad \text{or} \quad 60\%.$$

There was a 60% decrease in the number of items sold per day.

Exercises 4.4

■ Find the portion (or percentage).

1. $r = 7\%, b = 170$ **2.** $r = 9\%, b = 250$

3. $r = 8\tfrac{1}{3}\%, b = 1200$ **4.** $r = 14\tfrac{2}{7}\%, b = 2800$

■ Find the base.

5. $p = 110, r = 5\%$ **6.** $p = 435, r = 3\%$

7. $p = 100, r = 14\tfrac{2}{7}\%$ **8.** $p = 600, r = 33\tfrac{1}{3}\%$

■ Find the rate.

9. $p = 60, b = 15$ **10.** $p = 90, b = 6$

11. $p = 60, b = 180$ **12.** $p = 30, b = 50$

■ Solve each of the following.

13. A chair that sells for $160 retail is on sale at 50% off. How much can be saved by purchasing the chair on sale?

14. How much can be saved by purchasing a $210 item at $33\frac{1}{3}$% off? (Use aliquot parts.)

15. In a math class of 28 students, $14\frac{2}{7}$% missed an exam. How many students missed the exam?

16. A calculator that sells for $25 is on sale for $20. What is the percent discount? Be careful. The portion saved is $5.

17. In a shipment of 500 items, 20 items were found to be defective. What percent were defective?

18. A $600 stereo is on sale at $100 off. What is the percent of discount?

19. If 20 people make up 10% of a club's membership, how many members does the club have?

20. If Kay saved $20 by purchasing an item that was reduced 40%, what was the item's original price?

21. Suppose that sales tax is 5% of the purchase price. If you buy an item and pay $15 in sales tax, what is the item's price?

22. A car is on sale for 15% off and the sale price is $3300. What was the original price?

23. A person borrows $100 and pays back $110. What percent of interest did he pay?

24. After advertising, sales went from 10 items per day to 25 items per day. What was the percent increase in sales?

25. The price per share of Positron Corporation stock decreased from $13 per share to $11 per share during today's trading. What was the percent decrease?

26. Given the following profit figures, find the rate of increase or decrease from
    a. 1980 to 1981,
    b. 1981 to 1982,
    c. 1982 to 1983.

Year	Profit
1980	$1,236,000
1981	$1,759,000
1982	$1,426,000
1983	$1,350,000

27. A 4-ounce hamburger shrank to 3.1 ounces after cooking. Find the percent decrease in weight.

28. Ira's grade went from 71 on the first exam to 83 on the second exam. Find the percent increase in his grade.

Review Exercises / Chapter 4

1. Express $\frac{14}{100}$ as a percent.

2. Express $\frac{3}{10}$ as a percent.

3. Express 2 as a percent.

4. Change 20% to a fraction and reduce.

5. Change 8.5% to a fraction and reduce.

6. Express $\frac{3}{4}$% as a decimal.

7. Change 9% to a decimal.

8. Express 0.025 as a percent.

9. Express 0.06 as a percent.

10. Express $\frac{1}{6}$ as a percent.

11. An item that sells for $39.95 is on sale at 15% off. What is the sale price?

12. Seventy percent of the Business Club's 200 members were present at the last meeting. How many attended?

13. If you pay 6% sales tax on a $23 purchase, how much is the tax?

14. A $40 item is on sale at $5 off. What is the percent saved?

15. If 40 people are $11\frac{1}{9}$% of the audience, how large is the audience?

16. A research firm found that 80% of those interviewed watched television sometime during the week. What fraction of those interviewed watched television?

17. Is 2.4% the same as $\frac{3}{125}$?

18. A stock decreased in value from $30 to $25. What is the percent decrease?

Chapter Test / Chapter 4

1. Define each of the following terms:

   a. percent **b.** aliquot part **c.** base

   d. portion **e.** percentage **f.** rate

2. Compute each of the following:

   a. 8% of 12   **b.** $7\frac{1}{2}$% of $963.86   **c.** 6.43% of 182.6

   d. 5.38% of 1.05   **e.** 12.639% of 8,150   **f.** .023% of 87.64

3. Compute each of the following. Round-off to the nearest hundredth.

   a. 14.73 is what percent of 86.954?

   b. .047 is what percent of .6358?

   c. 24.06 is what percent of 734.123?

   d. 12.35 is 18.24% of what?

   e. .43 is .035% of what?

   f. 94.703 is 36.82% of what?

4. If you pay $13,682 in income tax on $49,875.28 of income, what percent of your income went for tax?

5. If the sales tax on a $354.21 purchase is $21.25, what is the tax rate?

6. Benny received a 7.24% raise. If his previous salary was $1486.50 per month, what is his current salary?

7. Change 21.3% to a decimal.

8. Change 0.185 to a percent.

9. Change $\frac{4}{9}$ to a percent.

10. Change $7\frac{1}{7}$% to a fraction.

11. Find the discount if a $1400 ring is on sale for $7\frac{1}{7}$% off.

12. A stock selling for $64 per share increased $12\frac{1}{2}$% in price. What is the new price per share?

13. If job applications increased from 86 to 98 per day, what is the percent increase?

14. Automobile sales decreased from 234,000 units to 186,000 units. What is the percent decrease?

15. Tanya spends 20% of her monthly income on rent of $350. What is her monthly income?

16. Zeta, Inc., reported a 30% increase in sales this year over last year. If sales last year were $150,000, what are sales this year?

17. If there are 49 business students in a class of 350 students, what percent are business students?

18. Seven is 5% of what number?

CHAPTER 5

Equations

INTRODUCTION

The idea of "equality" occurs in many everyday situations. We know that 50 cents equals one-half dollar, four quarts equals 1 gallon, or 12 inches equals 1 foot. Such statements are made to indicate that two things have the same value, amount, or quantity. Such statements are called *equations*. They occur frequently in business operations.

In this chapter we begin by defining an equation and explaining what is meant by "the solution of an equation." Then the process for determining the solution is presented.

5.1 Defining an Equation

Definition

What is an equation?

An *equation* is a mathematical statement containing an equal ($=$) symbol. It means that the quantity on the left side of the $=$ has the same value as the quantity on the right side.

The simplest equation is one that involves only numerals such as $2 + 4 = 6$. You have used equations of this type many times in the first few chapters.

Another type of equation is one that contains an "unknown quantity" represented by a literal number as in the equation $A + 4 = 6$.

Definition

unknowns

Literal numbers used in equations are frequently called *unknowns* or *variables*.

conditional equation

An equation that contains one literal number is called a *conditional equation*.

The equation $A + 4 = 6$ is conditional. Both sides are *equal* only if A *is* 2. They are *not equal* if A *is* 5. That is, the statement $A + 4 = 6$ is an equation *under the condition* that A is 2.

Definition

a solution

The value of the literal number (or unknown) that makes the equation "true" (i.e., makes both sides equal) is called a *solution* of the equation.

In the example $A + 4 = 6$, the solution is 2, since replacing A by 2 makes the equation true. Sometimes the solution is expressed by the equation $A = 2$ (read A is two or A equals two).

When a literal number is placed next to a numeral (or another literal number) with no operation sign between them, the two numbers are "understood" to be *multiplied together*.

Consider the equation $2x + 5 = 13$. The numeral 2 and the literal number x are multiplied together; that is, $2x$ means 2 times x.

The solution to $2x + 5 = 13$ is 4 because when x is 4,

$$(2)(4) + 5 = 13$$

$$8 + 5 = 13$$

$$13 = 13$$

That is, 4 makes both sides equal. Conversely, the number 3 is *not* a solution of the equation $2x + 5 = 13$. Replacing x with 3, we have

$$2(3) + 5 = 13$$

$$6 + 5 = 13$$

$$11 = 13 \quad \text{which is not true}$$

Since 11 does not equal 13, 3 definitely *is not* a solution to the equation.

Example 1

a. Is 4 a solution to the equation $3x - 2 = 10$?
b. Is 2 a solution to the equation $4 + x = 7$?

SOLUTION

a. $3x - 2 = 10$

Replacing x with 4,

$$3(4) - 2 = 10$$

$$12 - 2 = 10$$

$$10 = 10$$

Yes, 4 is a solution, because 10 does equal 10.

b. $4 + x = 7$

Replacing x with 2,

$$4 + 2 = 7$$
$$6 = 7$$

No, 2 is not a solution, because 6 does not equal 7.

Exercises 5.1

■ For each of the following equations, determine if the given value of the literal number is a solution.

1. $x + 5 = 9$, $x = 4$ **2.** $x - 3 = 10$, $x = 13$

3. $2x + 1 = 10$, $x = 3$ **4.** $3x - 2 = 8$, $x = 5$

5. $\frac{1}{2}x - 7 = 0$, $x = 14$ **6.** $\frac{1}{3}x + 5 = 10$, $x = 15$

7. $I = (100)(0.05)(2)$, $I = 10$ **8.** $S = (20)(0.5)$, $S = 15$

9. $\frac{2}{3}y + \frac{1}{2} = 1\frac{1}{2}$, $y = \frac{3}{2}$ **10.** $\frac{4}{5}z - \frac{1}{4} = \frac{3}{4}$, $z = \frac{5}{4}$

11. $7x = 21$, $x = 3$ **12.** $9x = 36$, $x = 4$

13. $2x + 3y = 13$, $x = 2$ and $y = 3$ **14.** $x - 4y = 2$, $x = 10$ and $y = 2$

■ Multiple choice: circle the correct answer.

15. Find the solution of $2x - 8 = 4$.
     a. 3   *b.* 2   *c.* 6   *d.* None of these

16. Solve for x: $\frac{1}{3}x - \frac{2}{3} = 1$.
     a. 0   *b.* 5   *c.* 3   *d.* None of these

5.2 Solving an Equation Containing One Unknown

Now that we know what the solution of an equation is, how is it found? That is, how do we solve an equation?

Definition

solving equations   An equation is *solved* when the unknown is isolated on one side of the equal sign (=) with all other quantities on the opposite side of the equal sign.

The isolation of the unknown on one side of the equal sign can be accomplished by the following operations.

operations involving
equations

> **Operations on Equations**
>
> The following operations may be performed on an equation without changing the equality relationship.
>
> 1. The same number may be added (or subtracted) to (or from) both sides of an equation. That is, if $a = b$, then

addition

$$a + c = b + c, \quad or$$

subtraction

$$a - c = b - c$$

multiplication

> 2. Both sides of an equation may be multiplied *or* divided by the same (nonzero) number.

division

Multiplication	*Division*
If $a = b$, then $(a)(c) = (b)(c)$	If $a = b$, then $a \div c = b \div c$

> 3. The *entire* right and left sides of an equation may be interchanged. That is, if $a = b$, then
>
> $$b = a$$

It is customary to get the unknown on the left side of the equal sign and the other numbers on the right. However, this is not required, since the sides may be interchanged (operation 3 above).

Example 1   Solve for the value of x in the equation $2x = 6$.

SOLUTION $2x = 6$. Since we are looking for the value of x (not $2x$), divide both sides of the equation by 2.

$$\frac{2x}{2} = \frac{6}{2}$$

By reducing the fractions,

$$x = 3$$

checking your work   To determine the accuracy (correctness) of the *number obtained*, replace the unknown in the original equation by the obtained number and simplify. If both sides of the equation are equal, the number obtained is the solution of the equation.

To check Example 1, put the number obtained (3) in the equation $2x = 6$. Then $(2)(3) = 6$. Since both sides are equal (i.e., $6 = 6$), the number obtained, 3, is the solution.

Example 2   Solve $3x - 2 = 10$.

SOLUTION $3x - 2 = 10$. Add 2 to both sides.

$$\frac{+2 = +2}{3x \quad = 12}$$ Divide both sides by 3.

$$\frac{3x}{3} = \frac{12}{3}$$ Simplify.

$$x = \frac{12}{3}$$

$$x = 4$$

To check: $3(4) - 2 = 10$

$$12 - 2 = 10$$

$$10 = 10$$

Since both sides are equal, the solution obtained, 4, is correct.

Example 3   Solve $\frac{1}{2}x + 3 = 13$.

SOLUTION $\frac{1}{2}x + 3 = 13$ Subtract 3 from both sides.

$$\frac{-3 = -3}{\frac{1}{2}x \quad = \quad 10}$$ Multiply both sides by two.

$$2(\tfrac{1}{2}x) = 2(10)$$ Simplify.

$$x = 20$$

To check: $\frac{1}{2}(20) + 3 = 13$

$$10 + 3 = 13$$

$$13 = 13$$ Since both sides are equal, 20 is the solution.

Equation with More than One Literal Number

Definition

literal equation   **An equation that contains two or more literal numbers is called a *literal equation*.**

Many business relationships are represented by such equations. The portion, rate, and base relationship $p = rb$ that you saw in Chapter 4 is an example of a literal equation. Sometimes you may need to rewrite the equation in another form, such as $r = \dfrac{p}{b}$. The process of changing the

equation $p = rb$ to the form $r = \dfrac{p}{b}$ is called *solving for r*.

solving literal
equations

Solving Literal Equations

To solve a literal equation for a specified literal number, isolate the desired number on one side of the equal sign and have everything else on the other side.

Since there are several literal numbers, the one for which you want to solve must be specified in the problem.

Example 4   Solve the formula $A = P + I$
a. for I **b.** for P

SOLUTION

    a. We are given $A = P + I$. By subtracting P from both sides, we get $A - P = I$ or $I = A - P$.

    b. To solve $A = P + I$ for P, subtract I from both sides. Hence, $A - I = P$ or $P = A - I$.

For formulas that contain several letters and terms, several steps may be required.

Example 5   Solve $A = P + Prt$ for t.

SOLUTION

$$A = P + Prt \qquad \text{Subtract } P \text{ from both sides.}$$

$$A - P = Prt \qquad \text{Divide both sides by } Pr; \text{ then}$$

$$\frac{A - P}{Pr} = \frac{Prt}{Pr}$$

Reducing, we obtain

$$\frac{A - P}{Pr} = t \qquad \text{or} \qquad t = \frac{A - P}{Pr}$$

If the formula given contains a fraction, multiply both sides of the equation by the denominator and reduce. This will remove the fraction and make the problem easier to solve.

Example 6   Solve $\dfrac{A}{B} - C = D$ for A.

SOLUTION   Multiply $\dfrac{A}{B} - C = D$ by B.

$$\cancel{B}\left(\dfrac{A}{\cancel{B}}\right) - BC = BD$$

$$A - BC = BD \qquad \text{Add } BC \text{ to both sides.}$$

$$A = BD + BC$$

Exercises 5.2

■ Solve each of the following equations.

1. $5x = 20$ **2.** $6x = 18$ **3.** $2x - 3 = 5$ **4.** $4B - 2 = 10$

5. $5x + 7 = 17$ **6.** $3x + 6 = 21$ **7.** $\frac{1}{2}x = 8$ **8.** $\frac{1}{4}N = 7$

9. $\frac{1}{2}x + 4 = 5$ **10.** $\frac{2}{3}x + 4 = 12$ **11.** $\frac{4}{5}w + 1 = 2$ **12.** $\frac{2}{5}w + 7 = 8$

13. $4x = 28$ **14.** $3y + 6 = 18$

15. $3x - 5 = 13$ **16.** $8A = 392$

17. $2x - 18 = 22$ **18.** $4x + 2 = x + 38$

19. $2x - 45 = 45 - 3x$ **20.** $\frac{1}{2}x = 25$

21. $3x = 2$ **22.** $4x + 1 = 10$

23. $3x - 5 = x + 2$ **24.** $4x - 6 = x + 5$

25. $-2x = 10 - 3x$ **26.** $4 - 2x = 8 - 4x$

27. $S = 2C$; solve for C.   **28.** $P = 2l + 2w$; solve for l.

29. $P = 2l + 2w$; solve for w.   **30.** $S = C + M$; solve for C.

31. $S = C + M$; solve for M.   **32.** $A = Pdt$; solve for P.

33. $A = Pdt$; solve for d.   **34.** $A = Pdt$; solve for t.

35. $D = \dfrac{C - S}{L}$; solve for L.   **36.** $D = \dfrac{C - S}{L}$; solve for S.

37. $D = \dfrac{C - S}{L}$; solve for C.   **38.** $A = P(1 + i)^n$; solve for P.

39. $p = rb$; solve for b.   **40.** $p = rb$; solve for r.

5.3 Solving Word Problems

It is a fact of life that most meaningful problems requiring mathematical solution begin in word form. A person who is well versed in both mathematics and language will frequently find the conversion from language (written or verbal) to mathematical (symbolic) statements a challenging task. One of the major difficulties arises because there are many words that mean the same (or almost the same) thing. In this section we will give the mathematical translation of some commonly used words. The goal is to translate a complete thought to a complete mathematical statement (equation) that can be solved by the methods presented earlier in this chapter.

The following table shows common words or phrases and their usual mathematical equivalent.

	Word Forms	*Key Words*	*Mathematical Form*
	Any unknown quantity or value that needs to be determined	unknown a number a quantity	$a, b, c, \ldots, x, y, z$ (any letter you choose may represent the unknown. x is probably the most commonly used literal number.)
$\oplus$	The *sum, total, increased, plus,* or *combined amounts* of any two quantities implies *addition*.	sum total increased plus add combine	$x + y$
$\ominus$	The *difference* of two quantities, minus, one quantity decreased by another, or one quantity *less* another implies *subtraction*.	difference minus less decrease subtract	$x - y$
$\otimes$	The *product* of two quantities, one quantity *times* another, or one amount *of* another amount implies *multiplication*.	product times of multiply	$(x)(y)$
$\oslash$	The *quotient* of two quantities, one quantity divided by another, or one quantity *per* another quantity implies *division*.	quotient per divide	$x \div y$
$\equiv$	The words *is, is equal,* or *results in* imply *equal*.	is equals results in	$x = y$

Example 1   Translate the following word statements into mathematical statements.

    a. The unknown quantity is seven.
    b. The total cost is the sum of fixed cost and variable cost.
    c. The car's mileage is 100 miles per 5 gallons of gas.
    d. Revenue is the product of selling price times number of units sold.
    e. Profit is the revenue less cost.

SOLUTION   *a.* If the unknown quantity is represented by x, then

$$\underbrace{x}_{\substack{\text{unknown} \\ \text{quantity}}} \quad \underbrace{=}_{\text{is}} \quad \underbrace{7}_{\text{seven}} \qquad \text{or} \qquad x = 7$$

b. If C = total cost
  F = fixed cost
  V = variable cost

then

$$\underbrace{C}_{\text{total cost}} \quad \underbrace{=}_{\text{is}} \quad \underbrace{F}_{\text{fixed cost}} \quad \underbrace{+}_{\text{plus}} \quad \underbrace{V}_{\text{variable cost}}$$

or

$$C = F + V$$

c. If x = mileage, then

$$\underbrace{x}_{\text{mileage}} \quad \underbrace{=}_{\text{is}} \quad \underbrace{100}_{\text{miles}} \quad \underbrace{\div}_{\text{per}} \quad \underbrace{5}_{\text{gallons}}$$

or

$$x = \frac{100 \text{ miles}}{5 \text{ gallons}}$$

$$= 20 \text{ miles/gallon}$$

Remember: the slash (/) is sometimes used as a division symbol or fraction bar. When it is used between two quantities such as miles and gallons, it is read "per."

d. Let R = revenue
  S = selling price
  N = number of units

Then

$$\underbrace{R}_{\text{revenue}} \quad \underbrace{=}_{\text{is}} \quad \underbrace{S}_{\substack{\text{selling} \\ \text{price}}} \quad \underbrace{\times}_{\text{product}} \quad \underbrace{N}_{\substack{\text{number of} \\ \text{units}}}$$

or

$$R = SN$$

Remember: the multiplication sign ($\times$) is "understood" to be between S and N.

e. Let P = profit
R = revenue
C = cost

Then

$$\underbrace{P}_{\text{profit}} \quad \underbrace{=}_{\text{is}} \quad \underbrace{R}_{\text{revenue}} \quad \underbrace{-}_{\text{less}} \quad \underbrace{C}_{\text{cost}}$$

or

$$P = R - C$$

If you know numerical values for all but one of the quantities in the mathematical statement, you can solve for the value of the remaining quantity (or unknown).

Example 2   If you increase 5 times a number by 10, the result is equal to 20. What is the number?

SOLUTION   First, translate the word statement to a mathematical statement.
Let x = the number. Then

$$\underset{\text{five times } x}{5x} \quad \underset{\text{increased}}{+} \quad \underset{\text{ten}}{10} \quad \underset{\text{is equal}}{=} \quad \underset{\text{twenty}}{20}$$

or

$$5x + 10 = 20$$

Now, solve the equation.

$$\begin{array}{rcr} 5x + 10 = & & 20 \\ -10 & & -10 \\ \hline 5x \quad = & & 10 \end{array}$$

$$\frac{5x}{5} = \frac{10}{5}$$

$$x = 2$$

The number is 2.

Example 3   This year Beta Company made $90,000, which was only $10,000 less than twice last year's profit. Find last year's profit.

SOLUTION   Let P = last year's profit. Hence, $90,000 = 2P - \$10,000$ solving,

$$90,000 = 2P - \$10,000$$
$$+\ \ 10,000 =\ \ \ \ \ +\ \ 10,000$$

$$100,000 = 2P$$

$$\frac{100,000}{2} = \frac{2P}{2} \text{ or } P = \$50,000$$

Exercises 5.3

■ Translate the following into mathematical statements.

1. Selling price is cost plus markup.

2. The amount of discount is the difference between original price and sale price.

3. The amount of simple interest is principal times rate times time.

4. The sale price is $\frac{3}{4}$ of the original price.

5. Average cost is cost per unit.

■ Translate each of the following into an equation and solve for the unknown.

6. A number plus itself is 4.

7. Three times a number is 18.

8. Half of a number is 6.

9. Three times a number decreased by 4 equals 2.

10. A number decreased by 6 equals one-half the number.

11. The result of increasing 4 times a number by 2 is 18.

12. Two times a number equals the number plus 4.

13. A number increased by twice itself is 24.

14. The $20 selling price is the cost plus $5 markup.

15. The amount of $100 is the result of combining the principal plus $10 interest.

16. The cost of an item plus 40 cents tax equals a total price of $8.30. Find the cost.

17. If you pay $12 for an item that was on sale for $3.00 off the regular price, what was the price?

18. A house and lot sold for $100,000 together. The value of the house is four times the value of the lot. What is the value of the lot?

19. This year Mecca Corp. made twice as much profit as last year. If the total profit for the two years is $300,000, what was last year's profit?

20. Mark's current salary plus one-half that amount equals $24,000. What is Mark's salary?

Review Exercises / Chapter 5

1. Is 8 a solution of $x + 6 = 14$?　　　**2.** Is 7 a solution of $2x + 3 = 17$?

3. Is 5 a solution of $3x - 5 = 12$?　　　**4.** Is $\frac{1}{2}$ a solution of $4x + 3 = 11$?

■ Solve each of the following.

5. $8x = 56$　　　　　　　　　　**6.** $\frac{1}{4}a = 3$

7. $3x - 7 = 20$　　　　　　　　**8.** $3x - 2 = x + 10$

9. $8 - x = 71 - 4x$　　　　　　**10.** $2x + 3 = 5$

11. $x - b = a$; solve for x.　　　**12.** $C = 3.14d$; solve for d.

13. $A = P + Prt$; solve for t.　　　**14.** $A = P + Prt$; solve for r.

■ Translate the following into mathematical statements.

15. One-half of the cost is $10. Find the cost.

16. Twice a number equals 16. Find the number.

17. Future value equals principal plus interest.

18. Future value minus discount equals net proceeds.

19. A number minus itself equals zero.

20. A number increased by 6 equals twice the number. Find the number.

21. This year's fuel cost of $7000 is $1000 more than three times last year's cost. Find last year's fuel cost.

22. Production cost of $8000 at Little and Company is $2000 more than three times last year's cost. What was last year's cost?

23. One-half of a number decreased by 8 equals 10. What is the number?

Chapter Test / Chapter 5

1. Define each of the following terms:
　　a. equation　　　　　**b.** unknown　　　　**c.** solution
　　d. conditional equation　　**e.** literal equation

2. Which of the following is a solution of $2x + 3 = 4x + 2$?
　　a. 2　　　**b.** $\frac{1}{2}$　　**c.** $\frac{1}{4}$　　　**d.** none of these

3. Solve $ax + 2b - z = y$ for

    a. z **b.** x **c.** y.

4. If one-half of a number is decreased by 5, the result is 5. Find the number.

5. Twice a number minus 3 equals the number plus one. Find the number.

6. If a company has $10,000 profit when revenue is $98,000, find the cost.

7. A house and lot sold for $120,000 together. If the value of the house is three times the value of the lot, what is the value of the lot?

8. Twice a number decreased by 3 equals the number increased by 8. What is the number?

9. Solve the equation $3x - 6 = 2x + 1$.

10. Three times a number decreased by itself is 6. Find the number.

■ Solve each of the following. Round off to the nearest hundredth.

11. $3.24x = 7.35$

12. $0.76y = 2.459$

13. $1.75x + 4.375 = 10.196$

14. $0.04x - 0.035 = 0.002x + 0.137$

15. $3.4x - 6.1y = 4.375$; solve for y.

16. $3.4x - 6.1y = 4.375$; solve for x.

Cumulative Review Exercises

Compute.

1. $\dfrac{1}{5} + \dfrac{2}{3}$

2. $\dfrac{7}{8} - \dfrac{1}{3}$

3. $\left(\dfrac{2}{3}\right)\left(\dfrac{3}{4}\right)$

4. $\dfrac{2}{3} \div \dfrac{3}{4}$

5. $23.718 + 14.65$

6. $72.369 - 15.428$

7. $(23.4)(1.075)$

8. $42.3 \div 1.5$

9. 20% of 80

10. 8 is what percent of 25?

11. 5 is 40% of what number?

12. $10\% + 0.8 - \dfrac{1}{2}$

Solve the following equations.

13. $5x = 60$

14. $3x + 2 = 26$

15. $2x - 8 = x + 7$

16. $A + B = C$; solve for A.

17. $ax + b = c$; solve for x.

18. $2x + 3y = 6$; solve for y.

Word problems: translate each of the following into a mathematical statement.

19. A number increased by 12 is 32. Find the number.

20. The result of decreasing twice a number by 3 is 5. Find the number.

21. Future value equals principal plus interest.

22. Sale price equals regular price less the discount.

23. B. A. Arceneaux's commission this month was $80 more than her commission last month. If her total commission for both months was $960, find her commission each month.

24. Find the statement balance:

Beginning balance	1,364.52
Deposits	835.99
Checks paid	1,627.94
Service charge	6.29

25. Is $\frac{13}{17}$ equivalent to $\frac{9}{13}$?

26. If you subtract the same nonzero number from both the numerator and denominator of a fraction, will you always get an equivalent fraction?

27. Express $\frac{3}{7}$ in higher terms with a numerator of 12.

28. A company budgets $\frac{1}{4}$ of its income for salaries and 20% of the salary budget goes to the data processing department. What fraction of the budget goes to pay salaries in the data processing department?

29. What is the multiplicative inverse of 6?

30. Convert $\frac{1}{18}$ to a percent.

31. In a recent shipment of 250 china plates, 14 were broken. What percent were broken?

32. If 24% of 3000 mathematics students made a grade of F, how many made a grade of F?

Part Two

Mathematics for Business

O V E R V I E W

This part of the text discusses some of the mathematical applications encountered in the business environment. The presentation is time-sequential; that is, the discussion proceeds in the order in which the applications are encountered in an ongoing business.

First, the business *purchases* (Chapter 6) the materials needed to continue operations. The discussion centers on the principal sales document (the invoice) for such purchases and the discounts frequently encountered in transactions between businesses. Next, the concepts of *pricing* (Chapter 7) the merchandise for resale to the ultimate consumer are discussed. Then comes the discussion on *inventory and overhead* (Chapter 8). How much merchandise is available to the business? What is its value? How can general expenses be equitably spread throughout the business? These questions are discussed before proceeding to the *depreciation* (or *cost recovery*) treatment (Chapter 9) of business property. A considerable amount of money can be spent to provide all the "nonsalable" things a business uses. The proper treatment of such costs is important to the business. Finally, our discussion covers the *financial statements* (Chapter 10), which show how successful the business has been in its effort to make a profit. Included are some analysis techniques that can be used to indicate the overall "economic health" of a business.

These chapters provide a general framework of how important mathematics can be in business operations. Careful study and practice will greatly increase your understanding of the business process, which affects us all daily.

CHAPTER 6

Purchasing

INTRODUCTION

Our business system is founded on selling (or its counterpart, purchasing). Businesses attempt to sell the goods and services that they have produced (or purchased from others) and make a profit on such sales. There are basically two types of sales:

1. *Retail sales*—Retail sales are sales made primarily to the general public, or to a buyer who will be the ultimate consumer of the purchased items.
2. *Trade sales*—Trade sales are sales made primarily between businesses. The purchasing business is not the ultimate user of the merchandise; the merchandise is generally resold to the consumer as a retail sale.

Refer to Figure 6.1, which shows the general type of trade and retail sales patterns.

Sales from a manufacturer to a wholesaler, from a wholesaler to a retailer, or from a manufacturer to a retailer are trade sales. Such sales are called trade sales because they are between firms in the same business or "trade."

Trade sales are the topic of this chapter. We will be discussing sales between businesses, where the purchasing business will be reselling the merchandise to the ultimate consumer. The basic document used in trade sales is the *invoice*. The invoice is a record of the sale, describing the merchandise purchased and other terms of the sale. The price the purchasing business will pay for merchandise may vary according to many factors. The amounts of such price variations are determined by *trade discounts* offered on trade sales. In addition, the selling business may offer additional *cash discounts* for early payment by the purchasing business. With this background, let us examine trade sales more closely.

Figure 6.1

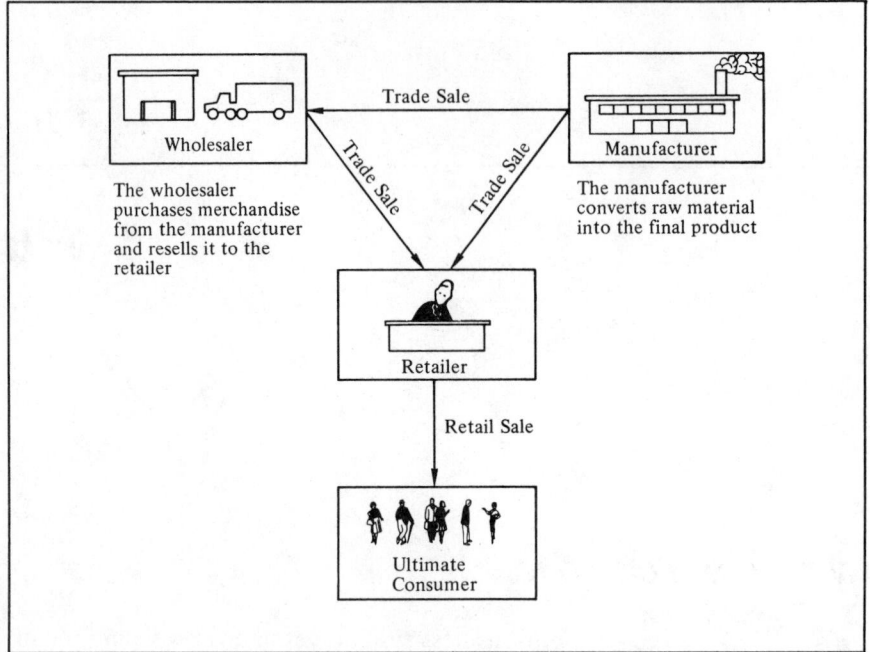

6.1 *The Invoice and List Price*

Invoice: a written record of sales between a supplier and buyer

One of the basic documents in trade sales is the *invoice*. The invoice is a written record of a sales transaction between businesses. It provides necessary information to both the seller and buyer. The seller can record the outflow of goods from his business and show money that he is to receive. The buyer can record goods coming into his business and have the necessary documentation to record paying money out when the seller is paid.

Extended price: total price for all items of the same type

Figure 6.2 shows and describes a typical invoice. You will notice in Figure 6.2 that the *extended* (or total) price for each item is found by multiplying the quantity of the item times the *unit price* per item. The invoice *total list price* is the sum of the extended price for all types of items.

Unit price: the suggested price to the retail consumer

Definitions

Total list price: the sum of all prices for all items

1. *Unit (list) price*—The unit or list price shown on an invoice is generally the suggested price to the retail consumer. It is the price at which the item is carried on the list of merchandise (or catalog) of a manufacturer or wholesaler. The list price is normally discounted to a retailer.
2. *Extended price*—The extended price on an invoice is the *total price for all units of a given item*. It is found by multiplying the number of items purchased by the price per item.
3. *Total list price*—The total list price on an invoice is the *sum of the extended prices for all items*. It represents the total cost to the buying company *before* discounts and adjustments.

Figure 6.2

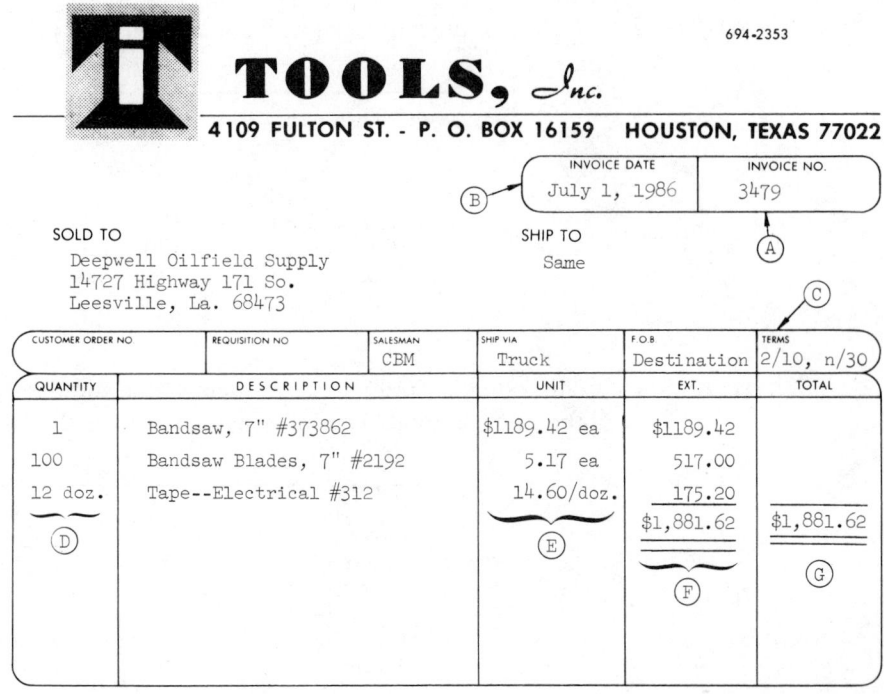

Courtesy of Mr. Frank D. Kleinworth, III, President, Tools, Inc.

The items identified by letter on the invoice show the following:

A. The invoice number whereby the transaction can be identified and traced if necessary.

B. The date of the invoice. This date will be used in determining possible discounts.

C. The terms of payment. This tells the buyer when he must pay in order to receive any offered discounts and how much the discounts will be.

D. The quantity of merchandise sold. This can be stated as ea. (each), doz. (dozen), gross (144 units), c (per 100), cwt (per hundredweight), and so on.

E. The selling price per unit. This price is usually the suggested retail price to the consumer and the price at which the supplier carries the product on his list of goods (or catalog). The term "list price" is frequently used. The selling price may be stated in terms of "per dozen," "per case," "per hundred," and so on. Be sure the unit price is in the same terms as the quantity before determining the total cost of all units.

F. The extension (or extended price) is the total amount to be paid for the items ordered. It is calculated by multiplying the quantity of items sold by the unit price per item.

G. This total is the sum of all extended prices. It is the total price of all items ordered on the invoice.

Note: This sample invoice *does not* include discounts or other items (such as taxes, freight, etc.) normally found on an invoice. These will be discussed later.

Example 1　Calculate the extended prices and total invoice price for the following invoice.

	Item	Quantity	Unit Price
a.	Steam iron	20	$8.75 ea.
b.	TV set, portable	6	$89.85 ea.
c.	Hair dryer	12	$6.30 ea.
d.	Hair spray	104 cases	$12.20/case
e.	Tissue	121 gross	$9.87/gross

SOLUTION　The extended price for each item is the number of units purchased times the price per unit. The total invoice price is the sum of all extended prices.

	Item	Quantity		Unit Price		Extended Price
a.	Steam iron	20	×	$8.75	=	$175.00
b.	TV set, portable	6	×	$89.85	=	$539.10
c.	Hair dryer	12	×	$6.30	=	$75.60
d.	Hair spray	104 cases	×	$12.20/case	=	$1268.80
e.	Tissue	121 gross	×	$9.87/gross	=	$1194.27
				Total price	=	$3252.77

You should be very careful in computing the extended price of an item. *The quantity ordered and the price per quantity must be the same.* For example, widgets may be priced in quantities of 100. Thus, 500 widgets priced at $10 per 100 widgets requires a conversion before calculating the extended price. We can either convert the quantity ordered into the same grouping as the price, or vice versa.

1. $\dfrac{500 \text{ widgets}}{100} \times \$10 \text{ per } 100 = \$50 \text{ extended price}$

That is, 5 groups of 100 widgets × $10 per group of 100 widgets = $50 extended price.

Or,

2. $500 \text{ widgets} \times \dfrac{\$10}{100} = \$50 \text{ extended price}$

That is, 500 widgets × $0.10 per widget = $50 extended price.

The extended price in either case is the same. However, you must have matching prices and quantities to correctly calculate the extended price.

Exercises 6.1

■ Calculate the extended price on the following purchases.

	Quantity Purchased	Price	Extended Price
Example:	100	$1/unit	$100
1.	12 doz.	$4/doz.	
2.	10,000	$0.07 ea.	
3.	4560 bushels	$0.75/bushel	
4.	96 bags	$3/bag	
5.	24 doz.	$0.50 ea.	
6.	1,000,000	$2.70/1000	
7.	2600	$38/100	
8.	5400	$19.60/doz.	

■ Calculate the total list price for the following invoices.

	Quantity		Price		Extended Price
Example:	100	×	$0.16 ea.	=	$16.00
	75	×	$2.90 ea.	=	$217.50
	4 doz	×	0.08\frac{1}{3}$ ea.	=	$4.00
			Total list price =		$237.50

	Quantity	Price	Extended Price
9.	1,500	$12.00/100	
	144	$22.00/doz.	
	11,000	$0.09 ea.	
		Total list price =	
10.	360 cases	$19.50/case	
	47,000	$3.50/100	
	1,080	$9.00/doz.	
		Total list price =	
11.	200 cases (15 units/case)	$3.75/unit	
	20 gross (144 units/gross)	$1.50/doz.	
	920	$2.00 ea.	
		Total list price =	
12.	40 tons	$295/ton	
	3700	$1.50 ea.	
	240 doz.	$0.50 ea.	
		Total list price =	

13. Two wholesalers have approached you concerning your requirements for machine parts. You will require 130,000 in the next three months. Wholesaler A offers these parts to you at $0.35 each. Wholesaler B offers you a price based on quantities as follows:

0–35,000	$0.55 ea.
35,001–70,000	$0.30 ea.
70,001–up	$0.25 ea.

As the purchasing manager, which wholesaler should you choose, and why?

14. Your regular supplier has informed you of a price increase in the cost of lubricants. It will now cost you $18.00 per dozen cans. A new supplier is trying to acquire your business. He is offering to sell you lubricant at $38.40 per case. Each case contains 24 cans. From whom should you purchase your next order, and why?

15. You placed an order for 10 dozen boxes of tissue (list price—$0.22 per box), 4 cases of paper towels (list—$2.60 per case), and 6 dozen disposable plates (list—$0.32 per dozen). What is the total list price of your invoice?

16. Which offers the better option:
  a. purchase of 20 gross at $1.16 per unit
  b. 240 cases (12 units per case) at $13.95 per case?

17. The Reagan Company is trying to promote a new line of products. They are offering you the opportunity to buy your first order at $12.64 per unit. Subsequent orders will cost $51.80 per case (4 units per case). How much will you save per unit on your initial purchase?

18. Effective December 1, the Magnus Supply House is increasing its price on color TVs to $378.46 (an increase of 9.1%). How much will you save (in dollars) on your current requirement of 12 TV sets if you order before December 1?

6.2 *Trade Discounts*

Trade discount: a reduction in the price of merchandise as an incentive for the buyer to purchase the merchandise

Wholesalers and manufacturers sell their merchandise to retailers in many geographic locations. They frequently use a catalog of their merchandise to show prospective buyers their products. This catalog acts as a "showroom" for the supplier. The prices for items are generally given in the catalog at their list price (or suggested retail price to the consumer). However, a supplier may wish to vary the price he charges his customers for merchandise. The prices may vary because of the quantity of merchandise purchased, competition within the geographic region, or other such reasons. Using trade discounts, a supplier can use one catalog for all customers and still vary the price charged for merchandise. The price of the merchandise will be decreased as the trade discount is increased.

Definition

A *trade discount* **is a reduction in the price of merchandise given by a seller to a buyer. Trade discounts are generally expressed as a percent of the list price. The amount of discount (or reduction in price) is subtracted from the list price to determine the actual cost of merchandise to the buyer.**

Trade discounts are a pricing mechanism. They are used by a seller to vary prices and compete for sales. There is no relationship between trade discounts and the time of payment for an invoice.

Net price: the actual cost of merchandise to the buyer. It is the list price less discounts.

The amount of the trade discount can be computed by multiplying the list price by the discount rate. The *net price* (or the actual selling price to the buyer) can be calculated by subtracting the amount of discount from the list price. If only the net price is required, it can be calculated by multiplying the list price by (100% − the discount rate).

Trade discount = list price × discount rate

Net price =
a. list price − trade discount, *or*
b. list price × (100% − discount rate)

Calculation of Trade Discount and Net Price

1. The amount of *trade discount* is equal to the list price multiplied by the discount rate.

$$\text{trade discount} = \text{list price} \times \text{discount rate}$$

2. The *net price* of the merchandise to the buyer is equal to:
a. the list price minus the trade discount, *or*
b. the list price times (100% minus the discount rate)

The list price multiplied by (100% − the discount rate) can be used when *only* the net price (not the amount of discount) is desired.

Example 1

The Handy Hammer Hardware Store has ordered $500 in merchandise (list price) from their supplier. If they are allowed a 25% trade discount, calculate the following:
a. The amount of the trade discount.
b. The net price of the merchandise.

SOLUTION

a. The amount of trade discount is the list price times the discount rate, or

$$\text{trade discount} = \$500 \times 25\% = \$125$$

b. The net price of the merchandise is the list price minus the trade discount, or

$$\text{net price} = \$500 - \$125 = \$375$$

If the amount of discount is not needed, the net price can be found by multiplying the list price times (100% − the discount rate), or

$$\text{net price} = \$500(100\% - 25\%)$$
$$= \$500(75\%)$$
$$= \$375$$

Series (or *chain*) *of discounts*: more than one trade discount applied to a product at the same time

Suppliers frequently find it advantageous to change their prices for promotional sales, seasonal trends, or other reasons. This can result in several discounts being offered on the same product at the same time. Such a *series* (or *chain*) *of discounts* is expressed as a percent of the list price; however, the second (and third) discount rate is applied to the net price determined from using the preceding discount rate.

Example 2

Calculate the net price on merchandise listing for $100 and having trade discounts of 30%, 20%, and 10%.

SOLUTION

a. $100 × 30% = $30   first discount (30%)
$100 − $30 = $70   first price

b. $70 × 20% = $14   second discount (20%)
$70 − $14 = $56   second price

c. $56 × 10% = $5.60   third discount (10%)
$56 − $5.60 = $50.40   net price

The net price is $50.40.

The order in which the discounts are taken is irrelevant because the base (or price in this case) changes. Normally, for ease of calculation, the larger discount is expressed first and taken first. Also, the net price resulting from these discount rates *is not* the same as adding the discount rates together before calculating the net price (i.e., 30% + 20% + 10% = 60%; 60% × $100 = $60 discount vs. the actual discount of $49.60).

Single equivalent discount rate: one discount rate that will yield the same discount amount as a series of trade discounts

Computation of the net price as shown above can be cumbersome. The net price resulting from a series of discounts can be found much more easily through the use of a *single equivalent discount rate*.

Single Equivalent Discount

A single equivalent discount percent is a discount rate which, when multiplied by the list price, will yield a discount equal to the discount resulting from applying all series discounts. It may be calculated as follows:

Step 1. Subtract each discount rate (in decimal form) from 1.0.
Step 2. Multiply the resulting differences together.
Step 3. Subtract the product from 1.0. The result is the single equivalent discount rate in decimal form.

Note: If only the net price, not the amount of discount, is required, the product from step 2 (the *single equivalent cost rate*) can be multiplied by the list price to yield the net price.

Let us verify the single equivalent discount rate using the data from Example 2.

Example 3   Find the net price on merchandise listing for \$100 and having trade discounts of 30%, 20%, and 10%. Use a single equivalent discount rate.

SOLUTION   **Step 1.**

1.00	1.00	1.00	$\left.\begin{array}{l}\end{array}\right\{$ Subtract each
−0.30	−0.20	−0.10	rate from 1.0.
0.70	0.80	0.90	

Step 2. $(0.70)(0.80)(0.90) = 0.504$ $\left\{\begin{array}{l}\text{Multiply the differences together;} \\ \text{this is the single equivalent cost} \\ \text{rate}\end{array}\right.$

Step 3.

$$
\begin{array}{l}
1.00 \\
-0.504 \\
\hline
0.496
\end{array}
\qquad \left\{\begin{array}{l}\text{Subtract the} \\ \text{product from 1.0.}\end{array}\right.
$$

The single equivalent discount rate is 0.496, or 49.6%. The discount and the net price would then be

$$\$100 \times 49.6\% = \$49.60 \quad \text{discount, and}$$

$$\$100 - \$49.60 = \$50.40 \quad \text{net price}$$

Since the net price only was required, we could have multiplied the list price by the single equivalent cost rate from step 2:

$$\$100 \times 0.504 = \$50.40 \quad \text{net price}$$

In summary, we can find the single equivalent discount rate by

single equivalent discount rate $= 1 - [(1 - \text{first discount rate}) \times (1 - \text{second discount rate}) \cdots]$

If only the net price is required, it can be obtained by

net price $=$ list price $\times [(1 - \text{first discount rate})(1 - \text{second discount rate}) \cdots]$

These calculations, while not difficult, can be tedious. Table XII contains the single equivalent discount rate and single equivalent cost rate associated with many common discount series.

Exercises 6.2

■ Calculate the trade discounts on the following.

	List Price	×	Trade Discount Rate	=	Trade Discount
Example:	\$100	×	25%	=	\$25.00
1.	\$25	×	10%	=	
2.	\$47.50	×	16%	=	

	List Price	×	Trade Discount Rate	=	Trade Discount
3.	$295	×	18%	=	
4.	$780	×	22%	=	
5.	$1080	×	36%	=	
6.	$19.95	×	20%	=	

■ Calculate the trade discounts and net price on the following.

	List Price	Trade Discount Rate	Trade Discount	Net Price
Example:	$100	25%	$25	$75 (i.e., $100 − $25)
7.	$47.50	10%		
8.	$1750	12%		
9.	$3800	30%		
10.	$10,750	20%		
11.	$130.00	15%		
12.	$780.00	25%		

■ Calculate the net price for the following.

	List Price	Trade Discount Rate	Net Price
Example:	$100	25%	$75 [i.e., $100 × (100% − 25%)]
13.	$140	15%	
14.	$1110	20%	
15.	$25,000	12%	
16.	$900	22%	

■ Calculate the single equivalent discount rates and net price on the following.

Example: Discounts of 10% and 5% on $100:

Step 1.
$$\begin{array}{cc} 1.00 & 1.00 \\ -0.10 & -0.05 \\ \hline 0.90 & 0.95 \end{array}$$

Step 2. $(0.90)(0.95) = 0.855$

Step 3. $1.000 − 0.855 = 0.145$, or 14.5% single equivalent discount rate

net price $= \$100 \times (0.855) = \$85.50$

17. Discounts of 10% and 5% on $750.

18. Discounts of 15% and 10% on $1250.

19. Discounts of 20% and 15% on $900.

20. Discounts of 25% and 20% on $2500.

21. Discounts of 30%, 20%, and 5% on $1500.

22. Discounts of 20%, 15%, and 10% on $800.

23. Discounts of 15%, 10%, and 5% on $2000.

24. Discounts of 10%, 10%, and 10% on $1000.

25. Jayco advertises discounts of 20%, 10%, and 5%. Jeffco advertises its discounts of 20% and 15%. Which company would you prefer to buy from? (That is, which company has the highest single equivalent discount rate?)

26. Monitor Boating Company is quoted discounts of 30% and 10% by its supplier. Merimac Marine's supplier offers 20%, 15%, and 5%. Whose supplier offers the better discount?

27. The Anderson Company paid a net price of $76.95 after discounts of 10%, 10%, and 5%. What was the list price of the item purchased?

28. The Baker's Dozen receives discounts of 30%, 15%, and 5%. If the net cost for supplies was $1130.50, how much did the supplies list for?

29. You have been offering your customers a 35% discount on your $400 radial arm saw. Your competitor is offering the saws for $247. What additional discount must you offer to meet that price? What single equivalent discount rate would that be?

30. The Good Company carries an item at $50.00 less 30%. The Great Company carries the same item at $60 less 20% and 10%. Which company offers the lowest net price? How much additional discount should the other company offer to meet the competition?

6.3 *Cash Discounts*

Cash discounts are frequently offered by suppliers to influence *when* their customers pay for goods purchased. Basically, the sooner the invoice is paid, the less the buyer must pay.

Definition

A *cash discount* is a reduction in the amount to be paid on an invoice if payment is made within a certain time period.

Cash discount: a reduction in the invoice price depending on when the invoice is paid

Cash discounts can be considered a financing mechanism. For the seller, receiving payment for invoices sooner results in more money available to manage the business. For the buyer, a cash discount results in a lower cost of merchandise and a potentially greater profit. Cash discounts are a powerful incentive for a buyer to pay invoices early. For example, a common invoice term is a 2% discount if the invoice is paid within 10 days from the invoice date; the net amount is due within 30 days. (This is written as 2/10, n/30 and read "two-ten, net-thirty.") The amount of cash discount is computed by multiplying the discount rate by the invoice amount.

Example 1

What will be the cash discount on an invoice of $100 having terms of 2/10, n/30 if payment is made on the eighth day? How much should be paid to the supplier?

SOLUTION

The discount is 2% if paid within 10 days. Since payment is made on the eighth day, the discount is allowed. The amount of discount is

$$\$100 \text{ (invoice amount)} \times 2\% = \$2.00$$

The amount sent to the supplier is

$$\$100 \text{ (invoice amount)} - \$2.00 \text{ (discount)} = \$98$$

Example 2

Using the data in Example 1, what will be the discount if payment is made on the 15th day?

SOLUTION

There will be no discount, because payment is not made in the 10-day discount period.

Cash discounts are allowed only for merchandise actually purchased. Therefore, it is frequently necessary to make adjustments to an invoice before calculating cash discounts. If merchandise is returned to the seller for some reason (damaged in shipment, wrong item, etc.), the cost of the returned merchandise must be subtracted from the invoice amount before calculating discounts. Freight or shipping charges are not subject to cash discounts; therefore, they must be subtracted from the invoice amount before calculating cash discounts. However, freight charges must be added back to the invoice amount (less appropriate discounts) to determine the total amount to be paid.

Example 3

Consider an invoice allowing a cash discount of 2/10, n/30 with a total invoice price of $515.00. This price includes $15.00 in freight charges. If the buyer returned $25.00 worth of merchandise because of shipping damage and paid the invoice on the seventh day, how much should be sent to the seller?

SOLUTION

cash discount =
(invoice total −
returns − freight) ×
discount rate

An adjustment must be made to the total price for freight and returned merchandise. Therefore,

$515.00	total price
− 15.00	freight charges
$500.00	net price of merchandise
− 25.00	returned merchandise
$475.00	amount subject to discount

Since payment is made within the discount period,

$475.00	amount subject to discount
× 0.02	2% discount rate
$ 9.50	amount of discount

The total amount to be paid is

$475.00	total of merchandise kept
− 9.50	cash discount
$465.50	
+ 15.00	freight charges
$480.50	total amount to be paid

The buyer should pay $480.50 for the invoice.

The calculation of cash discounts can be viewed as two separate problems:

1. Will the invoice be paid in time to qualify for a discount? (This is a problem of determining correct *dates*.)
2. What amount of money would be paid after allowances for discounts, returned merchandise, and so on?

Example 3 discusses the amount of an invoice after the necessary adjustments for freight, returned merchandise, and so on. However, the determination of dates warrants further discussion.

Ordinary dating method: the discount period for cash discounts begins from the date of the invoice

The *ordinary dating method* is encountered most frequently in business. Under this method, the discount period is counted from the date of the invoice. For example, an invoice dated April 17 with terms of 2/10, n/30 must be paid on or before April 27 (April 17 + 10 days = April 27) to qualify for a discount. To determine the last day of the discount period, the number of days in the discount period can be added to the invoice date. The resulting date is the last date of the discount period. Of course, when the discount period crosses the end of a month, the length of the month must be considered in determining the discount period.

We can also determine the last day of the discount period by using an *exact-day calendar* (Table IX, page 573). The exact-day calendar assigns a specific number (1 through 365) to each day during the year.* That is, January 1 is day 1 and December 31 is day 365. In order to calculate the last date of the discount period, we do the following (using an invoice dated March 26 with terms of 2/10, n/30 as an example).

1. Determine the exact day of the invoice date from the exact-day calendar (March 26 is day 85).
2. Add the days in the discount period to the exact day of the invoice date (85 + 10 days in the discount period = 95).
3. Convert the exact day from step 2 to its calendar date. That calendar date is the last date of the discount period. (Day 95 on the exact-day calendar corresponds to April 5; therefore, the last date for obtaining the discount is April 5.)

* The exact-day calendar assigns 366 days in leap years.

Use of the exact-day calendar eliminates the need to consider the length of the month involved when calculating discount periods.

R.O.G. (*receipt of goods*): cash discount terms where the discount period begins when the goods are received

Not all discount periods begin on the date of the invoice. In some cases, the discount period may begin the day the goods are received. Such discount terms would be written "2/10, n/30 R.O.G." and mean a 2% discount if paid within 10 days after receipt of goods (the "R.O.G.") The net amount is due 11 to 30 days after receiving the goods. R.O.G. dating is usually used (1) when there is a long time interval between the order and delivery of goods, or (2) when the goods ordered are susceptible to damage in shipment and should be inspected before invoice payment. Another dating period that may be encountered is the "end of the month" (E.O.M.). Discount terms of "$1\frac{1}{2}$/10, n/30 E.O.M." for an invoice dated May 12 means a $1\frac{1}{2}$% discount if paid within 10 days of the end of May (i.e., by June 10); the net amount is due within 30 days of the end of May (i.e., June 30). Generally, if an invoice is dated after the 25th of the month, the E.O.M. applies to the end of the following month. That is, an invoice dated August 26 with E.O.M. terms would begin its discount period on October 1.

E.O.M. (*end of month*): cash discount terms where the discount period begins at the end of the month

---

Example 4

Stafford Tool Company purchased goods amounting to $370 on May 10 at terms of 3/10, n/30 R.O.G. If the goods were received on May 19, when will the discount period expire? How much must be paid assuming that the discount is taken and there are no returns, freight charges, and so on?

SOLUTION

Since May 29 is 10 days after the goods were received (May 19), Stafford Tool Company may take the 3% discount if the invoice is paid on or before May 29. The discount is (3%)($370) = $11.10; the amount due is $358.90.

Example 5

Assume the information given in Example 4. The terms of the invoice are 3/10, n/30 E.O.M. When will the discount period expire and what amount is due?

SOLUTION

The discount period would end 10 days after the end of May, or June 10. The discount and amount due would be the same: $11.10 discount and $358.90 due.

Exercises 6.3

■ Compute the last day of the discount period on the following invoices.

	Invoice Date	Terms	Last Day of Discount
Example:	May 13	2/10, n/30	May 23
1.	July 20	$1\frac{1}{2}$/15, n/30	
2.	Feb. 24	7/30, n/60	
3.	Mar. 10	2/25, n/45	

4.	Aug. 7	1/20, n/30
5.	Sept. 15	2/10, n/30 E.O.M.
6.	Nov. 20	1/15, n/30 E.O.M.

■ Compute the cash discount and amount due on the following invoices. Assume that all are paid in the discount period, that there are no returns, and that there are no additional charges (freight, etc.).

	Invoice Total	Terms	Discount	Amount Due
Example:	$200.00	2/10, n/30	$4.00 ($200 × 2%)	$196.00 ($200 − $4)
7.	$1800.00	$1\frac{1}{2}$/15, n/30		
8.	$700.00	2/10, n/30		
9.	$1100.00	3/10, n/45		
10.	$4850.00	2/30, n/60		
11.	$2000.00	n/30		
12.	$3800.00	1/10, n/30		
13.	$2000.00	5/10, n/60		
14.	$1500.00	$1\frac{3}{4}$/10, n/30		

■ Compute any applicable discounts and amounts due for the following invoices based on information given.

	Invoice							
	Date	Paid	Terms	Invoice Total	Returned Mdse.	Freight	Discount	Amount Due
Example:	3-15	3-22	2/10, n/30	$100	$25	0	$1.50 [($100 − $25) × 2%]	$73.50 ($75.00 − $1.50)
15.	11-23	12-1	2/10, n/30	$525	0	$25		
16.	4-24	5-11	1/20, n/45	$800	$100	0		
17.	6-16	6-30	$1\frac{1}{2}$/15, n/30	$900	$60	$40		
18.	8-9	9-7	1/30, n/60	$1400	$200	$75		
19.	1-24	2-4	2/10, n/30	$1800	$200	$100		
20.	11-21	12-16	2/25, n/60	$2725	$300	$125		

21. You have invoices from two of your suppliers. The one from Jack's Athletic Wear is for $500 and is dated August 1. It has terms of 2/10, n/30. There was no freight and no returns. The invoice from Re-Tred Sports Shoes is dated July 17 for $650.00. It has terms of $1\frac{1}{2}$/30, n/60; freight of $40; and returns of $110.00. Today is August 9 and you have only $550 to pay suppliers. Which invoice should you pay, and why?

22. An invoice dated May 4 for $200.00 states sales terms of 2/10, n/30. How much should you pay on May 12 if the shipping charges were $20.00 and you are returning $30.00 in damaged merchandise?

23. You sent an invoice dated August 28 in the amount of $450.00 to the Reliable Store. It billed shipping charges of $35.00 and carried terms of 2/10, n/30 E.O.M. On October 8 you received a check in the amount of $368.20 and returned merchandise totaling $75.00. How much does the Reliable Store still owe you?

24. You placed an order on March 12 for supplies. On March 20 you received an invoice totaling $1136.42 with terms of 2/10, n/30 R.O.G. On April 5 your order arrived. By when must you pay the invoice to obtain the discount? How much should you pay assuming all three of the following:

    a. you pay in time to take the discount,

    b. you did not return any goods, and

    c. shipping charges of $127.40 were included in the original invoice amount?

Review Exercises / Chapter 6

1. Calculate the total invoice price for the following order.

Quantity	Unit Price
12 gross	$0.12 ea.
10 cases	$3.70 ea.
(12 per case)	
22	$2.86 ea.
10,000	$22.00/100
25 bags	$1.89/bag

2. Calculate the net price paid for an invoice totaling $1250.00 (list price). The trade discount is 30%. What is the discount?

3. Compute the single equivalent discount rate for

    a. Discounts of 12%, 20%, and 25%.

    b. Discounts of 18%, 22%, and 28%.

4. Your normal supplier gives you a 20% "regular" discount on merchandise. He is also giving you a seasonal discount of 15% on winter coats. After you tell him what his competitor is offering, he agrees to give you another 15% discount on the coats. What will you pay for the coats if they list for $89.95? What is the single equivalent discount rate? What is the discount?

5. What cash discount is available on an invoice totaling $213.78 and dated March 20 if

    a. the discount terms are $1\frac{1}{2}$/10, n/30 and today is March 28?

    b. the discount terms are $2\frac{1}{2}$/10, n/30 and today is March 31?

6. You received an invoice for $12,750 on August 11. In reviewing your records, you found that you returned $1450 in damaged merchandise. The invoice terms are 3/10, n/30 E.O.M. Today is September 8. Freight charges are $300. How much should you pay?

7. A manufacturer's net price on a household appliance is $38.96 and the price listed in the catalog is $55.65. What are the discount and the discount rate?

8. A supplier offers you a trade discount of 8% in addition to a previously offered discount of 28%. What is your cost on an item that lists for $86.50?

9. Your hardware manager is purchasing lawn mowers on which the manufacturer has offered discounts of 5%, 15%, and 10%. What is the single equivalent rate of those discounts? What is your net price assuming the mowers list for $189.50?

10. The So-low Music Company is offering a piano discounted at 8%, 22%, and 10%. The Ten Ear Piano Company has the identical instrument with discounts of 10%, 15%, and 12%. From which should you buy? How much will you save on a piano listing for $2400?

11. You received a bill dated April 15 with terms of 2/10, n/30. The bill totals $187.35, which includes $22.14 in shipping charges. You return $36.50 in merchandise on April 22, and today (April 24) you are writing a check to pay the bill. How much should that check be?

12. You received an invoice dated September 12 in the amount of $163.24. It billed shipping charges of $18.62 and carried terms of $1\frac{1}{2}$/10, n/30 E.O.M. By what date must you pay the invoice to receive the discount? How much discount will you receive if you have returned $48.74 in merchandise?

Chapter Test / Chapter 6

1. Define the following terms

a. retail sale	**b.** trade sale
c. invoice	**d.** trade discount
e. single equivalent	**f.** cash discount
g. discount rate	**h.** net price

2. Compute the total list price for the following invoice.

Quantity	Price	Extended Price
1000	$10.00/100	
38	18.76/each	
108	11.56/doz.	
144	4.67/case	
	(12 per case)	
	Total list price	

3. You must buy supplies for your printing operation. The Best Company has quoted you a price of $0.38 per linear foot for paper stock; the A-1 Company offers a similar quality paper for $1.11 per linear yard. Which would you choose? Why?

4. In each of the following, find the single equivalent discount rate, the amount of trade discount, and the net price of the item.

List Price	Trade Discounts	Single Equivalent Discount Rate	Amount of Discount	Net Price
a. $3765	15% and 15%			
b. $1946	10%, 10%, and 5%			
c. $48.75	15%, 15%, and 5%			
d. $89.95	20%, 5%, and 5%			
e. $147.50	35%, 20%, and 5%			

5. Paragon Company offers an item for sale at $136.50. Pinnacle Company has the same article for sale at $133.77. How much discount must Paragon offer to be competitive (i.e., to match Pinnacle's price)?

6. Paragon Company (problem 5) offered the item at a list price of $136.50 less discounts of 10% and 15%. What discount must Pinnacle offer off its list price of $133.77 in order to match Paragon's price? Give both the amount and the rate.

7. The Magic Fan paid $112.37 for a ceiling fan after receiving discounts of 10%, 20%, and 5%. What is the list price of the fan?

8. You have a snowblower in your catalog listing for $375. You are offering trade discounts of 15% and 10%. One of your customers wants to buy some of the blowers and makes the following statement: "To simplify calculations, let's just add the discounts and multiply by 25% to calculate the discount." Do you agree? Discuss the reasons for your answer.

9. You received an invoice in the amount of $2876.90 for merchandise purchased. The invoice was dated June 22 and had terms of 3/5, n/30. It included shipping charges of $68.45. After inspecting the merchandise, you found that $178.60 worth of merchandise was the wrong item; you returned that amount on June 24. Today (June 26) you are paying the invoice. How much should you send?

10. Your net cost for merchandise ordered is $3746.28. The invoice is dated May 19 with terms of $1\frac{1}{2}/15$, n/30. Assuming the seller pays the freight charges and you keep all the merchandise

    a. what is your potential cash discount?

    b. what is the trade discount on the merchandise?

    c. how much should you remit on June 4?

11. You are planning your purchases for next month. You wish to purchase merchandise listing for a total of $6395.95. The seller is offering discounts of 20% and 10%. You always pay within the discount interval allowed by the supplier (2/10, n/30) and shipping charges on similar orders have cost about $75. How much should you plan to spend for this purchase?

CHAPTER 7

Pricing:
Markup and Markdown

INTRODUCTION

trade sales
retail sales

In Chapter 6 we mentioned two types of sales: *trade sales* from a supplier to another business who was not the ultimate consumer, and *retail sales* made to the general consumer or to the ultimate user of the merchandise. Trade sales were discussed in Chapter 6. In this chapter our discussion will concern retail sales.

Prices change constantly. They move up or down according to inflation, supply, demand, time of the year, and so on. A retailer is constantly faced with the question: "How much should I charge for my product?" Logically, what do we know about the selling price? If we want to make a profit, we have to sell merchandise for more than we paid for it. Let's look at what we paid for the merchandise. From Chapter 6 we know how to calculate the amount paid the supplier. But there are other expenses involved in obtaining the merchandise and preparing it for sale (such as freight costs, taxes, storage costs in a warehouse, and assembly costs). The sum of all these expenses represents the actual *cost* of the product. Does this mean that we can price the product above the cost and make money? Not necessarily. What about other business expenses, such as employee salaries, building and equipment expenses, utilities, taxes, and insurance? These expenses (commonly known as *overhead* expenses) must be paid before the business makes a profit. And, finally, we must earn a reasonable profit for our efforts. Therefore, we can calculate the selling price of the product by adding the product cost and that product's share of the overhead expense and profit requirements:

Cost: the sum of all expenses necessary to acquire and prepare a product for sale

$$\text{selling price} = \text{cost} + \text{overhead} + \text{profit}$$

With this background, let us look a little deeper into the pricing of products.

7.1 *Markup*

Markup: that portion of a product's selling price which contributes toward overhead expenses and profit

Customarily, the overhead and profit contribution portion of the selling price is called the *markup* (the terms *markon* and *gross profit* are also used). From Figure 7.1 we can now get a complete picture of the selling price of a product.

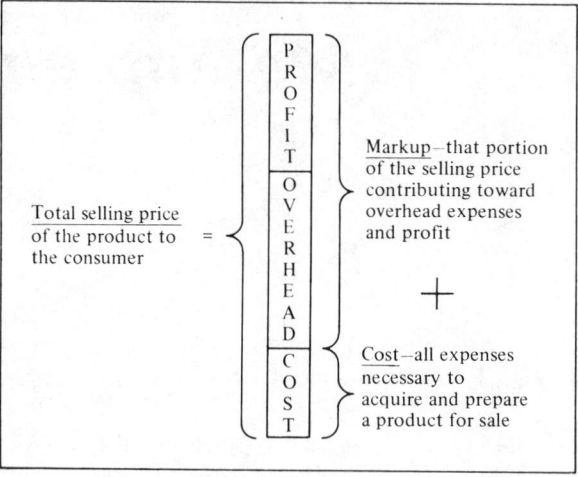

Figure 7.1 gives us the basic pricing equation with which we will be working.

selling price =
cost + markup

Selling Price of a Product

   The selling price of a product is equal to the cost of the product plus the markup, or

$$S = C + M$$

where S = selling price
        C = cost
        M = markup
with S, C, and M expressed in dollars and cents.

To illustrate this pricing process, review Example 1.

Example 1   An item costs $10.00 to acquire and prepare for sale. The product has a markup of $5.00 (to cover operating expenses and profit). What is the selling price?

SOLUTION In this example $C = \$10.00$ and $M = \$5.00$. Therefore,

$$S = C + M$$

$$= \$10.00 + \$5.00$$

$$= \$15.00$$

The selling price is $15.00.

Of course, we can solve the pricing equation for any unknown (S, C, or M) if the other two values are known.

Markup by itself may be misleading. Suppose that you are told that product A and product B both have a markup of $1.00. Which would you prefer to handle? You really need additional information to answer that question. Suppose that product A costs you $40.00 and product B costs you $5.00. You invest $40.00 for product A and receive $1.00 toward expenses and profit [i.e. a 2.5% return on investment ($1.00 ÷ $40.00)]. Product B returns 20% ($1.00 ÷ $5.00). Obviously, you would prefer to sell product B, because it contributes a greater percent toward overhead and profit.

You can easily see the advantage of expressing markup as a percent. When markup is expressed as a percent, it is referred to as the *markup rate*. Markup can be expressed as a percent of *either selling price or cost* (i.e., either the selling price or cost may be the base for the markup rate).

Markup rate: markup expressed as a percent of either the cost or selling price of a product

The markup rate may be calculated by simply dividing the markup (in dollars) by either the cost (in dollars) or the selling price (in dollars), depending on which base you choose. The result is converted to percent by multiplying by 100. That is,

Markup rate based on cost (M_C):

markup rate based on cost = markup ÷ cost

$$M_C = \frac{M}{C}$$

Markup rate based on selling price (M_S):

markup rate based on selling price = markup ÷ selling price

$$M_S = \frac{M}{S}$$

where M = markup, dollars
C = cost, dollars
S = selling price, dollars

Example 2 Anderson Electric Company purchases light bulbs for $0.40. The markup is $0.10. Compute the markup rate based on (**a**) selling price, and (**b**) cost.

SOLUTION   *a.* The light bulbs sell for $0.50 (i.e., cost of $0.40 + markup of $0.10). Therefore, the markup rate based on selling price is

$$M_S = \frac{\$0.10}{\$0.50}$$

$$= 0.20$$

$$= 20\%$$

b. The markup based on cost is

$$M_C = \frac{\$0.10}{\$0.40}$$

$$= 0.25$$

$$= 25\%$$

Why do we use the markup rate with two different bases? The choice of base is largely determined by the individual business. Since the cost of merchandise is readily identifiable from invoices, many businesses (especially small retailers) find it convenient to price the product with a markup based on cost. Many other businesses prefer to use a markup based on selling price. The sales figure (the total of all selling prices) is used as a base for many business comparisons. Sales tax, sales commissions, and many financial statement comparisons (in Chapter 10) are based on sales. Also, markup based on selling price allows quick calculation of gross profit from daily cash register tapes.

Pay close attention to the base used for the markup rate. You will notice from Example 2 that the markup rates are quite different. As you would expect, the markup rate on cost is a larger percent since the denominator (cost only) is less than the selling price denominator.

Exercises 7.1

■ Solve for the missing quantity in the following problems based on the selling price equation (selling price = cost + markup).

	Selling Price	=	Cost	+	Markup
Example:	($22.50)	=	$20.00	+	$2.50
1.	?	=	$14.60	+	$2.10
2.	$29.95	=	?	+	$4.60
3.	$11.65	=	$9.49	+	?
4.	$12.99	=	?	+	$2.16
5.	?	=	$0.96	+	$0.19
6.	$24.75	=	$18.90	+	?

7. You purchased a supply of yo-yos for $0.59 each. Each one should contribute $0.30 for recovery of operating expenses and profit. What should you charge customers?

8. The Discount Barn has a special on dog leashes. They are selling for $1.79. The supplier informed you that the Barn paid $0.89 each for the leashes. How much is the contribution to operating expenses and profit?

9. Skinnum's Quick Stop believes they can sell backscratchers for $0.19 each. Each backscratcher must be marked up $0.08. What is the most Skinnum can pay for backscratchers?

10. The *Yellow Journal* newspaper made an error in our newspaper advertisement. They listed the sale price of an item as $18.88 instead of $19.99. If we paid $12.15 for the item and must mark the item up at least $6.60, can we still honor the ad at the printed price?

■ Compute the markup rate based on cost (M_C) and selling price (M_S) given the following information.

	Selling Price	Cost	Markup	Markup Based on Selling Price	Markup Based on Cost
Example:	$20.00 = ? Solve for ($15):		+ $5	? 25% $\left(\text{i.e., } \dfrac{\$5}{\$20}\right)$	? 33.33% $\left(\text{i.e., } \dfrac{\$5}{\$15}\right)$
11.	$100	$80	?	?	?
12.	?	$60	$10	?	?
13.	$300	?	$50	?	?
14.	$19.95	$14.60	?	?	?
15.	$1500	?	$250	?	?
16.	$60	$40	?	?	?

17. Hooker's Bait Stand charges $0.60 a dozen for minnows that cost $0.35 a dozen. What is the markup rate based on (**a**) selling price, and (**b**) cost?

18. The Pit Stop has auto tires on sale for $39.95 each. If the tires are marked up $8.95, what is the markup rate based on (**a**) selling price, and (**b**) cost?

19. The Nic Nac Shoppe prices its merchandise at 30% above cost (i.e., the markup rate based on cost is 30%). What are the markup and selling price on an item that cost the shop $15?

20. Wing-jets are selling for $25.00 and have a 25% markup based on selling price. What are the markup and cost of Wing-jets?

21. The Hard Ware Store purchases hand saws from their supplier at a 40% discount off the list price of $25.00. They sell the saws at a 15% discount (off the list price) to their customers.

    a. What cost and selling price does the Hard Ware Store have on the saws?

    b. What is the markup rate based on cost? selling price?

22. The O.K. Corral received a shipment of saddle blankets; the blankets had a total list price of $200 for 20 blankets (excluding shipping). Shipping charges totaled $15.00. What would be the proper markup and selling price of each blanket if the Corral receives a 35% discount from list price and requires a 25% markup on cost?

23. What should the selling price be on merchandise listing for $40.00 (and on which you receive discounts of 20% and 10%) if you require a markup based on cost of 20%?

7.2 *Pricing*

　　　　Now that we know the variables involved in determining the selling price, we are ready to begin the pricing process. We will develop a pricing factor and apply it to the cost to determine the selling price. However, you know from Section 7.1 that the markup rate based on cost is different from the markup rate based on selling price. Therefore, the factors and the way we use them to determine the selling price will differ depending on the base of the markup rate.

rules for pricing

　　　　There are two general rules we can use (regardless of the base used for the markup rate) in developing the pricing factors.

Rule 1. The pricing factors are based on the equation

$$\text{selling price} = \text{cost} + \text{markup}$$

Rule 2. Set the base used for the markup rate at 100% in the equation

$$\text{selling price } \% = \text{cost } \% + \text{markup } \%$$

This equation is simply an expression of

$$\text{selling price} = \text{cost} + \text{markup}$$

stated in percent form.

With these two general rules in mind, let us begin our pricing discussion.

Markup Based on Cost

　　　　Suppose that a retailer purchases a product for $200. His markup rate (based on cost) is 30%. How much should he charge for the product? Using our two general rules, we can quickly calculate the selling price.

Rule 1		*Rule 2*
cost	100%	(i.e., cost base = 100%)
+ markup	+ 30%	(markup rate)
= selling price	= 130%	selling price

Thus, we can calculate the selling price as a percent of the cost: that is, the selling price is 130% of the cost, or $260.00 ($200.00 cost × 130% = $260.00).

From this general example we can determine a formula for pricing a product when the markup is based on cost.

calculating the
selling price when
the markup rate is
based on cost

Selling Price (Markup Based on Cost)

The selling price of a product can be determined by multiplying the cost of the product by a pricing factor composed of the sum of 100% and the markup rate based on cost.

selling price = cost × (100% + markup rate based on cost)

Example 1   Wonder World has a markup rate of 35% based on cost. How much should they charge for a toy costing $5.00?

SOLUTION   Using the markup base (cost) as 100%, we have

$$
\begin{array}{ll}
\text{cost} & 100\% \\
+\text{ markup} & 35\% \\
\hline
=\text{ selling price} & 135\%
\end{array}
$$

The selling price is 135% of the cost, or

$$\text{selling price} = \$5.00 \times 135\% = \$6.75$$

The toy should be sold for $6.75.

Example 2   Whiznat's buys shoes for $25.00 a pair. If the markup rate is 20% based on cost, how much should the shoes be sold for?

SOLUTION   Again, the markup base (cost) is assigned the value of 100%.

$$
\begin{array}{ll}
\text{cost} & 100\% \\
+\text{ markup} & 20\% \\
\hline
=\text{ selling price} & 120\%
\end{array}
$$

The selling price is 120% of cost, or

$$\text{selling price} = \$25.00 \times 120\% = \$30.00$$

The selling price of the shoes is $30.00.

Markup Based on Selling Price

Suppose that our retailer purchases a product for $200.00. The markup rate is 25% based on selling price. What should the selling price be? Using our two general rules, we can calculate the cost as a percent of the selling price and then determine the actual selling price.

Rule 1		*Rule 2*
cost	cost %	(unknown)
+ markup	+ 25%	(markup rate based on selling price)
= selling price	= 100%	(selling price base = 100%)

or, cost % + 25% = 100%. Solving for the cost percent, we have

$$\text{cost \%} = 100\% - 25\%$$
$$= 75\%$$

That is, 75% of the selling price is the cost. We know that the product cost $200.00 and that the cost is 75% of the selling price. Therefore, we have

$$75\% \times \text{selling price} = \$200.00$$

$$\text{selling price} = \$200.00 \div 75\%$$

$$= \$266.67$$

The process is a complicated explanation of an operation that can be simplified greatly. If we remember that the base of the markup rate is always equated to 100% (in this case, the selling price), we can calculate the selling price directly by dividing the cost by 100% minus the markup rate (based on selling price). If you go back through the example above, you will see that that is exactly what we did.

calculating the
selling price when
the markup rate is
based on selling
price

Selling Price (Markup Based on Selling Price)
    The selling price of a product can be determined by dividing the cost by a pricing factor composed of 100% minus the markup rate based on selling price.

$$\text{selling price} = \frac{\text{cost}}{100\% - \text{markup rate based on selling price}}$$

Example 3

What is the selling price of an item costing $49.00 if the retailer has a markup rate of 30% based on selling price?

SOLUTION

$$\text{Selling price} = \frac{\text{cost}}{100\% - \text{markup rate}}$$

$$= \frac{\$49}{100\% - 30\%}$$

$$= \frac{\$49}{70\%} = \frac{\$49}{0.70}$$

$$= \$70.00$$

The item should sell for $70.00.

Example 4

Edwards & Sons paid $375 each for a shipment of color TV sets. If they have a markup rate of 25% based on selling price, what should the sets retail for?

SOLUTION

$$\text{Selling price} = \frac{\text{cost}}{100\% - \text{markup rate}}$$

$$= \frac{\$375}{100\% - 25\%} = \frac{\$375}{75\%}$$

$$= \$500.00$$

The retail price of each set should be $500.00.

In summary, you can easily determine a pricing factor by determining the base of the markup rate and setting that base equal to 100% in the equation

$$\text{selling price } \% = \text{cost } \% + \text{markup } \%$$

The resulting pricing factor can be multiplied by (for cost-base problems) or divided into (for selling price-base problems) the cost to determine the selling price.

Markup rates based on cost and on selling price each have particular circumstances in which the use of one is more desirable than the other. Even though a markup rate on one base is normally used by a business, there might be occasions where the markup rate on the other base would be helpful. Therefore, the ability to convert from one markup base to the other would be most helpful.

converting
markup
bases

Formulas for converting markup rates from a cost base (M_C) to a selling price base (M_S), and vice versa, can be developed.

markup rate from
selling price to cost
base

To convert markup rates *from a selling price* base *to a cost* base, divide the markup rate based on selling price by 100%—the markup rate based on selling price. That is,

$$M_C = \frac{M_S}{100\% - M_S}$$

markup rate from cost to selling price base

To convert markup rates *from a cost* base *to a selling price* base, divide the markup rate based on cost by $1 +$ the markup rate based on cost. That is,

$$M_S = \frac{M_C}{100\% + M_C}$$

These formulas allow us to easily convert from one markup base to the other, as illustrated in the following examples.

Example 5

The Acme Brick Company has a 20% markup rate based on selling price. What is the corresponding markup rate based on cost?

SOLUTION

The markup rate based on selling price (M_S) is 20% and we want to determine the markup rate based on cost (M_C):

$$M_C = \frac{M_S}{100\% - M_S}$$

$$= \frac{20\%}{100\% - 20\%}$$

$$= \frac{0.20}{0.80} = 0.25 = 25\%$$

The Acme Brick Company has a 25% markup rate based on cost.

Example 6

Delta Industries has a 35% markup rate based on the cost of its electronic components. Convert the markup rate to a selling price base.

SOLUTION

The markup rate based on cost (M_C) is 35%. We want to determine a markup rate based on selling price (M_S).

$$M_S = \frac{M_C}{100\% + M_C}$$

$$= \frac{35\%}{100\% + 35\%}$$

$$= \frac{0.35}{1.35} = 0.259 = 25.9\%$$

Delta Industries has a 25.9% markup rate based on selling price.

Markup Allowing for Spoilage

Many businesses handle products that will spoil with time. Florists, bakeries, dairy and produce suppliers, and others lose part of their product to spoilage before it is sold. The markup applied to these products must allow for such spoilage.

Example 7   The Sour Dough Bakery bakes 10 dozen sweet rolls. The baker expects 10% of the rolls to become stale and be thrown away. If the rolls cost the baker $1.80 per dozen and he wants a markup of 50% (based on cost), what should he charge for a dozen sweet rolls?

SOLUTION   The 10 dozen sweet rolls will cost the baker $18.00 (10 dozen × $1.80 per dozen). The selling price for the sweet rolls can be calculated by

$$\text{selling price} = \text{cost} \times (100\% + \text{markup rate})$$
$$= \$18.00 \times (100\% + 50\%)$$
$$= \$18.00 \times 150\%$$
$$= \$27.00$$

That is, the baker must receive $27.00 from the sale of all sweet rolls to obtain a 50% markup based on cost.

Although 10 dozen rolls were baked, 10% (or 1 dozen) will be thrown away. Therefore, the $27.00 must be received for the sale of only 9 dozen rolls. The selling price should be

$$\$27.00 \div 9 \text{ dozen} = \$3.00 \text{ per dozen}$$

Therefore, the sweet rolls should be priced at $3.00 per dozen to provide a markup rate of 50% based on cost *and* provide for 10% spoilage.

The obvious question arises: Why should a retailer have more merchandise than he expects to sell? Customers usually will not return to a business that does not have the items they want. Stocking a slight excess of merchandise can keep customers returning *and* provide additional profit when there is unexpected demand.

Example 8   The Kiln Pottery Shop makes specialized cups that cost $0.50 each to make. The potters have found that 25% of the cups will have slight blemishes. These cups can be sold, but they are sold as "seconds" for $0.60 each. What should the cups sell for assuming a 50% markup based on cost and production of 100 cups at a time?

SOLUTION   Actual cost for 100 cups is $50.00 (i.e., 100 cups × $0.50 each). The total selling price of the cups (allowing for a 50% markup) will be

$$\text{selling price} = \text{cost} \times (100\% + \text{markup rate})$$
$$= \$50.00 \times (100\% + 50\%)$$
$$= \$50.00 \times 150\%$$
$$= \$75.00$$

That is, $75.00 must be received from the sale of *all* cups to provide the appropriate markup. However, 25 cups (25% × 100 cups) will be blemished and sold for $0.60 each, or a total of $15.00 (25 cups × $0.60 each). The remaining cups must sell for $75.00 − $15.00, or $60.00.

$$(75 \text{ cups})(\text{selling price}) = \$60.00$$

$$\text{selling price} = \frac{\$60.00}{75} = \$0.80$$

The normal selling price of the cups should be $0.80.

Exercises 7.2

■ Compute the selling price for the following items when the markup rate is based on cost.

Item	Cost	Markup Rate	Selling Price
Example:	$75.00	15%	$86.25 [$75 × (100% + 15%)]
1.	$90.00	12.5%	
2.	$3850	15%	
3.	$800	18%	
4.	$1100	22%	
5.	$7.60	20%	
6.	$28,000	7½%	
7.	$630	25%	
8.	$1750	30%	

■ Compute the selling price for the following items assuming that the markup rate is based on selling price.

Item	Cost	Markup Rate	Selling Price
Example:	$75.00	25%	$100 [$75 ÷ (100% − 25%)]
9.	$210	30%	
10.	$9500	5%	
11.	$1800	10%	
12.	$255	15%	
13.	$37,500	25%	
14.	$2400	20%	
15.	$2870	18%	
16.	$324	28%	

■ Convert the following markup rates from a selling price base to a cost base, or vice versa (as required).

	Markup Rate Based on Selling Price (M_S)	Markup Rate Based on Cost (M_C)
17.	10%	?
18.	?	15%
19.	30%	?
20.	?	35%
21.	40%	?
22.	?	45%

23. Acme Company purchased picture frames at $3.25 each. What price should they charge if their markup rate (on cost) is 40%? What is the markup?

24. The Trike Motor Kids Shop has a markup rate of 35% (on selling price). How much should they price playsuits costing $6.50? What is the markup?

25. Klassic Kars purchased a car for $2700. If their markup rate (on selling price) is 10%, what would you expect to pay for the car?

26. Molly's Apparel marks up merchandise 45% based on cost. What will they charge for a dress costing $17.50?

27. You have an opportunity to purchase merchandise for $8.00 per unit. Your markup rate is 25% on selling price. If you feel the most you can charge per unit is $10.80, should you purchase the merchandise? Why or why not?

28. The Foundary has a 20% reject rate on castings from process 13. These rejects are discarded. The castings cost $20.00 each and are produced in 500-lot batches. Assuming a 30% markup on cost, what should each casting be sold for?

29. One out of every 5 tires produced by the Big Wheel Company has a blemish. These blemished tires sell for $20.00 each. Assuming a cost of $20.00 per tire and a markup rate of 40% based on cost, what should the tires normally sell for?

30. Crocks Pots Company produces 2000 pots a day. Five percent are rejected and discarded. Another 15% of the total must be sold as "seconds" for $4.00 apiece. If the pots cost $3.00 apiece to make, and the company wants a 40% markup on cost, what do the pots normally sell for?

31. You sell all merchandise at a markup rate of 28% based on selling price. A new supplier is trying to convince you to handle his product. He claims you can mark it up 34% based on cost. Should you try his product?

32. In analyzing the sales of electric newtons in your two stores you find that store manager A is selling newtons at 38% markup on cost. Store manager B reports selling newtons at 30% markup on selling price. You have a limited number of newtons to give each store. Where should you send the most? Why?

7.3 *Markdowns*

The selling price of a product can be a changeable thing. It can go *down* as well as up. Some of the common reasons for lowering a selling price might include the following:

1. An excess quantity of goods in inventory because of overbuying or poor customer demand.
2. Damaged merchandise (due to fire, water, etc.).
3. Competition from other merchants.
4. Introduction of newer models or lines of merchandise.

Markdown: a reduction in the selling price of merchandise

Markdown is the term given to a reduction in selling price.

Definition

Markdown is the difference, in dollars, between the original selling price and the new (reduced) selling price.

Markdown rate: the amount of markdown divided by the original selling price

The principles involved in markdown are basically the same as those used in markup. The amount of markdown can be found by subtracting the new selling price from the original selling price. Markdown can be expressed as a percent. It is then called the *markdown rate* and expresses the amount of markdown using the *original* selling price as a base. That is, the markdown rate is the amount of markdown divided by the original selling price (expressed as a percent). As in markup calculations, *markdown is a dollar amount and markdown rate is a percent*.

Definition

The *markdown rate* is the amount of markdown divided by the original selling price. The result is generally expressed as a percent.

Example 1

Jeff's Men's Wear has a sale on men's suits. Suits originally selling for $150 were reduced to $100. What are (*a*) the markdown, and (*b*) the markdown rate?

SOLUTION

a. The markdown is the original selling price minus the new selling price, or

$150   original selling price
−$100   new selling price
────
$ 50   markdown

The markdown is $50.00.

b. The markdown rate is the markdown divided by the original selling price, or

$$\text{markdown rate} = \frac{\$50}{\$150}$$

$$= 0.33\tfrac{1}{3}$$

$$= 33\tfrac{1}{3}\%$$

Example 2   The Sleepy Daze Mattress Company went out of business. They sold their inventory (with a retail value of $22,500) for $15,800. What was the markdown rate?

SOLUTION   The amount of markdown is $6700 (i.e., $22,500 − $15,800). The markdown rate will be

$$\frac{\$6700}{\$22,500} = 0.2978$$

$$= 29.78\%$$

The markdown rate on the mattresses is 29.78%.

Example 3   Kay's Bow Teak has a 40% reduction in the price of winter coats. These coats originally sold for $175. What is the sale price of the coats?

SOLUTION   We can solve this problem in either of two ways.

a. Since the markdown rate is 40%, the coats are now selling for 60% of the original price (i.e., 100% original selling price − 40% markdown rate). The sale price is then 60% of the original price, or

$$\text{sale price} = (\$175)\,(60\%)$$

$$= \$105$$

b. We can calculate the markdown and subtract it from the original price. We know the markdown rate (40%) and the original price ($175). We also know that

$$\text{markdown rate} = \frac{\text{markdown}}{\text{original selling price}}$$

or

$$40\% = \frac{\text{markdown}}{\$175}$$

$$\text{markdown} = (\$175)\,(40\%)$$

$$= \$70$$

The sale price is the original price minus the markdown, or

$$\text{sale price} = \$175 - \$70$$
$$= \$105$$

Exercises 7.3

■ Compute the required information in the following problems.

	Original Selling Price	−	Markdown	=	New Selling Price
Example:	$150	−	$70	=	$80
1.	$350		?		$275
2.	$87.50		$17.75		?
3.	?		$97.50		$495.00
4.	$19.95		?		$15.00
5.	?		$48.00		$372.00
6.	$995.00		$135.00		?

■ Calculate the missing information given in the following problems.

	Original Selling Price	−	Markdown	=	New Selling Price	Markdown Rate
Example:	$500	−	$100	=	$400	$20\% \left(\dfrac{\$100}{\$500}\right)$
7.	$1250		?		$1000	?
8.	?		$250		$750	?
9.	$800		$200		?	?
10.	?		$47.50		$427.50	?
11.	$9.95		?		$7.50	?
12.	$2400		$800		?	?
13.	$1800		?		?	50%
14.	?		$100		?	25%

15. You see an advertisement telling of a "giant 60% reduction" on lamps. They are "now only $30.00." What did the lamps originally sell for?

16. "All merchandise cut $33\frac{1}{3}\%$. Ladies dresses originally priced from $75.00 to $150." What is the price range of dresses during the sale?

17. "This is a real bargain. This $200 watch is only $140. That's a 35% savings." Is the salesperson correct in saying this?

18. You are told that you may buy the entire stock of tennis shoes from a sporting goods supplier at a 55% reduction. If the tennis shoes were originally valued at $3250, how much should you pay?

19. Lamps which usually retail for $35.00 were sold at a special price of $25.00. What percent markdown did the store allow, and how much above or below cost did the lamps sell for if the regular retail price had a markup rate of 20% based on selling price?

20. The Discount Barn paid $50.00 for barbecue grills. Their normal markup is 25% based on cost. The "clearance sale" price on these grills was 30% off the regular price. What were the sale price and dollar savings on the grill?

Review Exercises / *Chapter 7*

1. What is the markup on an item costing $38.50 and selling for $49.95? What is the markup rate based on (**a**) cost, and (**b**) selling price?

2. A coat selling for $42.50 has a 20% markup rate based on selling price. What are the retailer's cost and markup?

3. The Little Shoppe prices its merchandise at 30% based on cost. For what price should they sell dolls purchased at $8.50 each?

4. What should you charge for lamps costing $30.00 if you want a 20% markup rate based on selling price?

5. The Athletic Supporter Shop is selling tennis racquets for $35.00. How much did the racquets cost the store manager if her markup rate is (**a**) 30% based on cost? (**b**) 25% based on selling price? Round to the nearest cent.

6. The Better Bakers produce bread at a cost of $0.30 per loaf. Of the 10,000 loaves produced daily, 25% will be returned from the grocers as "old" bread. If the bakery requires a 50% markup based on cost, what price should the bread be sold for? What would your answer be if one-half of the returned loaves were sold at a "day-old" outlet for $0.30 per loaf?

7. You are adding jogging suits to your merchandise line. Action Wear suits can be marked up 30% based on cost and Go-Gettum suits can be marked up 25% based on selling price. Assuming equal quality, which should you choose to sell? Why?

8. "All merchandise slashed $33\frac{1}{3}$%. Suits that were $210 to $150 now $170 to $120!" Are the statements made in this ad true?

9. Mack has $400 with which to buy shirts for his men's store. His markup rate based on selling price is 25%. If the shirts sell for $14.95, how many shirts can Mack purchase? How much change will remain from the $400?

10. The markup rate based on selling price is 30°. If the selling price is $269.95, what is the markup?

11. A retailer sold a pair of binoculars that cost him $48.50 for $62.75. What were (**a**) his markup, (**b**) the markup rate based on cost, and (**c**) the markup rate based on selling price?

Chapter Test / Chapter 7

1. Define the following terms.
  a. markup rate   **b.** markdown
  c. markdown rate   **d.** markup

2. Al's Men's Wear sells dress shirts that cost him $7.85 for $11.95. What is Al's
  a. markup?
  b. markup rate based on cost?
  c. markup rate based on selling price?

3. Mr. Adams feels that he can sell garden hoses in his hardware store for a maximum of $8.98. If his required markup is $1.65, how much will he be willing to pay for a case of 20 garden hoses?

4. The Baroque Furniture Company manager purchased a dining room suite for 40% of its $699.50 list price. He sold it for 80% of its list price. What is
  a. the net cost of the furniture?
  b. the markup on the dining room suite?
  c. the markup rate based on cost?
  d. the markup rate based on selling price?

5. The Sound Warehouse manager marks her stereo receivers up 60% based on cost. How much should a receiver costing $89.80 sell for?

6. The manager of Les Mesdames shop prices his maternity clothes at 45% based on selling price. What will each dress sell for if an order of 10 identical dresses costs $520.30?

7. Your store carries a line of men's shoes that are priced at 35% based on cost. The salesman for a competing firm is offering a comparable line of shoes which he says can be priced at 25% based on selling price. If your current line costs you $21.88 per pair, which line should you handle?

8. The Artillery Linen Mills makes bath towels in lots of 5000. The towels cost $2.00 each to make. The production line at the Mills usually experiences a 10% defect rate in the production of towels; however, these seconds can be sold at $1.70 each in the Mills' outlet store. If the markup rate is 30% based on cost, what should the towels be priced for?

9. A lawn mower regularly priced at $189.95 is on sale for $125.00.
  a. What are the markdown and markdown rate?
  b. If the original price was set using a markup rate of 25% based on cost, how much is the hardware store making or losing?

10. Your competitor is going out of business. He has offered you his entire inventory at 35% below his cost. The inventory has a retail value of $62,400 and the competitor used a markup rate of 30% based on selling price. What price should you pay for the inventory?

11. The Best Interiors Shop received a shipment of 5 chairs with a list price of $375 each. The chairs are subject to a 25% trade discount and freight and insurance charges totaled $165 for the entire shipment. Assuming a 40% markup rate (based on cost), what should each chair sell for?

CHAPTER 8

Inventory and Overhead

INTRODUCTION

Definition

Inventory: goods held for sale to customers

Inventory is the name given to the merchandise held by a business manager for sale to his customers. For a manufacturer, inventory also includes partially completed merchandise and the raw materials that will be used in producing merchandise.

From this definition of inventory, we can see that inventory is defined more by the intended use of an item than by the item itself. For example, a pickup truck can be a piece of business equipment (for a florist who uses it to deliver flowers) or part of an inventory (for an automobile dealership).

Inventory management is of vital importance to a business. Inventory usually represents the single largest operating expenditure. A retailer must have enough merchandise on hand, as customers seldom return to a business that does not have what they want to buy. However, a retailer cannot afford to have money "tied up" in merchandise that is not selling within a reasonable length of time. Proper inventory management is a "balancing act" between having the merchandise required to satisfy most customers and spending as few business dollars as possible (see Figure 8.1).

The first step in inventory management is to determine the physical amount of inventory a business actually has. Most businesses use one of two inventory methods:

Perpetual inventory: inventory system recording all in and out inventory activity

1. *Perpetual inventory*—Under this inventory method, detailed records are kept about merchandise going into and out of inventory. Since all changes are recorded, the inventory quantity is available at all times. Inventory records are generally verified yearly by making a physical count of inventory (a procedure called *taking inventory*). This method offers good inventory control because the inventory quantity is constantly available; however, the detailed record keeping requires considerable effort and expense.

Figure 8.1

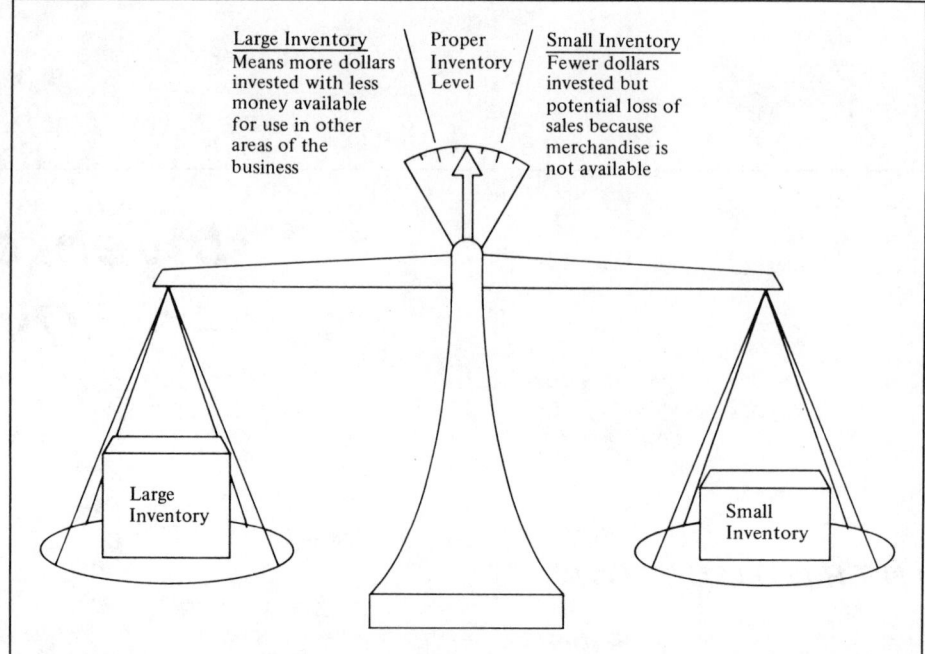

Large Inventory
Means more dollars invested with less money available for use in other areas of the business

Proper Inventory Level

Small Inventory
Fewer dollars invested but potential loss of sales because merchandise is not available

Periodic inventory: inventory system recording only incoming inventory activity

2. *Periodic inventory*—Under this method, records are kept only on goods coming into inventory. A physical count of inventory is made once a year. Last year's inventory count plus all purchases during the year provides the total quantity of goods available for sale. Subtracting the current year's inventory count gives the quantity of goods sold during the year. For example,

inventory, Dec. 31, 1984
+ purchases, All Year 1985

= goods available for sale 1985
− inventory, Dec. 31, 1985

= goods sold during 1985

The periodic method requires less record keeping than the perpetual method; however, there is much less inventory control.

Inventory valuation: placing a dollar value on goods remaining in inventory

Once the quantity of inventory has been determined, the problem of *inventory valuation* arises. Suppose that the same type of item is purchased several times during the year—at a different price each time. What is the value of that item in inventory? Inventory valuation seeks to answer that question.

Definition

Inventory valuation **is the process of placing a dollar value on the quantity of goods in inventory.**

The first section of this chapter discusses some of the most common ways of inventory valuation. The second section discusses methods of estimating the value of inventory. Such estimates are useful to "check" quantities under the perpetual or periodic inventory system and to provide reasonably close (and quick) inventory values for special purposes. The remaining sections discuss "special interest" items about inventory and ways to distribute "overhead" expenses, such as utilities, taxes, and insurance, throughout the business.

8.1 *Inventory Valuation*

Once the quantity of goods in inventory is determined, we are faced with the problem of placing a value on the goods. We will discuss four major methods of inventory valuation:

1. Specific identification.
2. Average cost.
3. First-in-first-out (FIFO).
4. Last-in-first-out (LIFO).

Specific Identification

Specific identification: each individual item is identified and its cost recorded

Specific identification is a simple method of inventory valuation used by retailers who handle readily identifiable merchandise. An automobile dealer can determine the value of his inventory simply by adding the cost of all cars he has in stock. The cars are easily identifiable and the cost associated with each one is known.

Example 1

The Farmer's Friend has the following tractors in inventory:

small tractor—purchased in January for $900
medium tractor—purchased in January for $3900
large tractor—purchased in March for $18,000

What is the value of the tractor inventory?

SOLUTION

All tractors (or units) in the tractor inventory are easily identifiable and the cost of each is known. The inventory value is simply the sum of all units. That is,

small tractor	$ 900
medium tractor	3,900
large tractor	18,000
Total	$22,800

The tractor inventory has a value of $22,800.

Inventory valuation is not so simple when the units in inventory cannot be easily identified and when the prices paid for the units vary.

Consider the purchase of tennis racquets made by Jocks Sporting Goods during the year.

March	100 racquets at $15.00 each
April	200 racquets at $16.00 each
May	300 racquets at $17.00 each
August	100 racquets at $17.50 each

If Jocks had 120 tennis racquets in inventory at the end of the year, what should the inventory value be? The value will vary depending on the valuation method used. Figure 8.2 gives a general idea of how the value will be determined under the various methods.

Figure 8.2

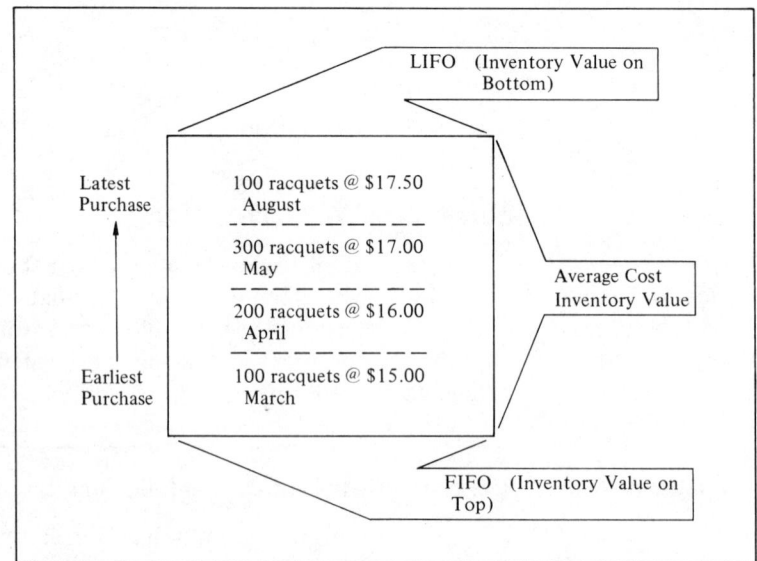

Average Cost

Average cost: the cost assigned to inventory units is the average cost for all purchases

Using the data from Figure 8.2, we can calculate the inventory value of Jocks' tennis racquets simply by determining an average cost of all racquets purchased and multiplying the remaining 120 racquets by that *average cost*.

August	100 racquets × $17.50 =	$ 1,750
May	300 racquets × $17.00 =	$ 5,100
April	200 racquets × $16.00 =	$ 3,200
March	100 racquets × $15.00 =	$ 1,500
Total	700 racquets	$11,550

The average cost per racquet is $11,550 ÷ 700 racquets = $16.50. Since 120 racquets remain in inventory, the inventory value by the average cost method is $1980 (i.e., 120 racquets × $16.50 average cost per racquet).

Example 2

Using average cost, what is the inventory value of 225 units assuming the following purchases during the year?

Purchase 4	400 units at $2.25 each
Purchase 3	800 units at $2.25 each
Purchase 2	700 units at $1.75 each
Purchase 1	500 units at $1.75 each

SOLUTION

The average unit cost is

Purchase 4	400 units at $2.25 =	$ 900
Purchase 3	800 units at $2.25 =	$1800
Purchase 2	700 units at $1.75 =	$1225
Purchase 1	500 units at $1.75 =	$ 875
Total	2400 units	$4800

$4800 \div 2400$ units = $2.00 average cost per unit

The inventory value is 225 units $\times$ $2.00 = $450.

First-In-First-Out (FIFO)

FIFO: The first goods purchased are the first sold. The inventory value is from the last purchase.

The *FIFO* inventory valuation method assumes a specific "flow" of inventory goods through the business. The first goods into the business are the first goods to be sold. Therefore, the goods remaining in inventory are the *last* goods purchased. Using Figure 8.2, we can see that goods would flow from the bottom to the top (i.e., the March purchase would be sold first, etc.). Therefore, the 120 racquets in inventory would be the 100 purchased in August plus 20 purchased in May. The value of the inventory would thus be

August	100 racquets at $17.50 =	$1750
May	20 racquets at $17.00 =	$ 340
	120 racquets valued at	$2090

Example 3

Using FIFO, what is the inventory value of 5500 units, assuming the following purchases during the year?

Purchase 4	4000 units at $8.50
Purchase 3	18,000 units at $8.00
Purchase 2	1500 units at $7.50
Purchase 1	13,000 units at $7.25

SOLUTION   Using FIFO, the first goods purchased would be the first goods sold. Therefore, the goods in inventory would be from the last purchases and the inventory value would be

Purchase 4	4000 units at $8.50 = $34,000
Purchase 3	1500 units at $8.00 = $12,000
Total	5500 units valued at $46,000

Last-In-First-Out (LIFO)

LIFO: The last goods purchased are the first sold. The inventory value is from the first purchase.

The *LIFO* inventory valuation method also assumes a specific "flow" of goods through the business. The last goods purchased are the first goods sold; hence, the goods remaining in inventory are the *first* goods purchased. Again, using Figure 8.2, we can see that goods will flow from the top (i.e., the August purchases will be sold first). Therefore, the 120 racquets in inventory would be the 100 purchased in March plus 20 purchased in April. The inventory value will be

March	100 racquets at $15.00 = $1500
April	20 racquets at $16.00 = $ 320
Total	120 racquets valued at $1820

Example 4   Using LIFO, what is the inventory value of 350 units, assuming that the following purchases were made during the year?

Purchase 4	200 units at $32.00
Purchase 3	400 units at $30.50
Purchase 2	300 units at $31.50
Purchase 1	300 units at $31.25

SOLUTION   Using LIFO, the last goods purchased would be the first goods sold. Therefore, the goods in inventory would be from the first purchases and the inventory value would be

Purchase 1	300 units at $31.25 = $9,375
Purchase 2	50 units at $31.50 = $1,575
Total	350 units valued at $10,950

Several items should be mentioned at this time.

1. The LIFO and FIFO methods assume a specific flow of goods *only* for valuation purposes. The actual item sold might come from any purchase during the year.
2. The methods of inventory valuation yield a different inventory value. Yet all are acceptable. Why are these methods so important

to a business? The basic effect is on the earnings of the business. The inventory value will affect the cost of goods sold during the year and this will change the company's earnings. This topic will be discussed more fully in Chapter 10.

3. The cost associated with inventory items should be the net cost (recall the treatment of discounts and sales returns in Chapter 7) plus costs incurred in ordering, handling, and storing the items.

4. Our discussion has been based only on what the inventory items cost. If the price of inventory items is currently below what was paid for them, the current (lower) price is used as their value. Inventory items are valued at whichever is lower: the actual cost of the item or the current market price of the item.

Exercises 8.1

■ Use the following inventory information on the Shaker Rattles Auto Company to answer questions 1–3.

Vehicle Number	Description	Invoice Cost
6302	Sedan—blue—4-door	$5890.00
6318	Sport Model-AS	$5135.00
6335	Pickup—green	$4860.00
6356	Sedan—yellow—2-door	$5125.00
6383	Pickup—red	$4695.00
6388	Hardtop—2-door	$3795.00

1. What is the total inventory value of the Shaker Rattles Auto Company?

2. What inventory value should the pickups carry?

3. Assuming that the company management wants no more than 25% of their dollar inventory in pickups, should they purchase another one? Explain.

■ Calculate the inventory values given the following information. Use the FIFO, LIFO, and average cost inventory methods in all problems.

	Purchases	Current Inventory Quantity	Inventory Value		
			Avg. Cost	FIFO	LIFO
Example:	Jan. 1—100 units at $1.00 Jan. 15—100 units at $1.10	50 units	$52.50 (50 at $1.05)	$55.00 (50 at $1.10)	$50.00 (50 at $1.00)
4.	Feb. 1—150 units at $2.25 Feb. 5—100 units at $2.60	60 units			

	Purchases	Current Inventory Quantity	Inventory Value		
			Avg. Cost	FIFO	LIFO
5.	Jan.—10,000 units at $0.68 Feb.—8000 units at $0.70 March—10,000 units at $0.72	4500 units			
6.	March 5—200 units at $6.00 March 20—100 units at $6.30 March 30—100 units at $6.50	45 units			
7.	June 20—10,000 units at $0.65 July 1—15,000 units at $0.70 July 12—10,000 units at $0.68	11,000 units			
8.	June—800 units at $22.00 July—600 units at $24.00 Aug.—600 units at $20.00	700 units			
9.	Aug. 1—1000 units at $2.35 Aug. 12—1200 units at $2.10 Aug. 30—1400 units at $2.00 Sept. 15—900 units at $1.90	1100 units			
10.	Sept.—20,000 units at $0.90 Oct.—30,000 units at $1.10 Nov.—25,000 units at $1.00 Dec.—10,000 units at $0.90	12,000 units			

11. The Handy Hammer Hardware Store purchased 3000 units of an item for its inventory in March at a cost of $0.65 per unit. In June, another 4000 units were purchased at a cost of $0.70 per unit. The final purchase of that item was made in November (6000 units at a cost of $0.75 each). On December 31, there were 3800 units in inventory. What is the value of that items inventory according to (**a**) average cost? (**b**) FIFO? (**c**) LIFO?

12. On January 1, there were 1000 units of an item in inventory valued at $1.50 each. In April, another 3000 items were purchased at $1.75 per item. There were two other purchases during the year (2500 in August at a cost of $1.70 per unit, and 3000 in October at a cost of $1.80 per unit). What is the value of the 1620 units in inventory on December 31 according to (**a**) average cost? (**b**) FIFO? (**c**) LIFO?

13. The beginning inventory was 300 units at $12.00 each. Purchases for the year were

March	1200 units at $14.00 each
June	600 units at $13.00 each
November	500 units at $13.50 each

What is the value of the 400 units in inventory on December 31 according to (**a**) average cost? (**b**) LIFO? (**c**) FIFO?

14. The inventory as of January 1 was 10,000 units valued at $0.10 each. Another 20,000 units were purchased in February at a cost of $0.12 each. The June shipment (of 15,000 units) was priced at $130 per thousand. The final order was received in October (12,000 units priced at $140 per thousand). What is the value of the 13,750 units in inventory on December 31 according to (**a**) average cost? (**b**) LIFO? (**c**) FIFO?

15. The beginning inventory was 9000 units valued at $0.30 each. Purchases during the year were

10,000 units at	$0.35 each
14,000 units at	$370 per thousand
11,000 units at	$365 per thousand

What is the value of the 12,000 units in inventory on December 31 according to (**a**) average cost? (**b**) LIFO? (**c**) FIFO?

16. The Everything Store added a new product to their inventory during the year. The first purchase was 300 units at $11.00 each. The next order was 250 units at $11.25. The final order of 350 units cost $11.35 apiece. What is the value of the 400 units in ending inventory according to (**a**) average cost? (**b**) LIFO? (**c**) FIFO?

8.2 *Estimating Inventory Values*

In Section 8.1 we discussed valuation of inventory when all items are known. That is, the actual quantity of inventory and the actual costs are available. In this section we will discuss two common methods of *estimating* the value of inventory.

Estimating the cost (i.e., value) of inventory is useful for several purposes:

1. To verify the validity of inventory cost obtained from normal inventory procedures.
2. To estimate the value of inventory between physical counts (for various management purposes).
3. To value the inventory when the quantity and price information normally used are not available.

The two estimating methods we will discuss are the *gross profit method* and the *retail method*.

The Gross Profit Method

gross profit
method—for
estimating inventory
value

The *gross profit method* of inventory estimation is used primarily to verify the reasonableness of inventory values obtained from other methods. It also provides a convenient way of estimating inventory values when it is impractical to make a physical inventory count. The gross profit method requires that all information be stated in terms of *cost* (versus retail value). The following relationship is the basis of the gross profit method:

$$
\begin{array}{ll}
\text{beginning inventory} & \text{(at cost)} \\
+ \text{ purchases} & \text{(at cost)} \\
- \text{ cost of goods sold} & \text{(at cost)} \\
\hline
= \text{ ending inventory} & \text{(at cost)}
\end{array}
$$

In an ongoing business, the beginning inventory (at cost) is known; it is the ending inventory of the previous period. The cost of merchandise purchased during the current period is readily available from invoices and supplier's records. The actual estimate made in the gross profit method is an estimate of the cost of goods sold. The cost of goods sold is estimated using the *markup rate and net sales* for the current period (net sales are sales adjusted for returns, allowances, etc.). When the cost of goods sold is subtracted from the sum of beginning inventory and purchases, the difference is an estimated ending inventory at cost.

You will recall from Chapter 7 that we calculated the selling price of merchandise in one of two ways; the method of calculation depended on the base of the markup rate. The selling price (when markup is based on cost) equals the cost multiplied by the sum of 100% plus the markup rate based on cost.

$$\text{selling price} = \text{cost} \times (100\% + \text{markup rate based on cost})$$

If the markup rate is based on selling price, the selling price is calculated as follows:

$$\text{selling price} = \frac{\text{cost}}{100\% - \text{markup rate based on selling price}}$$

We can restate these equations in terms of cost as follows:

$$\text{cost} = \frac{\text{selling price}}{100\% + \text{markup rate based on cost}}$$

or

$$\text{cost} = \text{selling price} \times (100\% - \text{markup rate based on selling price})$$

Since net sales and cost of goods sold are the sums of the selling prices and costs (respectively) for all merchandise sold, we can calculate the cost of goods sold as follows:

$$\text{cost of goods sold} = \frac{\text{net sales}}{100\% + \text{markup rate based on cost}}$$

or

$$\text{cost of goods sold} = \text{net sales} \times (100\% - \text{markup rate based on selling price})$$

We can now use the appropriate formula (depending on the base of the markup rate) to estimate the cost of goods sold. With this information, we can easily calculate the ending inventory value. The following examples show how.

Example 1 Wholesale Hardware Company had an inventory of $240,000 on December 31, 1985. So far in 1986, the company has purchased $295,000 worth of merchandise. Sales for 1986 to date have been $450,000. If the company has a 25% markup rate based on cost, estimate the current inventory value.

SOLUTION We can estimate the value of the inventory as follows:

> beginning inventory
> + purchases
> − cost of goods sold
> = ending inventory

We know the beginning inventory ($240,000) and the amount of purchases ($295,000), but we must calculate the cost of goods sold. We can do this using the markup rate (based on cost) and the sales information.

$$\text{cost of goods sold} = \frac{\text{net sales}}{100\% + \text{markup rate based on cost}}$$

$$= \frac{\$450,000}{100\% + 25\%}$$

$$= \frac{\$450,000}{125\%}$$

$$= \$360,000$$

The ending inventory value would then be estimated as follows:

beginning inventory	$240,000
+ purchases	+ 295,000
− cost of goods sold	− 360,000
= ending inventory	$175,000

The current estimated inventory value of the Wholesale Hardware Company is $175,000.

Example 2   The Chic Chick Shop had an inventory of $40,000 at the end of the previous year. So far this year, the store manager has purchased $95,000 worth of merchandise. Sales for the current year have been $150,000. If the store has a 20% markup based on selling price, estimate the current inventory value.

SOLUTION   In calculating the cost of goods sold when markup is based on selling price, we have

$$\text{cost of goods sold} = \text{net sales} \times (100\% - \text{markup rate based on selling price})$$

$$= \$150,000 \times (100\% - 20\%)$$
$$= \$150,000 \times 80\%$$
$$= \$120,000$$

The ending inventory value can then be estimated as:

beginning inventory	$40,000
+ purchases	+ 95,000
− cost of goods sold	− 120,000
= ending inventory	$15,000

The estimated inventory value of the Chic Chick Shop is currently $15,000.

As you can see from Examples 1 and 2, the processes for estimating the ending inventory are identical. The only difference is how you estimate the cost of goods sold. The method used in estimating the cost of goods sold depends on whether the markup rate is stated using cost or using selling price as the base.

If you feel more comfortable with one of the formulas, you can solve all problems by converting the markup rate to the base you choose (if a conversion is required). You may recall from Section 7.2, Example 5, that a 25% markup rate based on cost equals a 20% markup rate based on selling price. You may use this conversion and rework Example 1 (using 20% markup based on selling price) and Example 2 (using 25% markup based on cost). The estimated inventory value will not change.

The Retail Method

The retail method of inventory estimation is generally used by large merchandising businesses that value their inventory and purchases at retail sales value instead of cost; such a valuation coincides with other key indications in their operation. For example, the effectiveness of a retail department is often measured by its retail sales per square foot of floor space in the store; and, commissions for sales employees are based on sales made. Therefore, inventory valuation at retail is in keeping with the "normal language" of the retail operation. Also, since most stores mark only the selling price on inventory items, use of the retail method gives an estimate of the inventory value without first counting the inventory and then referring to the purchase invoices to determine its cost (a tedious task when one considers the number of items involved in a retail business).

The retail method requires rather extensive record keeping of the selling price of merchandise at the time it is purchased, as well as markups and markdowns after purchase.

The retail method is similar to the gross profit method in the manner of calculation. It is calculated as follows:

$$
\begin{array}{ll}
\text{beginning inventory} & \text{(at retail)} \\
+ \text{ purchases} & \text{(at retail)} \\
- \text{ net sales} & \text{(at retail)} \\
\hline
= \text{ ending inventory} & \text{(at retail)}
\end{array}
$$

Notice that all values are in terms of retail price; therefore, we subtract net sales instead of the cost of goods sold (as in the gross profit method). We now have an inventory value at retail; however, we must convert it to a cost basis for reporting purposes. We can make that conversion from retail value to cost by again using the selling price formulae from Chapter 7.

The retail method assumes that all inventory items have a similar markup rate. If the inventory is composed of groups of merchandise having different markup rates, the retail method should be applied to each group separately using the appropriate markup rate. The sum of all such calculations will give the total inventory value.

Example 3

The Big Man's Shop had an inventory valued at $8500 (retail) at the end of last year. So far this year, they have purchased goods with a retail value of $18,000, and net sales have totaled $22,000. What is the approximate value of the current inventory if the markup rate is 30% based on selling price?

SOLUTION

In the retail method, all values are stated at retail price. Therefore, we calculate an ending inventory at retail value; then we convert to cost.

$$
\begin{array}{lr}
\text{beginning inventory} & \$8,500 \\
+ \text{purchases} & +18,000 \\
- \text{net sales} & -22,000 \\
\hline
= \text{ending inventory (at retail)} & \$4,500
\end{array}
$$

The current inventory value is $4500 *at retail*. Since inventory values should be stated *at cost* for financial reporting, we must convert the $4500 retail value to a cost figure, using the markup rate.

We can calculate the cost of the inventory using the same formulae we developed in pricing (Section 7.2).

If the markup rate is 30% based on selling price, we can convert to cost using the selling price formula when markup is based on selling price.

$$\text{selling price (or retail value in this case)} = \frac{\text{cost}}{100\% - \text{markup rate based on selling price}}$$

$$\$4500 = \frac{\text{cost}}{100\% - 30\%}$$

$$\text{cost} = \$4500 \times 70\%$$

$$= \$3150$$

Therefore, the value of the current inventory at cost is $3150.

Example 4   The Modern Woman's Shop had an ending inventory last year valued at $7400 (retail). Purchases so far this year have a retail value of $26.200: and net sales to date are $29,100. What is the approximate value of the current inventory if the markup rate is 40% based on cost:

SOLUTION   The ending inventory at retail value can be calculated as follows:

beginning inventory	$7,400
+ purchases	26,200
− net sales	29,100
= ending inventory (at retail)	$4,500

If the markup rate is 40% based on cost, we can convert to cost using the selling price formula when markup is based on cost.

$$\text{selling price (or retail value)} = \text{cost} \times (100\% + \text{markup rate based on cost})$$

$$\$4500 = \text{cost} \times (100\% + 40\%)$$

$$\text{cost} = \frac{\$4500}{140\%}$$

$$= \$3214.29$$

Therefore, the value of the current inventory at cost is $3214.29.

Again we should note that, if we preferred, we could use only the markup rate based on selling price formula to compute cost (by converting markup based on cost to markup based on selling price) or only the markup rate based on cost formula (converting M_S to M_C). Using only one formula and converting the markup rate (if required) or using the two formulas as shown in these examples is a matter of choice.

Frequently, you will be required to calculate a *cost ratio* of the inventory from known information about current purchases and inventories. That is, you must develop the ratio of cost to retail sales value without knowing the markup rate directly.

Example 5

The inventory for Ajax Appliances on September 1 was $28,000 at cost and $54,000 at retail. Purchases for September cost $27,000 but had a retail value of $46,000. Net sales in September were $75,000. Estimate the value of the inventory at the end of September.

SOLUTION

The total goods available for sale in September were as follows:

	Cost	Retail
beginning inventory (Sept. 1)	$28,000	$54,000
+ purchases (during Sept.)	27,000	46,000
= total goods available for sale	$55,000	$100,000

We can use this information to calculate the ratio of cost to retail value.

$$\frac{\text{cost}}{\text{retail}} = \frac{\$55,000}{\$100,000} = 55\%$$

That is, cost represents 55% of the retail value. We can now solve for the ending inventory and estimate its value at cost using this information. The inventory remaining at retail is the total goods available for sale less the September sales, or

$100,000
$- 75,000$
$\overline{\$25,000}$ ending inventory (at retail)

The ending inventory at cost is the retail value times the cost ratio, or

Cost $= \$25,000 \times 55\%$
$= \$13,750$

The value of the inventory at the end of September is $13,750 (at cost).

Keep one point in mind when using the retail method. The retail method puts all values at the selling price or retail values. As we know, the selling prices may change over the life of the inventory. These changes must be allowed for to properly value the inventory at cost (which will not change). Basically, increases in retail price (or markups) must be added to the calculation and reductions in retail price (or markdowns) subtracted to properly value inventory.

Example 6 You know the following information about the Helping Hands Hardware Store.

1. Retail inventory value at the end of last year—$28,000.
2. Purchases this year—$76,000.
3. As a result of customer demand, prices on lawn mowers were reduced for a total of $3000 below normal, but prices on garden supplies were $4000 above normal.
4. Sales to date total $89,000.
5. The markup rate (based on selling price) is 30%.

Calculate an approximate value for the current inventory.

SOLUTION

Beginning inventory	$28,000
+ purchases	+$76,000
+ markups	+$ 4,000
− markdowns	−$ 3,000
− sales	−$89,000
= inventory (at retail)	$16,000

Inventory value at cost is $16,000 × (100% − 30%) = $11,200.

Exercises 8.2

■ Use the gross profit relationship

beginning inventory + purchases − cost of goods sold = ending inventory

to obtain the missing information.

	Beginning Inventory (at Cost)	+	Purchases (at Cost)	−	Cost of Goods Sold	=	Ending Inventory (at Cost)
Example:	$10,000	+	$2200	−	?	=	$3700
					Ans. $8500		
					($10,000 + $2200 − $3700)		
1.	?		$2750		$6800		$1800
2.	$9200		?		$10,450		$7400
3.	$12,000		$21,000		$19,200		?
4.	$5600		$12,750		?		$4750

	Beginning Inventory (at Cost)	Purchases (at Cost)	Net Sales	Markup Rate	Cost of Goods Sold	Ending Inventory (at Cost)
Example:	$10,000	$30,000	$45,000	25% (on selling price)	$33,750 [$45,000 sales × (100% − 25%)]	$6250 ($10,000 + $30,000 − $33,750)
5.	$15,000	$35,000	$65,000	30% (on selling price)	?	?
6.	$48,000	$164,000	$238,000	25% (on selling price)	?	?
7.	$13,450	$29,600	$37,900	20% (on selling price)	?	?
8.	$29,000	$76,500	$100,000	35% (on selling price)	?	?
9.	$22,000	$96,400	$109,200	40% (on cost)	?	?
10.	$117,000	$232,600	$330,750	35% (on cost)	?	?
11.	$89,650	$172,400	$233,220	38% (on cost)	?	?
12.	$204,150	$1,616,000	$1,592,500	30% (on cost)	?	?

13. Marlin's Store had a beginning inventory of $18,200. Purchases and net sales for the year were $32,000 and $56,000 respectively. Estimate the ending inventory value of Marlin's Store if the markup rate is (**a**) 40% based on selling price, (**b**) 45% based on cost.

14. Ginger's Snap Shop had $31,700 in inventory on January 1. Purchases for the year to date were $84,900 and net sales have totaled $146,000. Estimate the current (ending) inventory assuming a markup rate of (**a**) 40% based on cost, (**b**) 30% based on selling price.

■ Use the retail method to calculate the ending inventory values (at cost).

	Beginning Inventory (at Retail)	Purchases (at Retail)	Net Sales	Ending Inventory (at Retail)	Markup Rate	Inventory (at Cost)
Example:	$2500	$12,500	$13,000	$2000 [($2500 + $12,500 − $13,000)]	20% (on selling price)	$1600 ($2000 × 80%)
15.	$19,400	$47,600	$58,000	?	30% (on selling price)	?
16.	$7850	$14,400	$13,900	?	35% (on selling price)	?
17.	$212,400	$1,417,200	$1,516,200	?	40% (on cost)	?
18.	$110,140	$987,620	$1,017,500	?	35% (on cost)	?

19. The Weeping Willow had a beginning inventory of $22,500 (at retail) and purchased merchandise with a retail value of $56,800 during the year. Net sales totaled $64,200. Estimate the ending inventory using the retail method assuming the markup rate is (**a**) 25% based on selling price, (**b**) 30% based on cost.

20. The Colony Shoppe had inventory valued at (retail) $36,900. Purchases with a retail value of $118,000 were made during the year, and net sales totaled $132,000. Use the retail method to estimate the ending inventory assuming a markup rate of (**a**) 50% on cost, (**b**) 40% on selling price.

21. What is the estimated inventory (at cost) at the end of August given the following information?

		Cost	*Retail*
Aug. 1	Inventory	$8,000	$10,000
Aug. 1–31	Purchases	$19,200	$24,000
Aug. 1–31	Sales		$28,000

22. The Happy Daze Company wants to determine their estimated inventory value for the July–September quarter. Can you help them given the following information?

	Cost	*Retail*
Inventory as of July 1	$28,125	$ 37,500
Purchases July–September	$139,500	$186,000
Sales		$204,000

23. Given the following information, calculate the ending inventory for Harley's Store.

	Cost	*Retail*
Beginning inventory	$6,440	$9,200
Purchases	$26,880	$38,400
Sales		$36,200
Markups		$800
Markdowns		$1,100

24. Find the ending inventory of the Shirt Shack for the month of September. On September 1, the inventory was valued at $4800 (retail). Purchases amounted to $3650 during the month. The Shack had to reduce prices by $350 on some items. September sales were $6200 and the company uses a 40% markup (on selling price).

8.3 Other Inventory Items

Inventory Turnover Ratio

Inventory turnover ratio: a measure of how effectively inventory is being managed

Because inventory requires so much capital from the operating budget, inventory management is an important item. The *inventory turnover ratio* is a measure of how efficiently the inventory is being handled. The inventory turnover ratio basically indicates the number of times the average inventory is sold (or "turned over") during the year. The higher the turnover, the more efficient the inventory management; that is, the more times the inventory was turned over, the shorter the time the business dollar was utilized without making a profit. Comparison of turnover ratios with previous years and similar businesses provides company management with a measure of how effective the inventory management procedures are.

Inventory Turnover Ratio

$$\text{inventory turnover (at cost)} = \frac{\text{cost of goods sold}}{\text{average inventory value (at cost)}}$$

$$\text{inventory turnover (at retail)} = \frac{\text{sales}}{\text{average inventory value (at retail)}}$$

Note: The average inventory value is simply the average inventory available to the business during the time period. It could be the total inventory value at the beginning and end of the year divided by 2; the total value for the quarters of the year divided by 4; and so on. The value of the inventory can be stated at cost or retail and the turnover determined by using the appropriate equation.

Example 1   Ripleys Company had $200,000 in sales last year. The inventory value (at retail) was $30,000 at the beginning of the year and $50,000 at the end of the year. What was the inventory turnover?

SOLUTION   The average inventory was

$$\frac{\$30,000 + \$50,000}{2} = \$40,000$$

The inventory turnover ratio (at retail) was

$$\text{inventory turnover} = \frac{\text{sales}}{\text{average inventory}}$$

$$= \frac{\$200,000}{\$40,000}$$

$$= 5 \text{ times}$$

Example 2   Given the following information, calculate the inventory turnover.

Inventory (at cost) Jan. 1	$13,000
Inventory (at cost) Dec. 31	$17,000
Purchases	$94,000

SOLUTION   The average inventory was

$$\frac{\$13,000 + \$17,000}{2} = \$15,000$$

Calculate the cost of goods sold by

beginning inventory	$13,000
+ purchases	+ $94,000
− ending inventory	− $17,000
= cost of goods sold	$90,000

The inventory turnover (at cost)

$$= \frac{\text{cost of goods sold}}{\text{average inventory value}}$$

$$= \frac{\$90,000}{\$15,000}$$

$$= 6 \text{ times}$$

Planning Purchases

Planned purchase amount: estimated sales + desired ending inventory − beginning inventory

Since a lengthy time is often required between ordering merchandise and actual delivery, careful planning must be done to have the desired quantity available at the right time. The actual quantity of merchandise to be ordered can be calculated. We can calculate the amount of inventory to be ordered for any given month by

Step 1. Estimating the sales for the month.

Step 2. Adding the amount of inventory desired at the end of the month.

Step 3. Subtracting the amount of inventory available at the beginning of the month.

Step 4. The result is the amount of planned purchase *at retail*. The ordering quantity at cost can be calculated using the markup rate.

Example 3   The Trusty Auto Parts store is trying to determine how much merchandise they should purchase for the month of June. They estimate June sales at $28,000. They will have $22,000 inventory on June 1 and want $26,000 inventory on June 30. The markup rate (based on selling price) is 30%. How much merchandise should be ordered for June?

SOLUTION   Purchases for June can be calculated by

estimated June sales	$28,000
+ desired ending inventory	+ $26,000
− beginning inventory	− $22,000
= planned purchases (at retail)	$32,000

To find the planned purchases at cost,

$$\text{cost} = \$32{,}000 \times (100\% - 30\%)$$

$$= \$32{,}000 \times 70\%$$

$$= \$22{,}400$$

Of course, this planning should be done far enough in advance to allow for ordering and delivery of merchandise by the desired time. This planning gives only the total amount that should be spent to purchase inventory items for the month. The actual quantities of specific items must be determined by the particular items that are (and are not) selling well.

Open-to-Buy

Proper planning of inventory purchases gives the total amount that should be spent for inventory during the month. Prudent management dictates that not all of this planned purchase amount be spent in advance. Some of it should be available to purchase (1) new products just being introduced, (2) merchandise offered at special discounts, (3) items that are selling extremely well, and so on. The *open-to-buy* amount is simply the planned purchase amount less merchandise already purchased or ordered.

Open-to-buy: the amount of money planned for inventory purchase which is not yet committed

> **Open-to-Buy**
>
> The open-to-buy amount of a business can be calculated by
>
> | | |
> |---|---|
> | planned purchase amount for the period | |
> | − merchandise ordered and received | |
> | − merchandise ordered but not received | |
> | = open-to-buy | |
>
> If the planned purchase amounts and ordered amounts are at retail, the open-to-buy amount at cost can be calculated using the markup rate.

Example 4   Using the data from Example 3 and the following information, calculate the open-to-buy amount for June.

  a. Merchandise ordered but not received $12,800 (at retail).
  b. Merchandise ordered and received $16,200 (at retail).

SOLUTION   The total planned purchase amount for the Trusty Auto Parts store was $32,000 at retail. Therefore,

planned purchase amount	$32,000
− merchandise ordered and received	− $16,200
− merchandise ordered but not received	− $12,800
= open-to-buy (at retail)	$ 3,000

The open-to-buy at cost is

$$\text{cost} = \$3000 \times 70\%$$
$$= \$2100$$

Exercises 8.3

■ Calculate the missing values below using the inventory turnover ratios.

	Inventory Turnover (at Cost)	Cost of Goods Sold	Average Inventory (at Cost)
Example:	4 times $\left(\dfrac{\$4000}{\$1000}\right)$	$4000	$1000
1.	?	$13,500	$2250
2.	?	$23,750	$4750
3.	5.5	?	$2780
4.	6.4	$43,520	?
5.	8.6	?	$14,950
6.	9.3	$206,925	?

	Inventory Turnover (at Retail)	Sales	Average Inventory (at Retail)
Example:	7 times $\left(\dfrac{\$280,000}{\$40,000}\right)$	$280,000	$40,000
7.	?	$46,875	$6250
8.	3.8	$30,020	?
9.	7.8	?	$8100
10.	?	$316,575	$47,250
11.	10.3	?	$14,280
12.	9.6	$179,040	?

13. The Why Not Shop had the following inventory valued (at cost) for the four quarters of last year.

Dec. 31, 1983	$19,250
March 31, 1984	$17,860
June 30, 1984	$21,350
Sept. 30, 1984	$21,800
Dec. 31, 1984	$18,990

Purchases for the year totaled $179,740. Calculate the inventory turnover rate.

14. Craig's Appliances had an inventory of $28,600 on January 1 and $21,400 on December 31 (at retail values). Sales for the year totaled $125,000. How often does Craig's inventory turn over?

15. The quarterly inventory values (at retail) were

1st quarter	$34,900
2nd quarter	$38,700
3rd quarter	$40,600
4th quarter	$36,800

Sales for the year totaled $169,875. What was the inventory turnover?

16. The Woodsman's Shop had sales of $80,400 last year. They purchased $130,000 in merchandise and had an inventory costing them $10,600 at the end of the year. Their beginning inventory cost $12,600. Calculate the cost of goods sold and the turnover rate.

■ Calculate the planned purchases and open-to-buy amounts given the following data. Answers should be at cost. Inventory and sales figures are shown at retail values.

17.

Beginning inventory	$28,700
Estimated sales	$96,000
Desired ending inventory	$26,000
Markup rate (on selling price)	30%
Merchandise ordered	$75,900 (at retail)

18.

Merchandise ordered but not received	$29,300 (at retail)
Markup rate (on selling price)	40%
Desired ending inventory	$18,600
Estimated sales	$48,700
Beginning inventory	$17,000

19.

Estimated sales	$147,000
Ending inventory desired	$21,000
Goods ordered and received	$39,000 (at retail)
Goods ordered and not received	$68,000 (at retail)
Beginning inventory	$18,600
Markup rate (on selling price)	35%

20.

Markup rate (on cost)	25%
Ending inventory desired	$16,000
Beginning inventory	$17,000
Estimated sales	$48,000

8.4 *Overhead*

In Chapter 7 we discussed some of the operating expenses a business manager has over and above the cost of the merchandise alone. Expenses such as building rent, utilities, maintenance, office supplies, taxes, insurance, and so on, are necessary expenses to operate the business. These expenses are generally classified as overhead expenses.

Definition

overhead expenses

Overhead expenses **are those expenses which contribute indirectly to operation of the business. They benefit the business as a whole and, as such, are not directly identifiable with a specific product or department.**

Since efficient company managers are constantly trying to determine unprofitable (and profitable) products and departments in the company, some method must be found to equitably divide the overhead costs. This division (or *allocation*) of overhead is usually done by a ratio. That is, a ratio of each product or department to the total organization is developed. The overhead expense is multiplied by the ratio to determine each department or product share. That is:

Step 1. $\dfrac{\text{product or department share}}{\text{total organization}} = \text{allocation ratio}$

Step 2. Total overhead expense × allocation ratio = department or product share.

Two of the more common allocation ratios are based on *department floor space* and *product sales value.*

Floor Space

The floor space an individual department has may be used to allocate overhead. The ratio of individual department floor space to the total floor space is multiplied by the total overhead in order to determine the individual department's share of overhead. Allocation by floor space assumes that the department having more floor space is generating more of the overhead expense; therefore, that department should pay proportionally.

Example 1   Overhead expenses for Allen Corporation in May were $100,000. The company has three departments with the following floor space:

Production	35,000 square feet
Accounting	5,000 square feet
Sales	10,000 square feet

Allocate the May overhead according to floor space.

SOLUTION   First, we determine the ratio of each department's floor space to the total
                floor space.

	Department Size (sq ft)	Ratio
Production	35,000	$\dfrac{35,000}{50,000} = 70\%$
Accounting	5,000	$\dfrac{5,000}{50,000} = 10\%$
Sales	10,000	$\dfrac{10,000}{50,000} = 20\%$
Total area	50,000	100%

These ratios can be multiplied by the total overhead to determine each
department's share

	Ratio	Allocated Overhead
Production	70% × $100,000 =	$ 70,000
Accounting	10% × $100,000 =	$ 10,000
Sales	20% × $100,000 =	$ 20,000
	100%	$100,000

Note: A good "check" on the allocation process is to total the ratios (to
100%) and the amounts allocated (to the total to be allocated) to prevent
a mathematical error. (A slight allowance for rounding may be required.)

Sales Value

The sales value of products produced is frequently used to allocate
overhead. Again, a ratio is developed and applied to the total overhead.

Example 2   The Babblin Brooks Company produces four products. Products A and C
sell for $3.00 each; product B for $4.00; and product D for $6.00. Factory
overhead for the month was $180,000 and production was as follows:

Product A	20,000 units
Product B	30,000 units
Product C	40,000 units
Product D	10,000 units

Allocate the factory overhead among the various products according to
sales value.

SOLUTION   First, we must determine a ratio for allocation.

	Units Produced	Selling Price	Sales Value	Ratio
Product A	20,000 units	× $3.00 =	$ 60,000	$\dfrac{\$60,000}{\$360,000} = \dfrac{1}{6}$
Product B	30,000 units	× $4.00 =	$120,000	$\dfrac{\$120,000}{\$360,000} = \dfrac{1}{3}$
Product C	40,000 units	× $3.00 =	$120,000	$\dfrac{\$120,000}{\$360,000} = \dfrac{1}{3}$
Product D	10,000 units	× $6.00 =	$ 60,000	$\dfrac{\$60,000}{\$360,000} = \dfrac{1}{6}$
Total			$360,000	$\dfrac{6}{6}$ or 100%

Now, applying the ratios against the overhead expenses to be allocated, we can determine the factory overhead to be allocated to each product.

	Ratio	Allocated Overhead
Product A	$\dfrac{1}{6} \times \$180,000 =$	$ 30,000
Product B	$\dfrac{1}{3} \times \$180,000 =$	$ 60,000
Product C	$\dfrac{1}{3} \times \$180,000 =$	$ 60,000
Product D	$\dfrac{1}{6} \times \$180,000 =$	$ 30,000
	$\dfrac{6}{6} = 100\%$	$180,000

Exercises 8.4

■ Allocate the overhead expenses according to floor space in the following problems.

Department	Floor Space (sq ft)	Ratio	Total Overhead	Department Overhead
Example: A	2,500	$\dfrac{2500}{10,000} = 25\%$	$ 20,000	$ 5,000 (i.e., 20,000 × 25%)

	Department	Floor Space (sq ft)	Ratio	Total Overhead	Department Overhead
	B	7,500	$\frac{7500}{10,000} = 75\%$		$15,000 (i.e., 20,000 × 75%)
		10,000	100%		$20,000
1.	Plant	40,000		$ 60,000	
	Sales	10,000			
	Accounting	10,000			
2.	Shipping	5,000		$ 25,000	
	Administrative	2,000			
	Sales	3,000			
	Production	10,000			
3.	A	750		$ 5,000	
	B	1,250			
	C	500			
4.	Large	19,250		$140,000	
	Medium	12,250			
	Small	3,500			
5.	Administrative	2,500		$ 46,000	
	Design	1,500			
	Production	6,000			

■ Allocate the overhead expense according to sales value in the following problems.

	Product	Units Produced	Selling Price	Sales Value	Ratio	Total Overhead	Allocated Overhead
Example:	1	10,000 ×	$1.00	= $10,000	$\frac{\$10,000}{\$20,000} = 50\%$	× $ 4,000	= $2,000
	2	5,000 ×	$2.00	= $10,000	$\frac{\$10,000}{\$20,000} = 50\%$	× $ 4,000	= $2,000
				$20,000	100%		$4,000
6.	A	20,000	$2.10			$16,000	
	B	17,000	$1.50				
	C	2,500	$3.00				
7.	1	60,000	$2.50			$22,000	
	2	30,000	$5.00				
8.	A	30,000	$6.00			$67,500	
	B	90,000	$2.00				
	C	60,000	$4.00				
9.	Good	20,000	$3.00			$45,000	
	Better	15,000	$4.00				
	Best	10,000	$6.00				
10.	Cheap	1,000	$2.00			$ 800	
	Cheaper	800	$1.25				
	Own risk	1,000	$1.00				
11.	Solids	50,000	$0.70			$ 2,200	
	Stripes	50,000	$0.30				

12. The Ranger Manufacturing Company has a total of 100 people in the following departments.

Department A	15 employees
Department B	35 employees
Department C	5 employees
Department D	45 employees

Can you help allocate $5000 in overhead expenses for employee benefits?

13. Drillco has $30,000 in maintenance overhead which must be allocated among three production lines. If the three lines have the following machines, how would you allocate the overhead?

Line 1	3 machines
Line 2	6 machines
Line 3	9 machines

Review Exercises / Chapter 8

1. The High Fi Stereo Center purchased their "Convair" speakers for the year as follows:

March 28	115 units at $37.00 each
June 12	245 units at $38.50 each
Sept. 29	230 units at $40.00 each
Nov. 3	130 units at $41.50 each

On December 31, there were 142 units in inventory. Value the inventory according to (**a**) average cost, (**b**) FIFO, and (**c**) LIFO. (**d**) The Convair speaker was replaced on January 15 with the Convair II. All Convairs are being sold by the manufacturer for $30.00. Will that affect your inventory value?

2. The Knit Shop's inventory (at cost) on January 1 was $29,500. During the year, purchases totaled $196,000 (at cost) and net sales were $310,500 (at retail). If the shop uses a 35% markup based on selling price, what would you estimate as the ending inventory value?

3. The Fashion Mall has total sales of $2,833,450 for the year to date. The beginning inventory and purchases (valued at selling price) were $190,290 and $2,860,395, respectively. Can you estimate the inventory value (at cost) if you know that the markup rate (on selling price) is 40%?

4. Using the answers you calculated in problems 2 and 3, calculate the inventory turnover ratios for the Knit Shop and the Fashion Mall.

5. Hip Shot's Hunting Supply store has an inventory valued at $46,500. They estimate sales for the coming month at $97,000 and want to end the month with an inventory of $38,400. Their normal markup rate is 30% (on selling price).

a. Calculate the planned purchase amount (at cost) for the month.

b. They are offered a "great buy" in $10,000 worth of guns. If they have ordered and paid for $49,000 in merchandise and ordered $12,000 more, can they make the buy without exceeding their planned purchases? How much are they short or over before the purchase?

6. Allocate $240,000 in overhead costs among the following four departments according to the amount of space they occupy in the building. The production department has 12,000 square feet, the sales department has 4000 square feet, the accounting department has 2000 square feet, and the shipping department has 2000 square feet.

7. The Whatta Deal Warehouse has added a new product to their inventory. The first purchase was 500 units at $3.75 per unit. The next order was 750 units at $3.80, and the last order was 425 units at $3.70. What is the value of the 510 units remaining in inventory according to (*a*) average cost? (*b*) LIFO? (*c*) FIFO?

8. The House of Wax had $14,250 (at cost) in the January 1 inventory. Purchases during the year cost $87,410 and net sales to date have been $127,000. Use the gross profit method to estimate the current (ending) inventory assuming a markup rate of (*a*) 30% based on selling price, (*b*) 40% based on cost.

9. Use the retail method to estimate the cost of the ending inventory given the following information.

Beginning inventory	$107,600 (at retail)
Purchases	$1,317,210 (at retail)
Net sales	$1,389,000

Assume a markup rate of (*a*) 35% based on cost, (*b*) 25% based on selling price.

10. The Zero Defeck Corporation had $10,000 in maintenance expense associated with 3 machines on a production line. Allocate the maintenance expense among these machines (according to usage) assuming the following production.

Machine 1409	37,500 units
Machine 1106	40,300 units
Machine 0099	22,200 units

Chapter Test / Chapter 8

1. Define the following terms:

a. inventory   *b*. LIFO

c. FIFO   *d*. open-to-buy

e. overhead

Calculate the inventory values in problems 2 and 3 using LIFO, FIFO, and the average cost method.

2. The New Shop opened on March 10. Purchases for the year were as follows:

> Feb. 12   2000 units at $3.75
> June 8   1000 units at $3.80
> Aug. 4   1500 units at $3.82
> Nov. 8   1000 units at $3.90

What value would the 1240 units in inventory at the end of the year have?

3. Henry's Supply House had 300 units of Tyline Cutters that cost $11.45 each in inventory on December 1 of last year. Purchases of Tyline Cutters for this year have been as follows:

> April   450 at $11.60
> Aug.   300 at $11.50
> Oct.   325 at $11.65

Value the 400 units remaining in inventory at the end of this year.

4. Calculate the cost of goods sold and use the gross profit method to estimate the current inventory value for the Handy Helper Store. The January 1 inventory value was $132,000 and purchases so far this year amount to $287,250. Sales (net) to date are $316,472.64. The store has a 32% markup based on cost.

5. Given the same data as in problem 4, what would the inventory value be if the markup rate were 25% based on selling price?

6. The Tres Chic Shop had in inventory at the end of last year dresses that would sell for $48,650. So far this year, they have purchased dresses that will sell for $137,600; net sales for the same time period are $153,950. What is the approximate value (cost) of the current inventory if the markup rate used in the store is 30% based on selling price?

7. What would be your estimate of the current inventory of the Tres Chic Shop (problem 6) if the markup rate were 35% based on cost?

8. The Wonderbar had a beginning inventory of $22,300 and an ending inventory of $26,800 at cost. Sales for the year were $98,270 and the markup rate is 35% based on selling price. Calculate the inventory turnover rate.

9. Everett's Truly Value Store estimates that sales in the third quarter will be $186,000. The inventory as of July 1 is estimated to be $42,300 at retail and they would like to have an inventory retailing for $48,650 as of September 30. Some purchases for the third quarter have already been made; goods costing $63,500 have been ordered. Of that amount ordered, $28,450 worth have been received. Goods at the Truly Value Store are marked up 25% based on cost. Calculate the amount of planned purchases for the third quarter and the open-to-buy amount as of this date.

10. FGM Manufacturing Company distributes its overhead expense according to the sales values of the product lines. Overhead expense in April was $142,000, with production as follows: product A, 10,000 units; product B, 20,000 units; product C, 40,000 units, and product Z, 5,000 units. The selling prices of the products are product A, $4.00 each; product B, 2 for $10.00; product C, $8.00 for a case of 10; and product Z, $5.60 each. Allocate April's overhead expense.

CHAPTER 9

Depreciation (Cost Recovery)

INTRODUCTION

When the owner of a business purchases a machine, building, or other asset, he acquires a "pool" of resources to use in producing income in the future. He must find a way to determine the cost of the asset's service as the service is withdrawn from the "pool" of resources and used in business operation. *Depreciation* is that part of an asset's cost that is deducted from revenue to provide for the services of the asset used in business operation.

Definition

depreciation

Depreciation is a measure of the cost of an asset's services as the asset is used in business operation. It is normally stated in terms of dollars for a given period of time.

Although we calculate a dollar amount of depreciation, that dollar amount may vary depending on a number of factors. There are several variables used in the calculation of depreciation; some of these variables have estimated values. In addition, there is more than one acceptable way to calculate depreciation.

Although the *depreciation concept* remained the same, the *depreciation process* changed significantly with the Economic Recovery Tax Act of 1981. That act changed existing depreciation rules and provided new methods of calculating *cost recovery* (the term used for depreciation under the Accelerated Cost Recovery System as outlined in the Tax Act of 1981). Why the term "cost recovery?" We noted that depreciation matched a portion of the assets' cost with the revenue generated by that asset. Therefore, we are "recovering" (for use in the business) those dollars of the assets' cost represented by the annual depreciation.

Our discussion in this chapter will include *both* depreciation and cost recovery (that is, the depreciation concept and its calculation before and after the Tax Act of 1981). We do this for the following two reasons:

1. Cost recovery is applicable only to assets placed in service during or after 1981. Assets placed in service prior to 1981 (i.e., 1980 or earlier) will be depreciated under the "old" depreciation methods. However, many of these pre-1981 assets will be in service for many years after 1981. Therefore, we need to know how to calculate depreciation for such assets as long as they are in service.

2. The depreciation methods prior to 1981 were used in developing the cost recovery method for 1981 and later. Thus, our understanding of depreciation methods will help us understand the cost recovery system.

We need the following terms to study the depreciation concept under the depreciation and cost recovery methods.

Definitions

depreciation terms

1. *Life*—**The life of an asset is its estimated span of usefulness. Life may be measured in terms of time (i.e., the number of years an asset will last) or in terms of output (i.e., the number of units produced, the number of miles driven, the number of hours operated, etc.).**

2. *Salvage* (**or scrap**) *value*—**Salvage value is the estimated amount for which the asset can be sold at the end of its useful life.**

3. *Accumulated depreciation*—**Depreciation is calculated on a yearly basis (i.e., number of dollars per year). Accumulated depreciation is the sum of all annual depreciation amounts from the date the asset was purchased to the present.**

4. *Book value*—**Book value is the value of the asset as reflected in the company's records (or books). It is the *initial cost* (purchase price) of an asset *minus* the *accumulated depreciation*.**

5. *Depreciation base*—**The depreciation base is the total dollar amount that will be depreciated over the life of the asset. It is the original cost of the asset minus the salvage value.**

6. *Accelerated Cost Recovery System* (*ACRS*)—**The ACRS is the method provided in the Economic Recovery Tax Act of 1981 for matching a portion of an assets' cost with the revenue the asset generated. ACRS applies only to assets placed in service during 1981 or later years.**

7. *Class life period*—**Under ACRS, assets are assigned to one of four periods known as class life periods. The class life period determines how much of the asset's cost will be recovered each year and for how many years cost recovery applies.**

The amount of depreciation or cost recovered will affect the company's earnings for the year. These amounts are considered an expense of operating; as such, they reduce the amount of profit the business makes (and the amount of income tax the business must pay). We will now examine several of the major methods used to estimate depreciation (for assets placed in service *before* 1981). Then we will discuss the cost recovery method for assets placed in service *during or after* 1981.

9.1 Straight-Line Depreciation Method (Prior to the Tax Act of 1981)

straight-line
depreciation

The *straight-line method* is the simplest method of depreciation. The amount of depreciation is the same for every year of the asset's life. The amount of yearly depreciation is equal to the depreciation base (i.e., the cost of the asset minus its salvage value) divided by the estimated life in years.

Annual Depreciation—Straight Line

The amount of annual depreciation using the straight-line method can be computed as follows:

$$\text{depreciation} = \frac{\text{cost} - \text{salvage}}{\text{life}} \quad \text{or} \quad D = \frac{C - S}{L}$$

where D = annual depreciation, dollars
C = asset cost, dollars
S = salvage value, dollars
L = service life, years

This amount remains constant for each year of the asset's life.

Example 1

Safe-T Movers Co. bought a truck for $8500. They estimate that they can use the truck for 4 years and then sell it for $500. What is the amount of yearly depreciation using the straight-line method?

SOLUTION

$$D = \frac{C - S}{L}$$

$$= \frac{\$8500 - \$500}{4 \text{ years}}$$

$$= \frac{\$8000}{4 \text{ years}}$$

$$= \$2000 \text{ per year}$$

Therefore, the yearly amount of depreciation is $2000.

Depreciation may be expressed as a rate (i.e., percent). The depreciation rate per year may be calculated by dividing the life of the asset into 1. For example, an asset with a 4-year life will have a 25% annual depreciation rate (i.e., $\frac{1}{4} = 0.25$ or 25%).

Depreciation Rate

The depreciation rate (i.e., percent) can be computed as follows:

depreciation rate =
$$\frac{1}{\text{Life}}$$

$$\text{rate of depreciation} = \frac{1}{L}$$

where L is the life of the asset, in years. This equation gives the depreciation rate as a decimal number. It can be converted to percent by multiplying by 100.

Example 2   The Flying Stork Baby Furniture Co. purchased a new delivery van for $7500. It has an estimated life of 5 years and a salvage value of $500. Calculate the annual depreciation and the depreciation rate.

SOLUTION   The annual depreciation

$$D = \frac{C - S}{L}$$

$$= \frac{\$7500 - \$500}{5 \text{ years}}$$

$$= \frac{\$7000}{5 \text{ years}}$$

$$= \$1400 \text{ per year}$$

The depreciation rate $= \frac{1}{5} = 0.20 = 20\%$ per year.

---

depreciation schedule   Depreciation is commonly shown in a *depreciation schedule*. The schedule shows the amount of annual depreciation, the accumulated depreciation (i.e., the sum of all of the amounts previously depreciated on the asset), and the book value of the asset (i.e., the original cost of the asset minus the accumulated depreciation). Figure 9.1 shows the depreciation schedule for the delivery van in Example 2.

Figure 9.1

Depreciation Schedule
Flying Stork Baby Furniture Co.
Delivery Van

Year	Annual Depreciation	Accumulated Depreciation	Book Value
1	$1400	$1400	$6100
2	$1400	$2800	$4700
3	$1400	$4200	$3300
4	$1400	$5600	$1900
5	$1400	$7000	$ 500 (salvage value)

Note several points about the depreciation schedule *under the straight-line method.*

1. The annual amount of depreciation is a constant-dollar value ($1400 per year).
2. The book value is calculated by subtracting the accumulated depreciation from the original cost. Hence, the accumulated depreciation and the book value for any year should total the original cost ($7500).
3. The book value in the last year of life is equal to the salvage value ($500).

Example 3

The A-1 Milling Company purchases a new lathe for $10,000. You know that the book value at the end of the service life is $1000 and the depreciation rate is $33\frac{1}{3}\%$ on a straight-line basis. Set up the appropriate depreciation schedule.

SOLUTION

The book value at the end of the service life is equal to the salvage value (i.e., $1000). Hence, the depreciation base of the lathe is $9000 ($10,000 original cost − $1000 salvage value). Since the depreciation rate is $33\frac{1}{3}\%$ (or $\frac{1}{3}$) on a straight-line basis, $\frac{1}{3}$ of the $9000 will be depreciated in each of 3 years. Hence, the annual depreciation on the lathe is $3000 ($\frac{1}{3} \times$ $9000).

Depreciation Schedule
A-1 Milling Company
Lathe

Year	Annual Depreciation	Accumulated Depreciation	Book Value
1	$3000	$3000	$7000
2	3000	6000	4000
3	3000	9000	1000 (salvage value)

Our previous examples assumed that the assets were purchased on January 1 and that depreciation was calculated for the entire year. Obviously, major equipment purchases are made throughout the year, and thus, we need to be able to calculate depreciation for only part of a year (i.e., the *partial-year* depreciation).

Partial-Year Depreciation—Straight-Line Method
   The amount of depreciation is found by multiplying the fraction of a year that the asset is owned by the amount of depreciation normally calculated for the first full year.

Example 4   The Shakey Bridge Construction Company purchased a new tractor for $14,000 on April 1. The tractor has an estimated life of 4 years with a salvage value of $2000. Compute the amount of depreciation for the partial year using straight-line depreciation.

SOLUTION   The annual amount of depreciation is

$$D = \frac{\text{cost} - \text{salvage}}{\text{life}}$$

$$= \frac{\$14{,}000 - \$2000}{4 \text{ years}}$$

$$= \frac{\$12{,}000}{4 \text{ years}}$$

$$= \$3000 \text{ per year}$$

Since the company purchased the tractor on April 1, they owned it for 9 months (i.e., $\frac{3}{4}$ of a year). Depreciation for the first year is $(\frac{3}{4})(\$3000) = \$2250$. The following 3 years are depreciated at the full $3000 per year. The depreciation for the last 3 months of year 4 is calculated as a partial year [i.e., $(\frac{1}{4})(\$3000) = \$750$].

---

amortization— depreciation for intangibles

The term "depreciation" is generally applied only to tangible assets (those with physical substance or "touchable"). The principle of depreciation is applied to intangible assets (such as patents, copyrights, etc.), but the proper term is *amortization*. The straight-line method is generally used to amortize such assets.

Exercises 9.1

■ Calculate the straight-line depreciation and the depreciation rate for items having the following characteristics (assume depreciation for a full year in problems 1–16.)

	Cost	Salvage Value	Life	Depreciation Amount	Rate
1.	$900	$100	4 years		
2.	$1250	$50	3 years		
3.	$2500	$100	12 years		
4.	$55,000	$5000	10 years		
5.	$4850	$350	9 years		
6.	$9600	$600	3 years		

7. The Wizard Widget Company purchased a widget press for $4500. It has an estimated life of 4 years and a salvage value of $500. What is the annual depreciation?

8. Grandmother's Tennis Shoe Shop had new display shelves built in the store at a cost of $2000. These shelves should last 10 years and have no salvage value when removed. What is the annual depreciation on the shelves?

9. The Light Company purchased a new generator for $150,000. What is the

10. Mac's Delivery Service acquired a new pickup for $6000. It has no salvage value and will be depreciated at $1500 per year. What is the depreciation rate?

11. Complete the following depreciation schedule.

Depreciation Schedule
Acme Company
Dumpster

Year	Annual Depreciation	Accumulated Depreciation	Book Value
1	$4,000	?	$18,000
2	?	$ 8,000	14,000
3	4,000	12,000	?
4	4,000	?	6,000
5	4,000	20,000	? (salvage value)

12. The Zebra Paint Company purchased a new paint mixer for $2500. It has a useful life of 4 years and annual depreciation of $500. Set up the appropriate depreciation schedule. What is the salvage value?

13. Mr. Clean Laundry has a new press that will have a salvage value of $750 at the end of its 6-year life. Annual depreciation is $500. How much did the press cost?

14. The book value of an asset is $2200. The asset cost $4500 and has a salvage value of $300. What is the accumulated depreciation?

15. Whiz-Mark Corporation has a machine that was purchased 3 years ago for $17,500. The estimated life and salvage value are 5 years and $2500. What is (**a**) the book value, and (**b**) the accumulated depreciation on the machine?

16. A farmer purchased a new tractor in 1979 at a cost of $48,000. He is depreciating it at $7000 per year. The salvage value is estimated at $6000.

    a. What is the useful life of the tractor?

    b. What is the annual rate of depreciation?

    c. What will be the book value at the end of 4 years?

■ Compute the depreciation for the partial year in the following problems. Use the straight-line depreciation method.

	Months of Use (Current Year)	Asset Cost	Salvage Value	Life (Years)	Total Depreciation (Current Year)
Example:	6	$5500	$500	5	$500 $\left(\text{i.e., } \dfrac{\$5500 - \$500}{5 \text{ years}} \times \dfrac{1}{2}\right)$
17.	6	$69,500	$9500	12	
18.	3	$4850	$350	9	
19.	9	$105,000	$5000	10	
20.	12	$42,000	$3000	3	

21. Whiznat Manufacturing Corporation purchased a new machine on July 1. It cost $127,500 and has a salvage value of $7500 at the end of its 20-year life. What is the depreciation at the end of the first year?

22. Compute the depreciation for the second year in problem 21.

23. The Magic Mirror purchased some new display shelves on April 1 for $1250. They should last 3 years and have a salvage value of $50. Set up the appropriate depreciation schedule.

24. On October 1, Major Company bought an asset for $16,650. It has a salvage value of $2250 and an estimated life of 12 years. What will be the depreciation at the end of the first year?

25. The Novelty Company paid $4000 for a patent on processing rubber gimmicks. The life of the patent is estimated at 10 years. How much should be amortized each year?

26. The Rather Strange Publishing Company purchased the copyright on a book entitled "Going Against the Breeze." They paid $10,000. If the copyright is worthless in 20 years, how much should be amortized in the current year? The copyright was purchased on July 1.

9.2 *Units-of-Production Depreciation Method (Prior to the Tax Act of 1981)*

units-of-production
depreciation

The units-of-production method of depreciation is similar to the straight-line method in that a constant amount is depreciated. However, where the straight-line method depreciates a constant amount per year of life, the units-of-production method depreciates a *constant amount per unit produced*.

The annual depreciation of the asset is then calculated by taking the amount of depreciation per unit produced and multiplying it by the number of units produced during the year.

The basic equation for depreciation per unit is the cost of the asset minus the salvage value, all divided by the service life in *units produced* or *hours of use*. That is,

depreciation per unit

$$\text{depreciation per unit} = \frac{\text{cost} - \text{salvage value}}{\text{life (in production units)}}$$

or

$$D = \frac{C - S}{L}$$

where L is the life in production units. The annual depreciation is calculated by multiplying the depreciation per unit times the number of units produced during the year.

$$\text{annual depreciation} =$$
$$(D \text{ per unit}) \times (\text{units produced during the year})$$

Example 1

A machine costing $75,000 has a salvage value of $5000 and an estimated service life of 350,000 units. Calculate the depreciation per unit, the annual depreciation, and set up a depreciation schedule. Assume the following production:

Year 1	150,000 units
Year 2	100,000 units
Year 3	75,000 units
Year 4	25,000 units

SOLUTION

$$\text{Depreciation per unit} = \frac{\text{cost} - \text{salvage}}{\text{life (in production units)}}$$

$$= \frac{\$75,000 - \$5000}{350,000 \text{ units}}$$

$$= \frac{\$70,000}{350,000 \text{ units}} = \$0.20 \text{ per unit}$$

The annual depreciation for the years would be:

Year 1	150,000 units × $0.20/unit or	$30,000
Year 2	100,000 units × $0.20/unit or	$20,000
Year 3	75,000 units × $0.20/unit or	$15,000
Year 4	25,000 units × $0.20/unit or	$ 5,000
	350,000 units	$70,000

and the depreciation schedule would be

Year	Annual Depreciation	Accumulated Depreciation	Book Value
1	$30,000	$30,000	$45,000
2	20,000	50,000	25,000
3	15,000	65,000	10,000
4	5,000	70,000	5,000 (salvage value)

The units-of-production method of depreciation for a partial year poses no special problem. Remember: depreciation is based on the number of units produced by the asset, not the length of time the asset is owned.

Partial-Year Depreciation—Units-of-Production Method

The amount of depreciation (for a partial year) is the number of units used during the partial year multiplied by the depreciation rate per unit.

Example 2

A machine purchased on June 3 produces 2000 units for the remainder of the year. If the depreciation rate per unit is $0.12, find the amount of depreciation.

SOLUTION   The amount of depreciation is (2000) ($0.12) = $240.

---

depletion—
depreciation for
natural resources

The principle of depreciation is also applied to natural resources (minerals, oil, gas, etc.), but the proper term for such depreciation is *depletion*. The units-of-production method is generally used, although special depletion schedules can be used for tax purposes.

Example 3

The Quicksilver Gold Mine Company paid $5,000,000 for a limestone quarry with an estimated yield of 1,200,000 tons of limestone. The estimated value of the land following mining operations is $200,000. The company extracted 200,000 tons of limestone this year. What depletion expense should be charged?

SOLUTION   The depletion base of the mine is the $5,000,000 cost less the $200,000 residual value, or $4,800,000. The value per ton for the entire mine is thus

$$\frac{\$4,800,000}{1,200,000 \text{ tons}} = \$4.00/\text{ton}$$

Depletion for the year would then be

$$200,000 \text{ tons} \times \$4.00/\text{ton} = \$800,000$$

Exercises 9.2

■ Calculate the depreciation per unit for the following items:

	Cost	Salvage Value	Estimated Total Units Produced	Depreciation per Unit
1.	$50,000	$5000	90,000	?
2.	$36,000	0	400,000	?
3.	$42,500	$500	70,000	?
4.	$405,000	$15,000	3,000,000	?
5.	$11,000	$1000	10,000	?
6.	$75,000	$15,000	1,200,000	?

■ Compute the annual amount of depreciation in the following conditions.

	Depreciation per Unit	Units Produced	Annual Depreciation
7.	$0.15	100,000	?
8.	$2.45	10,000	?
9.	$0.125	185,000	?
10.	$0.50	22,500	?
11.	$0.30	196,000	?
12.	$0.65	89,500	?

13. Machine A has an estimated life of 200,000 hours. It cost $48,000 and will have a salvage value of $4000. It was used for 80,000 hours this year. Compute the depreciation.

14. The AB Company has an asset acquired at a cost of $22,750. This asset should produce 110,000 units and have a salvage value of $750. If this year's production was 30,000 units, what should the depreciation be?

15. The Ace Wrecker Company has used its wrecker 50,000 miles this year. If the wrecker cost $9500 and has a $1000 salvage value at the end of its 100,000-mile life, what should the depreciation be?

16. The Golden Hammer Hardware Store purchased a delivery pickup for $8450. The estimated service life of the pickup is 150,000 miles with a salvage value of $950. The pickup lasted five years (and 150,000 miles) and was driven as follows:

Year 1	35,000 miles
Year 2	32,500 miles
Year 3	30,000 miles
Year 4	27,500 miles
Year 5	25,000 miles

Show the appropriate depreciation schedule.

■ Compute the depreciation for the partial year in the following problems. Use the units-of-production depreciation method.

	Months of Use (Current Year)	Units Produced (Current Year)	Depreciation per Unit	Total Depreciation (Current Year)
Example:	6	30,000	$0.05	$1500 (i.e., 30,000 × $0.05)
17.	8	100,000	$0.02	?
18.	$5\frac{1}{2}$	18,500	$0.01	?
19.	10	98,700	$0.10	?
20.	$6\frac{1}{2}$	16,000	$0.25	?

21. An asset costing $9635 has a production life of 30,000 units and a salvage value of $635. It was acquired on June 1 and produced 4850 units in the remainder of the year. What is the yearly depreciation?

22. Wonder Widget Company acquired a new press which has an estimated life of 500,000 units. The press cost $120,000 and has a salvage value of $20,000. The press was purchased on April 1 and produced a monthly average of 10,000 units for the rest of the year. What is the depreciation expense?

23. The Lucky Strike Uranium Company purchased a mine for $10,000,000. The company estimates that the mine will yield 500,000 tons of ore over its life. How much depletion expense can the company take assuming 75,000 tons of ore were extracted in the current year?

24. The Dry Hole Oil Company purchased an oil well for $25,000. They anticipate pumping a total of 10,000 barrels of oil from the well. What is the depletion allowance for this year assuming removal of 4000 barrels of oil?

25. The Boulder Gravel Company purchased a new quarry for $450,000. Estimated output of the quarry is 10,000 tons. The quarry was purchased on April 1 and output for the current year was 2750 tons. What is the depletion expense?

9.3 *Sum-of-the-Years-Digits Depreciation Method (Prior to the Tax Act of 1981)*

accelerated
depreciation—
charging more
depreciation in the
early years of an
asset's life

The sum-of-the-years-digits method of depreciation is a method of *accelerated* depreciation. That is, the asset is depreciated at a different *rate* for each year of its life. More depreciation is charged in the earlier years of the asset's life than in later years.

Accelerated depreciation assumes that the economic benefit derived from the asset is greater in the earlier years of its service life; hence, more depreciation should be charged in those early years. In reality, accelerated depreciation reduces the amount of income tax payable by the company when the asset is new. For this reason, it is used by many companies.

The depreciation base under the sum-of-the-years-digits will be the same as the depreciation base under the previous methods (i.e., cost minus salvage value). However, the straight-line and units-of-production methods use a constant amount of depreciation, such as dollars per year or dollars per unit, respectively. In the sum-of-the-years-digits method, the *rate* of depreciation (and hence the amount of depreciation) changes from year to year (with the larger amounts first). The rate of depreciation for each year will be a fraction that can be calculated (as the name implies) from the sum-of-the-years-digits.

First, put the estimated number of years of service life in a column labeled "*Year*." Second, make a new column by reversing the order of the years, putting the number of the last year first, and counting downward. This column is labeled "*Digit*." Third, the numbers in the "*Digit*" column are totaled to get the *sum of the* (*years*) *digits*. Then, the rate of depreciation will be a fraction having the sum of the digits as the denominator and the digit from the "*Digit*" column as the numerator.

For an asset with a service life of 5 years, we have

Note: the sum of the digits 1 through n is

$$\text{sum} = \frac{n(n + 1)}{2}$$

Year	Digit	Depreciation Rate
1	5	$\frac{5}{15}$
2	4	$\frac{4}{15}$
3	3	$\frac{3}{15}$
4	2	$\frac{2}{15}$
5	1	$\frac{1}{15}$
Total =	15	$\frac{15}{15} = 1$

Note that the total of the depreciation rates always equals 1. This fact may be a useful check.

> To compute the *amount of depreciation in any year*, multiply the depreciation rate for that year times the depreciation base.

Example 1   An asset costing $18,000 has an estimated life of 5 years and a salvage value of $3000. Find the amount of depreciation for each year and make a depreciation schedule using the sum-of-the-years-digits method.

SOLUTION   The amount to be depreciated is $15,000 (i.e., $18,000 − $3000). The annual depreciation can be calculated as follows:

Year	Digit	Depreciation Rate	Amount of Depreciation (for Each Year)
1	5	$\frac{5}{15}$	($\frac{5}{15}$ × $15,000 =) $ 5,000
2	4	$\frac{4}{15}$	($\frac{4}{15}$ × $15,000 =) $ 4,000
3	3	$\frac{3}{15}$	($\frac{3}{15}$ × $15,000 =) $ 3,000
4	2	$\frac{2}{15}$	($\frac{2}{15}$ × $15,000 =) $ 2,000
5	1	$\frac{1}{15}$	($\frac{1}{15}$ × $15,000 =) $ 1,000
	15	$\frac{15}{15} = 1$	$15,000

Note that the amounts of depreciation are larger at the beginning of the asset's service life.

The depreciation schedule is as follows:

Year	Annual Depreciation	Accumulated Depreciation	Book Value
1	$5,000	$ 5,000	$13,000
2	4,000	9,000	9,000
3	3,000	12,000	6,000
4	2,000	14,000	4,000
5	1,000	15,000	3,000
			(salvage value)

Again, note that the accumulated depreciation at the end of the asset's life is equal to the depreciation base ($15,000) and that the book value remaining is the salvage value ($3000).

Partial-year depreciation using the sum-of-the-years-digits method requires that the depreciation generated by the depreciation rate be spread over two calendar years. Why? The sum-of-the-years-digits method requires that the amount depreciated over the first 12 months the asset is owned be equal to the depreciation rate (for the first year) times the depreciation base. However, in the case of a partial year, the first 12 months of ownership occurs in 2 calendar years. The same principle applies to the following years.

Partial-Year Depreciation—Sum-of-the-Years-Digits Method

First, set up the depreciation schedule for the sum-of-the-years-digits method as before.

The first year's depreciation is the fraction of the year the asset is owned multiplied by the depreciation for the first full year.

The depreciation for the second year is computed in two parts:

Step 1. The remaining fraction of the first year is multiplied by the amount of depreciation for the first year (even though you are working on the second year).

Step 2. The remaining part (or fraction) of the second year is multiplied by the amount of depreciation for the second year.

The total amount of depreciation for the second year is the sum of the amounts found in steps 1 and 2.

This process is repeated for all succeeding years.

Example 2   An asset is purchased on April 1 for $18,000. The asset has a life of 4 years and a salvage value of $2000. If the asset is depreciated by the sum-of-the-years-digits method, find the first (partial) year's depreciation and the second year's depreciation.

SOLUTION   The rate (fractions) for the sum-of-the-years-digits method and yearly depreciation are as follows:

Year	Digit	Rate (Fractions)		Annual Depreciation
1	4	$\frac{4}{10}$	$\times$ $16,000 =	$ 6,400
2	3	$\frac{3}{10}$	$\times$ $16,000 =	$ 4,800
3	2	$\frac{2}{10}$	$\times$ $16,000 =	$ 3,200
4	1	$\frac{1}{10}$	$\times$ $16,000 =	$ 1,600
		10	Total depreciation =	$16,000

If the asset had been owned for the entire first year, the depreciation would have been $6400. Since the asset was owned for only 9 months (i.e., $\frac{3}{4}$ of a year), the *first year's* depreciation is $(\frac{3}{4})(\$6400) = \$4800$. This is the depreciation for April 1–December 31 of the first year. Under the sum-of-the-years-digits method, the first 12 months of the asset's life must be depreciated at a rate of $\frac{4}{10}$. Since we have used only the first 9 months, the remaining 3 months ($\frac{1}{4}$ year) must be applied in year 2. Hence, the depreciation for year 2 is the remainder of year 1 times the year 1 depreciation plus the remaining fraction of year 2 times the year 2 depreciation:

$$(\tfrac{1}{4} \text{ from year 1})(\$6400 \text{ year 1 depreciation}) = \$1600$$
$$\text{plus } (\tfrac{3}{4} \text{ from year 2})(\$4800 \text{ year 2 depreciation}) = \$3600$$
$$\overline{}$$
$$\text{Total} = \$5200$$

Year 2 depreciation is $5200. Depreciation for following years would be calculated in the same manner.

Exercises 9.3

■ Complete the table of depreciation rates for the years shown. Use the sum-of-the-years-digits depreciation method. Assume depreciation for a full year in all problems unless given information to the contrary.

		Year	Digit	Depreciation Rate
Example:	2 years	1	2	$\frac{2}{3}$
		2	1	$\frac{1}{3}$
			3	$\frac{3}{3}$
1.	3 years	1		
		2		
		3		
2.	4 years	1		
		2		
		3		
		4		
3.	5 years	1		
		2		
		3		
		4		
		5		
4.	6 years	1		
		2		
		3		
		4		
		5		
		6		

5. What annual depreciation will be charged on an asset having a cost of $12,000, a salvage value of $2000, and a life of 4 years?

6. The DeTour Construction Co. purchased a piece of road machinery for $62,500. It has an estimated life of 10 years, at which time it can be sold for $7500. What will the annual depreciation be for the first 4 years?

7. Set up a depreciation schedule for an asset costing $25,000 and having a 6-year life. Its salvage value is $4000.

Give the depreciation rate and dollar amounts of depreciation in the following problems.

	Year	Asset Cost	Salvage Value	Life	Depreciation Rate	Dollar Depreciation
Example:	5	$16,000	$1000	5	$\frac{1}{15}$	$1000
8.	3	$22,000	$2000	4		
9.	6	$40,000	$4000	8		
10.	4	$110,000	0	10		
11.	7	$155,000	$20,000	9		
12.	5	$8350	$550	12		

13. What will be the depreciation in the eighth year of an asset that cost $123,000, has a salvage value of $13,000, and has a life of 10 years?

14. Tree Top Airways acquired a new plane for $10,000,000. It should last for 7 years and have a salvage value of $1,600,000. What will be the depreciation in the fourth year?

15. Compute the depreciation in the third year for an asset costing $72,500 and having a 6-year life. Salvage on the asset is $9500.

16. Shake 'N Movers purchased a new computer to handle their bookkeeping functions. It cost $28,000 and has an estimated life of 4 years. Salvage value is estimated at $2000. Assuming the computer was purchased on June 30, use the sum-of-the-year-digits depreciation method to prepare a depreciation schedule.

17. The Helping Hands Cleaning Service purchased a new floor polisher for $850. It was purchased on July 1 and has an estimated life of 3 years. Salvage value at that time should be $250. Helping Hands uses the sum-of-the-years-digits method of computing depreciation. Prepare the appropriate depreciation schedule.

18. Prepare a sum-of-the-years-digits depreciation schedule for an asset purchased on April 1 for $18,000. It has a 5-year life and a $3000 salvage value.

19. An asset was purchased October 1, 1979, for $10,000. It has an estimated life of 5 years and a salvage value of $1000. If the asset is depreciated by the sum-of-the-years-digits method, compute the depreciation schedule.

20. The Wonder World Company purchased a new machine on July 1, 1980, for $22,500. It has an estimated life of 4 years and an estimated salvage value of $2500. Compute the accumulated depreciation and book value for the machine (assuming the sum-of-the-years-digits method) at the end of 1981 and 1982.

9.4 *Declining-Balance Depreciation Method (Prior to the Tax Act of 1981)*

The declining-balance method of depreciation is an accelerated method of depreciation (as was the sum-of-the-years-digits method). Recall that the sum-of-the-years-digits method used a *variable rate* (fraction) for each year times a *constant amount* (cost less salvage value). The declining-balance method uses a *constant rate* times a *variable amount* each year. The *variable amount* is the (declining) book value of the asset.

The first step in the declining-balance method of depreciation is to determine the *depreciation rate*.

finding the declining-balance rate

Declining-Balance Rate of Depreciation

Step 1. The number 1 is divided by the estimated years of service life. That is, compute $\dfrac{1}{L \text{ (in years)}}$, where L is the service life of the asset. (This value may be expressed as a fraction, decimal, or percent.)

Step 2. The value of $\dfrac{1}{L}$ is multiplied by a factor ranging from 1.25 (or 125%) to 2.00 (or 200%). (The factor used depends on the tax laws that are applicable to the particular asset.) The resulting product is the declining-balance rate of depreciation.

Note that the value of $\dfrac{1}{L}$ is simply the depreciation rate in the straight-line method. The rate most commonly used for the declining-balance method is the *double-declining-balance* rate or twice the straight-line rate.

Example 1   Find the straight-line rate and the 200% (double) declining-balance rate for assets having lives of 4, 5, 10, and 20 years.

SOLUTION

Years of Life	Straight-Line Rate (1/L)	Double-Declining-Balance Rate (200%)
4	$\frac{1}{4}$ or 0.25 or 25%	0.5 or 50%
5	$\frac{1}{5}$ or 0.20 or 20%	0.4 or 40%
10	$\frac{1}{10}$ or 0.10 or 10%	0.2 or 20%
20	$\frac{1}{20}$ or 0.05 or 5%	0.1 or 10%

As with most rates, the declining-balance rates are usually stated in percent. Of course, the decimal forms are used in actual computation. The amount of depreciation for each year is determined as follows:

Depreciation—Declining-Balance Method

The amount of depreciation is found by multiplying the declining-balance rate (which is constant throughout the life of an asset) times the book value of the asset at the beginning of the year.

Remember, the *book value* is the *original cost minus the accumulated depreciation*. The book value decreases or declines each year; hence the name of the method. Also, *no salvage value is considered in computing depreciation by the declining-balance method*. However, if the salvage value is known, it must be considered in a special way.

Example 2   Stafford Packing Company purchases a forklift truck for $13,000. It has an estimated life of 4 years and a salvage value of $750. Calculate the amount of depreciation for each year and show the results in a depreciation schedule. Use the double-declining-balance rate.

SOLUTION   For an asset with an estimated life of 4 years, the straight-line rate is $\frac{1}{4}$ (or 25%). Hence, the double-declining-balance rate is 2 × 25%, or 50%.

The amount of depreciation for the first year is 50% times $13,000, or $6500. The book value for the first year is the cost (i.e., $13,000). Hence, the book value for the second year is $6500 (i.e., $13,000 − $6500).

The amount of depreciation for the second year is 50% times $6500, or $3250. Hence, the book value for the third year is $3250 (i.e., $6500 − $3250), and so on.

This amount can be represented in a depreciation schedule as shown in Figure 9.2.

Figure 9.2

**Depreciation Schedule
Stafford Packing Company
Forklift**

Year	Book Value (Beginning of Year)	Depreciation Rate	Current Year's Depreciation	Accumulated Depreciation	Book Value (End of Year)
1	$13,000	50%	$6,500	$ 6,500	$6,500
2	6,500	50%	3,250	9,750	3,250
3	3,250	50%	1,625	11,375	1,625
4	1,625	50%	875[a]	12,250	750

[a] The last year's depreciation must be adjusted to account for the proper salvage value when using the declining-balance method. The actual computation of the fourth year's depreciation would be $812.50. A book value or salvage value of $812.50 would be left at the end of the fourth year ($1625 − $812.50). The actual salvage value is only $750; hence, $875 must be depreciated in year 4.

[Strictly speaking, the declining-balance method does not allow full depreciation of the assets' cost unless the depreciation method for the asset is changed to the straight-line method at some point in the assets' life. This point normally will be when the straight-line method (calculated on the estimated life remaining and the salvage value at the time the change is made) exceeds the declining-balance depreciation. However, any undepreciated amount can be recovered as a loss when the asset is disposed of; therefore, we have shown the depreciation as adjusted in the schedule.]

To calculate declining-balance depreciation for a partial year, we need to adjust only the first full year's depreciation for the length of time the asset is owned. All following years can be calculated in the normal manner since the partial year's ownership in the first year will be reflected in the book value for all following years.

Partial-Year Depreciation—Declining-Balance Method

The amount of depreciation is found by multiplying the fraction of the year that the asset is owned by the amount of depreciation normally calculated for the first full year.

Example 3

An asset costing $10,000 is purchased on July 1. The asset is depreciated over 5 years using the double-declining-balance method. Find the depreciation for the partial year and the following year.

SOLUTION

The straight-line rate is $\frac{1}{5}$, or 20%. Therefore, the double-declining-balance rate is (2)(20%), or 40%.

The depreciation for the first full year would be (40%) ($10,000) = $4000. However, the company only had the asset for 6 months (i.e., $\frac{1}{2}$ year). Thus, the partial-year depreciation is

$$(\tfrac{1}{2})(\$4000) = \$2000$$

The book value for the second year has declined to $8000 (i.e., $10,000 initial cost − $2000 partial-year depreciation). At a rate of 40%, the second year's depreciation is

$$(40\%)(\$8000) = \$3200$$

Exercises 9.4

■ Find the straight-line and the 200% (double) declining-balance rate of depreciation for assets having the lives shown.

	Years of Life	Straight-Line Rate (1/L)	Double-Declining-Balance Rate 200%)
Example:	4	$\frac{1}{4}$ or 0.25 or 25%	0.50 or 50%
	3		
2.	5		
3.	6		
4.	8		
5.	25		
6.	30		

■ Compute the current year's depreciation and end-of-the-year book value for assets having the following. Assume depreciation for a full year unless given information to the contrary.

	Book Value (Beginning of Year)	Depreciation Rate	Current Year's Depreciation	Book Value (End of Year)
Example:	$10,000	50%	$5000	$5000
7.	$4000	75%		
8.	$9000	30%		
9.	$15,000	$33\frac{1}{3}\%$		
10.	$16,000	25%		
11.	$12,500	50%		
12.	$100,000	8%		

■ Calculate the depreciation rate, the first year's depreciation, the accumulated depreciation, and end-of-year book value in the following problems. Use the double-declining-balance rate and assume that the book value at the beginning of the year is the purchase price. Calculate depreciation for a full year unless given information to the contrary.

	Purchase Price	Asset Life	Depreciation Rate	Current Year's Depreciation	Accumulated Depreciation	Book Value (End of Year)
Example:	$5000	4	$\frac{1}{4} \times 200\% = \frac{1}{2}$	$2500 ($\frac{1}{2} \times \$5000$)	$2500	$2500 ($5000 − $2500)
13.	$6000	3				
14.	$20,000	5				
15.	$18,000	6				
16.	$8000	8				

17. Machine A initially cost $8000. It has a life of 3 years with no salvage value. Set up a depreciation schedule using the 150% declining-balance rate.

18. A Whammo press has a useful life of 4 years. Show the proper depreciation schedule assuming an initial cost of $18,000 and no salvage value. Use the double-declining-balance rate.

19. The Little Dynamo costs $30,000 new. It will last 5 years and has a $5000 salvage value. What would the appropriate depreciation schedule be using the 150% declining-balance rate?

20. Adam's Apple Orchard purchased an apple-picking machine for $12,000. It will last 4 years and can then be sold for $950. Show the depreciation schedule using the double-declining-balance method.

21. Use the 150% declining-balance rate to show a depreciation schedule for an asset costing $80,000 and having a salvage value of $15,000 at the end of its 6-year life.

22. An asset cost $50,000 and has a useful life of 5 years. The salvage value at the end of its life is estimated at $6000. Use the 175% declining-balance method to show the appropriate depreciation schedule.

■ Compute the depreciation for the partial year in the following problems. Use the declining-balance method. Also show the book value at the end of the year.

	Months of Use (Current Year)	Asset Cost	Depreciation Rate	Current Year's Depreciation	Book Value (End of Year)
Example:	6	$10,000	50%	$2500 [i.e., ($10,000 × 50%)$\frac{1}{2}$]	$7500 (i.e., $10,000 − $2500)
23.	4	$9000	$33\frac{1}{3}$%		
24.	9	$16,000	25%		
25.	8	$18,000	$66\frac{2}{3}$%		
26.	6	$20,000	40%		

27. Using the 200% declining-balance rate, set up a depreciation schedule for an asset purchased on July 1 for $30,000. The estimated life is 5 years and there is no salvage value.

28. Set up a depreciation schedule for an asset costing $12,000 with a 4-year life. Salvage value is $950. Use the 200% declining-balance rate. The asset was purchased on May 1.

9.5 Accelerated Cost Recovery System (ACRS) (After the Tax Act of 1981)

The Accelerated Cost Recovery System (ACRS) was formed by the Economic Recovery Tax Act of 1981. Members of Congress and the President felt that the depreciation procedures existing before that act were overly complicated and did not allow enough depreciation to encourage business expansion. Consequently, they replaced those procedures for depreciation with a much faster method of "cost recovery"—the "*Accelerated Cost Recovery System.*" Several things should be noted about ACRS:

1. ACRS provides for a much greater annual cost recovery than any of the previous depreciation methods. It combines accelerated cost recovery methods with drastically reduced asset lives (in comparison with the life under previous depreciation methods). Therefore, the time required to recover fully the cost of an asset is reduced *and* more of the cost is recovered earlier in the asset's life.

2. ACRS applies only to assets placed in service *during or after 1981.* Assets placed in service in 1980 or before must be depreciated using the "old" depreciation methods.

3. Partial-year cost recovery does not apply under ACRS. The tables used for calculation include a "half-year convention;" that is. they assume that all assets are owned for one-half of the year in which they were purchased.

4. The "depreciation base" under ACRS is the *entire cost* of the asset.* The salvage value *is not* subtracted from the asset's cost to determine the total amount that will be recovered over the asset's life.

5. All assets are grouped into one of four *life classes*. These life classes determine the length of time over which the cost of the asset will be recovered. The amount of cost recovered is calculated using data from tables for the appropriate life class.†

6. Although ACRS applies only to assets acquired during or after 1981, its use for such assets *is not* mandatory. Taxpayers who do not wish to use ACRS may use the straight-line method to recover cost.‡

7. No recovery of cost is allowed in the year of an asset's disposition, that is, when it is taken out of service.

8. Before the Tax Act of 1981, taxpayers were given the option of taking *additional first-year depreciation*. This option allowed up to 20% of an asset's cost (subject to certain dollar limitations) to be immediately depreciated in the first year (only) of an asset's life. Under ACRS, additional first-year depreciation is no longer allowed. In its place, ACRS allows a portion of the asset's cost to be treated as a currently deductible expense. This "expensing" provision is also subject to certain dollar limitations and becomes effective in 1982 and thereafter.

Under ACRS, the cost of assets is recovered over a 3-year, 5-year, 10-year, or 15-year period. The recovery period (or life) depends on the type of asset purchased. Examples of assets included in these four life classes are as follows:

1. *Three-Year Assets*—This life class includes *automobiles, light-duty trucks, machinery and equipment used for research and experimentation*, and *special tools* used in producing products.

2. *Five-Year Assets*—This life class includes *heavy-duty trucks, production-line machinery, office furniture, machines*, and other *equipment*.

3. *Ten-Year Assets*—This life class includes *public utility property* that, prior to ACRS, had an *average life of 18.5 to 25 years*. It also includes *railroad tank cars, manufactured homes*, and *theme and amusement park structures*.

*The 1981 Tax Act was amended in 1982 and the "depreciation base" may change slightly if the asset qualifies for an investment tax credit.

† The 1981 Tax Act provided three sets of tables for cost recovery. These tables applied to assets placed in service in 1) 1981–1984, 2) 1985, and 3) 1986 and thereafter. However, the 1981 Tax Act was amended in 1982; at that time the tables for 1985 and later were revoked. Those tables provided even more liberal cost recovery benefits.

‡ There are special tax consequences that apply to some assets where, in certain situations, the taxpayer would pay less taxes by using the straight-line method. However, we will leave this discussion to the students of accounting.

4. *Fifteen-Year Assets*—This life class includes *public utility property* that, prior to ACRS, had an *average life of more than 25 years.* It also includes most *real property*—buildings, houses, structures, etc. (*Note:* Although real property is included in the 15-year life class, the table for cost recovery of real property is different. We will discuss this later.)

Computing Cost Recovered Under ACRS

To calculate the cost recovered each year under ACRS, we simply multiply the cost of the asset (remember, we *do not* subtract the salvage value under ACRS) by a mandated percent. The percent depends upon two things:

1. The life class of the asset.
2. The number of years the asset has been in service.

These factors determine the percent we recover for the year.

For Assets Acquired in 1981 and Thereafter

The cost recovery table for these assets is based on the 150% declining-balance depreciation method in the early years of life with a conversion to the straight-line method in later years. The table includes the "half-year convention" for the first year of the asset's life. Figure 9.3 shows the cost recovery table for assets acquired in 1981 and thereafter.

Figure 9.3   **For Assets Acquired in 1981 and Thereafter**

Year of Asset's Life	Annual Cost Recovery Percent for Asset Life Class			
	3-Year	5-Year	10-Year	15-Year
1	25	15	8	5
2	38	22	14	10
3	37	21	12	9
4		21	10	8
5		21	10	7
6			10	7
7			9	6
8			9	6
9			9	6
10			9	6
11				6
12				6
13				6
14				6
15				6

Let us now see how we use the table to calculate the cost recovered on an asset.

Example 1   In November 1981, the manager of the Dough Boy Bakery bought $14,000 worth of baking equipment (i.e., production equipment). How much cost should be recovered for the equipment in (*a*) the first year? (*b*) the third year? (*c*) the last year of the asset's table life?

SOLUTION   First we must determine the life class of the equipment. Production equipment falls into the 5-year life class. Now that we know which life class (or column) to use, we can easily calculate the recovered cost.

   a. In the first year, we see that 15% of the asset's cost is recovered, or

$$\$14,000 \times 15\% = \$2100$$

   Notice that we did not make any adjustment for salvage value or because the asset was purchased in November. (Remember that the entire cost is recovered and that the table automatically adjusts the first-year recovery percent to allow for partial-years ownership.)

   b. The cost recovered in the third year would be

$$\$14,000 \times 21\% = \$2940$$

   c. The cost recovered in the last year (year 5) is

$$\$14,000 \times 21\% = \$2940$$

Example 2   What would be your answer to part (*c*) of Example 1 if the asset was removed from service during the fifth year (December 1986)?

SOLUTION   No cost would be recovered. Cost recovery is not allowed in the year in which the asset is taken out of service.

Example 3   In 1985, the owner of the Goner Company purchased office furniture for $13,750. In 1986, he purchased a new company car that cost $11,200. How much total cost will be recovered on both of these assets in 1987?

SOLUTION   First, we must determine the life class of the assets. The office furniture has a 5-year life class. The car has a 3-year life class. Next, we must determine which year of the asset's life is generating the current recoverable cost. The furniture was purchased in 1985 (year 1 of its life) and so 1987 is year 3 of its life. Likewise, the car is in year 2 of its life. With the following information:

Asset	Asset Life Class	Year of Life
Office furniture	5	3
Car	3	2

we can read the recovery percent and calculate the amount recovered (by multiplying the cost times the recovery percent).

Asset	Cost Recovery Percent	Cost	Cost Recovered
Office furniture	21	× $13,750	= $2887.50
Car	38	× $11,200	= $4256.00
		Total	$7143.50

Therefore, the total cost recovered on these assets in 1987 is $7143.50.

From Example 3, we can develop a set of steps allowing us to calculate cost recovery under ACRS.

To calculate ACRS cost recovered:

Step 1. Determine the life class of the asset.

Step 2. Determine which year of the asset's life is generating the current recoverable cost, that is, the cost recovery we are calculating.

Step 3. Use the data from steps 1–2 to determine the recovery percent.

Step 4. Calculate the annual cost recovered by multiplying the cost of the asset by the recovery percent.

Because both depreciation and cost recovery methods will be in effect for several years following the Tax Act of 1981, we might encounter problems as shown in Example 4.

Example 4   The Mill Run Company began a process of expansion in 1979. On April 1, 1980, company management purchased a $20,000 machine for use on the production line. It has an estimated life of 6 years and an estimated salvage value of $2000. In October 1982, they purchased an identical machine for $23,500. It is estimated to have the same life and a salvage value of $2800. Calculate the total cost recovered on these machines in 1983. The company has historically used the straight-line depreciation method for production equipment; however, they have used the ACRS method since the Tax Act of 1981.

SOLUTION   The machine purchased in 1980 falls under the old depreciation method. Therefore, depreciation for that machine is calculated using the straight-line method.

$$\text{depreciation} = \frac{\$20,000 - \$2000}{6 \text{ years}} = \$3000 \text{ per year}$$

Machine 2 (purchased in October 1982) falls under ACRS and in the 5-year life class. Cost recovered in 1983 is for the second year of the machine's life; therefore, using the ACRS table we find that the cost recovery rate for machine 2 is 22%. The cost recovered for machine 2 is

$$\$23,500 \times 22\% = \$5170$$

The total cost recovered for these production machines in 1983 is

Machine 1 (1980)	$3000
Machine 2 (1982)	5170
Total	$8170

The cost of real property (houses, buildings, structures, etc.) is recovered using the same basic ACRS principles we have discussed.[1] However, we use a different recovery table for real property. The table for real property (Figure 9.4) *does not* use the half-year convention. Since the cost of real

**Figure 9.4   ACRS Table for Real Property
(Other Than Low-Income Housing)**

Year of Recovery	Percent											
	Jan.	Feb.	March	April	May	June	July	Aug.	Sept.	Oct.	Nov.	Dec.
1	12	11	10	9	8	7	6	5	4	3	2	1
2	10	10	11	11	11	11	11	11	11	11	11	12
3	9	9	9	9	10	10	10	10	10	10	10	10
4	8	8	8	8	8	8	9	9	9	9	9	9
5	7	7	7	7	7	7	8	8	8	8	8	8
6	6	6	6	6	7	7	7	7	7	7	7	7
7	6	6	6	6	6	6	6	6	6	6	6	6
8	6	6	6	6	6	6	5	6	6	6	6	6
9	6	6	6	6	5	6	5	5	5	6	6	6
10	5	6	5	6	5	5	5	5	5	5	6	5
11	5	5	5	5	5	5	5	5	5	5	5	5
12	5	5	5	5	5	5	5	5	5	5	5	5
13	5	5	5	5	5	5	5	5	5	5	5	5
14	5	5	5	5	5	5	5	5	5	5	5	5
15	5	5	5	5	5	5	5	5	5	5	5	5
16	0	0	1	1	2	2	3	3	4	4	4	5

property is usually a significant portion of business investment, partial-year ownership is calculated more accurately. We still apply a recovery

[1] Note that only the cost of the structure itself can be recovered. There is *no* cost recovery on the value of the land.

percent to the cost of the property, and the recovery percent is still dependent on the year of property life that is generating the recovery. *To determine the recovery percent, choose the column under the month in which the asset was initially acquired, and we use those recovery percents for the entire life of the asset.* Consider the following example.

Example 5

The Golden Circles Hamburger Palace opened in July 1984. The building cost $120,000 and the owner uses ACRS whenever possible.

    a. What is the life of the building?
    b. What amount of cost will be recovered in the first year of the building's life?
    c. The fourth year?
    d. The eighth year?
    e. The 16th year?

SOLUTION

    a. Buildings have a 15-year life under ACRS.
    b. To determine the cost recovered in the first year, we use Figure 9.4 and read the recovery percents under the "July" column since the building was put in service in July. The first-year's recovery percent under the July column is 6%. Therefore, the cost recovered is

$$\$120,000 \times 6\% = \$7200$$

    c. The fourth year's recovery percent under the July column is 9%, so that cost recovered is

$$\$120,000 \times 9\% = \$10,800$$

    d. The eighth year's recovery percent is 5%, therefore,

$$\$120,000 \times 5\% = \$6000$$

    e. Cost recovered in year 16 is

$$\$120,000 \times 3\% = \$3600$$

Note: Don't be confused by cost recovery in the 16th year from an asset having a 15-year life. Recall our discussion of partial-year depreciation under the old depreciation methods. We are only recovering costs for 15 years; however, since we are recovering only one-half a year in the first year of recovery (the building was used from July to December 1984), we need to recover the other one-half year (January to June) in the 16th calendar year.

The table for real property is based on the 175% declining-balance method for early years of asset life. Later years' recovery rates are based on the straight-line method.

Exercises 9.5

■ Supply the missing information in the following problems. Assume ACRS is used in all problems.

Type of Asset	Life Class	Year of Life	Recovery Percent
Example: Automobile	? (3-year)	2	38 (Figure 9.3 for the second year of the 3-year life class.)
1. Research equipment	?	3	?
2. Office furniture	?	2	?
3. Production-line equipment	?	1	?
4. Generators for the electric company (formerly depreciated over 30 years)	?	9	?
5. An "over-the-road" tractor truck	?	3	?
6. Delivery pickups	?	2	?
7. Railroad tank car	?	8	?
8. Special equipment for producing drilling equipment	?	2	?
9. Business computer system	?	3	?
10. Lathe	?	4	?

11. The Major Company acquired a new testing device used in its research on a new product. The device was acquired in September 1982 at a cost of $12,000. What cost should be recovered on the device in 1984?

12. The Miner Corporation bought (at a cost of $27,500) a production robot for use in the manufacturing process. This robot was acquired in November 1985. Previous robots had a life of 7 years with salvage value approximately equal to 10% of their original cost. What cost is recovered (**a**) in 1985? (**b**) in 1986?

13. The Volt Air Electric Co-op purchased a generator in March 1987 for $135,400. Generators of this type had a life expectancy (prior to ACRS) of 22 years and salvage value was estimated at 12.5% of initial cost. What cost recovery should be charged on this generator (**a**) in 1987? (**b**) in 1991? (**c**) in 1993?

14. The X-Country Movers purchased a new, heavy moving van for $97,000. The van was purchased in August 1982, and should be worth approximately $4000 at the end of its useful life. Calculate the cost recovered on this van (**a**) in 1982, (**b**) in 1984, and (**c**) in 1987.

15. The Captain's Cleaners purchased a new bookkeeping processor in 1985 for $13,700. The processor was purchased in July and should have a salvage value of $1200 at the end of its life. Show the cost recovered in a depreciation schedule form.

16. The Magnus Lab purchased a device used in experiments for the Defense Department. The device cost $46,400 and should have a parts (scrap) value of $2400 at the end of its life. Assuming the device was purchased in February 1982, set up the appropriate cost recovery schedule.

17. The Tinker Bell Telephone Company is installing a new telephone switching system. The system (to be installed in mid-1983) will cost $2,300,000. Historically, equipment of this type had an average life of 30 years. Compute the cost recovered on this system (**a**) in 1985, (**b**) in 1987, and (**c**) in 1996.

18. The Busy Weaver Textile Company has acquired (in 1985) a computerized loom used in the production of textiles. The loom cost $116,400. How much of that cost will be recovered (**a**) in 1985? (**b**) in 1987? (**c**) in 1989? (**d**) in 1990? (**e**) in the year the asset is removed from service?

19. The owner of the Hot Spot Messenger Service purchased her first messenger car on April 1, 1980 for $7250. Estimated life was 4 years with a salvage value of $250. In June 1981, she purchased her second car for $7875. The owner uses straight-line depreciation, and ACRS where possible. Assuming these two cars constitute Hot Spot's "fleet," how much "depreciation" should be charged to automobiles (**a**) in 1981? (**b**) in 1982? (**c**) in 1983? (**d**) in 1984?

20. On July 1, 1979, the manager of Mr. Wizard's Computer Shoppe purchased some office furniture at a cost of $4800. The furniture is being depreciated on the sum-of-the-years-digits method (the estimated life is 7 years and salvage value is estimated at $600). In 1981, he purchased an additional $6200 in office furniture (for which he has chosen ACRS). How much "depreciation" expense should be charged to these furniture purchases (**a**) in 1981? (**b**) in 1983? (**c**) in 1985? (**d**) in 1986?

21. The Rapid Reproducer Company opened a new store in October 1983. Company management purchased the building at a cost of $176,500. Assuming ACRS, calculate the annual cost recovered on this building and its book value (**a**) for 1983, (**b**) for 1984, and (**c**) for 1985.

22. Slim Lord purchased an apartment house in April 1981. The apartment house cost $272,400 and the cost is being recovered through ACRS. How much cost recovery should be charged to the apartment house (**a**) for 1981? (**b**) for 1983? (**c**) for 1987? (**d**) for 1992?

23. Micro Processors, Inc., management acquired a new factory building in September 1984 at a cost of $350,000. Set up a cost recovery schedule showing the first 5 years of the building's life. Management has used ACRS whenever possible.

24. L. Ashby purchased a ski condominium in Colorado on January 1, 1972 for $28,000. In March of 1982, she purchased a waterfront condominium in Florida for $117,500. Both pieces of property are used exclusively for rental; therefore, their costs can be recovered as a business expense. The ski condo has an estimated life of 25 years with a $3000 salvage value. The waterfront condo has an estimated life of 30 years with no salvage value. How much cost is recovered (total) on both pieces of property assuming the straight-line method and ACRS (if applicable) (**a**) in 1986? (**b**) in 1989? (**c**) in 1992? (**d**) in 1996?

Review Exercises / Chapter 9

1. Bull's Dozer Works bought a new dozer for $35,000. It has a salvage value of $5000 at the end of its useful life. The dozer is now 2 years old and has a book value of $25,000. What are (**a**) the annual depreciation assuming the straight-line method, (**b**) the accumulated depreciation, and (**c**) the estimated life of the dozer?

2. A casting mold for a fabricating company has an estimated life of 2000 units with no salvage value. The mold was used to produce 1800 units this year and depreciation for the year was $4500 (using the units-of-production method). How much did the mold cost initially?

3. What are the annual and accumulated depreciation on a 3-year-old metal press costing $20,000 with a salvage value of $2500? The estimated life is 7 years and the sum-of-the-years-digits depreciation method is used.

4. Use a 150% declining-balance depreciation rate to show the depreciation schedule for an asset costing $80,000 and having a salvage value of $15,000 at the end of its 6-year life.

5. Sta-dri Plumbing purchased a new truck on October 1. The truck cost $12,500 and has an estimated salvage value of $2500 at the end of its 4-year life. Prepare a depreciation schedule using the sum-of-the-years-digits method of depreciation.

6. The Nash Company uses the units-of-production depreciation method on their plant equipment. On July 28, 1979, they purchased a new lathe for $28,000. It has an estimated life of 200,000 units (approximately 8 years) and a salvage value of $2000. What will be the total depreciation on the lathe assuming that production was (**a**) year 1—42,000 units, (**b**) year 2—36,417 units, and (**c**) year 3—22,905 units?

7. In 1985 John Jones purchased a new car for use in his business. The car cost $11,300 and that cost will be recovered using ACRS. How much cost will be recovered (**a**) in 1985? (**b**) 1986? (**c**) in 1987? (**d**) in 1988?

8. In 1982 the World Wide Company purchased $13,700 in office furniture. The following year they purchased two new cars (one for $10,350 and one for $9640). Assuming the company uses ACRS whenever possible, how much cost will be recovered (**a**) in 1982? (**b**) in 1984? (**c**) in 1985? (**d**) in 1986?

9. In 1980 (October 1) A. L. Edwards bought a production machine for $14,600. It has an estimated life of 6 years and an estimated salvage value of $2600. He purchased a similar machine in December 1981 for $16,900. Compute the total cost recovered on these machines (using ACRS when possible; otherwise using straight line depreciation) (**a**) for 1981), (**b**) for 1982, (**c**) for 1984, and (**d**) for 1986.

10. J. Jones purchased a rental house in September 1984 for $36,900. Assuming the use of ACRS, what amount of cost will be recoverable (**a**) in 1984? (**b**) in 1989? (**c**) in 1992? (**d**) in 1999? (**e**) in 2000?

Chapter Test / Chapter 9

1. Define the following terms.
   a. depreciation
   b. accumulated depreciation
   c. cost recovery
   d. book value
   e. depreciation schedule
   f. accelerated depreciation
   g. half-year convention

2. Wilco Inc. purchased a new machine 2 years ago today (January 1) for $44,250. The estimated life and salvage value of the machine are 5 years and $4250 respectively. The company uses the straight-line method of depreciation. What is
   a. the book value?
   b. the accumulated depreciation?
   c. the annual depreciation?

3. The Precisely Manufacturing Company purchased a new drill press for $22,670. The press was purchased on October 10, 1980, and has an estimated salvage value of $670 at the end of its 1,100,000-unit production life. Calculate the depreciation as of December 31, 1980, if the company uses the units-of-production depreciation method. Production on the press was 122,400 units.

4. The Miner Company acquired a machine on January 1, 1980, at a cost of $22,700. The machine has a 6-year life and an estimated salvage value of $1700. What was the depreciation at the end of 1980 and 1981 if the company used the sum-of-the-year-digits depreciation method?

5. Use the double-declining-balance depreciation method to calculate the first and second year of depreciation on an asset purchased on January 1, 1980, for $10,600. Estimated salvage value at the end of its 4-year life is $1200.

6. The Lowmas Company acquired an asset on April 1, 1980, at a cost of $27,000. The asset has a 6-year life and an estimated salvage value of $2395. Use the double-declining-balance depreciation method to calculate the depreciation for 1980 and 1981.

7. Jetco Inc. acquired an asset on October 1, 1980, at a cost of $18,000. It has an estimated life of 5 years and a salvage value of $3000. Calculate the depreciation for 1980 and 1981 if the company uses the sum-of-the-years-digits depreciation method.

8. The Elite Laundry purchased a new commercial washer on November 1, 1982, at a cost of $14,800. Such washers normally have a salvage value of approximately 15% of initial cost. Show the cost recovered in 1982 and 1983 assuming the Elite Laundry uses ACRS.

9. The Micro Company acquired (on May 10, 1985) a new device used for research and development work. The device cost $28,750. How much cost will be recovered (under ACRS)

      a. in 1985?　　*b.* in 1987?　　*c.* in 1988?

10. Rappco Incorporated purchased a new warehouse in October 1985. The warehouse cost $284,750 and the cost is being recovered under ACRS. How much cost will be recovered

      a. in 1985?
      b. in 1989?
      c. in 1992?
      d. in 1998?
      e. in 2000?

CHAPTER 10

Financial Statements and Distribution of Profits

INTRODUCTION

For the last four chapters we have followed a business through the processes used in operating and (hopefully) making a profit. In this chapter we get to the "bottom line" (i.e., we see the result of the business efforts during the last year). We will examine the two primary financial reports of a business: the balance sheet and the income statement.

We will begin with the *balance sheet* because a company has a balance sheet first; in fact, at the instant the company is *formed*, there is a balance sheet. The balance sheet is a *statement of financial position*. It shows

1. Everything of value to the company (its *assets*).
2. And who owns them:
    a. Creditors (*liabilities* to the company), *or*
    b. The owners of the business (the *owners' equity* in the business).

The balance sheet represents the status of the company at a particular instant in time. In an ongoing business, the balance sheet shows the cumulative effects of all previous years of operation. As such, it is basically a historical record.

The *income statement* is a report of the result of current operations. It shows the success (or failure) of the business for the current time period by presenting

1. The total amount of money received (*revenue*).
2. The amount of money spent (*expenses*) in order to receive the revenue.
3. The excess amount of revenue over expenses (which is a profit), or the excess amount of expenses over revenue (which is a loss).

At the end of the year, the effects of the income statement are combined with the balance sheet to accurately represent the status of the company as of the end of the year. Figure 10.1 shows the relationship of the income statement and the balance sheet.

Figure 10.1

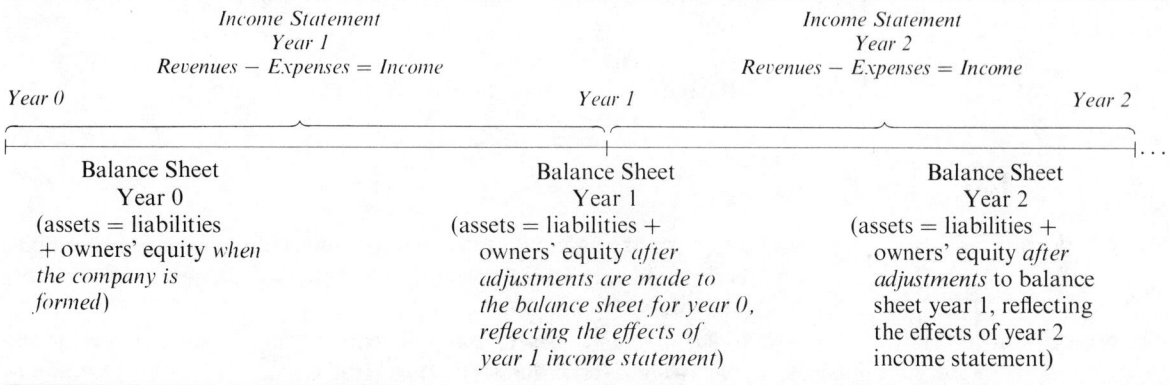

Finally, we will discuss methods of analyzing the financial statements to obtain a general idea of the "economic health" of a business. This examination can be done for only one time period (*vertical analysis*) or for several time periods (*horizontal analysis*). We will also discuss some of the comparisons that can be made from financial statements which are of particular interest to potential investors.

10.1 *The Balance Sheet (or Statement of Financial Position)*

Suppose that you have $50. You meet a friend and he lends you another $50. You now have $100, right? Yes and no. A true statement of your financial position would be

you have   you owe   you own
$$\$100 \quad = \quad \$50 \quad + \quad \$50$$

That statement reflects the total amount of money at your command ($100), the amount of that total that you owe ($50), and the amount of that total that is yours ($50). That statement is also the fundamental accounting equation on which the balance sheet is based.

Assets and liabilities are generally classified as *current* or *noncurrent*. The distinctions between the two are useful as indicators of the general economic health of the business.

assets = liabilities +
owners' equity

> **Assets   =   Liabilities   +   Owners' Equity**
>
> (you have)   (you owe)   (you own)
>
> where
>
> 1. *Assets* are economic resources from which the business expects a future benefit.
> 2. *Liabilities* are obligations to be settled in the future by transfer of assets or services of the business.
> 3. *Owners' equity* is the interest (or assets) the owners have in a business after all liabilities are paid.

Definitions

current assets

Current assets are assets that are readily convertible into cash. Examples are cash, marketable securities, inventories, and short-term notes and accounts owed to the business.

noncurrent assets

Noncurrent assets are assets that will require longer than one year or one business cycle (whichever is longer) before conversion into cash.* Examples are buildings, equipment, and land.

current liabilities

Current liabilities are liabilities that the company must settle using current assets. Examples are accounts owed to suppliers, wages, taxes, and other operating expenses.

noncurrent liabilities

Noncurrent liabilities are liabilities that will not require settlement using current assets. Examples are long-term debts such as mortgages or bonds not maturing for several years.

Review the balance sheet shown in Figure 10.2 for the Ace Company.

You should note that the noncurrent assets that are depreciable (buildings and equipment) are shown on the balance sheet net of depreciation (i.e., at current book value). Also, the owners' equity section of the balance sheet may be shown in different ways, depending on whether the business is individually owned, a partnership, or a corporation.

The information presented in the balance sheet is fine. However, there is something else we can do to make the information easier to use. We can take each category and calculate the percent it represents of the whole. That is, express all asset amounts as a percent of total assets, and all liabilities and owners' equity as a percent of total liabilities and owners' equity. This process is called *vertical analysis*.

Definition

vertical analysis

Vertical analysis expresses the components of a financial statement as a percent of the whole for a single time period.

---

*A business cycle is the length of time required for a business to take cash, invest in inventory, sell the inventory, and collect the money from sales. In essence, it is the time to go from cash to cash through the cycle of business operations.

Example 1

Using vertical analysis, what percent of Ace Company assets are (*a*) in cash and (*b*) in inventory? (*c*) What percent do accounts payable represent? (Use Figure 10.2.)

SOLUTION

Cash and inventory will be expressed as a percent using total assets (or $150,000) as a base. Accounts payable will be a percent using total liabilities and owners' equity as a base. Since assets = liabilities + owners' equity, the base for accounts payable will also be $150,000.

a. $\dfrac{\text{cash}}{\text{total assets}} = \dfrac{\$10,000}{\$150,000} = 0.0666 = 6.7\%$

b. $\dfrac{\text{inventory}}{\text{total assets}} = \dfrac{\$18,000}{\$150,000} = 0.12 = 12\%$

c. $\dfrac{\text{accounts payable}}{\text{total liabilities + owners' equity}} = \dfrac{\$22,000}{\$150,000} = 0.1466 = 14.7\%$

Figure 10.2

ACE COMPANY
Balance Sheet
As of December 31, Current Year
Assets

Current assets	
Cash	$ 10,000
Marketable securities	5,000
Accounts receivable	32,000
Inventory	18,000
Total current assets	$ 65,000
Noncurrent assets	
Land	$ 38,000
Building (net of depreciation)	26,000
Equipment (net of depreciation)	21,000
Total noncurrent assets	$ 85,000
Total assets	$150,000

Liabilities and Owners' Equity

Current liabilities	
Accounts payable	$ 22,000
Notes payable	10,000
Total current liabilities	$ 32,000
Noncurrent liabilities	
Mortgage	$ 56,500
Bonds payable	24,000
Total noncurrent liabilities	$ 80,500
Total liabilities	$112,500
Owners' equity	$ 37,500
Total liabilities and owners' equity	$150,000

Vertical analysis allows company management and potential investors some insight into how well the company is progressing. How? Consider inventory as an example. In Chapter 8 we learned that an excessive inventory is a poor utilization of company money. If the inventory percent is high (as compared with other companies in the same type of business), company management should take corrective action.

Now that we know how to calculate the appropriate percents, review Figure 10.3. It gives the balance sheet for Ace Company, showing a complete vertical analysis.

Note that individual categories may be added or subtracted to obtain subtotals in the balance sheet. This is also true of the percents, since they are expressed using the same number as base.

Vertical analysis is effective in analysis for a single time period. However, we can obtain a much better picture of how the business is doing

Figure 10.3

ACE COMPANY
Balance Sheet
December 31, Current Year
Assets

Current assets		*Percent*
Cash	$ 10,000	6.7
Marketable securities	5,000	3.3
Accounts receivable	32,000	21.3
Inventory	18,000	12.0
Total current assets	$ 65,000	43.3
Noncurrent assets		
Land	$ 38,000	25.3
Building (net of depreciation)	26,000	17.3
Equipment (net of depreciation)	21,000	14.0
Total noncurrent assets	$ 85,000	56.7[a]
Total assets	$150,000	100

Liabilities and Owners' Equity

Current liabilities		
Accounts payable	$ 22,000	14.7
Notes payable	10,000	6.7
Total current liabilities	$ 32,000	21.3[a]
Noncurrent liabilities		
Mortgage	$ 56,500	37.7
Bonds payable	24,000	16.0
Total noncurrent liabilities	$ 80,500	53.7
Total liabilities	$112,500	75
Owners' equity	$ 37,500	25
Total liabilities and owners' equity	$150,000	100

[a] Error due to rounding.

by comparing data for the current time period with data for previous time periods. Such a comparison is known as *horizontal analysis.*

Definition

horizontal analysis

Horizontal analysis **compares corresponding items of a financial statement for two or more time periods.**

Horizontal analysis is most useful in identifying trends in the performance of the company. When calculating percents under horizontal analysis, the figures for the *earlier time period should be used as the base.* Figure 10.4 gives an example of horizontal analysis for the current year and

Figure 10.4

ACE COMPANY
Comparative Balance Sheets
As of December 31, Current Year and Previous Year

			Increase (Decrease)		Percent	
	Current Year	*Previous Year*	*Amount*	*Percent*	*Current Year*	*Previous Year*
Current assets						
Cash	$ 10,000	$ 12,000	$ (2000)	(16.7)	6.7	9.0
Marketable securities	5,000	3,000	2000	66.7	3.3	2.2
Accounts receivable	32,000	26,000	6000	23.1	21.3	19.4
Inventory	18,000	22,000	(4000)	(18.2)	12.0	16.4
Total current assets	$ 65,000	$ 63,000	$ 2000	3.2	43.3	47.0
Noncurrent assets						
Land	$ 38,000	$ 38,000	0	0	25.3	28.4
Buildings (net)	26,000	16,000	10,000	62.5	17.3	11.9
Equipment (net)	21,000	18,000	3,000	16.7	14.0	13.4
Total noncurrent assets	$ 85,000	$ 71,000	$14,000	19.7	56.7[a]	53.0[a]
Total assets	$150,000	$134,000	$16,000	11.9	100	100
Current liabilities						
Accounts payable	$ 22,000	$ 20,000	$ 2000	10	14.7	14.9
Notes payable	10,000	12,000	(2000)	(16.7)	6.7	9.0
Total current liabilities	$ 32,000	$ 32,000	0	0	21.3[a]	23.9
Noncurrent liabilities						
Mortgage	$ 56,500	$ 57,000	$ (500)	(0.9)	37.7	42.5
Bonds payable	24,000	26,000	(2000)	(7.7)	16.0	19.4
Total noncurrent liabilities	$ 80,500	$ 83,000	$ (2500)	(3.0)	53.7	61.9
Total liabilities	$112,500	$115,000	$ (2500)	(2.2)	75	85.8
Owners' equity	$ 37,500	$ 19,000	$18,500	97.4	25	14.2
Total liabilities and owners' equity	$150,000	$134,000	$16,000	11.9	100	100

[a] Error due to rounding.

previous year of the Ace Company. The format shown is that of a comparative balance sheet.

Note: In presenting this information, we will follow the accounting convention of designating negative amounts or decreases by using parentheses, ( ). For example, a $2000 decrease from the previous year will be indicated as ($2000).

You will recall from the introduction to this chapter that the balance sheet for the current year (in Figure 10.4) is the balance sheet for the previous year *adjusted* for the current year's operations. By using horizontal analysis, we know that the current year's operations were quite good (total assets increased 11.9%, total liabilities decreased 2.2%, and owners' equity increased 97.4%). In addition, we can obtain an idea of what company management is doing with money from operations (buying buildings, securities, and equipment, and paying debts). You can now see the value of horizontal analysis in examining a company.

Summary

The balance sheet reflects the economic state of a business at a given point in time. It tells what the business has, how much is owned by creditors, and how much is owned by the owners of the business. The balance sheet is based on the fundamental accounting equation of

$$\text{assets} = \text{liabilities} + \text{owners' equity}$$

Vertical analysis is performed on the financial statement of a business by expressing the component parts as a percent of the whole for a *single time period*. Horizontal analysis compares like categories of the business over *two or more* time periods.

Exercises 10.1

■ Use the fundamental accounting equation of assets = liabilities + owners' equity to complete the following:

	Assets	Liabilities	Owners' Equity
1.	$1,487,000	?	$446,100
2.	?	$963,500	$386,900
3.	$22,987,000	$17,106,000	?
4.	?	$42,250	$21,980
5.	$876,400	$535,400	?
6.	$10,225,000	?	$4,728,000

7.

Assets		Liabilities and Owners' Equity	
Cash	$ 12,500	Accounts payable	$ 32,000
Accounts		Notes payable	20,000
receivable	30,000	Mortgage payable	40,000
Inventory	?	Owners' equity	?
Buildings	45,000		
Equipment	22,000		
		Total liabilities	
Total assets	$137,500	and owners' equity	$137,500

8.

Assets		Liabilities and Owners' Equity	
Cash	?	Accounts payable	$ 22,850
Accounts		Notes payable	?
receivable	$ 22,900	Owners' equity	68,300
Inventory	48,200		
Buildings	38,900		
Equipment	18,650		
		Total liabilities	
Total assets	$143,450	and owners' equity	$143,450

9. Complete the vertical analysis and missing information on the following balance sheet. Round percents to the nearest tenth.

		Percent
Current assets		
Cash	$ 38,000	
Accounts receivable	88,000	
Inventory	106,000	
Total current assets	?	
Land	64,000	
Building (net)	147,600	
Equipment (net)	31,400	
Total noncurrent assets	?	
Total assets	?	100
Current liabilities		
Accounts payable	$ 84,000	
Notes payable	14,800	
Total current liabilities	?	
Noncurrent liabilities		
Mortgage	$128,500	
Bonds payable	167,700	
Total noncurrent liabilities	?	
Total liabilities	?	
Owners' equity	$ 80,000	
Total liabilities and owners' equity	?	100

10. Complete the vertical analysis and missing information on the following balance sheet, rounding all percents to the nearest tenth.

		Percent
Current assets		
Cash	$ 106,400	_____
Accounts receivable	?	_____
Notes receivable	28,900	_____
Inventory	237,600	_____
Total current assets	609,300	_____
Noncurrent assets		
Land	$ 129,900	_____
Buildings (net)	406,800	_____
Equipment (net)	?	_____
Total noncurrent assets	$1,161,300	_____
Total assets	?	100
Current liabilities		
Accounts payable	$ 143,200	_____
Notes payable	78,800	_____
Taxes	80,500	_____
Total current liabilities	?	_____
Noncurrent liabilities		
Mortgage payable	?	_____
Bonds payable	746,000	_____
Total noncurrent liabilities	$ 938,200	_____
Total liabilities	$1,240,700	_____
Owners' equity	$ 529,900	_____
Total liabilities and owners' equity	?	100

11. Complete the missing information and perform a horizontal analysis on the following balance sheet.

	Current Year	Previous Year	Increase (Decrease) Amount	Increase (Decrease) Percent	Percent Current Year	Percent Previous Year
Current assets						
Cash	$ 68,500	?	_____	_____	_____	_____
Marketable securities	48,900	36,400	_____	_____	_____	_____
Accounts receivable	153,000	127,600	_____	_____	_____	_____
Inventory	?	182,100	_____	_____	_____	_____
Total current assets	$464,000	$?	_____	_____	_____	_____
Noncurrent assets						
Land	$ 78,000	$ 78,000	_____	_____	_____	_____
Buildings (net)	226,900	205,900	_____	_____	_____	_____
Equipment (net)	?	147,300	_____	_____	_____	_____
Total noncurrent assets	$486,000	$?	_____	_____	_____	_____
Total assets	$950,000	$850,200	_____	_____	100	100

Current liabilities							
Accounts payable	$126,400	$118,800					
Notes payable	32,200	?					
Taxes	58,500	47,600					
Total current liabilities	$217,100	$206,600					
Noncurrent liabilities							
Mortgage	$242,400	$249,300					
Bonds payable	?	292,700					
Total noncurrent liabilities	?	?					
Total liabilities	$748,500	$748,600					
Owners' equity	$201,500	?					
Total liabilities and owners' equity	$950,000	$850,200					100	100

12. Complete the missing information and perform a horizontal analysis on the following balance sheet.

	Current Year	Previous Year	Increase (Decrease) Amount	Increase (Decrease) Percent	Percent Current Year	Percent Previous Year
Current assets						
Cash	$ 212,800	$ 187,900				
Accounts receivable	?	501,900				
Notes receivable	57,800	61,700				
Inventory	475,200	439,200				
Total current assets	$1,218,600	?				
Noncurrent assets						
Land	$ 259,800	$ 198,400				
Buildings (net)	?	1,004,000				
Equipment (net)	1,249,200	?				
Total noncurrent assets	$2,322,600	$2,635,400				
Total assets	$3,541,200	?			100	100
Current liabilities						
Accounts payable	$ 286,400	$ 242,100				
Notes payable	157,600	161,900				
Taxes	?	183,000				
Total current liabilities	?	587,000				
Noncurrent liabilities						
Mortgage	$ 384,400	$ 392,200				
Bonds payable	1,492,000	1,473,600				
Total noncurrent liabilities	$1,876,400	$1,865,800				
Total liabilities	$2,481,400	$2,452,800				
Owners' equity	$1,059,800	?				
Total liabilities and owners' equity	$3,541,200	?			100	100

10.2 *The Income Statement*

The income statement shows the result (i.e., profit or loss) of operating a business for a given period of time. The time period may vary according to the needs of management; however, an income statement will at least be prepared annually for financial reporting purposes. The income statement basically matches revenue and expenses in order to determine the income for the period.

$$\text{revenue} - \text{expenses} = \text{income}$$

The basic calculation of the income statement is simply an extension of the markup formula from Chapter 7.

Income Statement	*Markup*
net sales = ⟵⟶	selling price =
cost of goods sold ⟵⟶	cost +
+ overhead expense ⎫ ⟵⟶	markup
+ net profit (or income) ⎭	

Since we are primarily interested in the net profit, the income statement expression is generally shown as

net sales
− cost of goods sold
= gross profit
− overhead expenses
= net profit (or loss)

Review the single-step income statement for the Lucky Company shown in Figure 10.5.*

Vertical and horizontal analyses are as beneficial for the income statements as they are for the balance sheet. *In analyzing the income statement, all categories are expressed using net sales as the base* (i.e., all categories are expressed as a percent of net sales). Just as in the balance sheet, the figures for the earlier year are used as the base for percent change (horizontal analysis). Mention should be made again concerning the computation of cost of goods sold (discussed in Section 8.2). Purchases made during the year are added to the inventory on hand at the beginning of the year to determine the goods available for sale during the year. By subtracting the goods in inventory at the end of the year, we can determine the cost of goods sold during the year. Review Figure 10.6,

---

*Income statements vary in format. The two formats most frequently encountered are the single-step and multiple-step formats. The *single-step format* groups all revenue in one category and all expenses in another to arrive at net income. The *multiple-step format* shows intermediate balances, such as gross profit, operating income, and income before taxes. Both forms will be used in this discussion.

Figure 10.5

```
                        LUCKY COMPANY
                        Income Statement
            For the Year Ended December 31, Current Year

Revenue
    Net sales                                          $1,000,000
    Interest earned                                         5,000
    Dividends received                                      7,500
                                                       _____
        Total revenue                                  $1,012,500
Expenses
    Cost of goods sold               $560,000
    Operating expenses                180,000
    Interest expense                   38,000
    Federal and state taxes           120,000
                                      _____
        Total expenses                                    898,000
                                                       _____
Net income                                             $  114,500
                                                       ==========
```

Figure 10.6

		Percent
CONOVER COMPANY		
Income Statement		
For the Year Ended December 31, Current Year		
Sales revenue		
Gross sales	$1,030,000	103
Less: sales returns and allowances	(30,000)	(3)
Net sales	$1,000,000	100
Cost of goods sold		
Beginning inventory	$ 92,000	
Purchases	665,000	
Less: returns and allowances	(23,500)	
Goods available for sale	$733,500	
Less: ending inventory	(83,500)	
Total cost of goods sold	$ 650,000	65
Gross profit on sales	$ 350,000	35
Operating expenses		
Salaries	$ 90,000	9.0
Rent	18,000	1.8
Utilities	8,000	0.8
Administrative	23,500	2.4
Depreciation	20,500	2.1
Total operating expenses	160,000	16[a]
Operating income	$ 190,000	19
Taxes	90,000	9
Net income	$ 100,000	10

[a] Error due to rounding.

showing a vertical analysis of a multiple-step income statement. Note the greater detail in calculation of net sales, cost of goods sold, gross profit, and so on.

The benefits explained for vertical analysis of the balance sheet apply to the income statement. Expense categories that are high (in comparison with other companies) warrant management investigation.

In Chapter 8 we mentioned that the value of the inventory will affect the financial statements. This can easily be seen from Figure 10.6. The "ending inventory" is subtracted from the "goods available for sale" to

Figure 10.7

CONOVER COMPANY
Comparative Income Statements
For the Years Ended December 31, Current Year and Previous Year

	Current Year	Previous Year	Increase (Decrease) Amount	Increase (Decrease) Percent	Percent Current Year	Percent Previous Year
Sales revenue						
Gross sales	$1,030,000	$920,000	$110,000	12.0	103	102.2
Less: sales returns and allowances	(30,000)	(20,000)	10,000	50.0	3	2.2
Net sales	$1,000,000	$900,000	$100,000	11.1	100	100
Cost of goods sold						
Beginning inventory	$ 92,000	$ 89,500	$ 2,500	2.8	9.2	9.9
Purchases	665,000	602,000	63,000	10.5	66.5	66.9
Less: returns and allowances	(23,500)	(20,500)	3,000	14.6	2.4	2.3
Goods available for sale	733,500	671,000	62,500	9.3	73.4[a]	74.6[a]
Less: ending inventory	(83,500)	(92,000)	(8,500)	(9.2)	8.4	10.2
Total cost of goods sold	650,000	579,000	71,000	12.3	65	64.3
Gross profit on sales	$ 350,000	$321,000	$ 29,000	9.0	35	35.7
Operating expenses						
Salaries	$ 90,000	$ 80,000	$ 10,000	12.5	9.0	8.9
Rent	18,000	15,000	3,000	20	1.8	1.7
Utilities	8,000	6,500	1,500	23.1	0.8	0.7
Administrative	23,500	18,500	5,000	27.0	2.4	2.1
Depreciation	20,500	17,000	3,500	20.6	2.1	1.9
Total operating expenses	160,000	137,000	23,000	16.8	16.0[a]	15.2[a]
Operating income	$ 190,000	$184,000	$ 6,000	3.3	19.0	20.4[a]
Taxes	90,000	88,000	2,000	2.3	9.0	9.8
Net income	$ 100,000	$ 96,000	$ 4,000	4.2	10.0	10.7[a]

[a] Error due to rounding.

determine the "cost of goods sold," which in turn is subtracted from "net sales" to determine "gross profit." Therefore, an inventory valuation method that gives inventory a lesser value will increase the cost of goods sold and reduce the gross profit. A higher ending inventory valuation will have the opposite effect. Since changing inventory valuation methods could allow manipulation of profits (and thereby taxes), government regulations require consistent use of the inventory valuation methods chosen.

Figure 10.7 shows a horizontal analysis of the current and previous years' income statements for the Conover Company. Its calculation is similar to that used for horizontal analysis of the balance sheet (again, the previous year's data are used as the base for calculating the percent change).

Figure 10.7 illustrates the value of horizontal analysis on the income statement. Net sales increased 11.1% for the current year. *However, net income only increased 4.2%.* The reason can be found in analyzing the operating expenses. They have increased much more than would normally be expected for the increase in sales. Such an analysis as this would give management a good idea of where to begin corrective action.

Summary

The income statement shows the result (profit or loss) of business operations for a period of time. An excess of revenue over expenses shows the profit; the excess of expenses over revenue shows the loss. Horizontal and vertical analysis may be performed on the income statement. Net sales for the year are used as the base in such analysis.

Exercises 10.2

1. Complete the following income statement including vertical analysis. Round answers to the nearest tenth.

			Percent
Sales revenue			
Gross sales		$982,000	——
Less: sales returns and allowances		(28,400)	
Net sales		?	100
Cost of goods sold			
Beginning inventory	$ 89,400		
Purchases	691,500		
Less: returns and allowances	(14,900)		
Goods available for sale	766,000		
Less: ending inventory	(?)		
Total cost of goods sold		$?	——
Gross profit on sales		$285,000	——

Operating expenses		Percent
Salaries	$?	____
Rent	18,000	____
Utilities	12,200	____
Supplies	8,700	____
Advertising	22,300	____
Depreciation	45,800	____
Administrative	12,100	____
Total operating expenses	$195,100	
Operating income	$?	____
Taxes	39,900	____
Net income	$?	____

2. Complete the following income statement including vertical analysis. Round answers to nearest tenth.

Sales revenue			Percent
Gross sales		$?	____
Less: sales returns and allowances		(72,400)	
Net sales	?	?	100.0
Cost of goods sold			
Beginning inventory	$123,200		
Purchases	?		
Less: returns and allowances	(25,000)		
Goods available for sale	?		
Less: ending inventory	(137,800)		
Total cost of goods sold		949,000	
Gross profit on sales		$511,000	____
Operating expenses			
Salaries	$ 73,400		
Depreciation	?		____
Rent	25,800		____
Administrative	24,100		____
Advertising	46,800		____
Total operating expenses		$?	15.0
Operating income		$?	____
Taxes		$ 73,000	____
Net income		$?	____

3. Complete the following income statements, including horizontal analysis. Round answers to the nearest tenth.

	Current Year	Previous Year	Increase (Decrease)		Percent	
			Amount	Percent	Current Year	Previous Year
Sales revenue						
Gross sales	$878,400	$859,800	$_____	_____	_____	_____
Less: sales returns and allowances	(13,400)	(14,800)	_____	_____	_____	_____
Net sales	$?	$?	$_____	_____	100.0	100.0
Cost of goods sold						
Beginning inventory	$ 78,400	$ 86,800	$_____	_____		
Purchases	630,400	639,750	_____	_____		
Less: returns and allowances	(18,800)	(14,400)	_____	_____		
Goods available for sale	$690,000	$?	$_____	_____		
Less: ending inventory	(84,500)	(78,400)	_____	_____		
Total cost of goods sold	$?	$633,750	$_____	_____	_____	_____
Gross profit on sales	$259,500	$?	$_____	_____	_____	_____
Operating expenses						
Salaries	$ 47,300	$?	$_____	_____	_____	_____
Rent	8,200	8,200	_____	_____	_____	_____
Utilities	6,900	7,100	_____	_____	_____	_____
Supplies	8,400	8,900	_____	_____	_____	_____
Advertising	?	13,400	_____	_____	_____	_____
Depreciation	12,200	12,800	_____	_____	_____	_____
Administrative	8,900	9,600	_____	_____	_____	_____
Total operating expense	$?	$114,600	$_____	_____	_____	_____
Operating income	$155,700	$ 96,650	$_____	_____		
Taxes	69,200	?	_____	_____		
Net income	$ 86,500	$ 57,700	$_____	_____	_____	_____

4. Complete the following income statements, including horizontal analysis. Round answers to the nearest tenth.

	Current Year	Previous Year	Increase (Decrease)		Percent	
			Amount	Percent	Current Year	Previous Year
Sales revenue						
Gross sales	$?	$2,984,500	$_____	_____	_____	_____
Less: sales returns and allowances	(144,800)	(157,500)	_____	_____	_____	_____
Net sales	$2,920,000	$?	$_____	_____	100.0	100.0
Cost of goods sold						
Beginning inventory	$ 246,400	$ 203,800	$_____	_____		
Purchases	?	1,943,400	_____	_____		
Less: returns and allowances	(50,000)	(48,200)	_____	_____		
Goods available for sale	$2,173,600	$?	$_____	_____		
Less: ending inventory	(275,600)	?	29,200	_____		
Total cost of goods sold	$1,898,000	?	$_____	_____	_____	_____

(table continues)

| | Current Year | Previous Year | Increase (Decrease) | | Percent | |
			Amount	Percent	Current Year	Previous Year
Gross profit on sales	$?	$ 974,400	$			
Operating expenses						
Salaries	$ 146,800	$ 152,400	$			
Depreciation	97,800	?				
Rent	51,600	50,400				
Administrative	48,200	51,300				
Advertising	?	97,800				
Total operating expense	$?	$?	$			
Operating income	$ 584,000	$ 519,400	$			
Taxes	$?	$ 132,400				
Net income	$ 438,000	$?	$			

10.3 Other Financial Analysis Techniques

There are many factors to be considered by a potential investor before investing in a company. Some of these cannot be reflected in any written document (things such as the company's overall management expertise, potential markets for the company's product, the company's share of existing markets, technological and environmental sensitivity, etc.). The financial statements of a company do, however, offer some valuable insight into a company's *past* performance. Although past performance is no guarantee of future performance, it is worthy of consideration.

Investors will be reviewing financial statements to try to answer two general questions about a company.

1. How is the company's *earning* performance (i.e., its ability to make a profit)?
2. What is the company's *financial condition*?

To answer these questions, certain ratios or comparisons may be calculated using financial statement data. While some are beneficial of their own accord, most calculations acquire much greater significance when compared with other companies in similar industries. Some of the major comparisons will be discussed in this section. Computations are done using the data found in the financial statements of the Bright Company (Figures 10.8 and 10.9).

Earning Performance

Return on Average Total Assets

The return on total assets is an indication of the productivity of assets. It is calculated by dividing the net income (from the income statement)

Figure 10.8

BRIGHT COMPANY
Comparative Balance Sheet
As of December 31, Current Year and Previous Year

	Current Year	Previous Year
Current assets		
Cash	$ 103,000	$ 98,300
Marketable securities	46,000	37,900
Accounts receivable	163,500	158,000
Notes receivable	35,000	35,000
Inventory	186,500	157,000
Total current assets	$ 534,000	$ 486,200
Noncurrent assets		
Land	$ 125,000	$ 125,000
Buildings (net)	420,800	285,000
Equipment (net)	198,000	178,500
Total noncurrent assets	$ 743,800	$ 588,500
Total assets	$1,277,800	$1,074,700
Current liabilities		
Accounts payable	$ 117,800	$ 105,300
Notes payable	83,000	71,000
Accrued liabilities	42,400	38,600
Total current liabilities	$ 243,200	$ 214,900
Noncurrent liabilities		
Mortgage	$ 248,000	$ 253,500
Bonds payable	240,000	260,000
Total noncurrent liabilities	$ 488,000	$ 513,500
Total liabilities	731,200	728,400
Owners' equity	546,600	346,300
Total liabilities and owners' equity	$1,277,800	$1,074,700

by the *average* total assets (from the balance sheet) for the period covered by the income statement.

**return on
total assets**

$$\text{return on total assets} = \frac{\text{net income}}{\text{average total assets}}$$

Example 1   The net income for Bright Company is $203,100 and the average total assets for the year are the total of the previous and current year divided by 2.

Figure 10.9

BRIGHT COMPANY
Comparative Income Statements
For the Years Ended December 31, Current Year and Previous Year

	Current Year	Previous Year
Sales revenue		
Gross sales	$1,984,000	$1,543,000
Less: sales returns and allowances	(28,000)	(24,500)
Net sales	$1,956,000	$1,518,500
Cost of goods sold		
Beginning inventory	157,000	143,200
Purchases	1,267,300	1,102,700
Less: returns and allowances	(27,700)	(25,800)
Goods available for sale	1,396,600	1,220,100
Less: ending inventory	(186,500)	(157,000)
Total cost of goods sold	1,210,100	1,063,100
Gross profit on sales	$ 745,900	$ 455,400
Operating expenses		
Salaries	$ 148,700	$ 122,800
Utilities	53,200	46,300
Advertising	58,600	45,900
Administrative	67,100	59,400
Depreciation	37,900	33,100
Total operating expense	$ 365,500	$ 307,500
Operating income ✓	$ 380,400	$ 147,900
Other revenue		
Interest	3,200	2,600
Dividends	2,200	800
Other expenses		
Interest expense ✓	19,700	13,400
Income before taxes	$ 366,100	$ 137,900
Income tax	163,000	68,200
Net income	$ 203,100	$ 69,700

SOLUTION

$$\text{Return on total assets} = \frac{\text{net income}}{\text{average total assets}}$$

$$= \frac{\$203,100}{(\$1,277,800 + \$1,074,700) \div 2}$$

$$= \frac{\$203,100}{\$1,176,250}$$

$$= 0.1727 \text{ or } 17.3\%$$

The higher the return on the average total assets, the more desirable the situation. The rate of return should be commensurate with the risk involved in the business. (Would you invest money in a business, taking the risk of failure, if you could earn the same rate of return in a savings account?)

Times Interest Earned (Before Taxes)

A company that finances its operations by borrowing money must pay the interest on such money. This computation shows how many times the company could have paid its interest commitments from current earnings. Such information is useful to both lenders (to know the relative safety of their loans) and owners of the business (since failure to pay such interest will have a negative effect on their holdings). *Times interest earned* can be calculated by dividing the operating income for the period by the amount of interest for the period.

times interest earned

$$\text{times interest earned} = \frac{\text{operating income}}{\text{interest charges}}$$

Example 2

SOLUTION

Bright Company paid $19,700 in interest charges for the current year.

$$\text{Times interest earned} = \frac{\text{operating income}}{\text{interest charges}}$$

$$= \frac{\$380,400}{\$19,700}$$

$$= 19.3 \text{ times}$$

There is no "standard" for the number of times interest earned. The higher the ratio, the better the company's performance in the view of lenders.

Operating Ratio

The *operating ratio* shows how much of the company sales dollar is used to pay for the cost of goods sold and operating expenses. It is calculated by dividing the cost of goods sold plus the operating expenses by the net sales.

operating ratio

$$\text{operating ratio} = \frac{\text{cost of goods sold} + \text{operating expenses}}{\text{net sales}}$$

Example 3

Bright Company had net sales of $1,956,000, cost of goods sold of $1,210,100, and operating expenses of $365,500.

SOLUTION $\text{Operating ratio} = \dfrac{\text{cost of goods sold} + \text{operating expenses}}{\text{net sales}}$

$$= \frac{\$1,210,100 + \$365,500}{\$1,956,000}$$

$$= 0.806 = 80.6\%$$

The higher the operating ratio, the more of each sales dollar that is required to cover expenses; therefore, the less money that is available for other liabilities and profit.

Earnings and Dividends per Share; Price–Earnings Ratio; Yield

These comparisons are of great interest to users of financial data. As such, it should be noted here that they are indicative of the company's earning performance. However, our discussion of them will be reserved for Chapter 15.

Financial Condition

A good earnings record is important. A weak financial condition looks less unfavorable with a good earnings record, as a company can *usually* work out of financial deficiencies. However, a company must be able to meet its obligations, to survive difficult times, and to change directions if necessary to continue operations. Analysis of financial condition can be considered within two time frames: the short term (less than one year or one business cycle, whichever is longer), and the long term (greater than one year or one business cycle).

Short-Term Financial Condition

short-term financial
strength indicators

The *short-term* financial strength of a company depends on two main factors: working-capital position and the ability to generate assets readily convertible to cash.

1. *Current* (*or working-capital*) *ratio*—The *working capital* of a business is the excess of current assets over current liabilities (i.e., working capital = current assets − current liabilities). The *current ratio* shows the relationship of current assets to short-term debt, or how effectively a company can pay its short-term debt.

current ratio $\text{current ratio} = \dfrac{\text{current assets}}{\text{current liabilities}}$

Example 4   Bright Company had current assets of \$534,000 and current liabilities of \$243,200.

SOLUTION

$$\text{Current ratio} = \frac{\text{current assets}}{\text{current liabilities}}$$

$$= \frac{\$534,000}{\$243,200}$$

$$= 2.2$$

A current ratio of 2.0 is generally considered to be the minimum acceptable level.

2. Quick (acid-test) ratio—The quick ratio is a more severe form of the current ratio. Only *quick* (or *liquid*) *assets* are divided by the current liabilities. Quick assets are those that are readily convertible into cash (such as cash, marketable securities, notes and accounts receivable). The less liquid current assets, such as inventory, are excluded because of the time required to convert into cash.

quick ratio

$$\text{quick ratio} = \frac{\text{quick assets}}{\text{current liabilities}}$$

Example 5

Bright Company's quick assets are

Cash	$103,000
Marketable securities	46,000
Accounts receivable	163,500
Notes receivable	35,000
Quick assets	$347,500

SOLUTION

$$\text{Quick ratio} = \frac{\text{quick assets}}{\text{current liabilities}}$$

$$= \frac{\$347,500}{\$243,200}$$

$$= 1.43$$

A quick ratio of 1.0 is generally considered to be the minimum acceptable level.

3. Inventory turnover—Inventory turnover has been thoroughly discussed in Chapter 8. It is the number of times that the inventory must be replaced during the period.

Example 6

We can calculate the inventory ratio (at cost) by dividing Bright Company's cost of goods sold by the average inventory for the period.

SOLUTION   Inventory turnover $= \dfrac{\text{cost of goods sold}}{\text{average inventory}}$

$$= \dfrac{\$1,210,100}{(\$186,500 + \$157,000) \div 2}$$

$$= \dfrac{\$1,210,100}{\$171,750}$$

$$= 7.0 \text{ times}$$

The higher the inventory turnover, the shorter the time interval between investment in inventory and sale of the product. Thus, the higher the turnover, the quicker the company can generate cash. Comparison with other companies in similar industries will give an idea of how effectively the inventory is being controlled.

4. *Accounts receivable turnover*—The accounts receivable turnover is an indicator of how efficiently the company is converting credit sales into cash. It is obtained by dividing the net sales for the period by the average accounts receivable:

accounts receivable
turnover

$$\text{accounts receivable turnover} = \dfrac{\text{net sales}}{\text{average accounts receivable}}$$

Example 7   The average accounts receivable for Bright Company was ($163,500 + $158,000) ÷ 2, or $160,750.

SOLUTION $\text{Accounts receivable turnover} = \dfrac{\text{net sales}}{\text{average accounts receivable}}$

$$= \dfrac{\$1,956,000}{\$160,750}$$

$$= 12.2 \text{ times}$$

The higher the accounts receivable turnover, the quicker the company is converting credit sales into cash. Comparison with other businesses should show how effectively the company is performing this function.

5. *Average age of accounts receivable*—This ratio indicates how current the company is keeping its collections. It is calculated by dividing the number of days in a year (365) by the accounts receivable turnover calculated in (4) above.

average age of
accounts receivable

$$\dfrac{\text{average age of}}{\text{accounts receivable}} = \dfrac{365}{\text{accounts receivable turnover rate}}$$

Example 8   The accounts receivable turnover from Example 7 was 12.2 times.

SOLUTION

$$\text{Average age of accounts receivable} = \frac{365}{\text{accounts receivable turnover rate}}$$

$$= \frac{365 \text{ days}}{12.2}$$

$$= 29.9 \text{ days}$$

If the average age of the accounts receivable is less than the company's normal credit period, collection procedures are being handled well.

Long-Term Financial Condition

long-term financial strength indicators

The *long-term* financial condition of a company can be analyzed through its *capital structure*, or where the company gets money to finance its operation.

1. *Debt ratio*—The debt ratio (generally expressed as a percent) tells how much of the total assets are owned by creditors. It is calculated by dividing the total short- and long-term debt by the total assets.

debt ratio

$$\text{debt ratio} = \frac{\text{total debt}}{\text{total assets}}$$

Example 9

Bright Company has a total debt of

Current liabilities	$243,200
Noncurrent liabilities	488,000
	$731,200

SOLUTION

$$\text{Debt ratio} = \frac{\text{total debt}}{\text{total assets}}$$

$$= \frac{\$731,200}{\$1,277,800}$$

$$= 0.572 = 57.2\%$$

Acceptable limits of debt financing can vary, so comparison with other companies is a good indicator of the company's standing.

2. *Equity ratio*—The equity ratio (expressed as a percent) tells how much of the total assets belong to the owners of the business. It is calculated by dividing the total owners' equity by the total assets (or subtracting the debt ratio, if calculated, from 100%).

equity ratio

$$\text{equity ratio} = \frac{\text{total owners' equity}}{\text{total assets}}$$

Example 10

Bright Company's owners have a total of $546,600 invested in the business.

SOLUTION

$$\text{Equity ratio} = \frac{\text{total owners' equity}}{\text{total assets}}$$

$$= \frac{\$546,600}{\$1,277,800}$$

$$= 0.428 = 42.8\%$$

Notice that we could also have calculated the equity ratio by subtracting the debt ratio (Example 9) from 100%.

$$\text{equity ratio} = 100\% - \text{debt ratio}$$

$$= 100\% - 57.2\%$$

$$= 42.8\%$$

The equity ratio indicates the protection of creditors by showing how much the owners of the business have invested. Again, comparison with other businesses would indicate how a given firm stands.

3. *Debt-to-equity ratio*—The debt-to-equity ratio (stated as a percent) indicates the relationship of borrowed and owners' capital. It is calculated by dividing the total debt by the total owners' equity.

debt-to-equity ratio

$$\text{debt-to-equity ratio} = \frac{\text{total debt}}{\text{total owners' equity}}$$

Example 11

Bright Company has total debt amounting to $731,200 and owners' equity of $546,600.

SOLUTION

$$\text{Debt-to-equity ratio} = \frac{\text{total debt}}{\text{total owners' equity}}$$

$$= \frac{\$731,200}{\$546,600}$$

$$= 1.34$$

That is, creditors have $1.34 in the Bright Company for every $1.00 the owners have invested.

This ratio should be compared with other businesses to determine a company's level of performance.

The essential information about the debt and equity relationship for any business can be determined from either the debt, equity, or debt-to-equity ratio. The choice of which one to use is an individual matter.

Summary

We have discussed many comparisons used in reviewing financial statements. They are some of the more common comparisons, but by no means are they all that are used. These comparisons have been summarized in Table 10.1.

TABLE 10.1

Ratio or Comparison	Method of Calculation	Significance
Earning performance		
1. Return on average total assets	$\dfrac{\text{net income}}{\text{average total assets}\ (\div 2)}$	Indicates the productivity of assets. The higher the return, the more desirable.
2. Times interest earned (before taxes)	$\dfrac{\text{operating income}}{\text{interest charges}}$	Indicates how effectively the company can pay interest charges from current operations.
3. Operating ratio	$\dfrac{\text{cost of goods sold} + \text{operating expenses}}{\text{net sales}}$	Indicates how much of the sales dollar is used to cover costs. The lower the ratio, the more desirable.
4. Earnings, dividends per share, price–earnings ratio, yield	Discussed in Chapter 15	
Financial condition		
Short term		
1. Current (working-capital) ratio	$\dfrac{\text{current assets}}{\text{current liabilities}}$	Indicates how effectively the company can pay its short-term debt. Ratio should be at least 2.0.
2. Quick (acid-test) ratio	$\dfrac{\text{quick assets}}{\text{current liabilities}}$	Indicates how effectively the company can pay its short-term debts from assets that are readily convertible to cash. Ratio should be at least 1.0.
3. Inventory turnover	Discussed in Chapter 8	Indicates how quickly the company is converting inventory to cash. The higher the turnover, the more desirable.
4. Accounts receivable turnover	$\dfrac{\text{net sales}}{\text{average accounts receivable}}$	Indicates how quickly the company is converting credit sales to cash. The higher the turnover, the more desirable.
5. Average age of accounts receivable	$\dfrac{365 \text{ days}}{\text{accounts receivable turnover rate}}$	Indicates the effectiveness of the company's collection procedures. Optimum is less than the normal credit period.
Long term		
1. Debt ratio	$\dfrac{\text{total debt}}{\text{total assets}}$	Indicates how much of the assets are financed by creditors.
2. Equity ratio	$\dfrac{\text{total owners' equity}}{\text{total assets}}$	Indicates how much of the assets are financed by owners.
3. Debt-to-equity ratio	$\dfrac{\text{total debt}}{\text{total owners' equity}}$	Indicates the relationship of borrowed to owners' capital.

Exercises 10.3

■ Show how you would calculate each of the following ratios or comparisons and tell from which financial statement you would obtain the data.

	Ratio or Comparison	Calculation	Financial Statements
Example:	quick ratio =	$\dfrac{\text{quick assets}}{\text{current liabilities}}$	balance sheet balance sheet

1. Return on average total assets

2. Times interest earned

3. Operating ratio

4. Current ratio

5. Accounts receivable turnover

6. Average age of accounts receivable

7. Debt ratio

8. Equity ratio

9. Debt-to-equity ratio

■ Mr. A. Rodriquez is considering buying the Great Company. He has taken the following information from the current financial statements. Can you help him analyze them?

    a. Owners' equity—$417,900

    b. Net sales for the period—$953,600

    c. Current assets—$382,900

    d. Operating expenses—$159,300

    e. Inventory—beginning—$203,600
                ending—$194,400

    f. Cost of goods sold—$599,800

    g. Current liabilities—$187,600

    h. Total liabilities—$378,900

    i. Quick assets—$194,300

    j. Total assets—beginning—$764,400
                 ending—$796,800

    k. Net income—$98,900

    l. Operating income—$194,500

    m. Interest paid—$22,400

    n. Accounts receivable—beginning—$122,900
                 ending—$107,800

10. What rate of return on total assets did the Great Company have for the current year?

11. How many times was the interest liability earned?

12. What is the operating ratio?

13. What is the current ratio?

14. How many times did the accounts receivable turn over?

15. What is the average age of accounts?

16. What is the debt ratio?

17. What is the equity ratio?

18. What is the debt-to-equity ratio?

19. What is the quick ratio?

20. What other information would you like to have for comparative purposes?

10.4 *Distribution of Profits*

In the preceding sections we learned how to identify the profit or loss aspect of business operations. The last thing we should discuss is how the profit or loss is transferred to the owners of the business. There are three basic kinds of businesses:

1. *Sole proprietorship*—This business is owned entirely by a single individual. He alone is responsible for the debts of the business and he alone receives the benefits from the profit or loss of the business.
2. *Partnership*—A partnership is a business having two or more persons as owners. They share the rewards and responsibility for the success of the business.
3. *Corporation*—A corporation is a legal entity created to own assets and be responsible for business operations. Ownership of a corporation is based on the shares of corporation stock owned by an individual.

Let us see how the profits of a business would be distributed to the owners of the business in these three cases.

Sole Proprietorship

sole proprietorship

The sole proprietorship is the simplest form of business. An individual uses his money (or the money he can borrow) to form a business. As the sole owner of the business, the proprietor receives *all* the profits of the business operation. However, should the business fail, the personal property of the proprietor can be taken to satisfy debts of the business. Obviously, there are no mathematical profit-distribution procedures required for a single owner.

Partnership

partnership

A partnership is a more complicated business arrangement than the proprietorship. Two or more owners (or *partners*) pool their resources, time, and talent to form a business. A partnership may be formed with only the agreement of the partners. However, to prevent misunderstandings at a later date, a formal, legal partnership agreement is usually drawn up and signed by all partners. This agreement will normally specify how much of the business each partner owns, how profits and losses are to be distributed, responsibilities of each partner, and so on. Just as there are some advantages to a partnership (increased assets and talent available from several partners), there are some disadvantages. The personal property of any partner may be used to pay creditors of the business. Any one partner can obligate the partnership to debt, and the personal property used to satisfy partnership debts can exceed the individual's amount of ownership in the business.

Partnerships may be formed by individuals to bring together any combination of talent and/or assets that they deem necessary. When the partnership agreement is signed, the partners mutually agree on how much of the business each partner owns. The partners will also agree on how profits and losses are to be distributed. The profit distribution may be different from the ownership agreement (i.e., a partner who works in the business full time may receive a larger share of the profit than the partner who contributes only money). The method of profit distribution may be limited only by the imagination of the partners. Any combination of distribution circumstances is possible.

distribution by equal shares

Equal Shares

The partners may agree to sharing the profit and loss equally.

Example 1

Mr. Jones and Mr. Bunker formed a partnership and agreed to distribute profit and loss equally between them. After their first year, they had a net profit of $5000. How much would each partner get?

SOLUTION

Each partner would receive an equal amount (or $\frac{1}{2}$ in this case) of the profit.

$$\text{Mr. Jones's share} = \frac{1}{2} \times \$5000 = \$2500$$
$$\text{Mr. Bunker's share} = \frac{1}{2} \times \$5000 = \$2500$$

In the absence of a formal partnership agreement, the law states that all profit and loss be shared equally among the partners. Therefore, a legal partnership document is necessary to distribute profits any other way.

Original Investment

distribution by original investment

The partners may choose to distribute profit and loss in accordance with how much each partner invested when the partnership was originally formed. In such a case, the ratio of each partner's initial contribution to the total initial investment would be applied to profit or loss figures.

Example 2

Mr. Adams, Mr. Baker, and Mr. Carlisle formed a partnership. Mr. Adams contributed $4500, Mr. Baker $1500, and Mr. Carlisle $1500. They agreed to distribute profits according to their original investment. How much of the $4000 first-year loss would each partner receive?

SOLUTION The partners contributed a total of $7500. Therefore, we must calculate a ratio of each partner's investment to the total. We can find each partner's share of the loss by multiplying that ratio by the $4000 loss.

$$\text{Mr. Adams:} \quad \frac{\$4500 \text{ investment}}{\$7500 \text{ total}} = 60\%$$

$4000 \text{ loss} \times 60\% = \$2400$ loss for Mr. Adams

$$\text{Mr. Baker:} \quad \frac{\$1500}{\$7500} = 20\%$$

$4000 \text{ loss} \times 20\% = \$800$ loss for Mr. Baker

$$\text{Mr. Carlisle:} \quad \frac{\$1500}{\$7500} = 20\%$$

$4000 \text{ loss} \times 20\% = \$800$ loss for Mr. Carlisle

We can verify our calculations by adding each partner's percent of ownership (to a total of 100%) and the individual losses (to a total of $4000).

Salary and Agreed Ratio

distribution by salary and agreed ratio
 The partners may agree to pay a salary to the partner managing the business. His salary will be deducted from the profits first; the remaining profit will be distributed to the partners in an agreed-upon ratio.

Example 3 Mr. Dickerson and Mr. Edwards formed a partnership. Mr. Dickerson quit his job to manage the partnership business. The partners agreed that Mr. Dickerson should receive a salary of $10,000 and that the remaining profits should be divided with 60% to Mr. Edwards and 40% to Mr. Dickerson. How will their $20,000 profit be distributed?

SOLUTION Mr. Dickerson will receive a $10,000 salary plus 40% of all profits in excess of $10,000. Therefore, he will receive

	Salary	$10,000
plus	Share of profit (i.e., $20,000 − $10,000 salary × 40% ratio)	4,000
	Mr. Dickerson	$14,000

Mr. Edwards will receive 60% of everything in excess of the $10,000 salary to Mr. Dickerson, so

$$(\$20,000 - \$10,000 \text{ salary}) \times 60\% = \$6000$$

Mr. Edwards's share is $6000. Again, we can check our calculations to ensure that the amount distributed totals the profit, or

$$\$14{,}000 + \$6000 = \$20{,}000$$

Interest on Investment and Agreed Ratio

distribution by
interest on
investment and
agreed ratio

Frequently when one partner contributes a significant amount of money to the partnership, the partners will agree to provide him with a stated return on investment. That return is subtracted from the profit and the remainder divided in accordance with an agreed ratio.

Example 4

Mr. Fox, Mr. Gerhl, and Mr. Higham formed a partnership in which Mr. Fox contributed $15,000, Mr. Gerhl $2500, and Mr. Higham $2500. Mr. Fox's involvement in the partnership was only to provide the money; Mr. Gerhl and Mr. Higham will manage the partnership. The partners agreed to give Mr. Fox an 8% return on investment with the remaining profits to be distributed as follows: Mr. Fox, 10%; Mr. Gerhl, 45%; and Mr. Higham, 45%. How would the $5000 profit be distributed?

SOLUTION

Mr. Fox is to receive 8% return on his $15,000 investment or $15,000 × 8% = $1200 plus 10% of everything in excess of $1200. Therefore, he will receive

Return on investment ($15,000 × 8%)	= $1200
plus share of profit [($5000 − $1200) × 10%]	= 380
Mr. Fox's share of profit	= $1580
Mr. Gerhl will receive [($5000 − $1200) × 45%]	= $1710
Mr. Higham will receive [($5000 − $1200) × 45%]	= $1710

To check, the total distributed is $1580 + $1710 + $1710 = $5000.

Example 5

Use the data from Example 4, but assume that the profits were only $200. What would be the distribution?

SOLUTION

The partners agreed to an 8% return on Mr. Fox's $15,000 investment, or that he would be paid $1200. Therefore, the $200 would go to Mr. Fox. However, the partners are now faced with a $1000 loss (i.e., the additional amount necessary to provide Mr. Fox his agreed-upon rate of return). This $1000 loss would be shared by the partners according to the agreed ratio, or

Mr. Fox's share	= 10% of $1000 loss =	$ 100 loss
Mr. Gerhl's share	= 45% of $1000 loss =	$ 450 loss
Mr. Higham's share	= 45% of $1000 loss =	$ 450 loss
	Total loss =	$1000

From the preceding examples, you can see that any combination agreeable to the partners is a valid way of distributing partnership profits.

corporation   ## *Corporation*

The corporation form of business is the most complex organization, since a new and legally accountable entity is created. The corporation is the safest form of business ownership. The liability of the corporation owner is limited only to the amount of money he has invested in his purchase of stock. The personal property of the corporation owner *is not* subject to use for paying creditors of the corporation.

Since there are numerous items that must be considered in the distribution of profits in a corporation, that portion of this discussion will be deferred until Chapter 15. After becoming familiar with the types of stock and the necessity for generating capital from within the corporation, corporate profit distribution will be much more meaningful.

Exercises 10.4

1. Distribute an $18,000 profit between two partners according to equal shares.

2. Distribute a $2000 loss among three partners on the basis of their original contribution. Ms. Murphy contributed $6000, Ms. Nixon $4000, and Ms. Oldfield $2000.

3. Mr. Petrich and Mr. Quince formed a partnership with each investing $5000. Since Mr. Petrich would be the primary manager of the partnership, they agreed to distribute profits with 70% to Petrich and the remainder to Quince. Distribute their profit of $8000.

4. Ms. Rutledge is to receive $12,000 per year as the managing partner of a business. After that, all profits are to be distributed equally among the three partners. Distribute an $18,000 profit.

5. Mr. South invested $20,000 of an investment totaling $30,000 in a partnership. The partners agreed that he is to receive a 9% return on his investment. All other profits will be distributed with 20% to Mr. South, and 40% each to his other partners, who will manage the business. Distribute a profit of $4800.

6. Mr. Trevino is the sole owner of a small business. How will his $5000 profit be distributed?

7. Mr. Ulrich and Mr. Valez formed a partnership with no formal agreement. Mr. Ulrich contributed $8000 of the capital and Mr. Velez $2000. Mr. Ulrich works approximately 40 hours per week at the business and Mr. Velez 20 hours. How will their $12,000 profit be distributed?

8. Don, Louis, and Charles formed a partnership. Don invested $3000, Louis $3000, and Charles $2000. Each is to receive a return of 5% on investment, with the remaining profit distributed by shares based on original investment. Distribute the $1400 profit.

9. Mr. Andrews invested $8000 into a partnership, and Mr. Bostich contributed $10,000. Their partnership agreement specified that Mr. Bostich will receive a salary of $7000 and that each will receive an 8% return on investment. All remaining profit will be shared equally. How will a profit of $12,000 be distributed?

10. Will and Abel each invested $10,000 in a partnership. Their partnership agreement provided for a 9% return on investment, a salary of $6000 for Will, a salary of $8000 for Abel, and equal distribution of excess profits. How will a profit of $22,000 be distributed?

Review Exercises / Chapter 10

1. Explain the difference between the balance sheet and the income statement.

2. Give the fundamental equation used to generate the balance sheet; the income statement.

3. Compute the missing information in the following:

Assets		Liabilities and Owners' Equity	
Cash	$187,500	Accounts payable	$ 148,700
Accounts receivable	347,600		
Inventory	?	Notes payable	200,000
Buildings	417,200	Mortgage	367,200
Equipment	98,900	Owners' equity	?
		Total liabilities	
Total assets	?	and owners' equity	$1,188,600

4. Compute the net profit given the following information: net sales, $120,000; cost of goods sold, $87,200; overhead expenses, $28,600.

5. Use the following information to analyze the "health" of the company as requested:

Net sales = $186,500   Cost of goods sold = $138,800
Current assets = $316,400   Operating expenses = $32,800
Average inventory = $36,200 (at cost)   Current liabilities = $289,400
Average accounts receivable = $42,800

Compute the following: (**a**) operating ratio, (**b**) current ratio, (**c**) inventory turnover, and (**d**) accounts receivable turnover.

6. Harry and James are partners. They invested $20,000 as follows: Harry $11,500 and James $8500. Their partnership agreement provided for a return on investment of 6%, salaries of $8000 for James and $7000 for Harry, and distribution of the excess in accordance with original investment. How much will each receive from profits of $18,000?

Chapter Test / Chapter 10

1. Define the following terms.

    a. assets   *b.* owners' equity

    c. revenue   *d.* liabilities

    e. expenses   *f.* balance sheet

    g. income statement   *h.* vertical analysis

    i. horizontal analysis

2. Vertically analyze the portion of the Fly By Day Airlines balance sheet shown below. (Round to the nearest tenth.)

		Answer
Current assets		
Cash	$12,000	_____
Marketable securities	4,000	_____
Accounts receivable	22,000	_____
Inventory	48,000	_____
Total current assets	$86,000	_____
Noncurrent assets		
Land	$112,500	_____
Buildings (net of depreciation)	46.500	_____
Equipment (net of depreciation)	5,000	_____
Total noncurrent assets	$164,000	_____
Total assets	$250,000	_____

3. Complete the following income statements, including horizontal analysis. (Round to the nearest tenth.)

	Current Year	Previous Year		*Answers*		
Sales revenue						
Gross sales	$146,500	$139,200	____	____	____	____
Less: sales returns and allowances	6,500	9,200	____	____	____	____
Net sales	?	$130,000	____	____	____	____
Cost of goods sold	?	75,000	____	____	____	____
Gross profit on sales	54,000	?	____	____	____	____
Operating expenses	36,000	34,000	____	____	____	____
Operating income	$18,000	$21,000	____	____	____	____

■ Given:

    Owners equity—$317,900

    Net sales for the period—$853,400

    Inventory—beginning—$183,600

              ending—$164,400

    Current liabilities—$114,250

    Total assets—beginning—$654,200

              ending—$687,100

    Interest paid—$14,650

    Accounts receivable—beginning—$87,400

                    ending—$79,200

    Current assets—$282,900

    Operating expenses—$74,300

    Cost of goods sold—$489,800

    Total liabilities—$288,600

    Quick assets—$94,300

    Net income—$48,600

    Operating income—$109,400

Calculate the following.

4. Rate of return on total assets

5. Times interest earned

6. Operating ratio

7. Current ratio

8. Debt ratio

9. Acid-test ratio

10. Accounts receivable turnover

11. Ms. Williams is to receive a salary of $12,000 for managing a partnership. Each partner is to receive a 10% return on investment with remaining profits distributed according to original investment. Distribute $48,000 in profits if the partnership consists of Ms. Williams ($25,000 investment), Ms. Owens ($75,000 investment), and Ms. Greer ($100,000 investment).

Cumulative Review Exercises

1. You are purchasing cans of cleaner. One supplier offers to sell to you at a cost of $18.50 per case (with 20 cans per case). Another supplier offers to sell you the same product at $11.34 per dozen cans. Which should you accept and why?

2. Calculate the net price only of a product if you receive discounts of 20%, 20%, and 20%. The product lists for $20.00 per unit.

3. What are the single equivalent discount rate and net price on an item listing for $2250 and having discounts of 20%, 10%, and 30%?

4. Outdoors, Inc., offers a lawn chair at $25 less 20%. Patio, Inc., offers a similar chair at $38 less 30% and 20%. Which company is offering the lower price? By how much?

5. Compute the cash discount available on an invoice totaling $1017.50 with terms of 3/10, n/30.

6. Trade discounts of 20% and 15% are allowed on the following items:

> 100 dozen red pencils at $0.48/doz. (list)
> 10 cartons paper at $12.85/carton (list)
> 1 gross rulers at $0.03 ea. (list)

These items were purchased on an invoice dated June 10 with terms of 2/10, n/30. If payment is made on June 18 and there are no returns or shipping charges, how much should be paid to the supplier?

7. The Sole Shack is selling tennis shoes for $19.95 per pair. If the markup is 30% based on selling price, what are the markup in dollars, and the cost of the shoes?

8. The Gallery estimates expenses at 25% of sales. They want to make a profit of 15% based on selling price. At what price should they sell a picture that cost them $50.00 (list) less a 10% trade discount?

9. A merchant received a shipment of 10 chairs. The freight cost was $75.00. The invoice total (list price), inclusive of freight, for the 10 chairs was $1775. If the merchant received discounts of 10% and 10% on the chairs, and his markup based on cost is 25%, what should each chair sell for? How much should he pay his supplier?

10. The Sand Castle Casting Company has a 20% defect rate on castings. Of that 20%, one-half can be sold for rejects at a price of $7.50 each. The other half must be discarded. The castings are made in lots of 100, and they cost $750 per lot to produce. Assuming that the company bases its markup at 30% on cost, what will the castings be sold for?

11. During a close-out sale, a $60 (regular price) pair of boots was advertised at a 45% reduction. The boots cost the seller $30 and selling expenses were 25% based on cost. What was the profit or loss?

12. Compute the value of 86,000 units remaining in inventory given the following purchases during the year:

April	136,000 units at $0.28 each
July	246,000 units at $0.31 each
Sept.	148,000 units at $0.27 each
Nov.	62,000 units at $0.32 each

Calculate according to (**a**) average cost, (**b**) FIFO, and (**c**) LIFO.

13. The Fig Leaf Shop had a clothing inventory of $35,000 on January 1. So far this year, the company has purchased $68,000 worth of merchandise (at cost) with net sales of $92,400. If the shop has a 25% markup based on *cost*, calculate the current inventory value using the gross profit method.

14. The Discount Mart has recorded the following information at retail levels: inventory of $138,600 as of January 1, purchases for the year of $368,900, and net sales of $437,200. Because of market fluctuations, the store management had marked merchandise up by $42,000 and down by $36,500 during the year. What would you estimate as the current inventory value if the Mart has a 35% markup rate based on selling price?

15. Assume that your answer to problem 14 is $96,400 (at cost). Use the remaining data in problem 14 to compute the inventory turnover.

16. The Hobby Kraft Shop is planning for inventory purchase in October. Sales for October are estimated at $26,900 and the manager wants an inventory of $18,700 (at retail) at the end of the month. Preliminary estimates put the September 30 inventory value at $14,680 (retail). The manager has already ordered $6200 (at cost) in inventory for October. If the markup rate based on selling price is 32%, how much *more* inventory (at cost) should the manager buy?

17. The Three Musketeers are three individuals who own a private plane for their business and pleasure. They must pay $100 per month for hangar storage and set aside $2600 a year for maintenance. They have agreed to allocate these "overhead" expenses according to the flying hours of each partner. How much should each partner pay if their flying hours for last year were: Dartran, 362 hours; Arty, 184 hours; Ports, 104 hours.

18. The Earth Mover Company has a grader whose current book value is $12,000. If the grader is 3 years old, is being depreciated according to the straight-line method, and has accumulated depreciation of $6000: (**a**) what is the salvage value assuming a 7-year life, and (**b**) how much did it cost?

19. The Overhead Express is depreciating a truck according to the miles driven. What was the annual depreciation last year if the truck was driven 92,000 miles? The truck cost $58,000 and has an estimated life of 550,000 miles. The salvage value is $3000.

20. Compute the first- and second-year depreciation on an asset purchased September 1 for $8600. The salvage value is $1100 and the life is 5 years. Use (*a*) the sum-of-the-years-digits, and (*b*) the double-declining-balance depreciation methods.

21. Give the total depreciation in the first year for an asset costing $12,000 and having an 8-year life. The salvage value is $1200. Assume that the asset was purchased on April 1 and it is depreciated by the sum-of-the-years-digits method.

22. Mr. Hernandez and Ms. Sanchez formed a partnership. Mr. Hernandez invested $8000 and Ms. Sanchez invested $12,000. They agreed to pay Mr. Hernandez a salary of $7200 and divide the remainder of the profits according to initial investment. How would a profit of $8600 be divided?

23. Three partners contributed the following amounts to a partnership: A, $18,000; B, $9000; and C, $6000. The partners agreed that A would receive 8% return on her investment, C would receive a salary of $8000, and B would receive 50% of the excess profits, with A and C receiving 25% each. How would a profit of $11,000 be divided?

24. Use the sum-of-the-years-digits method of depreciation to calculate a depreciation schedule for an asset costing $2,360.00 and having a 4-year life. The asset was purchased on May 1 and has no salvage value.

25. Mr. Goldman and Mr. Silverman each invested $14,000 in a partnership. Their partnership agreement provided for a 10% return on investment to each, a salary of $8000 to Mr. Goldman, and a salary of $10,000 to Mr. Silverman. Any excess profits were to be divided 60% to Mr. Goldman and 40% to Mr. Silverman. How will a profit of $32,685 be divided?

26. Calculate the net price paid for an item listing for $3600 if you are offered discounts of 10%, 12%, and 6%. The manufacturer bills you for the item on May 7 with terms of 2/10, n/30 R.O.G. The bill includes $260 freight charges. You received the item on May 28. On or before what date must you pay to obtain the discount? How much should you pay assuming you take the discount?

27. What should you charge for an item costing $64.60 if you want a 25% markup rate based on selling price? If you later mark the item down 30% from its regular price, how much above or below cost will the item sell for?

28. The March Hare had an inventory value (at cost) on January 1 of $14,265.00. During the year, purchases totaled $163,364.00 (at cost) and net sales (at retail) were $206,410.00. If the shop uses a 30% markup based on cost, what would you estimate as the ending inventory value?

29. The Weaver Mills is expanding their textile-producing capacity. On July 1, 1980, they purchased a $35,000 machine for use on the production line. It has an estimated life of 6 years and an estimated salvage value of $5000. In September 1982, the company purchased an identical machine for $40,000. Calculate the total cost recovered on these machines in 1984. The company has historically used the straight-line depreciation method; however, company management has used ACRS whenever possible.

30. On May 3, 1984, the Locus Company purchased a new building for business use. The building cost $240,000 and company management uses ACRS whenever possible. What amount of cost will be recovered in (**a**) the first year of the buildings life? (**b**) the fifth year? (**c**) the tenth year?

31. The Crush Movers purchased a new, heavy-duty moving van in April 1985 at a cost of $94,000. The van should be worth approximately $6000, at the end of its life. How much of the van's cost will be recovered under ACRS (**a**) in 1985? (**b**) in 1987? (**c**) in 1989? (**d**) in 1990?

Part Three

Mathematics of Money

O V E R V I E W

This part of the text focuses on money. Money is an asset; it has value to the one who possesses it. One measure of the value of money is what it will buy. Another measure of the value of money (and the one we will be concerned with in this part of the text) is the additional money that it will generate. This additional money is commonly called *interest*.

Suppose that you borrow $1000. You expect to pay interest for use of the money. The amount of interest paid depends on the interest rate charged, the time you use the money, and the method of repayment of the loan.

In Chapters 11 and 12 it is assumed that the loan (principal plus interest) is to be repaid in a *single* payment. Under this condition, the amount of interest may be computed by one of two different methods, depending on which one is specified by the lender. The methods are simple interest (Chapter 11), and bank discount (Chapter 12). Compound interest is discussed in Chapter 13.

If you choose to repay the loan by installments of two or more equal payments, the material in Chapter 14 is needed to find the amount of interest, the amount of the regular payments you must make, and the amount of interest contained in each payment.

On the other hand, you may have money and want to invest it in stocks or bonds. In this case you want to compute the interest yielded on your investment. Stocks and bonds are the subjects of Chapter 15.

CHAPTER 11

Simple Interest

INTRODUCTION

At one time or another, most people (and businesses) need money that they do not have. It may be needed to purchase special equipment, to take advantage of "special buys," or cash discounts, or just to take a vacation. In such a case. the solution might be to borrow the money. Borrowing allows a person to use money that he would not ordinarily have. However, the borrower must pay for the privilege of using the money. Why? Because money is an asset just as a building is. As such, its ownership is worth something. The owner of a building receives rent from a person using the building. The owner of money receives rent (called *interest*) from the person using the money.

Since ownership of money has value, the length of time involved in money transactions is important. For example, would you rather have someone pay you $10 today or a year from today? If you had the money today, you could invest it for the next year and receive interest for your ownership of the money. Thus, the $10 you have today is worth more than the $10 one year from today. The interest received represents the *time value* of money: that is, money received today is worth more than the same amount received later because of the interest that can be earned. With these concepts in mind, let us examine the transactions of borrowing, and lending money.

11.1 Making a Loan

An individual borrows a sum of money today. The amount borrowed is called the *principal* or *present value* (present value because money owned today is worth exactly the amount you have—there is no interest involved). The borrower must pay interest for the use of money. Then, at some time in the future, the borrower must repay the amount borrowed (principal) *plus* the interest (for use of the money). The money to be repaid (principal plus interest) is called the *future value* or *maturity value* of the loan (future value because the money borrowed will be increased by the interest paid). Frequently, a loan is referred to as a *note*.

Similarly, if a person owns money, he expects to invest it and have it earn interest. The amount invested is also called the *principal* (present value); the amount of money he will have in the future is called the *future value* or *maturity value* of the investment.

Promissory Notes

One of the most common types of loans is the *promissory note*. In such a note, you borrow money and sign a note or "promise" to pay back the principal plus specified interest on the maturity date. Such notes are extremely flexible, as they may be made at any time and mature at any time.

A promissory note must contain the following items:

1. The amount borrowed.
2. The loan date.
3. The name of the borrower.
4. The name of the lender.
5. The amount to be repaid.
6. The method of repayment.
7. The interest rate.
8. The borrower's signature.
9. The signature of a witness or notary.

These are shown in the sample note, Figure 11.1.

Promissory notes can be either *secured* or *unsecured*. For example, suppose that you wish to borrow $1000 from the bank. The banker may lend you the $1000 based only on your signature promising to repay the money plus interest. The note is called an *unsecured note* because the banker has nothing except your word that you will repay the loan. However, the banker

Figure 11.1
Sample
Promissory Note

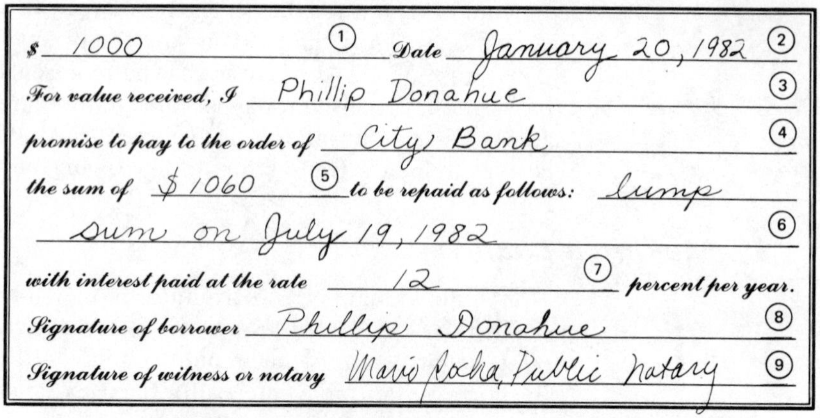

$ __1000__   ① Date __January 20, 1982__ ②
For value received, I __Phillip Donahue__ ③
promise to pay to the order of __City Bank__ ④
the sum of __$1060__ ⑤ *to be repaid as follows:* __lump__
__sum on July 19, 1982__ ⑥
with interest paid at the rate __12__ ⑦ *percent per year.*
Signature of borrower __Phillip Donahue__ ⑧
Signature of witness or notary __Mario Rocha, Public Notary__ ⑨

may require that you sign over to the bank ownership of something you own pending repayment of the loan. For example, you might have to sign over the title of your car to the bank as "insurance" that the note will be repaid. If you fail to repay the note, the bank can claim your car and dispose of it to recover the money you borrowed. Such a note is called a *secured note*. That asset which you sign over to the bank is called *collateral*. A note that is not repaid on time is said to be in *default*.

The amount of the promissory note is its *face value*. The face value is treated as the principal (*P*) for the purpose of computing interest. (The face value of Phillip Donahue's note on the previous page is $1000.)

Definitions

loan date and
maturity date
term

The date on which the money is borrowed is called the *loan date*. The date on which the money is to be repaid is called the *maturity date* or *due date*.

The time between the loan date and the maturity date is called the *term* of the loan.

A note made for less than 1 year is generally called a *short-term* note. Whether the note is a loan or investment is a matter of perspective. To the borrower, it is a loan; to the lender, it is an investment. The terminology of loan date, due date, term, and so on, is the same either way. We will view problems from both perspectives in this chapter.

11.2 Simple Interest

There are many methods of computing interest on borrowed money. The method used can change the amount of interest paid (or earned). Some common methods are simple interest, bank discount, interest compounded periodically, and interest compounded continuously. We begin with simple interest because it is conceptually and computationally the least difficult.

simple interest

Simple Interest

Interest that is computed on the principal (only) is called *simple interest*.

The amount of simple interest is computed for any principal by the formula

$$I = Prt$$

where I = amount of interest, dollars
      P = principal (invested or borrowed), dollars
      r = simple interest rate, percent
      t = time the money is used or term of the loan

Note: Time *must be* expressed in years or fractions of years to use the formula.

In Section 11.1, Phillip Donahue borrowed $1000 for 180 days at 12% simple interest and agreed to repay $1060. How did the loan officer at City Bank compute the amount of interest ($60) charged Mr. Donahue?

If the term of a loan is given in days, it must be converted to a fraction of a year by putting the number of days in the term *over* the number of days in a year. This requires special consideration.

Two types of years are used in business. One is called an *ordinary interest year*; the other is called an *exact interest year*.

How long is a year?

An *ordinary interest year* has 360 days.
An *exact interest year* has 365 days.

Interest on notes and bonds issued by business firms and most bank notes is calculated on the basis of 360 days (i.e., an ordinary interest year). The 360-day ordinary interest year is used to simplify calculations. It also results in a slightly higher amount of interest (the interest on the other 5 days normally included in the exact year).

Interest paid on U.S. government obligations is calculated on the basis of 365 days (i.e., an exact interest year).

The number of days in the year (360 or 365) must be specified in the problem.

The interest City Bank charged Phillip Donahue was computed as follows:

$$I = \$1000 \times 12\% \times \frac{180}{360} = \$60$$

Note that City Bank used an ordinary (360-day) year.

Example 1

Determine the amount of interest on a $100 loan at 6% simple interest for 180 days. Use an *ordinary interest year* (360 days).

SOLUTION

In this problem, $P = \$100$ and $r = 6\%$. Since the loan is for 180 days, t is obviously a fraction. Using an ordinary interest year of 360 days, we have $t = \frac{180}{360}$ or $t = \frac{1}{2}$ year. Hence,

$$I = Prt$$

$$= \$100\,(6\%)\left(\frac{180}{360}\right)$$

$$= \$100\,(0.06)\,(0.5)$$

$$= \$3.00$$

Note: Calculation may be done using decimals or fractions.

Example 2

Determine the interest on a loan of $100 at 6% simple interest for 180 days. Use an *exact interest year* (365 days).

SOLUTION

$P = \$100$, $r = 6\%$, and $t = \frac{180}{365}$. Hence.

$$I = Prt$$

$$= \$100(6\%)\left(\frac{180}{365}\right)$$

$$= \$100(0.06)\left(\frac{180}{365}\right)$$

$$= \$2.96 \quad \text{(rounded to the nearest cent)}$$

Compare the amounts of interest in Examples 1 and 2. Although the principal ($100), rate (6%), and time (180 days) are the same, the amounts of interest are different ($3.00 versus $2.96). The amount of interest using an exact year (365 days) is less than the amount computed using an ordinary year (360 days). The larger amount of interest is one reason why institutions in the business of lending money use the ordinary interest year. For large amounts of money, the difference can be considerable.

The Overseas Import Company borrowed $9735 for 60 days at 6% simple interest. If interest is based on an *ordinary* year, then

$$I = \$9735 \times 0.06 \times \frac{60}{360}$$

$$= \$9735 \times 0.01$$

$$= \$97.35$$

The product of $0.06 \times \frac{60}{360}$ always equals 0.01. Therefore, the amount of interest in a 60-day, 6% problem is always 0.01 of the principal. If $8650 were borrowed, the interest would be $86.50. This is called the *60-day, 6% method* for determining interest.

60-day, 6% method

Variations of the 60-Day, 6% Method

People who work extensively with simple interest frequently use variations of the 60-day, 6% method for computing interest at other rates and times. For example, if you borrow $1000 at 6% for 180 days, you can find the interest for 60 days ($10, i.e., 1% of the note) and multiply by 3 to adjust for the 180-day term, which is 3 times as long as 60 days. The interest on $1000 at 6% for 180 days is $30 (= 3 × $10).

Suppose that you borrow $500 at 12% for 60 days. The interest at 6% would be $5 (= $500 × 0.01). Since the interest rate being charged is twice 6% (or 12%), the amount of interest is $10 (= 2 × $5). Computing the amount of interest for 60 days at 6% and adjusting this amount to take into account the actual interest rate and time is one of the "tricks of the trade" used by loan officers. However, it cannot be used for an exact (365-day) year.

Other rates and terms giving $I = 1\%$ of P are 8% for 45 days, 4% for 90 days, and 2% for 180 days.

Occasionally, the term of a loan is given in months. In this case, a year is 12 months. The number of days is of no concern. The time t is the number of months in the term *over* 12 months, which gives us the time in years.

Example 3   Madaline borrowed $500 at 9% simple interest for 4 months. How much interest did she pay?

SOLUTION $P = \$500$, $r = 9\%$, and $t = \frac{4}{12}$ year. Hence,

$$I = Prt$$

$$= \$500(9\%)\left(\frac{4}{12}\right)$$

$$= \$500(0.09)\left(\frac{1}{3}\right)$$

$$= \$15$$

Madaline paid $15 interest.

If the values of any three of the four quantities in the formula $I = Prt$ are known, the remaining quantity can be determined by solving the equation (using the procedure presented in Chapter 5). Examples 4 and 5 illustrate this process.

Example 4   Robert has $300 to invest at 6% simple interest. How long will it take to earn $18 in interest?

SOLUTION $P = \$300$, $r = 6\%$, and $I = \$18$. Hence,

$$I = Prt$$
$$\$18 = \$300(6\%)t$$

The length of time can be determined by solving the equation for t.

$$\$18 = \$300(0.06)t$$

$$= \$18t$$

$$1 = t$$

Remember: t is always expressed in years or fractions of a year. Hence, $t = 1$ means that the time is 1 year. Hence, Robert will earn $18 in interest in 1 year.

Example 5

a. If the principal is $500, the amount of interest is $80, and the time is 2 years, find the interest rate.

b. If the amount of interest is $40, the rate of interest is 8%, and the time is 4 years, find the principal.

SOLUTION

a. By substituting the values given for I, P, and t in $I = Prt$, we have

$$\$80 = \$500(r)(2)$$
$$= \$1000r$$
$$\frac{80}{1000} = r$$
$$0.08 = r \quad \text{or} \quad r = 8\%$$

b. By substituting the values given for I, r, and t in $I = Prt$, we have

$$\$40 = P(8\%)(4)$$
$$= P(0.08)(4)$$
$$= P(0.32)$$
$$\frac{\$40}{0.32} = P \quad \text{or} \quad P = \$125$$

Exercises 11.2

■ Find the amount of interest (I) for each of the following loans. Use an *ordinary* interest year where appropriate.

1. $P = \$100$, $r = 6\%$, $t = 2$ years.

2. $P = \$100$, $r = 6\%$, $t = 6$ months.

3. $P = \$100$, $r = 6\%$, $t = 60$ days.

4. $P = \$500$, $r = 5\%$, $t = 2$ years.

5. $P = \$800$, $r = 8\%$, $t = 2$ years.

6. $P = \$500$, $r = 10\%$, $t = 2$ years.

7. $P = \$1000$, $r = 6\%$, $t = 240$ days.

8. $P = \$1000$, $r = 6\%$, $t = 180$ days.

9. $P = \$1000$, $r = 6\%$, $t = 2$ years.

10. $P = \$2000$, $r = 8\%$, $t = 270$ days.

11. $P = \$5000$, $r = 9\%$, $t = 1$ year.

12. $P = \$10,000$, $r = 9\%$, $t = 1\frac{1}{2}$ years.

■ Find the interest earned on each of the following investments. Use an *exact* interest year where appropriate.

13. $1000, $r = 6.39\%$, $t = 5$ years.

14. $500, $r = 8.30\%$, $t = 73$ days.

15. $1000, $r = 12\%$, $t = 146$ days.

16. $850.75, $r = 10\%$, $t = 2$ years.

17. $10,000, $r = 7.3\%$, $t = 15$ days.

18. $500, $r = 14.6\%$, $t = 75$ days.

19. Richard purchased a $1000 bond that pays 8.5% simple interest each year. How much interest will be paid in 4 years?

20. Bob borrowed $500 at 12% simple interest. If he repays the loan in 60 days, how much interest does he owe?

21. Karen's charge account has an unpaid balance of $100. If she is charged 18% simple interest per year, how much interest will she owe in 60 days?

■ Find the missing values in the following table. (Some equation solving is required.)

	Interest, I	Principal, P	Interest Rate, r	Time, t
22.	$20	$100	5%	?
23.	$4.80	$80	?	1 year
24.	$100	?	10%	2 years

25. Find the amount of interest earned on $600 at $5\frac{1}{4}\%$ for 4 years.

26. What interest rate would yield $120 interest on $1000 in 2 years?

27. How long would it take to earn $80 on a principal of $200 at 5% simple interest?

11.3 *Future Value; Present Value*

Our primary concern so far has been to find the amount of interest due on a specified principal for different simple interest rates and time periods. However, when you borrow money, you must repay the principal plus the

future value

> **Future Value**
>
> The future value (A) of a loan is equal to the money borrowed (principal) plus the interest; that is,
>
> $$A = P + I$$
>
> where A = future value
> P = principal (or present value)
> I = amount of interest, dollars

interest. The amount of the *principal plus interest* is called the *future value* of the loan (or investment).

Definition

An *interest-bearing note* **is one for which you borrow the principal or present value and repay principal plus interest.**

The note "bears interest" in that interest is paid at the *end* of the term (on the due date). (This point will be more meaningful when we discuss notes in which the interest is paid at the *beginning* of the term; these are called non-interest-bearing notes.)

Example 1

Craig borrowed $600 for 90 days at 18% simple interest. What future value will he have to pay in 90 days?

SOLUTION

First, we find the interest *I*.

$$I = Prt$$

$$= \$600(18\%)\left(\frac{90}{360}\right)$$

$$= \$27$$

The future value is

$$A = P + I.$$

$$= \$600 + \$27$$

$$= \$627$$

Therefore, Craig must repay $627 in 90 days.

You will notice that we used two steps in Example 1 to determine the amount of money to be repaid. First, the amount of interest was computed according to the formula $I = Prt$. Second, the future value was computed using the formula $A = P + I$. Since the I in both formulas is the same, we may develop a new formula for determining A without calculating I separately. We do this by substituting Prt for I in $A = P + I$.

$$A = P + I$$

$$= P + Prt$$

$$= P(1 + rt)$$

This formula may be considered a shortcut since it does not involve two steps.

The next two examples illustrate use of this formula.

Example 2   Find the future value of a loan of $800 at 12% simple interest for 6 months.

SOLUTION $A = P(1 + rt)$; $P = \$800$, $r = 12\% = 0.12$, and $t = \frac{6}{12}$ or $\frac{1}{2}$ year.

$$A = \$800\left[1 + (0.12)\left(\frac{1}{2}\right)\right]$$

$$= \$800[1 + 0.06]$$

$$= \$800[1.06]$$

$$= \$848$$

Brackets [ ] are interpreted the same as parentheses ( ). They are used to avoid confusion by having too many sets of parentheses in the same problem.

The future value is $848.

Example 3   Kay invested $900 at 9% simple interest for 2 years. What is the future value of her investment?

SOLUTION $A = P(1 + rt)$

$$= \$900[1 + (9\%)(2)]$$

$$= \$900[1 + (0.09)(2)]$$

$$= \$900[1 + 0.18]$$

$$= \$900[1.18]$$

$$= \$1062$$

Kay will have $1062.

Present Value

Suppose a company knows that $10,000 will be needed to pay for a shipment of merchandise that will be arriving in 90 days. If the company can make a short-term investment at 6% simple interest, how much should it invest *now* to have $10,000 in 90 days? In other words, what is the present value of $10,000 at 6% simple interest for 90 days?

present value

Present Value
$$P = \dfrac{A}{1 + rt}$$
where P = present value (or principal) A = future value (or maturity value) r = simple interest rate t = time (or term), years

One approach would be to substitute the known values in the formula $A = P(1 + rt)$ and solve for P (present value). An alternative is to solve the equation explicitly for P and determine a new formula for present value.

We can use the formula to find present value of $10,000 at 6% simple interest for 90 days. Here $r = 6\% = 0.06$, $t = \frac{90}{360} = \frac{1}{4}$ year, assuming an ordinary year.

$$P = \frac{\$10,000}{1 + (0.06)\left(\frac{1}{4}\right)}$$

$$= \frac{\$10,000}{1 + 0.015}$$

$$= \frac{\$10,000}{1.015}$$

$$= \$9852.22$$

If the company invests $9,852.22 now, it will have the future value of $10,000 to pay for the merchandise when it arrives.

Example 4   Elizabeth wants *to have* $1000 in 2 years. She has an opportunity to invest her money at 8% simple interest. How much must she invest now to have $1000 2 years from now?

SOLUTION   Since Elizabeth wants to have $1000 in the future, $A = \$1000$. The time is $t = 2$ years and $r = 8\% = 0.08$. Hence,

$$P = \frac{A}{1 + rt}$$

$$= \frac{\$1000}{1 + (0.08)(2)}$$

$$= \frac{\$1000}{1 + 0.16}$$

$$= \frac{\$1000}{1.16}$$

$$= \$862.07$$

Elizabeth must invest a present value or principal of $862.07 to have a future value of $1000.

Remember the time value of money. The present value is *always less* than the future value.

Exercises 11.3

■ Find the amount (*A*) to be repaid for each of the following loans. Use an *ordinary* interest year where appropriate.

1. $P = \$100$, $r = 10\%$, time $= \frac{1}{2}$ year.

2. $P = \$100$, $r = 10\%$, time $= 2.5$ years.

3. $P = \$100$, $r = 10\%$, time $= 90$ days.

4. $P = \$300$, $r = 8\%$, time $= \frac{1}{4}$ year.

5. $P = \$300$, $r = 8\%$, time $= 2$ years, 3 months.

6. $P = \$300$, $r = 8\%$, time $= \frac{1}{2}$ year.

■ Find the present value of each of the following.

7. $A = \$1000$, $r = 9\%$, time $= 2$ years.

8. $A = \$1000$, $r = 9\%$, time $= 8$ months.

9. $A = \$1000$, $r = 9\%$, time $= 90$ days.

10. $A = \$1600$, $r = 12\%$, time $= 1$ year, 3 months.

11. $A = \$1600$, $r = 6\%$, time $= 1\frac{1}{2}$ years.

12. $A = \$1600$, $r = 10\%$, time $= \frac{1}{4}$ year.

■ Find the future value (*A*) of each of the following investments. Use an *exact* interest year where appropriate.

	Principal Invested	Time	Interest Rate	Future Value
13.	$700	2 years	9%	_____
14.	$900	6 months	10.5%	_____
15.	$1000	$\frac{1}{2}$ year	12.6%	_____
16.	$2000	73 days	8%	_____
17.	$1800	9 months	8%	_____
18.	$4000	45 days	7.3%	_____

19. Gene bought a living room suite for $850. He agreed to pay in 5 months at 12% simple interest. How much will he pay for the furniture?

20. Mr. Ford's house payment is presently $300 per month. Because of increases in taxes and insurance, he expects the payment to increase at 10% next year. What will Mr. Ford's payment be next year?

21. Find the future value of an investment of $2000 for 3 years at 8% simple interest.

22. Find the future value of an $800 investment for 5 years at 6% simple interest.

23. Kay purchased a car for $1800 at 9% simple interest. If she pays for the car in 6 months, how much will she need?

24. A $1000 certificate of deposit (CD) pays 6.39% simple interest for 3 years. What is the future value of the CD?

■ Find each missing value in the following table. (Finding r and t will require solving equations.)

	A	P	r	t
25.	$2000	?	10%	10 years
26.	$400	$200	5%	?
27.	$300	$200	?	5 years

28. Find the future value of $600 at 12% simple interest in 6 months.

29. What principal would yield $1120 at 6% in 2 years?

30. How long will it take for $300 to grow to $600 at 10% simple interest?

11.4 Calendar Dates

Two methods of referring to days of the year are used in business. The one that is most familiar to the layman is the use of the month, day, and year, such as January 3, 1980. The day of the week on which the date falls can be determined by looking at a 1980 calendar. (It is a Thursday.) A business (such as a bank) that is not open on weekends or holidays would use this system for scheduling work, vacations, and so on.

Another way to refer to dates is to number the days of the year consecutively from 1 to 365 (or 366 for leap year). Then January 3 is day 3, May 5 is day 125, December 31 is day 365 (ignoring leap year). A business such as a computer or data processing company that operates every day would use the consecutive-day (or *exact-day*) numbering system for scheduling work.

The conversion from one system to the other is facilitated by use of an *exact-day calendar* (Figure 11.2). It is extremely helpful in working with short-term notes to be able to use both methods and to be able to convert between them.

The number of days between the loan date and due date (or term) can easily be determined by using the exact day of the dates. Suppose that a note made on January 3 is due on May 5. What is the term?

using an exact-day
calendar

> To use an exact-day calendar, we observe that the left-hand column is labeled "Day of Month." We place a ruler or other straightedge at the given date and read across until we come to the column headed by the given month. The number found is the exact day of the given calendar date.

Thus, to find the exact day of May 5, we place a straightedge along the row with 5 on the left and read across to May. The exact day is 125. Similarly, the exact day of September 20 is 263.

Suppose that you borrow money on January 3, which is day 3, and wish to repay it on May 5, day 125. How do you find the term of the note? We can use the following procedure.

Figure 11.2   Exact-Day Calendar (Excluding Leap Year)

Day of Month	Jan.	Feb.	Mar.	Apr.	May	June	July	Aug.	Sept.	Oct.	Nov.	Dec.
1	1	32	60	91	121	152	182	213	244	274	305	335
2	2	33	61	92	122	153	183	214	245	275	306	336
3	3	34	62	93	123	154	184	215	246	276	307	337
4	4	35	63	94	124	155	185	216	247	277	308	338
5	5	36	64	95	125	156	186	217	248	278	309	339
6	6	37	65	96	126	157	187	218	249	279	310	340
7	7	38	66	97	127	158	188	219	250	280	311	341
8	8	39	67	98	128	159	189	220	251	281	312	342
9	9	40	68	99	129	160	190	221	252	282	313	343
10	10	41	69	100	130	161	191	222	253	283	314	344
11	11	42	70	101	131	162	192	223	254	284	315	345
12	12	43	71	102	132	163	193	224	255	285	316	346
13	13	44	72	103	133	164	194	225	256	286	317	347
14	14	45	73	104	134	165	195	226	257	287	318	348
15	15	46	74	105	135	166	196	227	258	288	319	349
16	16	47	75	106	136	167	197	228	259	289	320	350
17	17	48	76	107	137	168	198	229	260	290	321	351
18	18	49	77	108	138	169	199	230	261	291	322	352
19	19	50	78	109	139	170	200	231	262	292	323	353
20	20	51	79	110	140	171	201	232	263	293	324	354
21	21	52	80	111	141	172	202	233	264	294	325	355
22	22	53	81	112	142	173	203	234	265	295	326	356
23	23	54	82	113	143	174	204	235	266	296	327	357
24	24	55	83	114	144	175	205	236	267	297	328	358
25	25	56	84	115	145	176	206	237	268	298	329	359
26	26	57	85	116	146	177	207	238	269	299	330	360
27	27	58	86	117	147	178	208	239	270	300	331	361
28	28	59	87	118	148	179	209	240	271	301	332	362
29	29	—	88	119	149	180	210	241	272	302	333	363
30	30	—	89	120	150	181	211	242	273	303	334	364
31	31	—	90	—	151	—	212	243	—	304	—	365

finding the term

> **Find the Time Between Loan Date and Due Date (Term)**
>
> **Step 1.** Find the exact-day number of the due date.
> **Step 2.** Find the exact-day number of the loan date.
> **Step 3.** Subtract to find the number of days between the two dates (i.e., the term).

The term of a note made on January 3 and due on May 5 is 125 − 3, or 122 days. Once we find the number of days, we use the fraction 122/360 or 122/365 as the value of t in the simple interest formula.

Example 1   Find the term of a note made on June 27 and due on September 15.

SOLUTION

Date	Day of Year
Step 1. September 15 (due date)	258
Step 2. June 27 (loan date)	− 178
Step 3. Subtract	80 days (term)

The term is 80 days.

The exact-day calendar is useful because it presents the calendar dates and days of the year in a single concise table. However, it does present some problems in practical situations. For example, if September 15 (in Example 1) falls on a weekend or some other day that the bank is closed, you could not repay the loan on that date. To avoid such problems, a current calendar is also needed. Fortunately, many calendars give dates both ways.

Example 2   Marie borrowed $800 at 10% simple interest on June 10. If she repays the loan on October 4, how much interest does she owe? Use an ordinary interest year.

SOLUTION $I = Prt$, where $P = \$800$ and $r = 10\%$. The time (t) in days is determined as follows:

Date	Day of Year
Step 1. October 4 (due date)	277
Step 2. June 10 (loan date)	− 161
Step 3. Subtract	116 days

Therefore, $t = 116$ days or $\frac{116}{360}$ year. Hence,

$$I = \$800(0.10)\left(\frac{116}{360}\right)$$

$$= \$25.78 \quad \text{(rounded to the nearest cent)}$$

(For notes made near the end of a year that come due in the following year, the number of days remaining in the year is added to the number of the due date in the following year.)

Determining the Due Date

Suppose that you know the *term* of the loan and the *loan date*. With this information, you can determine the due date. Robert makes a loan on August 10 that is to be repaid in 90 days. What is the maturity date? The following procedure for determining the maturity date may be used.

Determining the Due Date

Step 1. Find the exact day of the loan date.

Step 2. Add the exact date and term to get the exact day of the due date.

Step 3. Use the exact-day calendar to determine the calendar date that the loan is due.

The procedure can be used to determine the due date of Robert's loan made on August 10 for 90 days as follows:

Date	Day of Year
Step 1. August 10 (loan date)	222
Step 2. Add	+ 90 days (term)
Step 3	312 → November 8 (due date)

Hence, Robert's loan is due to be repaid on November 8.

Example 3

A 60-day loan is made on March 10. Find the due date.

SOLUTION

Date	Day of Year
Step 1. March 10 (loan date)	69
Step 2. Add	+ 60 days (term)
Step 3	129 → May 9 (due date)

Example 4

A $600, 90-day note at 8% simple interest is made on June 3. If the loan is repaid in 74 days, find the date on which the money is repaid and the amount of interest paid. Use an ordinary interest year.

SOLUTION

Date	Day of Year
Step 1. June 3 (loan date)	154
Step 2. Add	$+$ 74 days (term)
Step 3	228 → August 16 (due date)

Hence, the money is repaid on August 16. The interest is

$$I = \$600(8\%)\left(\frac{74}{360}\right)$$

$$= \$600(0.08)\left(\frac{74}{360}\right)$$

$$= \$9.87$$

Terms Expressed in Months

To find the maturity date of a loan where time is expressed in months, simply count the number of months in the term. The maturity date falls on the same day of the month as the loan date with one exception: If the due date is a nonexistent day (such as February 30), the loan falls due on the last day of the month.

Example 5 Find the maturity date of a 6-month loan made on April 8.

SOLUTION

Month	Number of Months Elapsed
April	0
May	1
June	2
July	3
August	4
September	5
October	6

Hence, the loan matures on October 8. Note that the month of April is counted as month 0 because the first full month of the loan falls in May on May 8.

Exercises 11.4

■ Find the number of days (i.e., the *term*) between the following loan dates and due dates. The loan date is given first.

1. February 3, April 11

2. June 3, August 12

3. January 10, May 15

4. January 3, March 3

5. April 10, October 10

6. June 10, December 10

7. March 10, May 31

8. June 21, July 22

9. August 10, November 12

10. January 5, 1978, and July 10, 1979

11. May 5, 1982, and August 30, 1983

12. March 15, 1981, and April 15, 1982

■ Find the maturity date for each of the following.

	Loan Date	Term	Maturity Date
13.	March 12	60 days	_____
14.	June 15	3 months	_____
15.	August 10	4 months	_____
16.	April 15	43 days	_____
17.	November 6	29 days	_____
18.	January 21	6 months	_____

■ Find the amount of interest and maturity value for each of the promissory notes. Use an *ordinary interest year*.

	Face Value	Simple Interest Rate, r	Loan Date	Maturity Date
19.	$1000	9%	Jan. 1	Mar. 2
20.	$1000	6%	Aug. 31	Sept. 30
21.	$200	12%	June 3	Aug. 2
22.	$100	12%	Dec. 1	Dec. 31
23.	$500	10%	Feb. 2	Mar. 10
24.	$400	5%	May 5	July 16

25. Robert bought a TV set from the Square Appliance Company for $500 and signed a 180-day promissory note at 10% simple interest on April 1. When is the note due, and how much will he owe?

26. On December 5, Jay was told that he had 45 days to complete a report. When is the report due?

27. A company borrowed $5000 at 8% simple interest on May 2. Forty-five days later the company repaid the loan. When and how much did the company repay?

28. Bob borrowed $500 for 3 months at 9% simple interest on March 15. Find the due date and maturity value.

Review Exercises / Chapter 11

1. Mario borrowed $750 at 6% simple interest for 60 days. How much interest did he pay?

2. Sue borrowed $800 for 90 days at 8% simple interest. What amount must she repay?

3. How much should be invested now to have $1000 in 2 years if the investment yields 10% simple interest?

4. The Korner Store borrowed $5000 for 60 days at 12% simple interest on February 10. What amount must the Korner Store repay and when is it due?

5. Susan invested $5000 at 9% for 3 years. How much will she have?

6. A loan is made on April 10 for a term of 5 months. When is it due to be repaid?

7. If Ralph invests $500 at 8% simple interest, how long will it take to earn $20 interest?

8. If an investment of $100 grows to $120 in 2 years, what is the interest rate?

9. If Bill has the option to borrow $10,000 for 270 days at 10% simple interest computed using an ordinary year or exact year, which should he choose?

10. Find the present value of $1200 at 9% for 8 months.

11. If $A = \$744$, $P = 600$, and $r = 12\%$, find t.

12. Fisher's Bait Shop borrowed $700 at 8% on March 21 and repaid the loan on June 19. How much interest was paid?

Chapter Test / Chapter 11

1. Define each of the following terms:

    a. principal   **b.** present value   **c.** interest

    d. loan date   **e.** maturity date   **f.** secured note *g.* unsecured note   *h.* ordinary year   *i.* exact year

j. simple interest   *k.* present value   *l.* interest-bearing note

m. term   *n.* short-term note   *o.* long-term note

p. collateral   *q.* default   *r.* face value

s. six-percent, sixty-day method   *t.* certificate of deposit

2. How much interest will be earned on a 6-month money market certificate for $14,638.24 at a simple interest rate of 12.086%?

3. How much interest will be earned on a $2\frac{1}{2}$-year CD of $3268.49 at 10.684%?

4. Find the future value of an $18,684.29 investment at 14.214% for 36 months.

5. If the maturity value of a $12,354.68 investment is $13,881.96 after 1 year, what was the interest rate?

6. If you invest in a money market certificate with a term of 182 days on January 26, what will be the maturity date?

7. Find the interest on $500 at 12% for 30 days using
   a. an ordinary year,
   b. an exact year.

8. Find the interest on $900 at 18% for 60 days using
   a. an ordinary year,
   b. an exact year.

9. How long would it take to double an investment at
   a. 5% simple interest,
   b. 10% simple interest,
   c. 20% simple interest?

10. If an $8000 investment grows to $9800 in 2 years, what is the simple interest rate?

11. If you invest $14,372 in a certificate of deposit at 13.862% simple interest for 182 days, how much interest will be earned? Use an exact year.

12. At 12% simple interest, how many days would it take to earn interest equal to 1% of the principal? Assume an ordinary year.

Simple (Bank) Discount

INTRODUCTION

We have commented that a borrower must pay interest for using a lender's money and that there are several methods for computing the amount of interest. The method called *simple (bank) discount* is the subject of this chapter.

You will see that the term "discount" is used in the same sense that it is when you purchase an item on sale. The selling price is discounted and you pay the lesser amount (sale price). When interest on a loan is charged as a bank discount, you borrow an amount of money and receive a lesser amount because the bank subtracts the (discount) interest immediately. Of course, the amount of the discount depends on the time you plan to use the bank's money and the discount rate. (Time was not involved in purchasing an item on sale.)

12.1 Bank Discount; Factoring

In Chapter 11, the amount of simple interest was based on the amount borrowed (the principal or present value P). However, the interest charged on many loans is based on the amount to be repaid (the future or maturity value A). This type of interest is called a *simple bank discount* or *discount*.

To illustrate the idea, suppose that you borrow $1000 from a bank for 1 year at a 9% discount. The bank will take 9% of $1000, or $90 from $1000, and give you $910. The amount you receive ($910) is called the *proceeds* or present value. Notice that the interest you pay is based on the $1000 to be repaid in 1 year, not the $910 you actually receive.

Definition

A promisory note in which interest is charged as a discount is called a *non-interest-bearing note*.

As with other forms of interest, the *rate of discount* is given in *percent*. The discount rate is denoted d. The following method may be used to compute bank discount.

bank discount

> **Computing Bank Discount (Interest)**
>
> Bank discount is interest that is based on the amount borrowed and to be repaid (not the amount received). It can be computed as follows:
>
> $$B = Adt$$
>
> where $B =$ amount of bank discount (interest), dollars
> $A =$ amount borrowed, dollars
> $d =$ discount rate, percent
> $t =$ time, years

We illustrate this procedure with an example.

Example 1   Charlotte borrowed $200 for 2 years at a discount rate of 5%. Find the amount of bank discount.

SOLUTION $B = Adt$

$= \$200(5\%)(2)$

$= \$200(0.05)(2)$

$= \$20$

Charlotte's note is discounted $20.

The amount of money actually received by the borrower can be computed by subtracting the interest (B) from the amount (A) of the loan. Thus, Charlotte receives $200 − $20, or $180.

In bank discount, the borrower receives the difference D between the amount borrowed and the amount of bank discount; that is,

$$D = A - B$$

where D = difference the *borrower actually receives*
$\quad\quad A$ = *amount borrowed* (or future value)
$\quad\quad B$ = *amount of bank discount*

All amounts are in dollar values.

In bank discount, the amount borrowed is the future value that must be repaid. The borrower actually receives a lesser amount.

Example 2

The owner of Jones Hardware store needed to borrow $5000 for 3 months to make a special purchase on chain saws. His banker agreed to the loan, and specified an 8% discount on the loan. Compute the bank discount and the amount of money received by Jones Hardware.

SOLUTION

The bank discount is computed with the formulas $B = Adt$ and $D = A - B$, where $A = \$5000$, $d = 8\% = 0.08$, and $t = \frac{3}{12}$ or $\frac{1}{4}$ year.

$$B = Adt$$

$$= \$5000(0.08)\left(\frac{1}{4}\right)$$

$$= \$100.00$$

The amount of money received by Jones Hardware is

$$D = A - B$$

$$= \$5000 - \$100$$

$$= \$4900$$

We used two steps in Example 2 to compute the amount of money received. First, the amount of discount was computed according to the formula $B = Adt$. Second, the amount received was computed by the formula $D = A - B$. Since B in both formulas is the same, we can develop a single formula for determining the amount of money received after discounting. Since $D = A - B$ and $B = Adt$, we can say that

$$D = A - Adt \quad \text{or} \quad D = A(1 - dt)$$

Since B is not computed separately, the formula is a shortcut.
Example 3 illustrates the use of the shorter formula.

Example 3   A company borrowed $500 for 9 months at a discount rate of 9%. How much
did the company receive? How much did the company repay?

SOLUTION   We have $A = \$500$, $d = 9\%$, and $t = \frac{9}{12}$ year.

$$D = A(1 - dt)$$

$$= \$500 \left[1 - (9\%) \left(\frac{9}{12} \right) \right]$$

$$= \$500 \, [0.9325]$$

$$= \$466.25$$

The company received $466.25; it repaid $500.

Suppose that the company in Example 3 *had to receive* $500. Then the
company would have to borrow more than $500 because the discount
(interest) is subtracted before the customer leaves the bank. In this case,
$500 would be the amount (D) that the company must receive. The amount
(A) that the company must borrow can be determined by replacing the
known values in $D = A(1 - dt)$ and solving for A. Hence, $D = A(1 - dt)$,
where $D = \$500$, $d = 9\%$, and $t = \frac{9}{12}$ year.

$$\$500 = A \left(1 - 9\% \times \frac{9}{12} \right)$$

$$= A(1 - 0.0675)$$

$$= A(0.9325)$$

$$\frac{\$500}{0.9325} = A \quad \text{or} \quad A = \$536.19$$

The company must borrow $536.19 in order to receive the needed $500.

To find A when D, d, and t are known, it is convenient to solve
$D = A(1 - dt)$ for A as follows:

$$D = A(1 - dt)$$

$$\frac{D}{1 - dt} = \frac{A(1 - dt)}{(1 - dt)}$$

$$A = \frac{D}{1 - dt}$$

Example 4 illustrates use of this formula.

Example 4

How much must you borrow at 10% discount for 6 months to receive $1000?

SOLUTION

$A = \dfrac{D}{1 - dt}$, where $D = \$1000$, $d = 10\%$, and $t = \frac{6}{12}$ year.

$$A = \frac{\$1000}{1 - 10\% \times \frac{6}{12}}$$

$$= \frac{\$1000}{1 - 0.05}$$

$$= \frac{\$1000}{0.95}$$

$$= \$1052.63$$

You must borrow $1052.63 in order to receive $1000.

As with all formulas, if all but one of the quantities are known, the remaining quantity may be determined by solving the equation for that quantity.

Factoring Accounts Receivable

Business assets such as the credit sales a business makes to its customers (the accounts receivable) may be discounted to a third party to obtain cash. Such discounting of accounts receivables is known as *factoring*. Factoring may be *with recourse* or *without recourse*. If accounts are sold *with recourse*, you (the seller) agree to pay your banker if your customer does not pay. Accounts sold *without recourse* shift the risk of nonpayment to the banker. As you would expect, there is a higher discount on accounts sold without recourse.

Factoring is a common business practice. It offers a business manager several advantages:

1. The risk of credit sales (and associated collection problems) can be shifted to a third party.
2. Money for business operations is obtained immediately.

The disadvantage is that the company does not receive the full value of its accounts.

Example 5

Stafford Electronics has $5000 in accounts receivable in 3 months. The accounts are factored (without recourse) to the ABC Finance Company at a 12% discount.

  a. How much does Stafford Electronics receive?
  b. What happens if one of the accounts is not paid on time?

SOLUTION

    a. The amount received by Stafford Electronics is

$$D = \$5000\left(1 - 12\% \times \frac{3}{12}\right)$$

$$= \$5000(1 - 0.03)$$

$$= \$5000(0.97)$$

$$= \$4850$$

    b. If one of the accounts is not paid, ABC Finance must attempt to collect, because the accounts were factored without recourse.

Exercises 12.1

■ In problems 1–14, the dollar value is the amount borrowed. Find the amount of discount (B) and the amount received by the borrower (D) for problems 1–7.

  1. $1000 for 1 year at 8%.

  2. $1000 for 2 years at 8%.

  3. $1000 for 5 years at 8%.

  4. $500 for 1 year at 10%.

  5. $500 for 26 weeks at 10%.

  6. $500 for 90 days at 10%. Use an *ordinary* interest year.

  7. $600 for 1.5 years at 5%.

■ In problems 8–14, find the amount the borrower receives.

  8. $600 for 3 years at 5%.

  9. $600 for 6 months at 5%.

10. $1000 for 73 days at 10%. Use an *exact* interest year.

11. $500 for 13 weeks at 7%.

12. $350 for 4 months at 9%.

13. $1175 for 2 years at 7%.

14. $2600 for $2\frac{1}{2}$ years at 6%.

■ In problems 15–18, the dollar value is the amount received by the borrower. What amount was borrowed in each?

15. $6000, 90 days, at 10% discount (use an ordinary year).

16. $300, 1 month, at 12%.

17. $1200, 6 weeks, at 13%.

18. $1000, 45 days, at 9%.

19. Socket Wrench Company borrowed $800 for 30 days at a 9% discount rate. How much did the company receive? How much did the company repay the lender?

20. Fred borrowed $600 at a discount rate of 6%. If he repaid the note 5 months later, how much interest did he owe?

21. A company borrowed $10,000 for 2 weeks at a 6.5% discount rate. How much did it receive?

■ Determine the missing values in the following table. (Solution of equations is required.)

	A	D	d	t
22.	?	$95	5%	1 year
23.	$500	?	10%	2 years
24.	$100	$84	8%	?

25. If you borrow $1000 for 6 months and receive $970, what is the discount rate?

26. If you borrow $200 and receive $152 at 8% discount, what is the term of the loan?

27. Bill borrowed $500 for 2 years and received $440. What discount rate was he charged?

28. A company factors accounts receivable that will be worth $10,000 in 6 months. If the discount rate is 6%, how much does the company receive?

29. A company factors $5000 in accounts receivable in 1 month at 9% discount. How much does the company receive?

30. Woods' Furniture factored accounts receivable in the amount of $8000 due in 4 months at a 12% discount. How much did the company lose by not holding the accounts until maturity?

12.2 *Discounting Interest-Bearing Notes*

One of the most common uses of the discount principal is its use in converting the short-term assets of a business into immediate cash. A business may *accept* a short-term note from one of its customers and *sell* it to a bank or other party. For example, you sell $1000 worth of merchandise to a customer and accept a promissory note for 90 days at 12% simple interest as his payment for the goods. At the end of 90 days customer A will owe you $1030.

Transaction between Customer and Company

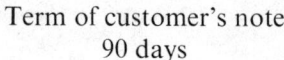

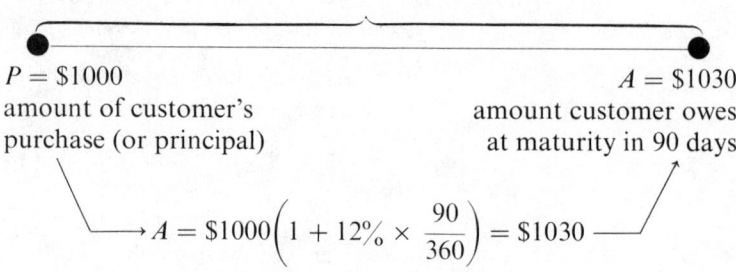

Term of customer's note
90 days

$P = \$1000$
amount of customer's
purchase (or principal)

$A = \$1030$
amount customer owes
at maturity in 90 days

$$A = \$1000\left(1 + 12\% \times \frac{90}{360}\right) = \$1030$$

After 30 days have passed, you have the opportunity to purchase some high-quality merchandise at a very favorable price. However, you do not have the cash required to make the purchase. You take the 90-day note of the customer to your banker and sell it to him for cash. Your banker agrees to buy the customer's note. However, since you are using the bank's money, you will pay interest. The interest comes in the form of a *discount* applied to the note. Your banker may require a discount of 8% on the note. In other words, the note worth $1030 in 60 days will be discounted by $13.73 $[B = \$1030(8\%)(\frac{60}{360})]$ and you will receive $1016.27 (i.e., $1030 − $13.73) cash for the note.

Transaction between Company and Bank after 30 Days Have Passed

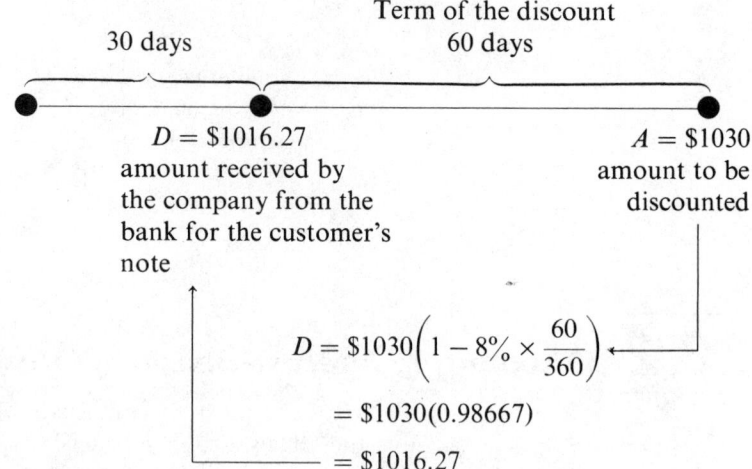

Term of the discount
60 days

30 days

$D = \$1016.27$
amount received by
the company from the
bank for the customer's
note

$A = \$1030$
amount to be
discounted

$$D = \$1030\left(1 - 8\% \times \frac{60}{360}\right)$$

$$= \$1030(0.98667)$$

$$= \$1016.27$$

The customer is not directly involved in the discounting transaction between the company and the bank. He will pay the full amount of $1030 for his purchase after 90 days as if nothing had happened.

In effect, the company and bank have divided the customer's $30 in interest.

The company gets $16.27 for the 30 days it held the note.

The bank gets $13.73 for the 60 days it held the note.

Computations in discounting interest-bearing notes involve two steps.

Discounting an Interest-Bearing Note

Step 1. Find the *future value* of the customer's note using $A = P(1 + rt)$.

Step 2. Compute the discounted amount (D) of the maturity value found in step 1. The time used is *what remains of the original term* at the time the note is sold (or discounted) to a third party.

Notes may be sold *with recourse* or *without recourse*.

The following examples illustrate the procedure; study them carefully.

Example 1   A customer purchases $500 worth of merchandise with a note at 10% simple interest for 6 months.

    a. Find the future value of the note. Two months later the company sells (discounts) the note to the bank (with recourse) at a 12% discount rate.

    b. How much will the company receive?

    c. What happens if the customer does not pay?

SOLUTION   *a.* The future value is $A = P(1 + rt)$, $P = \$500$, $r = 10\%$ simple interest, and $t = \frac{6}{12}$ year.

Step 1. $A = P(1 + rt)$

$$= \$500\left[1 + (10\%)\left(\frac{6}{12}\right)\right]$$

$$= \$500[1 + 0.05]$$

$$= \$500[1.05]$$

$$= \$525 \text{ at maturity}$$

b. Remember that the amount $A = \$525$ is to be discounted in the next step. $D = A(1 - dt)$, $d = 12\%$ discount rate, and $t = \frac{4}{12}$ year.

Step 2. $D = \$525\left[1 - (12\%)\left(\dfrac{4}{12}\right)\right]$ ***Note:*** $t = \frac{4}{12}$ year is the time remaining until the maturity date. It is the difference in the term ($\frac{6}{12}$ year) and the elapsed time ($\frac{2}{12}$ year).

$\qquad\qquad = \$525[1 - 0.04]$

$\qquad\qquad = \$525[0.96]$

$\qquad\qquad = \$504$

The company receives $504 for the customer note.

c. The *company must pay* the bank if the customer does not pay, because the note was discounted *with recourse*.

Example 2   Beth's Boutique accepted a $100 note for 90 days at 10% simple interest. After 50 days, the note was sold to the bank (without recourse) at a discount rate of 18%. How much does Beth's Boutique receive for the customer's note?

SOLUTION   If Beth's Boutique had held the note, the future value would have been $A = P[1 + rt]$, $P = \$100$, $r = 10\%$ simple interest rate, and $t = \frac{90}{360}$ year.

Hence,

$$A = \$100\left[1 + (10\%)\left(\frac{90}{360}\right)\right]$$

$$= \$102.50$$

Let $A = \$102.50$ for the discount step. $D = A(1 - dt)$, $A = \$102.50$, $d = 18\%$ discount rate, and $t = \frac{40}{360}$ year. (Since 50 days have passed, 40 days remain.)

$$D = \$102.50\left[1 - (18\%)\left(\frac{40}{360}\right)\right]$$

$$= \$102.50[1 - 0.02]$$

$$= \$102.50[0.98]$$

$$= \$100.45 \quad \text{net proceeds}$$

Beth's Boutique received $100.45 for the note.

Exercises 12.2

■ Use the following information to find the maturity value A and the discounted amount D in problems 1–4.

1. $P = \$1000$
   simple interest rate $= 8\%$
   term of note $= 1$ year
   discount rate $= 10\%$
   discount term $= \frac{1}{2}$ year

2. $P = \$2000$
   simple interest $= 9\%$
   term of note $= 8$ months
   discount rate $= 12\%$
   discount term $= 3$ months

3. $P = \$5000$
  simple interest rate $= 6\%$
  term of note $= 180$ days
  discount rate $= 9\%$
  discount term $= 40$ days

4. $P = \$1000$
  simple interest rate $= 6\%$
  term of note $= 60$ days
  discount rate $= 9\%$
  discount term $= 20$ days

5. Mr. Tebo purchased a new minicomputer for $1000 from the Small Computer International and signed a 9% interest-bearing note for 4 months.

a. What will he owe at maturity?

Three months later Small Computer International has the opportunity to purchase plastic buttons and knobs at an attractive price. The company discounts Mr. Tebo's note to Big State Bank at a 12% discount rate.

b. How much does Small Computer International receive?

6. Stick's Furniture Company sold $10,000 worth of chairs and accepted a 120-day note at 12% simple interest. Thirty days later Stick's sold the note to the Rich Finance Company at a 16% discount. How much did Rich Finance give Stick's for the note?

7. Miss Stern purchased 500 gizmos from the Miscellaneous Company for $800. She signed a 90-day promissory note at 9% simple interest to pay for the merchandise.

a. How much will she need to repay the note?

Sixty days after selling the gizmos, the Miscellaneous Company has the opportunity to acquire some cheap gadgets. At that time the company discounts the note to the Interplanetary Bank at a 12% discount with recourse.

b. How much did the Miscellaneous Company receive for Miss Stern's note?
c. How much interest was earned by the Miscellaneous Company?
d. How much interest was earned by the bank?
e. What happens if Miss Stern does not pay?

8. Craig's Car Parts is holding a promissory note that will be worth $150 at maturity in 3 months. If Craig's discounts the note to the bank at an 8% discount, how much is received?

9. On March 1, Mr. Jones purchased $2000 worth of merchandise from Smith Supply Company and signed a 9% interest-bearing note for 90 days.

a. What is the maturity value of Jones' note?
b. What is the due date?

On April 24, Smith Supply discounted Jones' note to the Outer City Bank and Trust at a 10% discount.

c. How much did Smith Supply receive?
d. How much did Smith Supply lose by not holding the note to maturity?

10. On January 2, Mrs. Dresswell purchased $1800 worth of apparel at the after Christmas sale of the Exclusive Threads Boutique. She agreed to pay in 270 days at 12% simple interest.

     a. What is the maturity value of Mrs. Dresswell's note?

     b. What is the due date of her note?

On July 1, Exclusive Threads discounted Mrs. Dresswell's note in order to begin purchasing their fall selection. The bank purchased the note at a 12% discount.

     c. How much did the bank give Exclusive Threads?

12.3 *Effective Rate of Interest*

As you are beginning to see, there are many methods for computing a dollar amount of interest. So far we have presented simple interest and bank discount. In later chapters, other methods, such as compound interest, will be presented. *All methods* of computing interest *have one thing in common.* An interest rate (given as a percent) is known and it is used as the basis for calculating the dollar amount of interest. This rate is called the *nominal* or *stated* interest rate. The nominal rate is *always an annual rate.* (The fact that nominal rates are annual rates is why formulas for computing interest must contain a separate quantity relating to time. The time is not always 1 year.)

the nominal or stated interest rate

On the other hand, *all methods* of computing interest *are different* in that the amount of interest computed will be different (even when the same *principal, nominal rate,* and *time* are used).

In order to compare the effects of computing interest in different ways, we need some way to reduce them to a common basis. The common basis of comparison is called the *effective rate.* The effective rate of interest takes into consideration the *total amount* of interest paid on the *actual amount* of money received for the *total time* the money is used without regard to the method used to determine these values. The *effective interest rate* is stated in terms of an equivalent *simple interest rate.* Hence, we use the simple interest formula to determine the effective rate of interest.

effective interest rate

Effective Rate of Interest

     The effective rate of interest is the *simple interest rate* that results from the simple interest formula

$$I = Prt$$

where I = dollar amount of interest paid *regardless* of the method of computation

       P = dollar amount of money *actually received* by the borrower

       r = effective (simple) interest rate

       t = length of time for which the money is used

If the interest is computed using simple interest, the *simple interest rate* for 1 year is the effective rate. If some other method (such as bank discount) is used to compute the interest, then the *effective rate* must be computed because it is not the same as the nominal rate.

For example, you borrow $1000 at a 6% discount rate for 1 year. The amount of interest is $60 (which is deducted from $1000) and you receive $940. (One year later you repay $1000.)

In essence, you borrowed $940 and paid $60 in interest for 1 year. If we put those values into the simple interest formula $I = Prt$, where $P = \$940$, $I = \$60$, and $t = 1$ year, the simple interest rate (r) can be determined.

$I = Prt$, so $60 = 940(r)(1)$. By dividing both sides of the equation by 940, we have $0.0638 = r$ or $r = 6.38\%$.

A revelation! What looked (on the surface) like a 6% interest rate is effectively 6.38%. That is, a 6.38% simple interest produces the same amount of interest as a 6% discount rate. The reason that the effective rate is higher is because you were charged interest on $1000 but only got to use $940.

Most methods of computing interest have an effective rate that is higher than the stated rate.

Example 1　　Elaine borrowed $800 for 1 year at a discount rate of 9%. Find the effective rate of the loan.

SOLUTION　　The amount of bank discount is $B = Adt$, where $A = \$800$, $d = 9\%$, and $t = 1$ year. Hence,

$$B = \$800(9\%)(1)$$

$$= \$72$$

Therefore, Elaine received $728 ($800 − $72). In other words, she borrowed $728 for 1 year and paid $72 in interest. To find the effective rate (r), use $I = Prt$, where $P = \$728$, $I = \$72$, and $t = 1$ year.

$$\$72 = \$728(r)(1)$$

$$= \$728r$$

$$0.0989 = r \quad \text{or} \quad r = 9.89\%$$

The effective rate of 9% discount is 9.89%.

Since we must always solve the simple interest formula for r to get the effective rate, we can solve for r in general:

$$I = Prt$$

$$\frac{I}{Pt} = \frac{Prt}{Pt}$$

effective rate
using dollar values
$$r = \frac{I}{Pt}$$

Example 2   John borrowed $300 from a friend and promised to repay $320 in 2 months. What is the effective rate?

SOLUTION   The amount of interest John agreed to pay is $20. Hence,

$$r = \frac{I}{Pt}$$

$$= \frac{\$20}{\$300 \times \frac{2}{12} \text{ year}}$$

$$= \frac{\$20}{\$50}$$

$$= 0.40 \quad \text{or} \quad 40\%$$

The effective rate is 40%.

Converting Nominal Rate to Effective Rate

annual percentage
rate

   The usual basis for converting a nominal rate (that is *not* given in terms of simple interest) to an effective rate is to base *all* calculations on a time of *one* year. When the effective interest rate is based on a time of 1 year, it is also called the *annual percentage rate* (APR).
   By combining the formulas for simple interest $A = P(1 + rt)$ and bank discount $D = A(1 - dt)$, it is possible to develop a formula that will *directly* convert *any* discount rate to the effective interest rate without using dollar values. However, we will not show the development.

Converting a Bank Discount Rate to the Annual Percentage Rate (APR)

$$r = \frac{d}{1 - d}$$

where r = annual percentage rate (APR)
      d = bank discount rate in decimal form

Note: Application of the formula always gives a decimal answer for r. It may be converted to a percent by moving the decimal point two places to the right and attaching the % symbol, as we have done before. Example 3 illustrates how the formula may be used.

Example 3   Find the annual percentage rate (APR) that is the equivalent of the following bank discount rates.

     a. $d = 5\%$
     b. $d = 10\%$

SOLUTION   ***a.*** $r = \dfrac{d}{1-d}$ where $d = 5\% = 0.05$

$$= \frac{0.05}{1 - 0.05}$$

$$= \frac{0.05}{0.95}$$

$$= 0.526 \quad \text{or} \quad 5.26\% \text{ APR}$$

     b. $r = \dfrac{d}{1-d}$ where $d = 10\% = 0.10$

$$= \frac{0.10}{1 - 0.10}$$

$$= \frac{0.1}{0.9}$$

$$= 0.1111 \quad \text{or} \quad 11.11\% \text{ APR}$$

Summary

If you have dollar values for I and P, use $r = \dfrac{I}{Pt}$ to get the effective rate. If you have the discount rate ($d\%$), use $r = \dfrac{d}{1-d}$ to get the effective (APR) rate.

Exercises 12.3

■ Determine the APR of each of the following *bank discount* rates.

1. 1% ***2.*** 2% ***3.*** 3% ***4.*** 4% ***5.*** 4.5% ***6.*** 6%

■ Determine the effective rates.

7. $P = \$100$, $I = \$10$, $t = 1$ year.   ***8.*** $P = \$500$, $I = \$40$, $t = 6$ months.

9. $P = \$1000$, $I = \$20$, $t = 90$ days.   ***10.*** $P = \$100$, $I = \$100$, $t = 5$ years.

11. $P = \$600$, $I = \$7.50$, $t = 45$ days.   ***12.*** $P = \$500$, $I = \$80$, $t = 2$ years.

13. Does 20% bank discount have an APR of 25%?

14. What is the effective rate of 12% simple discount?

15. A company purchased $1000 in goods. It can save $20 if paid in 10 days. The total amount is due in 30 days. What is the effective rate if the company does not take the discount? (*Hint*: The company is, in effect, charging itself $20 for the use of $1000 for 20 days.)

16. If you invest $100 for 6 months and earn $4 in interest, what is the effective rate of interest?

17. Gene paid $60 for the use of $500 for 1 year. Find the effective rate.

18. The Interplanetary Bank charges 8.3% discount on a loan. What is the annual percentage rate?

Review Exercises / Chapter 12

1. The Snack Shop borrowed $10,000 for 5 years at 8% discount. Find the amount of interest paid.

2. Nelson borrowed $500 for 60 days at 6% bank discount. How much did he actually receive?

3. Speedy Delivery signed a 120-day note at 9% bank discount. If the amount actually received was $850, how much was borrowed?

4. If you borrow $2000 at 10% bank discount for 270 days, how much will you receive?

5. Carolyn borrowed $2000 for 180 days and received $1940. What discount rate was she charged? What effective rate?

6. Use the following information to find the maturity value and discounted amount.

$P = \$4000$
simple interest rate $= 9\%$
term of note $= 4$ months
discount rate $= 12\%$
discount term $= 1$ month

7. Hope Wrightwell purchased a new typewriter for $600 from Modern Office Supply and signed a 45-day promissory note at 10% simple interest. Thirty days later Modern Office Supply discounted the note to Cooley Bank at 14%. How much did Modern Office Supply receive for Ms. Wrightwell's note?

8. The Delta Loan Company will lend $800 for 6 months for $50 interest. What is the effective rate of interest?

9. Find the effective rate of 8% bank discount.

10. Sue can borrow $1000 for 1 year at either 10% simple interest or 10% bank discount. Which should she choose? Why?

Chapter Test / Chapter 12

1. Define each of the following terms:

    a. bank discount   **b.** non-interest-bearing note

    c. factoring   **d.** nominal interest rate

    e. stated interest rate   **f.** effective rate

    g. annual percentage rate **h.** simple discount

 2. Find the amount of interest on a $7835.68 loan at 6.358% simple discount for 98 days. How much did the borrower actually receive?

3. Find the annual percentage rate of a discount rate of 8.439%.

4. Determine the effective rate if $P = \$60$, $I = \$7$, and $t = 9$ months.

5. A customer purchases $2000 worth of merchandise with a note at 12% simple interest for 6 months.

    a. Find the future value of the note.

Three months later you discount the customer's note to a finance company at a 15% discount.

    b. How much will you receive from the finance company for the note?

6. If you borrow $5000 for 9 months and receive $4550, find the discount rate.

7. If you borrow $4000 and receive $3780 at an 11% discount, what is the term of the loan?

8. Find the amount of the discount when $3600 is borrowed for 8 months at a 9% discount.

9. In problem 8, what amount is to be repaid at the end of 8 months?

10. A company borrows $8000 for 4 weeks at a 12% discount. How much is received?

11. What is the APR equivalent to a 6.5% discount rate?

12. What is the APR equivalent to a 9.3% discount rate?

CHAPTER 13

Compound Interest

INTRODUCTION

Suppose that you want to open a savings account and deposit $1000. You find that all of the savings and loan institutions in your area pay $5\frac{1}{4}\%$ per year on regular passbook accounts and that they all pay *compound interest*. However, they all compound interest differently.

Institution A pays $5\frac{1}{4}\%$ compounded annually

Institution B pays $5\frac{1}{4}\%$ compounded semiannually

Institution C pays $5\frac{1}{4}\%$ compounded quarterly

Institution D pays $5\frac{1}{4}\%$ compounded daily

Institution E pays $5\frac{1}{4}\%$ compounded continuously

If you leave your $1000 on deposit for 2 years, will there be a difference in the amount of interest you will earn, even though all institutions advertise the same *nominal* or *stated rate*? Yes, there is a difference. In this chapter we will examine what the difference is, why it occurs, and how to compute the amount of interest in each case.

The point of view generally taken in this chapter is that of an individual who is depositing or borrowing money at compound interest as opposed to the business point of view taken in the previous chapters. Of course, the principles discussed apply for businesses as well.

There are two types of compound interest: *interest compounded for specific periods* (i.e., periodically) and interest compounded *continuously*. Periodically compounded interest is presented first. At the end of the chapter, all types of compound interest rates will be compared by means of *effective rates*.

13.1 *Future Value at Compound Interest*

What is meant when a bank advertises interest compounded quarterly? How does compound interest differ from simple interest? To show the distinction between compound interest and simple interest, we begin by reviewing simple interest.

Example 1 Suppose that $100 is deposited in an account paying 5% simple interest. How much money will be in the account at the end of 5 years?

SOLUTION The amount in the account at the end of 5 years may be computed as follows:

$$A = P(1 + rt)$$
$$= \$100[1 + (0.05)(5)]$$
$$= \$100[1 + 0.25]$$
$$= \$100[1.25]$$
$$= \$125$$

Remember: this amount could have been computed by finding the interest for each year separately and adding the results.

Year 1: $I = \$100(0.05)(1) = \$\ 5$
Year 2: $I = \$100(0.05)(1) = \ \ 5$ Note that all
Year 3: $I = \$100(0.05)(1) = \ \ 5$ computations are
Year 4: $I = \$100(0.05)(1) = \ \ 5$ based on $P = \$100$.
Year 5: $I = \$100(0.05)(1) = \ \ 5$

Total interest $\$25$

Therefore, the total $I = \$25$ and the total amount

$$A = P + I$$
$$= \$100 + 25$$
$$= \$125$$

compound interest   In the case of *compound interest*, the interest earned *is added to the principal* for the computation of future interest payments. Suppose that at the end of 1 year you receive $5 interest on your original deposit. If the interest is added to the principal, then the second year's interest will be $105 × (0.05) = \$5.25$ in interest. This is called compound interest. Study the following example carefully.

Example 2   Suppose that $100 is deposited in an account paying 5% *compounded annually*. How much money will be in the account at the end of 5 years?

SOLUTION   The interest at the end of year 1 (i.e., the end of the first compounding period) will be $5:

$$\text{Year 1:} \quad I = \$100(0.05)(1) = \$5$$

The principal for year 2 becomes the principal plus the interest of year 1 ($100 + $5 = $105). Hence, the interest for year 2 is

$$\text{Year 2:} \quad I = \$105(0.05)(1) = \$5.25$$

Therefore, the second year's interest is greater than the first year's interest ($5.25 vs. $5.00). The cumulative effect of compounding can be seen as follows:

$$
\begin{aligned}
\text{Year 1:} \quad & I = \$100(0.05)(1) & = \$\ 5.00 \\
\text{Year 2:} \quad & I = (\$100 + \$5)(0.05)(1) & = \ 5.25 \\
\text{Year 3:} \quad & I = (\$100 + \$5 + \$5.25)(0.05)(1) & = \ 5.51 \\
\text{Year 4:} \quad & I = (\$100 + \$5 + \$5.25 + \$5.51)(0.05)(1) & = \ 5.79 \\
\text{Year 5:} \quad & I = (\$100 + \$5 + \$5.25 + \$5.51 \\
& \qquad + \$5.79)(0.05)(1) = & 6.08 \\
\hline
& \text{Total interest} & \$27.63
\end{aligned}
$$

Note that all computations are based on $P = P + I$ for previous periods. Therefore, the total $I = \$27.63$ and the total amount

$$A = P + I$$
$$= \$100 + \$27.63$$
$$= \$127.63$$

Let us compare Examples 1 and 2. At the end of 5 years, the account paying 5% interest compounded annually (Example 2) has $127.63. The account paying 5% simple interest (Example 1) has only $125.00. Thus, we see that compounding resulted in a greater amount of interest ($2.63 more).

In general, when using compound interest, the next period's interest is computed on a *new principal*, which is the *sum* of the *principal* and *interest* of the previous period.

Example 3   Karen deposited $500 in an account paying 6% compounded annually. How much will be in the account at the end of 3 years?

SOLUTION
$$
\begin{aligned}
\text{Year 1:} \quad & I = \$500(0.06)(1) = \$30 \\
& A = \$500 + 30 = \$530 \\
\text{Year 2:} \quad & I = \$530(0.06)(1) = \$31.80 \\
& A = \$530 + 31.80 = \$561.80
\end{aligned}
$$

Year 3: $I = \$561.80(0.06)(1) = \$33.71$
$A = \$561.80 + 33.71 = \$595.51$

Hence, Karen will have $595.51 at the end of 3 years. If the account paid 6% *simple* interest, Karen would have only $590.00.

Definition

compounded interest

Interest calculated on both the principal and interest previously earned is called *compounded interest*.

Clearly, if one has the option to deposit money at a particular simple interest rate or at the same compound interest rate, the compound interest rate would be preferable because of the greater *yield*. (Would your decision be different if you were borrowing money?)

Our previous examples have dealt with interest compounded annually (once a year). Compounding periods do not have to be yearly. The most commonly used compounding periods are annually, semiannually (every 6 months), quarterly (every 3 months), monthly, daily, and continuously. For example, when interest is compounded quarterly, each quarter becomes one *compounding period*.

Definition

compounding period

The interval of time over which interest is computed or the interval between interest payments is called the *compounding period*.

Compounding periods are also called interest periods or conversion periods.

When interest is compounded more than once a year, we need to know the interest rate per compounding period (denoted i). To find i, the following procedure may be used.

interest rate per
period

> ### Interest Rate per Compounding Period
>
> When the compounding period is less than 1 year, the stated interest rate per year must be converted to the *interest rate per period*. This change is done by dividing the stated interest rate (i.e., yearly interest rate) by the number of compounding periods in one year. If
>
> S = stated rate of interest per year
>
> K = number of compounding periods per year
>
> then the interest rate per compounding period is
>
> $$i = \frac{S}{K}$$

For example, an account paying 6% interest per year compounded quarterly will pay

$$\frac{6\% \text{ annual interest}}{4 \text{ periods per year}} = 1.5\% \text{ interest per period}$$

Example 4   Jay earns $1000 during the summer. He deposits the money in an account paying 6% per year compounded quarterly. How much will he have at the end of 1 year?

SOLUTION   In order to get the interest rate per period, we must divide the stated interest rate by the number of compounding periods per year.

$$\text{Interest per period } i = \frac{\text{stated interest rate } (S)}{\text{no. of compounding periods/year } (K)}$$

$$= \frac{6\%}{4}$$

$$= 1.5\% \quad \text{or} \quad 0.015 \text{ (in decimals)}$$

The amount of interest for each of the four periods (quarters) is computed as follows:

Period 1: $I = \$1000(0.015)(1)$ $= \$15.00$
Period 2: $I = (\$1000 + 15)(0.015)(1)$ $= 15.23$
Period 3: $I = (\$1000 + 15 + 15.23)(0.015)(1)$ $= 15.45$
Period 4: $I = (\$1000 + 15 + 15.23 + 15.45)(0.015)(1) =$ 15.69

Total interest $\$61.37$

The future value (A) of Jay's account (in 1 year) is the sum of the principal and interest. Therefore,

$$A = P + I$$

$$= \$1000 + \$61.37$$

$$= \$1061.37$$

Jay will have $1061.37 at the end of 1 year.

Suppose that you wish to know the amount of money in an account at the end of 20 years with interest compounded quarterly. By our previous method, this solution would require 80 computations. There should be a quicker way—and there is. The following formula can be used for finding the future value (A) in a compound interest problem.

future value

Future Value at Compound Interest

$$A = P(1 + i)^n$$

where A = future value, dollars
P = original principal, dollars
i = interest rate per period, percent
n = number of periods per year multiplied by the number of years

---

The number (n) is the *total number* of periods in the term that money earns compound interest.

Let us see how Example 3 could be solved using the future value formula.

Example 5   Karen deposited $500 in an account paying 6% compounded annually. How much will be in the account at the end of 3 years?

SOLUTION $A = P(1 + i)^n$, where $P = \$500$, $i = \dfrac{6\% \text{ per year}}{1 \text{ period/year}} = 6\%$ per period, and $n =$ (1 period/year)(3 years)

$$A = \$500(1 + 6\%)^3$$

$$= \$500(1 + 0.06)^3$$

$$= \$500(1.06)^3$$

$$= \$500(1.06)(1.06)(1.06)$$

$$= \$595.51$$

Hence, Karen will have $595.51 in her account at the end of 3 years.

Similarly, we could use the formula $A = P(1 + i)^n$ to find the future value of Jay's investment in Example 4.

The formula $A = P(1 + i)^n$ provides a nice, concise way to solve a compound interest problem. However, computing the value of $(1 + i)^n$ for large values of n is tedious unless one has access to a good calculator. Since large values of n are common, we used a computer to produce the values of $(1 + i)^n$ for many commonly used values of i and n. Use of a table (Table I, p. 528) saves a lot of computation. The following procedure illustrates the use of Table I.

How to Use Table I

Step 1. Determine the value of $i\%$ and n periods appropriate for the given problem.

Step 2. Read down the column under the appropriate value of $i\%$ until you get to the number that corresponds to the appropriate value of n (denoted on the far left side of the table). The value found is that of the expression $(1 + i)^n$.

Step 3. Multiply the principal by the value found in the table to determine the future value.

When using Table I, there is no need to convert $i\%$ to a decimal. This was taken into account in constructing the table.

Example 6   Using Table I, find the values of $(1 + i)^n$, where

     a. $i = 2\%, n = 30$
     b. $i = \frac{3}{4}\%, n = 10$
     c. $i = 3\frac{1}{2}\%, n = 17$

SOLUTION

     a. By looking down the 2% column to the 30th row, we find $(1 + 2\%)^{30} = 1.81136$.

     b. By looking down the $\frac{3}{4}\%$ column to the 10th row, we find $(1 + \frac{3}{4}\%)^{10} = 1.07758$.

     c. By looking down the $3\frac{1}{2}\%$ column to the 17th row, we find $(1 + 3\frac{1}{2}\%)^{17} = 1.79468$.

Note that stated interest rates are on an annual basis. That is, 5% interest compounded semiannually is understood to be 5% interest *per year* compounded semiannually.

Example 7   When Jeff was born, his father put \$1000 in a savings account paying 5% compounded semiannually. How much will be in his account on Jeff's 18th birthday?

SOLUTION   The future value $A = P(1 + i)^n$, where

$$P = \$1000$$

$$i = \frac{5\% \text{ per year}}{2 \text{ periods per year}} = 2\frac{1}{2}\% \text{ per period}$$

$$n = (2 \text{ periods per year})(18 \text{ years}) = 36 \text{ periods}$$

$$A = \$1000(1 + 2\tfrac{1}{2}\%)^{36} \qquad \text{from Table I}$$

$$= 1000(2.43253)$$

$$= \$2432.54$$

Hence, Jeff will have \$2432.54 on his 18th birthday.

___

To emphasize the reason why savings institutions advertise the number of times interest is compounded each year, we offer the following example.

___

Example 8   Find the future value of \$1000 in 1 year at each of the following compound rates.

  a. 12% compounded semiannually
  b. 12% compounded quarterly
  c. 12% compounded monthly

SOLUTION   *a.* For 12% compounded semiannually,

$$i = \frac{12\%}{2} = 6\% \text{ per period}$$

$$n = (1 \text{ year})(2 \text{ periods per year}) = 2 \text{ periods}$$

Therefore,

$$A = \$1000(1 + 6\%)^2 \qquad \text{by Table I}$$

$$= \$1000(1.12360)$$

$$= \$1123.60$$

b. For 12% compounded quarterly,

$$i = \frac{12\%}{4} = 3\% \text{ per period}$$

$$n = (1 \text{ year})(4 \text{ periods per year}) = 4 \text{ periods}$$

Therefore,

$$A = \$1000(1 + 3\%)^4 \qquad \text{by Table I}$$

$$= \$1000(1.12551)$$

$$= \$1125.51$$

c. For 12% compounded monthly,

$$i = \frac{12\%}{12} = 1\% \text{ per period}$$

$$n = (1 \text{ year})(12 \text{ periods per year}) = 12 \text{ periods}$$

Therefore,

$$A = \$1000(1 + 1\%)^{12} \qquad \text{by Table I}$$
$$= \$1000(1.12682)$$
$$= \$1126.82$$

Even though the same stated rate (12%), principal ($1000), and time (1 year) were used, the future values are different:

$1123.60 for semiannual compounding
$1125.51 for quarterly compounding
$1126.82 for monthly compounding

The future value increases as the number of compounding periods per year increases, even though the stated rate, principal, and time are exactly the same.

Now we see why institution X advertises that it compounds interest more frequently than institution Y. The informed saver knows he will earn more interest at institution X.

Daily Compounding

It has become commonplace for financial institutions to pay interest compounded daily. Daily compounding presents no new conceptual problems but does *require* a calculator with exponential capability. Most institutions use the 360/365 method for computing interest compounded daily. They use 360 days in a year for determining the periodic rate ($i\%/360$), but pay interest for 365 (or 366) days.

Suppose that you invest $10,000 for 365 days at 13.682% compounded daily. How much will you have? The future value is

$$A = P(1 + i)^n$$

where $P = \$10,000$

$$i = \frac{13.682\%}{360}$$

$$n = 365$$

Hence,

$$A = \$10,000\left(1 + \frac{0.13682}{360}\right)^{365}$$
$$= \$10,000(1 + 0.00038006)^{365}$$
$$= \$10,000(1.00038006)^{365}$$
$$= \$10,000(1.1487724)$$
$$= \$11,487.72$$

Therefore, you will have $11,487.72.

Since many institutions still pay $5\frac{1}{4}\%$ interest on regular savings account, we offer the following example.

Suppose that you deposit $100 in an account paying $5\frac{1}{4}\%$ compounded daily. How much will be in the account after 170 days? The future value $A = P(1 + i)^n$, where

$$P = \$100 \text{ principal}$$

$$i = \frac{5.25\%}{360}$$

$$n = 170 \text{ days (periods)}$$

Therefore, $A = \$100\left(1 + \dfrac{5.25\%}{360}\right)^{170}$

using Table II

Since computation of the $(1 + i\%)^n$ factor in daily compounding is not practical (without the use of a calculator or computer), we have prepared Table II (p. 535). Table II gives the value of $(1 + i\%)^n$ for $5\frac{1}{4}\%$ compounded daily for periods of 1 to 365 days. To find the desired value, read the number immediately to the right of the particular number of days (n) that the money is left on deposit. Multiply the value found by the principal to get the future value.

For $P = \$100$ at $5\frac{1}{4}\%$ compounded daily for 170 days, we have

$$A = \$100(1.024751656)$$

$$= \$102.48$$

Example 9   If Bob deposits $300 in an account paying $5\frac{1}{4}\%$ compounded daily, how much will he have in 43 days?

SOLUTION   By using Table II,

$$A = \$300(1.00620365) \text{ for 43 days} \quad \text{or}$$

$$= \$301.86$$

Continuous Compounding

We have seen that compound interest yields a greater return on an investment than the same simple interest rate. Further, we concluded that compounding more often (i.e., more times per year) would increase the return. For a fixed principal, an interest rate of 5% compounded quarterly will yield a greater amount than 5% compounded semiannually (given the same amount of time). Furthermore, 5% compounded monthly will yield a greater amount than 5% compounded quarterly, and so on.

The greater the number of compounding periods per year, the greater the amount of interest earned.

Although the idea of compounding continuously seems rather abstract, the formula is really very simple and many savings and loan companies do advertise interest computed in this manner.

Future Value for Interest Compounded Continuously

$$A = Pe^{st}$$

where A = future value
 P = original principal
 e = 2.71828 (a constant number)
 s = stated rate of interest
 t = time in years (or fractions of a year)

The continuously compounded interest formula can be derived (mathematically) from the periodically compounded interest formula, but calculus is required. Therefore, the development is omitted.

Since we know the principal (P) that we are depositing and want to find the future value (A), the question becomes, how does one calculate the value of e^{st}? As before, we have prepared a table of values of e^{st} for certain values of st (Table III, p. 537).

Use of Table III

Step 1. Put the appropriate values of P, s, and t (for your problem) into the continuously compounded interest formula.

Step 2. Compute the value of the exponent st using decimals.

Step 3. Read down the left column of Table III until you find your particular value. The number immediately to the right is the value of e^{st}.

Step 4. Put the value found in Table III in place of e^{st} in your problem and multiply by the principal to obtain the future value.

Example 10   We have $1000 invested for 1 year in an account paying 12% and compounding continuously. How much will be in the account at the end of the year?

SOLUTION   The amount can be computed by the formula

$$A = Pe^{st}$$

$$= \$1000(e)^{(12\%)(1)}$$

$$= \$1000(e)^{(0.12)(1)}$$

$$= \$1000(e)^{0.12} \quad \text{by Table III}$$

$$= \$1000(1.12750)$$

$$= \$1127.50$$

There will be $1127.50 in the account at the end of 1 year.

If we compare the future value of Example 10 ($1127.50) with the values obtained in Example 8, we see that the future value is yet larger than compounding monthly ($1126.82).

Rule of 72

In financial planning one frequently wants to know how long a time is needed to double the value of an investment. If the investment's interest is compounded annually, the rule of 72 is a useful (and reasonably accurate) rule of thumb.

> ### Rule of 72
>
> The number of years required to double an investment at $x \%$ compounded annually is $\dfrac{72}{x}$.

For example, at 6% compounded annually, your investment would double in approximately 12 years $(= \frac{72}{6})$.

To check, a $100 investment at 6% compounded annually would be $A = \$100 (1 + 6\%)^{12} = \$100(2.01220) = \$201.22$. If interest were 9% compounded annually, approximately 8 years would be required to double the investment. Of course, if interest is compounded more frequently (than annually), less time (than shown by the rule of 72) is required.

Exercises 13.1

■ Find the value of $(1 + i)^n$ for each of the following. Use Table I.

1. $(1 + 5\%)^8$ **2.** $(1 + 6\%)^{10}$ **3.** $(1 + 4\frac{1}{2}\%)^{20}$ **4.** $(1 + \frac{3}{4}\%)^{30}$

■ Find the future value of the following.

5. $P = \$1000$ at 9% compounded monthly for 2 years.

6. $P = \$1000$ at 10% compounded semiannually for 4 years.

7. $P = \$100$ at 6% compounded annually for 2 years.

8. $P = \$100$ at 6% compounded semiannually for 2 years.

9. $P = \$100$ at 6% compounded quarterly for 2 years.

10. $P = \$100$ at 6% compounded monthly for 2 years.

11. $P = \$1000$ at $5\frac{1}{4}\%$ compounded annually for 20 years.

12. $P = \$800$ at $5\frac{1}{4}\%$ compounded annually for 10 years.

13. $P = \$10,000$ at 9% compounded monthly for 3 years.

14. If you invest $900 on April 10 at 12% compounded monthly, how much will you have on October 10?

15. Miss Bailey invests $2000 at 9% simple interest for 2 years. How much will she have? How much would she have if she invested the money at 9% compounded quarterly?

16. Beth purchases a certificate of deposit for $5000 that pays 7.5% compounded semiannually if held for 10 years. How much will the certificate be worth in 10 years?

17. Mr. Roberts buys a piece of equipment for $10,000 and agrees to pay 8% compounded quarterly. How much will he owe if he plans to pay for the equipment at the end of $1\frac{1}{2}$ years?

18. The population of a town is 10,000. If the town's projected growth is a rate of 2% compounded annually, what will be its population in 10 years?

19. A man kept a $2 bill for 40 years. He could have deposited it at 5% compounded annually. How much did he lose?

20. An expert claims that a certain piece of land will increase in value at 5% compounded annually. If the land is currently worth $4000, how much will it be worth in 10 years?

21. You are offered $2000 now or $2100 1 year from now. If money is worth 6% compounded monthly, which should you accept?

22. You have the option to invest at 8% compounded annually or 8% compounded monthly. Which would give the greatest future value?

T-II { **23.** Find the future value of $1000 invested at $5\frac{1}{4}\%$ compounded daily for 90 days.

24. Find the future value of $800 invested at $5\frac{1}{4}\%$ compounded daily for 235 days.

25. On March 3, Angela opened a savings account paying $5\frac{1}{4}\%$ compounded daily. If her initial deposit was $500 and she made no further deposits, what is the balance of her account on September 1?

26. Find the future value of $10,000 at $5\frac{1}{4}\%$ compounded daily for 160 days.

■ Find the values of e^{st} for each of the following.

27. $e^{0.27}$ **28.** $e^{1.42}$ **29.** $e^{(7\%)(2)}$ **30.** $e^{(3\%)(10)}$

■ Find the future values:

31. $P = \$1000$, $s = 6\%$ compounded continuously, time $= 3$ years.

32. $P = \$500$, $s = 5\%$ compounded continuously, time = 4 years.

33. $P = \$800$, $s = 4\%$ compounded continuously, time = 6 months.

34. $P = \$100$, $s = 8\%$ compounded continuously, time = 18 months.

35. Jay invested $200 at 4% compounded continuously. How much will he have in 3 years?

36. Robert borrows $100 and promises to pay 6% compounded continuously. How much will he owe in 6 months? How much interest will he pay?

37. A savings and loan company pays $5\frac{1}{4}\%$ compounded continuously. If you deposit $100, how much will you have in 4 years?

38. If you have the option to borrow $1000 at 8% compounded continuously or 8% compounded quarterly, which would you choose? Why?

39. If you invest $1000 at 5% compounded continuously, how much will you have in 3 years?

40. Suppose that you have $100 to invest for 2 years. Which would give the greatest future value, 5% compounded continuously or $5\frac{1}{4}\%$ compounded annually?

41. Find the future value of a $6000 investment at 11.589% compounded daily for 280 days.

42. Find the future value of a $5000 investment at 12.641% compounded daily for 545 days.

43. How long will it take to double your investment at
    a 12% compounded annually,   *b* 18% compounded annually?

44. Find the future value of $1000 invested at 8% compounded annually for 9 years. Does the investment double?

13.2 *Present Value at Compound Interest*

In preceding sections, we determined the *future value* (*A*). In those problems we were given the present value or principal (*P*), the stated interest rate, and the time.

In this section we wish to change our point of view. That is, we want to find the present value or principal (*P*) when we know the *desired* future value (*A*), interest rate, and time. This procedure is useful when we wish to know the required outlay *now* in order to have a specific amount in the future.

For example, you might want to take a vacation in 2 years and you know you will need $3000. How much must you deposit now in a savings account paying 4% compounded quarterly to have the desired $3000 in 2 years assuming that you plan to make no further deposits?

We can develop a formula for finding the present value by solving the compound interest formula $A = P(1 + i)^n$ for the present value or principal *P*.

present value

> ## *Present Value at Periodically Compounded Interest*
>
> $$P = \frac{A}{(1 + i)^n}$$
>
> where P = present value (or original principal deposited)
> A = future value (desired)
> i = interest rate per period
> n = number of periods per year multiplied by the number of years

Example 1 illustrates the use of the present value formula. Since division is required, a calculator will be helpful.

Example 1

How much money should be invested today at 6% compounded quarterly in order to purchase a $1200 lathe in 2 years?

SOLUTION

Using the formula $P = \dfrac{A}{(1 + i)^n}$ we have $A = \$1200$, $i = 6\%$ per year $\div$ 4 periods per year or 1.5% per period, and $n = 4$ periods per year for 2 years or 8 periods. Therefore,

$$P = \frac{\$1200}{(1 + 1.5\%)^8} \qquad \text{by Table I}$$

$$= \frac{\$1200}{1.12649}$$

$$= \$1065.26$$

Thus, $1065.26 invested today at 6% compounded quarterly for 2 years will yield $1200.

Certainly, the answer in Example 1 seems reasonable. By depositing $1065.26 presently, the interest earned will bring our balance up to $1200 in 2 years. Consequently, the present value (P) is less than the future value (A) by the amount of interest earned. (Remember: present value is always less than future value.)

Example 2

Kay wants to take a vacation in 2 years. The trip will cost her $3000. How much must she deposit today in an account paying 4% compounded quarterly to pay for the trip?

SOLUTION In this case, $P = \dfrac{A}{(1 + i)^n}$, where $P = ?$, $A = \$3000$,

$$i = \frac{4\% \text{ yearly}}{4 \text{ compound periods/year}} = 1\% \text{ per period}$$

and $n = (4 \text{ periods per year})(2 \text{ years}) = 8$ periods. Hence,

$$P = \frac{\$3000}{(1 + 1\%)^8} \qquad \text{by Table I}$$

$$= \frac{\$3000}{1.08286}$$

$$= \$2770.44$$

Therefore, Kay must deposit $2770.44 today in order to pay for her trip.

One of the most common uses of present and future values is to determine the best course of action from alternative choices. Consider the following example.

Example 3 A customer of Addicks Company has been forced into bankruptcy. In order to settle the account owed to Addicks Company, the company has been offered their choice of the following by the customer:

    a. $10,000 cash paid today.
    b. Securities that will mature in 2 years with a future value of $12,000 at maturity.

Addicks management believes the current interest rate is 8% compounded quarterly. Which option should they choose?

SOLUTION There are two possible approaches to this problem. The company may find the *future value* of $10,000 at 8% compounded quarterly and compare that amount with $12,000. Alternatively, the company may also find the *present value* of $12,000 at 8% compounded quarterly and compare that amount with $10,000. Either approach should give the proper decision.

Approach 1. Future value of $10,000: $A = P(1 + i)^n$, where $A = ?$, $P = \$10,000$, $i = \frac{8}{4}\%$ or 2% per period, and $n = (2)(4) = 8$ periods.

$$A = \$10,000(1 + 2\%)^8$$

$$= 10,000(1 + 0.02)^8$$

$$= 10,000(1.17166)$$

$$= \$11,716.60$$

Since $10,000 will be worth $11,716.60 in 2 years, Addicks manager should choose option (**b**): $12,000 in 2 years. The company will receive $283.40 more under option (**b**).

Approach 2. Present value of $12,000:

$$P = \frac{A}{(1 + i)^n}$$

$$= \frac{\$12,000}{(1 + 2\%)^8}$$

$$= \frac{\$12,000}{1.17166}$$

$$= \$10,241.89$$

The present value (of $12,000 due in 2 years) is $10,241.89. This is $241.89 more than the $10,000 today under option (**a**). Hence, the best choice would be option (**b**).

Just as we calculated the present value where interest was compounded per period, we may calculate the present value where interest is compounded continuously.

Present Value at Continuously Compounded Interest

$$P = \frac{A}{e^{st}}$$

where P = present value or original principal
   A = amount or future value
   e = 2.71828 (a constant number)
   s = stated rate of interest
   t = time in years (or fractions of a year)

Example 4   A certificate of deposit paying 6% compounded continuously for 4 years has matured. Its current value is $15,890. What amount was invested 4 years ago?

SOLUTION   In this example, P (original principal) = ?, A = $15,890, s = 6%, and t = 4 years.

$$P = \frac{A}{e^{st}}$$

$$= \frac{\$15,890}{e^{(6\%)(4)}}$$

$$= \frac{\$15,890}{e^{(0.06)(4)}}$$

$$= \frac{\$15,890}{e^{0.24}} \quad \text{by Table III}$$

$$= \frac{\$15,890}{1.27125} = \$12,499.51$$

Hence, $12,499.51 was originally invested.

Exercises 13.2

■ Compute each of the following.

1. $\dfrac{1}{(1 + 3\%)^5}$ **2.** $\dfrac{1}{(1 + 5\%)^4}$ **3.** $\dfrac{1}{e^{(3\%)(10)}}$ **4.** $\dfrac{1}{e^{(2.5\%)(4)}}$

■ Find the present value of each of the following.

5. $A = \$100$, 7% compounded semiannually, 3 years.

6. $A = \$100$, 7% compounded quarterly, 3 years.

7. $A = \$100$, 7% compounded continuously, 3 years.

8. $A = \$500$, 8% compounded quarterly, 1 year.

9. $A = \$500$, 8% compounded quarterly, 2 years.

10. $A = \$500$, 8% compounded quarterly, 3 years.

11. How much must Craig deposit now in order to have $2000 in 2 years if he can get
     a. 9% compounded annually?
     b. 9% compounded quarterly?
     c. 9% compounded continuously?

12. Charlotte wants to purchase a bond that will be worth $1000 in 5 years. If the bond pays 10% compounded semiannually, how much should she pay?

13. How much should be deposited in a savings account that pays 5% compounded continuously if you want to have $10,000 20 years from now?

14. An antique car has been increasing in value at a rate of 6% compounded continuously. It is currently worth $1200. What was its value 5 years ago?

15. Which has the greatest present value, $300 now or $330 in 2 years if money is worth 6% compounded quarterly?

16. Which has the greatest present value, securities that will be worth $1000 in 2 years that pay 8% compounded quarterly or securities that will be worth $1000 in 2 years that pay 6% compounded semiannually?

13.3 *Effective Rate of Interest*

We know from Chapter 12 that the nominal or stated rate of interest is the one that is used as the basis for computing the amount of interest earned and that the effective rate is the simple interest rate that would produce the same (dollar) amount of interest in the same length of time. Further, if we restrict the time to 1 year, the effective rate is also called the annual percentage rate (APR). In Chapter 12 we found the effective rate of bank discount. Now we want to find the effective rate of compound interest.

Suppose a savings institution advertises that it pays 5% per year compounded quarterly, which yields an effective interest rate of 5.095%. That is, a deposit of $1000 at *5% per year compounded quarterly* will yield an amount (A) of $1050.95 at the end of 1 year. This may be verified as follows: $A = P(1 + i)^n$, where $P = \$1000$, $i = \dfrac{5\%}{4} = 1\frac{1}{4}\%$ per period, $n = (1)(4) = 4$ periods. Hence,

$$A = \$1000(1 + 1\tfrac{1}{4}\%)^4$$
$$= \$1000(1.05095)$$
$$= \$1050.95$$

The same deposit of $1000 in an account paying *5.095% simple interest* will yield the identical amount of $1050.95. That is, $A = P(1 + rt)$, where $P = \$1000$, $r = 5.095\%$, and $t = 1$ year. Hence,

$$A = \$1000[1 + (5.095\%)(1)]$$
$$= \$1000(1.05095)$$
$$= \$1050.95$$

Therefore, for a given principal ($1000 above), 5% per year compounded quarterly has an *effective rate* (i.e., equivalent simple interest rate) of 5.095%.

The following formula can be used to determine the effective rate of any compound interest rate (except continuously compounded interest). Proof of the formula is left as an exercise.

effective rate of
compound interest

> ### *Effective Rate of Periodically Compounded Interest*
> ### *Annual Percentage Rate* (APR)
>
> $$r = (1 + i)^n - 1$$
>
> where r = effective rate
> $\quad\quad i$ = interest rate per period (or stated rate divided by number of periods per year)
> $\quad\quad n$ = number of compounding periods in 1 year
>
> The values of $(1 + i)^n$ are found in Table I.

The formula can now be used to show that 5% per year compounded quarterly has an effective rate of 5.095% per year.

$$r = (1 + i)^n - 1$$

where

$$i = \frac{5\% \text{ per year}}{4 \text{ periods/year}} = 1\tfrac{1}{4}\% \text{ per period}$$

and

$$n = 4 \text{ periods per year}$$

$$r = (1 + 1\tfrac{1}{4}\%)^4 - 1 \qquad \text{by Table I}$$

$$= (1.05095) - 1$$

$$= 0.05095$$

$$= 5.095\%$$

Hence, 5% per year compounded quarterly has an equivalent simple interest rate (APR) of 5.095%.

Example 1   Find the APR that is equivalent to 12% per year compounded semiannually.

SOLUTION $r = (1 + i)^n - 1$, where $i = \dfrac{12\% \text{ per year}}{2 \text{ periods/year}}$ or 6% per period, and $n = 2$ periods (in a year).

$$r = (1 + 6\%)^2 - 1$$

$$= 1.1236 - 1$$

$$= 0.1236$$

$$= 12.36\%$$

Hence, 12% per year compounded semiannually has an effective interest rate of 12.36%.

Note that the effective rate is generally greater than the stated compound interest rate. Remember that the greater the number of compounding periods per year, the greater the yield on your investment (when all other things are equal); hence, the greater the effective rate. To verify this fact, let us work Example 2 using 12% compounded monthly (instead of semiannually as in Example 1).

Example 2 Find the APR that is equivalent to 12% per year compounded monthly.

SOLUTION $r = (1 + i)^n - 1$

$= (1 + 1\%)^{12} - 1$

$= 1.12682$

$= 0.12682 - 1$

$= 12.68\%$

Hence, 12% per year compounded monthly has an effective interest rate of 12.68%. Compare this with the 12.36% effective rate when interest is compounded semiannually (Example 1).

From the preceding examples, we would expect the greatest effective rate from interest compounded continuously. The formula for the effective interest rate for continuous compounding may be developed as follows. The amount (A) in simple interest is $A = P(1 + rt)$. The amount (A) in interest compounded continuously is $A = Pe^{st}$. Therefore, $P(1 + rt) = Pe^{st}$. Dividing both sides by P, we have $1 + rt = e^{st}$. Since $t = 1$ year, $1 + r = e^s$. Solving for r, $r = e^s - 1$.

effective rate of
interest
compounded
continuously

> **Effective Rate at Continuously Compounded Interest**
> **Annual Percentage Rate (APR)**
>
> $$r = e^s - 1$$
>
> where r = effective interest rate
> e = 2.71828 (a constant number)
> s = stated annual interest rate

The value of e^s is found by using Table III. Find s under the st column (since $t = 1$) and read the number immediately to the right.

Example 3 Find the effective rate of 12% per year compounded continuously.

SOLUTION $r = e^s - 1$

$= e^{12\%} - 1$

$= e^{0.12} - 1$ by Table III

$= 1.1275 - 1$

$= 0.1275$

$= 12.75\%$

Hence, 12% per year compounded continuously has an effective rate of 12.75%. Compare this with Example 2 (compounding monthly). Does the effective rate increase with a greater number of compounding periods?

It has been stated in this chapter that interest compounded continuously has a greater effective rate than interest compounded for any other number of times per year.

For example, 12% compounded continuously has a greater effective rate than 12% compounded semiannually, quarterly, or monthly. However, the effective rate of 12% compounded daily using the 360/365 method is higher than 12% compounded continuously. That is,

$$r = \left(1 + \frac{12\%}{360}\right)^{365} - 1 = 12.9354\%$$

The effective rate of 12% compounded continuously is 12.75%.

As a final revelation, find the effective rate of 12% bank discount.

For 12% bank discount,

$$r = \frac{d}{1-d} \qquad \text{where } d = 12\% = 0.12$$

$$= \frac{0.12}{1 - 0.12}$$

$$= \frac{0.12}{0.88}$$

$$= 0.13636 \quad \text{or} \quad 13.636\%$$

For the same stated rate, bank discount has a much higher effective rate than even daily compounding. Could this be why lenders use simple (bank) discount for charging interest on loans?

Exercises 13.3

■ Find the effective rates of each of the following.

1. 6% compounded semiannually.

2. 6% compounded quarterly.

3. 6% compounded monthly.

4. 6% compounded continuously.

5. 6% bank discount.

6. 9% compounded semiannually.

7. 9% compounded quarterly.

8. 9% compounded monthly.

9. 9% compounded continuously.

10. 9% bank discount.

11. Find the effective rate of $5\frac{1}{4}\%$ compounded daily.

12. Which has the greater effective rate, 19% compounded continuously or 20% compounded quarterly?

13. Find the effective rate of 10% compounded daily.

14. Find the effective rate of 18% compounded daily.

Review Exercises / Chapter 13

■ Compute each of the following.

1. $(1 + 4\%)^{25}$ **2.** $(1 + \frac{1}{2}\%)^{40}$ **3.** $e^{0.32}$ **4.** $e^{0.54}$

5. $\dfrac{1}{(1 + 5\frac{1}{2}\%)^{10}}$ **6.** $\dfrac{1}{e^{0.25}}$

■ Find the future value of each of the following.

7. $P = \$500$ at 24% compounded quarterly for 3 years.

8. $P = \$500$ at 24% compounded monthly for 3 years.

9. $P = \$500$ at 24% compounded continuously for 3 years.

■ Find the present value of each of the following.

10. $A = \$600$ at 12% compounded semiannually for 4 years.

11. $A = \$600$ at 12% compounded monthly for 4 years.

12. $A = \$600$ at 12% compounded continuously for 4 years.

13. Find the effective rate of 10% compounded semiannually.

14. Find the effective rate of 10% compounded continuously.

15. If Miss Jones invests $900 at 8% compounded quarterly for 3 years, how much will she have?

16. Mr. Brown wants to have $1000 in 5 years. How much should he deposit now in an account paying $5\frac{3}{4}\%$ compounded annually to have the desired amount?

17. Suppose you signed a contract that will pay you $2000 in 3 years. You are given the option of accepting $1700 now as full payment of the contract. If money is worth 8% compounded quarterly, what should you do?

18. Robert deposits $750 at 8% interest compounded semiannually for 8 years. How much will he have?

19. How much will Robert have in 16 years?

20. Using the formula for simple interest $A = P(1 + rt)$ and the formula for compound interest $A = P(1 + i)^n$, develop the formula for effective rate $r = (1 + i)^n - 1$. (*Hint:* A in both formulas is the same. Assume a time of 1 year.)

21. Find the effective rate of daily compounding based on a 365-day year. How does it compare with continuous compounding? Use a rate of 10%.

Chapter Test / Chapter 13

1. Define each of the following.
- **a.** compound interest
- **b.** compounding period
- **c.** nominal interest rate
- **d.** effective interest rate
- **e.** rule of 72
- **f.** present value
- **g.** number e

2. Find the future value of a $10,000 investment for 20 years at 6% compounded annually.

3. Find the interest earned on an $8000 investment at 12% compounded quarterly for 9 years.

4. Find the future value of a $1000 investment for 90 days at
- **a.** $5\frac{1}{4}$% compounded daily,
- **b.** 8% compounded daily.

5. How much must be invested today to have $8000 in 5 years if the interest is 10% compounded annually?

6. How long will it take to double your investment at 24% compounded annually?

7. Find the future value of a $5000 investment at 8% compounded continuously for 10 years.

8. Find the effective rate (APR) of
- **a.** 6% compounded monthly,
- **b.** 6% compounded daily,
- **c.** 6% compounded continuously.

9. How much must you invest at 9% compounded continuously for 6 years in order to have $3826.42?

10. If you want to have $4000 in 2 years, how much must you invest at 16% compounded quarterly?

CHAPTER 14

Amortizing a Debt

INTRODUCTION

A debt is any amount of money owed. The debt could be owed for money borrowed (a loan) or for merchandise bought (a purchase). In Chapters 11, 12, and 13, the future value of the debt (principal plus interest) was paid by a *single payment* made at the end of the term.

However, you might want to repay a debt (principal plus interest) through a *series* (or two or more) *equal payments made at regular* (equal) *intervals of time.*

Definition

amortization
    A debt in which principal and interest are repaid by a series of equal payments made at equal intervals of time is said to be *amortized*.

The system for repaying an amortized debt is called an *amortization plan*, *installment plan*, or *level-payment plan*. Different names are used to communicate different aspects of amortization plans. Amortize means "to extinguish" the debt (i.e., to repay it). Installment means "in part" (i.e., to repay in parts). Level-payment means "equal amounts." Summarizing, an amortization plan extinguishes (or repays) a debt in several installments (or parts) through several equal (or level) payments. Car loans are common examples of amortization plans.

In amortizing a debt, three things are of primary concern:

1. How much are the regular payments?
2. How much of each payment is interest?
3. What is the effective rate of interest?

We will concentrate on answering these questions.

The discussion is organized according to the way interest is being charged. One section is allotted to each of the commonly used methods.

1. Interest charged given in dollar values.
2. Interest charged as a percent per year add-on.
3. Interest charged as a *percent compound interest per year* (i.e., an ordinary annuity).

In each case, we will know the principal (or present value) of the debt and the number of regular payments required. Other applications are considered in Section 14.5.

14.1 Repaying a Debt—Interest in Dollar Values

Suppose that you borrow $240 (principal). The lender charges you $7.20 in interest (*I*). You want to repay the principal plus interest in three equal payments made at regular intervals of time (such as every month). How much is each payment? The formula for determining the amount of each payment (denoted *R*) is just as you would expect it to be.

Amount of Regular Payment—Dollar Value Interest

$$R = \frac{P + I}{n}$$

where R = amount of each payment
P = principal in dollars
I = total amount of interest in dollars
n = number of regular equal payments

We refer to payments as "regular" to emphasize that they are paid at equal intervals of time such as every month.

Definition

installment cost

The total amount repaid on a loan ($P + I$) is called the *installment cost*.

Example 1   Kay borrowed $240 to be repaid in three equal payments over the next 3 months. She is charged $7.20 interest by the lender. Find the amount of each payment.

SOLUTION $P = \$240$ (principal borrowed)
$I = \$7.20$ (interest charged)
$n = 3$ (number of regular payments)

Therefore,

$$R = \frac{\$240 + \$7.20}{3}$$

$$= \frac{\$247.20}{3}$$

$$= \$82.40$$

The amount of each payment is $82.40.

Since the amount of interest may be deducted on your income tax, you would like to know the amount of interest contained in each payment, particularly if the payments fall in two different years.

Also, if you want to repay the loan before the end of the term, you would like to know how much interest you paid and, consequently, how much interest you saved. In short, there are many good reasons for wanting to know how much interest is contained in each payment.

Interest per Payment—Level Method

Remember, there are two points of view in a loan problem: that of the borrower and that of the lender. As the borrower, it seems fair and logical that the interest should be divided evenly among the payments. That is, if three payments are to be made, $\frac{1}{3}$ of the interest should be included in each payment. This is an accepted (but not common) way of apportioning interest called the *level method*.

level method

> **Amount of Interest per Payment—Level Method**
>
> If there are n payments to be made, the amount of interest for each payment in the level method is $\frac{1}{n} \times I$, where I is the total amount of interest charged.

Let us return to Kay's loan (in Example 1).

Interest per Payment—Level Method (Example 1)

Number of Each Payment	Fraction of Interest per Payment—Level Method	Amount of Interest per Payment
1	$\frac{1}{3}$	$(\frac{1}{3} \times \$7.20) = \$2.40$
2	$\frac{1}{3}$	$(\frac{1}{3} \times \$7.20) = \$2.40$
3	$\frac{1}{3}$	$(\frac{1}{3} \times \$7.20) = \$2.40$
Number of payments, $n = 3$		Total $I = \$7.20 \cdot$

Interest per Payment—Rule of 78's

From the lender's point of view, you would like to get as much of the interest as possible as soon as possible. In this case, you would like to apportion the interest per payment in such a way that the early payments in the term contain large amounts of interest. Consequently, the later payments contain very little interest. A method for accomplishing this is called the "rule of 78's." Since the leader is in control of the money, this is probably the most commonly used method of determining the interest per payment. The method is somewhat more difficult (computationally) then the level method.

rule of 78's

Note: the sum of the numbers 1 through n is
$$\frac{n(n + 1)}{2}$$

Interest per Payment—Rule of 78's

Let n be the number of regular payments. The *fraction of interest* per payment is determined by the following procedure:

Step 1. Find the sum of the payment numbers: $1 + 2 + 3 + 4 + \cdots + n$. This is the denominator of each of the fractions.

Step 2. Put the *last payment number* over the sum (from step 1). The fraction obtained $\left(\dfrac{n}{\text{sum}}\right)$ is the fraction of the interest (I) allotted to the *first payment*.

Put the next-to-last payment number over the sum $\left(\dfrac{n-1}{\text{sum}}\right)$; this is the fraction of I that is allotted to the second payment. Continue listing the payment numbers in reverse order, putting each over the sum in step 1.

As with the level method, the *fraction* of interest for each payment is *multiplied* by the total dollar amount of interest (I), to get the *amount* of interest contained in each payment.

The rule of 78's is difficult to read, but in fact is easy to do. Let us return to Kay's loan (in Example 1).

Interest per Payment—Rule of 78's (Example 1)

Payment Number	Fraction of Interest per Payment—Rule of 78's	Amount of Interest per Payment
1 ⟶ $\frac{3}{6}$	The *numerators* are	$(\frac{3}{6} \times \$7.20) = \$3.60$
2 ⟶ $\frac{2}{6}$	the payment *numbers*	$(\frac{2}{6} \times \$7.20) = \$2.40$
3 ⟶ $\frac{1}{6}$	in *reverse order*	$(\frac{1}{6} \times \$7.20) = \$1.20$
Sum of payment numbers is 6		Total $I = \$7.20$

This is the denominator of each of the fractions

For $n = 12$,

$$\text{sum} = \frac{12(12 + 1)}{2} = 78$$

By using the rule of 78's for determining the fractions, the larger fractions occur first and the smaller fractions later. The rule of 78's gets its name from the fact that a loan of 12 payments would give denominators of 78 (i.e., $1 + 2 + 3 + 4 + \cdots + 12 = 78$). [Loans to be paid monthly for 1 year (12 payments) are common.] Of course, the rule of 78's *method* can be used no matter what the number of payments. For this reason, the name is somewhat misleading.

Example 2

Joy borrowed $600 to be repaid in 6 monthly payments. She is charged $63 interest by the lender.

    a. Find the regular payment.
    b. Find the interest per payment—level method.
    c. Find the interest per payment—rule of 78's.

SOLUTION

    a. $R = \dfrac{P + I}{n}$

$$= \frac{\$600 + \$63}{6}$$

$$= \frac{\$663}{6}$$

$$= \$110.50$$

Each of the 6 payments is $110.50.

    b. Level method

Number of Each Payment	Fraction	Amount of Interest per Payment
1	$\frac{1}{6}$	$(\frac{1}{6} \times \$63) = \$10.50$
2	$\frac{1}{6}$	$(\frac{1}{6} \times \$63) = \$10.50$
3	$\frac{1}{6}$	$(\frac{1}{6} \times \$63) = \$10.50$
4	$\frac{1}{6}$	$(\frac{1}{6} \times \$63) = \$10.50$
5	$\frac{1}{6}$	$(\frac{1}{6} \times \$63) = \$10.50$
6	$\frac{1}{6}$	$(\frac{1}{6} \times \$63) = \$10.50$
Number of payments, $n = 6$		Total $I = \$63.00$

    c. Rule of 78's

Number of Each Payment	Fraction	Amount of Interest per Payment
1	$\frac{6}{21}$	$(\frac{6}{21} \times \$63) = \$18.00$
2	$\frac{5}{21}$	$(\frac{5}{21} \times \$63) = \$15.00$
3	$\frac{4}{21}$	$(\frac{4}{21} \times \$63) = \$12.00$
4	$\frac{3}{21}$	$(\frac{3}{21} \times \$63) = \$\ 9.00$
5	$\frac{2}{21}$	$(\frac{2}{21} \times \$63) = \$\ 6.00$
6	$\frac{1}{21}$	$(\frac{1}{21} \times \$63) = \$\ 3.00$
Sum of payment numbers is 21		Total $I = \$63.00$

$$\text{sum} = \frac{6(6 + 1)}{2} = 21$$

Under the level method, if Joy paid off the loan after making two payments she would have paid $21 in interest.

By the rule of 78's, if Joy paid off the loan after making two payments, she would have paid $33 in interest. It is clear why lenders prefer the rule of 78's method.

Effective Rate

Truth-in-lending legislation requires that loans where interest is charged in dollar amounts, the borrower must be told the effective rate of interest that he is being charged. This allows the borrower to compare loans from different institutions on a common basis. The U.S. government has tables available to consumers that give effective rates.

These Annual Percentage Tables (developed by the Federal Reserve Board) come in two volumes. They can be used for a wide variety of rates and numbers of payments. We include only six pages. These pages are for *monthly* payment plans having an APR from 10% to 37.75% (Table VIII, p. 562).

How to Use the APR Tables

Step 1. Compute the amount (x) of interest per $100 financed.

$$x = \frac{I}{P} \times 100$$

where

I = total interest charged

P = present value or principal financed

Step 2. Note the number (n) of monthly payments in the term of the loan.

Step 3. Read across the row corresponding to the number of payments until you find the value of x. The percent at the top of the column containing x is the APR.

Note: If the exact value of x is not in the table, use the closest value to x in the table that is *larger* than x. By choosing the larger value, you will not (illegally) understate the APR.

Now, let us find the effective rate of Kay's loan in Example 1.

Step 1. $x = \dfrac{\$7.20}{\$240} \times 100 = 3.00$

Step 2. Note that $n = 3$.

Step 3. Reading across from $n = 3$ (in Table VIII), the closest value to 3.00 that is larger is 3.01. The annual percentage rate (at the top of the column) is 18%.

If the Federal Reserve tables are not available, the following formula may be used to approximate the APR.

effective rate

> **Effective Interest Rate Using Dollar Values**
> **Annual Percentage Rate (APR)**
>
> The effective interest rate (r) for an amortization plan is
>
> $$r = \frac{(2)(K)(I)}{(P)(n+1)}$$
>
> where r = effective interest rate
> K = number of payments per year
> I = amount of interest, dollars
> P = principal or amount borrowed
> n = number of payments during the term of the loan

Note that the formula contains only dollar values and numbers. No percents (rates) are needed. This formula gives r in decimal form. It can be converted to a percent by multiplying by 100 and attaching a % symbol.

The only peculiar number in the formula is K. K is the number of payments that would be made in 1 year *if* the term were long enough. Even for a 3- or 6-month loan, $K = 12$ because there are 12 months (payments) in a year.

K is 12 for monthly payments, 4 for quarterly payments, 1 for annual payments. (The *actual number* of payments to be made is n.)

The effective rate of interest on Kay's loan in Example 1 is

$$r = \frac{(2)(12)(\$7.20)}{(\$240)(3+1)}$$

$$= \frac{172.8}{960}$$

$$= 0.18 \quad \text{or} \quad 18\%$$

Development of the approximation formula is based on the assumption that the interest is distributed among the payments by the level method. Since this is *not* the usual method of distributing interest, the formula gives only an approximation of the APR. Consider the following example.

Example 3   Find the effective rate for a loan advertised as follows:

> 48-month loan
> $3000
> for only $82.50
> a month

SOLUTION

The installment cost is $82.50 \times 48 = \$3960$. Therefore, the interest (I) is $960 (i.e., $3960 − $3000). $K = 12$ payments per year and $n = 48$ payments. By the formula, we have

$$r = \frac{(2)(12)(\$960)}{(\$3000)(48 + 1)} = \frac{23{,}040}{147{,}000} = 0.1567 = 15.67\%$$

By the Federal Reserve Board APR table, we have:

Step 1. $\quad x = \dfrac{\$960}{\$3000} \times 100 = 32$

Step 2. $\quad n = 48$

Step 3. Reading across from $n = 48$, the closest value to 32 (that is larger than 32) is 32.37. The APR at the top of that column is 14.5%.

Notice that 14.5% is considerably less than the value of 15.67% given by the formula.

Many installment plans have payment periods other than monthly (i.e., quarterly, semiannually, or annually). For these plans, we must use the formula to determine the effective rate. (Recall, the tables given in this text are for monthly plans only.)

Example 4

Thelma borrowed $900. She made *quarterly* payments for 2 years. The installment cost was $1100.

   a. Find the amount of each payment.
   b. Find the effective rate.

SOLUTION

   a. Thelma made 4 payments per year (K) for 2 years, or 8 payments (n). Therefore, each payment was

$$\frac{\$1100}{8} = \$137.50$$

   b. The amount of interest (I) is $200 ($1100 repaid − $900 borrowed). Hence, the effective rate of Thelma's loan is

$$r = \frac{(2)(4)(\$200)}{(900)(8 + 1)} = \frac{1600}{8100} = 0.1975 \quad \text{or} \quad 19.75\%$$

Because of the complexity of the formula for finding the effective rate r, you will probably want to use a calculator. If so, the following version of the formula might be advantageous. It assumes that you have a four-function ($\oplus$, $\ominus$, $\otimes$, $\oslash$) calculator with algebraic logic and an $\ominus$ key.

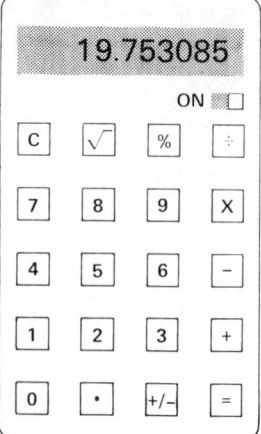

To use the formula, just enter the numbers and operations as they occur from left to right. Upon punching the ⊖ key, the value of $r\%$ will be displayed.

Effective Rate Formula—Calculator Version

$$200 \otimes K \otimes I \oplus P \oplus (n + 1) \ominus \rightarrow \text{displayed value is } r\%$$

The number 200 in the formula comes from the 2 in the other version times 100, to give the answer in percent.

For Thelma's loan in Example 4, we have

$$200 \otimes 4 \otimes \$200 \oplus \$900 \oplus 9 \ominus \rightarrow 19.75\% \text{ (rounded)}$$

Purchases

If the debt incurred is a purchase (as opposed to a loan), the amount of interest is usually called a *carrying charge*. It is called a carrying charge because the store selling the merchandise "carries" the customer's note, in effect making a loan to the customer.

In the case of a purchase, the principal is the cash price of the item *minus* any down payment made by the customer.

All the topics discussed in this section apply to purchases just as they do to loans.

Exercises 14.1

1. A debt is to be repaid in 5 equal monthly payments over the next 5 months.
   a. Find the fractions for computing the amount of interest each month by the level method.
   b. Find the fractions for the rule of 78's.

2. A debt is to be repaid in 8 equal monthly payments over the next 8 months.
   a. Find the fractions for computing the amount of interest each period by the level method.
   b. Find the fractions for the rule of 78's.

3. William borrowed $300 to be repaid in 6 equal monthly payments over the next 6 months. He was charged $21 interest.
   a. Find the amount of each payment.
   b. Find the interest per period—level method.
   c. Find the interest per period—rule of 78's.
   d. Find the effective rate by the formula and table.
   e. If he pays off the loan after making 3 regular payments, how much interest did he pay by the level method? By the rule of 78's?

4. Craig borrowed $600 to be repaid in 4 equal monthly payments over the next 4 months. He was charged $45 interest. Answer parts *a* through *e* of problem 3.

5. Richard purchased a washing machine for $450. He paid $50 down and amortized the balance for 12 months. The carrying charge was $96.

    a. How much were his monthly payments?

    b. He paid off the machine after making 6 payments. How much interest did he pay by the rule of 78's?

    c. What was the effective rate of interest? (Use the formula.)

6. Linda purchased a television set for $800. She paid $200 down and amortized the balance for 3 months. The carrying charge was $30.

    a. Find the monthly payment.

    b. Find the amount of interest contained in each payment by the rule of 78's.

    c. Find the effective rate by the formula and table.

7. The EZ Loan Company ran the following ad:

> Borrow $4427.47 for only $119.92 per month for 48 months.

    a. Find the installment cost.

    b. Find the dollar amount of interest.

    c. Find the effective rate by the formula and table.

8. Check the effective interest rate given in the following ad.

> Sale price—$3680.00, $500 down payment, total payments $4070.40, 48 months, 12.67% APR.

9. Suppose that you are a lender. If the borrower pays all of the payments on time over the entire term of the loan, which way of apportioning interest (level method or rule of 78's) would give you the greatest return?

10. Suppose that you are a lender. If the borrower pays off his loan after making 2 regular payments, which way of apportioning interest would give you the greatest return?

14.2 *Amortizing a Debt—S% per Year Add-on*

    Add-on interest is one of the simplest methods for determining the amount of interest due. Suppose that you want to purchase a car for $5000. The bank at which you borrow the money charges 4% per year add-on. The amount of interest per year is 4% of $5000, or $200 per year. You want to amortize the debt over 3 years, so you will pay $600 interest.

    The bank adds on the $600 interest to the $5000 principal, so $P + I = \$5600$. If the principal plus interest is to be repaid in monthly installments for 3 years (36 months), the amount of each payment is

$$R = \frac{P + I}{n}$$

$$= \frac{\$5000 + \$600}{36}$$

$$= \$155.56 \text{ per month}$$

Now, let us find the effective rate. The effective rate is

$$r = \frac{(2)(K)(I)}{P(n + 1)}$$

where $K = 12$, $I = \$600$, $P = \$5000$, and $n = 36$.

$$r = \frac{(2)(12)(\$600)}{\$5000(36 + 1)} = \frac{14,400}{185,000} = 7.784\%$$

The effective rate of 4% per year add-on is 7.784%, almost twice the stated rate. Why so high? Remember: the interest was computed on the entire principal of $5000. However, you do not have use of the entire amount for 3 years. As payments are made, part of each one goes to repay the principal, so you owe less and less of the principal, but you were charged as if you owed the $5000 the whole time. The result is an effective rate that is unexpectedly high.

Amortizing a Debt at S% per Year Add-on

Step 1. Compute the dollar amount of interest.

$$I = Pst$$

where P = principal
s = stated add-on rate per year
t = time, years or fraction of a year

Step 2. Compute the regular payment.

$$R = \frac{P + I}{n}$$

where P = principal
I = interest (from step 1)
n = number of regular payments

Step 3. The effective rate can be determined by the formula

$$r = \frac{(2)(K)(I)}{P(n + 1)}$$

The interest may be apportioned among the payments by the level method or rule of 78's.

Example 1   Marie borrowed $1000 for 2 years at 5% per year add-on to be repaid in 24 monthly installments.

> **a.** Find the amount of interest she was charged.
> **b.** Find the amount of each payment.
> **c.** Compute the effective rate.

SOLUTION   **a.** The amount of interest is 5% per year for 2 years, or

$$I = \$1000(5\%)(2) = \$100$$

b. $R = \dfrac{P + I}{n}$

$$= \frac{\$1000 + \$100}{24}$$

$$= \$45.83 \text{ per month}$$

c. The effective rate is

$$r = \frac{(2)(12)(\$100)}{\$1000(24 + 1)} = \frac{2400}{25,000} = 9.6\%$$

Exercises 14.2

■ Find the payment for each of the following loans.

1. Principal = $1000
   Add-on rate = 8%
   12 monthly payments

2. Principal = $2000
   Add-on rate = 6%
   6 monthly payments

3. Principal = $5000
   Add-on rate = 5%
   24 monthly payments

4. Principal = $800
   Add-on rate = 6%
   8 quarterly payments

5. Principal = $1000
   Add-on rate = 9%
   6 semiannual payments

6. Principal = $10,000
   Add-on rate = 4%
   5 annual payments

7. Gene borrowed $800 for 2 years at 6% per year add-on. The debt is to be repaid in 24 monthly payments. Find the amount of each payment and the effective rate.

8. Work problem 1 where the loan is to be repaid in 8 quarterly payments.

9. A car sells for $3200. If you pay $200 down and amortize the balance to be repaid monthly over the next 18 months at 5% per year add-on, what are the monthly payments?

10. Sue borrowed $500 for 1 year at 8% per year add-on to be repaid monthly. Find the effective rate.

11. Suppose that you borrow $1000 for 4 months to be repaid monthly. Find the interest at 9% add-on and the monthly payment.

12. Suppose that you borrow $1000 for 2 years to be repaid monthly. Which interest rate would result in smaller payments: $224 interest or 10% per year add-on?

13. If you borrow $100 for 3 months at 8% per year add-on, how much interest is charged? Find the amount of interest in each payment by the rule of 78's. What is the regular payment?

14. If you borrow $400 to be repaid in 3 monthly payments at 5% per year add-on, how much are the payments? Find the amount of interest in each payment by the level method and rule of 78. What is the effective rate?

14.3 *Amortizing a Debt—S% Compound Interest per Year*

Suppose that you borrow money (principal) at $S\%$ per year *compound interest* to be repaid in n regular payments. What is the amount (R) of each regular payment? How much of each payment is interest?

Since there are payments to be made and interest to be compounded, two types of periods are involved: (1) payment periods and (2) compounding periods.

Definition

ordinary annuity

An *ordinary annuity* is an installment plan (based on compound interest) in which the *payment period and compounding period correspond*.

That is, in an *ordinary* annuity, if the regular payments are made monthly, the interest is compounded monthly. If the payments are made quarterly, the interest is compounded quarterly.

There are other types of annuities in which the periods do not coincide. For example, the payment might be monthly and the compounding periods quarterly. These special cases are not presented here.

The formula for determining the amount of the regular payment for an ordinary annuity is as follows:

Regular Payment—Ordinary Annuity

The formula for determining the amount of the regular payment (R) for an ordinary annuity is

$$R = P\left[\frac{i(1 + i)^n}{(1 + i)^n - 1}\right]$$

where R = amount of each payment
P = original principal
i = interest rate per period
n = number of periods in the term of the annuity

It is evident that this formula is based on compound interest since it contains the expression $(1 + i)^n$. In computing R, you will want to look up values of $(1 + i)^n$ in Table I.

Remember, when working with compound interest i and n have special meaning.

Definition

The interest rate per period (i) for compound interest is

$$i = \frac{\text{stated rate of compound interest } (S)}{\text{number of compound periods/year } (K)}$$

The number of periods (n) is found by multiplying the *number of periods per year times the number of years* (in the term of the installment plan).

Example 1   Mac borrowed \$5000. Consider his payments to be an ordinary annuity at 12% compound interest per year compounded monthly. If the term of the annuity is 4 years, what will be the monthly payment?

SOLUTION   The principal $P = \$5000$. The interest rate per period is

$$i = \frac{12\% \text{ per year}}{12 \text{ monthly payments}} = 1\% \text{ per period}$$

The number of periods (and payments) is $n = 48$ (i.e., 12 per year $\times$ 4 years). (The number of payments is equal to the number of periods in an ordinary annuity.) Substituting these values into the formula for R, we have

$$R = \$5000\left[\frac{(1\%)(1 + 1\%)^{48}}{(1 + 1\%)^{48} - 1}\right] \qquad \text{by Table I}$$

$(1 + 1\%)^{48} = 1.61222$, so

$$R = \$5000\left[\frac{(0.01)(1.61222)}{1.61222 - 1}\right]$$

$$= \$5000\left[\frac{0.0161222}{0.61222}\right]$$

$$= \$5000[0.0263339]$$

$$= \$131.67$$

Mac's monthly payment is \$131.67 for 48 months.

Tables of Value for $\left[\dfrac{i(1 + i)^n}{(1 + i)^n - 1}\right]$ *(Table IV)*

Computation of $\left[\dfrac{i(1 + i)^n}{(1 + i)^n - 1}\right]$ can be tedious and time consuming even using a calculator. Values have been computed for various values of i and n. These are given in Table IV—Payment Needed to Amortize a Debt of 1. If values of i and n (appropriate for your problem) are given in Table IV, you may simply look-up the result.

How To Use Table IV

Step 1. Determine the value of $i\%$.
Step 2. Determine the number of periods n.
Step 3. Look across from the value of n (on the left) and underneath the value of $i\%$ (on the top). The number found is the value of

$$\left[\frac{i(1 + i)^n}{(1 + i)^n - 1}\right].$$

For Mac's loan in Example 1, $i = 1\%$ and $n = 48$. In Table IV, we find

$$\left[\frac{1\%(1 + 1\%)^{48}}{(1 + 1\%)^{48} - 1}\right] = 0.026334$$

This is the same result (rounded to six decimal places) that we found using the formula and Table I.

Example 2

Robert borrowed $1000 from the Sharp Loan Company at 24% per year compounded monthly. What is the amount of his monthly payment (R) if the term of the loan is 2 years?

SOLUTION

We can compute the amount of Robert's monthly payment by

$$R = P\left[\frac{i(1 + i)^n}{(1 + i)^n - 1}\right],$$

where

$$P = \$1000, \qquad i = \frac{24\%}{12} = 2\%$$

per period and $n = (12)(2) = 24$ periods (payments). Therefore,

$$R = \$1000\left[\frac{2\%(1 + 2\%)^{24}}{(1 + 2\%)^{24} - 1}\right].$$

By Table IV

$$\left[\frac{2\%(1 + 2\%)^{24}}{(1 + 2\%)^{24} - 1}\right] = (0.052871)$$

So

$$R = \$1000[0.052871]$$
$$= \$52.87 \text{ per month for 2 years}$$

Effective Rate

Effective Rate of an Ordinary Annuity
Annual Percentage Rate (APR)

The effective rate of an ordinary annuity is *equal* to the nominal (or stated) rate.

We can verify this for Examples 1 and 2 using the APR Table (Table VIII).

For Mac's loan in Example 1,

$$x = \frac{\$1320.16}{\$5000} \times 100 = 26.40$$

and $n = 48$. By Table VIII, the APR $= 12.00\%$.

For Robert's loan in Example 2,

$$x = \frac{\$268.88}{\$1000} \times 100 = 26.89$$

and $n = 24$. By Table VIII, the APR $= 24.00\%$.

As noted previously, some annuities have payment periods other than monthly (i.e., quarterly, semiannually, or annually). These periods pose no special problems, as shown in Example 3.

Example 3   The Smith Manufacturing Company bought a new machine for $20,000. They borrowed the money at 8% compounded quarterly. Find the *quarterly* payment required to pay for the machine in 10 years.

SOLUTION $P = \$20,000$, $i = \dfrac{8\%/\text{year}}{4 \text{ quarters}} = 2\%$ per quarter, and $n = 40$ (i.e., 4 periods per year $\times$ 10 years). (Remember: the period is quarterly, not monthly.)

$$R = \$20,000 \left[\frac{2\%(1 + 2\%)^{40}}{(1 + 2\%)^{40} - 1} \right] \quad \text{By Table IV, we have}$$

$$= \$20,000[0.03655]$$

$$= \$731.11 \text{ quarterly payment for 10 years.}$$

Amortization Schedule

We can combine the previous concepts to make a chart that completely describes a loan. Such a chart is called an *amortization schedule*.

Definition

amortization
schedule

An *amortization schedule* is a chart that shows the payment number, the amount of each regular payment (R), the amount repaid on the principal, and the part of each payment that is interest.

If you have ever bought a house or land, you probably received an amortization schedule. The procedure for making such a schedule is shown in the next example (Example 4). In an ordinary annuity, the amount of R must be determined before constructing the schedule.

Example 4

Make an amortization schedule for a loan of $1000 at 12% compound interest to be repaid in 12 monthly installments. Find the effective rate. Assume an ordinary annuity.

SOLUTION

First compute the monthly payment (R). $P = \$1000$, $i = \dfrac{12\%}{12} = 1\%$ per period, and $n = 12$. So

$$R = \$1000\left[\frac{(1\%)(1 + 1\%)^{12}}{(1 + 1\%)^{12} - 1}\right]. \quad \text{By Table IV, we have}$$

$$= \$1000[0.088849]$$

$$= \$88.85$$

The calculation of the numbers in the amortization schedule is shown on the table on the following page. The columns have been identified alphabetically (i.e., A through D). The manipulation on these columns to determine the correct entries is shown immediately above the line for payment 1.

Amortization Schedule
(12% Compound Interest, $i = 1\%$)

Payment Number	Principal Remaining Col. A	Amount of Payment R Col. B	Amount of Interest Paid Col. C	Amount Paid on Principal Col. D
Computations Made By	Previous Months Col. A–Col. D	Computed— Remains Constant	Col. A × Interest Rate (1%)	Col. B–Col. C
1	$1000.00	$ 88.85	$10.00	$ 78.85
2	$ 921.15	$ 88.85	$ 9.21	$ 79.64
3	$ 841.51	$ 88.85	$ 8.42	$ 80.43
4	$ 761.08	$ 88.85	$ 7.61	$ 81.24
5	$ 679.84	$ 88.85	$ 6.80	$ 82.05
6	$ 597.79	$ 88.85	$ 5.98	$ 82.87
7	$ 514.92	$ 88.85	$ 5.15	$ 83.70
8	$ 431.22	$ 88.85	$ 4.31	$ 84.54
9	$ 346.68	$ 88.85	$ 3.47	$ 85.38
10	$ 261.30	$ 88.85	$ 2.61	$ 86.24
11	$ 175.06	$ 88.85	$ 1.75	$ 87.10
12	$ 87.96	$ 88.84[a]	$ 0.88	$ 87.96
Total		$1066.19	$66.19	$1000.00

[a] The last payment adjusted by $0.01 due to errors in rounding.
The effective interest rate (r) is 12%.

Example 5   A loan of $500 is to be paid in six monthly payments at 18% compound interest. Find the amount of the regular payments (R) and make an amortization schedule. Find the effective rate.

SOLUTION $P = \$500$, $i = \dfrac{18\%}{12} = 1.5\%$ per month, and $n = (12)(1/2) = 6$ periods. Therefore,

$$R = \$500\left[\frac{1.5\%(1 + 1.5\%)^6}{(1 + 1.5\%)^6 - 1}\right]. \quad \text{By Table IV, we have}$$

$$= \$500[0.175525]$$

$$= \$87.76 \text{ per month for 6 months}$$

Amortization Schedule
(18% Compound Interest, $i = 1.5\%$)

Payment Number	Principal Remaining (Col. A)	Amount of Payment R (Col. B)	Amount of Interest (Col. C)	Amount Paid on Principal (Col. D)
1	$500.00	$ 87.76	$ 7.50	$ 80.26
2	$419.74	$ 87.76	$ 6.30	$ 81.46
3	$338.28	$ 87.76	$ 5.07	$ 82.69
4	$255.59	$ 87.76	$ 3.83	$ 83.93
5	$171.66	$ 87.76	$ 2.57	$ 85.19
6	$ 86.47	$ 87.77	$ 1.30	$ 86.47
Total		$526.57	$26.57	$500.00

The effective rate is 18%.

Note that in an ordinary annuity, the earlier payments contain larger amounts of interest than later payments, as was the case with the rule of 78's.

Consumer Credit

To compute the amount of interest (column C) in an amortization schedule, you multiply the periodic rate ($i\%$) by the principal remaining (or unpaid balance). This is the method of computing the interest due each period (usually 1 month) for most "revolving" change accounts and credit cards.

For example, if you have a balance of $100 subject to a $1\frac{1}{2}\%$ interest rate, you pay $1.50 interest. If you make a $10 payment on the account, $1.50 goes to pay the current interest charge; the remaining $8.50 reduces the principal to $91.50 ($100 − $8.50). As you make further charges and payments, the principal and interest are adjusted accordingly. The methods of computing the actual amount subject to interest charges vary considerably among retailers and credit card institutions.

Home Mortgages and Creative Financing (Calculator Required)

We find an important application of debt amortization in the purchase of a home. The traditional method of financing the purchase of a home requires a down payment (usually 5 % to 25 % of the purchase price) with the remainder of the price borrowed from a lender at a fixed rate and amortized over a set number of years (usually 20–40 years).

Example 6

The Kings purchased a new home for $125,000. They paid 20 % down and amortized the balance over 30 years at 15 %.
 a. How much was their down payment?
 b. How much is their monthly payment.

SOLUTION

Their down payment was $(20\%)(\$125,000) = \$25,000$. Hence, they amortized $100,000. Their payment

$$R = \$100,000\left[\frac{1.25\%(1 + 1.25\%)^{360}}{(1 + 1.25\%)^{360} - 1}\right]$$

$$= \$100,000[0.01264444]$$

$$= \$1264.44$$

The Kings' monthly payment on principal and interest is $1264.44.

Most financial lending institutions making home loans want to protect their investment. Therefore, they require that the homeowner insures the house against damage. To guarantee that homeowners maintain insurance and pay their taxes (failure to pay taxes could result in a forced sale of the home at below market prices), most lenders require an *escrow account*. This simply means that the home owner is required to pay an additional sum of money into a special account each month. The money in the escrow account is used by the lender to pay the insurance premiums and property taxes. The amount of money paid into the escrow account each month usually changes on a periodic basis to reflect the cost of home insurance and taxes. Assume the Kings' lendor required a $200 per month escrow payment. Their total monthly house payment would be $1464.44 ($1264.44 principal and interest plus $200 taxes and insurance).

Other traditonal mortgage plans include Federal Housing Administration (FHA) loans. These are attractive because the current down payment is 3 % of the first $25,000 and 5 % of the value over $25,000. If the Kings had gotten an FHA loan, their down payment would have been $5750. However, their monthly payment would be higher because they would have borrowed (and be amortizing) $119,250. (Their escrow payment would not change since taxes and insurance are based on the value of the home, not the amount amortized.)

Another common home loan is a Veteran's Administration (VA), loan which is only available to qualified veterans of the U.S. armed forces. Under the VA program, no down payment is required and the interest rate might be lower then the rate from other sources.

Creative Financing

Due to high interest rates and high prices of homes, many persons cannot afford to buy a home financed in the conventional ways. Hence, many "creative financing" methods have been (and are being) devised. We will mention a few of these.

The adjustable mortage loan (AML) is fairly popular. Under AML there is no limit on how much the interest rate can change over the life of the loan and it can be changed every month. However, most institutions adjust the rate every 6 months. The interest rate is governed by some independent interest index, such as Treasury bills. If the Kings had an AML and after 6 months interest rates fell to 12%, their interest rate, and hence their payment, would be lowered.

Another creative financing method is the variable rate mortgage. Under VRM, the rate can be adjusted up or down by one-half percent per year with a maximum increase of $2\frac{1}{2}\%$ over the life of the loan. If the Kings had a VRM, the maximum rate would be $17\frac{1}{2}\%$.

The graduated payment mortgage (GPM) is particularly appealing to younger buyers. The GPM allows lower payments for the first 3–5 years, with larger payments after the initial period (when the owners income will have increased). In GPM loans, the early payments might not cover the interest due; therefore, the additional interest is added to the principal. After the first few years of a GPM loan, the owner may actually owe more than he borrowed!

The balloon mortgage is a financing plan favored by owners who are selling and financing the sale themselves and by buyers who are not planning to hold the property for the full term of the loan. In a balloon mortgage loan, the payment is computed based on a fixed rate over a 25- or 30-year term. However, at the end of a preset period of time (usually 5 years) the remaining (unpaid) balance is due in full. This is the "balloon payment." At this time, the buyer must pay off the loan. This method is attractive to the seller because he does not have to wait 25 or 30 years to collect.

If a balloon mortgage is negotiated with a financial institution that guarantees to refinance the balance due at the (then) current interest rate, the mortage is called a "rollover mortgage."

There is almost no limit to the "creative methods" of financing a home. Some others that you might want to investigate are the shared appreciation mortgage (SAM), reverse annuity mortgage (RAM), and flexible loan insurance program (FLIP).

Exercises 14.3

1. **a.** Find the regular payment necessary to amortize a debt of $1000 for 6 months at 9% per year compounded monthly.

   b. Find the dollar amount of interest.

   c. Find the effective rate.

2. **a.** Find the regular payment necessary to amortize a debt of $1000 for 2 years at 8% per year compounded quarterly.

   b. Find the dollar amount of interest.

   c. Find the effective rate.

3. **a.** In order to take advantage of a cash discount, the Socket Wrench Company borrowed $2000 to be paid over the next 3 months at 12% compounded monthly. Find the amount of each payment.

   b. Make an amortization schedule for the loan.

   c. If the cash discount amounted to $200, did the company do the right thing in borrowing the money?

4. **a.** The Windy Boat Company borrowed $4000 to be repaid over the next 4 months at 6% compounded monthly. Find the amount of their monthly payment.

   b. Make an amortization schedule for the loan.

   c. What is the effective rate?

5. If the rule of 78's were used to apportion the dollar amount of interest in problem 3, would the interest per payment be the same as that in the amortization schedule (3b)?

6. Apportion the dollar amount of interest in problem 4 by the rule of 78's. Is it the same as that shown in the amortization schedule?

7. Suppose that you are the lender. If the loan is to be paid off halfway through the term, would you prefer that the interest on an annuity be apportioned as shown in the amortization schedule or by the rule of 78's? (Base your answer on the result in problem 5.)

8. Richard amortized $5000 of the cost of a new car at 18% compounded monthly. If the term of the loan is 42 months, find his monthly payments.

9. Which yields the greater interest on $1000 for 1 year, interest at 12% per year add-on or 12% compounded and paid monthly?

10. Find the semiannual payment to amortize a principal of $4000 at 10% compounded semiannually for 2 years. Make an amortization schedule for the loan.

11. Seth currently owes $200 on his Interplanetary Bank Credit Card, which charges $1\frac{1}{2}\%$ per month on the unpaid balance. He wants to amortize the debt over the next 4 months. Assuming he makes no further purchases with the card, what are his monthly payments?

12. Gene's credit card balance was $800 in January. He made a $200 payment. Assume the credit card account charges 2% per month on the unpaid balance.

> *a*. What will his February statement show the balance to be?
> *b*. If he makes no charges or payment in February, what will be the balance on his March statement?
> *c*. If no payment is made on a credit card account, is the interest compounded?

13. The current balance of your Customer Credit Card account is $1273.82. It is subject to a 2% interest rate. You decide to make a $225.48 payment.

> *a.* How much interest do you owe?
> *b.* How much of the payment goes to reduce the principal?

14. Suppose you owe $1387.50 on your Merry-Go-Round Charge account, which is subject to a $1\frac{1}{2}$% charge. If you make a $20 payment, how much will go to reduce the principal?

15. The Otto family is purchasing a new home listing for $82,000. They got a conventional 17.25% loan, requiring 20% down with the balance amortized over 25 years.

> *a.* How much is the down payment?
> *b.* How much is the monthly payment on principal and interest?

16. If the Otto family in problem 15 had gotten an FHA loan,

> *a.* How much would the down payment be?
> *b.* What would be the monthly payment on principal and interest?

17. If the Otto family in problem 15 had gotten a VA loan:

> *a.* What would the down payment be?
> *b.* What would be the monthly payment on principal and interest.

18. If the Otto family's monthly escrow payment were $180 with an FHA loan, what would it be with a VA loan?

19. If the Otto family had gotten a balloon mortgage requiring 20% down and the payment based on 17.25% amortized over 25 years, what would be the principal and interest payment?

20. The Youngs purchased a new home listing for $55,000. They paid $5000 down and amortized the balance over 30 years at 12%.

> *a.* Calculate their monthly principal and interest payment.

Suppose that the Youngs loan was a GPM with fixed payments of $500 per month over the first 5 years.

> *b.* What will be the remaining balance of the Youngs' mortgage at the end of five years?

21. *a.* If you amortized $100,000 over 25 years at 18%, what would be your monthly principal and interest payment?
> *b.* What would be the total amount paid over the 25-year term of the loan?

22. *a.* If you amortized $100,000 over 25 years at 12%, what would be your monthly principal and interest payment?
> *b.* What would be the total amount paid over the 25-year term of the loan?

23. *a.* If you amortized $100,000 over 25 years at 6%, what would be your monthly principal and interest payment?

b. What would be the total amount paid over the 25-year term of the loan?

24. a. Does the sum of the payments in problems 22 and 23 equal the payment in problem 21?

   b. Does the sum of the totals repaid in problems 22 and 23 equal the total repaid in problem 21?

14.4 Sinking Fund

Suppose that you are *anticipating* an expenditure. For example, you want to take a vacation in 2 years and it will cost $5000. You want to put away (deposit) a certain amount each month for the next 2 years (24 months) so that you *will have* $5000. If your savings account pays 6% compounded monthly, how much must you deposit each month?

In business math terminology, you want to establish an annuity whose future value (F) is $5000 and need the amount of the regular payment (R).

sinking fund

Such a system of saving money is called a *sinking fund*. Sinking funds are frequently used by business to have money for future expenditures in much the same way. In a sense, a sinking fund is simply a savings account. However, unlike ordinary savings accounts, sinking funds are established to have a definite future value after a certain (specified) amount of time.

Amount of the Regular Payment to Have a Specified Future Value

$$R = F\left[\frac{i}{(1 + i)^n - 1}\right]$$

where R = amount of the regular payment
  F = specified future value
  i = interest rate per period
  n = number of payments and compounding periods

Find the values of $(1 + i)^n$ in Table I.

This is an ordinary annuity; the payment periods and compounding periods must be the same.

Example 1   You want to have $5000 in 2 years. What is the amount of the regular payment that you must make monthly into an account paying 6% compounded monthly?

SOLUTION $F = \$5000$, $i = \dfrac{6\%}{12} = \tfrac{1}{2}\%$ per month (period), and $n = (12 \text{ periods per year}) \times$ (2 years) $= 24$ periods. Hence,

$$R = \$5000\left[\frac{\tfrac{1}{2}\%}{(1 + \tfrac{1}{2}\%)^{24} - 1}\right] \qquad \text{by Table I}$$

$$= \$5000\left[\frac{0.005}{1.12716 - 1}\right]$$

$$= \$5000\left[\frac{0.005}{0.12716}\right]$$

$$= \$5000[0.0393205]$$

$$= \$196.60$$

You must save $196.60 each month to have $5000 in 2 years at 6% compounded monthly.

Since you were earning interest, the total amount deposited is *less than* $5000. At $196.60 per month for 24 months, you deposited $4718.40 ($= \$196.60 \times 24$). The difference in the $5000 future value and $4718.40 is interest earned, namely $281.60.

The sinking-fund formula may be restated for calculator usage.

```
196.6027
```

Sinking Fund—Calculator Version

$$F \otimes i \otimes 0.01 \oplus (\text{Table I value} - 1) \ominus \; \to R$$

Enter the numbers and operations from left to right as they occur in the formula. When $\ominus$ is punched, the value displayed is R. It should be rounded to the nearest cent.

For Example 1, we have

$$\$5000 \otimes 0.5 \otimes 0.01 \oplus 0.12716 \ominus \to \$196.60$$

Example 2   The Expander Company plans to open a new office in 3 years at an expected cost of $10,000. They can make quarterly deposits in securities that pay 12% compounded quarterly. What amount must be deposited each quarter to have the money to open the new office?

SOLUTION $F = \$10,000$, $i = \dfrac{12\%}{4} = 3\%$ per quarter (period), and $n = (4$ quarters per year$)(3$ years$) = 12$ periods. Hence,

$$R = \$10,000 \left[\frac{0.03}{(1 + 3\%)^{12} - 1} \right] \qquad \text{by Table I}$$

$$= \$10,000 \left[\frac{0.03}{1.42576 - 1} \right]$$

$$= \$10,000 \left[\frac{0.03}{0.42576} \right]$$

$$= \$10,000[0.0704622]$$

$$= \$704.62 \text{ must be deposited each quarter}$$

In business, a sinking fund might be established at institution B to pay off a debt that will be due later to institution A.

Example 3   Fisher's Hood Company borrowed $10,000 from the Interplanetary Bank at 8% per year compounded quarterly. The debt is to be repaid (principal plus interest) by a *single payment* in 2 years. In order to have the money to pay the debt, Fisher's establishes a sinking fund at Town Savings Association which pays 6% compounded monthly. What monthly deposit must Fisher's make into the sinking fund in order to have the money to pay Interplanetary Bank?

SOLUTION   The future value of the bank loan is $A = P(1 + i)^n$, where $P = \$10,000$, $i = 2\%$ per period, and $n = 8$ periods.

$$A = \$10,000(1 + 2\%)^8 \qquad \text{by Table I}$$

$$= \$10,000(1.17166)$$

$$= \$11,716.60$$

The loan is not an annuity, because there is only one payment to be made.

The amount $A = \$11,716.60$ is the future value needed by Fisher's; hence, this is the future value (F) of the sinking fund established at Town Savings. The value of each monthly deposit made at Town Savings is $R = F \left[\dfrac{i}{(1 + i)^n - 1} \right]$, where $F = \$11,716.60$, $i = \frac{1}{2}\%$ per period, and $n = 24$ periods.

$$R = \$11,716.60 \left[\frac{\frac{1}{2}\%}{(1 + \frac{1}{2}\%)^{24} - 1} \right]$$

$$= \$11,716.60 \left[\frac{0.005}{1.12716 - 1} \right]$$

$$= \$460.70$$

By depositing \$460.70 each month for 2 years, Fisher's account at Town Savings will have the \$11,716.60 necessary to pay the Interplanetary Bank. At the end of 2 years, Fisher's takes the money out of the savings account, pays the bank, and hence clears the debt.

Tables of Value of $\left[\dfrac{i}{(1+i)^{n}-1}\right]$ (Table V)

Values of $\left[\dfrac{i}{(1+i)^{n}-1}\right]$ have been computed for various values of i and n. These are recorded in Table V, Payment Needed Each Period for a Sinking Fund to Amount to 1. To use Table V, follow the procedure given for Table IV.

For the sinking fund in Example 1, $i = \frac{1}{2}\%$ and $n = 24$. By Table V,

$$\left[\frac{\frac{1}{2}\%}{(1+\frac{1}{2}\%)^{24}-1}\right] = 0.039321$$

For the sinking fund in Example 2, $i = 3\%$ and $n = 12$. By Table V,

$$\left[\frac{3\%}{(1+3\%)^{12}-1}\right] = 0.070462$$

(Compare these values with those computed using Table I and the formula.)

Exercises 14.4

1. How much must be deposited each month into an account paying 12% compounded monthly to have \$1000 in 2 years?

2. How much must be deposited each quarter into an account paying 5% compounded quarterly to have \$1000 in 2 years?

3. Find the quarterly payment required to have \$10,000 in 5 years if you earn 8% compounded quarterly.

4. Find the semiannual payment required to have \$10,000 in 5 years if you can earn 8% compounded semiannually.

5. John wants to save a certain amount each month to purchase a new car costing \$5000 in 18 months. If he can earn 6% compounded monthly, how much must he save each month?

6. The Far Sight Company is planning a \$1,000,000 expansion in 5 years. Their financial analyst says that they can earn 12% compounded quarterly. What quarterly investment must be made to have the money for the planned expansion?

7. Leaky's Boat Company borrowed \$5000 due in 2 years at 12% compounded quarterly from High State Bank. They want to establish a sinking fund at Secondary Savings which pays 4% compounded quarterly. What quarterly deposit must Leaky's make into the sinking fund to have the money to pay High State Bank?

8. Shore's Land Company borrowed $100,000 due in 5 years at 10% compounded semiannually. How much must Shore's deposit each quarter into a sinking fund paying 8% compounded quarterly to have the money to repay the loan?

9. A city sold bonds that will have to be retired at a cost of $500,000 in 20 years. A sinking fund paying 5% compounded annually is established. What annual payment must the city make?

10. Semiannual deposits are made into a sinking fund paying 6% compounded semi-annually. Find the regular payment if the fund is to have $8000 in 10 years.

11. How much must be deposited each month into an account paying 15% compounded monthly to have $10,000 in 5 years?

12. How much must be deposited each quarter for 2 years in an account paying 12% compounded quarterly to have the same amount as $3000 deposited now in an account paying 8% compounded semiannually?

14.5 *Other Applications of Annuities*

In Section 14.3, we knew the present value or principal (P) to be amortized and needed to determine the regular payment (R). Of course, if we knew the regular payment (R), we could determine the principal (P) (given a specific interest rate and the term of the note or investment).

Suppose that you are to receive an inheritance. You have your choice of receiving $10,000 at the end of each year for the next 10 years (an annuity amounting to $100,000) or the present value of the annuity based on the current interest rate of 10% compounded annually. If you elect to receive the present value of the inheritance, how much will you receive?

The essence of the problem is that you know the regular payment ($R = \$10,000$ per year), the interest rate ($i = 10\%$ compounded annually), and the term of the annuity ($n = 10$ years); you want to find the present value P. The problem can be solved by applying the formula

$$R = P\left[\frac{i(1 + i)^n}{(1 + i)^n - 1}\right].$$

and solving for P. Hence,

$$\$10,000 = P\left[\frac{10\%(1 + 10\%)^{10}}{(1 + 10\%)^{10} - 1}\right].$$

Since Table IV does not contain $i = 10\%$, we must use the formula and Table I. By Table I, $(1 + 10\%)^{10} = 2.59374$.

$$\$10,000 = P\left[\frac{(0.1)(2.59374)}{(2.59374) - 1}\right]$$

$$= P(0.1627828)$$

Solving for P,

$$\frac{\$10,000}{0.1627828} = P \quad \text{or} \quad P = \$61,431.55$$

If you choose to receive the present value of the annuity (of ten $10,000 payments), you will get $61,431.55. The present value is simply the amount of money that (deposited now at 10% compounded annually for 10 years) will grow to be the same value as all of the payments and interest they could earn at 10%. (As usual, the present value is less than the future value.)

Example 1 Action Shoes retained a local accounting firm to do bookkeeping and tax work. The contract called for $1000 per quarter for 5 years.

The management of Action Shoes has been unhappy with the accounting firm's service and decides to pay off the contract, which has 4 years remaining. If Action Shoes must pay the present value of the contract at today's interest rate of 14% compounded quarterly, how much will be paid?

SOLUTION $R = \$1000$ per quarter, $i = \dfrac{14\%}{4} = 3\tfrac{1}{2}\%$, and $n = 16$ (4 quarters per year for 4 years remaining in the contract).
Therefore,

$$\$1000 = P\left[\frac{3\tfrac{1}{2}\%(1 + 3\tfrac{1}{2}\%)^{16}}{(1 + 3\tfrac{1}{2}\%)^{16} - 1}\right]$$

By Table IV, we have

$$\$1000 = P[0.082685]$$

$$\frac{\$1000}{[0.082685]} = P$$

and

$$P = \$12{,}094.09.$$

It will cost Action Shoes $12,094.09 to pay off the accounting firm's contract. This is equivalent to paying $16,000 (at $1000 per quarter for the remaining 16 quarters) as scheduled.

Saving for the Future

In Section 14.4, we knew the future value (F) of an annuity and determined the regular payment (R) that we must save to achieve the desired future value. Of course, if we knew R, we could solve for F (given a specific interest rate and time).

Suppose that you put $1000 per quarter into a savings plan paying 9% compounded quarterly. How much would you have after 15 years? We can apply the formula

$$R = F\left[\frac{i}{(1 + i)^n - 1}\right]$$

and solve for F, since $R = \$1000$ per quarter, $i = \dfrac{9\%}{4} = 2\frac{1}{4}\%$ per quarter, and $n = 4 \times 15 = 60$ quarters,

$$\$1000 = F\left[\frac{2\frac{1}{4}\%}{(1 + 2\frac{1}{4}\%)^{60} - 1}\right]$$

$$\$1000 = F\left[\frac{0.0225}{3.80013 - 1}\right]$$

$$\$1000 = F[0.0080353]$$

Solving for F,

$$\frac{\$1000}{0.0080353} = F \quad \text{or} \quad F = \$124,450.22$$

You would have $\$124,450.22$ at the end of 15 years. (*Note*: Since $2\frac{1}{4}\%$ is not in Table V, we had to use the formula and Table I.)

Example 2   Joan has elected to contribute $100 per month to her employer's pension fund. If the fund pays 15% compounded monthly, how much will she have in 5 years?

SOLUTION $R = \$100$ per month, $i = \dfrac{15\%}{12} = 1\frac{1}{4}\%$ per month, and $n = 5 \times 12 = 60$ months. Therefore,

$$\$100 = F\left[\frac{1\frac{1}{4}\%}{(1 + 1\frac{1}{4}\%)^{60} - 1}\right]$$

Since $i = 1\frac{1}{4}\%$ is in Table V, we have

$$\$100 = F(0.011290)$$

Solving for F,

$$\frac{\$100}{0.011290} = F \quad \text{or} \quad F = \$8857.40$$

Joan will have $8857.40 in the pension fund after 5 years.

The formulas we used to solve Examples 1 and 2 can be restated so that division is not necessary.

Present Value of an Ordinary Annuity

$$P = R\left[\frac{(1 + i)^n - 1}{i(1 + i)^n}\right]$$

The values of $\left[\dfrac{(1 + i)^n - 1}{i(1 + i)^n}\right]$ are given in Table VI.

Future Value of an Ordinary Annuity

$$F = R\left[\frac{(1 + i)^n - 1}{i}\right]$$

The values of $\left[\dfrac{(1 + i)^n - 1}{i}\right]$ are given in Table VII.

If your problem requires values of i and/or n that are not contained in Tables VI and VII, use Table I and the formulas.

Example 3 Consider an ordinary annuity of $1000 per year for 5 years at 8% compounded annually.

  a. Find the present value of the annuity.
  b. Find the future value of the amount found in part **a**. (*Hint:* This is a lump sum invested at 8% compounded annually for 5 years. See Section 13.1.)
  c. Find the future value of the annuity.
  d. Compare the answers of parts **b** and **c**.

SOLUTION **a.** $R = \$1000$, $i = 8\%$, $n = 5$. Therefore,

$$P = \$1000\left[\frac{(1 + 8\%)^5 - 1}{8\%(1 + 8\%)^5}\right]$$

By Table VI,

$$P = \$1000\,[3.99271]$$

$$P = \$3{,}992.71$$

b. $P = \$3{,}992.71$, $i = 8\%$, and $n = 5$. Therefore,

$$A = \$3992.71\,(1 + 8\%)^5$$
$$= \$3992.71\,(1.46933)$$
$$= \$5866.60$$

c. $R = \$1000$, $i = 8\%$, and $n = 5$. Therefore,

$$F = \$1000 \left[\frac{(1 + 8\%)^5 - 1}{8\%} \right]$$

By Table VII,

$$F = \$1000 \, [5.866601]$$

$$F = \$5866.60$$

d. The answers to parts **b** and **c** are equal. The present value of an annuity will grow (principal plus interest) to equal the future value of the annuity (payments plus interest).

Exercises 14.5

1. If $R = \$600$, $i = 12\%$ compounded semiannually, and $n = 10$, find the present value (P) of the annuity.

2. If $R = \$800$ and $i = 18\%$ compounded quarterly for 3 years, find P.

3. If $R = \$100,000$ and $i = 8\%$ compounded semiannually for 5 years, find P.

4. If $R = \$600$, $i = 12\%$ compounded semiannually, and $n = 10$, find the future value (F) of the annuity.

5. If $R = \$800$ and $i = 18\%$ compounded quarterly for 3 years, find F.

6. If $R = \$10,000$ and $i = 8\%$ compounded semiannually for 5 years, find F.

7. a. Find the present value of an annuity of $100 payments made each month for 4 years at 12% compounded monthly.
  b. If you invest the amount found in part **a** at 12% compounded monthly for 4 years, how much will you have?
  c. Find the future value of the annuity in part **a**.

8. a. Find the present value of an annuity of $100 payments made each month for 4 years at 18% compounded monthly.
  b. If you invest the amount found in part **a** at 18% compounded monthly for 4 years, how much will you have?
  c. Find the future value of the annuity in part **a**.
  d. If the interest rate is increased, how will it affect the present value of an annuity (assuming all other values remain constant)?
  e. If the interest rate is increased, how will it affect the future value of an annuity (assuming all other values remain constant)?

9. If Carol has 14 car payments of $200 per month remaining to be paid, how much is required to pay off the car today? Assume the loan was at 15% compounded monthly.

10. A contract calls for payments of $2000 per quarter for 5 years with an additional $10,000 due at the end. Find the present value of the contract if the interest rate is 16% compounded quarterly. (*Hint:* Find the present value of the annuity, then find the present value of the $10,000 lump sum, and add.)

11. A contract calls for payments of $500 per month for 2 years and a $4000 lump sum to be paid at the end of 3 years. Find the present value of the contract if the interest rate is 9% compounded monthly.

12. a. Terry Rich wants to establish a scholarship for business students at Metropolis University. A $10,000 scholarship is to be awarded each year for 5 years. If the University Scholarship Board can invest money at 6% compounded annually, how much must Terry Rich donate?

    b. If the Board could get a higher interest rate, how would it affect Terry Rich's donation?

13. Find the future value of an annuity of $500 payments made seminannually for 10 years at 8% compounded semiannually.

14. Find the future value of an annuity of $500 payments made seminannually for 10 years at 12% compounded semiannually.

15. If a person saves $300 per quarter for 6 years at 20% compounded quarterly, what will be the final amount?

16. If a person saves $1000 semiannually for 10 years at 8% compounded semiannually, then invests the resulting amount at 6% compounded continuously for 10 more years, what will be the final amount?

Review Exercises / Chapter 14

1. Jill borrowed $600 to be repaid in 3 monthly payments. She was charged $39 interest.

    a. Find the amount of each payment.
    b. Find the interest per month by the level method.
    c. Find the interest per month by the rule of 78's.
    d. Find the effective rate.
    e. If she repays the loan after 2 months, how much interest did she pay by the level method?
    f. By the rule of 78's?

2. Work problem 1 using interest charged as 24% add-on interest.

3. Ron borrowed $500 at 18% per year compounded monthly. The term of the loan is 3 months.

    a. Find the amount of each payment.
    b. Make an amortization schedule.
    c. Find the dollar amount of interest.
    d. Find the effective rate.

4. Sue wants to save a certain amount each month to purchase furniture costing $1000 in 12 months. If she can earn 12% compounded monthly, how much must she save each month?

5. Duke's Camera Shop borrowed $5000 for 3 years at 5% per year add-on. The loan is to be repaid in 36 monthly payments.
   a. Find the dollar amount of interest.
   b. Find the installment cost.
   c. Find the amount of each payment.
   d. Find the effective rate.

6. Find the payment necessary to amortize a debt of $6000 for 4 years at 9% per year compounded monthly.

7. What quarterly deposit into a sinking fund paying 4% compounded quarterly is necessary to have $10,000 in 8 years?

8. Suppose that the interest on a 24-month loan is apportioned by the rule of 78's. What denominator is used for the fractions of interest?

Chapter Test / Chapter 14

1. Define each of the following terms:
   a. amortization   b. installment plan
   c. installment cost   d. level-payment plan
   e. carrying charge   f. annuity
   g. ordinary annuity   h. effective rate
   i. amortization schedule   j. sinking fund

2. Find the monthly payment required to repay a $3000 loan in 30 months if interest is charged as follows:
   a. 10% carrying charge
   b. 6% add-on
   c. 9% compounded monthly.

3. A debt is to be repaid in 7 equal monthly payments. Find the fractions used for computing the amount of interest each month by the rule of 78's.

4. Suppose you borrow $1000 and make quarterly payments for 2 years. If the amount of interest is $180, what is the effective rate of interest?

5. Find the amount of interest on a $12,000 loan for 5 years at 8% add-on.

6. Find the monthly payment required to pay off the loan in problem 5.

7. Find the effective rate of interest in problem 5.

8. Suppose you borrow $12,000 for 5 years at 12% compounded monthly. Find the monthly payment.

9. Find the effective rate in problem 8.

10. Find the quarterly deposit required to have $20,000 in 5 years at 16% compounded quarterly.

11. Find the future value of an annuity of $250 payments made monthly for 2 years at 12% compounded monthly.

12. Find the present value of a contract calling for payments of $4000 per quarter for 5 years if money is worth 16% compounded quarterly.

13. Your Merry-Go-Round charge account shows a $486.52 balance subject to a 2% interest charge. If you make a $100 payment, how much will go toward reducing the principal?

14. If you save $500 per month for 3 years at 18% compounded monthly, how much will you have?

CHAPTER 15

Stocks and Bonds

INTRODUCTION

One of the fundamental problems a business faces is how to obtain necessary money to begin and continue operations. A company can obtain money (or *financing*) in two ways:

equity financing

1. The company owners can contribute money to the company for use in business operations. This method is known as *equity* or ownership financing and is commonly represented by *stock* transactions. Money is given to the business for use in operations, and the stock received makes the purchaser an owner of the business.*

debt financing

2. Company management can borrow the necessary money for the business from outside lenders. This method is known as *debt* financing and is commonly represented by *bond* transactions.† The bond received by a lender is essentially an "I.O.U." from the company.

Each type of financing has its own advantages and disadvantages. We will examine each type.

15.1 *Bonds*

When a business issues bonds, it is giving a promissory note to the investor (or bond purchaser) in exchange for the cost of the bond. Bonds issued by businesses are called *corporate bonds*. Bonds issued by cities are

---

*A major source of financing is money generated by business operations which is reinvested in the business. This is equity financing, because such money is "given" back to the company by virtue of it not being received by the stockholders as dividends.

†Debt financing also includes "notes" signed on behalf of the business for borrowing money. The mathematics involved in notes has been discussed previously.

called *municipal bonds*. Bonds have the following properties:

definition of bond
terms

1. *A specified interest*—**The bond holder receives money that represents interest for the use of his money. This interest is stated on the bond as a fixed amount (in dollars) or as a percent of the value of the bond. When the interest is stated as a percent of the bond's value, the interest percent is known as the *coupon rate* or *nominal yield*.**
2. *A maturity date*—**On this date the business agrees to repay the amount of money borrowed (*principal*) to the bondholder.**
3. **A *face value* (or *denomination*) is the amount of money borrowed (*principal*) and payable to the bondholder at the maturity date. The face value amount appears on the face of the bond. Bonds are generally issued in $1000 denominations.**

A bondholder becomes a creditor to the business, and he has a priority claim on the assets and earnings of the business. Bond interest (yearly) and face value amounts (at maturity) must be paid regardless of the financial condition of the business. Money can be paid to the business owners (i.e., stockholders) only after all bond expenses are met. If the business must be *liquidated* (i.e., all business assets converted into cash and the operation of the business ended), bondholders receive their money before any payment to the stockholders. Hence, bondholders have a more secure position in insuring the return of money loaned to the business. However, since they are not owners of the business, bondholders receive no additional benefits from exceptional performance of the company. A bondholder will receive only the amounts outlined in the bond he purchased.

bond interest =
coupon rate × face
value

The annual amount of interest paid on a bond is calculated by multiplying the *coupon rate* by the *face value* of the bond. When bond interest is paid more than once a year, the amount of each interest payment can be calculated by dividing the annual interest paid by the number of times each year interest is paid.

Example 1   Tinker's Toy Company issues bonds with a face value of $1000 due and payable in 10 years with a 9% (simple) interest rate. What is the annual amount of interest payment to the bondholder?

SOLUTION   The face value of the bond is $1000 and the coupon rate is 9%. Hence, the amount of interest (I) each year is

$$I = (\$1000 \text{ face value})(9\% \text{ coupon rate})(1 \text{ year})$$

$$= (\$1000)(0.09)(1)$$

$$= \$90 \text{ annual interest}$$

The $90 annual interest in Example 1 will be paid to the bondholder each year for 10 years. In the 10th year the bondholder will also receive $1000, since the bond has matured. Thus, we can see that a bond derives its value from two factors:

1. A sequence of regular payments representing interest.
2. A lump-sum payment (the face value) at maturity.

Example 2   The city of Sunnydale issued bonds in $1000 denominations with a coupon rate of $5\frac{1}{4}\%$ per year paid on June 30 and December 31. Find the amount of interest on a $1000 bond on June 30.

SOLUTION   The annual interest paid on the bond is

$$I = \$1000(5\tfrac{1}{4}\%)$$

$$= \$1000(0.0525)$$

$$= \$52.50 \text{ (per year)}$$

Since interest payments are made twice a year, the amount of interest paid on June 30 is one-half of the annual amount (i.e., $\$52.50 \div 2 = \$26.25$).

Example 3   The Hy Water Utility District issued $1,000,000 in 7% bonds of $1000 denomination. What amount of interest is paid to bondholders each year?

SOLUTION   Since the water district issued $1,000,000 in bonds at 7% per year, the annual amount of interest is

$$I = \$1,000,000(7\%)$$

$$= \$1,000,000(0.07)$$

$$= \$70,000 \text{ (per year)}$$

Exercises 15.1

■ Calculate the annual interest received by a bondholder having each of the following bonds.

	Face Value of Bond	Coupon Rate	Annual Interest
Example:	$1000	10%	$100 (i.e., $1000 × 0.10)
1.	$1000	$8\frac{1}{2}\%$	
2.	$1000	6%	
3.	$1000	$4\frac{3}{4}\%$	

	Face Value of Bond	Coupon Rate	Annual Interest
4.	$1000	7.75%	
5.	$1000	9%	
6.	$500	7%	
7.	$1000	6.25%	
8.	$1000	5.50%	
9.	$10,000	4%	
10.	$1000	$9\frac{1}{4}$%	

■ Interest on the following bonds is paid as shown. Calculate the amount of interest paid *each period* by the bond.

	Face Value of Bond	Coupon Rate	Interest Paid	Amount Received per Period
Example:	$1000	8.4%	Semiannually	$42.00 [i.e., ($1000 × 0.084) ÷ 2]
11.	$1000	4.4%	Semiannually	
12.	$1000	10%	Quarterly	
13.	$1000	5.85%	Annually	
14.	$1000	$9\frac{1}{2}$%	Semiannually	
15.	$1000	6%	Quarterly	
16.	$500	$7\frac{1}{4}$%	Annually	
17.	$100	$2\frac{3}{4}$%	Annually	
18.	$1000	8%	Quarterly	
19.	$1000	5%	Semiannually	
20.	$1000	4.8%	Quarterly	

21. The city of Flat issued $10,000,000 in city services bonds. The bonds are of $1000 denominations and mature in 20 years. The coupon rate is 5.25% paid annually. What is the interest expense on these bonds for 1 year?

22. The Whitewater River Authority has some $1000 bonds ($4\frac{3}{4}$%) outstanding. Interest is payable April 1 and October 1. If you own one of these bonds, how much interest will you receive per year?

15.2 Investing in Bonds

Premiums and Discounts

Bonds are long-lived instruments; that is, the date of maturity is usually several years after the date of issuance. The current yield on a bond is equal to the annual interest (which is fixed) divided by the cost of the bond.

bond yield

> ### Current Yield of Bonds
>
> The current yield of bonds can be calculated by dividing the annual interest payment by the purchase price of the bond. Or,
>
> $$Y_c = \frac{I}{P}$$
>
> where Y_c = current yield
> I = annual interest payment
> P = purchase price of the bond
>
> Current yield is usually stated as a percent.
>
> *Note:* The purchase price (P) may (or may not) be equal to its face value.

Example 1   Acme Investments purchased a $1000 bond paying $75 per year in interest. The price of the bond was $1000. What is the current yield?

SOLUTION   Since $I = 75 and $P = 1000, the current yield

$$Y_c = \frac{$75}{$1000}$$

$$= 0.075 \quad \text{or} \quad 7.5\%$$

The interest rate on a bond is set at the time the bond is issued. This coupon rate will not vary over the life of the bond. Suppose that 20-year bonds are issued with a coupon rate of 9% in denominations of $1000. These bonds would have a current yield of 9% (i.e., $90 ÷ $1000). However, in 5 years, the yield for comparable bonds might be 12%. How could such 9% bonds compete in a market where the current yield is 12%?

The yield on a bond depends on two things:

1. The annual interest paid on the bond (which is fixed).
2. The purchase price of the bond.

Therefore, to change the yield on a bond (and make it competitive in the money market), the purchase price of the bond must change. The amount paid will be the amount necessary to adjust the current yield so that it is comparable to current interest rates.

Example 2   The city of Summit issued 3% bonds of $1000 denomination in 1955. How much would an investor be willing to pay for one of these bonds if comparable bonds are now yielding 9%?

SOLUTION   The annual interest payment on a single bond is \$30 (i.e., \$1000 $\times$ 3%) per year. We want a current yield of 9%. We can use $Y_c = \dfrac{I}{P}$, where $I = \$30$, $Y_c = 9\%$, and P is unknown. Therefore,

$$9\% = \frac{\$30}{P}$$

and, solving for P,

$$P = \frac{\$30}{0.09}$$

$$= \$333.33$$

Hence, an investor would be willing to pay \$333.33.

---

discount: a
reduction in bond
price

We see that when the prevailing interest rate is higher than the coupon rate, investors will not pay face value for the bond. They will *discount* the bond's face value to a price that results in a current yield comparable to the market. The discount in Example 2 is \$666.67 (i.e., \$1000 face value − \$333.33 purchase price).

Conversely, the yield on comparable bonds might fall below the coupon rate of a given bond issue. We would then expect the investor to pay more than the face value.

Example 3   The Z Corporation issued 10% bonds of \$1000 denomination in 1971. Comparable bonds now yield 8%. What price would investors be willing to pay for Z Corporation bonds?

SOLUTION   The annual interest payment on a single bond is \$100. We want a current yield of 8%. We can use $Y_c = \dfrac{I}{P}$ when $I = \$100$, $Y_c = 8\%$, and P is unknown. Therefore,

$$8\% = \frac{\$100}{P}$$

and, solving for P,

$$P = \frac{\$100}{8\%}$$

$$= \frac{\$100}{0.08}$$

$$= \$1250$$

Hence, an investor would be willing to pay \$1250.

Figure 15.1

42 THE WALL STREET JOURNAL, Thursday, January 14, 1982

CORPORATION BONDS
Volume $21,830,000

(A) (B) Bonds		(C) Cur Yld	(D) Vol	(E) High	Low	Close	(F) Net Chg
AMF	10s85	12.	38	83⅜	83¼	83¼	−1¾
AMInt	9⅜95	23.	5	41	41	41	−1
ARA	4⅝s96	cv	13	47¾	47¾	47¾	− ¼
AbbtL	6¼93	11.	4	56⅞	56⅞	56⅞	+1⅝
AlaBn	16.95s99	17.	11	101⅛	100	100	.....
AlaBnc	9½84	11.	7	87⅛	87⅛	87⅛	+ ⅛
AlaP	8½s01	16.	10	52	52	52	+ ⅞
AlaP	8¼s03	16.	1	51⅞	51⅞	51⅞	+1⅝
AlaP	9¾s04	17.	64	59½	58	58	− ¼
AlaP	8¾07	16.	15	54	54	54	+1⅛
AlaP	9¼07	16.	1	56⅜	56⅜	56⅜	− ⅛
AlaP	9⅝08	17.	10	58	58	58	+ ⅞
AlaP	15¼10	17.	12	90⅜	88½	88½	.....
AlaP	17⅜11	18.	97	99	97	97⅞	− ⅜
AlaP	18¼89	17.	78	107¾	104	105	−2¾
AlskH	18⅜01	..	3	103	103	103	−1½
Alexn	5½96	cv	3	48	48	48	− ½
Allgl	9s89	14.	3	66	66	66	− ⅞
Allen	6s87	cv	5	84	84	84	−1
AlsCha	10.35s99	16.	2	65	65	65	−4
Alcoa	6s92	11.	10	55⅛	55⅛	55⅛	.....
Alcoa	9s95	14.	24	66¼	66⅛	66⅛	− ¼
AluCa	9½95	15.	10	64⅜	64⅜	64⅜	+ ⅛
AMAX	8s86	10.	1	79	79	79	.....
AMAX	8½84	9.6	40	88⅛	88⅛	88⅛	−1⅞
AFoP	4.8s87r	7.7	10	62⅛	62⅛	62⅛	.....
AForP	5s30	15.	15	34½	32⅛	32½	−2

New York Exchange Bonds

Wednesday, January 13, 1982

Total Volume $22,030,000

SALES SINCE JANUARY 1

1982	1981	1980
$172,713,000	$152,355,000	$150,751,000

	Domestic Wed	Domestic Tues	All Issues Wed	All Issues Tues
Issues traded	828	883	832	892
Advances	293	253	294	256
Declines	367	450	369	454
Unchanged ..	168	180	169	182
New highs ...	6	4	7	4
New lows	32	26	32	27

Dow Jones Bond Averages

−1980− High	−1980− Low	−1981− High	−1981− Low	−1982− High	−1982− Low		WEDNESDAY −1982−	WEDNESDAY −1981−	WEDNESDAY −1980−
76.61	60.96	65.78	54.99	57.23	56.66	20 Bonds	56.66 − .13	65.77 + .67	73.86 + .05
78.63	59.40	66.18	53.61	55.68	54.83	10 Utilities	54.83 − .25	65.47 + .44	73.33 + .22
74.92	61.55	66.15	56.32	58.95	58.31	10 Industrial	58.50	66.07 + .90	74.40 − .11

Dow Jones bond averages reprinted by permission of Dow Jones & Company, Inc.; all rights reserved.

A. This column gives the company name in abbreviated form. AMF is AMF Incorporated.

B. This column identifies the bond issue. The interest rate and maturity date are used. For example, "10s85" means a bond maturing in 1985 having a 10% coupon rate.

C. This column gives the current yield of the bond. For example, the AMF bond yield is

$$\frac{(\$1000)(0.10)}{\$832.50 \text{ close price}} = 0.120 \quad \text{or} \quad 12.0\%$$

D. This column gives the number of bonds that were sold during the day. AMF sold 38 bonds.

E. The High, Low, and Close columns give the highest and lowest price of the bonds during the day and the price of the bond when the bond exchange closed for the day. AMF sold as high as $83\frac{3}{8}$ ($833.75), as low as $83\frac{1}{4}$ ($832.50), and closed at $83\frac{1}{4}$ ($832.50).

F. This column gives the change in closing price from the previous day's close. AMF was down $1\frac{3}{4}$ from the previous day, so the previous day's close was $83\frac{1}{4} + 1\frac{3}{4}$ or 85 ($850.00).

---

premium: an increase in bond price

In this case, investors are willing to pay a *premium* to obtain a bond with a coupon rate that is higher than current market interest rates. The premium in Example 3 is $250 (i.e., $1250 purchase price − $1000 face value).

bond price is stated
as a percent of face
value

Bond prices are stated as a percent of the bond's face value. For example, a bond price of "97" on a $1000 face value bond means the bond is selling for $970 ($1000 face value × 97%). A bond price stated at "105" would be selling for $1050 ($1000 face value × 105%).

In order to completely familiarize yourself with the concepts that have been discussed about bonds, see Table 15.1.

TABLE 15.1

Bond	Face Value of Bond	Quoted Market Price	Coupon Rate	Bond Dollar Cost	Bond Premium (Discount)	Current Yield
A	$1000	102	8%	$1020 (a)	$20 (b)	7.84% (c)
B	$1000	96	9.5%	$960 (d)	−$40 (e)	9.90% (f)

Computation

Bond A: (a) $1000 face value × 102% market price quote = $1020 bond cost.
 (b) $1020 bond cost − $1000 face value = $20 premium.
 (c) [(8% coupon rate) ($1000 face value)] ÷ $1020 bond cost = 7.84%.

Bond B: (d) ($1000 face value) (96% market price) = $960.
 (e) $1000 face value − $960 market cost = $40 discount or −$40.
 (f) [($1000 face value) (9.5% coupon rate)] ÷ $960 bond cost = 9.90%.

We have discussed the variations in the selling price of bonds and why they occur. The actual "market" for bonds can be determined by reviewing the financial pages of any large newspaper. The current selling price (and other pertinent data) from activity on the New York Exchange will be reported. Review Figure 15.1, an excerpt from *The Wall Street Journal*, giving bond information.

Average Annual Yield to Maturity

Our previous discussions concerning yields on bonds have been in terms of current yield, that is, the amount of interest paid (by the bond) divided by the purchase price of the bond. Now consider the case of an investor who buys a bond and holds it to maturity. He is interested in the overall rate of return on his investment. This rate can be measured by the bond's *average annual yield to maturity* (Y_m).* *The yield to maturity relates the average annual return of the bond and the average amount invested.*

Definition

average annual
return

The *average annual return of a bond* is the fixed amount of interest "adjusted" by any applicable discount or premium.

---

* The total yield to maturity of a bond can be calculated by considering the "stream" of interest payments (an annuity), any premium or discount involved, and the value of the bond at maturity. The total yield can be approximated by the average annual yield, which is much easier to calculate.

For example, if a 10-year, $1000 bond with a 10% coupon rate was purchased for $950 (i.e., at a $50 discount), the investor will receive the face value of $1000 at maturity. Hence, the $50 "increase" in the bond price must be considered. The $50 increase in the bond's price over the 10-year life of the bond equates to a $5 per year increase (i.e., $50 discount ÷ 10 years = $5 per year). Thus, the average annual return on the bond is $100 of fixed interest *plus* the $5 per year increase in the bond's value or $105 per year.

discount accumulation

The $5 per year increase in the bond's value is called *discount accumulation*, because the $50 discount is accumulated over the 10-year life of the bond.

Conversely, a bond purchased at a premium must reflect the excess price of the bond (over its face value). A $1000 bond (10% coupon rate and 10-year life) that is purchased for $1100 (i.e., at a $100 premium) will lose $100 in value over the next 10 years or $10 per year. The average annual return on the bond thus becomes $100 per year in interest *minus* $10 per year premium, or $90. The $10-per-year decrease is called the *premium*

premium amortization

amortization.

The word "adjusted" in the definition of average annual return means *addition* when the bond is purchased at a discount and *subtraction* when the bond is purchased at a premium.

Definition

average amount invested

The *average amount invested* is the *sum* of the face value of the bond and the price the investor paid for the bond *divided* by 2.

For example, if a $1000 bond is purchased for $900, the *average amount invested* is $\dfrac{\$1000 + \$900}{2} = \$950$. Similarly, if a $1000 bond is purchased for $1050, the *average amount* invested is $\dfrac{\$1000 + \$1050}{2} = \$1025$.

Average Annual Yield to Maturity (Y_m) of a Bond

$$Y_m = \frac{\text{average annual return}}{\text{average amount invested}}$$

where   average annual return = dollars of fixed interest per year
plus discount accumulation *or*
minus premium amortization
average amount invested = sum of the bonds' face value and
the price paid by the bondholder all
divided by 2

Example 4   J. J. Jones purchased two bonds. Both have a 5-year remaining life and a 10% coupon rate. He paid $980 for Bond A and $1030 for Bond B. Calculate the yield to maturity for each. Assume a $1000 face value for each.

SOLUTION   Bond A has a $100 annual interest payment (i.e., $1000 × 10%). The *discount accumulation* is $4 per year (i.e., the $20 discount divided by 5 years). Hence, the average annual yield is $100 per year + $4 per year, or $104 per year.

$$\text{The average annual investment is } \frac{\$1000 \text{ face value} + \$980 \text{ price}}{2} = \$990.$$

Therefore, the yield to maturity is

$$Y_m = \frac{\$104}{\$990} = 0.1051 \text{ or } 10.51\%$$

Bond B has an annual interest payment of $100 per year. The *premium amortization* is $6 per year (i.e., the $30 premium divided by 5 years). The average annual yield is $94 per year (i.e., $100 per year − $6 per year).

$$\text{The average annual investment is } \frac{\$1030 + \$1000}{2}, \text{ or } \$1015.$$

Therefore, the yield to maturity is

$$Y_m = \frac{\$94}{\$1015} = 0.0926 \text{ or } 9.26\%$$

There is one remaining item to consider. All previous discussions of bonds assumed that a bond was purchased or sold at the time interest was paid. What happens when a bond is purchased 3 months *after* the last interest payment? The bond buyer will get the full amount of interest at the next payment of interest and the seller will receive nothing. The seller has earned the interest for 3 months because his money was being used for that period of time. The seller receives his interest from the bond buyer in the form of an *adjusted* bond sales price.

Definitions

accrued interest   *Accrued interest* is the amount of interest earned by the owner of a bond from the date of the last interest payment until the date the bond is sold. It is computed by multiplying the annual amount of interest times the fraction of a year the bond was owned and for which no interest has been received.

adjusted bond price   The *adjusted selling price* of a bond is the market price of the bond plus the accrued interest.

Example 5   Mr. Jones owns a $1000 bond with a coupon rate of 10%, which pays annual interest on September 30. He sells the bond on January 1. If the quoted market price of the bond is 98, what amount should Mr. Jones receive?

SOLUTION   The selling price of the bond on January 1 would be $1000 face value × 0.98, or $980. The annual amount of interest for the bond is $1000 face value × 10% coupon rate, or $100. Since Mr. Jones owned the bond from September 30 to January 1, he should receive interest for 3 months, or $\frac{1}{4}$ of a year. That is, Mr. Jones should receive $(\frac{1}{4})(\$100) = \$25$ accrued interest. Hence, the selling price of the bond should be $980 + $25, or $1005.

Example 6   A $10,000 municipal bond has a coupon rate of 5% with interest paid on June 30 and December 31.

    a. If the bond is sold on July 31, what is the *accrued interest*?

    b. If the bond is quoted at a market price of 103, what is the adjusted sales price?

SOLUTION   *a.* The annual amount of interest is $10,000 × 5%, or $500. Since the interest is paid twice a year, each interest payment is $250.

      Since the bond is sold on July 31, 1 month after interest is paid, the accrued interest is $(\frac{1}{6})(\$250) = \$41.67$.

    b. The market value of the bond is $(\$10,000)(103\%) = \$10,300$. Therefore, the *adjusted sales price* is $10,300 + $41.67, or $10,341.67.

Exercises 15.2

■ Compute the premium or discount on the following bonds.

	Face Value	Current Selling Price	Premium (Discount)
Example:	$1000	$985	($15) (i.e., $1000 face value − $985 current price)
1.	$1000	$1030	
2.	$1000	$945	
3.	$1000	$995	
4.	$1000	$1015	
5.	$1000	$1000	

■ Compute the current yield on the following bonds.

	Purchase Price	Annual Interest Paid	Current Yield
Example:	$1000	$50	5.0% $\left(\text{i.e., } \dfrac{\$50 \text{ interest}}{\$1000 \text{ price}}\right)$
6.	$950	$95	
7.	$1030	$85	
8.	$960	$60	
9.	$500	$75	
10.	$1042	$125	

■ Compute the current selling price on the following bonds assuming that the current market interest rate is 9.5%.

	Face Value	Coupon Rate	Current Price
Example:	$1000	8.5%	$894.74 $\left(\text{i.e., } \dfrac{\$85 \text{ interest}}{0.095 \text{ rate}}\right)$
11.	$1000	$10\frac{3}{4}\%$	
12.	$1000	6.25%	
13.	$1000	8.75%	
14.	$500	$4\frac{3}{4}\%$	
15.	$1000	12%	
16.	$1000	$9\frac{1}{4}\%$	

■ Compute the missing information for the following bonds. Round to the nearest tenth.

	Face Value	Quoted Market Price	Coupon Rate	Bond Premium (Discount)	Current Yield
17.	$1000	$985	8%		
18.	$1000		10%	$10	
19.		$460	6.5%	($40)	
20.	$1000		9.25%	($5)	
21.		$675	5.5%	($325)	
22.	$500	$490	$8\frac{3}{4}\%$		

23. HiGear Trucking Company issued $1000 face value bonds in 1973 with a coupon rate of $10\frac{1}{2}\%$. What amount would an investor pay if the current interest rate is 9.5%? What is the premium or discount?

24. You have the option of investing your money in a savings certificate paying 8% or of buying a bond of the High Flyer Aircraft Company. The bond is selling for $975 and has a coupon rate of 7.9% of its $1000 face value. Which would you choose in order to get the greatest current return?

25. Bond A has a current yield of 9%. The bond has a face value of $1000 and is currently selling for $1050. What is the coupon rate on bond A?

26. Zero Corporation bonds of $1000 face value have a coupon rate of 7.5%. The current market quote on these bonds is 97. What is the current yield?

■ Compute the premium or discount and average annual return on the following bonds.

	Face Value	Coupon Rate	Purchase Price	Premium (Discount)	Years to Maturity	Average Annual Return
Example:	$1000	8%	$980	($20)	4	$85 [i.e., ($1000 × 0.08) + ($20 ÷ 4)]
27.	$1000	12.5%	$1060		5	
28.	$1000	$9\frac{3}{4}$%	$1010		2	
29.	$1000	7.5%	$960		10	
30.	$500	6%	$470		5	
31.	$1000	$8\frac{1}{2}$%	$988		4	
32.	$1000	9%	$994		3	

■ Compute the average amount invested for the following bonds.

	Face Value	Purchase Price	Average Amount Invested
Example:	$1000	$980	$990 $\left(\text{i.e., } \dfrac{\$1000 + \$980}{2}\right)$
33.	$1000	$990	
34.	$1000	$1030	
35.	$500	$520	
36.	$1000	$960	
37.	$1000	$984	
38.	$100	$104	

■ Calculate the yield on the following bonds held to maturity.

	Face Value	Coupon Rate	Purchase Price	Years to Maturity	Yield to Maturity
Example:	$1000	10%	$1020	2	8.9%
					$\left[\text{i.e.,}\ \dfrac{(\$1000 \times 0.10) - (\$20 \div 2)}{(\$1000 + \$1020) \div 2}\right]$
39.	$1000	8.5%	$980	4	
40.	$1000	$7\frac{1}{4}$%	$960	5	
41.	$500	4.5%	$400	4	
42.	$1000	10.6%	$1018	3	
43.	$1000	9.9%	$1006	6	
44.	$100	8%	$97	3	

45. Y Not Corporation bonds having a 7.9% coupon rate are currently selling for 92. What is the yield to maturity of their $1000 bonds that have a remaining life of 4 years?

46. Delta Company $1000 bonds have a 10-year life from date of issuance and an $8\frac{3}{4}$% coupon rate. The current market rate on these bonds is 96. The bonds were issued 6 years ago. What would be your yield to maturity if you purchased one of these bonds today?

47. You have some money to invest. You have decided to invest in one of two bonds. Bond A has a coupon rate of $9\frac{1}{4}$% and matures in 6 years. Its quoted price is 97. Bond B has a coupon rate of 10.5% and matures in 4 years. Its quoted price is 104. If both bonds have a face value of $1000 and you plan to keep them until they mature, which bond should you buy? Why?

48. The $1000 bonds of Deep Water Corporation have a market quotation of 104. They mature in 8 years and have a coupon rate of 16%. What would be the yield to maturity on one of these bonds purchased today?

■ Compute the adjusted selling price of the following bonds using the data given.

	Face Value	Quoted Price	Coupon Rate	Dividends Paid	Months since Last Dividend	Adjusted Selling Price
Example:	$1000	103	10%	Semiannually	3	Accrued interest = $100 \times \frac{1}{4}$ = $ 25
						Quoted price = 1030
						$1055
49.	$1000	96	7.2%	Quarterly	2	
50.	$1000	103	6.0%	Semiannually	4	
51.	$1000	106	14.4%	Quarterly	1	
52.	$1000	98	12.0%	Quarterly	2	

	Face Value	Quoted Price	Coupon Rate	Dividends Paid	Months since Last Dividend	Adjusted Selling Price
53.	$1000	99	8.4%	Quarterly	1	
54.	$1000	102	11.0%	Semiannually	3	
55.	$1000	100	13.2%	Quarterly	1	
56.	$1000	99	9.6%	Quarterly	2	
57.	$1000	98	6.0%	Semiannually	5	
58.	$1000	104	10.8%	Quarterly	1	

59. A municipal bond of $1000 face value has a coupon rate of 5.5%. It pays interest semiannually on April 1 and October 1. What will be the total bond interest cost to the city from January to December 31 (per bond)?

60. Mr. Adams has a $1000 face value bond with a coupon rate of 8%. The market quote on the bond is 99. Interest is paid quarterly and was last paid on March 31. On May 15, he offers to sell you the bond for $1010 (i.e., the face value plus accrued interest). Did he state a fair price? Explain.

15.3 *Stock*

Stocks represent owner (or equity) financing. When a business is formed, the owners contribute money to the business for operations. In exchange, they receive shares of stock representing their portion of ownership in the business. As owners of the business, stockholders acquire two things bondholders (creditors) do not have:

1. *Risk*—Stockholders receive a return on their investment (or residual portion of the business if liquidated) *only* after all monies owed to bondholders have been paid. In fact, they receive their returns only after *all* creditor obligations have been paid.
2. *Control*—Stockholders retain the right to manage their business. They do this through their votes at stockholders' meetings.

Several terms used with stocks should be defined:

Definitions

Dividends—Dividends are a return to the stockholder on his investment in the business. Dividends are paid from profits of the business.

Share—A share of stock represents one unit of ownership. It is a fractional part of the total ownership of the business.

Shares outstanding—The outstanding shares of stock represent the total ownership of the company (i.e., the number of shares held by the owners).

Earnings—Earnings are the profits from the operation of the business.

Par value—Par value is the dollar "worth" assigned to each share of stock.

There are two major classifications of stock.

preferred stock

1. *Preferred stock*—Preferred stock has priority over other stock on the assets and earnings of the business (though its priority is behind bonds). Preferred stock might be viewed as a "hybrid bond," since it may have some or all of the following characteristics which greatly reduce risk:

a. Preferred stock has a stated value (par value) which is the amount due to preferred stockholders if the business is liquidated.

b. Preferred stock has a specified dividend, frequently stated as a percent of par value. This dividend must be paid to preferred stockholders before *any* dividends are paid to other stockholders. Payment of these dividends is not guaranteed, however. It is dependent on the success of the business.

c. Preferred stock may have *cumulative* dividends (i.e., *cumulative preferred stock*). This means any dividends not paid on preferred stock in previous years must be paid to preferred stockholders before any dividends are paid to nonpreferred stockholders.

d. Preferred stock may be *convertible* to other stock. The *conversion rate* (i.e., the number of shares of other stock received per share of preferred stock) is stipulated when the preferred stock is issued.

common stock

2. *Common stock*—Common stock represents the remaining ownership of the business. Common stockholders receive dividends only after all debts to creditors and dividends to preferred stockholders have been paid. In the event of liquidation, common stockholders receive a return of their investment only after all other obligations of the company have been paid. Common stock may or may not have a par value. In either case, it is of little value in the case of common stock.

In Chapter 10, we discussed distribution of profits for a sole proprietorship and partnerships. We will now discuss the distribution of profits for a corporation. This distribution comes in the form of dividends. We will be using the concepts previously discussed.

Example 1

The Fox Company has 10,000 shares of 8% preferred stock ($100 par value) and 100,000 shares of common stock outstanding. The company earned $600,000 last year. The company management feels that $350,000 must be reinvested in the business.

a. How much money is available for dividends?
b. How much money will be paid to preferred stockholders?
c. How much money is available for dividends to common stockholders?
d. How much dividend will be paid per share of common stock?
e. How much did Fox Company earn per share of common stock?

SOLUTION

a. Fox Company earned $600,000. Of this amount, $350,000 must be reinvested. Hence, $250,000 ($600,000 − $350,000) is available for dividends.

b. Preferred stockholders will receive a dividend of 8% of the par value of preferred stock. That is, $100 par value × 8% = $8.00 dividend per preferred share. There are 10,000 shares of preferred stock; hence $80,000 (10,000 shares × $8.00 dividend) will be paid to preferred stockholders.

c. Since dividends for common stockholders are paid only after dividends to preferred stockholders, then

$250,000	available for dividends
− 80,000	dividends on preferred stock
$170,000	available for dividends on common stock

d. There is $170,000 available for dividends for 100,000 shares of common stock. Hence, the dividend per share of common stock will be

$$\frac{\$170,000}{100,000} \quad \text{or} \quad \$1.70 \text{ per share of common stock}$$

e. The earnings per share of common stock is $600,000 ÷ 100,000 shares of common stock or $6.00 per share.
Note: Earnings per share is an important figure which is frequently encountered.

Exercises 15.3

■ Use the following information for Baker Manufacturing Company in Problems 1–5.

Baker Manufacturing Company
   Earnings for the year—$3,000,000
   Amount reinvested in the business—$2,000,000
   Preferred stock—20,000 shares of 6% ($100 par value)
   Common stock—500,000 shares

1. What are the earnings per share of common stock for Baker Manufacturing?

2. What total amount will be paid to preferred shareholders?

3. How much money is available for dividends on common stock?

4. What is the dividend per share of common stock?

5. What is the dividend per share of preferred stock?

■ The Anders Company has 1000 shares of 7% preferred stock ($100 par value) and 25,000 shares of common stock. Earnings per share of common stock were $4.00. The company management reinvested 75% of total earnings in the business. All remaining money was paid as dividends. Use this information in working problems 6–9.

6. What were the total earnings for the company?

7. What was the dividend per share of common stock?

8. What amount was paid as dividends to preferred stockholders?

9. What amount was reinvested in the business?

15.4 *Investing in Stocks*

When we discussed investing in bonds, we made little mention of the actual mechanics of how the bond sales were accomplished. That discussion was reserved until now; bond sales are handled in a manner similar to stock sales, and since stock sales represent a larger volume of transactions, we will discuss them. The sale of stock is accomplished basically like any other sales transaction—an owner of stock sells to a buyer of stock at a mutually agreeable price. However, since owners and potential buyers of stock are few (in relation to the total population) and are located all over the country, the actual sale is made through designated representatives (*stock brokers*) in *stock markets*. The New York Stock Exchange (NYSE) and American Stock Exchange (ASE) are the major organized stock markets. They are physical entities with designated members and an elected, governing body. Most of the larger stock brokerage firms (such as E. F. Hutton, Merrill Lynch, and Paine Weber) are members of the exchanges and can buy and sell securities on those exchanges. For example, an E. F. Hutton customer in Houston might want to sell 100 shares of stock in American Telephone and Telegraph (AT&T). At the same time, a Merrill Lynch customer in San Francisco might want to buy 100 shares of AT&T. Each firm's broker would communicate his customer's request to the firm's representatives on the exchange in New York. The exchange members with "sell orders" offer shares of stock for sale; these shares of stock are bid for by the members with "buy orders." The stock exchanges essentially operate as *auction markets*.

Stocks that are traded less frequently or that have fewer stockholders (the majority of the stocks in terms of the number of companies issuing stock) are traded in the *over the counter* (OTC) markets. The OTC markets consist of (1) some stockbrokers who hold inventories of over the counter stocks and who are said to "make a market" for these stocks, and (2) the numerous brokers who act as agents in bringing buyer and seller together.

Although most stock transactions occur through brokers, the sale transaction can be made directly between the buyer and seller.

Stockbrokers, as any agents, charge for their services. This charge (or *brokerage commission*) is dependent on several factors:

1. The brokerage firm involved—The larger brokers usually have market analysts and research members to assist in advising clients about buying and selling particular stocks. "Discount" brokers, on the other hand, simply execute buy/sell orders in accordance with your instructions; no market research advice is available.
2. The size of the stock transaction—Stocks are usually sold in *lots* of 100 shares. Any sale of less than 100 shares (an *odd lot* sale) has a higher broker's fee. Closely related to the size of the transaction in shares is the size of the transaction in dollars. A transaction of 100 shares at $100 per share (or $10,000) will have less brokerage cost (percentage-wise) than a transaction of 100 shares at $5 per share (or $500).

With this background in mind, let us examine some stock transactions.

Example 1   Ms. Ringo wants to purchase 100 shares of General Motors stock. She placed an order with her broker to buy 100 shares at the current price. Ms. Ringo's broker purchased the stock at $55 per share. He charged a brokerage commission of $100.
  a. How much did Ms. Ringo pay in order to buy stock?
  b. What was her total cost per share?

SOLUTION   *a.* Ms. Ringo paid:

$55 per share × 100 shares = $5500
plus a brokerage fee   =   100
or a total of $5600

  b. The total cost per share was $5600 ÷ 100 shares = $56 per share.

Every investor has a reason for investing his money in one stock rather than another. The primary reason is to increase the value of his holdings. The potential for an increase in value comes from two factors:

1. A change in the market price of the stock. The old adage of "buy low, sell high" is still the investor's goal.
2. The rate of return (or yield) on the stock through dividend payments.

We will now examine some measures used by investors in making investment decisions.

Definitions

If the price per share has increased above the purchase price, the purchaser is said to have a *gain* on the stock.

If the price per share has decreased below the purchase price, the purchaser is said to have a *loss* on the stock.

stock gain or loss

Gain and loss are measured in dollar values.

The *percent gain or loss* on investment is the gain or loss per share of stock divided by the original purchase price per share; that is,

$$\frac{\text{gain or loss per share}}{\text{original price per share}} = \text{percent gain or loss}$$

Example 2

A share of common stock in the Winged Aircraft Company was quoted at $32 per share. A week later the same stock was quoted at $27 per share. Find the amount of loss and the percent loss.

SOLUTION

The amount of loss per share is $5 (i.e., $32 − $27). The percent loss is $\frac{\$5}{\$32} = 0.156$, or 15.6%.

Example 3

Jason bought 100 shares of stock at $15 per share. He kept it for 1 year and sold it for $25 per share. His brokerage commission was $45 when he bought and $60 when he sold the stock. What was the amount of gain per share and the percent gain?

SOLUTION

The cost of the stock was $15.00 per share plus $0.45 commission (i.e., $45 ÷ 100 shares) or $15.45 per share. The amount realized from the sale of the stock was $2440 ($25.00 × 100 shares = $2500 *less* the brokerage commission of $60). Therefore, the price received per share at the time of sale was $24.40 ($2440 ÷ 100 shares).

The amount of gain per share is

$$
\begin{array}{lll}
& \text{Selling price} & \$24.40 \\
\text{less} & \text{Purchase price} & 15.45 \\
\hline
& & \$8.95
\end{array}
$$

and the percent gain is $\frac{\$8.95}{\$15.45} = 0.5793$ or 57.9%.

If the stockholder receives a dividend, it must be considered in the calculation. The amount of the dividend per share must be *added* to the change in price per share (i.e., the gain or loss) *before* dividing by the original cost per share.

Example 4

David purchased 100 shares of stock at $20 per share and paid a brokerage commission of $35. He kept it for 1 year and sold it for $23 per share. His selling brokerage commission was $45. During the year, he received a dividend of $1 per share. Find the percent gain on investment.

SOLUTION   The gain per share of stock is the amount received from the sale of the stock less the original cost. That is,

Amount Received	*Original Cost*
$23.00 (selling price)	$20.00 (purchase price)
− 0.45 (brokerage +	0.35 (brokerage
commission, i.e.,	commission, i.e.,
$45 ÷ 100 shares)	$35 ÷ 100 shares)
$22.55	$20.35

To the gain per share of $2.20 (i.e., $22.55 − $20.35) we must add the dividend of $1.00 per share. The percent gain is thus $\dfrac{\$2.20 + \$1.00}{\$20.35} = 0.157$ or 15.7%.

Investors consider the current rate of dividend payments in making investment decisions. Dividends are related to the price of the stock to obtain a yield (or rate of return) on investment.

Definition

stock yield   The *yield (or rate of return) on a stock* **is the current dividend divided by the current market price. The yield is given as a percent.**

Example 5   A Corporation stock is selling for $27 a share. It pays a dividend of $1.17 per share. B Company pays $2.00 per share in dividends and is selling for $52.50. Which stock has the greatest yield (or rate of return)?

SOLUTION   The yield on each stock is the dividend divided by the market price. Hence, the respective yields are:

	A Corp.	*B Corp.*
$\text{Yield} = \dfrac{\text{dividend}}{\text{market price}}$		
=	$\dfrac{\$1.17}{\$27.00}$	$\dfrac{\$2.00}{\$52.50}$
=	0.0433	0.0381
=	4.33%	3.81%

Hence, A Corporation has a greater yield.

As you would expect, the market for stock changes daily. The stock activity on the major exchanges is reported daily in the financial section of most large newspapers. Figure 15.2 shows the information given on stock activity by *The Wall Street Journal.*

Figure 15.2

44 THE WALL STREET JOURNAL, Thursday, January 14, 1982

Wednesday's Volume
56,890,160 Shares; 122,600 Warrants

TRADING BY MARKETS

	Shares	Warrants
New York Exchange	49,130,000	122,600
American Exchange	....	....
Midwest Exchange	2,951,200	....
Pacific Exchange	1,986,800	....
Nat'l Assoc. of Securities Dealers	1,242,960	....
Philadelphia Exchange	900,600	....
Boston Exchange	354,200	....
Cincinnati Exchange	195,400	....
Instinet System	129,000	....

NYSE – Composite

Volume since Jan. 1:	1982	1981	1980
Total shares	435,008,722	500,516,675	453,026,500
Total warrants	867,200	1,442,300	1,647,300

New York Stock Exchange

Volume since Jan. 1:	1982	1981	1980
Total shares	372,070,262	443,049,795	402,271,740
Total warrants	867,200	1,442,300	1,647,100

MOST ACTIVE STOCKS

	Open	High	Low	Close	Chg.	Volume
Amer T&T	60	60¼	58⅞	59	− ¾	1,154,700
IBM	57⅞	58¼	57	57⅜	− ⅛	914,400
Permian	11	11	10¾	10¾	− ⅛	762,100
Woolworth	18	18⅛	17½	17½	− ⅝	699,900
Exxon s	30	30½	29⅞	30⅛	+ ⅛	556,300
SuperOil s	32	32⅝	31¾	32⅛	+ ¼	549,800
StdOilInd	46⅜	47⅝	45⅜	45⅞	− ⅜	498,500
WarnrCom	54⅞	55½	54⅛	54½	+ ⅛	487,200
AmaxInc	41¼	42	39	40½	− 3⅛	455,900
RCA	17¼	17¼	16⅝	16¾	− ⅝	451,600
Sony Corp	16⅞	16⅞	16	16⅛	− ⅝	429,000
Gen Motors	39	39⅝	37⅞	38	− ¼	388,600
Smithkline	62½	62½	59¼	59½	− 3⅛	388,500
LTV Corp	14⅝	15	13¾	14	− ⅝	386,000
Tandy s	32⅞	33⅛	32⅛	32⅛	− ½	370,200

NYSE-Composite Transactions

Wednesday, January 13, 1982

Quotations include trades on the American, Midwest, Pacific, Philadelphia, Boston and Cincinnati stock exchanges and reported by the National Association of Securities Dealers and Instinet

(A) 52 Weeks High	Low	(B) Stock	(C) Div.	(D) Yld %	(E) P-E Ratio	(F) Sales 100s	(G) High	low	Close	(H) Net Chg.
		– A–A–A –								
14¼	6⅛	AAR	.44	5.7	8	23	8	7¾	7¾	− ¼
52¼	33⅝	ACF	2.76	7.6	11	281	36⅜	35½	36⅛	+ ⅝
28½	19⅜	AMF	1.36	6.1	25	1725	23⅞	22¼	22¼	− 1¾
16⅞	3⅜	AM Intl		..	..	243	4⅜	4⅛	4⅛	− ⅛
7¾	3¾	APL		..	..	28	4¾	4¾	4¾	− ⅛
37¼	23¾	ARA	2	7.6	7	25	27¼	26¼	26¼	− ¼
61	40	ASA	5a	13.	..	808	39¾	d38⅜	38½	− 1⅞
36⅝	11½	AVX	.32	2.5	..	107	13¼	12⅝	12⅝	− ⅛
32¼	23⅝	AbtLb s	.72	2.8	13	660	26¼	25½	25⅞	+ ½
31	17¼	AcmeC	1.40	6.6	9	31	21⅜	21⅛	21⅛	− ⅛
6¾	4	AdmDg	.04	.9	6	18	4½	4½	4½	.....
16⅛	12¾	AdaEx	1.88e	13.	..	29	14¾	14⅝	14¾	....
7⅛	4⅜	AdmMI	20e	3.4	6	40	5⅞	5⅞	5⅞	+ ⅛
31	14	AMD s		..	23	1753	16⅝	15⅞	15⅞	− ⅜
47⅝	30	AetnLf	2.32	5.6	7	836	42⅜	41⅜	41⅜	− ⅞
21	13⅞	Ahmns	1.20	8.9	338	191	13⅞	d13½	13½	− ⅜
4⅜	2⅛	Aileen		..	..	3	2⅞	2¾	2¾	− ⅛
48⅞	34	AirPrd	.80	2.3	8	190	35⅞	35⅜	35⅜	− ⅜
22	8¾	AirbFrt	.60	6.7	12	16	9	8⅞	9	− ⅛
15½	9¼	Akzona	.80	7.9	9	107	10¼	10	10⅛	.....
22½	17	AlMoa n		..	22	131	17⅞	17¾	17⅞	.....
27¼	23¼	AlaP pfA	3.92	16.	..	40	24½	23¾	24½	+ ¼
6⅞	5½	AlaP dpf	.87	15.	..	21	5¾	5¾	5¾	.....
61½	53	AlaP pf	9	16.	..	z50	55	55	55	− ⅛
17	13⅛	Alagsco	1.60	10.	5	1	15⅜	15⅜	15⅜	.....
34½	15½	AlskInt	.60	3.8	4	183	17	16	16	− ⅜
38⅞	22⅝	Albany	1.20	4.7	7	2	25½	25½	25½	.....
16¼	9¾	Alberto	.50	4.2	8	22	12	11¾	12	+ ⅜
29⅝	20¼	Albtsn	.88	3.5	8	13	25½	25	25	− ½
40	19⅝	Alcan	1.80	8.8	5	1061	20⅞	20⅜	20⅜	− ⅜
21⅝	16⅜	AlcoSt	s1.08	5.9	6	40	18⅞	18⅜	18⅜	− ½
18⅜	9⅜	Alexdr		..	..	47	9⅜	d 9¼	9⅜	.....
50¼	27½	AllgCp	1.08	2.3	8	20	47½	47⅛	47⅛	− ⅜
22¾	17⅝	AlgCp pf	2.86	15.	..	4	19½	19	19	− ½
55⅜	27⅝	AlgInt	1.40	5.1	7	143	28⅜	d27¼	27¼	− 1⅛
77	74⅝	Algi pfC	11.25	15.	..	156	75	d74¼	74¼	− ½
17¼	13⅛	AllgPw	2.16	13.	5	870	16½	16¼	16⅜	.....

A. The "52 Weeks High-Low" column gives the highest and lowest price for which the stock has sold within the last 52 weeks. Prices are given in $\frac{1}{8}$'s of a dollar. Alcan Aluminum sold for a high of \$40.00 (i.e. 40) and a low of \$19.63 (i.e. $19\frac{5}{8}$) during the last 52 weeks.

B. The "Stocks" column gives the name of the company, frequently in abbreviated form. "Alcan" is the company of Alcan Aluminium Ltd.

C. The "Div." column shows the dividend (in dollars) the company is currently paying. Alcan Aluminium is paying \$1.80 per share of stock.

(continued on p. 364)

D.   The "Yld %" column gives the current yield of the stock, that is, the current dividend divided by the current market price, expressed as a percent. Alcan Aluminum is yielding

$$\frac{\$1.80 \text{ dividend}}{\$20.38 \text{ current price}} = 0.0883 \quad \text{or} \quad 8.8\%$$

E.   The "P-E Ratio" column gives the price-to-earnings ratio of the company. It is obtained by dividing the current price of the stock by the earnings per share of the company. Alcan Aluminum stock is currently selling for five times more than the company is earning on each share.

F.   The "Sales 100s" column gives the volume of stock sold for the day. The figure shown must be multiplied by 100 to obtain the actual number of shares sold. Alcan Aluminum had 106,100 shares traded on January 13.

G.   The "High, Low, Close" columns give the highest and lowest price of the stock during the day's trading, and the price at the close of the exchange. Alcan Aluminum sold as high as $20.88 (i.e., $20\frac{7}{8}$) as low as $20.38 (i.e., $20\frac{3}{8}$) and was selling for $20.38 (i.e., $20\frac{3}{8}$) when the exchange closed.

H.   The "Net Chg." column tells the change in the stock's price at the close of the day vs. the close on the previous day. Alcan Aluminum closed $0.38 (i.e. $\frac{3}{8}$) lower on January 13 than it was on January 12 (i.e., it closed at $20.75 or $20\frac{3}{8} + \frac{3}{8} = 20\frac{3}{4}$ on January 12).

Exercises 15.4

■ Compute the amount and percent of gain or loss on the following stocks. Ignore brokerage commissions in problems 1–8.

	Stock	Purchase Price	Current Price	Amount of Gain (*Loss*)	Percent Gain (*Loss*)
Example:		$100	$105	$5 (i.e., $105–$100)	5% (i.e., $5 gain ÷ $100 purchase price)
1.	A	$76	$38		
2.	B	$12	$16		
3.	C	$22	$22		
4.	D	$47.50	$95		
5.	E	$75	$50		
6.	F	$90	$99		

7.   If stock A had paid a $3.80 dividend, what would have been the correct answer?

8.   If stock F had paid a $4.50 dividend, what would have been the correct answer?

9. Assuming the brokerage commission for 100 shares of stock B was $35 to buy and $42 to sell, what would have been the correct answer?

10. Assuming the brokerage commission for 100 shares of stock D was $65 to buy and $135 to sell, what would have been the correct answer?

11. Marsha purchased 100 shares of Boomer Corporation stock for $78.50 per share plus brokerage commission ($85). Six months later she sold the stock for $84.75 per share from which she had to pay $95 in brokerage commission. During the 6 months, she received a dividend of $0.25 per share. What was her gain on the stock (amount and percent)?

12. Allen bought 100 shares of Nova Manufacturing Company for $2335 (inclusive of brokerage commission). During the year he held the stock, he received $0.75 per share in dividends. He then sold the stock for $19.50 per share, not including brokerage commission of $47. What was his gain or loss (amount and percent)?

■ Calculate the rate of return on the following stocks.

	Stock	Current Price	Dividend	Yield or Rate of Return
Example:		$50	$5	$10\% \left(\text{i.e., } \dfrac{\$5}{\$50} \right)$
13.	K	$18	$1.80	
14.	L	$130	$1.30	
15.	M	$87	$4.35	
16.	N	$19	$0.38	
17.	O	$56	$4.20	
18.	P	$72	$2.88	
19.	Q	$33	$2.64	
20.	R	$287	$1.44	

■ Choose the best stock to buy in order to get the greatest yield.

		Stock A	Stock B	Stock C
Example:	Price	$48.50	$92.25	$13.50
	Dividend	$3.65	$7.85	$1.00
	Yield	$\dfrac{\$3.65}{\$48.50} = 7.5\%$	$\dfrac{\$7.85}{\$92.25} = 8.5\%$	$\dfrac{\$1.00}{\$13.50} = 7.4\%$
21.	Price	$192.00	$36.00	$19.75
	Dividend	$7.80	$2.10	$1.80
22.	Price	$43.50	$18.75	$64.50
	Dividend	$0.75	$1.10	$2.05
23.	Price	$19.25	$28.25	$47.00
	Dividend	$0.25	$1.00	$3.60
24.	Price	$134.00	$78.50	$38.75
	Dividend	$2.75	$4.00	$2.10

15.5 Stocks vs. Bonds—Summary

Let us review some of the advantages and disadvantages of stocks vs. bonds. We will do so by viewing several categories from the viewpoint of both the stockholder and the bondholder.

Category	Stock (Equity)	Bond (Debt)
Risk	Stock has a greater risk, since obligations to all creditors (including bondholders) must be fulfilled before stockholders receive any return. This risk is true in liquidation or dispersion of operating profits (dividends). In addition, preferred stockholders take precedence over common stockholders.	Bondholders have less risk since their claims on the business (as represented by the face value of the bond or bond dividend) must be paid prior to dispersal of any money to stockholders. Bonds also have a definite maturity date, at which time the business must pay the face value.
Income	Stockholders have a variable income. The amount they receive depends on how the business did in the operating year. If earnings were poor, they may receive nothing; however, if earnings were good, they may receive a significant return.	Bondholders receive a fixed income in the amount stated by the bond. They *must* receive this amount regardless of the earnings of the company. However, they do not receive any additional income if the business has a year of superior earnings.
Control	Stockholders retain the right to control the direction of the business through their votes. Hence, management of the business rests with them or the management personnel they elect.	Bondholders usually have no voting rights; hence they have no control over the operation of the business.

Review Exercises / Chapter 15

1. Wonder Works' latest bond issue carries a 10.8% coupon rate on $1000 bonds. Interest is paid quarterly at the end of the calendar quarter (i.e., March, June, etc.). If you purchased a bond on October 1, how much interest would you receive for the year?

2. Bonds on the Y Company are selling at a $50 premium. The bonds have a 10.5% coupon rate and are of $500 face value. What rate are the bonds currently yielding?

3. A $10,000 bond having a coupon rate of 12% is currently quoted on the market at 104. Interest is paid semiannually on April 1 and October 1. What would be a fair price for the bond on September 1? (Ignore brokerage commissions.)

4. Alpha Manufacturing bonds have a 7.2% coupon rate on the $500 face value. The current market quote is 97. Interest is paid annually on December 31. What should the bond sell for on October 1? (Ignore brokerage commissions.)

5. Which stock has the greatest yield?

	Stock A	Stock B	Stock C
Price	$27.50	$213.80	$2.00
Dividend	$ 2.50	$ 5.60	$0.38

6. You own a $1000 bond with a coupon rate of $8\frac{3}{4}\%$. How much interest will you receive each time dividends are paid if dividends are paid (**a**) annually (**b**) semiannually, (**c**) quarterly?

7. The Blue Sky Company issued $1000 bonds in 1978 with a coupon rate of $8\frac{1}{2}\%$. How much should an investor pay for a bond today if the current interest rate is $14\frac{1}{4}\%$? How much is the premium or discount? (Ignore brokerage commissions.)

8. The Limited Horizons Corporation bonds have a coupon rate of $6\frac{1}{4}\%$. The $1000 bonds are currently quoted at $86\frac{1}{2}$. What is the yield to maturity for the bonds if their remaining life is 6 years?

9. You own a $1000 bond with a coupon rate of $7\frac{3}{4}\%$. The market quote on the bond is 92 and interest is paid semiannually (on April 1 and October 1). If you sell the bond today (June 1), how much should you receive? (Ignore brokerage commissions.)

10. The Magnus Company stock is currently selling for $37.50 per share. Assuming that the brokerage commission for 100 shares is $40, what would be your cost per share if you bought 100 shares?

11. Drillco Inc. stock is now selling for $12.25 per share. Nine months ago, it was selling for $18.50. Dividends during this period totaled $0.60 per share. If brokerage commissions were $42 to buy and $35 to sell, how much would you have lost if you had purchased 100 shares?

12. Nathan bought 200 shares of HAL Computing Corporation for $10,600 (inclusive of brokerage commission). Today he sold 100 shares for $48.75 per share and paid a brokerage commission of $105. If his dividends were $0.85 per share, how much did Nathan make or lose on HAL Computing?

Chapter Test / Chapter 15

1. Define the following terms
    a. coupon rate   **b.** face value
    c. premium   **d.** yield to maturity
    e. discount   **f.** dividends
    g. accrued interest   **h.** brokerage commission

2. Quinto Corporation $1000 face value bonds are selling to yield 12.5%. If the coupon rate is 9.5%, what is the current market price of Quinto bonds?

3. You wish to purchase one of two bonds. Bond A is selling for a $10 premium (on its $1000 face value). It has a coupon rate of 9.75%. Bond B also has a $1000 face value but is selling at an $80 discount. The coupon rate on bond B is 8.5%. Which bond would you buy (ignoring brokerage commission) to obtain the maximum current yield?

4. The J&B Value Company issued $1000 bonds which now have 6 years of remaining life and are quoted on the market at 94. The coupon rate is 8.0%. What would be your yield to maturity on one of these bonds, ignoring brokerage commission?

5. On September 1, you purchase a $1000 face value bond issued by the Bummer Corporation. It has a 10% coupon rate with interest paid on the calendar quarter. The bond is currently quoted at 98. Assuming a brokerage commission of $10, how much should you pay for the bond?

■ The Paragon Company has 10,000 shares of 8% ($100 par value) preferred stock and 50,000 shares of common stock outstanding. This year's earnings per share of common stock were $6.50. Company management reinvested $145,000 in the business; the remaining earnings were paid as dividends. Given this information, answer questions 6–8.

6. What were the total earnings of the Paragon Company?

7. What was the total amount paid in dividends to preferred stockholders? What was the dividend per share?

8. What were the total amount and the amount per share paid to common stockholders as dividends?

9. Elisha purchased 100 shares of Lotsa Luky Company. She paid $22.50 per share plus a brokerage commission of $105 on the sale. She recently sold the stock for $24.75 per share with a brokerage commission of $120. What was her gain or loss on this stock (amount per share and percent)?

10. Ralph bought 100 shares of Wilder Corporation for $2875 (inclusive of brokerage commission). During the year he held the stock, he received a dividend of $0.68 per share. He sold the stock for $30.50 per share, not including the brokerage commission of $130. What was his gain or loss (amount per share and percent)?

11. You purchased a stock (100 shares) for $22.25 per share and paid a brokerage commission of $80. The company paid its annual dividend of $1.26 per share just prior to your purchase. At what price per share will you sell the stock if you want to receive a total return of 20%? (Assume you sell before dividends are paid again and that the selling brokerage commission will total $130.)

Cumulative Review Exercises

1. If money is worth 6% compounded quarterly, would you prefer to have $1000 now or $1055 a year from now?

2. Which of the following interest rates would you prefer to pay? Which would you prefer to charge?

    a. 8% simple interest.
    b. 8% bank discount.
    c. 8% compounded semiannually.
    d. 8% compounded quarterly.
    e. 8% compounded continuously.

3. A $600 purchase is to be repaid in 5 equal monthly payments over the next 5 months with a $30 carrying charge.

    a. Find the amount of each payment.
    b. Find the interest per payment by the rule of 78's.
    c. Find the effective rate.

4. A $600 loan is to be repaid in 5 equal monthly payments at a rate of 9% per year compounded monthly. Make an amortization schedule.

5. Linda wants to purchase a new living room suite that sells for $1200. She plans to make 12 monthly payments over the next year. Stick's Furniture has a $100 carrying charge. Wood's Furniture charges interest at an effective rate of 18%. Where should she purchase the furniture?

6. Mr. Rich has $950 to invest. He can purchase a 10-year bond with a face value of $1000 and a coupon rate of 5% at a market quote of 95 or he can put his money in a savings account paying 6% simple interest. If he can hold the bond to maturity, which investment would give the greatest return?

7. A stock purchased for $50 per share was sold a year later at $52 per share. During the year, the stock paid a dividend of $0.50 per share. Find the percent gain.

8. An investor can purchase stock X selling for $30 per share with a current dividend of $1 per share or stock Y selling for $50 per share with a current dividend of $1.80 per share. Which has the greatest rate of return?

9. Suppose that you borrow $2000 at 5% bank discount to be repaid in 1 year. The money you receive is invested at $5\frac{1}{4}$% compounded daily. Will you make any money; if so, how much?

10. What quarterly deposit must be made into an account paying 6% compounded quarterly to have $600 in 18 months?

11. How long will it take to double your money if it is invested at 8% compounded annually? Use the rule of 72.

12. Find the future value of $2500 invested for 365 days at 10.55% compounded daily. Assume the daily rate is based on a 360-day year.

13. Find the annual percentage rate of 9% compounded daily using the 360/365 method.

14. What is the present value of a 5-year contract paying $2000 quarterly if the current interest rate is 20% compounded quarterly?

15. If you save $50 per month for 3 years at 12% compounded monthly, what will be the future value?

16. Suppose that you sell $2000 worth of merchandise and accept a 9-month promissory note at 16% simple interest. Three months later, you discount the note to the finance company at a 12% discount. How much do you receive for the note?

17. What is the term of a loan made on June 13 and due on November 17?

18. If you purchase a new car for $14,000 and pay interest of 5% add-on for 5 years, what will be your monthly payment?

19. If you purchase a new car for $14,000 and pay interest of 9% compounded monthly for 5 years, what will be your monthly payment?

20. Find the APR for the loan in problem 20.

21. Find the APR of 15% compounded continuously.

22. Find the APR of 15% compounded daily based on a 365-day year.

23. Find the APR of 15% compounded daily based on a 360-day year.

24. The EZ Corporation bonds have a current yield of 12%. The bonds have a $1000 face value and are currently selling for $1125. What coupon rate do the bonds carry?

25. The $1000 face value bonds of Zero Company have a market quotation of 98. They mature in 4 years and have a coupon rate of 10%. What would be the yield to maturity if you purchased one of these bonds?

26. William James purchased a $1000 face value bond with a coupon rate of 9.5%. Interest is paid semiannually, and it was last paid on December 31. On April 1, William sold the bond (the market price was 99) and paid $15 in brokerage commission. How much should he receive from the sale of the bond?

27. Jose purchased 100 shares of Grand Corporation for $62.50 per share plus a brokerage commission of $195. Eight months later, he sold the stock for $88.50 per share less $225 in brokerage commission. During this period, Jose received a dividend of $0.35 per share. What was Jose's gain (amount and percent) per share of stock?

28. Celeste bought 200 shares of Magco Inc. for $8612 (inclusive of her brokerage commission). She sold 100 shares for $45.25 per share, and she paid a selling brokerage commission of $160 on the sale. If Celeste's dividends during the time she owned the stock were $1.20, how much (amount and percent) did she make or lose per share of Magco?

Part Four

Mathematics in Everyday Living

O V E R V I E W

This section is oriented toward some of the mathematical problems encountered in daily living. Chapter 16 (Wages and Adjustments) discusses the ways in which an employee may be compensated for his work. In addition, the various deductions that are withheld by the employer are mentioned.

Having earned the money, an individual is faced with many decisions on how to spend it. The remaining chapters discuss two of the "certainties" of these decisions—death and taxes. Sales taxes, property taxes, and income taxes (Chapter 17) are presented to aid in understanding how the individual supports some of the governmental services with which he is provided. Chapter 18 (Insurance) presents some of the alternatives an individual may consider to protect himself and his heirs from financial hardship in case things do not go "as planned."

CHAPTER 16

Wages and Adjustments

INTRODUCTION

Employees and employers share a common (and significant) interest in the compensation plan of a business. For the employee, the amount received as "pay" represents an exchange for a major part of his nonsleeping time. For the employer, payroll can represent a significant portion of the business operating expense. The ways employees can be paid are limited only by the imaginations of the employees and employers. Pay can be based on (1) the number of hours worked, (2) the amount of work done, (3) specific duties assigned, or (4) any combination of these methods.

We will consider compensation from the employee's viewpoint: how much the employee earns (his *gross pay*) and how much he takes home (his *net pay*) after all deductions are subtracted. We will also consider compensation from the employer's viewpoint. The employer's expenses for employee compensation can include much more than the amount paid to the employee. The employer must pay certain taxes and frequently provides fringe benefits (such as hospitalization insurance, life insurance, and pension benefits) which can increase employee compensation expenses significantly.

16.1 Salaries

A salary is the compensation generally given for the performance of specified duties. The salary is paid for performance of the job. Most salaries assume that the job will require approximately 40 hours per week to complete. If the employee requires more time in which to complete the job, he is usually expected to work without extra pay.

Definition

salary

A *salary* is compensation paid an employee for the performance of specified duties or responsibilities. Compensation is based on completion of the duties, regardless of the time required.

Gross pay: the amount paid before deductions

At this time, we will consider only gross pay. *Gross pay* is the amount paid an employee before any deductions (for taxes, insurance, etc.) are subtracted. Gross pay is easily calculated under a salary compensation plan. Salaries are generally stated as a fixed number of dollars per month or per year. Although a salary may be dollars per month or year, employees frequently receive their paychecks at different time intervals. That is, the

pay period

pay period (or length of time between checks) is generally monthly (once a month), semimonthly (twice a month), biweekly (every 2 weeks), or weekly.

Definitions

Gross pay is that amount earned by an employee before any deductions (for taxes, insurance, union dues, savings bonds, etc.) are subtracted.

A *pay period* is the length of time between employee checks. The most common pay periods are as follows:

1. Monthly (once a month, or 12 times a year).
2. Semimonthly (twice a month, or 24 times a year).
3. Biweekly (every 2 weeks, or 52 weeks per year ÷ 2 weeks = 26 times a year).
4. Weekly (once a week, or 52 times a year).

Example 1

Mr. D. D. Ray is a foreman for the local manufacturing company and receives a salary of $14,400 per year. What is his gross pay if he receives a check:

a. monthly?
b. semimonthly?
c. biweekly?
d. weekly?

SOLUTION

a. Monthly gross pay is the yearly salary divided by 12 months, or

$$\frac{\$14,400 \text{ per year}}{12 \text{ months per year}} = \$1200 \text{ per month}$$

b. Semimonthly gross pay is the yearly salary divided by 24 pay periods per year, or

$$\frac{\$14,400 \text{ per year}}{24 \text{ pay periods per year}} = \$600 \text{ twice a month}$$

c. Biweekly gross pay is the yearly salary divided by 26 pay periods (i.e., 52 weeks per year ÷ 2 weeks per pay period), or

$$\frac{\$14,400 \text{ per year}}{26 \text{ pay periods per year}} = \$553.85 \text{ every 2 weeks}$$

d. Weekly gross pay is the yearly salary divided by 52 pay periods (i.e., 52 weeks per year), or

$$\frac{\$14,400 \text{ per year}}{52 \text{ pay periods per year}} = \$276.92 \text{ per week}$$

Gross pay per period for salaried employees can easily be converted from one pay period to another. The easiest way is to convert the given rate per pay period to a yearly basis, then divide the yearly rate by the desired number of pay periods.

Example 2   A salaried employee receives $500 gross pay every 2 weeks (i.e., biweekly). What is his gross pay

    a. yearly?
    b. monthly?
    c. semimonthly?
    d. weekly?

SOLUTION

a. There are 26 biweekly pay periods in a year (i.e., 52 weeks per year ÷ 2 weeks per pay period = 26 pay periods). The employee receives $500 in gross pay per pay period. Therefore, his yearly salary is $500 per pay period times 26 pay periods, or $13,000 per year.

b. The monthly gross pay is the yearly salary divided by 12 months per year, or

    $13,000 ÷ 12 = $1083.33 per month

c. The semimonthly gross pay is the yearly salary divided by 24 pay periods (i.e., 2 pay periods per month), or

    $13,000 ÷ 24 = $541.67 twice a month

d. The weekly gross pay is the yearly salary divided by 52 pay periods (i.e., 52 weeks per year), or

    $13,000 ÷ 52 = $250.00 per week

The obvious question arises, "Why would I want to convert my salary to another pay period? I know how much I make." We noted the possible differences in pay periods (i.e., weekly, biweekly, etc.). However, most major bills (house note, car payment, charge cards, etc.) are on a monthly basis. Auto and home insurance may be on a monthly, quarterly, or semiannual basis. Being able to convert wages from the basis received to the basis for bills allows us to budget the correct amount from our wages in order to pay bills. Such conversions may also be helpful in considering alternatives between jobs offering wages based on different pay periods.

Exercises 16.1

■ Use the information given to complete the following table.

	Gross Pay Received				
	Yearly	Monthly	Semimonthly	Biweekly	Weekly
Example:	?	?	$600	?	?
Solution:	$600 × 24 = $14,400	$14,400 ÷ 12 = $1200		$14,400 ÷ 26 = $553.85	$14,400 ÷ 52 = $276.92
1.	$18,000				
2.		$2000			
3.			$300		
4.				$300	
5.					$225
6.			$800		
7.	$30,000				
8.		$1800			
9.				$600	
10.					$285

11. Mr. Lee receives a salary of $22,000 per year. What amount will he have to meet his monthly expenses?

12. You have been offered two jobs. One pays $1650 monthly and the other pays $750 biweekly. Which job will pay the most?

13. Alvin is paid $525 every 2 weeks. He applies for a car loan but is told that he must make $13,500 per year to qualify for the loan. Does he make enough?

14. Joseph earns $1500 semimonthly. His brother John makes $700 per week. John tells Joe to start working for John's company and "get a pay raise." Is John correct?

15. Frank receives $575 biweekly. He wants to buy a new car but feels his car notes cannot exceed 10% of his monthly pay. What is his maximum car note?

16. The Admiral Company pays a starting salary of $1200 per month. Ensign, Inc., pays $275 per week and boasts of having "the highest starting pay in town." Is this true?

17. The Alexanders want to buy a new house. They want to keep their monthly house payment below 1 week's pay for Mr. Alexander. If Mr. Alexander earns $26,000 per year, what is their maximum monthly house payment?

18. You now earn $700 biweekly. Can you increase your income by changing to a job paying $18,000 per year?

19. The Exclusive Club will not consider anyone earning less than $38,000 per year for membership. Can Adam apply for membership if he earns $750 per week?

20. What monthly amount will a person earning $800 biweekly have to cover his expenses?

16.2 Hourly Wages

Many employees are paid according to the number of hours they work. Time on the job is the main factor in determining an hourly employee's gross pay. An hourly employee's gross pay is simply the number of hours worked times the employee's rate of pay per hour.

gross pay at hourly rates

> **Gross Pay of Hourly Employees**
>
> The gross pay of hourly employees is the number of hours worked times the employee's rate of pay per hour: or
>
> gross pay = hours worked × rate per hour

Example 1   Calculate the gross pay of an hourly employee who worked 36 hours for the week. His hourly rate is $4.25 per hour.

SOLUTION   Gross pay = hours worked × rate per hour

$$= 36 \times \$4.25$$

$$= \$153.00$$

The employee earned $153.00 for the week.

Hourly wages are seldom so simple. Pay by the hour generally involves extensive record keeping to properly determine the amount of time an employee is on the job. Time on the job may be recorded to the nearest $\frac{1}{4}$ hour of work completed. That is, an employee working from 8:00 A.M. until 12:20 P.M. (noon) would be paid for $4\frac{1}{4}$ hours. Frequently, one encounters time on the job measured by "punching" a time clock. In such cases, time worked is often computed to the nearest tenth of an hour (i.e., 6-minute increments).

overtime   Another factor affecting the gross pay of an hourly employee is *overtime* (i.e., that amount of time worked in excess of the normal work week). Most labor agreements (and federal standards) consider a normal work week to be 5 working days of 8 working hours each. Any hours worked in excess of the normal work week are paid at an overtime rate. The overtime rate is usually $1\frac{1}{2}$ or 2 times the normal hourly rate of pay. Overtime is usually paid for time worked in excess of a given number of hours per week; however, it can be for time worked in excess of a given number of hours per day.

Example 2   Joe Dawson worked the following hours last week.

Monday	8:00 A.M.–12:05 P.M.; 1:05 P.M.–5:00 P.M.
Tuesday	7:55 A.M.–11:55 A.M.; 1:00 P.M.–4:55 P.M.
Wednesday	8:00 A.M.–12:00 P.M.; 12:55 P.M.–5:05 P.M.
Thursday	7:30 A.M.–12:25 P.M.; 1:00 P.M.–5:45 P.M.
Friday	7:45 A.M.–11:50 A.M.; 12:30 P.M.–5:15 P.M.

Assuming that Joe's company calculates work time to the nearest $\frac{1}{4}$ hour *completed*, how many hours did Joe work last week?

SOLUTION   Joe's work time would be calculated as follows. Remember that only time worked for $\frac{1}{4}$ hour (or 15 minutes) will be counted; no *partial* $\frac{1}{4}$ hour counts.

Monday	8:00 A.M.–12:05 P.M.	4 hr
	1:05 P.M.–5:00 P.M.	$3\frac{3}{4}$ hr
		$7\frac{3}{4}$ hr
Tuesday	7:55 A.M.–11:55 A.M.	$3\frac{3}{4}$ hr
	1:00 P.M.–4:55 P.M.	$3\frac{3}{4}$ hr
		$7\frac{1}{2}$ hr
Wednesday	8:00 A.M.–12:00 P.M.	4 hr
	12:55 P.M.–5:05 P.M.	4 hr
		8 hr
Thursday	7:30 A.M.–12:25 P.M.	$4\frac{3}{4}$ hr
	1:00 P.M.–5:45 P.M.	$4\frac{3}{4}$ hr
		$9\frac{1}{2}$ hr
Friday	7:45 A.M.–11:50 A.M.	4 hr
	12:30 P.M.–5:15 P.M.	$4\frac{3}{4}$ hr
		$8\frac{3}{4}$ hr

Joe's total work time for the week would then be

$$\text{Monday} + \text{Tuesday} + \text{Wednesday} + \text{Thursday} + \text{Friday} =$$
$$7\frac{3}{4} + 7\frac{1}{2} + 8 + 9\frac{1}{2} + 8\frac{3}{4} = 41\frac{1}{2} \text{ total hours}$$

Example 3   Using the hours from Example 2, what would be Joe's gross pay if his hourly wage is $5.50 and overtime in excess of a 40-hour week is paid at time and a half (i.e., $1\frac{1}{2}$ times the normal rate)?

SOLUTION   To determine the proper gross pay, the hours worked must be classified into "normal" hours and "overtime" hours. Each group of hours is multiplied by the proper rate per hour. The total of the two groups will be the gross pay.

"Normal" hours	40 hr × $5.50/hr	= $220.00
"Overtime" hours	$1\frac{1}{2}$ hr × ($5.50 + $2.75)	= 12.38
Total		$232.38

Example 4   Joe's company pays overtime at $1\frac{1}{2}$ times the hourly wage for all time worked in excess of 8 hours per day. Using the hours in Example 2 and an hourly wage of $5.50, how much is Joe's gross pay?

SOLUTION   This problem is solved like Example 3; however, the hours of each day are classified as normal or overtime. The appropriate rates are multiplied by the hours and the total is the gross pay.

	Normal Hours	Overtime Hours
Monday	$7\frac{3}{4}$	0
Tuesday	$7\frac{1}{2}$	0
Wednesday	8	0
Thursday	8	$1\frac{1}{2}$
Friday	8	$\frac{3}{4}$
Total	$39\frac{1}{4}$	$2\frac{1}{4}$

Multiplying the hours by the rate per hour, we have

Normal wages	$39\frac{1}{4}$ hr × $5.50/hr	= $215.88
Overtime wages	$2\frac{1}{4}$ hr × ($5.50 + $2.75)	= 18.56
Total		$234.44

Joe's total gross pay is $234.44 for the week. Compare this with the overtime paid by the week (Example 3).

Example 5   Erik's company records time worked to the nearest tenth of an hour using a time clock. Last week Erik worked the following hours:

Sun.	Mon.	Tues.	Wed.	Thur.	Fri.	Sat.
Off	8.2	7.9	Off	8.3	8.2	7.8

Erik's basic rate of pay is $8.80 per hour and his company pays time and a half for Saturday work and time worked in excess of 8 hours per day. Calculate Erik's gross pay.

SOLUTION   First, we must classify the hours Erik worked into normal and overtime hours.

	Normal Hours	Overtime Hours
Monday	8.0	0.2
Tuesday	7.9	—
Thursday	8.0	0.3
Friday	8.0	0.2
Saturday	—	7.8
Total	31.9	8.5

Multiplying the hours by the rate per hour, we have

Normal wages $31.9 \times \$8.80$ $= \$280.72$
Overtime wages $8.5 \times (\$8.80 + \$4.40) =$ 112.20

                                         Total $392.92

Erik's gross pay for the week is $392.92.

minimum wage

The rate of pay per hour for employees will vary significantly depending on the level of skill required by the job. However, the U.S. Congress has passed the Fair Labor Standards Act, which sets a minimum wage rate per hour for many employees. This rate will vary depending on congressional action.

Exercises 16.2

■ Calculate the gross pay of an employee using the data shown. Overtime is not to be paid.

	Hours Worked per Week	Rate per Hour	Gross Pay
Example:	40	$4.00	$160.00 (i.e., 40 × $4)
1.	39	$5.75	?
2.	40	$6.15	?
3.	40	$4.30	?
4.	$37\frac{1}{2}$	$5.70	?
5.	$38\frac{1}{4}$	$3.80	?
6.	$39\frac{1}{4}$	$7.12	?

■ Compute the hours worked (to the nearest $\frac{1}{4}$ hour of time worked) on the following employees.

	Employee	Monday	Tuesday	Wednesday	Thursday	Friday	Total
7.	James	7:20A–11:45A 12:30P–4:50P	7:30A–12:05P 12:55P–5:00P	8:00A–12:10P 1:05P–5:20P	8:10A–12:20P 12:55P–4:50P	7:45A–11:55A 12:40P–5:35P	?
8.	Rodney	5:45A–11:00A 11:40A–4:30P	7:05A–11:25A 12:30P–4:45P	7:15A–11:05A 12:00P–4:20P	8:00A–12:00P 12:45P–5:05P	7:30A–11:45A 12:30P–5:10P	?
9.	Richard	8:30A–12:25P 1:05P–5:35P	8:15A–11:47A 12:32P–5:04P	8:09A–11:42A 12:31P–5:41P	7:59A–12:02P 1:04P–5:21P	8:02A–11:51A 12:42P–5:08P	?
10.	Joann	7:30A–12:03P 12:59P–4:57P	8:00A–11:55P 12:45P–5:05P	7:57A–12:22P 1:15P–4:50P	8:00A–12:15P 1:30P–5:25P	8:20A–11:40A 12:30P–5:35P	?

■ Calculate the gross pay in the following problems. Overtime is paid at $1\frac{1}{2}$ times normal pay for all hours in excess of 40 per week.

	Hours Worked	Normal Rate of Pay	Gross Pay
11.	36	$5.70	?
12.	$42\frac{1}{2}$	$6.60	?
13.	$40\frac{3}{4}$	$8.40	?
14.	$39\frac{1}{4}$	$4.80	?
15.	44	$4.50	?
16.	$42\frac{1}{2}$	$5.80	?

17. Calculate the gross pay for the employees on the Shiner Company payroll. Overtime is paid at the rate of $1\frac{1}{2}$ times the normal rate for time worked in excess of 40 hours per week.

Employee	M	T	W	T	F	S	Tot. Hr	Reg. Hr	O.T. Hr	Reg. Rate	Total Wage
Dale, J.	8	8	$7\frac{3}{4}$	$8\frac{1}{2}$	$9\frac{1}{2}$	0		40		$4.60	
Mumfry, E.	$7\frac{1}{2}$	$7\frac{3}{4}$	9	$7\frac{1}{2}$	$8\frac{3}{4}$	4		40		$8.20	
Starr, B.	8	$8\frac{1}{4}$	$8\frac{3}{4}$	$8\frac{1}{2}$	$8\frac{1}{2}$	8		40		$6.20	

18. Warren worked the following hours last week: Sun.–off; Mon.–$8\frac{1}{2}$ hr; Tues.–$7\frac{3}{4}$ hr; Wed.–off; Thurs.–9 hr; Fri.–$8\frac{1}{4}$ hr; Sat.–$8\frac{3}{4}$ hr. If his normal rate of pay is $6.90 per hour and time in excess of 40 hours is paid at time and a half rate, how much did Warren earn?

19. Melanie received $247 last week. She worked her normal workweek of 38 hours. This week she worked 40 hours. How much will she receive if overtime is paid at time and a half of regular rate?

20. Estella worked Monday through Friday last week and received $240 gross pay. She is scheduled to work Monday through Saturday this week. How much will she receive if overtime pay in excess of 40 hours is $1\frac{1}{2}$ straight time? (All days are 8-hours days.)

21. Compute the weekly pay of the following employees. Overtime (in excess of 40 hours per week) is paid at time and a half. Sunday work is paid at double time and holiday work is paid at $1\frac{1}{2}$ straight time. Overtime hours begin accumulating only after 40 hours per week are worked.

Employee	S	M	T	W[a]	T	F	S	Hourly Rate
C. Thomas	6	8	$7\frac{1}{4}$	—	$7\frac{3}{4}$	8	8	$4.60
M. Doutery	—	9	$8\frac{1}{2}$	$7\frac{1}{2}$	$8\frac{1}{4}$	$7\frac{3}{4}$	—	$5.80
L. Charms	—	$7\frac{3}{4}$	8	8	—	$8\frac{1}{4}$	8	$6.20

[a] National holiday—July 4.

22. Compute the weekly pay of the following employees. Overtime (in excess of 8 hours per day) and weekend work (Saturday and Sunday) are paid at time and a half of regular rate.

Employee	S	M	T	W	T	F	S	Hourly Rate
J. Banks	6.8	8.2	7.8	9.2	8.3	—	—	$8.80
M. Charles	—	7.8	9.6	8.4	7.9	8.2	—	$9.00
V. Doren	—	—	8.1	7.9	8.6	9.4	7.5	$10.60
L. Bailey	7.8	—	8.6	—	9.4	8.1	7.8	$10.20
T. Warner	—	7.6	8.3	8.4	9.2	—	8.0	$9.60
D. Michel	—	10.4	9.8	7.8	—	—	8.0	$9.80

16.3 *Piece Rate*

Some employees are paid strictly in proportion to the amount of work they do. The more work the employee does, the more he gets paid. Such employees are on a *piece-rate* pay system.

Definition

piece-rate pay

A *piece-rate pay system* is one in which the employee is paid according to the number of units produced.

The gross pay of a piece-rate employee can be determined by multiplying the number of units produced by the amount paid per unit.

Example 1

Harold Black is paid $0.07 for each door stop he produces. Last week he produced 3000. How much is his gross pay for the week?

SOLUTION

Harold produced 3000 door stops at $0.07 each; therefore, his gross pay is

$$3000 \text{ units} \times \$0.07 \text{ per unit} = \$210.00$$

There are many variations of the piece-rate plan. Since there is a federal minimum wage in many businesses (see Section 16.2), most piece-rate plans provide for an hourly rate of pay either (1) the minimum wage, or (2) the units produced times the rate per unit. The employee is paid the greater amount. There are also *bonus* or *incentive* plans, which reward an employee for greater than normal production. Such bonus plans usually set a normal number (or *standard*) of units the average employee can produce in a given time period. The employee is paid more for units produced above the standard amount. For example, the first 3000 door stops (Example 1) might be the weekly standard and are paid at $0.07 per unit. The next 500 door stops might be paid at a rate of $0.09 per unit.

Example 2   The Foundry starts its new employees at a rate of $3.75 per hour or $0.15 per unit produced. What will be the gross pay for John Jay on his first 4-hour shift if his production is as shown?

Hour 1	Hour 2	Hour 3	Hour 4
20 units	23 units	26 units	27 units

SOLUTION   Since there is a minimum rate of $3.75 per hour, John will receive either $3.75 per hour or the units he produced times $0.15 per unit—whichever is greater.

	Minimum	Piece-Rate Plan	Gross Pay
Hour 1	$3.75	20 × $0.15 = $3.00	$ 3.75 (minimum)
Hour 2	$3.75	23 × $0.15 = $3.45	$ 3.75 (minimum)
Hour 3	$3.75	26 × $0.15 = $3.90	$ 3.90 (piece rate)
Hour 4	$3.75	27 × $0.15 = $4.05	$ 4.05 (piece rate)
Total pay for the first shift			$15.45

Example 3   The Machine Shop pays a minimum wage of $4.50 per hour or $0.25 per unit produced. The standard rate is 20 units per hour. For all units above standard, employees are paid $0.29. Calculate the gross pay for an employee having the following production:

Hour 1	Hour 2	Hour 3
17	19	23

SOLUTION   This problem is solved like Example 2; however, the bonus production possibility must be considered.

	Minimum	Units at Standard Rate	Units at Bonus Rate	Gross Pay
Hour 1	$4.50	17 units × $0.25 = $4.25		$ 4.50 (minimum)
Hour 2	$4.50	19 units × $0.25 = $4.75		$ 4.75 (piece rate)
Hour 3	$4.50	20 units × $0.25 = $5.00	3 units × $0.29 = $0.87	$ 5.87 (piece rate plus bonus)
		Total gross pay for the 3 hours		$15.12

Note that in hour 1 the minimum wage was used since it was greater than the actual production rate. In hour 2, actual production exceeded the minimum rate; therefore, the actual production rate was used. In hour 3, the employee produced enough units to qualify for a bonus. The gross pay for that hour is the sum of the units produced at the standard rate plus the units above the standard quantity times the bonus rate.

Exercises 16.3

■ Compute the gross pay for the following piece-rate production periods.

	Units per Hour	Rate per Unit	Gross Pay per Hour
Example:	20	$0.42	$8.40 (i.e., 20 × $0.42)
1.	17	$0.55	
2.	29	$0.15	
3.	35	$0.16	
4.	14	$0.45	
5.	23	$0.20	
6.	105	$0.05	

7. Trent Adams' work station has a production capacity of 800 units per day. Yesterday he produced 680 units. He is paid by the unit at the rate of $0.05 per unit. How much did he earn yesterday?

8. Lee Huang is paid $0.20 for all units he produces. Last week he produced 1275 units. What was his gross pay?

9. Markovitch Company pays $0.08 per unit or $3.60 per hour, whichever is greater. Jonathan started today and his production for the morning was as shown:

        Hour 1—22 units   Hour 3—45 units
        Hour 2—32 units   Hour 4—48 units

What was his gross pay for the morning?

10. Nelson Manufacturing pays its category I employees $240.00 per week or on a piece rate of $0.04 per unit produced, whichever is greater. Last month Mary produced 5500 units in week 1, 5800 units in week 2, 6100 units in week 3, and 6000 units in week 4. What was her gross pay for the month?

11. The O.T. Shine Company pays a minimum wage of $4.80 per hour for production personnel. As an incentive, a rate of $0.40 per unit is paid for production up to (and including) 15 units per hour. Production in excess of 15 per hour is paid at $0.50 per unit. E. Beaver's production for the morning was:

        Hour 1—14 units   Hour 3—12 units
        Hour 2—16 units   Hour 4—18 units

Calculate his gross pay for the morning.

12. Your employer offers you a choice of pay plans. The first is a guaranteed $285 per week. The second is payment of $0.05 for each unit you produce. If you produce in excess of 6250 units per week, he will pay you $0.06 for *all* units produced. You know your normal rate of production (approximately 6000 units per week). Which method would you choose to get the largest gross paycheck?

13. You are paid on a piece rate of $0.02 per unit for the first 3950 units per day. Units 3951 and up are paid at the rate of $0.03 per unit. You wish to earn $100 tomorrow. How many units must you produce?

14. The Best Company pays $0.25 per unit for production-line employees. All employees who produce in excess of 1000 units per week receive an additional $0.03 for each unit produced. Calculate the gross pay of employees having the following production levels:

Name	M	T	W	T	F	Total	Gross Pay
Aldrin, E	182	147	168	176	189		
Majors, A	201	207	246	258	213		
Thomas, W.	89	136	148	177	132		
Williams, J.	138	149	192	187	193		

15. The Fly By Day Company pays production employees $0.25 per unit for the first 800 units, $0.30 per unit for the next 300 units, and $0.35 for all units above that. In addition, the company has a minimum-wage level of $200.00 per week. What is the gross pay for the following employees?

Name	M	T	W	T	F	Total	Gross Pay
Allen, B	191	143	178	182	191		
Camp, D.	178	192	204	256	262		
Erwin, B.	92	128	152	167	140		
Flores, H.	210	214	266	272	236		

16.4 *Commissions*

Many employees are paid in accordance with the amount of business they generate for their company. Salespersons, for example, are frequently paid a percent of the amount of sales they have. Pay in such cases is on a *commission* basis.

Definition

commission

A *commission* is payment to an employee based on the amount of net sales the employee generates for the company.

The gross pay to a commissioned employee is calculated by multiplying the commission rate by the amount net sales (i.e., total sales less sales returns) during the time period.

Example 1

I. M. Eager is paid on a commission basis. He receives 10% of the amount he sells. Last week, Mr. Eager sold $3500 worth of merchandise. What is his gross pay?

SOLUTION

Gross pay on a commission basis is found by multiplying the commission rate by the amount sold. Therefore, Mr. Eager's gross pay for the week is

$$\$3500 \text{ sales} \times 10\% \text{ commission} = \$350 \text{ gross pay}$$

straight and graduated commissions

Commissions can take several forms. The *straight commission* is used in Example 1. Straight commissions pay a stated percent regardless of the level of sales. *Graduated commissions* may be paid to provide more pay for higher levels of sales. The employee usually receives a higher percent commission for higher sales volumes. Commissions are frequently combined with salaries. Such a plan protects the employee from extremely poor sales periods, yet provides a reward for outstanding efforts.

Example 2

John Jay receives a graduated commission of 10% of the first $5000 sold, 12% of the next $7500 sold, and 15% of sales above these amounts. Last month John sold $18,000 worth of merchandise. What is his gross pay?

SOLUTION

John's gross pay can be calculated by multiplying the appropriate percents and dollar amounts. These are as follows:

Percent		Sales		Commission
10%	×	$ 5,000	=	$ 500
12%	×	$ 7,500	=	$ 900
15%	×	$ 5,500	=	$ 825
		$18,000		$2,225

John receives a total commission of $2225 for selling $18,000 worth of merchandise.

Example 3

Salespeople at the Camel-ot Car Company receive a salary of $250 per week plus a commission of 5% of the sales they make. What would be the gross pay of a salesperson selling $10,000 in cars during the last 2 weeks?

SOLUTION

The gross pay received would be the sum of the salary plus the commission. In this case,

Salary	2 weeks × $250 per week	= $ 500
Commission	5% × $10,000 sales	= $ 500
	Gross pay for the 2 weeks	$1000

Exercises 16.4

■ Calculate the salaries of the following employees based on the sales and commission rates shown.

	Weekly Sales	*Commission Rate*	*Gross Wage*
Example:	$1000	10%	$100 (i.e., $1000 × 10%)
1.	$1800	15%	
2.	$2250	18%	
3.	$3650	9%	
4.	$4195	7%	
5.	$820	35%	
6.	$1635	20%	

7. Arthur Burns is paid a salary of $100 per week plus 12% commission on sales he makes. During the last 4 weeks he sold $12,000 in merchandise. What is his gross pay?

8. How much gross pay will Ms. Lester make for September? She receives a monthly salary of $400 plus 18% of all sales. She sold $14,955 in merchandise for the month.

9. Agnes Smith is paid on a graduated commission. She receives 12% of sales for the first $2500 sold, 14% of sales for the next $2500 sold, and 16% for sales in excess of $5000. Her total sales for March were $6000. What was her gross pay?

10. A. Larsen is the manager of an auto parts store. He receives a salary of $300 per month plus 2% of sales in excess of $10,000. He receives 3% of sales in excess of $50,000. How much can he expect to make if sales last month were $60,000?

11. Andrew Hardy received gross pay of $1000 last month. He is paid a salary of $500 per month plus a commission on all sales in excess of $5000 per month. What is his commission rate if sales last month were $10,000?

12. Ms. Beecher is paid on a commission basis. She received $1575 last month for sales of $52,500. What is her commission rate?

13. Cleo Masoni is paid on a commission basis. He receives 3% of sales up to $20,000 and 4% of sales above $20,000. In addition, he receives a $500 bonus if sales exceed $60,000. Last month he sold $61,000 in merchandise. What did he earn?

14. Mr. Cesank receives a 6% commission as a real estate broker. Last month he received $3600 for selling a home. How much did the home sell for?

15. Ms. Angelo receives a salary of $400 per month plus a commission of 3% of sales in excess of $10,000. However, any merchandise returned is not subject to a commission. Her sales last month were $28,000; however, her customers returned $3000 in merchandise. How much did Ms. Angelo receive?

16. Archie McIntyre receives a 6% commission on all sales he makes. He receives $500 at the first of the month as a "draw" (or advance commission) against the month's sales. This month he sold $48,600 in merchandise. How much should his paycheck be?

17. Ms. Hebert manages the women's-wear department of a large store. She receives a salary of $300 per month, 2% commission on her sales, and 0.3% commission on sales for the other employees she supervises. Last month she sold $16,380 in merchandise and the *total* sales for her department were $97,640. How much did Ms. Hebert earn?

18. The department manager of the automotive department receives a salary of $400 per month plus a 3% commission on her own sales. She also receives a 0.2% commission on all sales of the department. Any returned merchandise is excluded before calculating her commission. How much did she receive last month if her sales were $18,800, the department sales were $186,200, and returned merchandise totaled $8980? (None of the returned merchandise was sold by the manager.)

16.5 Adjustments to Wages

Our discussion in the first part of this chapter centered on gross pay. Let us now discuss *net pay* or the employee's actual "take-home pay" after all deductions are made. There are basically two types of deductions from gross pay: (1) required deductions (Social Security and income tax primarily), and (2) voluntary deductions (insurance, savings bonds, credit union, etc.).

Definition

net pay

Net pay **(or take-home pay) is the employee's gross pay minus all deductions.**

Required Deductions

Federal Insurance Contributions Act (F.I.C.A.)

Social Security (or F.I.C.A.)

The Federal Insurance Contributions Act (F.I.C.A.) was enacted as an emergency measure during the depression of the 1930s. It is commonly known as the Social Security Act. The rationale underlying this act assumed that employees and employers would pay a certain amount of salary into a fund from which eligible recipients would receive monthly benefit payments. Eligible recipients include retired and disabled workers, widows/widowers and dependent children of deceased workers, and persons qualifying for Medicare.

The F.I.C.A. fund is financed by employers and employees through contributions at rates established by legislative action.

The actual amount contributed by an employee can be calculated by multiplying the applicable F.I.C.A. rate by the amount earned. There is a "maximum amount" or earnings level above which F.I.C.A. taxes are not paid. For example, F.I.C.A. taxes may be paid at the rate of 6.7% of the first

$31,800. Earnings above $31,800 are not subject to F.I.C.A. taxes. The maximum earnings levels are set by legislative action just as the F.I.C.A. rates are, hence, they are subject to change yearly.

Example 1

Albert earned $27,500. Assuming a rate of 6.7% up to a maximum of $30,000, what should his contribution under F.I.C.A. be?

SOLUTION

Albert earned less than the $30,000 maximum income limit, so his entire salary would be subject to the 6.7% contribution; that is,

$$\$27,500 \times 6.7\% = \$1842.50$$

Albert paid $1842.50 as his share under F.I.C.A.

Example 2

If Albert had earned $35,000, what would his contribution under F.I.C.A. have been?

SOLUTION

Albert's contribution would have been the maximum of $2010.00 (i.e., $30,000 × 6.7%). The $5000 in excess of the F.I.C.A. limit would not have been taxed.

The amount an employee pays is only one-half of the contribution to the F.I.C.A. fund. Employers are required to contribute an amount equal to the employee's contribution. The employee contribution can be calculated using a withholding table furnished by the federal government or by multiplying the employees salary by the appropriate percent. The F.I.C.A. deductions are made from each paycheck at the proper percent until the earnings maximum is reached.

Example 3

Armando's gross pay for December was $3000. His earnings to date were $32,000. What would be the F.I.C.A. withholding assuming an F.I.C.A. rate of 6.7% and a maximum earnings level of $33,600?

SOLUTION

Armando is only $1600 (i.e., $33,600 − $32,000) away from the maximum earning limit for F.I.C.A., hence only $1600 would be subject to the 6.7% withholding: or

$$\$1600 \times 6.7\% = \$107.20 \text{ F.I.C.A. deduction}$$

income tax

Federal Income Tax

In 1913 the Congress of the United States was authorized (by the 16th Amendment to the Constitution) to tax incomes of U.S. citizens. Funds raised through such taxation are used to support various federal programs (national defense, social services, etc.) outlined in the national budget. This budget must be approved by the U.S. Congress, which, as duly elected representatives of the people, certifies that money spent as outlined represents the "will of the people."

withholding tax

Income taxes are due once a year, April 15, for income earned in the preceding year. Since income taxes represent a significant amount of money for the average individual, the *withholding tax* was initiated. Through the withholding tax, a certain amount of each employee's pay is "withheld" by the employer and turned over to the government as partial payment of the employee's income tax for the year. Such a plan avoids a heavy, once-a-year tax burden on the individual and provides the government with operating money throughout the year.

The amount of money withheld by the employer varies depending on four things: (1) the employee's gross earnings, (2) the employee's marital status (married or single), (3) the number of exemptions (or dependents) the employee is entitled to claim, and (4) the length of the employee's pay period. The federal government provides income tax withholding tables which direct the employer in the amount to withold depending on the employee's status in the four items mentioned (see Table X, p. 574).* These tables are only approximations of the income tax the employee will owe at the end of the year. The employee may have to pay additional money (or receive money back as a refund), depending on the amount that has been withheld and the actual tax circumstances of the employee. Our discussion here will be limited to calculating the proper withholding amount by using the withholding tables.

Example 4   Ms. Powitzsky earned $910 for the last 2 weeks. She is married and claims two exemptions. Using the tables in Table X, p. 574, how much should be withheld from her earnings?

SOLUTION   We know all four of the required items about Ms. Powitzsky:

> *1.* Income—$910.
> *2.* Marital status—married.
> *3.* Exemptions—two.
> *4.* Pay period—biweekly.

First, we find the table labeled "Married Persons—Biweekly Payroll Period." Then we find Ms. Powitzsky's gross pay in the column headed "And the wages are." Finally, we read across the "wages" line to the column showing the appropriate number of exemptions, or "withholding allowances." Thus, we see that $158.40 should be withheld for a married employee earning $910 biweekly and claiming two exemptions.

---

* The tables in Table X are *not* a complete set. They are representative samples of the ones you will encounter. In addition, these withholding tables change frequently. Be sure you have the current tables when making calculations.

MARRIED Persons — **BIWEEKLY** Payroll Period

And the wages are—		And the number of withholding allowances claimed is—										
At least	But less than	0	1	2	3	4	5	6	7	8	9	10 or more
		The amount of income tax to be withheld shall be—										
$880	$900	$170.00	$160.90	$152.80	$144.70	$136.70	$128.60	$120.50	$113.10	$105.90	$98.70	$91.40
900	920	176.40	167.20	158.40	150.30	142.30	134.20	126.10	118.10	110.90	103.70	96.40
920	940	182.80	173.60	164.40	155.90	147.90	139.80	131.70	123.60	115.90	108.70	101.40
940	960	189.20	180.00	170.80	161.50	153.50	145.40	137.30	129.20	121.20	113.70	106.40
960	980	195.60	186.40	177.20	167.90	159.10	151.00	142.90	134.80	126.80	118.70	111.40

Example 5

Lucas had $3100 in gross earnings for the last month. He is single and claims one exemption. How much withholding tax should he pay for the month?

SOLUTION

From Table X we find the tax table headed "Single Persons—Monthly Payroll Period." Since Lucas' pay exceeds the maximum covered by the table, we must calculate the withholding tax as directed at the bottom of the table. That is, the tax for a single person claiming one exemption should be

a. 36% of the excess over $2960, or
  ($3100 − $2960) × 36% = $ 50.40
plus
b. the maximum amount shown in the table
  for one exemption, or   822.10
  Total withholding tax $872.50

SINGLE Persons — **MONTHLY** Payroll Period

And the wages are—		And the number of withholding allowances claimed is —										
At least	But less than	0	1	2	3	4	5	6	7	8	9	10 or more
		The amount of income tax to be withheld shall be-										
$760	$800	$117.50	$103.80	$90.00	$77.40	$66.20	$54.90	$43.70	$32.40	$22.10	$12.10	$2.10
800	840	127.00	112.60	98.80	85.10	73.40	62.10	50.90	39.60	28.50	18.50	8.50
840	880	136.60	121.60	107.60	93.90	80.60	69.30	58.10	46.80	35.60	24.90	14.90
880	920	146.20	131.20	116.40	102.70	88.90	76.50	65.30	54.00	42.80	31.50	21.30
920	960	155.80	140.80	125.80	111.50	97.70	84.00	72.50	61.20	50.00	38.70	27.70
		36 percent of the excess over $2,960 plus—										
$2,960 and over		844.60	822.10	799.60	777.10	754.60	732.10	709.60	687.10	664.60	642.10	619.60

Voluntary Deductions

voluntary deductions: made at the employee's request

The employer may withhold additional money from the employee's gross pay and use it as directed by the employee. Such deductions are usually at the employee's discretion. The most frequently encountered deductions are money withheld for (1) state income taxes (which may be mandatory), (2) insurance, (3) credit unions, (4) community funds or United Way donations, (5) U.S. savings bonds, (6) union dues, and (7) stock options or savings plans. The amounts and frequency of these deductions will vary greatly, hence we will not discuss them in detail.

Mention should be made of additional employer "deductions." We noted that the employer contributes an amount equal to the employee contribution for F.I.C.A. The employer must also pay federal and state unemployment taxes. These taxes contribute to the fund from which individual unemployment compensation is paid.

Deductions withheld by the employer for F.I.C.A. and income tax withholding must be paid to the federal government monthly (for most businesses). The voluntary deductions are paid to the appropriate organizations in accordance with agreements between the employer and the organization.

You recall that an employee's net (or take-home) pay is the gross pay minus all deductions. Now that we know how to calculate F.I.C.A. and withholding tax, we can easily calculate net pay. Since voluntary deductions are an individual item, they must be treated as they occur.

Example 6   Mr. Nelson's gross pay for the last 2 weeks of June is $900.00. He is married and claims four dependents. His earnings to date total $13,950. He contributes $12.50 each paycheck to the United Way, and buys an $18.75 savings bond. Calculate Mr. Nelson's net pay if his F.I.C.A. rate is 6.7% and the earnings maximum is $33,600.

SOLUTION   Mr. Nelson's gross pay is $900. F.I.C.A. will be 6.7% on the entire amount since he has not earned the $33,600 maximum.

$$\$900 \times 6.7\% = \$60.30 \text{ F.I.C.A.}$$

Witholding tax for a married employee earning $900 biweekly and claiming four deductions is $142.30 (Table X).

Mr. Nelson's net pay is

$900.00	gross pay
− 60.30	F.I.C.A.
− 142.30	withholding
− 12.50	United Way
− 18.75	savings bonds
$666.15	net pay

Example 7   Ms. O'Hare earned $2500 last month. She is well below the maximum F.I.C.A. limit and her F.I.C.A. percent is 7.15%. She is single and claims one deduction. She contributes 10% of her gross pay to a company savings plan, $25.00 to the Community Chest, and buys a $37.50 savings bond each month. What is her net pay for the month?

SOLUTION   Ms. O'Hare's net pay is

$2500.00	monthly gross pay
− 178.75	F.I.C.A. (7.15% × $2500)
− 656.50	withholding (tax table for single taxpayer earning $2500 monthly)
− 250.00	savings plan (10% × $2500)
− 37.50	savings bond
− 25.00	Community Chest
$1352.25	net pay

Exercises 16.5

■ Calculate the F.I.C.A. and withholding tax for the following employees. Use Table X as necessary. Ignore F.I.C.A. maximums.

	Employee	Gross Pay	F.I.C.A. Rate	F.I.C.A. Tax	Withholding Tax
1.	J. G. Greene; single, no deductions claimed	$1800 monthly	6.7%		
2.	Alex Liston; married, 3 deductions	$3220 monthly	6.7%		
3.	Andrea Elston; married, 2 deductions	$1150 biweekly	7.15%		
4.	Mary Ann Carpenter; single, 1 deduction	$935 biweekly	6.7%		
5.	Alvin Littlefield; single, 3 deductions	$2325 monthly	6.7%		
6.	Monty McWilliams; married, 6 deductions	$375 weekly	7.05%		
7.	Melanie Marshall; married, 4 deductions	$1120 semimonthly	6.7%		
8.	Edwena Napoli; single, 2 deductions	$750 semimonthly	6.7%		
9.	Teddy Lasiter; single, no deductions	$750 weekly	7.15%		
10.	Barbara Evans; married, 4 deductions	$2020 biweekly	6.13%		

11. For the 2 weeks ending June 26, Earl worked 43 and $44\frac{1}{2}$ hours, respectively. His rate of pay is $6.80 per hour with time and a half for everything in excess of 40 hours per week. Earl is married and claims 3 deductions. If his earnings to date are $13,800 and he buys an $18.75 savings bond per payday, what is Earl's *net* pay? The F.I.C.A. rate is 6.7% with a $30,000 maximum.

12. Dr. Lopez is paid a salary of $4000 per month from the hospital. He is married and claims 4 deductions. He has earned $30,000 so far this year. Dr. Lopez contributes $1\frac{1}{2}$% of his salary to the United Fund and 10% to a savings plan. What is his net pay for the month? The F.I.C.A. rate is 7.15% and the maximum level is $37,500.

13. Mr. Anderson works on a commission of 10% of his sales. His November sales were $33,650. Mr. Anderson is single, claims 1 deduction, and has earned $38,000 to date. Assuming that he has no voluntary deductions, calculate his net pay. The maximum F.I.C.A. level is $39,600 and the F.I.C.A. rate is 7.15%.

14. Ms. Johnson receives a salary of $200 per week plus 4% of her sales. She sold $5500 for the week ended February 25. If Ms. Johnson is married, claims no deductions, and has earned a total of $3500 to date, what is her net pay? She has voluntary deductions totaling $26.00 per week. The F.I.C.A. rate is 6.7% and she is well below the F.I.C.A. maximum level.

15. Mr. Neuman is paid $0.30 for each unit he produces up to 1000 per week. He receives $0.35 per unit for all units in excess of 1000. For the week ended November 27, Mr. Neuman produced 1150 units. If he is married, claims 3 deductions, and has earned $31,000 so far, what is his net pay? He pays $30 per week to the credit union and contributes $20 per week to a savings plan. The F.I.C.A. rate is 6.7% up to a maximum of $30,000.

Review Exercises / Chapter 16

1. You have been offered two jobs: one pays $800 semimonthly and the other pays $740 biweekly. Which should you choose to receive the highest pay?

2. Charles worked the following schedule last week:

Sun.	Mon.	Tues.	Wed.	Thurs.	Fri.	Sat.
8 hr	off	$8\frac{3}{4}$ hr	$7\frac{1}{4}$ hr	off	9 hr	$7\frac{1}{4}$ hr

He makes $6.80 per hour and receives $1\frac{1}{2}$ time for overtime (in excess of 40 hours per week) and Saturday work, and double time for Sunday work. Calculate his gross pay.

3. You receive a guaranteed minimum weekly pay of $300. However, you are eligible for piece-rate pay at the rate of $0.03 per unit for the first 4500 units and $0.04 for the next 6000 units. Units 10,501 and up are paid at the rate of $0.045. What would your gross pay be for a week when you produced 9500 units?

4. Ms. Nance receives a graduated commission of 5% of the first $8000 in sales and 7% of sales exceeding $8000 per month. Sales exceeding $20,000 per month are paid at a 10% commission rate. How much must she sell to earn $1500 next month?

5. Mr. Feneolio has earned $34,500 to date. Calculate his net pay assuming that (1) the F.I.C.A. rate is 7.05% on the first $35,400, (2) he is married and claims 4 dependents, (3) he receives a salary of $500 plus 10% of sales above $10,000 every 2 weeks, and (4) voluntary deductions were $120. Sales for the 2 weeks were $19,100.

6. Which job should you choose to receive the highest rate of pay: one paying $312.50 per week or one paying $650 semimonthly?

7. Mr. Bradford receives $450 for his regular 40-hour week. How much will he receive if he worked 46.5 hours last week and his company pays for overtime at $1\frac{1}{2}$ straight time?

■ Find the gross pay in the following problems:

	Rate/Hr.	Hours at Regular Time	Hours at Time-and-a-half
8.	$6.48	38	4.5
9.	$8.37	40	8.75
10.	$9.16	35	6.25

11. A salesperson accepts a job that pays on a commission basis only. However, the person is given a $500 *monthly draw* (or advance to be repaid from commissions earned). The commission rate is $7\frac{1}{2}$% of sales in excess of $4250 per month. If the salesperson sold $18,965 in merchandise last month, by how much did the commission earnings exceed the draw?

12. A real estate broker receives 6% commission on the sales of homes. What was her commission on three homes selling for $58,250, $76,850, and $93,265?

13. For the month of July, Allan sold $28,362 in merchandise. He receives $1075 per month plus $5\frac{1}{2}$% of all sales in excess of $12,750. He is married and claims 3 deductions. If his earnings to date are $18,675 and he buys an $18.75 savings bond every payday, what is his net pay? The F.I.C.A. rate is 6.7% with a $30,000 maximum. (Use Table X.)

Chapter Test / Chapter 16

1. Define the following terms.
  a. salary   **b.** gross pay   **c.** net pay
  d. pay period   **e.** commission   **f.** deductions

2. Convert gross pay of $940 semimonthly to an amount
  a. per week, **b.** biweekly, **c.** per month, **d.** per year.

Round to the nearest cent if necessary.

3. Hank worked the following hours last week:

Mon.	Tues.	Wed.	Thur.	Fri.	Sat.
$8\frac{1}{4}$	$7\frac{3}{4}$	$8\frac{1}{2}$	$9\frac{1}{4}$	—	8

Hank earns $8.20 per hour and is paid time and a half for work on weekends (Saturday and Sunday) and for overtime in excess of 8 hours per day. Calculate Hank's gross pay.

4. Eloise received $384 last week for her normal 40-hour week. How much will she receive this week for working 43.5 hours if all overtime (in excess of 40 hours per week) is paid at time and a half?

5. You are paid piece rate for your production at the Alpha Company. You receive $0.04 per unit for the first 1700 units each day, and $0.05 per unit for units 1701 and above. How many units must you produce each day next week (an average of the 5 working days) in order to earn $395.25?

6. Elena receives a salary of $500 per month plus a commission of 5% on everything she sells (net) and 0.5% of the total net sales of the department she manages. How much did she receive last month if her net sales were $4000 and the net sales for the department were $72,400?

7. Calculate Elizabeth's contribution to F.I.C.A. last month if her gross salary was $3200. She has earned $32,000 to date, the F.I.C.A. limit is $34,000, and the F.I.C.A. tax rate is 6.85%.

8. Use the federal withholding tax tables to compute the withholding tax on the following:
   a. A single person, 2 deductions, earning $671.20 per week
   b. A married person, 4 deductions, earning $4150 per month
   c. A single person, 1 deduction, earning $1420 semimonthly

9. Eileen is paid $0.07 per unit for each unit she produces. Last week she produced 6217 units. Calculate her net pay for the week if she is married, claims 2 deductions, and has no voluntary deductions. She is well below the F.I.C.A. maximum (which has a 7.15% rate).

10. Ms. Evans receives a salary of $850 per month plus a commission of 11% on all net sales in excess of $10,000. She is single, claims 1 deduction, and is well below the F.I.C.A maximum. Last month, she sold $22,180 in merchandise but had $1480 in sales returned. What is her net pay if the F.I.C.A. tax rate is 7.15%? She contributes 12% of her gross pay to a company savings plan and gives 1% of her gross salary to the United Fund.

CHAPTER 17

Taxes

INTRODUCTION

Taxation is the process whereby governmental organizations obtain money from the people for the provision of goods and services to benefit the general society. Such money (*taxes*) is spent in accordance with the wishes of the people through spending programs authorized by elected representatives.

The concept of taxation is not new. Ancient Athens obtained revenue from taxes on aliens and slaves. Early Roman citizens paid poll taxes. Under Emperor Augustus, Roman taxation was expanded to land and inheritances; later emperors expanded taxes to even more objects, such as wheat, wine, oil, wood, salt; and bachelors. Taxation in the early years of the United States was primarily in the form of excises on specific goods and activities (snuff, sugar, distilling process, etc.). During the Civil War, Congress introduced income and inheritance taxes; these were abandoned after the war in favor of alcohol and tobacco taxes. On February 25, 1913, the Sixteenth Amendment to the U.S. Constitution became effective. This amendment gave Congress the power "to lay and collect taxes on incomes, from whatever source derived, without apportionment among the several States." The federal income tax authorized under this amendment is the major source of governmental revenue today.

From this brief history you can see the variety of ways in which governmental authorities can raise money. The *sales tax* (on transactions between a buyer and seller) and *property tax* (on ownership of property) are the primary financing means for state and local governments. The *income tax* represents the primary means of financing for the federal government. The income taxation process is a complicated one; it changes almost daily (through Congressional action and/or tax court rulings). Therefore, our discussion of income tax is aimed at familiarizing you with the basic concepts and processes. *Although the procedures presented applied at the time this book was published, you should be aware of current tax laws at the time you calculate your taxes.*

17.1 *Sales Tax*

Sales tax: tax paid
by the purchaser of
merchandise

Many state legislatures have adopted a tax on retail sales in order to finance state spending. The selling firm collects the appropriate tax from the buyer at the time of the sale; the amount collected as tax is then paid to the state at periodic intervals. In many locations, city governments are allowed to add city sales taxes to the state sales taxes in order to obtain money.

In most instances, the amount of the sales tax is stated as a percent of the selling price. On sales of less than a dollar, the tax rate may be set on a nonpercentage basis simply to eliminate errors in rounding. Most retail establishments have sales tax charts enabling sales personnel to "read" the amount of sales tax due without calculation (see Figure 17.1). Sales taxes on larger purchase amounts are usually calculated as a straight percent.

Example 1

Juanita purchased a new skirt for $17.95. The sale is subject to a 5% sales tax.

    a. How much tax will Juanita pay? (Use Figure 17.1.)
    b. What total amount will Juanita pay for the skirt?

SOLUTION

    a. From Figure 17.1, we see that sales from $17.90 through $18.09 have a tax of $0.90.
    b. Juanita will pay the sales price of $17.95 plus the sales tax of $0.90 or a total of $18.85.

Example 2

While she was shopping, Juanita purchased a chair selling for $149.95. Of the 5% sales tax, 4% goes to the state and 1% to the city.

    a. How much tax will Juanita pay on the chair?
    b. How much tax will the state receive? the city?
    c. How much will Juanita pay as the total price?

SOLUTION

    a. The sales tax on the chair will be the 5% tax rate times the selling price of the chair, or

$$\text{tax} = \$149.95 \times 5\% = \$7.50$$

    b. The state will receive 4% of the selling price as tax and the city 1%.

$$\text{State tax} = \$149.95 \times 4\% = \$6.00$$
$$\text{City tax } = \$149.95 \times 1\% = \$1.50$$
$$\text{Total} \quad \$7.50$$

c. Juanita will pay the sum of the selling price and tax for the chair, or

total = $149.95 + $7.50 = $157.45

Figure 17.1

5%

Amount of Sale	Tax	Amount of Sale	Tax
.10 — .29	.01	10.10 — 10.29	.51
.30 — .49	.02	10.30 — 10.49	.52
.50 — .69	.03	10.50 — 10.69	.53
.70 — .89	.04	10.70 — 10.89	.54
.90 — 1.09	.05	10.90 — 11.09	.55
1.10 — 1.29	.06	11.10 — 11.29	.56
1.30 — 1.49	.07	11.30 — 11.49	.57
1.50 — 1.69	.08	11.50 — 11.69	.58
1.70 — 1.89	.09	11.70 — 11.89	.59
1.90 — 2.09	.10	11.90 — 12.09	.60
2.10 — 2.29	.11	12.10 — 12.29	.61
2.30 — 2.49	.12	12.30 — 12.49	.62
2.50 — 2.69	.13	12.50 — 12.69	.63
2.70 — 2.89	.14	12.70 — 12.89	.64
2.90 — 3.09	.15	12.90 — 13.09	.65
3.10 — 3.29	.16	13.10 — 13.29	.66
3.30 — 3.49	.17	13.30 — 13.49	.67
3.50 — 3.69	.18	13.50 — 13.69	.68
3.70 — 3.89	.19	13.70 — 13.89	.69
3.90 — 4.09	.20	13.90 — 14.09	.70
4.10 — 4.29	.21	14.10 — 14.29	.71
4.30 —. 4.49	.22	14.30 — 14.49	.72
4.50 — 4.69	.23	14.50 — 14.69	.73
4.70 — 4.89	.24	14.70 — 14.89	.74
4.90 — 5.09	.25	14.90 — 15.09	.75
5.10 — 5.29	.26	15.10 — 15.29	.76
5.30 — 5.49	.27	15.30 — 15.49	.77
5.50 — 5.69	.28	15.50 — 15.69	.78
5.70 — 5.89	.29	15.70 — 15.89	.79
5.90 — 6.09	.30	15.90 — 16.09	.80
6.10 — 6.29	.31	16.10 — 16.29	.81
6.30 — 6.49	.32	16.30 — 16.49	.82
6.50 — 6.69	.33	16.40 — 16.69	.83
6.70 — 6.89	.34	16.70 — 16.89	.84
6.90 — 7.09	.35	16.90 — 17.09	.85
7.10 — 7.29	.36	17.10 — 17.29	.86
7.30 — 7.49	.37	17.30 — 17.49	.87
7.50 — 7.69	.38	17.50 — 17.69	.88
7.70 — 7.89	.39	17.70 — 17.89	.89
7.90 — 8.09	.40	17.90 — 18.09	.90
8.10 — 8.29	.41	18.10 — 18.29	.91
8.30 — 8.49	.42	18.30 — 18.49	.92
8.50 — 8.69	.43	18.50 — 18.69	.93
8.70 — 8.89	.44	18.70 — 18.89	.94
8.90 — 9.09	.45	18.90 — 19.09	.95
9.10 — 9.29	.46	19.10 — 19.29	.96
9.30 — 9.49	.47	19.30 — 19.49	.97
9.50 — 9.69	.48	19.50 — 19.69	.98
9.70 — 9.89	.49	19.70 — 19.89	.99
9.90 — 10.09	.50	19.90 — 20.10	1.00

You probably have noticed that the tax computation is simply the *base* × *rate* = *percentage* formula from Chapter 4. In this case, it is

sales tax = selling
price × tax rate

$$\text{selling price} \times \text{tax rate} = \text{tax}$$
$$\text{(base)} \quad \times \quad \text{(rate)} \; = \text{(percentage)}$$

The amount paid by the customer is the selling price plus the tax. Using these relationships, we can solve for any unknown in a sales transaction.

Example 3   Sales tax of $0.60 was paid on the purchase of a lamp. If the tax rate is 3%, what was the price of the lamp? How much did the buyer pay?

SOLUTION   Tax paid is calculated according to

$$\text{selling price} \times \text{tax rate} = \text{tax}$$

$$\text{selling price} \times 3\% \quad = \$\,0.60$$

$$\text{selling price} \qquad = \frac{\$\,0.60}{3\%}$$

$$= \$20.00$$

The lamp was priced at $20.00. The buyer paid the selling price plus the tax, or $20.60 (i.e., $20.00 + $0.60) for the lamp.

Example 4   Ms. Jackson paid a total (including a 5% sales tax) of $57.75 for a new blender. What was the price of the blender?

SOLUTION   We know that the total paid for the blender is the sum of the selling price and the tax. We also know that the tax is 5% of the selling price. Therefore,

$$\text{selling price} + \text{sales tax} \qquad\qquad = \text{total price}$$

$$\text{selling price} + (5\% \times \text{selling price}) = \$57.75$$

$$105\% \times \text{selling price} = \$57.75$$

$$\text{selling price} = \frac{\$57.75}{105\%}$$

$$= \$55.00$$

The selling price of the blender is $55.00. The sales tax is $2.75. Note that the sales tax is 5% of the selling price, *not* the total price. Consequently, this problem *cannot* be solved by taking 5% of the total and subtracting that amount from the total paid (i.e., $57.75 × 5% = $2.89; $57.75 − $2.89 = $54.86; see the difference).

Exercises 17.1

■ Calculate the sales tax on the following sales. Use the tax rate indicated.

	Purchase Price	Tax Rate	Sales Tax
Example:	$18.65	4%	$0.75
			(i.e., $18.65 × 4%)
1.	$2.16	$3\frac{1}{2}\%$	
2.	$98.60	4%	
3.	$18.29	Figure 17.1	
4.	$47.25	5%	
5.	$189.95	$4\frac{1}{2}\%$	
6.	$286.50	6%	

7. Jerry purchased a new football priced at $29.95. He must pay a $3\frac{1}{2}\%$ state sales tax and $\frac{1}{2}\%$ city sales tax. How much will Jerry pay

    a. for state tax?
    b. for city tax?
    c. for the football?

8. A dress is priced at $39.85 in Wanda's Shop. The Chic Shop (across the county line) is charging the same price but the sales tax there is 1% lower. How much would you save by purchasing the dress at the Chic Shop?

9. What sales tax is due on an item selling for $175? The sales tax is 5%.

10. Wood Brothers collects $4\frac{1}{2}\%$ sales tax on their sales. How much tax should they pay the state if they collected tax on sales of $22,982.75?

11. A 3% tax totaling $1.18 was paid on an item you recently purchased. What was the price of the item?

12. Maurice purchased a new desk priced at $169.85. State sales taxes are 3% and the city sales tax is 1%. How much did Maurice pay for the desk?

13. You recently purchased a gift on which the tax was $1.00. You cannot remember the price of the gift, but the sales tax rate is 5%. Can you calculate the price of the gift?

14. You are about to pay for a new canoe. The salesman has rung up the purchase price of $325 + $15.63 sales tax (at the $4\frac{1}{2}\%$ tax rate). Is he correct?

15. Mary Jo bought some dress material for herself and her friend. The friend is to pay Mary Jo for her material. Mary Jo paid a total of $19.89. She remembers that her material was priced at $11.25 before the 3% sales tax. How much does Mary Jo's friend owe her?

16. Wonder World Toys sold $18,667.27 before taxes last month. If the state sales tax is $4\frac{1}{2}\%$ and the city sales tax is $\frac{1}{2}\%$, how much should Wonder World pay each taxing authority for last month's sales?

17. James paid a total of $124.80 for automotive parts. What was the actual price of the parts if the tax rate on sales is 4%?

18. Leonard's check register shows a total of $88.58 paid for a purchase. What amount was tax if the tax rate is 3%?

19. Tax on a purchase (at 5%) was $5. What was the purchase price and the total paid?

20. What is the amount of sales tax on a purchase totaling $175.10 if the tax rate is 3%?

21. Eloise paid sales tax of $2.70 on a purchase the total price of which was $92.70. What is the tax rate?

17.2 *Property Tax*

The revenue for most county and city governments is obtained primarily through property taxes. Property taxes may be applied to real property (land, houses, buildings, etc.) and personal property (cars, jewelry, furniture, etc.). The amount of tax paid is dependent on two factors:

assessed value

1. *Assessed property value*—Property has an assessed value for tax purposes. That value is generally expressed as a percent of the fair market value of the property. For example, a house may have a fair market value of $40,000. The assessed value for tax purposes may be 50% of fair market value, or $20,000.

tax rate

2. *Tax rate*—The tax rate per $1 of assessed value is set by various governmental authorities. The tax rate may be expressed as a percent, as an amount per $100, as amount per $1000, or in mills (i.e., in $\frac{1}{1000}$'s of a dollar). Mills are simply a different expression of the amount per $1000.

The tax rate is computed by the governmental authority after the required budget for the coming year is known. For example, if the county budget for the next year is $2,000,000 and the assessed property value totals $100,000,000, the tax rate is computed as follows:

$$\text{tax rate} = \frac{\text{total taxes required}}{\text{total assessed value}}$$

$$= \frac{\$2,000,000}{\$100,000,000}$$

$$= 0.02$$

This tax rate may be stated as 2%, $2 per $100, $20 per $1000, or 20 mills. Normally, the tax rate will not be an even number. When the tax rate is not an even number, the final digit used is always rounded upward, regardless of the size of the following digit. For example, a tax rate of 0.014436 rounded to percent would be 1.45% even though normal rounding rules would be 1.44%. Mills are rounded upward to the nearest whole mill. The assessed value can be changed in either of two ways. The fair market value may be changed to reflect changes in conditions, or the percent of fair market value used for assessed value may be changed. These changes are originated by the appropriate taxing authority.

The actual amount of property tax can be calculated by multiplying the assessed values by the tax rate.

property tax = assessed value × tax rate

$$\boxed{\text{property tax} = \text{assessed value} \times \text{tax rate}}$$

Example 1   Walker County tax requirements for the coming year total $12,000,000. If the assessed value for property tax totaled $335,000,000, what is the tax rate? Express the rate as a percent, dollars per $100, dollars per $1000, and mills.

SOLUTION
$$\text{Tax rate} = \frac{\text{total taxes required}}{\text{total assessed value}}$$

$$= \frac{\$12,000,000}{\$335,000,000}$$

$$= 0.0358208$$

The tax rate is 0.0358208, or 3.59%.
The rate per $100 is $0.0359 \times \$100 = \$3.59$.
The rate per $1000 is $0.0359 \times \$1000 = \$35.90$.
The rate in mills is $0.0359 \times 1000 = 36$ mills (as mills are rounded to the next whole mill).

Example 2   Mr. McCarroll owns a house in Walker County (Example 1). His house has a *fair market value* of $50,000. The assessed valuation rate is 45% of fair market value. What is Mr. McCarroll's county tax?

SOLUTION   Mr. McCarroll's house has an assessed value of $22,500 (i.e., $50,000 × 45%). The amount of property tax is the assessed value times the tax rate, or

$$\text{property tax} = \text{assessed value} \times \text{tax rate}$$

$$= \$22,500 \times 3.59\%$$

$$= \$807.75$$

Mr. McCarroll's county taxes are $807.75 for the year.

We can solve for any unknown in the equation of

$$\text{property tax} = \text{assessed value} \times \text{tax rate}$$

if we know the other two factors. When solving for the assessed value, remember that the answer will be stated in terms of the tax rate; that is, the assessed value will be in $100 units when the tax rate is per $100, in $1000 units when the tax rate is per $1000, and so on. Consequently, a conversion might be required.

Example 3

Property taxes for a house assessed at $23,000 were $805. What is the tax rate in percent?

SOLUTION

Property tax = assessed value × tax rate

$$\$805 = (\$23,000)(\text{tax rate})$$

$$\text{Tax rate} = \frac{\$805}{\$23,000}$$

$$= 0.035 \quad \text{or} \quad 3.5\%$$

Example 4

Ms. Gobel paid $1190 in taxes on her house. The tax rate is $42.50 per $1000 and the house is assessed at 70% of fair market value. What is the fair market value of Ms. Gobel's house?

SOLUTION

Property tax = assessed value × tax rate

$$\$1190 = \text{assessed value} \times \$42.50$$

$$\text{Assessed value} = \frac{\$1190}{\$42.50}$$

$$= 28$$

Since the tax rate is in dollars per $1000, the assessed value represents 28 units of $1000, or an assessed value of $28,000. However, the assessed value is only 70% of fair market value, so

$$\text{Fair market value} \times 70\% = \$28,000$$

$$\text{Fair market value} = \frac{\$28,000}{70\%}$$

$$= \$40,000$$

Exercises 17.2

■ State the following tax rates in terms of percent, dollars per $100, dollars per $1000, and mills. When appropriate, round your answer.

	Tax Rate	*Percent*	*Dollars/$100*	*Dollars/$1000*	*Mills*
Example:	0.0400	4 (0.0400 × 100)	$4 (0.0400 × $100)	$40 (0.0400 × $1000)	40 (0.0400 × 1000)
1.	0.0385				

Tax Rate	Percent	Dollars/$100	Dollars/$1000	Mills
2. 0.0250				
3. 0.0395				
4. 0.0415				
5. 0.0522				
6. 0.0560				

■ Calculate the assessed value of the following property given the fair market value and percent of fair market value used to assess property.

	Fair Market Value	Valuation Percent	Assessed Value
Example:	$50,000	50%	$25,000 (i.e., $50,000 × 50%)
7.	$72,500	45%	
8.	$19,800	30%	
9.	$36,200	55%	
10.	$48,000	60%	
11.	$104,000	35%	
12.	$87,250	40%	

13. The Lower River Authority requires $500,000 in tax revenue next year. If property within its jurisdiction is assessed at $12,500,000, what is the tax rate? State as a percent, per $100, per $1000, and in mills.

14. Summit City requires $4,500,000 to operate in the coming year. If property in the city has an assessed value of $300,000,000, what is the tax rate per $1000?

15. Canyon County has property with an estimated fair market value of $40,000,000. What is the tax rate (in percent) if the county requires $100,000 in revenue and property is assessed at 50% of market value?

16. The East Independent School District has a tax rate of $3.00 per $100 of assessed valuation. If the revenue for the coming year is $150,000 and property is assessed at 40% of fair market value, what is the total fair market value of property in the school district?

17. What amount of property tax will be due on a house assessed at $28,000 if the tax rate is $4.25 per $100 of assessed value?

18. City property is taxed at $15.75 per $1000 of assessed value. What tax is due on a building assessed at $100,000?

19. Mr. Traver owns a home with a fair market value of $95,000. If the tax rate is 5.6% of assessed value and property is assessed at 35% of fair market value, how much tax will he pay?

20. Calculate the tax due on a $29,000 house assessed at 60% of market value. The tax rate is $3.75 per $100.

21. Ms. Womack paid $1787.50 in taxes on her rental property. If the tax rate is 0.025 and rental property is assessed at 55% of fair market value, what is the fair market value of Ms. Womack's rental property?

22. The Municipal Utility District tax on a home was $270.00. What is the fair market value if the tax rate is $30 per $1000 and homes are assessed at 30% of fair market value?

23. The Elite Laundry and Cleaners paid $3200 in property tax. If the property is assessed at $80,000, what is the tax rate?

24. Property tax on the Corner Store was $3000. What is the tax rate in mills if the store is assessed at $60,000?

25. Polly Alvarado paid $2250 in property tax on her home. What are the assessed value and fair market value of her home if the tax rate is 3.75% and property is assessed at 60% of fair market value?

17.3 *Federal Income Tax*

The Sixteenth Amendment to the United States Constitution gave the federal government the power to tax the incomes of U.S. citizens. This taxation power has provided the federal government with its main source of revenue. In Chapter 16, we discussed how money was withheld from an employee's paycheck in order to pay the income tax owed to the government (refer to Section 16.5). However, the amount of money withheld was an *estimated* amount required to pay the taxes owed by the "average" citizen in certain income and family status categories.

In this section, we will discuss how to calculate the actual taxes you owe. We will discuss the general process under laws existing at the time this book was published. While this process will apply in general, there are many "special situations" that affect the calculation of income tax. Therefore, you should thoroughly review current tax laws or seek professional help when actually preparing your income tax.

In general, the federal income tax is a graduated, progressive tax. That is, the amount of tax you pay is a percentage of the income you earn; also, the percent tax you pay increases as your income increases. Whether or not a U.S. citizen has to pay income taxes depends on the income earned, age, and marital status of that citizen. Before beginning our discussion, we should understand some of the terminology applicable to income taxes.

Definitions

gross income   **Gross income is all income received (in the form of money, property, and services) that is not exempt from taxes. It includes wages, salaries, tips, commissions, most stock dividends, interest received, rent and royalties, and other income from all sources. There are some exclusions from gross income. Examples of these exclusions are gifts, inheritances, Social Security benefits received, interest on state and local government bonds, and other items as outlined by tax laws.**

adjusted gross income

Adjusted gross income is the income after certain "adjustments to income" are subtracted from the gross income. These adjustments include items such as employee business expenses (i.e., expenses necessary to earn income), contributions to retirement plans (Individual Retirement Accounts, Keogh), alimony paid, disability income received, and an allowance for married couples (both of whom work).

taxable income

Taxable income is the adjusted gross income minus itemized deductions (if applicable) and an allowance for exemptions. (See the definition of deductions and exemptions below.)

deductions

Deductions from income are allowed for payments made for specified purposes. For example, gifts to churches and charities, interest paid on home mortgages and other notes, taxes on property, casualty and theft losses in excess of $100, and other specified payments may be deducted from income in order to determine the amount of income that is taxable. These deductions may be *itemized*; however, you may choose not to itemize and accept the standard deductions that are built into the tax tables.

exemptions

Exemptions are allowances made for persons supported by the income earned. For example, you may claim one exemption for yourself, one for your spouse (if married), and one for each dependent person in your household. Persons who are age 65 or older may claim an additional exemption, as may persons who are blind.

The actual determination of income tax due can be calculated by the following steps.

1. Determine the taxable income by
   a. Gross income

   $$\frac{-\text{ adjustments to income}}{= \text{ adjusted gross income}}$$

   b. Adjusted gross income

   $$\frac{-\text{ itemized deductions (or zero if deductions are not itemized)} \text{ and the allowance for exemptions}}{= \text{ taxable income}}$$

2. Read the taxable income into the appropriate tax table. The tax tables vary according to marital and tax filing status. The figure obtained from the table is the income tax owed to the federal government.

The actual reporting of income taxes is usually done on one of three forms. Form 1040A (sometimes known as the *short form*) is used by persons making less than $50,000 per year who receive income only from wages, salaries, interest, dividends, tips, or unemployment compensation. Form 1040EZ is used by single taxpayers who meet the basic requirements of Form 1040A but who claim no dependents or exemptions for being age 65 or more or blind.

The standard Form 1040 is used by taxpayers who cannot, by law, use the other forms. Taxpayers using Form 1040 include persons who

1. make more than $50,000 per year,
2. itemize deductions,
3. are married but file their tax returns separately, or
4. are specifically required to use Form 1040 for other reasons.

Business income is taxed as well as personal income. Income earned by sole proprietors and partners in a partnership is taxed as personal income to the individuals involved. However, corporations are separate, legal entities. As such, they are taxed on their corporate earnings and must file separate corporate income tax returns.

The following examples will help clarify the calculation of income tax owed.

Example 1   Henry is single with no other dependents. He received a salary of $19,800 last year and has elected not to itemize deductions when filing his income tax. Calculate the tax Henry owes.

SOLUTION   First, we must compute Henry's taxable income.

$19,800	gross income
− 0	adjustments to income
= 19,800	adjusted gross income
− 0	deductions (since Henry is not itemizing his deductions)
− 1,000	exemption allowance (the current exemption allowance is $1000 for each exemption)
= $18,800	taxable income

We can determine Henry's income tax by reading the taxable income into the tax table (Figure 17.2).* Reading in the "$18,800–$18,850" line to the "single" column heading (Henry's status), we find that Henry's tax is $3730.

Example 2   Marcia is a sales representative. She earned a salary of $15,000 plus sales commissions totaling $18,000. In addition, she received a bonus of $4500 for her outstanding sales record. To earn this money, Marcia had to spend $7000 of her own money for traveling expenses. Marcia is divorced and has a son. How much does Marcia owe in taxes if her itemized deductions exceed the "standard" deductions by $2100? †

---

* Figure 17.2 gives only one page of the income tax tables. The remaining tax tables we shall use are shown in Table XI on pp. 583–588.

† All tax tables have a "built-in" allowance for deductibles. You may deduct only the amount of itemized deductions that exceed the deductions provided in the table.

Figure 17.2

Tax Table (Continued)

If line 34 (taxable income) is— At least	But less than	Single	Married filing jointly *	Married filing separately	Head of a household
			Your tax is—		
16,250	16,300	2,950	2,302	3,546	2,772
16,300	16,350	2,965	2,314	3,564	2,785
16,350	16,400	2,980	2,326	3,582	2,798
16,400	16,450	2,995	2,337	3,601	2,811
16,450	16,500	3,009	2,349	3,619	2,824
16,500	16,550	3,024	2,361	3,637	2,837
16,550	16,600	3,039	2,373	3,655	2,849
16,600	16,650	3,054	2,385	3,674	2,862
16,650	16,700	3,069	2,397	3,692	2,875
16,700	16,750	3,083	2,409	3,710	2,888
16,750	16,800	3,098	2,420	3,729	2,901
16,800	16,850	3,113	2,432	3,747	2,914
16,850	16,900	3,128	2,444	3,765	2,926
16,900	16,950	3,143	2,456	3,783	2,939
16,950	17,000	3,158	2,468	3,802	2,952
17,000					
17,000	17,050	3,172	2,480	3,820	2,965
17,050	17,100	3,187	2,491	3,838	2,978
17,100	17,150	3,202	2,503	3,856	2,991
17,150	17,200	3,217	2,515	3,875	3,003
17,200	17,250	3,232	2,527	3,893	3,016
17,250	17,300	3,246	2,539	3,911	3,029
17,300	17,350	3,261	2,551	3,930	3,042
17,350	17,400	3,276	2,563	3,948	3,055
17,400	17,450	3,291	2,574	3,966	3,068
17,450	17,500	3,306	2,586	3,984	3,081
17,500	17,550	3,320	2,598	4,003	3,093
17,550	17,600	3,335	2,610	4,021	3,106
17,600	17,650	3,350	2,622	4,041	3,119
17,650	17,700	3,365	2,634	4,062	3,132
17,700	17,750	3,380	2,646	4,083	3,145
17,750	17,800	3,395	2,657	4,104	3,158
17,800	17,850	3,409	2,669	4,126	3,170
17,850	17,900	3,424	2,681	4,147	3,183
17,900	17,950	3,439	2,693	4,168	3,196
17,950	18,000	3,454	2,705	4,189	3,209
18,000					
18,000	18,050	3,469	2,717	4,210	3,222
18,050	18,100	3,483	2,728	4,232	3,235
18,100	18,150	3,498	2,740	4,253	3,247
18,150	18,200	3,513	2,752	4,274	3,260
18,200	18,250	3,529	2,764	4,295	3,274
18,250	18,300	3,546	2,776	4,317	3,290
18,300	18,350	3,562	2,788	4,338	3,305
18,350	18,400	3,579	2,800	4,359	3,320
18,400	18,450	3,596	2,811	4,380	3,336
18,450	18,500	3,613	2,823	4,402	3,351
18,500	18,550	3,630	2,835	4,423	3,366
18,550	18,600	3,646	2,847	4,444	3,381
18,600	18,650	3,663	2,859	4,465	3,397
18,650	18,700	3,680	2,871	4,486	3,412
18,700	18,750	3,697	2,883	4,508	3,427
18,750	18,800	3,713	2,894	4,529	3,443
18,800	18,850	3,730	2,906	4,550	3,458
18,850	18,900	3,747	2,918	4,571	3,473
18,900	18,950	3,764	2,930	4,593	3,489
18,950	19,000	3,781	2,942	4,614	3,504

If line 34 (taxable income) is— At least	But less than	Single	Married filing jointly *	Married filing separately	Head of a household
			Your tax is—		
19,000					
19,000	19,050	3,797	2,954	4,635	3,519
19,050	19,100	3,814	2,965	4,656	3,535
19,100	19,150	3,831	2,977	4,678	3,550
19,150	19,200	3,848	2,989	4,699	3,565
19,200	19,250	3,865	3,001	4,720	3,580
19,250	19,300	3,881	3,013	4,741	3,596
19,300	19,350	3,898	3,025	4,762	3,611
19,350	19,400	3,915	3,037	4,784	3,626
19,400	19,450	3,932	3,048	4,805	3,642
19,450	19,500	3,949	3,060	4,826	3,657
19,500	19,550	3,965	3,072	4,847	3,672
19,550	19,600	3,982	3,084	4,869	3,688
19,600	19,650	3,999	3,096	4,890	3,703
19,650	19,700	4,016	3,108	4,911	3,718
19,700	19,750	4,032	3,120	4,932	3,733
19,750	19,800	4,049	3,131	4,954	3,749
19,800	19,850	4,066	3,143	4,975	3,764
19,850	19,900	4,083	3,155	4,996	3,779
19,900	19,950	4,100	3,167	5,017	3,795
19,950	20,000	4,116	3,179	5,038	3,810
20,000					
20,000	20,050	4,133	3,191	5,060	3,825
20,050	20,100	4,150	3,202	5,081	3,841
20,100	20,150	4,167	3,214	5,102	3,856
20,150	20,200	4,184	3,226	5,123	3,871
20,200	20,250	4,200	3,239	5,145	3,887
20,250	20,300	4,217	3,253	5,166	3,902
20,300	20,350	4,234	3,267	5,187	3,917
20,350	20,400	4,251	3,280	5,208	3,932
20,400	20,450	4,267	3,294	5,230	3,948
20,450	20,500	4,284	3,308	5,251	3,963
20,500	20,550	4,301	3,322	5,272	3,978
20,550	20,600	4,318	3,336	5,293	3,994
20,600	20,650	4,335	3,350	5,314	4,009
20,650	20,700	4,351	3,363	5,336	4,024
20,700	20,750	4,368	3,377	5,357	4,040
20,750	20,800	4,385	3,391	5,378	4,055
20,800	20,850	4,402	3,405	5,399	4,070
20,850	20,900	4,419	3,419	5,421	4,086
20,900	20,950	4,435	3,433	5,442	4,101
20,950	21,000	4,452	3,446	5,463	4,116
21,000					
21,000	21,050	4,469	3,460	5,484	4,131
21,050	21,100	4,486	3,474	5,506	4,147
21,100	21,150	4,503	3,488	5,527	4,162
21,150	21,200	4,519	3,502	5,548	4,177
21,200	21,250	4,536	3,516	5,569	4,193
21,250	21,300	4,553	3,529	5,590	4,208
21,300	21,350	4,570	3,543	5,612	4,223
21,350	21,400	4,586	3,557	5,633	4,239
21,400	21,450	4,603	3,571	5,654	4,254
21,450	21,500	4,620	3,585	5,675	4,269
21,500	21,550	4,637	3,598	5,697	4,285
21,550	21,600	4,654	3,612	5,718	4,300
21,600	21,650	4,670	3,626	5,739	4,315
21,650	21,700	4,687	3,640	5,760	4,330
21,700	21,750	4,704	3,654	5,782	4,346

If line 34 (taxable income) is— At least	But less than	Single	Married filing jointly *	Married filing separately	Head of a household
			Your tax is—		
21,750	21,800	4,721	3,668	5,803	4,361
21,800	21,850	4,738	3,681	5,824	4,376
21,850	21,900	4,754	3,695	5,845	4,392
21,900	21,950	4,771	3,709	5,866	4,407
21,950	22,000	4,788	3,723	5,888	4,422
22,000					
22,000	22,050	4,805	3,737	5,909	4,438
22,050	22,100	4,821	3,751	5,930	4,453
22,100	22,150	4,838	3,764	5,951	4,468
22,150	22,200	4,855	3,778	5,973	4,483
22,200	22,250	4,872	3,792	5,994	4,499
22,250	22,300	4,889	3,806	6,015	4,514
22,300	22,350	4,905	3,820	6,036	4,529
22,350	22,400	4,922	3,833	6,058	4,545
22,400	22,450	4,939	3,847	6,079	4,560
22,450	22,500	4,956	3,861	6,100	4,575
22,500	22,550	4,973	3,875	6,121	4,591
22,550	22,600	4,989	3,889	6,142	4,606
22,600	22,650	5,006	3,903	6,164	4,621
22,650	22,700	5,023	3,916	6,185	4,637
22,700	22,750	5,040	3,930	6,206	4,652
22,750	22,800	5,056	3,944	6,227	4,667
22,800	22,850	5,073	3,958	6,249	4,682
22,850	22,900	5,090	3,972	6,270	4,698
22,900	22,950	5,107	3,986	6,293	4,713
22,950	23,000	5,124	3,999	6,317	4,728
23,000					
23,000	23,050	5,140	4,013	6,341	4,744
23,050	23,100	5,157	4,027	6,365	4,759
23,100	23,150	5,174	4,041	6,389	4,774
23,150	23,200	5,191	4,055	6,414	4,790
23,200	23,250	5,208	4,069	6,438	4,805
23,250	23,300	5,224	4,082	6,462	4,820
23,300	23,350	5,241	4,096	6,486	4,836
23,350	23,400	5,258	4,110	6,510	4,851
23,400	23,450	5,275	4,124	6,535	4,866
23,450	23,500	5,292	4,138	6,559	4,881
23,500	23,550	5,310	4,151	6,583	4,898
23,550	23,600	5,329	4,165	6,607	4,916
23,600	23,650	5,348	4,179	6,631	4,934
23,650	23,700	5,367	4,193	6,656	4,951
23,700	23,750	5,387	4,207	6,680	4,969
23,750	23,800	5,406	4,221	6,704	4,987
23,800	23,850	5,425	4,234	6,728	5,005
23,850	23,900	5,444	4,248	6,752	5,022
23,900	23,950	5,464	4,262	6,776	5,040
23,950	24,000	5,483	4,276	6,801	5,058
24,000					
24,000	24,050	5,502	4,290	6,825	5,076
24,050	24,100	5,521	4,304	6,849	5,094
24,100	24,150	5,541	4,317	6,873	5,111
24,150	24,200	5,560	4,331	6,897	5,129
24,200	24,250	5,579	4,345	6,922	5,147
24,250	24,300	5,598	4,359	6,946	5,165
24,300	24,350	5,618	4,373	6,970	5,182
24,350	24,400	5,637	4,386	6,994	5,200
24,400	24,450	5,656	4,400	7,018	5,218
24,450	24,500	5,675	4,414	7,043	5,236

*This column must also be used by a qualifying widow(er).

Continued on next page

SOLUTION   First, we compute the tax table income. Marcia's gross income is

$15,000   salary
+ 18,000   commission
+   4,500   bonus
—————
= $37,500

Her adjusted gross income is

$37,500
−   7,000   business expense (adjustments to income)
—————
= $30,500

and her taxable income is

$30,500
− 2,100   excess itemized deductions
− 2,000   exemptions ($1000 each for Marcia and her son)
—————
$26,400

Marcia qualifies as the head of a household since she is providing support for her son, therefore, we use that column in the tax table (see Table XI on p. 583). Reading across the $26,400–$26,450 income level, we find that Marcia owes taxes of $5929.

———————————————

In Chapter 16, we calculated the tax withheld, and in this chapter the tax owed. Now we should bring the two together to determine whether the income tax withheld matches the tax owed. In January of each year, an employee receives a form (Form W-2) from his employer. Included on this form are the amount of money earned by the employee, the Social Security tax paid, and the amount of income tax withheld by the employer. Of course, the income tax withheld has already been paid to the government by the employer. When the income tax forms are filed, if the employee has paid in more taxes through withholding than he owes, he receives money back (a *tax refund*). If he owes more tax than the amount withheld, he must pay the additional amount by April 15 of the year following the tax year. Let us illustrate the concept by referring to Example 6 in Section 16.5 (p. 392).

———————————————

Example 3   Assume Mr. Nelson (Example 6, p. 392) earned the same amount all year ($900 every two weeks). The four dependents he claims are himself, his wife, and their two children. If the Nelsons have no income other than Mr. Nelson's pay and they file their taxes together (jointly), how much additional tax do the Nelsons owe? They are not itemizing their deductions.

SOLUTION   Mr. Nelson earned $23,400 for the year ($900 biweekly × 26 pay periods) and has paid $3699.80 in taxes (from the withholding table for married persons, biweekly pay period, with four exemptions the withholding tax is $142.30 per pay period). We can calculate the Nelsons' income tax owed as follows:

$23,400   gross income

−   0   adjustments to income

= $23,400   adjusted gross income

−   0   deductions (since the Nelsons are not itemizing)

−   4000   exemptions ($1000 for Mr. Nelson, Mrs. Nelson, and each child)

$19,400   taxable income

Reading the $19,400 into the tax tables under the "married filing jointly" column, we find that the Nelson's owe $3048 in taxes. The Nelsons will be getting a tax refund since they have paid more tax than they owe.

$3699.80   tax paid (i.e., $142.30 withholding × 26 pay periods)

− 3048.00   tax owed

$651.80   tax refund

Exercises 17.3

■ Calculate the required information in the following problems. Assume $1000 is allowed as the reduction in income for each exemption.

	Gross Income	Adjustments to Income	Adjusted Gross Income	Excess Itemized Deductions	Number of Exemptions	Taxable Income
Example:	$30,000	$4000	$26,000 ($30,000 − $4,000)	$2000	3	$21,000 [$26,000 − ($2000 + 3($1000))]
1.	$27,000	0	?	0	4	?
2.	$41,240	$3000	?	$1585	3	?
3.	$35,940	$1800	?	$2246	4	?
4.	$22,360	0	?	$1170	2	?
5.	$38,942	$2682	?	$3412	3	?
6.	$44,210	$3096	?	$2648	4	?

Classify each of the following items in the appropriate category.

Item	Gross Income	Adjustment to Income	Deduction
Example: Salary			
7. Interest received			
8. Interest paid			
9. Stock dividend			
10. Business expense			
11. Property taxes			
12. Contribution to an Individual Retirement Account			
13. Rental from property owned			
14. Donations to the church			
15. Alimony paid			
16. Disability income received			

■ Calculate the income tax owed on the following taxable incomes. Use the tax tables shown in Table XI on pp. 583–588.

	Taxable Income	Tax Status	Income Tax
Example	$28,840	Single	$7352
17.	$46,224	Married, filing jointly	?
18.	$36,430	Single	?
19.	$28,312	Married, filing separately	?
20.	$19,061	Single	?
21.	$29,318	Head of household	?
22.	$30,928	Married, filing jointly	?

■ Assume an allowance of $1000 per exemption in the following problems. Also assume married filing jointly unless given information to the contrary.

23. James received a salary of $32,400 for the year. His income from an oil well royalty was $3600. James is married, has 2 children, and does not itemize his deductions. Calculate his income tax.

24. Erin received a salary of $24,000 and a commission of $12,000. She is single (the only exemption) and itemized her deductions (the excess deductions she had totaled $2200). What is her income tax?

25. Marie earned a total of $29,150 for the year. She contributed $2000 into an Indivi-dual Retirement Account. She is single; however, she supports her daughter and is classified as the head of a household. Assuming Marie did not itemize her deductions, how much tax will she owe?

26. Johnathon works on a salary plus commission basis. For the year, his salary was $20,000 and his commission totaled $18,000. He also received $1100 in stock dividends and $400 in interest from a savings account. Johnathon itemized his deductions (his excess deductions totaled $3417) and is married with 3 children. How much income tax will he owe?

27. Hilda received a total of $9800 for the year. She is retired and $5800 of that amount came from Social Security. The remaining $4000 was stock dividends and interest received on savings. She is single, over 65, and does not itemize deductions. What is her income tax? (*Hint:* Recall that a person over age 65 receives an additional exemption.)

28. Wayne received a salary of $31,450 and rental income of $3965. He contributed $1500 into an Individual Retirement Account, and his excess itemized deductions were $2942. Wayne is married and has 1 child. Calculate his income tax.

29. Wilma received the following income: salary—$28,400; stock dividends—$350; and royalty income—$3940. She spent $4200 in business expense necessary to earn her income and chose to itemize her deductions (the excess itemized deductions were $1916). If she contributed $2000 into a Keogh retirement plan, what is her income tax? She is single with no other dependents.

30. Elena has paid $8070 in withholding tax during the year. Her earnings total $36,920 (from all sources). She contributed $2000 into an Individual Retirement Account and her excess itemized deductions are $3712. Elena is single with no other dependents. How much additional tax does she owe?

31. Thomas earned $18,000 in salary and $22,000 in commission last year. His em-ployer withheld $8540 in taxes for the year. Thomas incurred $3200 in necessary business expense and he chooses not to itemize deductions. Thomas is married and has 1 child. How much will he receive as a tax refund?

Review Exercises / Chapter 17

1. After the 6% city sales tax was added, a television sold for $496.61. How much was the marked price of the television? How much tax was included in the purchase price?

2. Ms. Sontag paid $166.77 for an airline ticket. This price included a 5% state sales tax and a 4% federal excise tax. Compute
   a. the cost of the ticket.
   b. the state sales tax.
   c. the federal excise tax.

3. Tax on a purchase (at 6%) was $7.20. What was the marked price and total paid for the purchased item?

4. A New Jersey resident paid $866.25 in property taxes. What was the assessed value of her property if the tax rate was $3.85 per $100?

5. Property assessed at $48,200 was taxed in the amount of $2048.50. What was the tax rate expressed as a percent?

6. A homeowner whose property was assessed at $28,000 paid $1050 in property taxes. The next year, the tax rate increased by $0.25 per $100 and the property tax was $1280. How much had the assessed value of the house increased?

7. The property tax on a building was $5040 when the tax rate was $120.00 per $1000. During the next year, the assessed value of the building increased by $10,000 and the tax rate changed. If the new tax was $6760, how much had the tax rate changed?

8. Mr. Lee paid $1815.10 in property tax on his home. What is the fair market value of his home if the tax rate is 44 mills and the house is assessed at 65% of fair market value?

9. Ms. James is married and the sole support of her husband and 2 children. She earned $36,920 in salary and commissions last year. She also received rental income of $4200 and stock dividends totaling $895. Ms. James contributed $2000 into an Individual Retirement Account and had excess itemized deductions of $3791. What is her income tax? (Assume a $1000 allowance for exemptions and filing jointly.)

10. Alex received $2200 in stock dividends, $4600 in rental income, and $19,200 in wages. Necessary business expenses totaled $1965. He is single and does not itemize deductions. How much income tax will he owe (assume $1000 per exemption)?

11. Grady received a salary of $29,200 and a commission of $13,680. Necessary business expenses were $2695 and he contributed $1800 into a Keogh retirement plan. Grady is married and has 3 children. His excess itemized deductions were $2206. How much income tax will he owe assuming he and his wife file a joint tax return (allow $1000 per exemption)?

12. William has paid $4085 in withholding tax for the year. He earned $26,460 in salary and received $1100 in stock dividends and interest. William is married, has 2 children, and he and his wife file a joint tax return. If William does not itemize his deductions, and exemptions are allowed at $1000 each, how much more does William owe in taxes?

Chapter Test / Chapter 17

1. Define the following terms.

    a. taxes   **b.** assessed value

    c. exemptions   **d.** fair market value

    e. gross income   **f.** adjusted gross income

    g. taxable income   **h.** deductions

2. The Children's World Store sold $23,287.18 in merchandise last week. How much sales tax do they owe
   a. the state whose sales tax rate is $4\frac{1}{2}\%$,
   b. the city whose sales tax rate is 1%?

3. Harry paid a total of $104.34 for a purchase. What was the actual cost of the merchandise if the sales tax rate is $4\frac{1}{2}\%$?

4. Tax on merchandise costing $37.95 was $2.28. What is the tax rate?

5. Montgomery County taxes property at $27.85 per $1000 of assessed value. What county tax is due on a building assessed at $96,800?

6. Calculate the property tax due on a home with a fair market value of $85,000. The tax rate is 3.65% and homes are assessed at 65% of market value for tax purposes.

7. Arthur Anderson paid $3277.50 in property tax on his home. What are the assessed value and fair market value of his home if the tax rate is $4.75 per $100 of assessed value and property is assessed at 60% of fair market value?

8. The property tax on a building was $31,500 when the tax rate was $140 per $1000. During the next year, the assessed value of the building increased by 50% and the tax rate changed. If the new tax is $37,125, how much had the tax rate changed?

9. Eloise received a salary of $28,900 and a commission of $4200. She is single and does not itemize her deductions. What is her income tax for the year (assuming $1000 per exemption)?

10. Guerimina received the following income: salary—$29,000; stock dividends—$1350; royalty income—$2200; and interest from savings accounts—$695. She incurred necessary business expenses totaling $3890 and contributed $2000 to an Individual Retirement Account. What is the income tax Guerimina owes if she is the sole support of her family (husband and 2 children)? Assume a $1000 deduction for each exemption and joint filing.

11. Jerry paid $7860 in income tax withholding during the year. His income consisted of $31,000 in salary and $4800 in commissions. He contributed $1400 into a Keogh plan and itemized his deductions (his excess deductions totaled $1876). Jerry is single. Assuming a $1000 deduction for exemptions, how much money does Jerry owe in taxes; or how much will he receive as a tax refund?

CHAPTER 18

Insurance

INTRODUCTION

Man is exposed to many events in his life; not all of them are desirable. Property losses (from fire, earthquakes, floods, etc.) and personal losses (physical disability or premature death) can have a severe financial effect on the individual or his heirs. While he cannot predict or prevent these undesirable events, the individual can do something to protect against the financial consequences involved. He can provide *insurance* against financial losses resulting from the events.

Definition

insurance

Insurance protects against financial loss by having the loss of the unfortunate few who experience the event paid as a result of the contributions of many who are exposed to the same event.

The key to insurance lies in the law of large numbers. As the number of people (or things) insured increases, so does the predictability of disastrous occurrence. Data accumulated on large numbers of similar people or things provide an accurate indicator of the actual number that will experience a disaster. With the actual number of occurrences available, it is possible to determine the contribution that each member must make.

Some of the major terms used in insurance are defined as follows:

insurance terms
defined

1. *Insured*—The insured is the one who carries insurance against a financial loss.
2. *Insurer* (or *underwriter*)—The insurer is the group (normally an insurance company) that agrees to pay the financial loss to the insured if a specific event occurs.
3. *Policy*—The insurance policy is the legal contract between the insured and insurer. It stipulates the events covered, maximum amounts to be paid, exclusions of coverage, and so on.

4. *Premium*—The premium is the amount of money paid by the insured to the insurer for coverage as provided in the policy. Premiums are normally stated as cost per year, although semi-annual, quarterly, and monthly costs are sometimes used.

5. *Beneficiary*—The beneficiary of an insurance policy receives the money paid by the insurer in the event of loss. The beneficiary may be the insured or someone he designates.

6. *Face amount*—The face amount of insurance is the maximum amount of coverage under the insurance policy. Payment for claims under the policy will be limited to the actual amount of loss or to the face amount, whichever is less. (*Note:* The face amount is always paid under life insurance policies.)

It is possible to insure almost anything or anyone. Our discussion in this chapter, however, will cover only the kinds of insurance you will normally encounter. These kinds are fire, motor vehicle, and life insurance.

18.1 *Fire Insurance*

Fire insurance provides insurance coverage against the financial loss resulting from fire or lightning damage. Additional insurance coverage for damage caused by smoke, water, windstorm, vandalism, and so on, can be purchased by *extended coverage* to the fire insurance policy. Fire insurance premiums are usually stated as cost per $100 of insurance coverage. Basic fire insurance coverage consists of two parts: (1) coverage of the *structure* or building, and (2) coverage of the *contents* of the building. Insurance costs for fire insurance on both the structure and contents are usually the same; however, extended coverage rates are normally higher on contents than on the structure. Our discussion in this chapter will center only on fire insurance without extended coverage. The principles are the same.

factors affecting cost of fire insurance

There are three basic factors that affect the cost of fire insurance:

1. *The structure or type of construction of the insured building*—certain types of construction will be less susceptible to fire and fire damage. A cinderblock structure with a fire-resistant roof will have a lower insurance cost than will a wooden frame house with a cedar shingle roof.

2. *The area (or key rate area, i.e., the location of the building)*—the geographic area in which the structure is located will affect the fire insurance premiums. Structures close to fire hydrants and/or fire stations in an area served by well-trained firefighters are less likely to incur major damage than structures in rural areas far from fire-fighting facilities.

3. *The class or use of the building*—structures are assigned a "class" by insurance companies depending on the use and equipment in the structure. A building used to manufacture or store combustible products is more likely to have a fire than is a building storing

metal pipe. Buildings having smoke/fire alarm systems and sprinkler systems are assigned a more favorable insurance class than are buildings with no fire-protection devices. Of course, homes have a separate class from businesses.

Figure 18.1 shows typical fire insurance premiums for residence property. (Notice how all three factors are considered in a single table to arrive at the rate.)

Figure 18.1

Class A Dwelling (1–2 Family) Rate per $100

Type of Structure	Area				
	1	2	3	4	5
Brick	0.102	0.146	0.202	0.252	0.313
Brick veneer	0.139	0.182	0.237	0.285	0.345
Asbestos and stucco	0.179	0.231	0.295	0.354	0.424
Frame	0.233	0.281	0.344	0.399	0.467

The fire insurance premium can be calculated by multiplying the insurance rate (obtained from a table similar to Figure 18.1) by the face amount of the insurance policy divided by 100 (since the rates are quoted per $100 of coverage).

$$\frac{\text{fire insurance}}{\text{premium}} = \frac{\text{insurance}}{\text{rate per } \$100} \times \frac{\text{face amount of policy}}{100}$$

Example 1   Mr. Anderson has taken out fire insurance on his new home. He wants to insure the house for $55,000 and the contents for $25,000. His home is brick and is in area 3. Using Figure 18.1 for a class A home, find his insurance premium.

SOLUTION   The fire insurance rates for house and contents are the same. Mr. Anderson wants coverage of $80,000 (i.e., $55,000 for the house and $25,000 for the contents). From Figure 18.1 we see that a brick house in area 3 has a rate of 0.202 per $100 of coverage. Thus, Mr. Anderson's insurance premium would be

$$\text{total premium} = (0.202) \times \left(\frac{\$80,000}{100}\right) = \$161.60$$

Fire insurance policies are normally written on an annual basis. Although 2- and 3-year policies (once common) are still written, the majority of fire insurance policies are based on a single year.

Short-Rate (or Pro Rata) Cancellation

canceling a fire
insurance policy
(short-rate
schedule)

There are occasions when fire insurance policies are in effect for less than a year. An owner may sell property and wish to discontinue insurance protection; or he may wish to change policies and companies for some reason. When a policy is canceled, the premium for the part of the year not used is returned to the policyholder. However, to cover policy handling costs, insurance companies charge a higher premium for those months of coverage used. To determine the actual premium cost of insurance for months covered, the annual premium is multiplied by a factor based on the number of months for which coverage was provided. Figure 18.2 shows a typical *short-rate cancellation schedule*.

**Figure 18.2
Short-Rate
Cancellation
Schedule**

Months of Coverage	Percent of Annual Premium	Months of Coverage	Percent of Annual Premium
1	14	7	67
2	27	8	74
3	36	9	81
4	44	10	87
5	52	11	94
6	60	12	100

You can see from Figure 18.2 that more than one-half of the premium is paid when coverage has been in effect only 5 months. The amount of refund the policyholder receives after cancellation will be the annual premium less the cost of coverage (at the short-rate schedule) for months used. (*Note:* If the *insurer* cancels the policy, short rates do not apply; the cost of each month's protection is $\frac{1}{12}$ of the annual premium.)

Example 2

A frame house (and contents) valued at $48,000 is located in area 5. Four months after renewing her insurance policy, the owner sells the home and cancels the policy.

    a. What annual premium did the owner pay?
    b. How much will she receive as a refund?

SOLUTION

    a. The rate per $100 for a frame home in area 5 is 0.467. The annual premium paid was

$$\text{annual premium} = 0.467 \times \frac{\$48,000}{100} = \$224.16$$

    b. The refund from cancellation is the annual premium less the cost of 4 months' insurance at short rates; or

$$\text{cost for 4 months} = \$224.16 \times 44\%$$
$$= \$98.63$$

$$\text{refund} = \$224.16 - \$98.63 = \$125.53$$

coinsurance   ## Coinsurance

Since most fires do not completely destroy the insured property, some property owners might wish to insure their property for less than its full value. That is, the owner of a $40,000 home might insure it only for $20,000 on the assumption that a fire would not do more than $20,000 worth of damage. Then the insurance company would pay the amount of loss or $20,000, whichever is less. However, in such a situation, the insurance company would be carrying most of the risk for premium payments of about one-half the value. To prevent such cases, most insurance companies have a *coinsurance clause* in their fire policies. This clause stipulates that the insurance company will pay the lesser of full damages or face amount *only* if the insurance coverage is at least 80% of the value of the property and contents. If the insurance coverage is less than 80%, the owner of the property is assumed to be a *coinsurer* with the insurance company. In essence, the insurance company will pay the smallest of the following amounts: (1) the amount of actual loss, (2) the face amount of the policy, or (3) the amount resulting from the coinsurance calculation. In coinsurance cases, insurance payments are made only in the ratio of actual insurance coverage to required insurance coverage. The property owner will be responsible for the remaining loss. The following example indicates the coinsurance clause.

Example 3   Allen Campbell has a home valued at $60,000. He purchased his fire insurance years ago and has not updated the coverage since. His fire insurance policy provides for coverage of $30,000. His home burned with an estimated loss of $20,000. How much will his insurance company pay if his policy has an 80% coinsurance clause?

SOLUTION   The required insurance coverage for $60,000 property under an 80% co-insurance clause is

$$\$60,000 \times 80\% = \$48,000$$

Allen's $30,000 coverage is less than $48,000, so Allen is a coinsurer of the property. The amount of coverage provided by the insurance company is in the ratio of insurance carried to insurance required, or

$$\frac{\$30,000 \text{ insurance carried}}{\$48,000 \text{ insurance required}} = 62.5\%$$

Since Allen is carrying only 62.5% of the required insurance, the insurance company will pay for only 62.5% of the loss, that is,

$$\$20,000 \text{ loss} \times 62.5\% = \$12,500$$

Allen's part of the loss (as coinsurer) will be the remaining $7500.

Multiple Insurance Coverage

insurance coverage
by several insurance
companies

There may be instances when the insurance coverage for property is provided by more than one insurance company. In such a case, each company pays damages equal to the percent coverage its policy is of the total insurance coverage.

Example 4

The Ace Chemical Company has insurance policies with three companies as follows:

First Insurance Company	$150,000
Second Insurance Company	$100,000
Third Insurance Company	$ 50,000
Total	$300,000

The Ace Company suffered fire damage amounting to $180,000. Assuming that the Ace Company had enough insurance coverage to avoid coinsurance restrictions, how much should each company pay?

SOLUTION

Each insurance company's ratio to total coverage can be calculated as follows:

First $\dfrac{\$150,000}{\$300,000} = \dfrac{1}{2}$

Second $\dfrac{\$100,000}{\$300,000} = \dfrac{1}{3}$

Third $\dfrac{\$50,000}{\$300,000} = \dfrac{1}{6}$

The amount paid by each company is found by applying these ratios to the total loss.

First pays $\frac{1}{2}$ × $180,000 loss $\quad= \$ \ 90,000$
Second pays $\frac{1}{3}$ × $180,000 loss $= \$ \ 60,000$
Third pays $\frac{1}{6}$ × $180,000 loss $\ = \$ \ 30,000$
Total paid $\qquad\qquad\qquad \$180,000$

Exercises 18.1

■ Compute the annual fire insurance premiums for the following insurance coverage.

	Annual Rate per $100	Face Amount of Policy	Annual Premium
Example:	$0.38	$10,000	$(\$0.38)\left(\dfrac{\$10,000}{100}\right) = \$38.00$

	Annual Rate per $100	Face Amount of Policy	Annual Premium
1.	$0.46	$15,000	
2.	$0.87	$26,000	
3.	$0.26	$112,000	
4.	$0.19	$94,500	
5.	$0.33	$58,600	
6.	$0.58	$49,200	

■ Use Figures 18.1 and 18.2 for the following problems where needed.

7. Calculate the annual insurance premium for a frame home in area 5. The policy amount should be $38,400.

8. What amount would you expect to pay for $45,000 of insurance coverage on a brick veneer home in area 3?

9. Mr. Allen purchased $28,000 insurance coverage on his brick home in area 1. Six months later he canceled the policy. What did the insurance cost him?

10. Ms. Mitchell feels her stucco home should have $38,000 insurance coverage. She lives in area 4. She is planning to sell the home in 3 months. If she does, how much will she pay for fire insurance?

11. Mr. Lowell lives in a brick veneer home in area 2. He wishes to insure his home for $42,500 and the household contents for $22,500. How much will he pay for insurance?

12. Mr. T. Jones renewed his fire insurance 6 months ago. He owns a frame home and contents valued at $62,500. His insurance company has decided to cancel all their policies in Mr. Jones' area (5). How much should Mr. Jones receive as a refund?

13. Ms. Laker has filed an insurance claim for the $15,000 in damage done to her $45,000 home by a fire. Her insurance policy has a face amount of $30,000 and an 80% coinsurance clause. How much will Ms. Laker's insurance company pay?

14. The Ajax Cleaners has $120,000 of insurance coverage on its plant and equipment valued at $300,000. A fire caused $100,000 worth of damage. If the insurance policy has an 80% coinsurance clause, how much will the policy pay for the claim? What amount will the cleaners have to pay?

15. How much will the owner of a $70,000 home have to pay on $40,000 of fire damage to his house? The face amount of the insurance policy is $60,000 and there is an 80% coinsurance clause.

16. A warehouse valued at $200,000 is covered by a $150,000 insurance policy. If the policy has a 75% coinsurance clause, how much will the insurance company pay on

    a. an $85,000 loss?
    b. a $140,000 loss?
    c. a total loss ($200,000)?

17. The Good Cheer Company has two insurance policies: one with Metropolis Insurance Company for $80,000 and one with Northern Company for $160,000. A fire did $180,000 in damage to the company. How much will each insurance company pay if all coinsurance requirements have been satisfied?

18. The Last Hurrah Entertainment Palace was damaged by fire. The $60,000 damage will be covered in total by the three companies providing the $100,000 insurance coverage on the Palace under the following policies: Allied Company—$50,000, Bankers Company—$25,000, and Consolidated Company—$25,000. How much should each company pay of the total claim?

19. The Active Company has $200,000 of insurance coverage with two companies: $80,000 with Mutual of Teneha and $120,000 with Rock of Ages. How much will each one pay on an $80,000 loss? There are no coinsurance exclusions.

18.2 *Motor Vehicle Insurance*

Motor vehicle insurance is carried by businesses and individuals to limit their financial loss through motor vehicle related accidents. It consists of three basic types of insurance:

types of motor vehicle insurance coverage

1. *Liability* — Liability insurance protects the vehicle owner against loss if he injures another person or damages another person's property.
2. *Collision* — Collision insurance protects only the vehicle of the policyholder from loss resulting in an accident (i.e., where two or more motor vehicles come together in a violent and unexpected manner).
3. *Comprehensive* — Comprehensive insurance protects the vehicle of the policyholder from loss caused by any event other than an accident (such as theft, fire, flood, etc.).

Other types of insurance are available but are more specialized in nature (emergency road towing, uninsured motorist, etc.). Motor vehicle insurance policies are normally issued for either 6 months or a year. There are many factors affecting the cost of insurance. Some of these factors are as follows:

1. How the vehicle is used (i.e., for pleasure, to work, for commercial purposes, etc.).
2. The location and distances traveled by the vehicle (i.e., in a large metropolitan area vs. a small community; commonly known as the *territory*).
3. The driving record, age, and sex of the principal drivers.
4. The type of vehicle and its age.

With so many factors involved, the rates charged by different companies can vary. Hence, comparative shopping for motor vehicle insurance is advisable.

Liability

Liability insurance protects the policyholder from losses through injury to other persons or damage to the property of others. The face amount of liability coverage shows three separate figures. The first figure is the maximum amount the insurance company will pay for bodily injury to any *one* person in an accident. The second figure is the maximum amount the insurance company will pay to *all* persons for bodily injury in a single accident. The third figure is the maximum amount the insurance company will pay for property damage (excluding the policyholder's property, which is covered by collision insurance) in a single accident. These face-amount figures are expressed without the "thousand dollar" indication. For example, a policy providing $5000 for bodily injury to one person, $10,000 for bodily injury to all persons, and $10,000 for property damage is written "5/10/10." Since premiums for larger amounts of liability coverage are reasonably priced, and since damage in excess of coverage must be paid by the policyholder, most vehicle owners carry more than the minimum coverage (5/10/5) required in most states.

Liability insurance rates depend on the amount of liability coverage, the *territory* (geographic location) in which the vehicle is driven, and the driver's *class* (i.e., age, sex, driving record, vehicle use, etc.). Figure 18.3 shows a table with typical liability insurance rates.

Figure 18.3

		Rate Schedule—Semiannual Bodily Injury and Property Damage (thousands)							
		Bodily Injury					**Property Damage**		
Territory	Driver Class	10/20	15/30	25/50	50/100	100/300	5	10	25
28	A	14.03	16.42	19.36	22.45	25.82	17.85	18.74	19.28
	B	14.45	16.91	19.94	23.12	26.59	18.28	19.19	19.74
	C	50.00	58.50	69.00	80.00	92.00	64.00	67.20	69.12
	D	23.80	27.85	32.84	38.08	43.79	30.18	31.69	32.59
29	A	14.45	16.91	19.94	23.12	26.59	17.00	17.85	18.36
	B	14.88	17.41	20.53	23.81	27.38	17.43	18.30	18.82
	C	51.50	60.26	71.07	82.40	94.76	61.00	64.05	65.88
	D	24.65	28.84	34.02	39.44	45.36	28.90	30.35	31.21

Example 1   Ms. Andretti purchased a new car and obtained 50/100/25 insurance coverage. Using Figure 18.3, calculate her semiannual insurance premiums. She lives in territory 28 and is a class C driver.

SOLUTION   The semiannual premium for 50/100 of bodily injury coverage is $80.00.

Twenty-five thousand dollars of property damage insurance is $69.12. Her semiannual insurance premium is the sum of the two, or

$$\text{premium} = \$80.00 + \$69.12 = \$149.12$$

Example 2   After buying her new car, Ms. Andretti has an accident in which she is judged at fault. She hit car A, forcing it into motor home B. The driver of car A is awarded $60,000 in bodily injury and $10,000 of property damage. The driver of motor home B is awarded $10,000 of bodily injury and $20,000 in property damage. How much will Ms. Andretti's insurance company pay and how much will she be responsible for?

SOLUTION   The total damage in the accident can be summarized as follows:

	Bodily Injury	*Property Damage*
Car A	$60,000	$10,000
Motor home B	$10,000	$20,000
Total	$70,000	$30,000

The insurance company will pay driver A only $50,000 in bodily injury damage (the maximum for one individual). It will pay driver B $10,000 (since the total payments for A and B are less than the total bodily injury limit of $100,000). The remaining $10,000 of bodily damage to driver A will be paid by Ms. Andretti. The insurance company will pay the maximum of $25,000 property damage, leaving Ms. Andretti to pay the remaining $5000.

Collision

Collision insurance provides coverage against physical damage to the insured's motor vehicle resulting from an accident. Premiums are dependent on the same variables as liability insurance. In addition, the value of the insured motor vehicle and the *deductible* amount must be considered. The deductible amount is the amount the insured must pay on every claim. For example, collision coverage with a $50 deductible means the insured pays the first $50; everything above that amount is paid by the insurance company. The value of the insured motor vehicle is based on the original cost less allowances for age and condition.

Comprehensive

Comprehensive insurance protects the insured's motor vehicle against damage from fire, theft, floods, and other "nonaccidental" disasters. Premiums for comprehensive insurance are based on the same variables as collision coverage (of course, the larger the deductible amount, the lower the premium).

Figure 18.4 gives some typical collision and comprehensive rates.

Figure 18.4

		Semiannual Rates—Passenger Automobiles Territory 28, 29, 32, 37 $50 Deductible									
		Vehicle Classification (New)									
	Age of	1		2		3		4		5	
Driver Class	*Vehicle (years)*	*Coll.*	*Comp.*	*Coll.*	*Comp.*	*Coll.*	*Comp.*	*Coll.*	*Comp.*	*Coll.*	*Comp.*
A	1	24.70	10.00	34.70	12.00	42.04	15.00	49.38	19.00	59.39	24.00
	2	23.36	9.00	32.70	11.00	40.04	14.00	46.71	17.00	56.05	22.00
	3	20.69	7.00	29.36	9.00	36.03	11.00	42.04	14.00	50.05	18.00
	4 or more	18.68	6.00	26.03	7.00	31.37	9.00	37.37	11.00	44.71	14.00
B	1	31.37	10.00	43.38	12.00	52.72	15.00	62.06	19.00	74.73	24.00
	2	29.36	9.00	41.37	11.00	50.05	14.00	59.39	17.00	70.73	22.00
	3	26.69	7.00	37.37	9.00	44.71	11.00	52.72	14.00	63.40	18.00
	4 or more	23.36	6.00	32.70	7.00	39.38	9.00	46.71	11.00	56.05	14.00
C	1	106.76	12.00	149.15	15.00	181.34	18.00	213.52	22.00	255.91	28.00
	2	101.27	11.00	142.09	13.00	171.92	16.00	202.53	20.00	243.35	26.00
	3	90.28	9.00	127.17	11.00	153.86	13.00	181.34	17.00	217.45	21.00
	4 or more	80.07	7.00	112.26	9.00	135.81	11.00	160.14	13.00	191.54	17.00

Example 3   Mr. Alden has a 2-year-old car in vehicle classification 1. His driver class is C. Based on Figure 18.4, how much will Mr. Alden pay for collision and comprehensive insurance coverage?

SOLUTION   Collision coverage for a class C driver with a 2-year-old car is $101.27 in vehicle class 1. Comprehensive insurance is $11.00, so Mr. Alden will pay the sum of the two, or $112.27 for 6 months of coverage.

Exercises 18.2

■ Use Figure 18.3 to compute the requested motor vehicle premiums given the following information:

	Liability Coverage	*Territory*	*Driver Class*	*Premium*
Example:	10/20/5	28	A	$31.88 (i.e., $14.03 + $17.85)
1.	15/30/10	29	C	
2.	100/300/25	28	B	
3.	25/50/25	29	A	
4.	50/100/10	29	D	
5.	15/30/25	28	C	
6.	10/20/10	28	B	

7. Edwanda Larnar lives in territory 29. She is in driver class C. What will be her *annual* insurance premium if she has $15,000 coverage for single bodily injury, $30,000 for total bodily injury, and property coverage of $10,000?

8. T. Allen Jamail has bodily injury coverage of $25,000 for one person and $50,000 for all persons in a single accident. His property damage coverage is $25,000. If he is in driver class B and lives in territory 29, what will be his semiannual insurance premium?

9. J. Ketchbaw is a class C driver in territory 28. He has coverage of 15/30/10. How much will his *annual* premium change when he moves into territory 29?

10. Kathy Partridge lives in territory 29 and is a class C driver. After her birthday, Kathy's driver class will change from class C to class D. How much will this change save her semiannually if she has 25/50/25 coverage?

11. Larry Pettit has liability coverage of 10/20/5. He was found at fault in an accident and the driver of the other car was awarded $8000 of bodily injury and $6000 of property damage. A passenger in the other car was awarded $13,500 of bodily injury. How much will Larry's insurance company pay and how much will Larry pay?

12. Ms. Pate has liability coverage of 25/50/25. She was at fault in a single-car accident that totally destroyed her $8000 automobile and did $28,000 damage to a shopping center. How much will her *liability* insurance pay on the claim?

■ Use Figure 18.4 to compute the requested collision and comprehensive insurance premiums given the following information.

	Driver Class	Age of Vehicle	Vehicle Classification	Collision Premium	Comprehensive Premium
13.	C	3	5		
14.	A	1	2		
15.	C	4	4		
16.	B	2	1		

17. Mr. Quon is a class B driver who owns a 3-year-old class 3 vehicle. How much does he pay for collision and comprehensive insurance semiannually?

18. The Adams family has two new vehicles in classification 2. Both drivers are class B drivers. What is the total annual collision and comprehensive insurance premium? (*Note:* New vehicles are assumed to be 1 year old or less for insurance rate purposes.)

19. Ms. Ganty has a 2-year-old class 4 vehicle. She is a class A driver. What is her semiannual collision and comprehensive insurance premium? Ms. Ganty was involved in an accident. Total damage to her car was $483.72. How much will her insurance company pay?

20. Elmer McGuirk has a new class 1 vehicle covered by a $100 deductible comprehensive policy. How much must he pay of $1225.00 in fire damage to his car?

■ Use Figures 18.3 and 18.4 to calculate the requested information in the following problems.

21. Mrs. Hooper purchased a new car (class 3). She is a class B driver and lives in territory 28. What is her semiannual automobile insurance premium for 25/50/25 liability coverage with $50 deductible on collision and comprehensive?

22. Mr. James Guehring received an annual premium notice on his 4-year-old class 2 vehicle. If Mr. Guehring is a class C driver living in territory 29, what is his total premium for liability (50/100/25), collision, and comprehensive coverages?

23. Calculate the total annual insurance premium on a class 1 automobile that is 1 year old. The driver is a class C driver and the primary location is territory 28. Liability coverage is 15/30/10. Will the insurance premium change next year? If so, by how much and why?

18.3 Life Insurance

Life insurance differs from other types of insurance in two major respects:

1. Most insurance policies provide payment *only if* the insured event occurs. Otherwise, no payment is made. In the case of life insurance, the question is not *whether* the insured event (death) will occur; rather, *when* it will occur.

2. Other types of insurance policies pay losses only up to the amount of loss or to the face amount of the policy, whichever is less. Life insurance policies pay the full face amount when death occurs.

Life insurance is usually intended to replace the financial support no longer available when the insured dies. The person(s) receiving the proceeds from a life insurance policy are designated by the insured in the policy. Therefore, life insurance allows the insured to replace the financial uncertainty of continued living with the certainty of what happens upon death.

The question of "when" the insured will die can be answered with a *mortality table*. Figure 18.5 shows and explains the *Commissioners' 1958 Standard Ordinary Table of Mortality*, which is currently used by most life insurance companies. This table assumes a population of 10,000,000 persons.

Example 1   Use Figure 18.5 (p. 431) to estimate how many 20-year-old people from a group of 100,000 will die during the current year. What age would you expect a 20-year-old person to attain before dying?

SOLUTION   We see that 20-year-old people have a death rate of 1.79 per 1000. Therefore, in a group of 100,000 persons, 179 (i.e., 1.79 × 100 groups of 1000) should die. A person aged 20 should expect to live another 50.37 years or attain age 70.37 years before dying.

Example 2   Assume that the group in Example 1 is age 60. What would your answer be?

SOLUTION At age 60 the death rate per 1000 rises to 20.34. Therefore, in a group of 100,000 people, 2034 will die during the year. However, a person age 60 can expect to live another 16.12 years or attain age 76.12 before dying.

You will notice that the death rate increases as age increases. That is what you would expect. Since the premium paid for life insurance is proportionate to the risk, you would also expect an older person to pay more for insurance than a younger person. That is exactly what happens, since an older person will pay into the insurance fund for fewer years.

The other major factor affecting the cost of life insurance is the type of policy purchased.* There are basically four types of life insurance policies.

types of life insurance policies

1. *Term*—Term life insurance is just as the name implies. It provides insurance protection only for the term of the policy (the usual term is 1 year with options to renew). If the insured dies within the term of the policy, the face amount is paid to the beneficiary. If the insured lives past the policy term, the policy is of no further value (unless the option to renew is exercised, usually at a higher rate).

2. *Ordinary life*†—Ordinary life insurance policies provide coverage for the lifetime of the insured. To maintain full coverage, the insured must continue paying premiums each year that he or she lives.

3. *Limited payment*†—Limited-payment policies are similar to ordinary life in that they provide insurance coverage for the lifetime of the insured. However, the number of payments the insured must make is limited to a specified length of time (usually 10 to 30 years).

4. *Endowment*—Endowment policies provide insurance coverage for a specified number of years. The beneficiary is guaranteed payment of the face amount should the insured die. The insured is guaranteed payment of the face amount of the policy if he lives the specified number of years.

5. *Universal*—Universal life policies are whole life policies, however they provide for a flexible premium schedule and adjustable death benefit. These variations arise from the way universal policies operate, a process we will discuss below.

The type of policy has a definite effect on the cost of insurance. Term policies have a lower cost since they provide coverage only for a year at a time. However, as a person gets older, the probability of dying increases; therefore, the cost of term insurance increases. Ordinary life insurance (as well as limited payment and endowment policies) are "level-pay" policies in that the annual insurance premium remains "level" or at a fixed rate. Ordinary life rates are higher than term rates during the earlier years but

---

* Additional factors such as health, occupation, smoker/non-smoker, and leisure pursuits (flying, skydiving, auto or boat racing, etc.) are extra premium considerations and will change the standard premium paid.

† The term "whole life" is often applied to ordinary and limited-payment insurance policies, because both provide coverage for the "whole life" of the insured.

much lower during the later years of life. Limited payment insurance rates are higher than ordinary life because the total costs for the insured are about the same; however, the total cost for a limited payment policy must be made in fewer years. Endowment policies have the highest rate because they must provide both insurance protection and an amount necessary to pay the face amount of the policy at the end of coverage. Universal life policies have a variable premium schedule because of the way the policy is designed.* From the preceding discussion (and Figure 18.6), you can see that the "whole life" policies charge a higher premium than term policies. In fact, annual ordinary life premiums for a 20-year-old male are $9.59 per $1000 of insurance coverage. Comparable term insurance does not approach that rate until the male is 51 years old (a term cost of $9.58 per $1000). Universal life policies are based on the "buy term insurance and invest the difference in premiums" concept. Each premium received, less applicable handling fees, accumulates in a holding account. Money in this holding account is invested by the insurance company, and interest (usually at rates comparable to current government obligations) is credited to the account monthly. The insurance protection is provided by term insurance whose premiums are paid by deductions from the holding account. The amount of money paid as a premium for universal life is flexible. There must be enough money in the account to pay for the term insurance. However, that money may come from premiums paid in or from interest earned. Also, since money invested by the insurance company is earning interest tax-free (under existing tax rulings), many policy holders choose to pay higher premiums to allow greater investment. Death benefits paid under universal life policies may also vary. The minimum paid is the amount of term insurance purchased; however, the insurance company may pay more depending on the amount of money in the holding account. Because universal life policies are new and there are *significant* tax advantages available to them, it is questionable whether they will be allowed to continue in their present form. Therefore, we will limit our discussion of them. However, universal life policies currently offer advantages that make them worthy of serious consideration when purchasing life insurance.

Insurance premiums vary slightly according to sex. Females have a longer life expectancy; therefore, their insurance premiums are slightly less than premiums for males. Insurance premiums are usually quoted at a rate per $1000 of coverage. That is, term life insurance for a female age 20 is $2.05 per $1000 annually. The premium for a $20,000 life insurance policy would be $41.00 per year (or $2.05 × 20). Figure 18.6 exemplifies the different items we have discussed and shows the effects of age, sex, and type of policy on the annual premium per $1000 of coverage.

---

* Universal life insurance policies are a new offering in the life insurance industry. They attempt to do three major things: (1) maximize the flexibility of death benefit and premium payments, even to the extent of temporarily suspending premium payments without canceling the policy; (2) provide a savings and investment vehicle that pays high interest rates and incurs (though large-scale investing) minimum expense; and (3) maximize the tax advantages allowable under existing regulations.

Figure 18.5
Commissioners'
1958 Standard
Ordinary Table of
Mortality

Commissioners' 1958 Standard Ordinary Table of Mortality

A B C D E

Age	Number Surviving at Each Age	Deaths in Year	Deaths per 1000 in Year	Expectation in Years	Age	Number Surviving at Each Age	Deaths in Year	Deaths per 1000 in Year	Expectation in Years
0	10,000,000	70,800	7.08	68.30	50	8,762,306	72,902	8.32	23.63
1	9,929,200	17,475	1.76	67.78	51	8,689,404	79,160	9.11	22.82
2	9,911,725	15,066	1.52	66.90	52	8,610,244	85,758	9.96	22.03
3	9,896,659	14,449	1.46	66.00	53	8,524,486	92,832	10.89	21.25
4	9,882,210	13,835	1.40	65.10	54	8,431,654	100,337	11.90	20.47
5	9,868,375	13,322	1.35	64.19	55	8,331,317	108,307	13.00	19.71
6	9,855,053	12,812	1.30	63.27	56	8,223,010	116,849	14.21	18.97
7	9,842,241	12,401	1.26	62.35	57	8,106,161	125,970	15.54	18.23
8	9,829,840	12,091	1.23	61.43	58	7,980,191	135,663	17.00	17.51
9	9,817,749	11,879	1.21	60.51	59	7,844,528	145,830	18.59	16.81
10	9,805,870	11,865	1.21	59.58	60	7,698,698	156,592	20.34	16.12
11	9,794,005	12,047	1.23	58.65	61	7,542,106	167,736	22.24	15.44
12	9,781,958	12,325	1.26	57.72	62	7,374,370	179,271	24.31	14.78
13	9,769,633	12,896	1.32	56.80	63	7,195,099	191,174	26.57	14.14
14	9,756,737	13,562	1.39	55.87	64	7,003,925	203,394	29.04	13.51
15	9,743,175	14,225	1.46	54.95	65	6,800,531	215,917	31.75	12.90
16	9,728,950	14,983	1.54	54.03	66	6,584,614	228,749	34.74	12.31
17	9,713,967	15,737	1.62	53.11	67	6,355,865	241,777	38.04	11.73
18	9,698,230	16,390	1.69	52.19	68	6,114,088	254,835	41.68	11.17
19	9,681,840	16,846	1.74	51.28	69	5,859,253	267,241	45.61	10.64
20	9,664,994	17,300	1.79	50.37	70	5,592,021	278,426	49.79	10.12
21	9,647,694	17,655	1.83	49.46	71	5,313,586	287,731	54.15	9.63
22	9,630,039	17,912	1.86	48.55	72	5,025,855	294,766	58.65	9.15
23	9,612,127	18,167	1.89	47.64	73	4,731,089	299,289	63.26	8.69
24	9,593,960	18,324	1.91	46.73	74	4,431,800	301,894	68.12	8.24
25	9,575,636	18,481	1.93	45.82	75	4,129,906	303,011	73.37	7.81
26	9,557,155	18,732	1.96	44.90	76	3,826,895	303,014	79.18	7.39
27	9,538,423	18,981	1.99	43.99	77	3,523,881	301,997	85.70	6.98
28	9,519,442	19,324	2.03	43.08	78	3,221,884	299,829	93.06	6.59
29	9,500,118	19,760	2.08	42.16	79	2,922,055	295,683	101.19	6.21
30	9,480,358	20,193	2.13	41.25	80	2,626,372	288,848	109.98	5.85
31	9,460,165	20,718	2.19	40.34	81	2,337,524	278,983	119.35	5.51
32	9,439,447	21,239	2.25	39.43	82	2,058,541	265,902	129.17	5.19
33	9,418,208	21,850	2.32	38.51	83	1,792,639	249,858	139.38	4.89
34	9,396,358	22,551	2.40	37.60	84	1,542,781	231,433	150.01	4.60
35	9,373,807	23,528	2.51	36.69	85	1,311,348	211,311	161.14	4.32
36	9,350,279	24,685	2.64	35.78	86	1,100,037	190,108	172.82	4.06
37	9,325,594	26,112	2.80	34.88	87	909,929	168,455	185.13	3.80
38	9,299,482	27,991	3.01	33.97	88	741,474	146,997	198.25	3.55
39	9,271,491	30,132	3.25	33.07	89	594,477	126,303	212.46	3.31
40	9,241,359	32,622	3.53	32.18	90	468,174	106,809	228.14	3.06
41	9,208,737	35,362	3.84	31.29	91	361,365	88,813	245.77	2.82
42	9,173,375	38,253	4.17	30.41	92	272,552	72,480	265.93	2.58
43	9,135,122	41,382	4.53	29.54	93	200,072	57,881	289.30	2.33
44	9,093,740	44,741	4.92	28.67	94	142,191	45,026	316.66	2.07
45	9,048,999	48,412	5.35	27.81	95	97,165	34,128	351.24	1.80
46	9,000,587	52,473	5.83	26.95	96	63,037	25,250	400.56	1.51
47	8,948,114	56,910	6.36	26.11	97	37,787	18,456	488.42	1.18
48	8,891,204	61,794	6.95	25.27	98	19,331	12,916	668.15	.83
49	8,829,410	67,104	7.60	24.45	99	6,415	6,415	1,000.00	

A. This column represents the age of the person.

B. The "number surviving" column shows the beginning population (10,000,000 persons) less the total deaths in previous years.

C. This column shows the number of persons expected to die during the current year.

D. This column shows the anticipated deaths per 1000 persons during the current year. It is calculated by dividing the yearly deaths by the number of persons living at the beginning of the year, expressed per 1000 persons.

E. This column shows the expected years of life remaining for a person having attained the age shown in column A.

Figure 18.6

INSURANCE PREMIUM TABLE
Annual Rate per $1000

	Term		Ordinary		Limited Pay[a]		Endowment[b]	
Age	Male	Female	Male	Female	Male	Female	Male	Female
16	$2.46	$2.05	$8.51	$8.02	$11.01	$10.41	$12.88	$12.53
17	2.46	2.05	8.76	8.26	11.30	10.68	13.37	13.02
18	2.46	2.05	9.03	8.52	11.60	10.97	13.88	13.53
19	2.46	2.05	9.30	8.78	11.90	11.26	14.41	14.06
20	2.46	2.05	9.59	9.05	12.22	11.56	14.97	14.62
21	2.46	2.05	9.89	9.33	12.53	11.86	15.54	15.18
22	2.46	2.05	10.19	9.62	12.86	12.18	16.13	15.76
23	2.46	2.05	10.52	9.92	13.20	12.50	16.75	16.39
24	2.46	2.05	10.86	10.24	13.55	12.84	17.41	17.04
25	2.46	2.05	11.21	10.57	13.92	13.19	18.11	17.74
26	2.46	2.05	11.59	10.91	14.31	13.54	18.82	18.43
27	2.46	2.05	11.98	11.27	14.71	13.91	19.55	19.15
28	2.46	2.05	12.39	11.64	15.12	14.30	20.33	19.92
29	2.46	2.05	12.82	12.03	15.56	14.70	21.17	20.74
30	2.46	2.05	13.28	12.44	16.01	15.12	22.05	21.60
31	2.49	2.09	13.77	12.86	16.50	15.55	22.94	22.45
32	2.52	2.13	14.28	13.31	17.01	16.01	23.89	23.37
33	2.56	2.17	14.82	13.78	17.54	16.48	24.91	24.34
34	2.61	2.22	15.39	14.27	18.11	16.98	25.99	25.37
35	2.69	2.29	15.99	14.79	18.70	17.50	27.15	26.48
36	2.78	2.36	16.64	15.34	19.34	18.05	28.36	27.63
37	2.90	2.46	17.32	15.91	20.02	18.63	29.66	28.87
38	3.09	2.63	18.04	16.51	20.72	19.23	31.05	30.19
39	3.35	2.85	18.80	17.13	21.47	19.87	32.53	31.60
40	3.69	3.14	19.59	17.79	22.25	20.53	34.13	33.13
41	4.06	3.45	20.44	18.49	23.06	21.18	35.87	34.79
42	4.44	3.77	21.33	19.22	23.90	21.87	37.74	36.58
43	4.83	4.11	22.27	19.99	24.79	22.58	39.76	38.50
44	5.25	4.46	23.27	20.80	25.72	23.33	41.97	40.61
45	5.70	4.84	24.32	21.65	26.70	24.10	44.38	42.91
46	6.18	5.25	25.44	22.59	27.74	24.95	47.07	45.55
47	6.70	5.70	26.63	23.58	28.84	25.84	50.06	48.47
48	7.25	6.16	27.89	24.63	30.00	26.78	53.36	51.71
49	7.90	6.72	29.22	25.73	31.22	27.76	57.06	55.33
50	8.68	7.38	30.62	26.89	32.51	28.80	61.21	59.40
51	9.58	8.05	32.13	28.21	33.88	29.98	66.53	64.70
52	10.59	8.79	33.73	29.61	35.34	31.24	72.62	70.78
53	11.66	9.56	35.43	31.09	36.90	32.57	79.70	77.85
54	12.76	10.34	37.22	32.67	38.54	33.99	88.04	86.18
55	13.89	11.11	39.13	34.33	40.30	35.49	97.97	96.11
56	15.08	11.91	41.18	36.23	—	—	—	—
57	16.36	12.76	43.36	38.25	—	—	—	—
58	17.82	14.27	45.67	40.40	—	—	—	—
59	19.63	16.33	48.13	42.70	—	—	—	—
60	22.04	18.88	50.74	45.14	—	—	—	—
61	24.58	20.63	53.54	47.83	—	—	—	—
62	27.14	22.26	56.51	50.71	—	—	—	—
63	29.72	23.77	59.68	53.78	—	—	—	—
64	32.31	25.14	63.05	57.07	—	—	—	—
65	35.10	26.57	66.64	60.58	—	—	—	—

[a]30-year pay.　[b]At age 65.

Example 3

Allen purchased a $10,000 ordinary life insurance policy when he graduated at age 22. How much is his annual insurance premium? (Use Figure 18.6.)

SOLUTION

The ordinary insurance rate for a male age 22 is $10.19 per $1000 of coverage. The cost for $10,000 of coverage would be

$$\$10.19 \times 10 = \$101.90 \text{ per year}$$

Example 4

If Allen had purchased a term insurance policy, what would his premium be?

SOLUTION

Term insurance costs $2.46 per $1000, or

$$\$2.46 \times 10 = \$24.60 \text{ for the year}$$

The rates shown in Figure 18.6 are indicative of the general range of insurance costs. *However, the cost of insurance varies greatly among companies.* Therefore, it pays to compare costs and benefits before buying insurance. Mention should be made of several other factors which have a definite bearing on the purchase of insurance. These items are as follows:

participating vs. nonparticipating insurance policies

1. Insurance policies are generally classified as *participating* or *nonparticipating* policies. Participating policies are usually sold by *mutual* insurance companies (i.e., by companies where the policyholders are the owners of the company). Since the policyholders own the company, any excess profits are returned to the policyholders in the form of dividends. These dividends may be used in several ways (to purchase additional insurance, to reduce the premium cost of the current year, or to be invested by the company at a stated interest rate much like a savings account). Nonparticipating policies are generally issued by stockholder-owned companies. As with any stockholder company, profits go to the stockholders. Frequently, the cost per $1000 of coverage charged by participating companies will be greater than the cost charged by nonparticipating companies. However, when the participating dividends are considered, the *net cost* of insurance is lower.

additional life insurance policy options

2. There are several optional items that can be purchased with life insurance. The *waiver of premium* option will guarantee payment of the annual premium on the insurance policy if the insured becomes totally and permanently disabled. The cost is relatively low (approximately $0.35 per $1000 for a male age 20; $1.36 per $1000 for a male age 40). The *double-indemnity benefit* provides payment of twice the face amount of the policy in the event of accidental death. This benefit costs approximately $1.01 per $1000 for a male age 20 and $1.04 per $1000 for a male age 40.

Nonforfeiture Options

Fire and auto insurance pay only in the event of disaster. If the disastrous event fails to occur, the premium for the policy has provided only the insurance coverage for the year—nothing else. Life insurance is

nonforfeiture options

different. Life insurance policy premiums usually generate benefits even if the insured does not die. These *nonforfeiture options* accrue to the insured over the life of the policy but are available to him only when he stops paying premiums and cancels his policy (ceasing insurance coverage). The primary benefit that accrues (in all policies except term) is a *cash value*. Insurance companies invest the policy premiums in various enterprises (in fact, insurance companies are one of the major lenders for investment borrowing). Since premiums are a relatively stable income flow, the companies can invest money in projects yielding very favorable returns. Part of the profits from these investments are returned to policyholders as cash value. Cash value is simply the amount of money (in cash) the policy holder could receive should the policy be canceled. Normally, a cash value does not begin to accrue until after two or three years so that the company can cover the expenses involved in writing the policy. This cash value may be taken by a policyholder in one of several ways when insurance coverage ceases:

1. *Cash*—The policyholder may receive the amount of money stated in the insurance policy as the cash value. (*Note:* This amount of money is available to an active policyholder through borrowing. The insured may borrow up to the amount of cash value from the insurance company at a stated interest rate which is usually lower than prevailing bank rates. If the loan and interest are repaid, the policy remains in effect at full face amount. If the loan has not been repaid, the amount of loan and interest will be deducted from the face amount when any claim is paid.)

Figure 18.7

	Nonforfeiture Options per $1000[a] (Policy Issued at Age 20)											
	Ordinary Life				Limited Pay—30 Years				Endowment (at 65)			
Years in Force	Cash Value	Paid-up Ins.	Ext. Term		Cash Value	Paid-up Ins.	Ext. Term		Cash Value	Paid-up Ins.	Ext. Term	
			Years	Days			Years	Days			Years	Days
1	—	—	—	—	—	—	—	—	—	—	—	—
2	—	—	—	—	—	—	—	—	$ 4.66	—	—	—
5	$ 21.51	$ 92.00	8	330	$ 32.83	$ 140.00	13	334	44.35	$ 150.00	18	100
10	77.04	284.00	22	109	105.02	388.00	27	55	118.80	346.00	29	92
15	130.39	416.00	24	255	178.40	570.00	30	29	194.92	487.00	30	$ 74[b]
20	191.83	530.00	24	274	264.10	730.00	30	334	283.97	609.00	25	$315[b]
40	493.61	823.00	17	331	600.02	1000.00	—	—	799.28	940.00	5	$925[b]
45	573.71	865.00	15	269	663.29	1000.00	—	—	1000.00	1000.00	—	—

[a]Cash value and paid-up insurance are per $1000 of face amount; extended term coverage is the same regardless of the face amount.

[b]Amount of money left after purchasing term insurance to the end of the endowment period. This amount is payable to the insured at age 65.

2. *Paid-up insurance*—The policyholder may use the cash value to make a one-time payment which will purchase a smaller amount of life insurance that will remain in effect for the rest of the insured's life.

3. *Extended term insurance*—The policyholder may use the cash value of the policy to purchase an amount of term insurance equal to the face amount of the expiring policy. The length of the term coverage will depend on the amount of cash value available and the age of the insured.

Again, it is important to note that none of these options apply to term insurance; they apply only to ordinary, limited payment, and endowment policies.

Figure 18.7 shows a typical table of nonforfeiture options on an insurance policy issued at age 20. By incorporating all of these features and costs, we can determine the net cost of insurance to an individual. Since dividends and cash value are actually a result of premiums, the net cost of insurance is less than the premiums paid. The net cost can be determined as shown below.

net cost of life insurance

Net Cost of Insurance

Participating Insurance Policies:

net cost = premiums − (cash value + dividends)

Nonparticipating Policies:

net cost = premiums − cash value

To further clarify and compare these insurance concepts, let us examine Figure 18.8. Using the data previously given on premium rates and cash values, let us compare the net cost of a $10,000 insurance policy purchased by James Allen at age 20. We will assume that all policies are held to age 65. (See Figure 18.8.)

Example 5

You are planning to buy a $15,000 ordinary life insurance policy and have been doing some comparative pricing based on your age (25). Company A has quoted you a rate of $10.03 per $1000 of coverage and the policy has a guaranteed cash value of $572.00 per $1000 at age 65. Company B has quoted a cost of $10.21 per $1000 and the guaranteed cash value of $564.00 per $1000 at age 65. However, Company B is a mutual company paying dividends and Company A is not. If the dividends paid by Company B will total $1839.00 at age 65 and you wish to minimize your net cost, which company should you choose?

Figure 18.8

Net Cost of Insurance—$10,000

Comparison of Term, Ordinary, Limited-Payment, and Endowment
for James Allen, Age 20

Term   *Cost*

The term insurance net cost would simply be the sum of the
term rates from age 20 through age 65 (Figure 18.6), multiplied
by 10 to convert the cost per $1000 to a $10,000 policy, or

$$\$414.99 \times 10 =$$ $4149.90

At age 65, all insurance coverage would cease and the term policy
would have no further value of any type. Although the $4149.90
represents the actual cost of term insurance, this approach ignores
the "stream of payments" effect represented by the yearly variations
between other rates and term rates. For example, the term policy
rate for the first year is $2.46 per $1000 vs. $9.59 per $1000 for
ordinary insurance (of course, limited payment and endowment
rates are higher). The $7.13 difference ($9.59–$2.46) could be
invested at prevailing interest rates to compound over the next
45 years. Because of the variables involved, we have not included
this calculation in our example; however, such a consideration
certainly should be undertaken in actual purchase decisions.

Ordinary Life

The premium for an ordinary life policy at age 20 is $9.59
per $1000. Thus, the cost for a $10,000 policy would be $9.59 ×
10, or $95.90. These premiums would be paid for 45 years before
attaining age 65. The cash value of an ordinary life policy would
be $573.71 per $1000 (Figure 18.7). The net cost of the policy
would be

Gross cost — $95.90 × 45 years	= $4315.50
Less cash value — $573.71 × 10	= $5737.10

Net cost   −$1421.60
    (or a return over cost of $1421.60)

James would also have all options shown in Figure 18.7 available
at age 65.

Limited Payment—30-Year

The premium for a 30-year limited-payment life policy is
$12.22 per $1000, or an annual premium of $12.22 × 10 =
$122.20 for $10,000. These payments would be made for only 30
years, however. Cash value at age 65 is $663.29 per $1000. The
net cost of the policy would be

Gross cost — $122.20 × 30 years	= $3666.00
Less cash value — $663.29 × 10	= $6632.90

Net cost   −$2966.90
    (or a return over cost of $2966.90)

Again, James would have several options available to him under
the insurance policy at age 65 (Figure 18.7).

Endowment—Age 65

The premium for an endowment policy to age 65 is $14.97 per $1000, or an annual premium of $149.70 (i.e., $14.97 × 10) for a $10,000 policy. Cash value at age 65 is $1000 per $1000 of policy value. The net cost of the policy would be

Gross cost − $149.70 × 45 years	= $ 6,736.50	
Less cash value − $1000 × 10	= $10,000.00	
Net cost		−$3263.50

(or a return over cost of $3263.50)

SOLUTION To determine the minimum cost, we need simply compute the net cost from each company on a $15,000 policy.

Company A (nonparticipating)

$$\begin{aligned}
\text{Net cost} &= \text{premiums} - \text{cash value} \\
&= (\$10.03 \times 15 \times 40 \text{ years}) - (\$572.00 \times 15) \\
&= \$6018 - \$8580 \\
&= -\$2562 \text{ (or a return of \$2562)}
\end{aligned}$$

Company B (participating)

$$\begin{aligned}
\text{Net cost} &= \text{premiums} - (\text{cash value} + \text{dividends}) \\
&= (\$10.21 \times 15 \times 40 \text{ years}) - [(\$564.00 \times 15) + \$1839] \\
&= \$6126 - \$10,299 \\
&= -\$4173 \text{ (or a return of \$4173)}
\end{aligned}$$

Therefore, you would choose Company B.

Settlement Options

options for receiving
life insurance
proceeds

The beneficiary of a life insurance policy has several options under which to collect death benefits. The first method is a lump-sum payment of the face amount of the policy; most insurance claims are settled in this manner. The beneficiary may, however, elect to receive the benefits as an *annuity*. You will recall from Chapter 14 that an annuity is a stream of constant payments at periodic intervals. The size of and length of time for annuity payments may vary according to the wishes of the beneficiary. In principle, the insurance company takes the death benefits (or *proceeds*) under the policy and invests them. The proceeds and the interest earned compose the amount of the total annuity to be paid. Some of the more common forms of annuities are as follows:

1. *Fixed amount*—The amount of the annuity is fixed at a certain level. That set amount is paid periodically (usually monthly) until the proceeds plus interest have been paid by the insurance company. The amount of payment is constant, the time paid is variable.

2. *Fixed period*—The length of time that the annuity is paid is fixed (in years). The insurance company will compute monthly annuity payments to be paid for the specified period of time. The time paid is thus fixed, while the amount paid is determined by the proceeds of the policy.

3. *Annuity for life*—The beneficiary will receive a monthly annuity for life. The amount received will be determined by the insurance company based on the sex and age of the beneficiary. The insurance company utilizes the mortality table to estimate the remaining life of the beneficiary, then adjusts the annuity amount based on the proceeds available and the expected length of payment. All payments stop with the death of the beneficiary.

4. *Annuity for life* (*guaranteed number of years*)—Payment of benefits under this annuity is similar to form 3 except that annuity payments are guaranteed for a specific number of years. Even if the beneficiary dies after the first year, annuity payments will continue to the beneficiaries or estate of the original beneficiary for the guaranteed time period. The payments under this method are slightly lower than the life annuity to compensate for a known payment period; however, this method is the most popular annuity choice. Guaranteed time periods usually range from 5 to 20 years.

These options are also available to endowment policyholders at policy maturity. You will recall that the mortality table assumes death by age 100. Consequently, life insurance death benefits are normally paid to the insured if still living at age 100. Figure 18.9 gives some representative figures showing monthly payments per $1000 of face amount for benefits received as an annuity.

Example 6

Dr. Angelo had a $50,000 life insurance policy. He died of a heart attack, and his wife has decided to receive the insurance proceeds as an annuity. Explain how the proceeds will be paid if Mrs. Angelo (age 50) chooses an annuity

    a. of $500 per month for as long as possible.
    b. for 15 years to be paid monthly.
    c. for the rest of her life.
    d. for the rest of her life but with a guaranteed payment of 10 years.

SOLUTION

    a. To determine the length of time Mrs. Angelo will receive monthly payments, refer to Figure 18.9-A. Reading down the "$500" column to the "$50,000 Policy Proceeds," we see that Mrs. Angelo (or her beneficiaries) will receive payment for 114 months.

    b. To determine the amount of monthly payments received by Mrs. Angelo for 15 years, we will use Figure 18.9-B. Reading down the "Monthly" column to the "15 Year" line, we see that Mrs. Angelo

Figure 18.9-A   Fixed Amount Unit Proceeds and Interest Exhausted

Number of Months That Payment Will Be Made for Different Amounts of Monthly Income and Amounts of Policy Proceeds

Policy Proceeds	$25	$50	$100	$200	$300	$400	$500	$600	$700	$800	$900	$1000
					Number of Months—3% Interest Guaranteed							
$ 5,000	274	114	53	25	16	12	10	8	7	6	5	5
10,000		274	114	53	34	25	20	16	14	12	11	10
15,000			186	82	53	39	31	25	21	19	16	15
20,000			274	114	72	53	42	34	29	25	22	20
25,000				149	93	67	53	43	37	32	28	25
30,000				186	114	82	64	53	45	39	34	31
35,000				228	137	98	76	62	53	46	40	36
40,000				274	161	114	88	72	61	53	47	42
45,000					186	131	101	82	69	60	53	47
50,000					214	149	114	93	78	67	59	53
60,000					274	186	142	114	96	82	72	64
70,000						228	171	137	114	98	86	76
80,000						274	203	161	134	114	100	88
90,000							237	186	154	131	114	101
100,000							274	214	175	149	129	114

Figure 18.9-B   Fixed Period—Payment per $1000 of Policy Proceeds

3% Interest Guaranteed
Installments Certain per $1000 of Policy Proceeds

Number of Years	Amount of Each Installment			
	Annual	Semiannual	Quarterly	Monthly
1	$1000.00	$503.70	$252.80	$84.47
2	507.39	255.57	128.27	42.86
3	343.23	172.88	86.77	28.99
4	261.19	131.56	66.03	22.06
5	212.00	106.78	53.59	17.91
6	179.22	90.27	45.31	15.14
7	155.83	78.49	39.39	13.16
8	138.31	69.67	34.96	11.68
9	124.69	62.81	31.52	10.53
10	113.82	57.33	28.77	9.61
11	104.93	52.85	26.53	8.86
12	97.54	49.13	24.66	8.24
13	91.29	45.98	23.08	7.71
14	85.95	43.29	21.73	7.26
15	81.33	40.97	20.56	6.87
16	77.29	38.93	19.54	6.53
17	73.74	37.14	18.64	6.23
18	70.59	35.56	17.85	5.96
19	67.78	34.14	17.13	5.73
20	65.25	32.87	16.50	5.51
25	55.76	28.09	14.10	4.71
30	49.53	24.95	12.52	4.18

Figure 18.9-C Annuity for Life and Annuity for Life—Guaranteed Payment
Monthly Payments per $1000 of Policy Proceeds

Female					
	Annuity for Life	Annuity—Guaranteed Monthly Payments for:			
Age of Benef.		60 mo.	100 mo.	120 mo.	240 mo.
35	3.40	3.39	3.38	3.37	3.30
36	3.44	3.43	3.41	3.40	3.33
37	3.47	3.46	3.45	3.44	3.36
38	3.51	3.50	3.49	3.48	3.40
39	3.55	3.54	3.53	3.52	3.43
40	3.60	3.59	3.57	3.56	3.47
41	3.64	3.63	3.61	3.60	3.51
42	3.69	3.68	3.66	3.65	3.55
43	3.74	3.73	3.71	3.70	3.60
44	3.79	3.78	3.76	3.75	3.64
45	3.84	3.83	3.81	3.80	3.69
46	3.90	3.89	3.87	3.85	3.74
47	3.96	3.95	3.93	3.91	3.79
48	4.02	4.01	3.99	3.97	3.84
49	4.09	4.08	4.05	4.04	3.90
50	4.16	4.15	4.12	4.10	3.96
51	4.24	4.22	4.19	4.17	4.02
52	4.32	4.30	4.27	4.25	4.08
53	4.40	4.38	4.35	4.33	4.14
54	4.49	4.47	4.43	4.41	4.21
55	4.58	4.56	4.52	4.50	4.28
56	4.67	4.65	4.61	4.58	4.34
57	4.77	4.75	4.70	4.67	4.40
58	4.88	4.85	4.80	4.77	4.47
59	4.99	4.96	4.90	4.87	4.54
60	5.10	5.07	5.01	4.97	4.60
61	5.23	5.19	5.13	5.08	4.67
62	5.37	5.33	5.25	5.20	4.74
63	5.52	5.47	5.38	5.33	4.81
64	5.67	5.62	5.52	5.46	4.87
65	5.84	5.78	5.67	5.60	4.94
66	6.02	5.95	5.83	5.75	5.00
67	6.22	6.14	6.00	5.90	5.06
68	6.43	6.34	6.17	6.06	5.11
69	6.66	6.55	6.36	6.23	5.17
70	6.91	6.78	6.55	6.40	5.22
71	7.17	7.02	6.75	6.58	5.26
72	7.46	7.28	6.97	6.76	5.30
73	7.77	7.56	7.18	6.95	5.34
74	8.11	7.85	7.41	7.14	5.37
75	8.47	8.16	7.64	7.33	5.40

Age of Benef.	Annuity for Life	Annuity—Guaranteed Monthly Payments for:			
		60 mo.	100 mo.	120 mo.	240 mo.
35	3.59	3.58	3.56	3.55	3.46
36	3.63	3.62	3.61	3.59	3.50
37	3.68	3.67	3.65	3.64	3.54
38	3.73	3.72	3.70	3.69	3.58
39	3.79	3.78	3.76	3.74	3.63
40	3.84	3.83	3.81	3.80	3.67
41	3.90	3.89	3.87	3.85	3.72
42	3.97	3.95	3.93	3.91	3.77
43	4.03	4.02	3.99	3.97	3.82
44	4.10	4.09	4.06	4.04	3.87
45	4.18	4.16	4.13	4.11	3.93
46	4.25	4.23	4.20	4.18	3.99
47	4.33	4.31	4.28	4.25	4.05
48	4.42	4.39	4.35	4.33	4.11
49	4.51	4.48	4.44	4.41	4.17
50	4.60	4.57	4.53	4.49	4.23
51	4.70	4.67	4.62	4.58	4.30
52	4.80	4.77	4.71	4.68	4.37
53	4.91	4.87	4.81	4.77	4.43
54	5.03	4.99	4.92	4.88	4.50
55	5.15	5.10	5.03	4.98	4.58
56	5.27	5.22	5.14	5.09	4.64
57	5.39	5.34	5.25	5.19	4.70
58	5.53	5.47	5.37	5.31	4.77
59	5.67	5.61	5.50	5.42	4.83
60	5.82	5.75	5.63	5.55	4.89
61	5.99	5.91	5.77	5.68	4.95
62	6.16	6.07	5.92	5.82	5.01
63	6.35	6.25	6.07	5.96	5.07
64	6.55	6.44	6.24	6.11	5.13
65	6.77	6.64	6.41	6.27	5.18
66	7.01	6.85	6.60	6.44	5.22
67	7.26	7.08	6.79	6.60	5.27
68	7.53	7.32	6.99	6.78	5.31
69	7.82	7.58	7.20	6.96	5.34
70	8.14	7.86	7.41	7.14	5.37
71	8.48	8.15	7.63	7.32	5.40
72	8.85	8.46	7.86	7.51	5.42
73	9.25	8.79	8.09	7.69	5.44
74	9.68	9.14	8.33	7.87	5.46
75	10.14	9.50	8.56	8.05	5.47

Male

will receive $6.87 per $1000 of proceeds per month. Therefore, Mrs. Angelo (or her beneficiaries) will receive

$6.87 × 50 (i.e., $50,000 proceeds) = $343.50

per month for 15 years.

c. To determine the annuity for life, we must use Figure 18.9-C for Females—age 50. Reading down the "Annuity for Life" column to the "Age 50" line, we find that Mrs. Angelo will receive $4.16 per month per $1000 of coverage for as long as she lives:

$4.16 × 50 = $208.00 per month

d. Using Figure 18.9-C for an annuity for life—10-year guarantee, we read down the "120 Months" column (i.e., 10 years × 12 months per year = 120 months) to the "Age 50" line. Mrs. Angelo will receive $4.10 per month per $1000 of coverage for as long as she lives, or $4.10 × 50 = $205.00. If she should die within the next 10 years, her beneficiaries will receive annuity payments for the remainder of the 10 years.

Exercises 18.3

■ Use Figure 18.6 to calculate the annual premiums on the following life insurance policies.

	Face Amount of Policy	Type of Policy	For: Sex	For: Age	Annual Premium
Example:	$2000	Term	M	16	$4.92 (i.e., $2.46 × 2)
1.	$5000	Limited Pay	F	31	
2.	$10,000	Ordinary	M	26	
3.	$20,000	Endowment	M	35	
4.	$25,000	Term	F	45	
5.	$50,000	Ordinary	M	38	
6.	$100,000	Limited Pay	F	29	

7. Elaine Gerhart purchased an ordinary insurance policy (face amount $20,000) at age 30. How much less would her annual premiums be if she had purchased the policy at age 25?

8. Andrew McCready purchased a 30-year limited-payment life insurance policy with coverage of $30,000. He is 27 years old. How much will he pay over the life of the insurance policy?

9. Mary Ellen Moreland is 45 years old. She wants life insurance of $50,000 for next year only when she will be traveling a lot. What is the least expensive insurance she can get, and how much will the coverage cost her?

10. What is the annual premium difference on a $10,000 ordinary policy and a $10,000 limited pay policy for a 33-year-old man?

■ Use Figures 18.6, 18.7, and 18.9 to work the following problems.

11. Mrs. Copeland purchased a $20,000 30-year limited-payment life insurance policy at age 20. How much did she pay in premiums over the life of the policy? What cash value does she now have in the policy (ignoring any dividends, and so on, and assuming age 60)?

12. How much paid-up insurance is available to the holder of a $10,000 ordinary life insurance policy purchased at age 20 if the policy has been in effect for 45 years?

13. Rose purchased a $25,000 endowment policy at age 20. The policy has been in force for 10 years. How much has she paid in and for how long could she obtain term insurance coverage if she chose to cancel the policy? If she chose term insurance, how much coverage would she have?

14. Mr. Alfred purchased a $20,000 30-year limited-payment insurance policy at age 20. On his 65th birthday, he decided to cancel the policy. What options are available to him? How much will he receive under each?

15. Calculate the net cost of a $25,000 ordinary life policy purchased by a male at age 20 and held to age 65. Assume that
   a. the policy has no dividends
   b. the policy has dividends of $2378 during the period

16. Ms. Frances purchased a limited-payment policy for 30 years when she was 20 years old. The policy has been in effect for 15 years. What is her net cost to date if the policy has a face amount of $10,000 and has paid dividends totaling $232.00?

17. Mrs. Dobraski's husband died leaving her $50,000 in life insurance death proceeds. If she chooses to receive an annuity of $500 per month, for how many months will she receive payment? If she chooses to receive monthly payments for 15 years, how much will they be?

18. Mr. Hobartsch is to receive $20,000 of death proceeds from his wife's insurance policy. He is 60 years old. How much will he receive per month if he chooses an annuity for life? If he wishes to guarantee payment of the annuity for at least 10 years, how much will he receive?

19. Ms. Ginther is the beneficiary of her sister's $30,000 life insurance policy. Her sister recently died and the death proceeds are to be paid to Ms. Ginther (age 40). Ms. Ginther would prefer a lifetime annuity but she feels she must receive at least $100 per month. Can she receive a lifetime annuity and still receive the $100 per month?

20. Mrs. Gutierrez was the beneficiary of her husband's $50,000 life insurance policy. He died when she was 45 years old. She elected to receive a lifetime annuity. How much had she received when she died at age 82?

21. Mr. Culver began receiving an annuity for his wife's death proceeds on a $10,000 policy when he was 55. He chose to receive the proceeds for a guaranteed 15 years. Would he have received more under an annuity for life if he lived to age 75?

Review Exercises / Chapter 18

■ Use the appropriate figures in Chapter 18 to obtain the necessary rate information.

1. How much will Mr. Hodges receive for $30,000 in fire damages to his $60,000 home? His policy has a face amount of $45,000 and there is an 80% coinsurance clause.

2. The We-Stor-It Warehouse is valued at $200,000 and carries insurance totaling $140,000. $85,000 of the insurance coverage is provided by the Great Western Company; the remainder by the Eastern Company. How much will each company pay for fire damages totaling $100,000 if there is an 80% coinsurance requirement?

3. Douglas purchased a new class 5 automobile. He is a class C driver and resides in territory 29. How much did he pay semiannually for 10/20/5 liability, comprehensive, and collision insurance ($50 deductible on the latter)? The first week he drove the car, he had an accident and was found at fault for $8000 in damages to the other vehicle and $12,000 in bodily injury to the single occupant of the other vehicle. Damage to his new car was $1850. How much will his insurance company pay for the accident and to whom?

4. Ms. Erwin's husband died at age 52, when she was 47 years old. She chose to receive the proceeds of his $50,000 ordinary, nonparticipating life insurance policy as a lifetime annuity guaranteed for 20 years. If Mr. Erwin purchased the policy at age 26, by how much will the guaranteed benefits exceed the payments made for the policy?

5. A business structure valued at $575,000 is covered by a $400,000 insurance policy. The policy has an 80% coinsurance clause. How much will the insurance company pay on:
  a. $230,000 loss?
  b. $400,000 loss?

6. The Progressive Company has $600,000 of insurance with three companies: $275,000 with Great North, $125,000 with Upper Midwest, and $200,000 with California General. The insured property suffers damages of $375,000. How much will each company pay assuming there are no coinsurance exclusions.

7. Calculate the total annual insurance premium on a class 1 automobile that is 2 years old. The driver is a class C driver and the primary location is territory 28. Liability coverage is 25/50/25.

8. Ms. Riley purchased a new (class 1) automobile. She is a class C driver and lives in territory 29. What is her total semiannual automobile insurance premium for 25/50/25 liability coverage and $50 deductible on collision and comprehensive?

9. Vanna Jo purchased $40,000 in ordinary life insurance at age 27. How much will she pay in annual premiums?

10. Mrs. Fullerton is the beneficiary of her husband's $50,000 life insurance policy. Her husband died when Mrs. Fullerton was 52 years old. Mrs. Fullerton would prefer a lifetime annuity but she feels she must receive at least $215 per month. Can she receive a lifetime annuity and still receive the $215 per month?

Chapter Test / Chapter 18

1. Define the following terms.

a. insurance

b. beneficiary

c. face amount

d. premium

e. coinsurance

f. collision insurance

g. comprehensive insurance

h. term insurance

i. endowment policy

j. annuity

2. Mr. Henry wishes to insure his home for $63,500 and the contents for an additional $19,700. His home is brick veneer and he lives in area 4. What is Mr. Henry's annual home insurance premium?

3. An asbestos and stucco home and its contents (valued at $72,300) are located in area 2. Six months after renewing the policy, the owner decides to change insurance companies and cancel his existing policy. How much refund will the owner receive?

4. Ms. Cline has a home valued at $75,000. Her fire insurance coverage is $52,000 and the policy has an 80% coinsurance clause. A fire caused an estimated $37,000 in damage to her home. How much will her insurance company pay for the damage (rounded to the nearest dollar)?

5. The Paragon Corporation has insurance policies with three companies as follows: Little Rock—$75,000; Big Boulder—$150,000; and Pebbleworth—$75,000. An explosion destroyed the corporation's plant (damage is estimated at $225,000). Assuming there were no coinsurance restrictions, how much of the damage will be covered by each company?

6. William is a class C driver living in territory 29. He is purchasing automobile insurance coverage for his 3-year-old class 5 vehicle. The insurance coverage is as follows: liability, 50/100; property damage, $25,000; and collision/comprehensive coverage with $50 deductible. What is his *annual* insurance premium?

7. Shortly after obtaining his insurance coverage, William (problem 6) had an automobile accident in which he was judged at fault. He hit two cars, doing $12,000 in damage to car 1 and $10,000 in damage to car 2. The driver of car 1 was awarded $60,000 in damages; the driver of car 2 received damages of $48,000. Damage to Williams car was $7850. Describe how William and his insurance company will settle all claims.

8. How much more will a 26-year-old male pay per year for a $50,000 limited payment life insurance policy than a 26-year-old female? How much less would a term insurance policy in the same amount cost for each?

9. You are planning to buy a $10,000 ordinary life insurance policy. Best Company has quoted you a rate of $10.22 per $1000 for your age group (age 25) and the policy has a guaranteed cash value of $704.00 per $1000 at age 65. Better Company has quoted you a cost of $10.30 per $1000 and the guaranteed cash value at age 65 is $675 per $1000. However, Better Company is a mutual company paying dividends. If the dividends paid by Better Company will total $300 at age 65 and you wish to minimize your cost, which company should you choose?

10. Mrs. Frank's husband died leaving her $100,000 in life insurance death proceeds. If she chooses to receive an annuity of $700 per month, for how many months will she receive payment? If she chooses to receive monthly payments for 25 years, how much will they be?

11. Ms. Sharp (age 47) is the beneficiary of her deceased husband's $50,000 life insurance policy. How much will she receive per month if she chooses an annuity for life? If she wishes to guarantee payment of the annuity for at least 20 years, how much will she receive?

Cumulative Review Exercises

1. George Evans is the department manager of the menswear department. He receives a salary of $250 a month plus a commission of 1% on his personal sales in excess of $2000. In addition, he receives $\frac{1}{2}$% of the sales above $10,000 for the total department. Calculate his gross pay for the month if he sold $4500 in merchandise and the department sales were $19,600.

2. How much did James earn (gross) working the following schedule last week:

Sun.	Mon.	Tues.	Wed.	Thurs.*	Fri.	Sat.
0	$8\frac{1}{4}$	$7\frac{3}{4}$	$7\frac{1}{4}$	$7\frac{3}{4}$	$8\frac{1}{2}$	8

* National holiday.

He earns $6.80 per hour with time and a half pay for overtime in excess of 8 hours per day and for Saturday work; Sundays and holidays are paid at double time.

3. You must earn $91 (gross wages) tomorrow to qualify for the Christmas bonus. If you receive $0.01 per unit for the first 3000 units, $0.015 for the next 3000 units, and $0.02 per unit for the next 4000 units, how many units must you produce?

4. Louis Hernandez is married and claims 3 deductions. He receives a salary of $650 per month and 5% of sales in excess of $7800. Last month his sales totaled $32,650. Compute his *net* pay if he contributes $18.75 each month to buy a savings bond, and $1\frac{1}{2}$% of his gross pay to the United Way. He has earned $34,000 to date and pays F.I.C.A. at 7.05% with a maximum earnings limit of $35,500.

5. What are the marked price and total paid on a sale involving $4.05 sales tax at a 6% tax rate?

6. The total price paid for new clothing was $136.21. If the tax rates are 5% for state and 1% for city, what was the marked price of the clothing, and how much tax will be paid to the city and state?

7. Ms. Surber paid $345.63 in property tax on her home. What is the fair market value of her home if the tax rate is 1.25% of assessed value (at a rate of 70%)?

8. A property owner paid tax of $8352 on his property at a tax rate of 87 mills. During the next year, the tax rate increased to 94 mills and the assessed value of the building changed. If the new tax amount was $10,152, how much had the assessed value of the building changed?

9. The Majestic Theater carries insurance totaling $200,000 on property valued at $260,000. Three insurers carry the policy as follows: A—$80,000; B—$70,000; and

C—$50,000. How much will each company pay for fire damage totaling $90,000, assuming an 80% coinsurance clause?

10. Mr. Landrum (age 52) is trying to decide how to receive the proceeds of his wife's $30,000 life insurance policy. He would like to receive an annuity of at least $160 per month for 20 years. Can he do so? If not, he will choose an annuity for life. How much will that annuity exceed the cost of premiums paid for Mrs. Landrum's ordinary nonparticipating policy if she purchased it at age 23 and died at age 53 and Mr. Landrum lives to age 65?

11. Calculate the total semiannual insurance premium on a class 2 automobile that is 2 years old. The driver is class C and the primary location is 28. Protection provided is 25/50/10. How much will the insurance premium change *next* year when a class A driver purchases the same coverage in the same location?

12. Elena worked the following schedule last week:

Sun.	Mon.	Tues.	Wed.	Thur.	Fri.	Sat.
Off	$7\frac{3}{4}$ hr.	$8\frac{1}{2}$ hr.	Off	$9\frac{1}{4}$ hr.	$8\frac{1}{4}$ hr.	$9\frac{1}{4}$ hr.

She makes $8.47 per hour with time and a half for all hours in excess of 36 per week. Calculate her net pay if she is single, claims 1 deduction, and has voluntary deductions totaling $42.65. She is well below the F.I.C.A. limit which is currently 7.15%.

 13. You receive a guaranteed minimum wage of $325 per week. You are eligible for a piece rate pay at the rate of $0.035 for the first 4250 units and $0.045 for the next 5000 units. Units 9251 and up are paid at the rate of $0.0475. What would your gross pay be for a week when you produced 8643 units?

14. Mr. Zuniga paid $1265.25 in taxes on his rental property. If the tax rate is 3% and the rental property is assessed at 58% of fair market value, what is the fair market value of the rental property? Round your answer to the nearest $100.

15. Angela paid $7.78 in tax (i.e., $7.77725) on a purchase. What was the purchase price and the total paid for the purchase if the tax rate is 4.5%.

16. The Highlander Shop has $150,000 of insurance coverage on its plant and equipment valued at $375,000. A fire caused $145,000 worth of damage. If the insurance policy has an 80% coinsurance clause, how much will the policy pay for the claim? How much will the owners of the Highlander have to pay?

17. Mr. Henricy was the beneficiary of his wife's $45,000 life insurance policy. She died when he was 54 years old. He elected to receive the proceeds as a lifetime annuity. How much had he received when he died at age 84? (Assume no partial years are involved.)

18. Erin is paid on a piece rate basis at her company. She receives $0.045 per unit for the first 1000 units produced each day, $0.055 for units 1001 through 1500, and $0.07 for units above 1501. How many units must she produce each day next week (assume a 5-day working week) in order to earn $448.25.

19. Jerome receives a salary of $375 per month plus a 6% commission on all his net sales in excess of $4800. He also receives a 0.75% override commission on the net sales of all the salesmen he supervises. Last month, Jerome sold $8196 in merchandise, $146 of which was returned. His salesmen sold $128,930 with only $1422 in returns. How much should Jerome earn as gross pay?

20. Adam worked the following schedule last week:

Sun.	Mon.	Tues.	Wed.	Thur.	Fri.	Sat.
8 hrs.	7.8 hrs.	8.4 hrs.	7.9 hrs.	—	8.1 hrs.	—

He makes $9.80 per hour. All time in excess of 40 hours per week is paid at time and a half; Sunday work is paid at double time. What is Adam's gross pay for the week?

21. Elisha receives a salary of $1345 every 2 weeks. She is single, claims 1 deduction, and is well below the F.I.C.A. maximum. What is her net pay for the last pay period if the F.I.C.A. tax rate is 7.05%? She contributes 1% of her gross pay to the United Fund and pays 8% of her gross pay into a company savings plan.

22. Todd paid a total of $145.43 for a purchase. What is the tax rate if the purchase itself cost $137.85?

23. Calculate the property tax due on Ms. Edmond's home. The home has a fair market value of $72,800. The tax rate is $42 per $1000 and homes are assessed at 70% of fair market value.

24. Mr. Erwin paid $2042.69 in property tax on his home. What are the assessed value and fair market value of his home if the tax rate is $3.80 per $100 of assessed value and the assessment ratio is 65%?

25. Natasha's income last year was as follows: salary—$28,200; stock dividends—$1840; royalty income—$3750; and interest from savings accounts—$990. She incurred necessary business expenses of $3960 and contributed $2000 to an Individual Retirement Account. Natasha is the sole support of her family (husband and daughter). How much additional tax does she owe if she has paid $4972 and the deduction for each exemption is $1000? (Assume married and filing jointly.)

26. A fire did $34,800 worth of damage to Mr. Edward's home. His home was valued at $69,000 and he had an insurance policy for $50,000 with an 80% coinsurance clause. How much of the damage will be paid by the insurance company?

27. Orange Computer Incorporated has $500,000 in insurance coverage with three firms as follows: Company A—$175,000; Company B—$125,000; and Company C—$200,000. A recent flood caused an estimated $190,000 in damage. Assuming no coinsurance restrictions, how much of the damage will each company pay?

28. Mrs. Nelson (age 54) is the beneficiary of her deceased husband's $60,000 life insurance policy.
   a. If she chooses to receive an annuity for life, how much will she receive monthly?
   b. Assuming she wishes to guarantee payment of the annuity for 10 years, how much will she receive per month?
   c. How much will she receive quarterly if she chooses to receive payments for the next 20 years?
   d. For how many months can she receive monthly payments of $500 per month?

Part Five

Mathematics for Presentation and Analysis of Information

O V E R V I E W

Suppose that you are in charge of production for a large manufacturing firm. Every day you receive vast amounts of information about production costs, labor costs, production levels, worker absenteeism, and numerous other things relating to your area of responsibility. How do you bring all of this information into focus so that it can be used effectively?

Two powerful mathematical tools used in presenting and analyzing information are graphs and statistics. In the following chapter, you will see how to interpret and construct some of the most common graphs and how they can be applied. Next, you will see how to describe a large amount of information with a single number called a statistic. Statistics are one of the most useful tools in managerial decision making. The final chapter (metric system) will allow you a glimpse of one of the challenges facing the business-person of the future.

CHAPTER 19

Graphs

INTRODUCTION

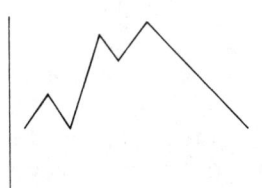

A philosopher once said "a picture is worth more than ten thousand words." In this age of mass communication and masses of new information, it follows that pictures are used to display information in a form that can be quickly and easily understood.

In this chapter we want to examine a particular type of picture called a *graph*. You can hardly pick up a newspaper or magazine without seeing a graph. Sometimes the graph consists of one or more lines, bars, or pictures. Each one is used in an attempt to show the relationship between quantities of presumed interest to the reader.

Graphs are no less important in business. The management of a business might use graphs to display information about the sales, profit, cost, budget, and so on, for its stockholders. Internally, one branch of a business might use graphs to depict information about its area to another branch of the business.

The four most commonly used types of graphs are presented in the following discussion. They are line graphs, bar graphs, pictograms, and circle graphs. The point of view taken in this chapter is that the reader has a *table of data* that is to be displayed by means of a graph.

19.1 *Line Graphs*

The Pocket Radio Company has determined the cost of producing radios at its new factory. The number of radios produced and the corresponding cost of production are shown in the following table.

Pocket Radio Company
Table of Data

Number of Radios Produced	Cost of Production
1000	$ 5,000
2000	$ 9,000
3000	$12,000
4000	$14,000
5000	$15,000

The plant supervisor wants to present the information to higher management by means of a line graph. How is the graph constructed?

Constructing a Line Graph

Step 1. The *first step* in constructing a line graph is to establish a "framework" in which to work. This framework is called a *coordinate system*. In the Pocket Radio example, there are two quantities being considered: number of radios, and cost of production. Therefore, two number lines called *axes* are needed. One axis is marked-off or "scaled" in number of radios produced; the other is marked-off in dollar cost of production.

The two axes are drawn perpendicular to each other, one horizontal and the other vertical.

The point of intersection of the two axes (at the corner) is called the *origin*. If we put units produced on the horizontal axis and production cost on the vertical axis, the coordinate system shown in Figure 19.1 results.

coordinate system

origin

Figure 19.1

Pocket Radio Company

Coordinate System

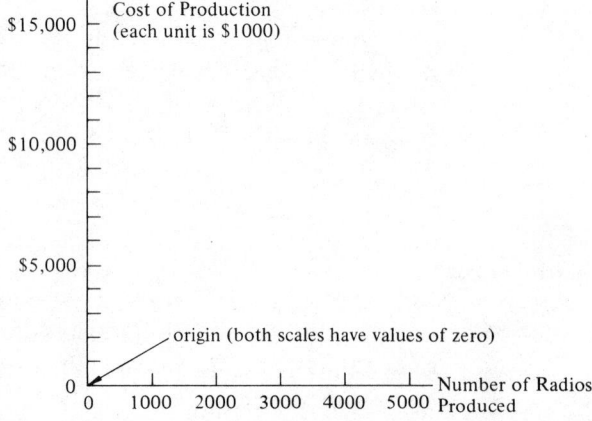

Step 2. After establishing the coordinate system, the *second step* is to transfer the data from the table to the coordinate system. This is done by *plotting points* that represent the information in the table.

Pocket Radio Company
Table of Data

Number of Radios Produced	Cost of Production
1000	$ 5,000
2000	$ 9,000
3000	$12,000
4000	$14,000
5000	$15,000

From the table we see that 1000 radios corresponds to a cost of $5000. To plot the point that represents this information, move vertically (above 1000) a distance that corresponds to $5000 on the vertical axis and "plot" a point.

For 2000 units, move vertically (above 2000) a distance that corresponds to $9000 on the vertical axis. Continue this process for production of 3000, 4000, and 5000 units. The (partial) graph shown in Figure 19.2 illustrates the points that represent the data.

Figure 19.2

Pocket Radio Company (Partial Graph
Showing Plotted Points)

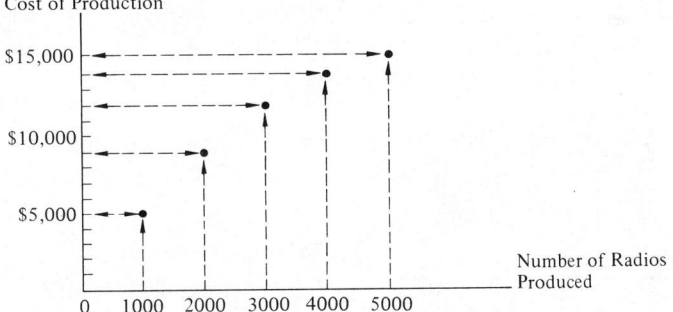

Note: The dashed construction lines in Figure 19.2 illustrate the plotting process. They do not appear on the completed graph.

Step 3. The *third* (and final) *step* is to connect the points with straight-line segments proceeding from left to right. That is, connect the point corresponding to 1000 radios to the point corresponding to 2000 radios. Then, connect the points corresponding to 2000 and 3000 radios, and so on until all points are connected. Figure 19.3 shows the completed graph results.

Figure 19.3

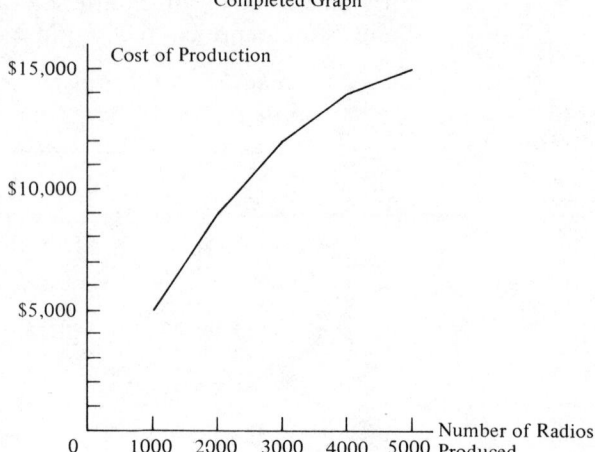

Pocket Radio Company
Completed Graph

Interpolation

Suppose that you wanted to estimate the cost of producing 1500 radios. You would locate 1500 (halfway between 1000 and 2000) and construct a vertical line intersecting the line graph. At the point of intersection, construct a horizontal line intersecting the vertical axis. The number found on the vertical axis is the estimated cost of producing 1500 radios. (The cost is $7000.)

interpolation   The process of determining values from the graph for levels of production not given in the table is called *interpolation*.

Example 1   The total number of units coming off an assembly line for an 8-hour shift is related to the number of hours the line has been in production.

Table of Data
Time versus Production

Hours, x	Units Produced, y
0	0
1	10
2	20
3	30
4	40
5	50
6	60
7	70
8	80

a. If the number of units produced is related to the time in hours as shown in the previous table, graph the data.

b. Estimate the number of units produced at $4\frac{1}{2}$ hours.

SOLUTION

a. To graph the data:

Step 1. Draw the coordinate system (Figure 19.4).
Step 2. Plot the data points (Figure 19.4).

Figure 19.4

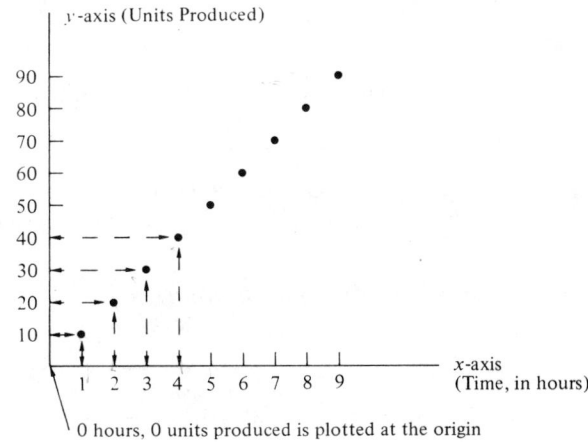

Production Data

0 hours, 0 units produced is plotted at the origin

Step 3. Complete the graph by connecting the points (Figure 19.5).

Figure 19.5

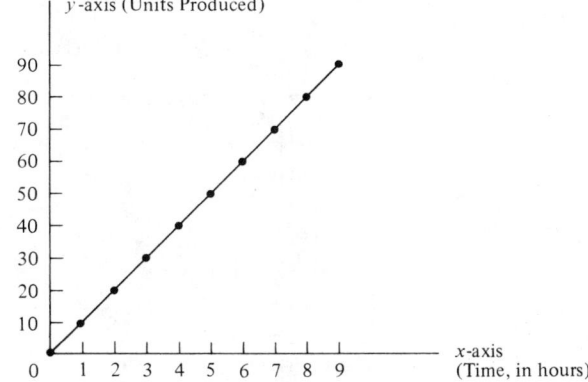

Production Data

b. Draw the vertical line at $4\frac{1}{2}$ hours. At the point of intersection, draw the horizontal line intersecting the vertical axis (Figure 19.6).

Figure 19.6

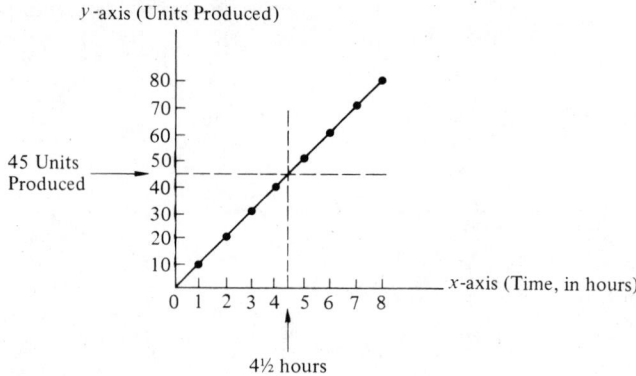

Production Data—Interpolation

The estimated number of units is 45.

Example 2   The production manager of Jones Industries collected the following data on the number of gadgets produced (x) and the associated cost of production (y).

Jones Industries
Production Figures

Number of Gadgets Produced, x	Cost of Production, y
100	$120
200	$140
300	$150
400	$170
500	$180

Figure 19.7

Jones Industries
Production Graph

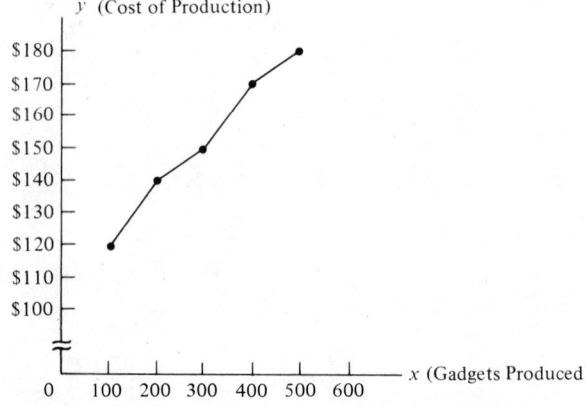

a. Construct a line graph omitting costs between 0 and $100.

b. Estimate the cost of producing 250 gadgets.

SOLUTION

a. Graph of data (Figure 19.7).

b. By interpolation, the estimated cost of producing 250 units is $145.

Graph Distortion

In constructing a line graph, the distance between values marked on the axes (the scale of the graph) is at the discretion of the person drawing the graph. The primary consideration is making the scale so that the picture will turn out to be of reasonable size. The only restriction is that the scale be consistent throughout. However, different choices of scale can have a significant effect on the visual impact of the final picture. Unless the same scale is used for both variables, the picture is distorted.

Suppose that the following data are to be graphed.

x	y
1	2
2	3
3	4
4	5

If the axes are scaled in *equal* units of distance for both x and y, we get a "true" picture of the relationship between x and y (see Graph I of Figure 19.8).

If the scale for y is marked using distances that are *twice* as large as those used for x, the graph of the relation appears to "rise" more steeply than if the same scale were used for both (see Graph II). The graph gives a distorted picture of the relationship.

If the values of y are scaled in units that are *half* as large as those

Figure 19.8

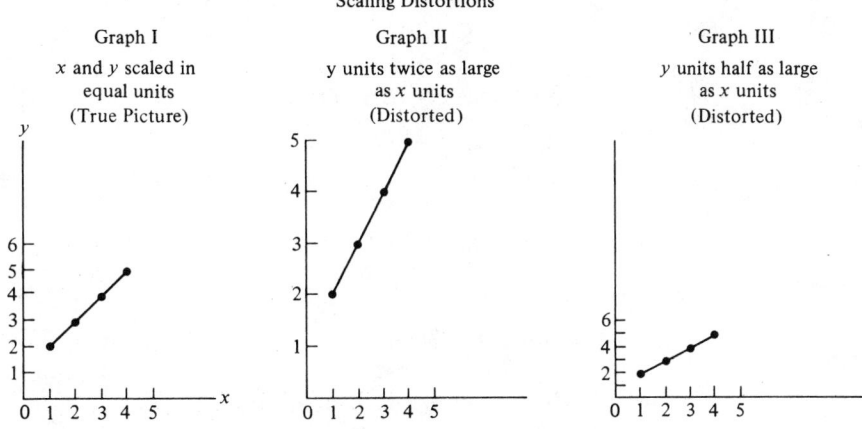

Scaling Distortions

Graph I	Graph II	Graph III
x and y scaled in equal units (True Picture)	y units twice as large as x units (Distorted)	y units half as large as x units (Distorted)

used for x, the graph will rise less steeply than if the same scale were used (see Graph III). Again, we get a distorted picture of the relationship.

Whenever possible, the same scale should be used for both axes. However, in displaying real data such as time versus production, this might not be practiced. In this case, the person constructing the graph should choose his scales to display the relation as clearly as possible in order not to mislead the reader.

Omitting part of an axis is also a type of distortion. Suppose that you must graph the following data.

x	y
1	50
2	55
3	60
4	65
5	70

Figure 19.9

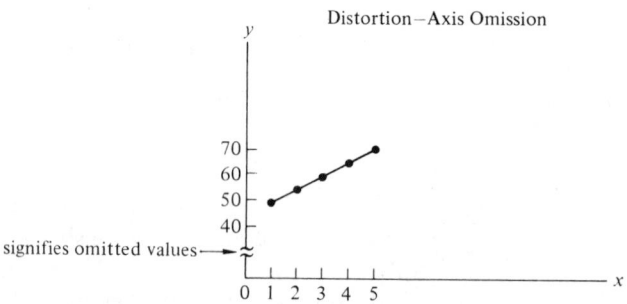

Since no values of y less than 50 are to be plotted, you might choose to omit the values between 0 and 40 by using the symbol " $\approx$." The graph would be as shown in Figure 19.9. Since the values between 0 and 40 have been omitted, the line is "lower" in the picture than it should be. This type of distortion is used to save space as in Example 2.

Graphing an Equation

Sometimes there is a consistent, predictable relationship between two variables. In this case, the relation between the two variables might be expressed in the form of an equation.

Suppose you are selling pipe for $2 per foot. The cost depends on the length of pipe sold. If we let x = the length of pipe and y = the cost of the pipe, then the equation $y = \$2x$ describes the relation. If you sell 1 foot, the cost $y = \$2(1) = \$2$. If you sell 5 feet, then $y = \$2(5) = \$10$. If you sell $6\frac{1}{2}$ feet, $y = \$2(6\frac{1}{2}) = \$13$ and so on. In short, we can use the equation to predict the cost of *any* length of pipe.

By choosing representative values of length (x), the corresponding cost can be computed. The results may be shown conveniently in a table.

x (length in feet)	y (cost in dollars)	
0	0	
1	2	
2	4	
3	6	
4	8	
...	...	and so on.

Figure 19.10

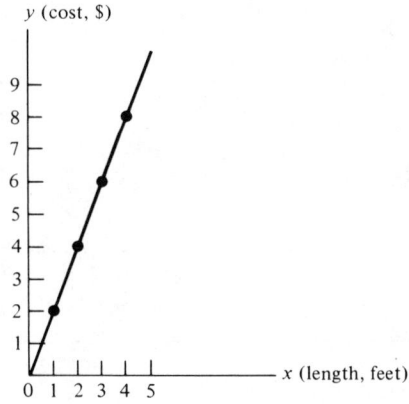

Line Graph of $y = \$2x$ (where $x =$ length and $y =$ cost).

Since the relationship is predictable, it is appropriate to extend the line beyond points that are actually computed and plotted. The extended line represents points that could have been plotted but were not.

Procedure For Graphing an Equation

Step 1. Select some appropriate values for one of the variables (such as x).
Step 2. Put each value of x into the equation and compute the corresponding value of y. Make a table.
Step 3. Draw the coordinate system and plot the points.
Step 4. Connect the points with a line.

Example 3   Brand X gasoline sells for $1.80 per gallon. The cost (y) of x gallons is $y = \$1.80x$. Graph the equation.

SOLUTION   **Step 1–2.** Choose values of x and compute values of y. Make a table.

x Gallons	y Cost
0	0
1	$1.80
2	$3.60
3	$5.40
4	$7.20
...	...

Step 3–4. Draw the coordinate system and plot the points. Since x may be *any number*, a line graph is drawn.

Figure 19.11

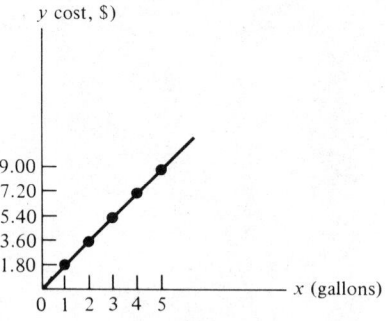

Exercises 19.1

■ Construct a line graph for each of the following.

1.

x	y
1	2
2	3
3	5
4	6
5	7

Estimate the value of y when $x = 3\frac{1}{2}$.

2.

x	y
2	3
4	4
6	7
8	6
10	12

Estimate the value of y when $x = 7$.

3.

Hours Worked, x	Money Earned, y
0	$ 0
10	$ 30
20	$ 60
40	$120
50	$165

Estimate the amount earned for 45 hours worked.

4.

Week of Production, x	Number of Cars Produced, y
0	0
5	5000
10	8000
15	14,000
20	18,000

Estimate the number of cars produced in 12 weeks.

5. Units Produced, x	Production Cost, y
1000	$ 500
2000	$1000
3000	$2000
4000	$2500
5000	$3000

Estimate the cost of 2500 units.

6. Units Sold, x	Revenue, y
100	$200
200	$400
250	$500
300	$600

Estimate the cost of 150 units.

7. An insurance company bases life insurance rates on the customer's age at the time the policy is purchased. The following table shows the customer's age and the corresponding annual premium for its basic $10,000 policy. Represent the information graphically.

Age of Insured, x	Amount of Annual Premium, y
20	$170
25	$180
30	$200
35	$220
40	$270

8. Suppose that you purchase a new automobile. The resale value decreases each year. The table shows the decrease in value of a car that cost $6,000 in 1975.

Year, x	Value, y
1975	$6,000
1976	$4,500
1977	$3,600
1978	$3,000

a. Graph the data.
b. Estimate the value halfway through the year 1977.

9. A business has an initial stock of 300 items. The number of items remaining at the end of each business day for a particular week is shown in the table.

Day	Items Remaining
1	280
2	250
3	250
4	210
5	200

a. Graph the data.
b. Estimate the number of items in stock after $1\frac{1}{2}$ days.

10. The units produced by an assembly line are related to the time of operation as shown in the table of data. Graph the data.

Hours	Units of Production
0	0
1	8
2	15
3	17
4	22
5	25

■ Graph each of the following equations.

11. $y = \$1x$ where x = length of plastic pipe in feet and y = cost.

12. $y = \$1.50x$ where x = gallons of gasoline and y = cost.

13. $y = \$1.20x$ where x = number of loaves of bread and y = cost.

14. $y = \$0.50x$ where x = number of ballpoint pens and y = cost.

15. Graph $y = 2x + 1$ where x may be *any non-negative number.*

16. Graph $y = x - 3$ where x may be any number greater than 3.

17. Fragrant perfume can be purchased in bulk from the manufacturer for $5 per ounce. Write an equation representing the cost (y) of x ounces of perfume and graph.

19.2 Bar Graphs and Pictograms

Bar graphs of numerical data are constructed by centering each bar at one of the numerical values and making its length represent the other numerical value. As with line graphs, two perpendicular axes are required. The following example illustrates the procedure for constructing a bar graph.

Suppose that the Korner Store had daily sales for the first 5 days of the month as shown in the table.

**Korner Store
Daily Sales**

Day	Total Sales Each Day
1	$10,000
2	$ 8,000
3	$10,000
4	$ 8,000
5	$14,000

The first step in making a bar graph is to draw the coordinate system marking days on the horizontal axis and sales on the vertical axis as shown in Figure 19.12.

Figure 19.12

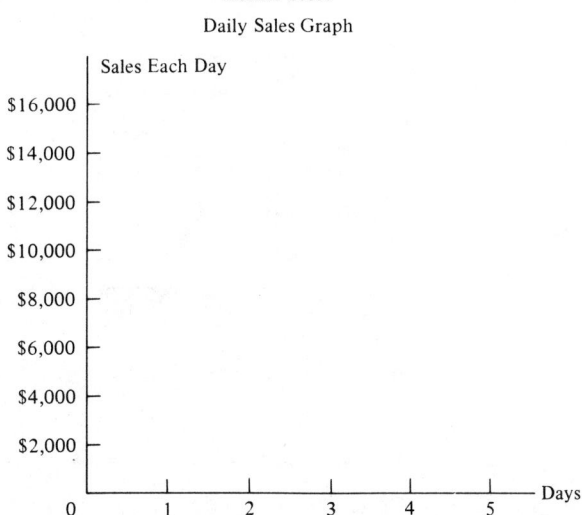

To transfer the data from the table to the graph, center a bar above (day) 1 and draw its length up to $10,000. Next, center a bar above 2 and draw its length up to $8000, and so on, until all five bars are constructed (Figure 19.13). The bars are usually shaded to contrast with the background, thus making the graph easy to read.

Figure 19.13

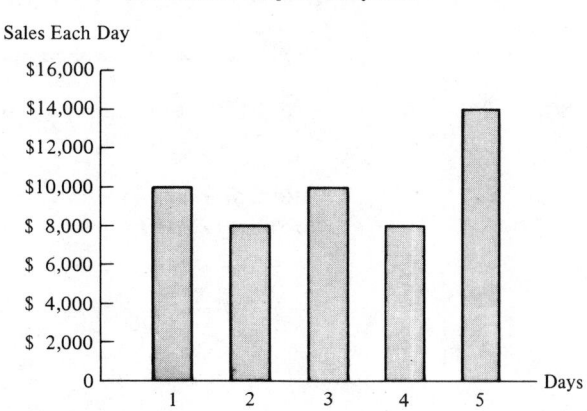

The bars may be drawn horizontally or vertically for numerical data. If days are marked on the vertical axis and sales on the horizontal, the (horizontal) bar graph of Figure 19.14 results.

Figure 19.14

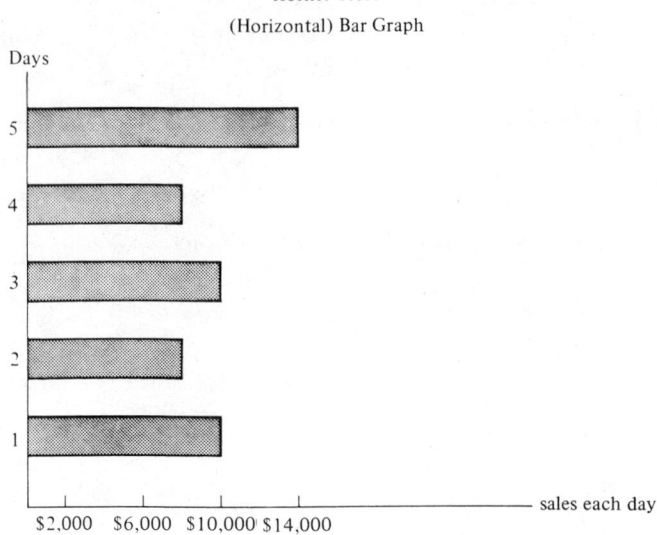

Korner Store
(Horizontal) Bar Graph

---

bar graph
construction

> **Constructing a Bar Graph Where Both Variables Are Numerical**
>
> **Step 1.** Decide whether you want a horizontal or vertical bar graph.
> **Step 2.** Draw the coordinate system.
> **Step 3.** Construct each bar centered at the value of one variable and
> draw its length equal to the value of the other variable. Shade
> each bar.

Each bar should be the same width in order not to distort the picture
of the relationship. The length of each bar is all that communicates value.

Example 1   The Verbage Publishing Company's profits for 5 recent years were as
follows:

**Verbage Publishing Company
Annual Profit**

Year	Profit
1975	$70,000
1976	$90,000
1977	$85,000
1978	$65,000
1979	$80,000

Construct a vertical bar graph with years on the horizontal axis.

SOLUTION   **Step 1.** The type of bar graph is stated in the problem.
Step 2. Draw the coordinate system (Figure 19.15).

Figure 19.15

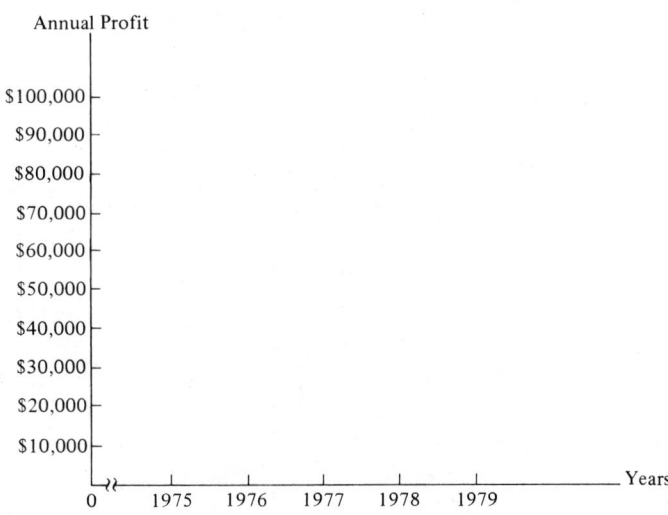

Step 3. Draw and shade the bars (Figure 19.16).

Figure 19.16

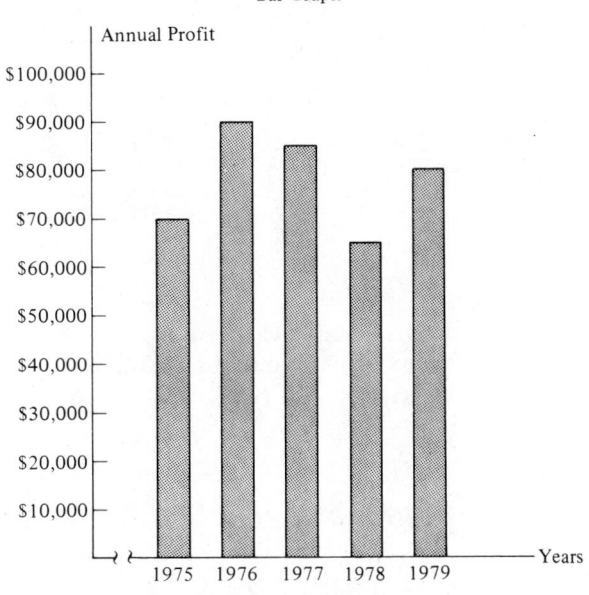

A bar graph may be drawn when *only one* of the variables is numerical. The other variable may be nominal (i.e., its "values" may simply be items identified by name).

The Metro Appliance Company sales of common appliances during its first year of operation were as follows:

Metro Appliance
First Year's Sales Data

Type of Appliance	Number Sold
Dishwashers	250
Refrigerators	350
Ranges	300
TV sets	400

The variable "type of appliance" is nominal. Its "value" consists of names. The variable "number sold" is numerical. A bar graph can be drawn for such data by centering each bar at the name and drawing its length to represent the number.

In this situation, the nominal variable is usually put on the vertical axis so that the name can be easily read (Figure 19.17).

Figure 19.17

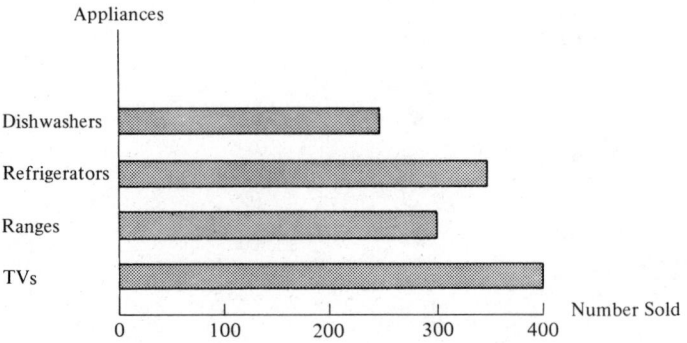

Metro Appliance
Bar Graph of First Year's Sales Data

When one variable is nominal, the arrangement of names is not important. If the Metro Appliance graph had TV sets first, it would still be correct.

Bar Graph Distortion

Bar graphs may be distorted by omitting part of the axis of a numerical variable in order to save space. In a bar graph this can be very misleading—more so than with a line graph.

Consider the salaries of Smith, Jones, and Brown.

Salaries

Name	Amount
Smith	$18,000
Jones	$20,000
Brown	$22,000

The bar graph should appear as shown in Figure 19.18.

Figure 19.18

Salary Bar Graph

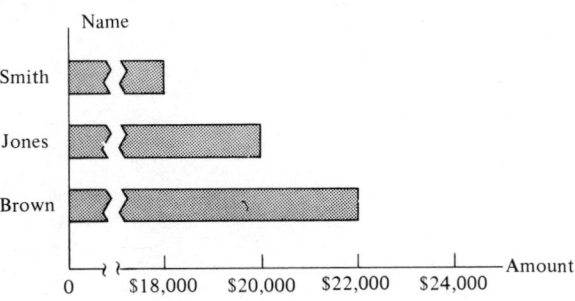

If we omit all the values less than $18,000, the graph shown in Figure 19.19 results.

Figure 19.19

Distorted Salary Bar Graph

From the distorted graph, it appears that Brown makes three times as much as Smith. Be alert for omissions in bar graphs.

Of course, making some bars wider than others would also be misleading. Also, the space between the bars should remain the same.

Pictograms

A pictogram is a modified horizontal bar graph in which each bar is replaced by a picture. In a pictogram each picture represents a certain quantity or amount; in a bar graph units of length are used to represent quantity.

Suppose that the Leaky Boat Company made 200 boats in 1978 and 300 boats in 1979. A bar graph could be used to depict the data (Figure 19.20). The quantity 300 is represented by 3 units of length; 200 is represented by 2 units of length. If the company used the picture of a boat to represent 100 boats, the pictogram shown in Figure 19.21 results.

Figure 19.20

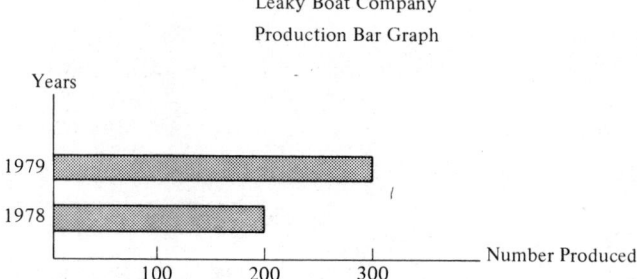

The advantage of a pictogram is its simplicity and visual appeal. Also, no axes are required. The main disadvantage is in interpretation. Suppose that the Leaky Boat Company produced 150 boats in 1977. The pictogram would show half a boat (Figure 19.22). To the reader (who does not have access to the exact figures), the partial picture could just as well represent 49 boats or 51 boats. Because of the problem of interpretation, pictograms are rarely used when precision is required.

Figure 19.21

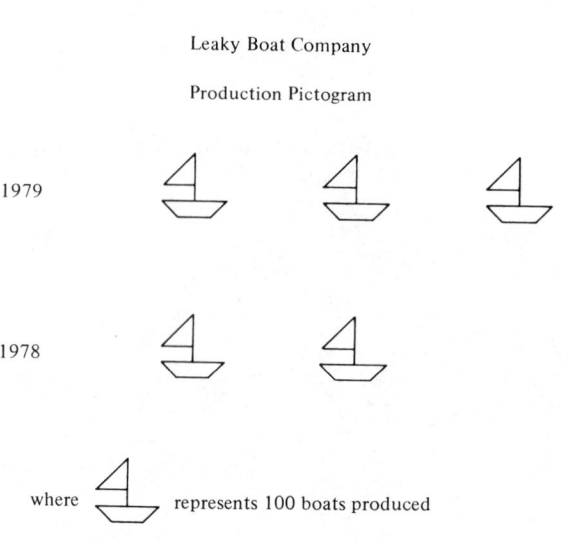

Figure 19.22

Exercises 19.2

1. **a.** Make a vertical bar graph for the following data.

Year	Revenue
1975	$1,000,000
1976	$1,500,000
1977	$2,000,000
1978	$1,250,000
1979	$2,500,000

b. Make a pictogram using ● to represent $1,000,000.

2. **a.** Make a vertical bar graph for the following.

Year	Earnings per Share
1978	$1.00
1979	$0.50
1980	$1.25

b. Make a pictogram using ■ to represent $1.00.

3. **a.** Make a horizontal bar graph.

Employee	Salary
A	$10,000
B	$12,000
C	$ 8,000

b. Make a pictogram using $ to represent $2000.

4. **a.** Make a bar graph.

Make of Car	Number Sold in July
Ford	50
Chevrolet	70
Dodge	40

b. Make a pictogram using 🚗 to represent 10 cars.

5.   **a.** Make a bar graph.

Week	Weekly Sales
1	$10,000
2	$12,000
3	$ 8,000
4	$16,000

b. Make a pictogram using ▲ to represent $4000.

6.   **a.** Make a bar graph.

Years	Annual Income
1978	$15,000
1979	$18,000
1980	$21,000

b. Make a pictogram using 🛍️($) to represent $3000.

19.3 Circle Graphs

The management of Industrial Machine Company has allocated 25% of next year's budget for labor costs, 20% for taxes, 10% for maintenance, and 45% for material and other costs. What type of graph may be used to display the budget allocation? How is it constructed?

The breakdown of a budget (or other whole quantity) may be represented by a *circle graph* or *pie graph*. A circle graph uses a circle to represent the whole quantity to be allocated. The circle is partitioned into pie-shaped slices called *sectors*. Each sector represents one of the parts into which the whole is divided.

sectors

To construct a circle graph, each item of data must be converted into a sector of the circle. The sizes of the sector are in the same ratio to the circle as the item of data is to the whole data. Items that make up a large part of the whole are represented by large "slices" and conversely, small items by small "slices."

Interpretation of a pie graph poses no particular problems. Each portion of the whole is clearly labeled and the percent of the whole is also shown on the graph. In fact, circle graphs are probably the most easily understood of all the types of graphs. Construction is the difficult task. It requires special instruments and some knowledge of geometry.

Needed Geometry

First, the circle (base) of the graph must be drawn. For this, we need a *compass*. A compass is a device that allows us to easily draw a perfect circle any size we desire.

compass

A circle is measured by subdividing it into 360 equal parts or 360 degrees. The symbol "°" is used to denote degrees. Thus, a circle has 360°. For measuring degrees, a *protractor* is needed. Sectors containing 30°, 90°, and 270° are shown in Figure 19.23.

protractor

Figure 19.23

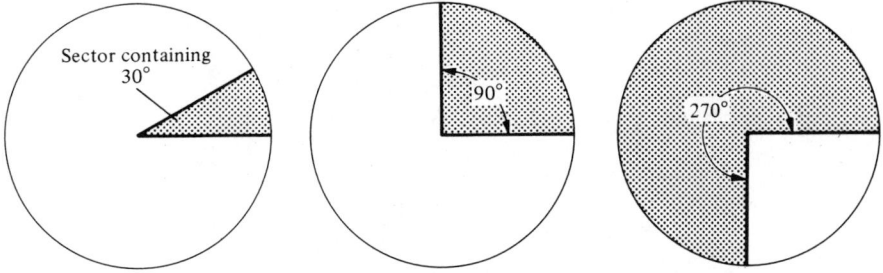

To measure angles with a protractor, place the pivot point (or hole) at the center of the circle with the base line (at 0°) along the radius. A radius is a line from the center of the circle to the edge of the circle (the circumference). Place a dot at the outer edge of the protractor at the appropriate number of degrees. Use the straightedge (ruler) to draw the other side of the angle. Use the newly drawn side of each angle as the "baseline" for constructing the next angle. The sides of the angle cut the circle into sectors.

Converting Data to Degrees

Each item in the data must be represented by a sector of the circle. Since the size of a sector is determined by the number of degrees it contains, each item of data must be converted to degrees.

A circle graph is used primarily to show the relation of parts making up a whole, so each item may be expressed as some percent of the whole. Therefore, 100% of the data equals 360° of the circle or 1% of the data = 3.6° of the pie. The degrees in a given sector equal the percent of data multiplied by 3.6.

Equation for Determining the Size of a Sector

$$y = 3.6\,x$$
where y = degrees in sector
x = percent of the (whole) data

The formula is developed so that we may use the value of $x\%$ without considering the % symbol, that is, only the value of x is needed.

Now let us return to the Industrial Machine Company budget.

Industrial Machine Company Budget

Item	Percent of Whole	Computation	Degrees in Sector
Labor	.25 ✗360	$y° = 3.6(25)$ or	90°
Taxes	20	$y° = 3.6(20)$ or	72°
Maintenance	10	$y° = 3.6(10)$ or	36°
Material and other costs	45	$y° = 3.6(45)$ or	162°
Total	100% of data	⟶	360° of circle

Figure 19.24   **Circle Graph of Industrial Machine Company Budget**

Procedure for Constructing a Circle Graph

Step 1. Convert all of the portions of the whole in the data or percents.

Step 2. Compute the number of degrees (y) for each percent (x) by the formula

$$y = 3.6x$$

As a check, make sure the percents total 100 and the degrees total 360.

Step 3. Draw a line from the center of the circle to the circumference (i.e., draw a radius).

Step 4. Use a protractor to measure the number of degrees alloted to each item in the data and label the sectors.

Example 1   The Jones family spends 20% of their income on rent, 15% on clothes, 10% on savings, 25% on taxes, and 30% on other things. Draw a circle graph of their budget.

Step 1. The data are already given in percents.

Step 2. Determine the number of degrees for each item.

$$y = 3.6(20) \text{ or } 72° \text{ rent}$$

$$y = 3.6(15) \text{ or } 54° \text{ clothes}$$

$$y = 3.6(10) \text{ or } 36° \text{ savings}$$

$$y = 3.6(25) \text{ or } 90° \text{ taxes}$$

$$y = 3.6(30) \text{ or } 108° \text{ other}$$

$$\overline{\quad\quad} \quad \overline{\quad\quad}$$

$$100 \quad\quad 360°$$

Step 3–4. Draw a circle and radius. Measure, draw, and label each sector.

Figure 19.25   Jones Family Budget

A circle graph is unique in that it is not susceptible to scaling distortions as were line and bar graphs. Since there are no axes, there can be no distortions. No matter how large the (base) circle is drawn, each sector is a proportional part of the whole. However, since a protractor is usually marked in one-degree units, it might be necessary to round-off some values to the nearest degree. This could cause a small distortion.

TABLE 19.1   Summary and Comparison of Graphs

Type of Graph	Type of Data	Form of Data	Advantages	Disadvantages
Line graph	Two variables, both numerical, *can be* interpreted between values	Table (or equation)	Shows trends, highs, and lows in the relation; allows interpolation	Can be distorted by scaling and omission of part of the axes
Bar graph	Two variables, both numerical, *cannot* be interpreted between values *or* one variable numerical, one nominal	Table	Can be used for nominal data	Can be distorted by scaling and omission of axes
Pictogram	Same as bar graph	Table	Visually appealing, easily understood	Difficult to interpret precisely
Circle	Numerical data about a whole	Table	Easily understood, difficult to distort	Cannot be used to graph equations

Exercises 19.3

■ Draw a circle for each of the following.

1. McBurney Manufacturing, Inc.

Budget	Distribution
Labor	40%
Material	20%
Taxes	10%
Other Costs	30%

2. Brown family budget

Utilities	10%
Food	20%
Automobile	5%
Insurance	10%
Other	55%

3. College student

Distribution of Time/Day	
Sleeping	40%
Eating	10%
Going to class	20%
Studying	10%
Free time	20%

4. Global sales distribution

U.S.	70%
Mexico	10%
Canada	15%
Other	5%

5. Metro Appliance Company

Sales distribution for March (1000 units)	
TV's	300
Refrigerators	250
Ranges	100
Vacuum cleaners	200
Other	150

6. University College employee breakdown
(100 employees)

Administration	18
Faculty	62
Staff	20

Review Exercises / Chapter 19

1. The Eaton Joint sells hamburgers, hot dogs, and fish sandwiches. Draw a bar graph of last week's sales.

Eaton Joint
Last Week's Sales

Food	Number Sold
Hamburgers	175
Hot dogs	150
Fish sandwiches	100

2. Suppose that the accumulated sales for the Korner Store for 1 week are as follows:

Day	Accumulated Sales
1	$10,000
2	$18,000
3	$28,000
4	$36,000
5	$50,000

Draw a line graph.

3. Small City College had 150 employees classified as follows:

Administration	18
Faculty	90
Professional staff	30
Other	12

Draw a bar graph of the data.

4. Draw a circle graph of the data in problems 1 and 3.

Chapter Test / Chapter 19

1. Define each of the following terms:

    a. graph   **b.** data   **c.** coordinate system
    d. axes   **e.** origin   **f.** plotting

g. interpolation   *h*. distortion   *i*. bar graph
j. pictogram   *k*. circle graph   *l*. circumference
m. radius   *n*. protractor   *o*. compass

2. Annual exploration expenditures of Dome Petroleum Limited for 6 recent years were as follows:

1975 $ 863,000
1976   785,000
1977   1,230,000
1978   1,605,000
1979   2,240,000
1980   2,800,000

a. Make a line graph of the data.

b. Compute the total expenditure.

c. Compute each year's expenditure as a percent of the total (found in *b*).

d. Make a bar graph of the percent data.

3. Big Burger sells hamburgers for $1.38 each.
   a. Write the equation relating the number of burgers sold (x) to the income (y) received.
   b. Graph the equation.

In 1980, 38% of unemployed persons were out of work for less than 5 weeks; 9% were out of work for 5 or 6 weeks; 12% were out of work for 7 to 10 weeks; 9% were out of work for 11 to 14 weeks; 32% were out of work for more than 14 weeks.
   a. Make a bar graph.
   b. Make a circle graph.

5. A retired couple spends $10,000 as follows: $2300 on food $2200 on housing; $1060 on transportation; $550 on clothing, $400 on personal care; $600 on medical care; and $2890 on other expenses.
   a. Make a horizontal bar graph.
   b. Make a circle graph.

6. Graph the equation $y = 2x - 3$ where x can be any nonnegative number.

7. Annual compensation for employees of Megation Manufacturing for 1982 were as follows:

Employee	Salary
3146	$28,000
2041	$20,000
7326	$26,000
0004	$16,000
1000	$ 8,000

a. Make a pictogram using $ to represent $4000.
b. Make a circle graph.
c. Make a bar graph.

CHAPTER 20

Statistics

INTRODUCTION

People in business are frequently confronted with the task of understanding and interpreting large amounts of information (called raw data). The first step in the understanding and interpreting process is data organization. Organization helps in understanding the data. For a deeper understanding and analysis of the data, certain quantities or measures (called statistics) can be computed based on the data.

Definition

statistic

A *statistic* is a single "measure" that describes or characterizes some aspect of the total data (information).

The statistics presented in Sections 20.2, 20.3, and 20.4 are called (collectively) by several names (depending on the author):

1. Measures of location.
2. Measures of center.
3. Measures of central tendency.

These measures characterize what is "typical" or "average" about the data. We will present three measures of location. Each characterizes what is "average" about the data; yet, each is different from the others in its use and calculation. They are called the *mean, median,* and *mode.* In Section 20.5 we discuss the *standard deviation.* The standard deviation is a measure of the dispersion or variation in the data. We also discuss the distribution of data, in particular, the normal distribution.

20.1 *Data and Their Organization*

Data are collections of related observations or measures about some topic of special interest to the businessperson. Each collection is called a *data set*. They can be acquired by current observation or from records kept for managerial purposes. The business manager then makes decisions based on analysis of the data by reasoning, discussion, or computation of statistical measures.

Raw Data

raw data

No matter how the data are to be analyzed, organization of the data is important. Before data are organized and analyzed, they are called *raw data*.

The Automated Beverage Company received complaints that one of its coffee dispensing machines (No. 823) was working improperly. It was supposed to dispense an average of 4 ounces per cup of coffee. In testing the machine, the service department collected the following data for 30 consecutive cups of coffee.

Automated Beverage Company
Raw Data—Machine 823
Ounces Dispensed—30 Cups

3.5	3.5	2.6	3.9	4.1	4.0
3.8	3.9	0	3.8	4.3	0
4.0	4.1	2.1	2.1	2.6	0
5.2	4.1	4.3	0	4.0	2.6
2.6	3.7	0	5.2	3.7	4.3

In raw form, the data are just a mass of numbers. Organizing the data would make them easier to analyze. Three methods are commonly used.

Data Array

data array

One of the simplest ways to organize data is to use a *data array*.
In a *data array*, the information is presented in tabular form with the numbers arranged *in order* from smallest to largest (or vice versa).

Automated Beverage Company
Data Array—Machine 823
Ounces Dispensed

0	2.1	2.6	3.8	4.0	4.3
0	2.1	3.5	3.8	4.0	4.3
0	2.6	3.5	3.9	4.1	4.3
0	2.6	3.7	3.9	4.1	5.2
0	2.6	3.7	4.0	4.1	5.2

The data array has some advantages over the raw data.

1. The smallest and largest values in the data are readily apparent. The data range from 0 to 5.2 ounces. From the range of values, maintenance personnel may observe that the machine is working erratically. It should dispense 4 ounces most of the time.

2. Values that occur most frequently are easily found. Maintenance might observe that the machine dispenses 0 ounces more often than any other amount—an indication that the machine needs attention.

A disadvantage is that the data array is still cumbersome because each observation is listed. In many (real) situations, hundreds or thousands of observations might be involved.

Frequency Distribution

frequency
distribution

A method of presenting data in a *compressed* (or shortened) form is by a *frequency distribution* or *frequency table*. This is particularly helpful when many observations occur repeatedly.

To make a *frequency distribution*, list each of the different values occurring in the data in a column (usually placed on the left). Put the number of times (or frequency) that each value occurs in a column (on the right).

Automated Beverage Company
Frequency Distribution—Machine 823

Ounces Dispensed	Frequency
0	5
2.1	2
2.6	4
3.5	2
3.7	2
3.8	2
3.9	2
4.0	3
4.1	3
4.3	3
5.2	2

The advantage of a frequency distribution is that it presents the data without the necessity of listing each value each time it occurs.

To make sure that all observations are included in the frequency distribution, *sum the frequencies*. The sum *should equal* the number of values in the data set being organized.

Grouping Data

grouping data

Occasionally, data are grouped into "classes" to emphasize a particular characteristic or pattern in the data. Suppose the Automated Beverage Company feels that any amount from 0 to 2.99 ounces is "underfilled,"

3 to 4.99 ounces is "acceptable," and 5 or more ounces is "overfilled." If working properly, the machine should dispense an "acceptable" amount every time.

The data for machine 823 could be "grouped" accordingly and shown in a *grouped frequency distribution*.

Automated Beverage Company
Grouped Frequency Distribution—Machine 823

Class *(oz)*	Frequency
0–2.99 (underfilled)	11
3–4.99 (acceptable)	17
5 or more (overfilled)	2

In this form, one might conclude that the machine dispensed an acceptable amount most of the time (17 times out of 30) but that it is not working properly.

A grouped frequency distribution has the advantage of displaying data in a very abbreviated form. However, there is a disadvantage. Grouping loses the detail; the exact values of the observations are not shown.

By making the classes "wider," fewer classes could be used, thus compressing the data even further. (Classes of "less than 4 ounces" and "4 or more ounces" would compress the Automated Beverage data even further.)

In practical work, the classes are established according to some external criteria imposed by the analyst. The criterion depends on the point of the analysis and varies from one application to another. The only (mathematical) rules for grouping data are that:

1. The classes are *all-inclusive* (no possible values in the data are omitted).
2. The classes are *mutually exclusive* (no observation may fall into two different classes).

A common grouping of data familiar to students is the A, B, C, D, F, I, W grading system. When grades are posted at the end of the semester, several students may have A's. But, the *exact* averages of the students in the "A group" are not known. One may have had 91, another 97.5, another 90.2. The detail is lost by grouping. However, the data are clearly organized, easily understood, and patterns are easily determined.

Grading fits the criteria for grouping data. All measures of performance fall into one of the groups A, B, C, D, F, I, or W. (The groups are all-inclusive.) Each measure of performance fits into a single group. (They are mutually exclusive.)

The data of the Automated Beverage Company relating to machine 823 consisted of numbers (of ounces dispensed). These *quantitative* or *numerical data* were grouped into classes of numbers (0 to 2.99, 3 to 4.99, 5 or more). However, groups or classes *are not restricted* to quantitative measures.

Suppose that the Public Opinion Poll asked 100 people if they thought their congressman was doing a good job. Forty said "yes," 35 said "no," and 25 had "no opinion." Each response may be considered as a "class," which may be illustrated graphically by a bar graph (Figure 20.1). Data consisting of *qualitative* "*measures*" (identified by name) are called *nominal* or *categorical data.*

Figure 20.1

Public Opinion Poll
Survey Response

Bar Graph

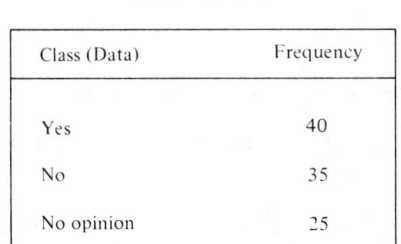

Class (Data)	Frequency
Yes	40
No	35
No opinion	25

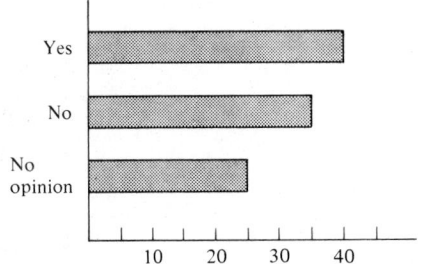

In spite of the obvious advantages of organizing data, sometimes this is not enough. Even an organized list of the cost of each item in inventory does not tell you the average cost of the inventory (which is a statistic called the mean). Calculations of statistics based on the data set are needed to provide a better understanding of the data.

Exercises 20.1

1. The number of units produced each day by Domestic Tractor Company's Boondock plant for the month of February was as follows:

**February Domestic Tractor Production
Boondock Plant**

2	3	2	6	2	4	2
2	6	3	0	1	5	3
5	1	1	5	3	3	2
0	4	4	3	2	0	7

Make a data array.

2. Make a frequency distribution for the data set in problem 1.

3. If 0 to 2 tractors produced is considered "low," 3 to 5 "average," 6 or more "high," make a grouped frequency distribution for the data in problem 1.

4. The Consumer Survey Company asked 25 homeowners if they insured their home with Company X, Company M, or other (O). The responses were: X, O, O, M, X, O, M, M, O, X, O, X, M, X, M, O, O, O, M, M, X, O, O, X, M. Make a frequency distribution for the responses.

5. *a.* What type of data is contained in problems 1–3?
b. What type of data is given in problem 4?

6. A class of 25 students made the following scores on a 5-point pop quiz.

Data set: 5, 2, 3, 1, 0, 2, 0, 5, 4, 3, 4, 2, 0, 4, 3, 1, 5, 2, 3, 5, 2, 1, 3, 4, 0

Make a data array.

7. Make a frequency distribution for the data in problem 6.

8. If scores of 0, 1, and 2 are "failing" and 3, 4, and 5 are "passing," make a grouped frequency distribution of the scores in problem 6.

9. Would it be correct to group the scores in problem 6 as follows: 0, 1, 2, 3 are failing; 3, 4, 5 are passing? Why?

10. Would it be correct to group the scores in problem 6 as follows: 0, 1, 2 are failing; 3 and 4 passing? Why?

11. The personnel manager of Positron Corporation did a study on worker absenteeism. The number of days missed by each employee last year was as follows: 2, 0, 1, 0, 0, 3, 14, 5, 2, 7, 6, 6, 3, 4, 3, 0, 2, 5, 11, 1. If 0 to 3 days is "low," 4 to 7 is "average," and 8 or more is "excessive," make a frequency distribution.

12. Graph the frequency distribution in problems 3, 4, 7, and 11.

20.2 Mean

Suppose that you have grades of 83, 97, and 75 on three tests. Your "average" grade is

$$\frac{83 + 97 + 75}{3} = 85$$

The average grade of 85 is a statistic. It is a single number that describes the "center" or "typical" level of performance. It is called the *mean* of the data.

Definition

the mean of data

The *mean of raw data* **is the arithmetic average of the numbers. It is found by summing *all* the values and dividing by the number of values.**

Clearly, the mean can only be used to describe numerical data. In fact, since the mean usually falls between numbers in the data set, it should "make sense" to interpret between values. The mean is the quantity you most frequently encounter as the "average." Strictly speaking, however, all measures of location are averages.

Example 1   In the past 5 days, John has spent 3, 2, 1, 4, and 2 hours preparing a financial report. Find the mean number of hours spent each day.

SOLUTION $\dfrac{3 + 2 + 1 + 4 + 2}{5} = \dfrac{12}{5} = 2.4$ hours per day.

John spent an "average" of 2.4 hours per day working on the report.

Example 2   The dividend per share of stock paid by Sigma, Inc., for each of the past 3 years is $1.00, $0.62, and $0.84. Find the mean dividend.

SOLUTION $\dfrac{\$1.00 + \$0.62 + \$0.84}{3} = \$0.82.$

Sigma, Inc., has paid a mean (or average) of $0.82 over the past 3 years.

Mean of a Frequency Distribution

The mean of the raw data 1, 3, 5, 5, 1, 3, 1, 5 is

$$\frac{1 + 3 + 5 + 5 + 1 + 3 + 1 + 5}{8} = \frac{24}{8} \quad \text{or} \quad 3 \text{ (mean)}$$

This raw data could be presented by a frequency distribution as follows:

Data	Frequency
1	3
3	2
5	3

Changing the presentation of the data from raw to a frequency distribution *will not change* the mean. However, it *does change* the computational procedure to be used.

Mean of a frequency distribution   Add the products of each value (in the data) times its frequency. Divide the total found by the sum of the frequencies.

Example 3   Compute the mean.

Data	Frequency
1	3
3	2
5	3

SOLUTION   It is convenient to multiply (from left to right) across the table, and produce a new column of products. Then find the sum and divide.

Data	Frequency	(Products)
1	3	$1 \times 3 = 3$
3	2	$3 \times 2 = 6$
5	3	$3 \times 5 = 15$
sum of frequencies = 8		sum of products = 24

$$\text{mean} = \frac{\text{sum of products (24)}}{\text{sum of frequencies (8)}} = 3$$

Pertinent business information is often presented in the form of a table that is essentially a frequency distribution, although it might not be labeled as such.

Example 4   Jock's Sport Shop purchased tennis racquets on three different occasions at different prices as shown. Find the mean cost of the racquets.

Cost per Racquet	Number of Racquets
$4	50
$5	100
$6	200

SOLUTION   The table is a frequency distribution where the cost per racquet is "data" and the number of racquets is "frequency."

Data	Frequency	(Products)
$4	50	$ 200
$5	100	$ 500
$6	200	$1200
sum = 350		sum = $1900

$$\text{mean} = \frac{\$1900}{350} = \$5.43 \text{ (rounded)}$$

The mean (average) cost of the racquets is $5.43.

The (arithmetic average) mean has several advantages.

1. It is a single number representing the entire quantitative data set.

2. It is familiar to most people and intuitively clear.
3. It always exists and is easily computed for moderately sized data sets.
4. The value of every observation is always taken into account.
5. It has many applications in inventory valuation, yield on stock, and so on.

For example, if you are estimating the value of inventory, you want a measure that reflects the value of each and every item. No cost is too small or too large to be considered.

The mean also has some disadvantages.

1. It cannot be used with qualitative data. You cannot average yes and no responses.
2. Since it does depend on every value in the data, it is profoundly affected by extreme values in the data set.

For example, a small company may have six employees, five of whom make $10,000 per year and one (the president) who makes $100,000 per year. The mean salary of the employees is

$$\text{mean} = \frac{5(\$10,000) + \$100,000}{6} = \$25,000$$

Does the mean reflect the "typical" salary of employees of the company? Of course not; five of the six make (much) less than that. Another measure is more appropriate in this context.

Exercises 20.2

■ Find the mean.

1. Data set: 1, 2, 4, 6, 7.

2. Data set: 2, 4, 5, 9, 13.

3. Data set: 0, 1, 3, 5, 1, 4, 2, 3, 5, 4, 2, 3, 6, 2.

4. Data set: 7, 2, 6, 8, 7, 9, 5, 7, 4, 8, 2, 3, 1, 2, 7.

5. | Value | Frequency |
|-------|-----------|
| $3 | 20 |
| $4 | 8 |
| $6 | 12 |

6. | Value | Frequency |
|-------|-----------|
| 5 | 10 |
| 7 | 20 |
| 8 | 30 |

7. Kay made the following grades on five math tests. Grades: 93, 16, 94, 89, 100. Find her mean grade. Does the mean reflect her typical performance?

8. A small class made the following scores on a 10-point quiz. Grades: 0, 6, 8, 4, 10, 10, 9, 8, 7, 7. Find the class mean.

9. Delta Company paid the following dividend per share of stock for each of the past 5 years. Find the mean dividend.

Year	Dividend
1976	$0.25
1977	$0.30
1978	$0.15
1979	0
1980	$0.40

10. Find the mean salary.

Employee	Salary
A	$10,500
B	$12,800
C	$16,000
D	$ 9,300

11. Long's Driving Range purchased 100 golf balls at $0.80 each, 200 at $0.70 each, and 300 at $0.85 each. Find the mean cost of the balls.

12. Finny's Fish Mart purchased 50 pounds of shrimp at $2 per pound, 100 pounds at $1.85 per pound, and 80 pounds at $2.25 per pound. What is the mean cost?

13. Opinion Poll Results

Response	Frequency
For	70
Against	20
Undecided	10

Can the mean be used to analyze these data?

14. Find the mean of each data set given in problems 1, 6, and 11 of Exercises 20.1.

20.3 *Median*

the median   The *median* is a single quantity that identifies the *most central* item or location in the data set. Unlike the mean, calculation of the median requires that the data be organized. Also, the method of calculation depends on whether the data set contains an odd number or even number of values.

> **Calculating the Median**
>
> **Step 1.** Put the data in order from smallest to largest value (or vice versa).
>
> **Step 2.** If the data set contains an *odd number* of values, the median is the middle value in the (ordered) list.
>
> If the data set contains an *even number* of values, the median is the *average* of the two middlemost numbers.

Example 1

    a. Find the median of the data set 1, 7, 2, 3, 10.

    b. Find the median of the data set 2, 8, 1, 6.

SOLUTION

    a. Put the values in order: 1, 2, 3, 7, 10. Since there is an odd number of values, the median is the middle number. Median = 3.

    b. Put the values in order: 1, 2, 6, 8. Since there is an even number of values, the median is the average of the two middlemost values:

$$\text{median} = \frac{2 + 6}{2} = 4$$

The median is a number above which (and below which) 50% of the data fall. It can be easily determined from a data array since the array (by definition) is an ordered list of all the values in the data set. The median amount of coffee dispensed by machine 823 in Section 20.1 is

$$\frac{3.7 \text{ oz} + 3.8 \text{ oz}}{2} = 3.75 \text{ oz}$$

The median has one advantage over the mean. The median *is not* affected by an extreme value in the data set. Consider the following data sets:

Data set one: 1, 2, 3, 7, 10.

    median = 3

$$\text{mean} = \frac{1 + 2 + 3 + 7 + 10}{5} = \frac{23}{5} = 4.6$$

Data set two: 1, 2, 3, 7, 100.

    median = 3

$$\text{mean} = \frac{1 + 2 + 3 + 7 + 100}{5} = \frac{113}{5} = 22.6$$

Changing the extreme score from 10 to 100 greatly changed the mean but had no effect on the median.

Recall the small company with six employees mentioned at the end of Section 20.2. Five employees made $10,000 per year and one made $100,000 per year. The data set is: $10,000; $10,000; $10,000; $10,000; $10,000; $100,000. The median salary is $10,000; the mean was $25,000. In this context, the median is a much better measure of the "typical" salary.

Other advantages of the median are:

1. It is easily understood and commonly used.
2. It always exists for quantitative data.
3. It can be used for a particular type of qualitative data where ratings or rankings are used.

If a supervisor ranks the performance of five people in his group as low, low, low, average, high, even though the data are qualitative (rather than quantitative), an ordering is implied. Since the data can be ordered, the median can be "computed." The median rank (given by the supervisor) is "low."

A disadvantage of the median is that it is relatively difficult to compute. The data must be ordered. This can be a tedious, time-consuming task for data sets of even moderate size.

Exercises 20.3

■ Find the median.

1. Data set: 7, 8, 11, 20, 100.

2. Data set: 2, 5, 83, 100, 1000.

3. Data set: 2, 3, 9, 10.

4. Data set: 7, 8, 12, 29.

5. Data set: 15, 1, 3, 9, 7.

6. Data set: 80, 100, 96, 54, 70.

7. Data set: 15, 2, 10, 23.

8. Data set: 83, 96, 72, 100.

9. Sam made grades of 82, 90, 76, 100, and 85 on 5 history tests. Find his median and mean grades.

10. A class made the following scores on a 5-point quiz: 2, 0, 1, 3, 5, 5, 4, 4, 2, 2. Find the class median and mean.

11. Beta International paid the following dividends.

Year	Dividend
1978	$0.64
1979	$0.32
1980	$0.50
1981	$0.39

Find the median and mean dividend.

12. The ratings of 6 employees on a scale of 1 to 10 were 8, 6, 5, 9, 10, and 7. Find the median and mean ratings.

13. Five different brands of canned peas were ranked good, good, better, better, and best. What is the median rating?

14. Can the mean be used for the data in problem 13?

15. Find the median and mean of the data in problem 11, Exercises 20.1.

20.4 Mode

the mode

The *mode* is the statistic used to indicate the "item" that occurs *most frequently* in the data set.

It can be used for both quantitative *and* qualitative data sets. If the data set contains numbers, the "item" that occurs most frequently will be a number (if there is one). If the data set is categorical or nominal, the "item" that occurs most frequently will be identified by name.

Remember the Public Opinion Poll survey (Section 20.1):

Data	Frequency
Yes	40
No	35
No opinion	25

The most frequently occurring "item" was "yes." Hence, "yes" is the mode of the qualitative data set.

Also in Section 20.1, we had a quantitative data set presenting the number of ounces of coffee dispensed by machine 823. The "item" that occurred most frequently was 0 ounces. Hence, the mode of the quantitative data set is zero.

Automated Beverage Company
Frequency Distribution—Machine 823

Ounces Dispensed		Frequency	
0	← mode	5	← largest
2.1		2	frequency
2.6		4	
3.5		2	
3.7		2	
3.8		2	
3.9		2	
4.0		3	
4.1		3	
4.3		3	
5.2		2	

Two special cases must be mentioned:

1. If all items occur equally often in the data set, there is *no* mode.
2. If two or more items occur equally often and more than all of the rest, the data set is multimodal.

The primary use of the mode in business is to identify the *most popular* item, *most frequently* made error, the *most commonly* held opinion, and so on.

Example 1   The Sports Shop sells four brands of tennis racquets. Sales last year were as follows:

Year's Sales

Brand	Number Sold
A	230
B	412
C	61
D	197

What is the mode?

SOLUTION   The mode is Brand B; it sold with the greatest frequency.

Example 2   Ten employees were rated on a scale from 1 to 20. The results were 1, 2, 5, 4, 13, 12, 10, 18, 7, and 19. What was the modal rating?

SOLUTION   Since each rating occurs equally often (one time), there is *no mode*.

The advantages of the mode are:

1. It can be used with qualitative data such as opinion polls or as a measure of popularity.
2. It is not affected by extreme values in quantitative data.
3. It is easily understood.

Some disadvantages are:

1. There is frequently no mode because many data sets contain no repeated values. This is particularly true in quantitative data sets measured to a high degree of accuracy.
2. It may not be unique. If a data set contains several modes, they may be difficult to interpret.
3. It is difficult to compute for large data sets (if it exists) because the data must be organized into a frequency distribution.

Exercises 20.4

■ Find the mode.

1. Data set: 1, 2, 1, 3, 4.

2. Data set: 2, 7, 10, 7, 8, 6, 5.

3. Data set: 1, 2, 3, 7, 10.

4. Data set: 2, 8, 9, 14, 15.

5. Data set: 1, 2, 4, 1, 3, 2.

6. Data set: 2, 7, 8, 7, 6, 3, 2, 5.

7. Sue made the following scores in math: 78, 62, 78, 84, 100. Find her mean, median, and mode score.

8. A class made the following score on a 5-point quiz: 2, 0, 5, 4, 5, 3, 2, 1, 5, 4. Find the class mean, median, and mode.

9. Make a frequency distribution for the following data. Find the mode.

Data set: 1, 2, 1, 3, 3, 2, 1, 4, 5, 1, 5, 3, 4, 2, 3

10. Find the mean and median of the data in problem 9.

11. A company has 2 employees making $12,000, 3 making $14,000, and 1 making $15,500. Find the mean, median, and mode of the salaries.

12. Metro Appliance sales for March were as follows:

Appliance	Number Sold
TV sets	100
Refrigerators	15
Ranges	20
Air conditioners	0

What is the mode?

13. Can the median be used to describe the data in problem 12?

14. The number of purchases made each day last week at the Teen Shop was 21, 32, 18, 25, 30, and 15. Find the mode, median, and mean number of purchases.

15. Find the mode for problem 11, Exercises 20.1.

16. Find the mode for problem 12, Exercises 20.3.

Range = Large − Small

20.5   *Standard Deviation and Normal Distribution*

The statistics presented thus far (mean, median, and mode) have all been measures of what is "typical" in a data set. As such, they describe only one aspect of the data. To have a more complete understanding of the data, we also need a measure of the dispersion or "scattering" of the data. For example, the following data sets have the same mean, median, and mode.

Data set A: 19, 20, 21
Data set B: 0, 20, 40

However, the data in set B are more scattered (more *dispersed*) than those in set A. We want a statistic that will characterize this difference in dispersion between the two sets.

One statistic commonly used to measure dispersion of data is the *range*. The range is simply the difference between the largest and smallest values in the data. The range of Data set A is $2(=21 - 19)$. The range of Data set B is $40(=40 - 0)$. Even though the range is an easily computed measure of dispersion, the most important measure of dispersion is the *standard deviation*. Computation of the standard deviation (S) requires subtraction, squaring, and finding the square root. Hence, it is advisable to have a calculator.

The Standard Deviation

The standard deviation (S) is computed as follows:

$$S = \sqrt{\frac{\text{sum of all } (x_i - \text{mean})^2}{N}}$$

where

x_i = each value in the data set
N = the number of values in the data set

To find the standard deviation of Data set A, we proceed as follows:

List Data x_i	Find Each Deviation $(x_i - \text{mean})$	Square Each Deviation $(x_i - \text{mean})^2$	
19	$19 - 20 = -1$	$(-1)^2 = 1$	$S = \sqrt{\dfrac{\text{sum} = 2}{N = 3}}$
20	$20 - 20 = 0$	$(0)^2 = 0$	$= \sqrt{0.66667}$
21	$21 - 20 = 1$	$(1)^2 = 1$	$= 0.816$
		sum = 2	

The mean = $\frac{60}{3} = 20$

(handwritten margin notes:) cal — $\sqrt{} \div 3$ $\leftarrow$ then press $\sqrt{x}$

Hence, the standard deviation of set A = 0.816, which means that the numbers in the data set are 0.816 unit different from their mean (on the average).

Now let's compare this with the standard deviation of set B.

To find the standard deviation of set B, we proceed as follows:

List Data x_i	Find Each Deviation $(x_i - \text{mean})$	Square Each Deviation $(x_i - \text{mean})^2$	
0	$0 - 20 = -20$	$(-20)^2 = 400$	$S = \sqrt{\dfrac{\text{sum} = 800}{N = 3}}$
20	$20 - 20 = 0$	$(0)^2 = 0$	$= \sqrt{266.6667}$
40	$40 - 20 = 20$	$(20)^2 = 400$	$= 16.33$
		sum = 800	

The mean = $\frac{60}{3} = 20$

Hence, the standard deviation of set B = 16.33, which means that the numbers in the data set are 16.33 units different from their mean (on the average).

As we can see, the standard deviation of set B is larger than the standard deviation of set A, characterizing the greater dispersion in the data.

Example 1　Suppose that two machines are producing ball bearings with an average (mean) diameter of 5 millimeters. The ball bearings produced by machine A have a standard deviation of 2 millimeters while those of machine B have a standard deviation of 0.01 millimeter. Which machine is working better?

SOLUTION　Machine B is working better. The standard deviation is smaller, which means that most ball bearings are close to the 5-millimeter diameter.

Example 2　Find the standard deviation of the following data set: 1, 2, 3, 1, 3.

SOLUTION

List Data x_i	Find Each Deviation $(x_i - mean)$	Square Each Deviation $(x_i - mean)^2$	
1	−1	1	$S = \sqrt{\dfrac{sum = 4}{N = 5}}$
1	−1	1	
2	0	0	$= \sqrt{0.8}$
3	1	1	$= 0.894$
3	1	1	
		sum = 4	

mean $= \frac{10}{5} = 2$

Hence, $S = 0.894$

An important advantage of the standard deviation over other measures of variation (such as the range) is that it characterizes the "interval" variation of the data. For example Data set C: 0, 5, 5, 5, 10; and Data set D: 0, 0, 0, 10, 10, have the same range (R = 10). However, the numbers in data set D are generally farther from their mean than those in data set C. This greater dispersion is reflected by a larger standard deviation ($S_C = \sqrt{10}$; $S_D = \sqrt{24}$).

Distribution of Data

In everyday discourse, we hear that something (some variable) is "normal" (or normally distributed). Statistically speaking, a data set is considered to be "normal" if certain percents of the data fall within a certain number of standard deviations of the mean and if the data are symmetric (i.e., there is the same number of values above and below the mean). Figure 20.2 shows a statistically normal distribution.

Figure 20.2

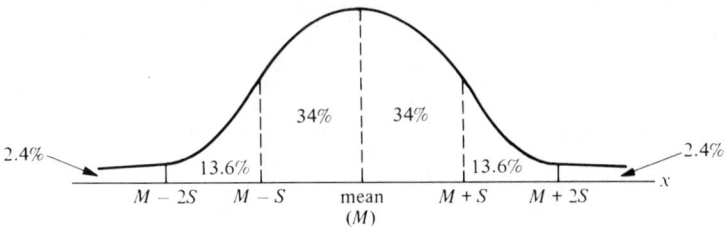

Normal Distribution (*M* = Mean, *S* = Standard Deviation)

From Figure 20-2, we can see that about 68% of "normal" data fall within one standard deviation of the mean. ✳

By knowing the distribution of normal data, we can make certain inferences and draw conclusions. For example, if we know the IQ scores of the students at this college are normally distributed with a mean of 120 and standard deviation of 10, then we can conclude that 34% of the students have an IQ from 120 to 130. Also, 34% have an IQ from 110 to 120 (see Figure 20.3).

Figure 20.3

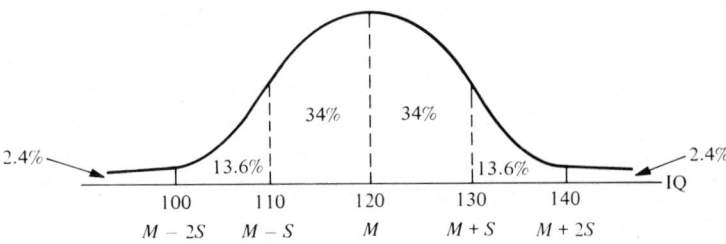

Normal Distribution of IQ (*M* = 120, *S* = 10)

We may also conclude that about 2.4% have an IQ over 140.

Example 3

The number of defective items produced on a certain assembly line is normally distributed with mean of 10 and standard deviation of 2.

a. What percent of the time will there be between 10 and 12 defectives?
b. What percent of the time will there be less than six defectives?

SOLUTION

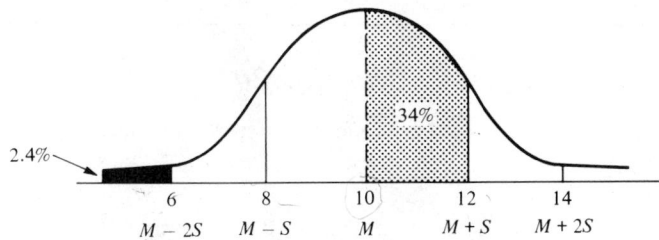

Figure 20.4

Normal Distribution of Defective (*M* = 10, *S* = 2)

a. 34%
b. 2.4%

Exercises 20.5

■ Find the standard deviation and range in problems 1, 2, 3, and 5.

1. Data set: 1, 2, 4, 6, 7.

2. Data set: 2, 4, 5, 9, 15.

3. Data set: 11, 12, 14, 16, 17.

4. Compare the mean and standard deviation of problems 1 and 3.

5. Data set: 4, 8, 10, 18, 30.

6. Compare the mean and standard deviation of problems 2 and 5.

7. If a class had a mean of 60 and standard deviation of zero on an exam, what can you conclude about all the scores?

8. If the stock of Stable Company averaged $10 per share with a standard deviation of $1 per share while the Rolling Company averaged $10 per share with a standard deviation of $4 per share, in which one would you rather invest?

9. If the mean number of units produced each day is 200 with a standard deviation of 20, what percent of the time will more than 220 units be produced?

10. The scores on a certain exam were normally distributed with a mean of 60 and a standard deviation of 10.
    a. In a class of 1000 students, how many made between 50 and 60?
    b. How many made less than 40?
    c. How many made more than 80?

11. In problem 1, what percent of the data fall within 1 standard deviation of the mean?

12. In problem 2, what percent of the data fall within 2 standard deviations of the mean?

13. If all of the values in a data set are doubled, what happens to the mean?

14. If all of the values in a data set are doubled, what happens to the standard deviation?

Review Exercises / Chapter 20

1. The following scores were made by 25 students on a 100-point exam in elementary statistics: 93, 81, 77, 85, 41, 79, 86, 98, 88, 71, 45, 86, 94, 92, 55, 49, 36, 49, 98, 69, 84, 68, 67, 92, 67.

    Scores of 90 to 100 were A, 80 to 89 were B, 70 to 79 were C, 60 to 69 were D, 0 to 59 were F.

    a. Find the mean.

    b. Find the median.

    c. Find the mode.

    d. Make a frequency distribution of the scores by grade.

    e. How many students passed?

    f. Graph the frequency distribution.

    g. Find the standard deviation.

    h. What percent of the scores fall within 1 standard deviation of the mean?

    i. How many scores fall above the mean?

    j. How many scores fall below the mean?

    k. Might these grades be considered normally distributed? Comment.

2. A clothing manufacturer is about to make 10,000 pairs of trousers with 32-inch waistbands. The marketing research department did a survey to determine the mean, median, and modal trouser length of persons with 32-inch waists. Which one of the lengths should the production supervisor use? Which measure would probably be the worst to use?

3. Find the mean of the following frequency distribution:

Value	Frequency
$1	10
$3	5
$4	8

4. What statistic is the *least* appropriate for the following data: 3, 3, 3, 3, 1000?

Chapter Test / Chapter 20

1. Define each of the following terms.

    a. raw data   *b.* data array   *c.* frequency distribution

    d. frequency table   *e.* all-inclusive   *f.* mutually exclusive

    g. quantitative data   *h.* numerical data   *i.* nominal data

    j. categorial data   *k.* mean   *l.* median

    m. mode   *n.* frequency   *o.* multimodal

    p. grouped data   *q.* standard deviation   *r.* normal distribution

2. The closing price per share of International Titanium for the past 10 consecutive days was:

$14\frac{3}{8}$, $14\frac{1}{4}$, $13\frac{7}{8}$, $15\frac{1}{8}$, $14\frac{1}{2}$, $13\frac{7}{8}$, $13\frac{1}{8}$, $12\frac{7}{8}$, $12\frac{1}{2}$, $11\frac{7}{8}$.

    a. Convert each closing price to a decimal.

    b. Find the mean of the data.

    c. Find the median.

    d. Find the mode.

    e. Find the price range.

f. Make a grouped frequency distribution using classes one dollar wide starting at $11.00.

g. Find the mean of the grouped frequency distribution.

h. Make a line graph of the data.

3. Find the mean and standard deviation of the following data set. Data set: 5, 5, 5, 5.

4. Find the mean and standard deviation of the following data set. Data set: 0, 5, 15, 20.

5. If 2 classes have the same mean on an exam but 1 class has a standard deviation of 5 while the other class has a standard deviation of 20, what can you say about their performance?

6. The number of absentees averages 20 per day with a standard deviation of 6 per day. What percent of the time is there between 14 and 20 employees absent?

7. If you add 5 to all the values in a data set, how will the mean be affected?

8. If you add 5 to all the values in a data set, how will the standard deviation be affected?

9. In a normal distribution of 100 grades, how many made more than the mean?

10. In a normal distribution with a mean of 50 and standard deviation of 10, what is the median?

CHAPTER 21

The Metric System

INTRODUCTION

In our modern society, almost everything we do is "measured." The time of day is measured in hours, minutes, and seconds; gasoline that we purchase is measured in gallons; distance we travel is measured in miles; and so on. The list is endless. Without measurement, society would not be able to function. In fact, a "common system" of measurement that is accepted and understood by all is a necessity. Without it, there would be a hopeless state of confusion.

The measurement system currently used in the United States is nearly the same as the one brought from England to the colonies in the seventeenth century. Distance is measured in miles, furlongs, rods, links, yards, feet, and inches; weight is measured in tons, pounds, and ounces; volume in barrels, bushels, pecks, quarts, and pints; temperature in degrees Fahrenheit; money in dollars and cents; area in acres, square yards, square feet, square inches, and so on.

Most of the rest of the world uses the International System of Units (SI), commonly called the metric system. It gets its name from the Greek word "metron" meaning "a measure." In the metric system length is measured in kilometers, meters, centimeters, and millimeters; volume is measured in liters or milliliters; weight is measured in metric tons, kilograms, grams; temperature is measured in degrees Celsius; area in hectares, square meters, and so on. These are measures that are not familiar to most Americans.

On December 23, 1975, President Gerald Ford signed into law the Metric Conversion Act of 1975. This act established a national policy for conversion to the metric system.

Proponents of the conversion have two basic arguments for conversion. First, since the rest of the world uses the metric system, our using it would facilitate international trade. Second, the metric system is "simpler" than the English system. Opponents argue that it will cost untold amounts of money to change to the "new" system.

In this chapter we will discuss units of length, weight, volume, and temperature within the metric system. Each section will discuss conversion from one unit to another *within* the metric system and conversion *between* the metric and English systems.

If and when conversion to the metric system takes place, the measurement of money (in dollars and cents) and time (in hours, minutes, and seconds) will remain the same. Also, electric power (measured in watts or kilowatts) will remain the same because it is the measure used in the metric system.

21.1 *Measures of Length*

The basic unit of length in the metric system is the *meter*. Scientifically, it is defined as 1,650,763.73 wavelengths in a vacuum of the red-orange line of the spectrum of krypton 86. In more familiar terms, a meter is approximately 39.37 inches.

The following chart shows some of the measures of length used in the metric system and their relationship to a meter.

Length in the Metric System

1 kilometer	= 1000 meters	
1 hectometer	= 100 meters	Longer distances
1 dekameter	= 10 meters	
1 meter	= 1 meter	(base unit)
1 decimeter	= $\dfrac{1}{10}$ meter	
1 centimeter	= $\dfrac{1}{100}$ meter	Shorter distances
1 millimeter	= $\dfrac{1}{1000}$ meter	

Of course, not all of these are commonly used in everyday situations. Hectometer, dekameter, and decimeter are used infrequently, as are rod and links in the English system.

They are all shown in the chart to illustrate why the proponents of the metric system claim that it is "simple." It is "simple" because every unit of length is some power of 10 times a meter. In other words, it is a decimal system. This makes conversion *within* the system very easy.

Further, the name of each unit gives a clue to its relationship to the basic unit (meter).

$$\text{"kilo" means } 1000 \rightarrow \text{kilometer (1000 meters)}$$

$$\text{"deci" means } \frac{1}{10} \rightarrow \text{decimeter}\left(\frac{1}{10}\text{ meter}\right)$$

$$\text{"centi" means } \frac{1}{100} \rightarrow \text{centimeter}\left(\frac{1}{100}\text{ meter}\right)$$

(Remember from Chapter 4 that "per centum," from which centi is derived, means divided by 100.)

$$\text{"milli" means } \frac{1}{1000} \rightarrow \text{millimeter}\left(\frac{1}{1000}\text{ meter}\right)$$

Compare this with the English system. If you take 1 foot as the basic unit of length, it must be multiplied by 12 to get inches. Feet must be divided by 3 to get yards. Feet must be divided by 16.5 to convert to rods. There is no uniform system of factors to convert from one unit to another within the English system. The reason for the "nonuniformity" of the English system is due to its historical development over many centuries (which is an interesting topic in itself, but one into which we will not go).

Conversion within the Metric System

Conversion between units can be done based on the definition of each unit in relation to the meter. However, the following table gives a quick method for conversion. To keep the discussion as painless as possible, we will use it. Commonly used abbreviations are also included.

Conversion of Common Metric Units of Length

When You Know the Number of	Multiply by	To Find the Number of
kilometers (km)	1000	meters (m)
centimeters (cm)	$\frac{1}{100}$	meters (m)
millimeters (mm)	$\frac{1}{1000}$	meters (m)
meters (m)	$\frac{1}{1000}$	kilometers (km)
meters (m)	100	centimeters (cm)
meters (m)	1000	millimeters (mm)

Example 1   Convert the following.

  a. 100 cm = _____ m.

  b. 50 mm = _____ m.

c. 2 km = _____ m.
d. 3 m = _____ cm.
e. 450 m = _____ km.
f. 0.5 m = _____ mm.

SOLUTION   Use the factors given in the conversion table.

a. $100 \text{ cm} \times \dfrac{1}{100} = 1 \text{ m.}$

b. $50 \text{ mm} \times \dfrac{1}{1000} = 0.05 \text{ m.}$

c. $2 \text{ km} \times 1000 = 2000 \text{ m.}$

d. $3 \text{ m} \times 100 = 300 \text{ cm.}$

e. $450 \text{ m} \times \dfrac{1}{1000} = 0.45 \text{ m.}$

f. $0.5 \text{ m} \times 1000 = 500 \text{ mm.}$

Metric-English Conversion

Again, the necessary conversion factors will be presented via table.

Conversion between Metric and English Units of Length

When You Know the Number of	Multiply by	To Find the Number of
inches (in)	25.4	millimeters (mm)
inches (in)	2.54	centimeters (cm)
feet (ft)	0.3048	meters (m)
yards (yd)	0.9144	meters (m)
miles (mi)	1.60934	kilometers (km)
millimeters (mm)	0.0393701	inches (in)
meters (m)	3.28084	feet (ft)
meters (m)	1.09361	yards (yd)
kilometers (km)	0.621371	miles (mi)

Example 2   Convert the following.

a. 2 in = _____ mm.
b. 5 mi = _____ km.
c. 100 mm = _____ in.
d. 2 m = _____ ft.

SOLUTION   **a.** $2 \text{ in} \times 25.4 = 50.8 \text{ mm.}$
b. $5 \text{ mi} \times 1.60934 = 8.0467 \text{ km.}$
c. $100 \text{ mm} \times 0.0393701 = 3.93701 \text{ in.}$
d. $2 \text{ m} \times 3.28084 = 6.56168 \text{ ft.}$

The following examples show metric measure of some familiar things.

Example 3   What is 55 miles per hour in kilometers per hour?

SOLUTION   55 mi × 1.60934 = 88.5137. Hence, 55 mph = 88.5 km per hour (approximately).

Example 4   An ordinary sheet of paper is $8\frac{1}{2}$ inches by 11 inches. What are its dimensions in centimeters?

SOLUTION $8\frac{1}{2}$ in × 2.54 = 21.59 cm wide
11 in × 2.54 = 27.94 cm long

Example 5   You need to loosen a $\frac{1}{4}$-inch bolt, but all of your tools are measured in mm. A wrench of what size in millimeters is needed?

SOLUTION $\frac{1}{4}$ in × 25.4 = 6.35 mm. The wrench would need to be 6.35 mm.

Examples 3, 4, and 5 show why conversion to the metric system is going to be a major problem. A "soft" conversion to the metric system would simply mean relabeling everything in metric units without actually changing the dimensions. However, having an 88.5-kph speed limit or paper that is 21.59 by 27.94 cm would be difficult to handle and remember. A "hard" conversion would be to change the size of things, such as making paper 22 by 28 cm (or 20 by 30 cm) so that "round" numbers are used. However, in many cases, this will require major modifications in equipment.

Exercises 21.1

1. 2.5 m = _____ cm.   **2.** 0.8 m = _____ mm.

3. 1532 m = _____ km.   **4.** 27 mm = _____ m.

5. 280 cm = _____ m.   **6.** 3.1 km = _____ m.

7. 10 in = _____ mm.   **8.** 36 in = _____ cm.

9. 6 ft = _____ m.   **10.** 2 yd = _____ m.

11. 20 mi = _____ km.   **12.** 50 mm = _____ in.

13. 5 m = _____ ft.   **14.** 10 m = _____ yd.

15. 80 km = _____ mi.

16. Find the length in meters of a board that is 8 ft long.

17. If you live 14 mi from work, what is the distance in kilometers?

18. What is the height in centimeters of a person 5 ft 2 in tall?

19. A standard doorway is $6\frac{1}{2}$ ft high. What is the height in cm?

20. Find the length in centimeters of curtains that are 84 in.

21.2 Measures of Weight

The discussion of "weight" in the metric system requires special consideration. The units used to measure *weight* are given in terms of *mass*. In everyday (nonscientific) work, mass and weight are treated as meaning the same thing, but some explanation is in order.

Roughly speaking, *mass* is the amount of material (or substance) that an object contains. Its mass causes it to have weight. *Weight* is the measure of the force that gravity exerts on the object. The relationship is direct— the more mass, the more weight.

Take your textbook, for example. It contains a certain amount of material (i.e., a certain mass). If you weigh the book (on earth) it will have a certain weight. If you weighed the book on the moon, it would have a different weight because the force of gravity is different. Either place, the mass is the same; the weight is not.

In scientific work, the distinction between mass and weight is crucial. You could build a spaceship with "spindly legs" that would collapse on earth but would be strong enough to support it on Mars (because the attraction of gravity is less, hence its weight on Mars is less).

By keeping this section down to earth (where gravity is practically the same everywhere), we can treat mass and weight as meaning the same thing.

The basic unit of mass or weight in the metric system is the *gram*. All other units are powers of 10 times a gram. The internationally accepted mass of 1 gram is $\frac{1}{1000}$ of a cylinder of platinum–iridium kept by the Bureau of International Weights and Measures in Sèvres, France. In more familiar terms, the cylinder weighs 2.20462 pounds.

Metric System Measures of Mass

1 kilogram	= 1000 grams	
1 hectogram	= 100 grams	Heavier weights
1 dekagram	= 10 grams	
1 gram	= 1 gram	(base unit)
1 decigram	= $\frac{1}{10}$ gram	
1 centigram	= $\frac{1}{100}$ gram	Lighter weights
1 milligram	= $\frac{1}{1000}$ gram	

Hectogram, dekagram, decigram, and centigram are rarely used as are drams and scruples in the English system. We will concentrate on conversion between common units.

Mass Conversions Within the Metric System

When You Know the Number of	Multiply by	To Get the Number of
kilograms (kg)	1000	grams (g)
milligrams (mg)	$\dfrac{1}{1000}$	grams (g)
grams (g)	$\dfrac{1}{1000}$	kilograms (kg)
grams (g)	1000	milligrams (mg)

Example 1   Convert the following.

   a. 2.5 kg = _____ g.
   b. 600 mg = _____ g.
   c. 150 g = _____ kg.
   d. 20 g = _____ mg.

SOLUTION   Use the table for conversion.

   a. 2.5 kg × 1000 = 2500 g.

   b. 600 mg × $\dfrac{1}{1000}$ = 0.6 g.

   c. 150 g × $\dfrac{1}{1000}$ = 0.15 kg.

   d. 20 g × 1000 = 20,000 mg.

Metric-English Conversion

When You Know the Number of	Multiply by	To Get the Number of
grams	0.035274	ounces (oz)
grams	15.4321	grains (gr)
kilograms	2.20462	pounds (lb)
grains	0.0648	grams
ounces	28.3495	grams
pounds	0.453592	kilograms

Example 2   Convert the following.

   a. 100 g = _____ oz.
   b. 50 g = _____ gr.
   c. 95 kg = _____ lb.
   d. 500 gr = _____ g.
   e. 4 oz = _____ g.
   f. 200 lb = _____ kg.

SOLUTION   Use the table for conversion.

   a. 100 g × 0.035274 = 3.5274 oz.
   b. 50 g × 15.4321 = 771.605 gr.
   c. 95 kg × 2.20462 = 209.44 lb.
   d. 500 gr × 0.0648 = 32.4 g.
   e. 4 oz × 28.3495 = 113.398 g.
   f. 200 lb × 0.453592 = 90.7184 kg.

The following examples show the metric equivalent of some familiar English measures.

Example 3   How many milligrams are in a 5-gr aspirin tablet?

SOLUTION   By using the metric–English table we have

$$5 \text{ gr} \times 0.0648 = 0.324 \text{ g}$$

To convert to milligrams,

$$0.324 \text{ g} \times 1000 = 324 \text{ mg}$$

There are 324 mg in a 5-gr aspirin tablet.

Example 4   Find the weight in kg of a person who weighs 180 lb.

SOLUTION   180 lb × 0.453592 = 81.65 kg.

Example 5   Find the weight in grams of an 8-oz steak.

SOLUTION   8 oz × 28.3495 = 226.796 g.

Exercises 21.2

■ Convert the following.

1. 2.8 kg = _____ g.   *2.* 725 mg = _____ g.

3. 1250 g = _____ kg.   *4.* 42 g = _____ mg.

5. 20 g = _____ oz.   *6.* 10 g = _____ gr.

7. 50 kg = _____ lb.   *8.* 100 gr = _____ g.

9. 16 oz = _____ g.   *10.* 100 lb = _____ kg.

11. A baby weighing 7 lb 9 oz weighs how many kg?

12. Find the weight in kg of a 3600-lb automobile.

13. Find the weight in grams of a 1-lb can of coffee.

14. Find the weight in kg of a person weighing 148.5 lb.

15. Find the weight in mg of a 1.5-gr tablet.

16. Convert $1\frac{1}{2}$ lb to grams.

21.3 *Measures of Volume and Temperature*

The basic unit of volume in the metric system is the *liter*. The liter is defined as a fluid volume equal to $\frac{1}{1000}$ of a cubic meter. The liter is a "derived" unit because it is defined in terms of another metric measure instead of something "absolute" (such as the wavelength of light emitted by a particular element). A liter is slightly larger than the familiar quart (1 liter = 1.05669 quarts).

Metric Measures of Volume

$$1 \text{ hectoliter} = 100 \text{ liters}$$
$$1 \text{ dekaliter} = 10 \text{ liters}$$
$$1 \text{ liter} \quad = 1 \text{ liter} \quad \text{(base unit)}$$
$$1 \text{ deciliter} \quad = \frac{1}{10} \text{ liter}$$
$$1 \text{ centiliter} = \frac{1}{100} \text{ liter}$$
$$1 \text{ milliliter} = \frac{1}{1000} \text{ liter}$$

Larger volumes

Smaller volumes

Of all the measures of volume, only liter and milliliter are commonly used.

Liter-Milliliter Conversion

When You Know the Number of	Multiply by	To Get the Number of
liters (l)	1000	milliliters (ml)
milliliters (ml)	$\dfrac{1}{1000}$	liters (l)

Example 1   Convert the following.

    a. 2.65 l = _____ ml.
    b. 450 ml = _____ l.

SOLUTION

    a. 2.65 l × 1000 = 2650 ml.

    b. 450 ml × $\dfrac{1}{1000}$ = 0.45 l.

The following chart shows the conversion between quarts and liters. Conversion between other commonly used measures, such as gallons, pints, and fluid ounces, will be done through these base units. A quart contains 32 fluid oz. in U.S. liquid measure.

Liter–Quart Conversion

When You Know the Number of	Multiply by	To Get the Number of
quarts (qt)	0.946353	liters (l)
liters (l)	1.05669	quarts (qt)

Example 2   Convert the following.

    a. 2 qt = _____ l.
    b. 3 l = _____ qt.

SOLUTION

    a. 2 qt × 0.946535 = 1.89307 l.
    b. 3 l × 1.05669 = 3.17 qt. (rounded)

Example 3   Convert the following.

    a. 2 l = _____ pints.
    b. 1 gal = _____ l.
    c. 60 fluid oz = _____ ml.

SOLUTION

a. First, convert 1 to qt.

$$2\ 1 \times 1.05669 = 2.1138 \text{ qt}$$

Since there are 2 pints per quart,

$$2 \times 2.11338 = 4.22676 \text{ pints in a liter}$$

b. 1 gal = 4 qt
4 qt $\times$ 0.946535 = 3.7854 l in a gallon

c. 60 fluid oz $\div$ 32 = 1.875 qt
1.875 qt $\times$ 0.946353 = 1.7744 l (rounded)
1.7744 l $\times$ 1000 = 1774.4 ml

There are 1774.4 ml in 60 fluid oz.

Temperature

In the metric system, temperature is measured in degrees Celsius. On the Celsius scale, 0° is the freezing point of water; 100° is the boiling point of water. On the more familiar Fahrenheit scale, water freezes at 32° and boils at 212°. Approximate equivalents between the Celsius (C) scale and Fahrenheit scales can be seen in Figure 21.1.

Figure 21.1

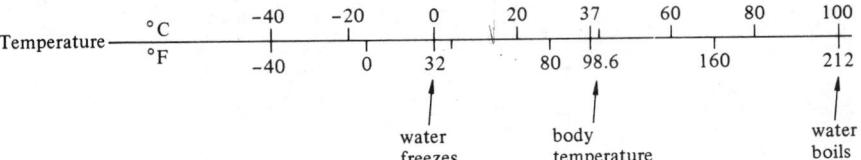

Since there are 100 divisions (degrees) between the freezing and boiling points of water on the Celsius scale and 180 divisions on the Fahrenheit scale, each degree Celsius represents a greater change in temperature.

The relation between degrees Celsius and Fahrenheit can be expressed by an equation or formula. We will give two versions of the formula to facilitate conversion both ways.

Celsius–Fahrenheit Conversion

If You Know Degrees	Compute	To Get Degrees
Celsius (C)	$F = \dfrac{9C + 160}{5}$	Fahrenheit (F)
Fahrenheit (F)	$C = \dfrac{5F - 160}{9}$	Celsius (C)

Example 4   Convert the following.

a. $40°C = \underline{\hspace{2cm}} F°.$
b. $90°F = \underline{\hspace{2cm}} C°.$

SOLUTION   a. Since we know C ($= 40°$),

$$F = \frac{9(40) + 160}{5}$$

$$= \frac{360 + 160}{5}$$

$$= \frac{520}{5}$$

$$= 104° \text{ Fahrenheit}$$

b. Since we know F ($= 90°$),

$$C = \frac{5(90) - 160}{9}$$

$$= \frac{450 - 160}{9}$$

$$= \frac{290}{9}$$

$$= 32.2° \text{ Celsius (rounded)}$$

Exercises 21.3

1. $3 l = \underline{\hspace{1.5cm}}$ ml.   **2.** $2.75 l = \underline{\hspace{1.5cm}}$ ml.   **3.** 835 ml $= \underline{\hspace{1.5cm}}$ l.

4. 50 ml $= \underline{\hspace{1.5cm}}$ l.   **5.** 5 qt $= \underline{\hspace{1.5cm}}$ l.   **6.** $5 l = \underline{\hspace{1.5cm}}$ qt.

7. $1 l = \underline{\hspace{1.5cm}}$ pints.   **8.** $2 l = \underline{\hspace{1.5cm}}$ fluid oz.   **9.** $\frac{1}{2}$ pint $= \underline{\hspace{1.5cm}}$ l.

10. $\frac{1}{2}$ gal $= \underline{\hspace{1.5cm}}$ l.

11. How many ml are in a 12-oz canned drink?

12. If it takes 4 qt to change the oil in an automobile, how many liters are required?

13. A pint of milk contains how many ml?

14. An imported car requiring 2 l of oil needs how many quarts?

15. What is the Celsius equivalent of $72°F$?

16. If the boiling point of a solution is $200°C$, what is it in degrees F?

17. What is $100°F$ in Celsius?

18. What is $20°C$ in Fahrenheit?

Review Exercises / *Chapter 21*

1. Find the length in centimeters of an object that measures 40 in.

2. How many inches long is a 120-mm cigarette?

3. The Strong Construction Company wants to purchase 1000 ft of cable from an overseas supplier that uses the metric system. How many meters of cable should be ordered?

4. Ralph jogged 5 km. How many miles did he go?

5. Find the weight in kilograms of a 5-lb bag of flour.

6. How many milliliters are contained in 1 pint of milk?

7. How many quarts are contained in a 1-l bottle of cola?

8. If the mean temperature of Thermal Island is 40°C, what is the temperature in degrees Fahrenheit?

9. If the freezing point of automobile coolant is −40°F, what is it in degrees Celsius?

10. If a light bulb is rated at 40 watts, what is its rating in metric units?

Chapter Test / *Chapter 21*

■ Convert each of the following:

1. 38 centimeters = _____ millimeters

2. 425 meters = _____ kilometers

3. 42 inches = _____ millimeters

4. 15 miles = _____ kilometers

5. 18 kilometers = _____ miles

6. 150 grams = _____ kilograms

7. 180 milligrams = _____ grams

8. 15 pounds = _____ kilograms

9. 12 grams = _____ ounces

10. 3 quarts = _____ liters

11. 10° Celcius = _____ °Fahrenheit

12. 60°Fahrenheit = _____ °Celsius

1. White's Milk Company revenue data.

Gallons Sold, x	Revenue, y
0	0
25	$ 50
50	$100
75	$150
100	$200
⋮	⋮

Make a line graph.

2. The ABC Corporation profit data.

Year	Profit
1978	$100,000
1979	$ 80,000
1980	$110,000

Make a bar graph.

3. The Food Store sales data.

Type of Merchandise	Dollar Sales for a Particular Week
Meat	$ 60,000
Dairy products	$120,000
Canned goods	$ 70,000
Perishables	$ 50,000
Other	$150,000

Make a bar graph.

4. Craig Manufacturing Company—1980 Budget:

Item	Percent of Total Budget
Labor	40
Taxes	10
Maintenance	5
Material cost	40
Other costs	5

Make a bar graph.

5. Find the mean, median, and mode of the following data set.

Data set: 10, 12, 20, 16, 17, 13

6. Find the mean of the following frequency distribution.

Value	Frequency
$ 6.00	20
$ 7.50	10
$10.00	30

7. Which is cheaper, a 2-l container or a 64-oz bottle of Tasty Cola? The price per ounce is $0.02. By how much?

8. If your car contains enough antifreeze for $-10°C$ protection, is it adequate for $5°F$? What protection is offered in $°F$?

9. An automobile jack is rated safe to 1000 kg. Should this jack be used to lift a truck weighing 2500 lb? How much difference is there?

10. Which distance is longer, $\frac{2}{3}$ mi or $\frac{4}{5}$ km? By how much?

11. Find the mean, median, and mode of the following data: 1.23, 0.87, 1.42, 0.99, 0.76, 1.02, 0.53, 1.98, 1.27, 0.93, 0.99, 1.07.

12. If the distance between Leesville and Alexandria is 96.56 kilometers, how many miles is it?

13. What is the length in miles of a 10,000 km race?

14. How many milliliters of tomato juice are contained in a 6 oz. can?

15. If a wine should be served at 53.4° Fahrenheit, what is the temperature in degrees Celsius?

16. If it cost Wordsworth Publishing Company $83,689.54 to publish a 495-page book, what was the average cost per page?

Glossary

Accelerated Cost Recovery System (ACRS). See depreciation.

Account Balance. The correct amount of money in a checking account allowing for all transactions that have taken place.

Accrued Interest. Interest earned but not yet paid on a bond, note, etc.

Accumulated Depreciation. The sum of all depreciation taken in previous years on an asset.

Adjusted Gross Income. The amount of money earned after allowances are made by the government for specific items (such as expenses necessary to earn money, contributions to retirement plans, etc.)

Aliquot Part. An exact divisor of a given number.

All-inclusive. No values omitted.

Amortization. To extinguish by equal payments at regular intervals.

Amortization Schedule. A table that completely describes a loan. It shows the payment numbers, principal remaining, amount of each payment, and interest.

Annual Percentage Rate (APR). Interest rate that will produce the same amount of interest (on a specific principal) in one year as the stated rate.

Annuity. A sequence of regular equal payments.

Assessed Value. The value assigned for tax purposes.

Asset. Items of value owned by a business (cash, stocks, buildings and machinery, etc.).

Axis. A line along which a coordinate is measured (pl. axes).

Balance Sheet. The accounting statement of financial position for a business as of a given point in time showing assets = liabilities + owners' equity.

Bank Discount. Interest charged on the entire principal which is immediately subtracted from the amount borrowed; also called simple discount.

Bank Reconciliation. The procedure for eliminating discrepancies between the bank's records and the accountholder's records on a checking account.

Bank Statement. The bank's record of all transactions to a checking account.

Bar Graph. Consists of parallel, equally spaced bars whose length is proportional to certain quantities given in the data.

Base. A quantity of which some percent is taken.

Beneficiary. The person or company receiving the money paid by an insurance company in the event of loss.

Bond. A written agreement of debt in which the company agrees to pay a fixed rate of interest (the coupon rate) for the specified time plus the principal borrowed (the face value of the bond) at a future date (the maturity date).

Book Value. The amount at which an asset is carried on the company's books. It is the cost less all depreciation.

Broken-Line Graph. Segments of straight lines that join points representing data.

Brokerage Commission. Amount of money paid by buyers and sellers to the agents who actually arrange for the purchase or sale of stocks, bonds, real estate, etc.

Cash Discount. A reduction in price offered by a seller for early payment of merchandise.

Cash Value. The value of an insurance policy (in cash) if the insured cancels the policy.

Categorical Data. Nonnumerical information.

Celsius Scale. Temperature scale in which the difference between the freezing and boiling point of water is divided into 100 units.

Chain (or Series) Discounts. Two or more trade discounts offered on a product at the same time.

Check. The document given by an account holder to remove previously deposited money from his checking account.

Check Register. The record kept by a checking account holder showing the amounts of money deposited and the amounts of checks given (and to whom and when).

Circle Graph. One in which portions of a whole are represented by sectors of a circle.

Circumference. The edge or boundary of a circle.

Coinsurance. Insurance protection provided jointly by the owner of property and an insurance company.

Collateral. Something of value used as security for repayment of a loan.

Collision Insurance. Insurance protection against accidental damage to the motor vehicle of the insured.

Commission. Payment to an employee based on the amount of sales generated by the employee.

Compass. A device for drawing circles.

Compounding Period. The length of time over which interest is computed.

Compound Interest. The interest due is added to the principal and therefore accumulates interest for all of the remaining periods.

Comprehensive Insurance. Insurance protection against nonaccidental damage to the motor vehicle of the insured.

Conditional Equation. One which is true for only certain values and not true for other values.

Coordinate System. Any method by which sets of numbers are used to represent a geometric object such as a line.

Corporation. A legally created entity engaged in a business enterprise. It is owned by stockholders.

Coupon Rate. The annual rate of interest stated as a percent of a bond's face value.

Data. Factual information or measurements.

Data Array. Data listed in numerical order.

Debt Financing. Financing a business by borrowing (bonds, notes, etc.).

Deductions. Reductions in the amount of pay received; reduction in the amount of taxable income.

Default. Failure to repay a note.

Degree. A unit of angular measure, 360 of which are contained in a circle; a unit of temperature.

Denominator. The number below the line in a fraction. It divides the numerator.

Depreciation. The accounting process of matching the cost of the asset with the income it produces. This process is known as accelerated cost recovery after the Economic Recovery Tax Act of 1981.

Depreciation Base. The cost of an asset minus its salvage value; the total amount to be depreciated.

Depreciation Schedule. A record of an asset's depreciation showing the total (accumulated) depreciation and the book value of the asset.

Difference. The result of subtracting one quantity from another.

Digits. The symbols 0, 1, 2, 3, 4, 5, 6, 7, 8, 9.

Discount. A reduction in the usual selling price of an item; also called a markdown; the difference between a bond's face value and its selling price when the selling price is lower.

Discount Rate. The percent reduction in the usual selling price of an item.

Discounted Note. See non-interest-bearing Note.

Distortion. To misrepresent.

Dividend. The quantity that is to be divided by another quantity. The money received from ownership of stock.

Divisor. The quantity by which the dividend is divided: in a fraction the divisor is the denominator.

e. A constant (approximately) equal to 2.71828 that is used in continuously compounded interest.

Effective Rate. Simple interest rate that yields the same amount of interest as the stated (nominal) rate.

Endowment (Insurance) Policy. Insurance coverage for a specified number of years whereby the insured is guaranteed payment of the policy if he lives or not.

Equation. A statement of equality between two expressions.

Equity Financing. Financing of a business enterprise obtained from owners of the business (through sale of stock shares, etc.).

Equivalent. Having the same value.

Exact Year. 365 days.

Exemptions. Allowances made in earned income for the status of the persons supported by the income.

Expenses. The amount of money spent in order to produce revenue. (See revenue.)

Extended Price. The total price for all items of the same type.

Face Amount. The maximum amount of insurance coverage as given by an insurance policy.

Face Value (of a Bond). The amount of money borrowed and payable to the bond holder at some (stated) time in the future.

Factoring. Selling of accounts receivable at a discount to a third party.

Factors. Quantities that are multiplied together.

Fahrenheit Scale. Temperature scale in which the difference between the boiling and freezing points of water is divided into 180 units.

Fair Market Value. The amount paid for goods or services by a willing buyer to a willing seller in a free market.

F.I.C.A. Tax (or Social Security Tax). Tax paid by the employee and employer to provide Social Security benefits.

FIFO. First-in-first-out method of valuing inventory.

Formula. A general rule or principle stated in mathematical language, usually an equation.

Fraction. A number expressed in the form a/b, where a and b are whole numbers and b is not zero.

Frequency. The number of items in each category of a data set.

Frequency Distribution. A table listing all values or classes of data and their corresponding frequency of occurrence in the data.

Frequency Table. See frequency distribution.

Future Value. Sum of principal plus interest; also called maturity value.

Graph. A drawing that shows the relationship between certain sets of numbers.

Gross Pay. Total compensation by an employer to an employee for services rendered; pay before any deductions are considered.

Gross Profit Method. A method for estimating inventory value based on the cost of merchandise.

Grouped Data. Data put into classes or categories for ease of interpretation.

Half-Year Convention. The allowance built-into the ACR tables that accounts for partial-years ownership of assets.

Horizontal Analysis. Expressing the component parts of a financial statement as a percent of the whole and comparing two or more time periods.

Income Statement. The financial report showing the economic success or failure of a business over a given period of time. (i.e., the difference between revenues and expenses).

Installment Cost. Total of price and interest on a credit purchase.

Installment Plan. Amortization plan. *See* Amortization.

Insurance. A contract under which an insurance company reimburses a business or individual for loss caused by a specified event.

Insurance Premium. The amount paid for insurance coverage.

Insured. A person or business on whom insurance protection is provided.

Insurer. The company agreeing to pay for financial loss if a specific event occurs.

Interest. Money paid for the use of money.

Interest-bearing Note. A note in which the interest is paid at maturity.

Interpolation. The process of finding the value between two known values.

Inventory. Merchandise held by a business for sale to its customers.

Inventory Turnover Ratio. A measure of the efficiency of inventory management.

Inventory Valuation. The process of assigning a dollar value to goods held in inventory.

Invoice. An itemized list of merchandise shipped in a sales transaction between businesses.

Level Method. A method of apportioning interest equally among the payments in amortization.

Level Payment Plan. See amortization.

Liabilities. Obligations owed by a company.

Liability Insurance. Economic protection against damages to the property or person other than the insured.

Life (Asset). The estimated span of usefulness (in terms of years, units, etc.).

LIFO. Last-in-first-out method of valuing inventory.

List Price. The original or "catalog" price at which merchandise is offered for sale to the ultimate consumer.

Literal Equation. A statement of equality between two expressions which contain two or more literal numbers.

Literal Number. A letter used to represent a number.

Loan Date. The date on which a loan is consummated: the beginning date for computation of interest.

Markdown. *See* Discount.

Markdown Rate. The markdown on merchandise expressed as a percent of the original price of the merchandise.

Markup. That portion of the selling price of an item that contributes toward the overhead expense and profit of a business.

Markup Rate. The markup on merchandise expressed as a percent of either the cost or the selling price of merchandise.

Maturity Date. The date upon which an obligation (note or bond) becomes payable in full.

Maturity Value. *See* Future Value.

Mean. The arithmetic average of quantitative data.

Median. The middle measurement of numerical data when ordered in size.

Metric System. System of measurement in which the meter is the fundamental unit of length and the gram is the fundamental unit of weight. Used almost universally for scientific work.

Minuend. The number from which another number is being subtracted.

Mixed Number. Understood sum of a whole number and fraction.

Mode. The most frequently occurring item in a data set.

Multimodal. Having two or more modes.

Multiplicative Inverse. *See* Reciprocal.

Mutually Exclusive. Two or more sets that have no quantities in common.

Negotiable Order of Withdrawal (NOW) Accounts. Accounts provided by financial institutions which offer the convenience of checking accounts and the interest-earning ability of savings accounts.

Net Pay. "Take-home" compensation to an employee for services rendered; pay after all deductions are made.

Net Price. The actual cost of merchandise to the buyer inclusive of all discounts.

Nominal Rate. The stated yearly rate.

Non-interest-bearing Note. A note in which the interest is charged as a discount.

Normal Distribution. Is symmetric about its mean and has about 68% of the data within 1 standard deviation of the mean and about 95% of the data within 2 standard deviations of the mean.

Note. Common name given to a loan agreement.

Numerator. The number above the line in a fraction.

Numerical Data. See quantitative data.

Open-to-Buy. The amount of planned inventory purchases not yet made or committed for.

Ordinary Annuity. One in which the compounding period for the interest and the payment period are the same.

Ordinary Year. 360 days.

Origin. Point on a coordinate system where axes intersect.

Overhead (Expenses). Expenses contributing to the overall operation of a business but which are not usually identifiable with a particular product or department.

Overtime. Time worked in excess of the normal workweek (generally paid at a higher rate of pay).

Owner's Equity. That portion of a company's assets that is owned by the owners, free of debt.

Partnership. A nonincorporated business enterprise having two or more owners; each owner may be liable in excess of his or her investment for the obligations of the enterprise.

Par Value. The assigned dollar worth on stock.

Pay Period. The length of time between employee checks.

Percent. Hundredths (e.g., 6 percent equals $\frac{6}{100}$).

Percentage. The result found by taking a percent of the base; also called portion.

Pictogram. Graph consisting of pictures.

Policy. The legal contract of insurance coverage between the insurer and the insured.

Portion. Part of a whole; percentage.

Premium. The amount paid for an insurance policy; the excess of a bond's cost over its face value.

Present Value. Principal (see principal).

Prime Number. A counting number that cannot be divided evenly by any counting number except 1 and the number itself.

Principal. Money on which interest is paid or charged.

Product. The answer to a multiplication problem.

Profit (Net). The amount actually made on a transaction after all expenses have been paid.

Promissory Note. A loan agreement containing a promise to pay and terms of payment.

Property Tax. A tax levied by governmental entities on real property (i.e., land, buildings, etc.) and personal property (cars, etc.).

Protractor. A device for measuring angles.

Qualitative Data. Data about qualities such as opinions, sex, marital status, or other nonnumerical characteristics.

Quantitative Data. Data consisting of measured or numerical quantities.

Quotient. The answer obtained in a division problem.

Radius. Line drawn from the center of a circle to its circumference.

Range. Difference between the largest and smallest numbers in a data set.

Rate. A percent.

Raw Data. Unorganized information.

Reciprocal. The number whose product with the given number is 1; also called the multiplicative inverse of the given number.

Retailer. A business selling products to the ultimate consumer instead of to another business.

Retail Method. A method of estimating inventory value based on the selling price of merchandise.

Revenue. The total amount of money received (usually by a business) during its course of operations.

Rounding-off. Deletion of digits in a decimal number after a certain place. The result is an approximation of the original number.

Rule of 72. States that money will double in $72/x$ years where x is the annual compound interest rate.

Rule of 78's. A method of apportioning interest among the payments in amortization such that the earlier payments contain more interest than later payments.

Salary. Money paid to an individual for the performance of specified duties.

Sales (Retail). Sales made to the general public or to the buyer who is the ultimate consumer of the purchased items.

Sales (Trade). Sales made between businesses; the purchaser is not the ultimate consumer of the purchased items.

Sales Tax. A tax levied by governmental entities on the sale of goods and services to the ultimate consumer.

Salvage (or Scrap) Value. The value of an asset at the end of its useful life.

Secured Note. One requiring collateral. (See collateral).

Selling Price. The price of merchandise to the buyer; the sum of cost plus markup.

Series (or Chain) Discounts. Two or more trade discounts offered on a product at the same time.

Settlement Options. Those choices available to a beneficiary for payment of insurance proceeds.

Short-Term Note. A note or loan made for less than 1 year.

Simple Discount. *See* Bank Discount.

Simple Interest. Interest computed on the original principal for the entire period.

Single Equivalent Discount. A single discount rate that will yield the same discount amount as a series of trade discounts.

Sinking Fund. Savings plan with a specified future value.

Six-Percent 60-Day Method. A method of computing simple interest by taking 1% of the principal and adjusting for the actual interest rate and time.

Sole Proprietorship. A nonincorporated business enterprise having a single owner.

Solution. A number that makes both sides of an equation equal.

Solving an Equation. Isolation of the unknown on one side of the equal symbol.

Standard Deviation. The most commonly used measure of dispersion in data; measures the average difference between data and its mean.

Statistic. A single quantity that characterizes some aspect of data.

Stock. The capital or ownership financing of a corporation in the form of transferable shares. Generally of two types: (1) preferred—having a stated value and a fixed rate of interest (dividend), and (2) common—receiving dividends only after all other obligations are satisfied.

Subtrahand. Number being taken from the minuend; the number being subtracted.

Sum. The answer to an addition problem; also called the total.

Taxable Income. The amount of money earned which is subject to taxation by the government.

Taxes. The amount of money collected by governmental organizations for the provision of goods and services to the general society.

Term. The time between the loan date and due date.

Term Insurance. Insurance protection provided only for the length of time stipulated in the insurance policy.

Terms. The numerator and denominator of a fraction.

Trade Discount. A reduction in the price of merchandise offered by one business to another as a method of changing prices.

Universal Life Insurance. A flexible premium, adjustable death benefit life insurance policy.

Unknown. A literal number whose value is implied and can be found by solving the equation.

Unsecured Note. One not requiring collateral. (See collateral).

Variables. A symbol used to represent an unspecified member of some set.

Vertical Analysis. Expressing the components of a financial statement as a percent of the whole for a single time period; used for comparative purposes.

Wholesaler. A business selling products to another business and not to the ultimate consumer.

Withholding Tax. An amount withheld by an employer from an employee's pay check to pay federal income taxes.

Yield. The return on invested money.

Yield-to-Maturity. The average annual return on a bond held to maturity; it relates the annual interest and premium (or discount) on the bond to the average investment in the bond.

Tables

		Pages
I.	Values of $(1 + i)^n$	528–534
II.	Values of $(1 + i)^n$ for $5\frac{1}{4}\%$ Compounded Daily	535–536
III.	Values of e^{st}	537
IV.	Payment Needed to Amortize a Debt of 1	538–543
V.	Payment Needed Each Period for a Sinking Fund to Amount to 1	544–549
VI.	Present Value of An Annuity of 1 per Period	550–555
VII.	Amount of An Annuity of 1 per Period	556–561
VIII.	Board of Governors' APR Tables—Volume 1	562–572
IX.	Exact-Day Calendar	573
X.	Federal Income Tax Witholding Table	574–582
XI.	Federal Income Tax Table	583–588
XII.	Single Equivalent Discount Rates for Series Discounts	589–593

TABLE I   Values of $(1+i)^n$

I N	$\frac{1}{4}\%$ .0025	$\frac{1}{2}\%$ .0050	$\frac{3}{4}\%$ .0075	1% .0100	$1\frac{1}{4}\%$ .0125	$1\frac{1}{2}\%$ .0150	$1\frac{3}{4}\%$ .0175	2% .0200	$2\frac{1}{4}\%$ .0225
1	1.00250	1.00500	1.00750	1.01000	1.01250	1.01500	1.01750	1.02000	1.02250
2	1.00501	1.01002	1.01506	1.02010	1.02516	1.03022	1.03531	1.04040	1.04551
3	1.00752	1.01508	1.02267	1.03030	1.03797	1.04568	1.05342	1.06121	1.06903
4	1.01004	1.02015	1.03034	1.04060	1.05095	1.06136	1.07186	1.08243	1.09308
5	1.01256	1.02525	1.03807	1.05101	1.06408	1.07728	1.09062	1.10408	1.11768
6	1.01509	1.03038	1.04585	1.06152	1.07738	1.09344	1.10970	1.12616	1.14283
7	1.01763	1.03553	1.05370	1.07214	1.09085	1.10984	1.12912	1.14869	1.16854
8	1.02018	1.04071	1.06160	1.08286	1.10449	1.12649	1.14888	1.17166	1.19483
9	1.02273	1.04591	1.06956	1.09369	1.11829	1.14339	1.16899	1.19509	1.22171
10	1.02528	1.05114	1.07758	1.10462	1.13227	1.16054	1.18944	1.21899	1.24920
11	1.02785	1.05640	1.08566	1.11567	1.14642	1.17795	1.21026	1.24337	1.27731
12	1.03042	1.06168	1.09381	1.12682	1.16075	1.19562	1.23144	1.26824	1.30805
13	1.03299	1.06699	1.10201	1.13809	1.17526	1.21355	1.25299	1.29361	1.33544
14	1.03557	1.07232	1.11028	1.14947	1.18995	1.23176	1.27492	1.31948	1.36548
15	1.03816	1.07768	1.11860	1.16097	1.20483	1.25023	1.29723	1.34587	1.39621
16	1.04076	1.08307	1.12699	1.17258	1.21989	1.26899	1.31993	1.37279	1.42762
17	1.04336	1.08849	1.13544	1.18430	1.23514	1.28802	1.34303	1.40024	1.45974
18	1.04597	1.09393	1.14396	1.19615	1.25058	1.30734	1.36653	1.42825	1.49259
19	1.04858	1.09940	1.15254	1.20811	1.26621	1.32695	1.39045	1.45681	1.52617
20	1.05121	1.10490	1.16118	1.22019	1.28204	1.34685	1.41478	1.48595	1.56051
21	1.05383	1.11042	1.16989	1.23239	1.29806	1.36706	1.43954	1.51567	1.59562
22	1.05647	1.11597	1.17867	1.24472	1.31429	1.38756	1.46473	1.54598	1.63152
23	1.05911	1.12155	1.18751	1.25716	1.33072	1.40838	1.49036	1.57690	1.66823
24	1.06176	1.12716	1.19641	1.26973	1.34735	1.42950	1.51644	1.60844	1.70577
25	1.06441	1.13280	1.20539	1.28243	1.36419	1.45094	1.54298	1.64061	1.74415
26	1.06707	1.13846	1.21443	1.29526	1.38124	1.47271	1.56998	1.67342	1.78339
27	1.06974	1.14415	1.22353	1.30821	1.39851	1.49480	1.59746	1.70689	1.82352
28	1.07241	1.14987	1.23271	1.32129	1.41599	1.51722	1.62541	1.74102	1.86454
29	1.07510	1.15562	1.24196	1.33450	1.43369	1.53998	1.65386	1.77584	1.90650
30	1.07778	1.16140	1.25127	1.34785	1.45161	1.56308	1.68280	1.81136	1.94939
31	1.08048	1.16721	1.26066	1.36133	1.46976	1.58653	1.71225	1.84759	1.99325
32	1.08318	1.17304	1.27011	1.37494	1.48813	1.61032	1.74221	1.88454	2.03810
33	1.08589	1.17891	1.27964	1.38869	1.50673	1.63448	1.77270	1.92223	2.08396
34	1.08860	1.18480	1.28923	1.40258	1.52557	1.65900	1.80372	1.96068	2.13085
35	1.09132	1.19073	1.29890	1.41660	1.54463	1.68388	1.83529	1.99989	2.17879
36	1.09405	1.19668	1.30864	1.43077	1.56394	1.70914	1.86741	2.03989	2.22782
37	1.09679	1.20266	1.31846	1.44508	1.58349	1.73478	1.90009	2.08068	2.27794
38	1.09953	1.20868	1.32835	1.45953	1.60329	1.76080	1.93334	2.12230	2.32919
39	1.10228	1.21472	1.33831	1.47412	1.62333	1.78721	1.96717	2.16474	2.38160
40	1.10503	1.22079	1.34835	1.48886	1.64362	1.81402	2.00260	2.20804	2.43519
41	1.10780	1.22690	1.35846	1.50375	1.66416	1.84123	2.03662	2.25220	2.48998
42	1.11056	1.23303	1.36865	1.51879	1.68497	1.86885	2.07227	2.29724	2.54600
43	1.11334	1.23920	1.37891	1.53398	1.70603	1.89688	2.10853	2.34319	2.60329
44	1.11612	1.24539	1.38926	1.54932	1.72735	1.92533	2.14543	2.39005	2.66186
45	1.11891	1.25162	1.39968	1.56481	1.74894	1.95421	2.18297	2.43785	2.72175
46	1.12171	1.25788	1.41017	1.58046	1.77081	1.98352	2.22118	2.48661	1.78299
47	1.12452	1.26417	1.42075	1.59626	1.79294	2.01328	2.26005	2.53634	2.84561
48	1.12733	1.27049	1.43140	1.61222	1.81535	2.04348	2.29960	2.58707	2.90964
49	1.13015	1.27684	1.44214	1.62835	1.83805	2.07413	2.33984	2.63881	2.97510
50	1.13297	1.28323	1.45296	1.64463	1.86102	2.10524	2.38079	2.69159	3.04204
51	1.13580	1.28964	1.46385	1.66108	1.88428	2.13682	2.42245	2.74542	3.11049
52	1.13864	1.29609	1.47483	1.67769	1.90784	2.16887	2.46484	2.80033	3.18048
53	1.14149	1.30257	1.48589	1.69446	1.93168	2.20140	2.50798	2.85633	3.25204
54	1.14434	1.30908	1.49704	1.71141	1.95583	2.23443	2.55187	2.91346	3.32521
55	1.14720	1.31563	1.50827	1.72852	1.98028	2.26794	2.59653	2.97173	3.40003
56	1.15007	1.32221	1.51958	1.74581	2.00503	2.30196	2.64197	3.03116	3.47653
57	1.15295	1.32882	1.53097	1.76327	2.03010	2.33649	2.68820	3.09179	3.55475
58	1.15583	1.33546	1.54246	1.78090	2.05547	2.37154	2.73524	3.15362	3.63473
59	1.15872	1.34214	1.55402	1.79871	2.08116	2.40711	2.78311	3.21670	3.71651
60	1.16162	1.34885	1.56568	1.81670	2.10718	2.44322	2.83181	3.28103	3.80013
61	1.16452	1.35559	1.57742	1.83486	2.13352	2.47987	2.88137	3.34665	3.88563
62	1.16743	1.36237	1.58925	1.85321	2.16019	2.51706	2.93180	3.41358	3.97306
63	1.17035	1.36918	1.60117	1.87174	2.18719	2.55482	2.98310	3.48185	4.06246
64	1.17328	1.37603	1.61318	1.89046	2.21453	2.59314	3.03531	3.55149	4.15386
65	1.17621	1.38291	1.62528	1.90936	2.24221	2.63204	3.08842	3.62252	4.24732

TABLE I   Values of $(1 + i)^n$ (continued)

I / N	$\frac{1}{4}\%$ .0025	$\frac{1}{2}\%$ .0050	$\frac{3}{4}\%$ .0075	1% .0100	$1\frac{1}{4}\%$ .0125	$2\frac{1}{2}\%$ .0150	$1\frac{3}{4}\%$ .0175	2% .0200	$2\frac{1}{4}\%$ .0225
66	1.17915	1.38982	1.63747	1.92846	2.27024	2.67152	3.14247	3.69497	4.34289
67	1.18210	1.39677	1.64975	1.94774	2.29862	2.71159	3.19746	3.76887	4.44060
68	1.18505	1.40376	1.66212	1.96722	2.32735	2.75227	3.25342	3.84425	2.54052
69	1.18802	1.41078	1.67459	1.98689	2.35644	2.79355	3.31036	3.92113	4.64268
70	1.19099	1.41783	1.68715	2.00676	2.38590	2.83545	3.36829	3.99956	4.74714
71	1.19396	1.42492	1.69980	2.02683	2.41572	2.87798	3.42723	4.07955	4.85395
72	1.19695	1.43204	1.71255	2.04710	2.44592	2.92115	3.48721	4.16114	4.96316
73	1.19994	1.43920	1.72540	2.06757	2.47649	2.96497	3.54823	4.24436	5.07483
74	1.20294	1.44640	1.73834	2.08824	2.50745	3.00945	3.61033	4.32925	5.18902
75	1.20595	1.45363	1.75137	2.10913	2.53879	3.05459	3.67351	4.41583	5.30577
76	1.20896	1.46090	1.76451	2.13022	2.57053	3.10041	3.73780	4.50415	5.42515
77	1.21198	1.46820	1.77774	2.15152	2.60266	3.14691	3.80321	4.59423	5.54721
78	1.21501	1.47554	1.79108	2.17303	2.63519	3.19412	3.86976	4.68612	5.67203
79	1.21805	1.48292	1.80451	2.19476	2.66813	3.24203	3.93748	4.77984	5.79985
80	1.22110	1.49034	1.81804	2.21671	2.70148	3.29066	4.00639	4.87544	5.93014

I / N	$2\frac{1}{2}\%$ .0250	$2\frac{3}{4}\%$ .0275	3% .0300	$3\frac{1}{4}\%$ .0325	$3\frac{1}{2}\%$ .0350	$3\frac{3}{4}\%$ .0375	4% .0400	$4\frac{1}{4}\%$ .0425	$4\frac{1}{2}\%$ .0450
1	1.02500	1.02750	1.03000	1.03250	1.03500	1.03750	1.04000	1.04250	1.04500
2	1.05062	1.05576	1.06090	1.06606	1.07122	1.07641	1.08160	1.08681	1.09202
3	1.07689	1.08479	1.09273	1.10070	1.10872	1.11677	1.12486	1.13300	1.14117
4	1.10381	1.11462	1.12551	1.13648	1.14752	1.15865	1.16986	1.18115	1.19252
5	1.13141	1.14527	1.15927	1.17341	1.18769	1.20210	1.21665	1.23135	1.24618
6	1.15969	1.17677	1.19405	1.21155	1.22926	1.24718	1.26532	1.28368	1.30226
7	1.18869	1.20913	1.22987	1.25092	1.27228	1.29395	1.31593	1.33824	1.36086
8	1.21840	1.24238	1.26677	1.29158	1.31681	1.34247	1.36857	1.39511	1.42210
9	1.24886	1.27655	1.30477	1.33355	1.36290	1.39281	1.42331	1.45440	1.48609
10	1.28008	1.31165	1.34392	1.37689	1.41060	1.44504	1.48024	1.51621	1.55297
11	1.31209	1.34772	1.38423	1.42164	1.45997	1.49923	1.53945	1.58065	1.62285
12	1.34489	1.38478	1.42576	1.46785	1.51107	1.55545	1.60103	1.64783	1.69588
13	1.37851	1.42287	1.46853	1.51555	1.56396	1.61378	1.66507	1.71786	1.77220
14	1.41297	1.46199	1.51259	1.56481	1.61869	1.67430	1.73168	1.79087	1.85194
15	1.44830	1.50220	1.55797	1.61566	1.67535	1.73709	1.80094	1.86699	1.93528
16	1.48451	1.54351	1.60471	1.66817	1.73399	1.80223	1.87298	1.94633	2.02237
17	1.52162	1.58596	1.65285	1.72239	1.79468	1.86981	1.94790	2.02905	2.11338
18	1.55966	1.62957	1.70243	1.77837	1.85749	1.93993	2.02582	2.11529	2.20848
19	1.59865	1.67438	1.75351	1.83616	1.92250	2.01268	2.10685	2.20519	2.30786
20	1.63862	1.72043	1.80611	1.89584	1.98979	2.08815	2.19112	2.29891	2.41171
21	1.67958	1.76774	1.86029	1.95745	2.05943	2.16646	2.27877	2.39661	2.52024
22	1.72157	1.81635	1.91610	2.02107	2.13151	2.24770	2.36992	2.49846	2.63365
23	1.76461	1.86630	1.97359	2.08675	2.20611	2.33199	2.46471	2.60465	2.75217
24	1.80873	1.91763	2.03279	2.15457	2.28333	2.41944	2.56330	2.71535	2.87601
25	1.85394	1.97036	2.09378	2.22460	2.36324	2.51017	2.66584	2.83075	3.00543
26	1.90029	2.02454	2.15659	2.29690	2.44596	2.60430	2.77247	2.95106	3.14068
27	1.94780	2.08022	2.22129	2.37155	2.53157	2.70196	2.88337	3.07648	3.28201
28	1.99649	2.13743	2.28793	2.44862	2.62017	2.80328	2.99870	3.20723	3.42970
29	2.04641	2.19621	2.35656	2.52820	2.71188	2.90841	3.11865	3.34353	3.58403
30	2.09757	2.25660	2.42726	2.61037	2.80679	3.01747	3.24340	3.48563	3.74532
31	2.15001	2.31866	2.50008	2.69520	2.90503	3.13063	3.37313	3.63377	3.91386
32	2.20376	2.38242	2.57508	2.78280	3.00671	3.24802	3.50806	3.78821	4.08998
33	2.25885	2.44794	2.65233	2.87324	3.11194	3.36982	3.64838	3.94921	4.27403
34	2.31532	2.51525	2.73190	2.96662	3.22086	3.49619	3.79431	4.11705	4.46636
35	2.37320	2.58442	2.81386	3.06304	3.33359	3.62730	3.94609	4.29202	4.66734
36	2.43253	2.65550	2.89828	3.16258	3.45027	3.76332	4.10393	4.47443	4.87738
37	2.49335	2.72852	2.98522	3.26537	3.57102	3.90445	4.26809	4.66460	5.09686
38	2.55568	2.80356	3.07478	3.37149	3.69601	4.05087	4.43881	4.86284	5.32622
39	2.61957	2.88065	3.16702	3.48107	3.82537	4.20277	4.61636	5.06951	5.56590
40	2.68506	2.95987	3.26204	3.59420	3.95926	4.36038	4.80102	5.28497	5.81636
41	2.75219	3.04127	3.35990	3.71101	4.09783	4.52389	4.99306	5.50958	6.07810
42	2.82099	3.12490	3.46069	3.83162	4.24126	4.69354	5.19278	5.74373	6.35161
43	2.89152	3.21084	3.56451	3.95615	4.38970	4.86954	5.40049	5.98784	6.63743
44	2.96381	3.29914	3.67145	4.08472	4.54334	5.05215	5.61651	6.24233	6.93612
45	3.03790	3.38986	3.78159	4.21748	4.70236	5.24161	5.84117	6.50763	7.24824

TABLE I   Values of $(1 + i)^n$ (**continued**)

I / N	$2\frac{1}{2}\%$ .0250	$2\frac{3}{4}\%$ .0275	3% .0300	$3\frac{1}{4}\%$ .0325	$3\frac{1}{2}\%$ .0350	$3\frac{3}{4}\%$ .0375	4% .0400	$4\frac{1}{4}\%$ .0425	$4\frac{1}{2}\%$ .0450
46	3.11385	3.48308	3.89504	4.35454	4.86694	5.43817	6.07482	6.78420	7.57441
47	3.19169	3.57887	4.01189	4.49607	5.03728	5.64210	6.31781	7.07253	7.91526
48	3.27149	3.67729	4.13225	4.64219	5.21359	5.85368	6.57052	7.37311	8.27145
49	3.35327	3.77841	4.25622	4.79306	5.39606	6.07319	6.83335	7.69647	8.64366
50	3.43711	3.88232	4.38390	4.94883	5.58492	6.30094	7.10668	8.01314	9.03263
51	3.52303	3.98908	4.51542	5.10967	5.78040	6.53722	7.39095	8.35370	9.43910
52	3.61111	4.09878	4.65088	5.27574	5.98271	6.78237	7.68658	8.70873	9.86386
53	3.70139	4.21150	4.79041	5.44720	6.19211	7.03670	7.99405	9.07885	10.30773
54	3.79392	4.32731	4.93412	5.62423	6.40883	7.30058	8.31381	9.46470	10.77158
55	3.88877	4.44632	5.08214	5.80702	6.63314	7.57435	8.64636	9.86695	11.25630
56	3.98599	4.56859	5.23461	5.99575	6.86530	7.85839	8.99222	10.28630	11.76283
57	4.08564	4.69423	5.39165	6.19061	7.10558	8.15308	9.35190	10.72347	12.29216
58	4.18778	4.82332	5.55339	6.39180	7.35428	8.45882	9.72598	11.17921	12.84530
59	4.29247	4.95596	5.72000	6.59954	7.61168	8.77603	10.11502	11.65433	13.42334
60	4.39979	5.09225	5.89160	6.81402	7.87809	9.10513	10.51962	12.14964	14.02739
61	4.50978	5.23228	6.06834	7.03548	8.15382	9.44657	10.94040	12.66600	14.65863
62	4.62252	5.37617	6.25039	7.26413	8.43920	9.80082	11.37802	13.20430	15.31826
63	4.73809	5.52402	6.43791	7.50021	8.73458	10.16835	11.83314	13.76549	16.00759
64	4.85654	5.67593	6.63104	7.74397	9.04029	10.54966	12.30647	14.35052	16.72793
65	4.97795	5.83201	6.82997	7.99565	9.35670	10.94527	12.79872	14.96042	17.48068
66	5.10240	5.99239	7.03487	8.25551	9.68418	11.35572	13.31067	15.59623	18.26731
67	5.22996	6.15718	7.24592	8.52381	10.02313	11.78156	13.84310	16.25907	19.08934
68	5.36071	6.32651	7.46330	8.80084	10.37394	12.22337	14.39682	16.95008	19.94836
69	5.49473	6.50049	7.68720	9.08686	10.73702	12.68174	14.97270	17.67046	20.84604
70	5.63210	6.67925	7.91781	9.38219	11.11282	13.15731	15.57160	18.42146	21.78411
71	5.77290	6.86293	8.15535	9.68711	11.50177	13.65071	16.19447	19.20437	22.76439
72	5.91722	7.05166	8.40001	10.00194	11.90433	14.16261	16.84225	20.02055	23.78879
73	6.06515	7.24558	8.65201	10.32700	12.32098	14.69371	17.51594	20.87143	24.58929
74	6.21678	7.44483	8.91157	10.66263	12.75221	15.24472	18.21657	21.75846	25.97795
75	6.37220	7.64957	9.17891	11.00916	13.19854	15.81640	18.94524	22.68320	27.14696
76	6.53151	7.85993	9.45428	11.36696	13.66049	16.40951	19.70305	23.64723	28.36857
77	6.69479	8.07608	9.73791	11.73639	14.13861	17.02487	20.49117	24.65224	29.64516
78	6.86216	8.29817	10.30005	12.11782	14.63346	17.66330	21.31081	25.69996	30.97919
79	7.03372	8.52637	10.33095	12.51165	15.14563	18.32567	22.16325	26.79221	32.37325
80	7.20956	8.76084	10.64087	12.91828	15.67573	19.01289	23.04977	27.93088	33.83005

I / N	$4\frac{3}{4}\%$ .0475	5% .0500	$5\frac{1}{4}\%$ .0525	$5\frac{1}{2}\%$ .0550	$5\frac{3}{4}\%$ .0575	6% .0600	$6\frac{1}{4}\%$ .0625	$6\frac{1}{2}\%$ .0650	$6\frac{3}{4}\%$ .0675
1	1.04750	1.05000	1.05250	1.05500	1.05750	1.06000	1.06250	1.06500	1.06750
2	1.09726	1.10250	1.10776	1.11302	1.11831	1.12360	1.12891	1.13422	1.13956
3	1.14938	1.15762	1.16591	1.17424	1.18261	1.19102	1.19946	1.20795	1.21648
4	1.20397	1.21551	1.22712	1.23882	1.25061	1.26248	1.27443	1.28647	1.29859
5	1.26116	1.27628	1.29155	1.30696	1.32252	1.33823	1.35408	1.37009	1.38624
6	1.32106	1.34010	1.35935	1.37884	1.39856	1.41852	1.43871	1.45914	1.47981
7	1.38382	1.40710	1.43072	1.45468	1.47898	1.50363	1.52863	1.55399	1.57970
8	1.44955	1.47746	1.50583	1.53469	1.56402	1.59385	1.62417	1.65500	1.68633
9	1.51840	1.55133	1.58489	1.61909	1.65395	1.68948	1.72568	1.76257	1.80016
10	1.59052	1.62889	1.66810	1.70814	1.74906	1.79085	1.83354	1.87714	1.92167
11	1.66607	1.71034	1.75567	1.80209	1.84963	1.89830	1.94813	1.99915	2.05138
12	1.74521	1.79586	1.84784	1.90121	1.95598	2.01220	2.06989	2.12910	2.18985
13	1.82811	1.88565	1.94486	2.00577	2.06845	2.13293	2.19926	2.26749	2.33767
14	1.91495	1.97993	2.04696	2.11609	2.19738	2.26090	2.33671	2.41487	2.49546
15	2.00590	2.07893	2.15443	2.23248	2.31316	2.39656	2.48276	2.57184	2.66390
16	2.10119	2.18287	2.26753	2.35526	2.44617	2.54035	2.63793	2.73901	2.84371
17	2.20099	2.29202	2.38658	2.48480	2.58682	2.69277	2.80280	2.91705	3.03567
18	2.30554	2.40662	2.51187	2.62147	2.73556	2.85434	2.97797	3.10665	3.24057
19	2.41505	2.52695	2.64375	2.76565	2.89286	3.02560	3.16410	3.30859	3.45931
20	2.51977	2.65330	2.78254	2.91776	3.05920	3.20713	3.36185	3.52364	3.69282
21	2.64993	2.78596	2.92863	3.07823	3.23510	3.39956	3.57197	3.75268	3.94208
22	2.77580	2.92526	3.08238	3.24754	3.42112	3.60354	3.79522	3.99661	4.20817
23	2.90765	3.07152	3.24421	3.42615	3.61783	3.81975	4.03242	4.25638	4.49222
24	3.04577	3.22510	3.41453	3.61549	3.82586	4.04893	4.28444	4.53305	4.79545

TABLE I   **Values of** $(1 + i)^n$ **(continued)**

I N	$4\frac{3}{4}\%$ .0475	5% .0500	$5\frac{1}{4}\%$ .0525	$5\frac{1}{2}\%$ .0550	$5\frac{3}{4}\%$ .0575	6% .0600	$6\frac{1}{4}\%$ .0625	$6\frac{1}{2}\%$ .0650	$6\frac{3}{4}\%$ .0675
25	3.19044	3.38635	3.59379	3.81339	4.04585	4.29187	4.55222	4.82770	5.11914
26	3.34199	3.55567	3.78246	4.02313	4.27848	4.54938	4.83673	5.14150	5.46468
27	3.50073	3.73346	3.98104	4.24440	4.52449	4.82234	5.13903	5.47570	5.83355
28	3.66701	3.92013	4.19005	4.47784	4.78465	5.11168	5.46022	5.83162	6.22731
29	3.84120	4.11613	4.41002	4.72412	5.05977	5.41838	5.80148	6.21067	6.64766
30	4.02365	4.32194	4.64155	4.98395	5.35071	5.74349	6.16407	6.61436	7.09637
31	4.21478	4.53804	4.88523	5.25807	5.65837	6.08810	6.54933	7.04430	7.57538
32	4.41498	4.76494	5.14171	5.54726	5.98373	6.45338	6.95866	7.50218	8.08672
33	4.62469	5.00319	5.41164	5.85236	6.32779	6.84059	7.39358	7.98982	8.63257
34	4.84430	5.25335	5.69576	6.17424	6.69164	7.25102	7.85568	8.50916	9.21527
35	5.07447	5.51601	5.99478	6.51382	7.07641	7.68608	8.34666	9.06225	9.83730
36	5.31551	5.79181	6.30951	6.87208	7.48330	8.14725	8.86832	9.65130	10.50131
37	5.56799	6.08141	6.64076	7.25005	7.91359	8.63608	9.42259	10.27863	11.21015
38	5.83247	6.38548	6.98940	7.64880	8.36862	9.15425	10.01150	10.94674	11.96684
39	6.10952	6.70475	7.35634	8.06948	8.84982	9.70350	10.63722	11.65828	12.77460
40	6.39972	7.03999	7.74255	8.51330	9.35868	10.28571	11.30205	12.41607	13.63888
41	6.70371	7.39199	8.14903	8.98154	9.89681	10.90285	12.00843	13.22312	14.55737
42	7.02213	7.76158	8.57686	9.47552	10.46587	11.55702	12.75895	14.08262	15.54000
43	7.35568	8.14966	9.02714	9.99667	11.06766	12.25045	13.55639	14.99799	16.58895
44	7.70508	8.55715	9.50107	10.54649	11.70405	12.98547	14.40366	15.97286	17.70870
45	8.07107	8.98500	9.99987	11.12655	12.37704	13.76460	15.30389	17.01109	18.90404
46	8.45444	9.43425	10.52487	11.73851	13.08871	14.59048	16.26038	18.11681	20.18006
47	8.85603	9.90597	11.07742	12.38413	13.84132	15.46590	17.27666	19.29441	21.54221
48	9.27669	10.40127	11.65899	13.06525	14.63719	16.39386	18.35645	20.54854	22.99631
49	9.71733	10.92133	12.27108	13.78384	15.47883	17.37749	19.50373	21.88420	24.54856
50	10.17891	11.46739	12.91531	14.54195	16.36886	18.42014	20.72271	23.30667	26.20559
51	10.66240	12.04076	13.59337	15.34176	17.31007	19.52535	22.01788	24.82160	27.97447
52	11.16887	12.64280	14.30702	16.18556	18.30540	20.69687	23.39399	26.43501	29.86275
53	11.69939	13.27494	15.05814	17.07576	19.35796	21.93868	24.85612	28.15328	31.87848
54	12.25511	13.93869	15.84869	18.01493	20.47104	23.25500	26.40963	29.98325	34.03028
55	12.83723	14.63562	16.68075	19.00575	21.64813	24.65030	28.06023	31.93216	36.32732
56	13.44700	15.36741	37.55649	20.05106	22.89289	26.12931	29.81399	34.00775	38.77941
57	14.08573	16.13578	18.47820	21.15387	24.20924	27.69707	31.67736	36.21825	41.39702
58	14.75480	16.94256	19.44831	22.31734	25.60127	29.35890	33.65720	38.57244	44.19132
59	15.45565	17.78969	20.46934	23.54479	27.07334	31.12043	35.76077	41.07964	47.17424
60	16.18980	18.67918	21.54398	24.83975	28.63006	32.98766	37.99582	43.74982	50.35850
61	16.95881	19.61313	22.67504	26.20594	30.27628	34.96691	40.37056	46.59356	53.75769
62	17.76435	20.59379	23.86548	27.64726	32.01717	37.06493	42.89372	49.62214	57.38634
63	18.60816	21.62348	25.11842	29.16786	33.85816	39.28882	45.57457	52.84758	61.25992
64	19.49205	22.70465	26.43714	30.77209	35.80500	41.64615	48.42298	56.28267	65.39496
65	20.41792	23.83989	27.82508	32.46456	37.86379	44.14492	51.44942	59.94104	69.80912
66	21.38777	25.03188	29.28590	34.25011	40.04095	46.79362	54.66501	63.83721	74.52123
67	22.40369	26.28347	30.82341	36.13387	42.34331	49.60123	58.08157	67.98663	79.55142
68	23.46786	27.59765	32.44164	38.12123	44.77805	52.57730	61.71167	72.40576	84.92113
69	24.58259	28.97753	34.14482	40.21789	47.35278	55.73194	65.56864	77.11213	90.65331
70	25.75026	30.42641	35.93743	42.42988	50.07557	59.07586	69.66668	82.12442	96.77241
71	26.97340	31.94773	37.82414	44.76352	52.95491	62.62041	74.02085	87.46251	103.30455
72	28.25463	33.54511	39.80991	77.22551	55.99982	66.37763	78.64715	93.14757	110.27760
73	29.59673	35.22237	41.89993	49.82292	59.21981	70.36029	83.56260	99.20216	117.72134
74	31.00257	36.98349	44.09967	52.56318	62.62495	74.58190	88.78526	105.65030	125.66753
75	32.47519	38.83266	46.41491	55.45415	66.22588	79.05682	94.33433	112.51757	134.15008
76	34.01776	40.77429	48.85169	58.50413	70.03387	83.80022	100.23023	119.83121	143.20521
77	35.63360	42.81301	51.41640	61.72185	74.06081	88.82824	106.49462	127.62024	152.87156
78	37.32620	44.95366	54.11576	65.11655	78.31931	94.15793	113.15053	135.91555	163.19039
79	39.09919	47.20134	56.95684	68.69796	82.82267	99.80740	120.22243	144.75006	174.20574
80	40.95640	49.56141	59.94707	72.47635	87.58497	105.79585	127.73633	154.15882	185.96463

I N	7% .0700	$7\frac{1}{4}\%$ .0725	$7\frac{1}{2}\%$ .0750	$7\frac{3}{4}\%$ .0775	8% .0800	$8\frac{1}{4}\%$ .0825	$8\frac{1}{2}\%$ .0850	$8\frac{3}{4}\%$ .0875	9% .0900
1	1.07000	1.07250	1.07500	1.07750	1.08000	1.08250	1.08500	1.08750	1.09000
2	1.14490	1.15026	1.15562	1.16101	1.16640	1.17181	1.17722	1.18266	1.18810
3	1.22504	1.23365	1.24230	1.25098	1.25971	1.26848	1.27729	1.28614	1.29503
4	1.31080	1.32309	1.33547	1.34794	1.36049	1.37313	1.38586	1.39868	1.41158

TABLE I   Values of $(1 + i)^n$ (continued)

I N	7% .0700	7¼% .0725	7½% .0750	7¾% .0775	8% .0800	8¼% .0825	8½% .0850	8¾% .0875	9% .0900
5	1.40255	1.41901	1.43563	1.45240	1.46933	1.48641	1.50366	1.52106	1.53862
6	1.50073	1.52189	1.54330	1.56496	1.58687	1.60904	1.63147	1.65415	1.67710
7	1.60578	1.63223	1.65905	1.68625	1.71382	1.74179	1.77014	1.79889	1.82804
8	1.71819	1.75057	1.78348	1.81693	1.85093	1.88549	1.92060	1.95629	1.99256
9	1.83846	1.87748	1.91724	1.95774	1.99900	2.04104	2.08386	2.12747	2.17189
10	1.96715	2.01360	2.06103	2.10947	2.15892	2.20942	2.26098	2.31362	2.36736
11	2.10485	2.15958	2.21561	2.27295	2.33164	2.39170	2.45317	2.51607	2.58043
12	2.25219	2.31615	2.38178	2.44910	2.51817	2.58902	2.66169	2.73622	2.81266
13	2.40984	2.48408	2.56041	2.63981	2.71962	2.80261	2.88793	2.97564	3.06580
14	2.57853	2.66417	2.75244	2.84343	2.93719	3.03383	3.13340	3.23601	3.34173
15	2.75903	2.85732	2.95888	3.06379	3.17217	3.28412	3.39974	3.51916	3.64248
16	2.95216	3.06448	3.18079	3.30123	3.42594	3.55505	3.68872	3.82709	3.97030
17	3.15881	3.28665	3.41935	3.55708	3.70002	3.84835	4.00226	4.16196	4.32763
18	3.37993	3.52494	3.67580	3.83275	3.99602	4.16584	4.34245	4.52613	4.71712
19	3.61653	3.78049	3.95149	4.12979	4.31570	4.50952	4.71156	4.92216	5.14166
20	3.86968	4.05458	4.24785	4.44985	4.66096	4.88155	5.11204	5.35285	5.60441
21	4.14056	4.34854	4.56644	4.79471	5.03383	5.28428	5.54657	5.82123	6.10881
22	4.43040	4.66381	4.90892	5.16630	5.43654	5.72023	6.01803	6.33058	6.65860
23	4.74053	5.00193	5.27709	5.56669	5.87146	6.19215	6.52956	6.88451	7.25787
24	5.07237	5.36457	5.67287	5.99811	6.34118	6.70300	7.08457	7.48690	7.91108
25	5.42743	5.75350	6.09834	6.46296	6.84847	7.25600	7.68676	8.14201	8.62308
26	5.80735	6.17063	6.55571	6.96384	7.39635	7.85462	8.34013	8.85443	9.39915
27	6.21387	6.61800	7.04739	7.50354	7.98806	8.50263	9.04905	9.62920	10.24508
28	6.64884	7.09781	7.57594	8.08507	8.62710	9.20409	9.81821	10.47175	11.16713
29	7.11425	7.61240	8.14414	8.71166	9.31727	9.96343	10.65276	11.38803	12.17218
30	7.61225	8.16430	8.75495	9.38681	10.06265	10.78541	11.55825	12.38448	13.26767
31	8.14511	8.75621	9.41157	10.11429	10.86766	11.67521	12.54070	13.46812	14.46176
32	8.71527	9.39103	10.11744	10.89815	11.73708	12.63842	13.60666	14.64658	15.76332
33	9.32534	10.07188	10.87625	11.74275	12.67604	13.68108	14.76322	15.92816	17.18202
34	9.97811	10.80210	11.69197	12.65282	13.69012	14.80977	16.01810	17.32187	18.72840
35	10.67658	11.58525	12.56886	13.63341	14.78533	16.03158	17.37964	18.83754	20.41396
36	11.42394	12.42518	13.51153	14.69000	15.96816	17.35418	18.85690	20.48582	22.25121
37	12.22361	13.32600	14.52489	15.82847	17.24561	18.78590	20.45974	22.27833	24.25382
38	13.07927	14.29214	15.61426	17.05518	18.62526	20.33574	22.19882	24.22768	26.43666
39	13.99481	15.32832	16.78533	18.37696	20.11528	22.01344	24.08572	26.34760	28.81596
40	14.97445	16.43962	18.04423	19.80117	21.72450	23.82955	26.13300	28.65302	31.40940
41	16.02266	17.63149	19.39754	21.33576	23.46246	25.79548	28.35431	31.16016	34.23625
42	17.14425	18.90978	20.85236	22.98928	25.33946	27.92361	30.76442	33.88667	37.31751
43	18.34435	20.28073	22.41629	24.77095	27.36662	30.22731	33.37940	36.85176	40.67608
44	19.62845	21.75109	24.09751	26.69070	29.55595	32.72106	36.21665	40.07628	44.33693
45	21.00244	23.32804	25.90482	28.75923	31.92042	35.42055	39.29506	43.58296	48.32725
46	22.47261	25.01932	27.84768	30.98807	34.47405	38.34274	42.63514	47.39647	52.67670
47	24.04569	26.83322	29.93626	33.38964	37.23198	41.50602	46.25913	51.54366	57.41761
48	25.72889	28.77863	32.18148	35.97734	40.21053	44.93026	50.19116	56.05373	62.58519
49	27.52991	30.86508	34.59509	78.76558	43.42738	48.63701	54.45740	60.95843	68.21786
50	29.45701	33.10280	37.18972	41.76991	46.90156	52.64956	59.08628	66.29229	74.35746
51	31.51900	35.50275	39.97894	45.00708	50.65369	56.99315	64.10861	72.09286	81.04963
52	33.72533	38.07670	42.97736	48.48513	54.70598	61.69508	69.55785	78.40099	88.34410
53	36.08610	40.83726	46.20067	52.25350	59.08246	66.78492	75.47026	85.26107	96.29506
54	38.61213	43.79796	49.66571	56.30314	63.80906	72.29468	81.88523	92.72141	104.96162
55	41.31498	46.97331	53.39064	60.66664	68.91378	78.25899	88.84548	100.83454	114.40816
56	44.20702	50.37888	57.39494	65.36830	74.42688	84.71535	96.39734	109.65756	124.70489
57	47.30151	54.03135	61.69956	70.43434	80.38103	91.70437	104.59112	119.25259	135.92833
58	50.61262	57.94862	66.32703	75.89300	86.81151	99.26997	113.48136	129.68719	148.16188
59	54.15550	62.14989	71.30155	81.77471	93.75643	107.45975	123.12727	141.03482	161.49644
60	57.94639	66.65576	76.64917	88.11224	101.25694	116.32517	133.59309	153.37536	176.03112
61	62.00263	71.48830	82.39785	94.94094	109.35749	125.92200	144.94850	166.79570	191.87392
62	66.34282	76.67120	88.57769	102.29886	118.10609	136.31056	157.26912	181.39033	209.14257
63	70.98681	82.22986	95.22101	110.22702	127.55458	147.55617	170.63700	197.26198	227.96540
64	75.95589	88.19152	102.36259	118.76961	137.75894	159.72955	185.14114	214.52240	248.48228
65	81.27280	94.58541	110.03978	127.97426	148.77965	172.90724	200.87813	233.29310	270.84568
66	86.96189	101.44285	118.29276	137.89226	160.68202	187.17208	217.95277	253.70625	295.22179
67	93.04923	108.79745	127.16472	148.57891	173.53658	202.61377	236.47876	275.90554	321.79174
68	99.56267	116.68527	136.70207	160.09377	187.41950	219.32940	256.57944	300.04727	350.75299
69	106.53206	125.14495	146.95472	172.50103	202.41306	237.42408	278.38869	326.30140	382.32076

TABLE I Values of $(1 + i)^n$ (continued)

I / N	7% .0700	7¼% .0725	7½% .0750	7¾% .0775	8% .0800	8¼% .0825	8½% .0850	8¾% .0875	9% .0900
70	113.98930	134.21796	157.97632	185.86986	218.60610	257.01155	302.05173	354.85277	416.72962
71	121.96855	143.94876	169.82454	200.27477	236.09458	278.21500	327.72612	385.90238	454.23528
72	130.50635	154.38504	182.56138	215.79606	254.98214	301.16773	355.58284	419.66883	495.11644
73	139.64179	165.57795	196.25348	232.52025	275.38071	326.01406	385.80738	456.38985	539.67691
74	149.41671	177.58235	210.97249	250.54056	297.41116	352.91021	418.60100	496.32396	588.24783
75	159.87588	190.45707	226.79542	269.95745	321.20404	382.02530	454.18208	539.75230	641.75230
76	171.06719	204.26520	243.80508	290.87915	346.90036	413.54238	492.78755	586.98061	698.89722
77	183.04189	219.07443	262.09045	313.42228	374.65238	447.65961	534.67448	638.34141	761.79796
78	195.85482	234.95732	281.74723	337.71249	404.62456	484.59152	580.12181	694.19627	830.35976
79	209.56465	251.99172	302.87827	363.88520	436.99452	524.57031	629.43216	754.93844	905.09213
80	224.23418	270.26112	325.59414	392.08630	471.95407	567.84735	682.93388	820.99554	986.55041

I / N	9¼% 0.925	9½% .0950	9¾% .0975	10% .1000	10¼% .1025	10½% .1050	10¾% .1075	11% .1100	11¼% .1125
1	1.09250	1.09500	1.09750	1.10000	1.10250	1.10500	1.10750	1.11000	1.11250
2	1.19356	1.19902	1.20451	1.21000	1.21551	1.22102	1.22656	1.23210	1.23766
3	1.30396	1.31293	1.32195	1.33100	1.34010	1.34923	1.35841	1.36763	1.37689
4	1.42458	1.43766	1.45084	1.46410	1.47746	1.49090	1.50444	1.51807	1.53179
5	1.55635	1.57424	1.59229	1.61051	1.62889	1.64745	1.66617	1.68506	1.70412
6	1.70031	1.72379	1.74754	1.77156	1.79586	1.82043	1.84528	1.87041	1.89583
7	1.85759	1.88755	1.91793	1.94872	1.97993	2.01157	2.04365	2.07616	2.10911
8	2.02942	2.06687	2.10492	2.14359	2.18287	2.22279	2.26334	2.30454	2.34639
9	2.21714	2.26322	2.31015	2.35795	2.40662	2.45618	2.50665	2.55804	2.61036
10	2.42222	2.47823	2.53539	2.59374	2.65330	2.71408	2.77611	2.83942	2.90402
11	2.64628	2.71366	2.78259	2.85312	2.92526	2.99906	3.07455	3.15176	3.23073
12	2.89106	2.97146	3.05390	3.13843	3.22510	3.31396	3.40506	3.49845	3.59418
13	3.15848	3.25374	3.35165	3.45227	3.55567	3.66193	3.77110	3.88328	3.99853
14	3.45064	3.56285	3.67844	3.79750	3.92013	4.04643	4.17650	4.31044	4.44836
15	3.76983	3.90132	4.03708	4.17725	4.32194	4.47130	4.62547	4.78459	4.94880
16	4.11854	4.27195	4.43070	4.59497	4.76494	4.94079	5.12271	5.31089	5.50554
17	4.49950	4.67778	4.86269	5.05447	5.25335	5.45957	5.67340	5.89509	6.12492
18	4.91571	5.12217	5.33681	5.55991	5.79181	6.03283	6.28329	6.54355	6.81397
19	5.37041	5.60878	5.85714	6.11591	6.38547	6.66627	6.95874	7.26334	7.58054
20	5.86717	6.14161	6.42821	6.72750	7.03999	7.36623	7.70681	8.06231	8.43335
21	6.40988	6.72506	7.05497	7.40025	7.76158	8.13969	8.53529	8.94916	9.38210
22	7.00280	7.36394	7.74282	8.14027	8.55715	8.99435	9.45283	9.93357	10.43759
23	7.65056	8.06352	8.49775	8.95430	9.43425	9.93876	10.46901	11.02626	11.61182
24	8.35823	8.82955	9.32628	9.84973	10.40126	10.98233	11.59443	12.23915	12.91815
25	9.13137	9.66836	10.23559	10.83470	11.46739	12.13548	12.84083	13.58546	14.37144
26	9.97602	10.58685	11.23356	11.91817	12.64280	13.40970	14.22122	15.07986	15.98823
27	10.89880	11.59260	12.32883	13.10999	13.93869	14.81772	15.75000	16.73 64	17.78690
28	11.90694	12.69390	13.53090	14.42098	15.36740	16.37358	17.44313	18.57989	19.78793
29	13.00833	13.89942	14.85016	15.86308	16.94256	18.09280	19.31826	20.62368	22.01407
30	14.21161	15.22030	16.29805	17.44939	18.67917	19.99255	21.39498	22.89228	24.49065
31	15.52618	16.66623	17.88711	19.19433	20.59379	22.09176	23.69494	25.41043	27.24585
32	16.96235	18.24952	19.63110	21.11376	22.70465	24.41140	26.24214	28.20558	30.31101
33	18.53137	19.98323	21.54513	23.22514	25.03187	26.97460	29.06317	31.30820	33.72099
34	20.24552	21.88163	23.64578	25.54765	27.59764	29.80693	32.18746	34.75210	37.51460
35	22.11823	23.96039	25.95124	28.10241	30.42640	32.93666	35.64761	38.57483	41.73500
36	24.16416	26.23663	28.48149	30.91265	33.54510	36.39500	39.47973	42.81806	46.43018
37	26.39935	28.72910	31.25843	34.00392	36.98348	40.21648	43.72380	47.52804	51.65358
38	28.84129	31.45837	34.30613	37.40431	40.77428	44.43921	48.42411	52.75612	57.46460
39	31.50911	34.44691	37.65098	41.14474	44.95364	49.10532	53.62970	58.55930	63.92937
40	34.42370	37.71937	41.32195	45.25921	49.56139	54.26138	59.39489	65.00082	71.12142
41	37.60789	41.30271	45.35084	49.78513	54.64143	59.95883	65.77984	72.15091	79.12258
42	41.08662	45.22647	49.77254	54.76364	60.24218	66.25450	72.85118	80.08750	88.02387
43	44.88713	49.52298	54.62536	60.24001	66.41700	73.21122	80.68268	88.89713	97.92655
44	49.03919	54.22766	59.95133	66.26401	73.22474	80.89840	89.35606	98.67581	108.94329
45	53.57531	59.37929	65.79469	72.89041	80.73027	89.39273	98.96184	109.53015	121.19940
46	58.53103	65.02032	72.21175	80.17944	89.00512	98.77897	109.60023	121.57846	134.83433
47	63.94515	71.19725	79.25240	88.19739	98.12814	109.15076	121.38225	134.95209	150.00319
48	69.86007	77.96098	86.97951	97.01712	108.18628	120.61158	134.43084	149.79682	166.87855
49	76.32213	85.36728	95.46001	106.71883	119.27537	133.27580	148.88216	166.27446	185.65238

TABLE I   Values of $(1 + i)^n$ (continued)

N	$9\frac{1}{4}\%$ 0.925	$9\frac{1}{2}\%$ .0950	$9\frac{3}{4}\%$ .0975	10% .1000	$10\frac{1}{4}\%$ .1025	$10\frac{1}{2}\%$ .1050	$10\frac{3}{4}\%$ .1075	11% .1100	$11\frac{1}{4}\%$ .1125
50	83.38192	93.47716	104.76735	117.39071	131.50109	147.27975	164.88699	184.56465	206.53827
51	91.09475	102.35749	114.98217	129.12978	144.97995	162.73308	182.61233	204.86676	229.77382
52	99.52101	112.08145	126.19293	142.04276	159.84039	179.82005	202.24316	227.40210	255.62337
53	108.72670	122.72919	138.49674	156.24703	176.22402	198.70115	223.98429	252.41632	284.38099
54	118.78392	134.38846	152.00016	171.87173	194.28698	219.56476	248.06260	280.18211	316.37385
55	129.77143	147.15536	166.82018	189.05890	214.20139	242.61906	274.72932	311.00214	351.96590
56	141.77528	161.13511	183.08514	207.96478	236.15702	268.09406	304.26272	345.21237	391.56205
57	154.88949	176.44295	200.93594	228.76125	260.36311	296.24393	336.97096	383.18572	435.61278
58	169.21677	193.20502	220.52719	251.63737	287.05032	327.34974	373.19533	425.33614	484.61921
59	184.86931	211.55950	242.02858	276.80110	316.47297	361.72123	413.31382	472.12311	539.13885
60	201.96972	231.65764	265.62637	304.48120	348.91144	399.70196	457.74505	524.05664	599.79196
61	220.65192	253.66512	291.52493	334.92932	384.67485	441.67066	506.95264	581.70286	667.26854
62	241.06222	277.76329	319.94860	368.42224	424.10402	488.04607	561.45004	645.69016	742.33624
63	263.36047	304.15080	351.14358	405.26445	467.57467	539.29090	621.80590	716.71606	825.84904
64	287.72130	333.04512	385.38007	445.79089	515.50105	595.91644	688.65002	795.55482	918.75704
65	314.33552	364.68440	422.95462	490.36997	568.33990	658.48765	762.67989	883.06583	1022.11719
66	343.41155	399.32941	464.19269	539.40695	626.59472	727.62884	844.66796	980.20306	1137.10535
67	375.17711	437.26570	509.45147	593.34763	690.82066	804.02985	935.46975	1088.02538	1265.02966
68	409.88099	478.80593	559.12297	652.68238	761.62975	888.45297	1036.03273	1207.70815	1407.34547
69	447.79497	524.29248	613.63744	717.95060	839.69678	981.74052	1147.40623	1340.55602	1565.67181
70	489.21600	574.10025	673.46708	789.74564	925.76568	1084.82326	1270.75238	1488.01715	1741.80986
71	534.46847	628.63976	739.13010	868.72018	1020.65663	1198.72968	1407.35823	1651.69901	1937.76343
72	583.90679	688.36053	811.19527	955.59218	1125.27391	1324.59627	1558.64922	1833.38586	2155.76175
73	637.91816	753.75476	890.28680	1051.15137	1240.61446	1463.67885	1726.20398	2035.05827	2398.28488
74	696.92558	825.36145	977.08974	1156.26648	1367.77740	1617.36510	1911.77087	2258.91464	2668.09186
75	761.39117	903.77077	1072.35596	1271.89310	1507.97455	1787.18840	2117.28619	2507.39520	2968.25214
76	831.81985	989.62897	1176.91063	1399.08237	1662.54190	1974.84315	2344.89441	2783.20862	3302.18042
77	908.76317	1083.64371	1291.65939	1538.99057	1832.95239	2182.20166	2596.97052	3089.36151	3673.67563
78	992.72375	1186.58983	1417.59615	1692.88959	2020.82996	2411.33279	2876.14481	3429.19122	4086.96405
79	1084.65993	1299.31584	1555.81174	1862.17850	2227.96497	2664.52271	3185.33032	3806.40219	4546.74738
80	1184.99095	1422.75082	1707.50334	2048.39630	2456.33103	1944.29755	3527.75327	4225.10632	5058.25635

TABLE II   *Values of $(1 + i)^n$ for $5\frac{1}{4}\%$ Compounded Daily*

Number of Days, n	Value of $(1 + i)^n$	n	$(1 + i)^n$	n	$(1 + i)^n$	n	$(1 + i)^n$
1	1.000143836	57	1.008231737	113	1.016385042	169	1.024604282
2	1.000287692	58	1.008376756	114	1.016531235	170	1.024751656
3	1.000431569	59	1.008521797	115	1.016677448	171	1.024899052
4	1.000575467	60	1.008666858	116	1.016823683	172	1.025046469
5	1.000719385	61	1.008811940	117	1.016969938	173	1.025193907
6	1.000863324	62	1.008957043	118	1.017116215	174	1.025341367
7	1.001007284	63	1.009102167	119	1.017262512	175	1.025488847
8	1.001151264	64	1.009247312	120	1.017408831	176	1.025636349
9	1.001295266	65	1.009392478	121	1.017555170	177	1.025783872
10	1.001439288	66	1.009537665	122	1.017701531	178	1.025931416
11	1.001583330	67	1.009682872	123	1.017847913	179	1.026078982
12	1.001727394	68	1.009828100	124	1.017994315	180	1.026226569
13	1.001871478	69	1.009973350	125	1.018140739	181	1.026374177
14	1.002015582	70	1.010118620	126	1.018287184	182	1.026521806
15	1.002159708	71	1.010263911	127	1.018433650	183	1.026669456
16	1.002303854	72	1.010409223	128	1.018580137	184	1.026817128
17	1.002448021	73	1.010554556	129	1.018726645	185	1.026964820
18	1.002592209	74	1.010699909	130	1.018873174	186	1.027112535
19	1.002736417	75	1.010845284	131	1.019019725	187	1.027260270
20	1.002880647	76	1.010990679	132	1.019166296	188	1.027408027
21	1.003024897	77	1.011136096	133	1.019312888	189	1.027555804
22	1.003169167	78	1.011281533	134	1.019459502	190	1.027703604
23	1.003313459	79	1.011426992	135	1.019606137	191	1.027851424
24	1.003457771	80	1.011572471	136	1.019752792	192	1.027999266
25	1.003602104	81	1.011717971	137	1.019899469	193	1.028147129
26	1.003746458	82	1.011863492	138	1.020046167	194	1.028295013
27	1.003890832	83	1.012009034	139	1.020192886	195	1.028442918
28	1.004035227	84	1.012154597	140	1.020339626	196	1.028590845
29	1.004179643	85	1.012300181	141	1.020486387	197	1.028738793
30	1.004324080	86	1.012445786	142	1.020633169	198	1.028886762
31	1.004468538	87	1.012591412	143	1.020779973	199	1.029034753
32	1.004613016	88	1.012737058	144	1.020926797	200	1.029182765
33	1.004757515	89	1.012882726	145	1.021073643	201	1.029330798
34	1.004902035	90	1.013028415	146	1.021220510	202	1.029478852
35	1.005046576	91	1.013174124	147	1.021367398	203	1.029626928
36	1.005191137	92	1.013319855	148	1.021514307	204	1.029775025
37	1.005335720	93	1.013465606	149	1.021661237	205	1.029923143
38	1.005480323	94	1.013611379	150	1.021808188	206	1.030071283
39	1.005624947	95	1.013757172	151	1.021955160	207	1.030219444
40	1.005769591	96	1.013902986	152	1.022102154	208	1.030367626
41	1.005914257	97	1.014048822	153	1.022249169	209	1.030515830
42	1.006058943	98	1.014194678	154	1.022396205	210	1.030664054
43	1.006203650	99	1.014340555	155	1.022543262	211	1.030812301
44	1.006348378	100	1.014486454	156	1.022690340	212	1.030960568
45	1.006493127	101	1.014632373	157	1.022837439	213	1.031108857
46	1.006637896	102	1.014778313	158	1.022984559	214	1.031257167
47	1.006782687	103	1.014924275	159	1.023131701	215	1.031405499
48	1.006927498	104	1.015070257	160	1.023278864	216	1.031553852
49	1.007072330	105	1.015216260	161	1.023426048	217	1.031702226
50	1.007217183	106	1.015362284	162	1.023573253	218	1.031850621
51	1.007362057	107	1.015508330	163	1.023720479	219	1.031999038
52	1.007506951	108	1.015654396	164	1.023867727	220	1.032147476
53	1.007651867	109	1.015800483	165	1.024014995	221	1.032295936
54	1.007796803	110	1.015946591	166	1.024162285	222	1.032444417
55	1.007941760	111	1.016092721	167	1.024309596	223	1.032592919
56	1.008086738	112	1.016238871	168	1.024456928	224	1.032741443

TABLE II   *Values of* $(1 + i)^n$ *for* $5\frac{1}{4}$% *Compounded Daily* (*continued*)

Number of Days, n	Value of $(1 + i)^n$	n	$(1 + i)^n$	n	$(1 + i)^n$	n	$(1 + i)^n$
225	1.032889988	261	1.038251862	297	1.043641570	333	1.049059256
226	1.033038554	262	1.038401199	298	1.043791683	334	1.049210149
227	1.033187142	263	1.038550558	299	1.043941817	335	1.049361062
228	1.033335751	264	1.038699939	300	1.044091973	336	1.049511998
229	1.033484382	265	1.038849341	301	1.044242151	337	1.049662955
230	1.033633034	266	1.038998764	302	1.044392350	338	1.049813934
231	1.033781707	267	1.039148210	303	1.044542571	339	1.049964935
232	1.033930401	268	1.039297676	304	1.044692813	340	1.050115957
233	1.034079117	269	1.039447164	305	1.044843077	341	1.050267001
234	1.034227855	270	1.039596674	306	1.044993363	342	1.050418067
235	1.034376614	271	1.039746205	307	1.045143670	343	1.050569154
236	1.034525394	272	1.039895757	308	1.045293999	344	1.050720264
237	1.034674195	273	1.040045331	309	1.045444350	345	1.050871395
238	1.034823018	274	1.040194927	310	1.045594722	346	1.051022548
239	1.034971863	275	1.040344544	311	1.045745115	347	1.051173722
240	1.035120729	276	1.040494182	312	1.045895531	348	1.051324918
241	1.035269616	277	1.040643843	313	1.046045968	349	1.051476136
242	1.035418524	278	1.040793524	314	1.046196426	350	1.051627376
243	1.035567454	279	1.040943228	315	1.046346907	351	1.051778637
244	1.035716406	280	1.041092952	316	1.046497409	352	1.051929920
245	1.035865379	281	1.041242698	317	1.046647932	353	1.052081226
246	1.036014373	282	1.041392466	318	1.046798478	354	1.052232552
247	1.036163389	283	1.041542256	319	1.046949044	355	1.052383901
248	1.036312426	284	1.041692066	320	1.047099633	356	1.052535271
249	1.036461485	285	1.041841899	321	1.047250243	357	1.052686663
250	1.036610565	286	1.041991753	322	1.047400875	358	1.052838077
251	1.036759666	287	1.042141628	323	1.047551529	359	1.052989512
252	1.036908790	288	1.042291526	324	1.047702204	360	1.053140970
253	1.037057934	289	1.042441444	325	1.047852901	361	1.053292449
254	1.037207100	290	1.042591384	326	1.048003619	362	1.053443950
255	1.037356287	291	1.042741346	327	1.048154360	363	1.053595473
256	1.037505496	292	1.042891329	328	1.048305122	364	1.053747017
257	1.037654726	293	1.043041334	329	1.048455905	365	1.053898584
258	1.037803978	294	1.043191361	330	1.048606710		
259	1.037953251	295	1.043341409	331	1.048757538		
260	1.038102546	296	1.043491478	332	1.048908386		

TABLE III   Values of e^{st} (s = stated rate, t = years)

st	e^{st}	st	e^{st}	st	e^{st}
0.00	1.00000				
0.01	1.01005	0.51	1.66520	1.01	2.74560
0.02	1.02020	0.52	1.68203	1.02	2.77319
0.03	1.03045	0.53	1.69893	1.03	2.80107
0.04	1.04081	0.54	1.71601	1.04	2.82922
0.05	1.05127	0.55	1.73325	1.05	2.85765
0.06	1.06184	0.56	1.75067	1.06	2.88637
0.07	1.07251	0.57	1.76827	1.07	2.91538
0.08	1.08329	0.58	1.78604	1.08	2.94468
0.09	1.09417	0.59	1.80399	1.09	2.97427
0.10	1.10517	0.60	1.82212	1.10	3.00417
0.11	1.11628	0.61	1.84043	1.11	3.03436
0.12	1.12750	0.62	1.85893	1.12	3.06485
0.13	1.13883	0.63	1.87761	1.13	3.09566
0.14	1.15027	0.64	1.89648	1.14	3.12677
0.15	1.16183	0.65	1.91554	1.15	3.15819
0.16	1.17351	0.66	1.93479	1.16	3.18993
0.17	1.18530	0.67	1.95424	1.17	3.22199
0.18	1.19722	0.68	1.97388	1.18	3.25437
0.19	1.20925	0.69	1.99372	1.19	3.28708
0.20	1.22140	0.70	2.01375	1.20	3.32012
0.21	1.23368	0.71	2.03399	1.21	3.35348
0.22	1.24608	0.72	2.05443	1.22	3.38719
0.23	1.25860	0.73	2.07508	1.23	3.42123
0.24	1.27125	0.74	2.09594	1.24	3.45561
0.25	1.28403	0.75	2.11700	1.25	3.49034
0.26	1.29693	0.76	2.13828	1.26	3.52542
0.27	1.30996	0.77	2.15977	1.27	3.56085
0.28	1.32313	0.78	2.18147	1.28	3.59664
0.29	1.33643	0.79	2.20340	1.29	3.63279
0.30	1.34986	0.80	2.22554	1.30	3.66930
0.31	1.36343	0.81	2.24791	1.31	3.70617
0.32	1.37713	0.82	2.27050	1.32	3.74342
0.33	1.39097	0.83	2.29332	1.33	3.78104
0.34	1.40495	0.84	2.31637	1.34	3.81904
0.35	1.41907	0.85	2.33965	1.35	3.85742
0.36	1.43333	0.86	2.36316	1.36	3.89619
0.37	1.44773	0.87	2.38691	1.37	3.93535
0.38	1.46228	0.88	2.41090	1.38	3.97490
0.39	1.47698	0.89	2.43513	1.39	4.01485
0.40	1.49182	0.90	2.45960	1.40	4.05520
0.41	1.50682	0.91	2.48432	1.41	4.09595
0.42	1.52196	0.92	2.50929	1.42	4.13712
0.43	1.53726	0.93	2.53451	1.43	4.17870
0.44	1.55271	0.94	2.55998	1.44	4.22069
0.45	1.56831	0.95	2.58571	1.45	4.26311
0.46	1.58407	0.96	2.61170	1.46	4.30596
0.47	1.59999	0.97	2.63794	1.47	4.34923
0.48	1.61607	0.98	2.66446	1.48	4.39294
0.49	1.63232	0.99	2.69123	1.49	4.43709
0.50	1.64872	1.00	2.71828	1.50	4.48169

TABLE IV   Payment Needed Each Period to Amortize a Debt of 1

Values of $\left[\dfrac{i(1 + i)^n}{(1 + i)^n - 1} \right]$

n	$\frac{1}{4}\%$	$\frac{1}{2}\%$	$\frac{3}{4}\%$	1%	$1\frac{1}{4}\%$
1	1.002500	1.005000	1.007500	1.010000	1.012500
2	0.501876	0.503753	0.505632	0.507512	0.509394
3	0.335002	0.336672	0.338346	0.340022	0.341701
4	0.251565	0.253133	0.254705	0.256281	0.257861
5	0.201503	0.203010	0.204522	0.206040	0.207562
6	0.168128	0.169595	0.171069	0.172548	0.174034
7	0.144289	0.145729	0.147175	0.148628	0.150089
8	0.126410	0.127829	0.129256	0.130690	0.132133
9	0.112505	0.113907	0.115319	0.116740	0.118171
10	0.101380	0.102771	0.104171	0.105582	0.107003
11	0.092278	0.093659	0.095051	0.096454	0.097868
12	0.084694	0.086066	0.087451	0.088849	0.090258
13	0.078276	0.079642	0.081022	0.082415	0.083821
14	0.072775	0.074136	0.075511	0.076901	0.078305
15	0.068008	0.069364	0.070736	0.072124	0.073526
16	0.063836	0.065189	0.066559	0.067945	0.069347
17	0.060156	0.061506	0.062873	0.064258	0.065660
18	0.056884	0.058232	0.059598	0.060982	0.062385
19	0.053957	0.055303	0.056667	0.058052	0.059455
20	0.051323	0.052666	0.054031	0.055415	0.056820
21	0.048939	0.050282	0.051645	0.053031	0.054437
22	0.046773	0.048114	0.049477	0.050864	0.052272
23	0.044795	0.046135	0.047498	0.048886	0.050297
24	0.042981	0.044321	0.045685	0.047073	0.048487
25	0.041313	0.042652	0.044016	0.045407	0.046822
26	0.039773	0.041112	0.042477	0.043869	0.045287
27	0.038347	0.039686	0.041052	0.042446	0.043867
28	0.037023	0.038362	0.039729	0.041124	0.042549
29	0.035791	0.037129	0.038497	0.039895	0.041322
30	0.034641	0.035979	0.037348	0.038748	0.040179
31	0.033565	0.034903	0.036274	0.037676	0.039109
32	0.032556	0.033895	0.035266	0.036671	0.038108
33	0.031608	0.032947	0.034320	0.035727	0.037168
34	0.030716	0.032056	0.033431	0.034840	0.036284
35	0.029875	0.031215	0.032592	0.034004	0.035451
36	0.029081	0.030422	0.031800	0.033214	0.034665
37	0.028330	0.029671	0.031051	0.032468	0.033923
38	0.027618	0.028960	0.030342	0.031761	0.033220
39	0.026943	0.028286	0.029669	0.031092	0.032554
40	0.026302	0.027646	0.029030	0.030456	0.031921
41	0.025692	0.027036	0.028423	0.029851	0.031321
42	0.025111	0.026456	0.027845	0.029276	0.030749
43	0.024557	0.025903	0.027293	0.028727	0.030205
44	0.024029	0.025375	0.026768	0.028204	0.029686
45	0.023523	0.024871	0.026265	0.027705	0.029190
46	0.023040	0.024389	0.025785	0.027228	0.028717
47	0.022578	0.023927	0.025325	0.026771	0.028264
48	0.022134	0.023485	0.024885	0.026334	0.027831
49	0.021709	0.023061	0.024463	0.025915	0.027416
50	0.021301	0.022654	0.024058	0.025513	0.027018
51	0.020909	0.022263	0.023669	0.025127	0.026636
52	0.020532	0.021887	0.023295	0.024756	0.026269
53	0.020169	0.021525	0.022935	0.024400	0.025917
54	0.019820	0.021177	0.022589	0.024057	0.025578
55	0.019483	0.020841	0.022256	0.023726	0.025251
56	0.019159	0.020518	0.021935	0.023408	0.024937
57	0.018845	0.020206	0.021625	0.023102	0.024635

TABLE IV **Payment Needed Each Period to Amortize a Debt of 1 (continued)**

$$\text{Values of } \left[\frac{i(1 + i)^n}{(1 + i)^n - 1} \right]$$

n	$\frac{1}{4}\%$	$\frac{1}{2}\%$	$\frac{3}{4}\%$	1%	$1\frac{1}{4}\%$
58	0.018543	0.019905	0.021326	0.022806	0.024343
59	0.018251	0.019614	0.021037	0.022520	0.024062
60	0.017969	0.019333	0.020758	0.022244	0.023790
61	0.017696	0.019061	0.020489	0.021978	0.023528
62	0.017431	0.018798	0.020228	0.021720	0.023274
63	0.017176	0.018543	0.019976	0.021471	0.023029
64	0.016928	0.018297	0.019731	0.021230	0.022792
65	0.016688	0.018058	0.019495	0.020997	0.022563
66	0.016455	0.017826	0.019265	0.020771	0.022341
67	0.016229	0.017602	0.019043	0.020551	0.022126
68	0.016010	0.017384	0.018827	0.020339	0.021917
69	0.015797	0.017172	0.018618	0.020133	0.021715
70	0.015590	0.016967	0.018415	0.019933	0.021519
71	0.015389	0.016767	0.018217	0.019739	0.021329
72	0.015194	0.016573	0.018026	0.019550	0.021145
73	0.015004	0.016384	0.017839	0.019367	0.020966
74	0.014819	0.016201	0.017658	0.019189	0.020792
75	0.014639	0.016022	0.017482	0.019016	0.020623
76	0.014464	0.015848	0.017310	0.018848	0.020459
77	0.014293	0.015679	0.017143	0.018684	0.020300
78	0.014127	0.015514	0.016981	0.018525	0.020144
79	0.013965	0.015354	0.016822	0.018370	0.019993
80	0.013807	0.015197	0.016668	0.018219	0.019847

n	$1\frac{1}{2}\%$	$1\frac{3}{4}\%$	2%	$2\frac{1}{2}\%$	3%
1	1.015000	1.017500	1.020000	1.025000	1.030000
2	0.511278	0.513163	0.515050	0.518827	0.522611
3	0.343383	0.345067	0.346755	0.350137	0.353530
4	0.259445	0.261032	0.262624	0.265818	0.269027
5	0.209089	0.210621	0.212158	0.215247	0.218355
6	0.175525	0.177023	0.178526	0.181550	0.184598
7	0.151556	0.153031	0.154512	0.157495	0.160506
8	0.133584	0.135043	0.136510	0.139467	0.142456
9	0.119610	0.121058	0.122515	0.125457	0.128434
10	0.108434	0.109875	0.111327	0.114259	0.117231
11	0.099194	0.100730	0.102178	0.105106	0.108077
12	0.091680	0.093114	0.094560	0.097487	0.100462
13	0.085240	0.086673	0.088118	0.091048	0.094030
14	0.079723	0.081156	0.082602	0.085537	0.088526
15	0.074944	0.076377	0.077825	0.080766	0.083767
16	0.070765	0.072200	0.073650	0.076599	0.079611
17	0.067080	0.068516	0.069970	0.072928	0.075953
18	0.063806	0.065245	0.066702	0.069670	0.072709
19	0.060878	0.062321	0.063782	0.066761	0.069814
20	0.058246	0.059691	0.061157	0.064147	0.067216
21	0.055865	0.057315	0.058785	0.061787	0.064872
22	0.053703	0.055156	0.056631	0.059647	0.062747
23	0.051731	0.053188	0.054668	0.057696	0.060814
24	0.049924	0.051386	0.052871	0.055913	0.059047
25	0.048263	0.049730	0.051220	0.054276	0.057428
26	0.046732	0.048203	0.049699	0.052769	0.055938
27	0.045315	0.046791	0.048293	0.051377	0.054564
28	0.044001	0.045482	0.046990	0.050088	0.053293
29	0.042779	0.044264	0.045778	0.048891	0.052115
30	0.041639	0.043130	0.044650	0.047778	0.051019

TABLE IV   *Payment Needed Each Period to Amortize a Debt of 1 (continued)*

$$\text{Values of} \left[\frac{i(1 + i)^n}{(1 + i)^n - 1} \right]$$

n	$1\frac{1}{2}\%$	$1\frac{3}{4}\%$	2%	$2\frac{1}{2}\%$	3%
31	0.040574	0.042070	0.043596	0.046739	0.049999
32	0.039577	0.041078	0.042611	0.045768	0.049047
33	0.038641	0.040148	0.041687	0.044859	0.048156
34	0.037762	0.039274	0.040819	0.044007	0.047322
35	0.036934	0.038451	0.040002	0.043206	0.046539
36	0.036152	0.037675	0.039233	0.042452	0.045804
37	0.035414	0.036943	0.038507	0.041741	0.045112
38	0.034716	0.036250	0.037821	0.041070	0.044459
39	0.034055	0.035594	0.037171	0.040436	0.043844
40	0.033427	0.034972	0.036556	0.039836	0.043262
41	0.032831	0.034382	0.035972	0.039268	0.042712
42	0.032264	0.033821	0.035417	0.038729	0.042192
43	0.031725	0.033287	0.034890	0.038217	0.042698
44	0.031210	0.032778	0.034388	0.037730	0.041230
45	0.030720	0.032293	0.033910	0.037368	0.040785
46	0.030251	0.031830	0.033453	0.036827	0.040363
47	0.029803	0.031388	0.033018	0.036407	0.039961
48	0.029375	0.030966	0.032602	0.036006	0.039578
49	0.028965	0.030561	0.032204	0.035623	0.039213
50	0.028572	0.030174	0.031823	0.035258	0.038865
51	0.028195	0.029803	0.031459	0.034909	0.038534
52	0.027833	0.029447	0.031109	0.034574	0.038217
53	0.027485	0.029105	0.030774	0.034254	0.037915
54	0.027151	0.028777	0.030452	0.033948	0.037626
55	0.026830	0.028461	0.030143	0.033654	0.037349
56	0.026521	0.028158	0.029847	0.033372	0.037084
57	0.026223	0.027866	0.029561	0.033102	0.036831
58	0.025937	0.027585	0.029287	0.032842	0.036588
59	0.025660	0.027314	0.025022	0.032593	0.036356
60	0.025393	0.027053	0.028768	0.032353	0.036133
61	0.025136	0.026802	0.028523	0.032123	0.035919
62	0.024888	0.026559	0.028286	0.031901	0.035714
63	0.024647	0.026325	0.028058	0.031688	0.035517
64	0.024415	0.026098	0.027839	0.031482	0.035328
65	0.024191	0.025880	0.027626	0.031285	0.035146
66	0.023974	0.025668	0.027421	0.031094	0.034971
67	0.023764	0.025464	0.027223	0.030910	0.034803
68	0.023560	0.025266	0.027032	0.030733	0.034642
69	0.023363	0.025075	0.026847	0.030562	0.034486
70	0.023172	0.024889	0.026668	0.030397	0.034337
71	0.022987	0.024710	0.026494	0.030238	0.034193
72	0.022808	0.024536	0.026327	0.030084	0.034054
73	0.022634	0.024367	0.026165	0.029936	0.033921
74	0.022465	0.024204	0.026607	0.029792	0.033792
75	0.022301	0.024046	0.025855	0.029654	0.033668
76	0.022141	0.023892	0.025708	0.029520	0.033548
77	0.021987	0.023743	0.025564	0.029390	0.033433
78	0.021836	0.023598	0.025426	0.029265	0.033322
79	0.021690	0.023457	0.025291	0.029143	0.033215
80	0.021548	0.023321	0.025161	0.029026	0.033112

n	$3\frac{1}{2}\%$	4%	$4\frac{1}{2}\%$	5%	$5\frac{1}{2}\%$
1	1.035000	1.040000	1.045000	1.050000	1.055000
2	0.526401	0.530196	0.533998	0.537805	0.541618
3	0.356934	0.360349	0.363773	0.367209	0.370654
4	0.272251	0.275490	0.278744	0.292012	0.285294

TABLE IV   *Payment Needed Each Period to Amortize a Debt of 1 (continued)*

Values of $\left[\dfrac{i(1+i)^n}{(1+i)^n - 1}\right]$

n	$3\frac{1}{2}\%$	4%	$4\frac{1}{2}\%$	5%	$5\frac{1}{2}\%$
5	0.221481	0.224627	0.227792	0.230975	0.234176
6	0.187668	0.190762	0.193878	0.197017	0.200179
7	0.163544	0.166610	0.169701	0.172820	0.175964
8	0.145477	0.148528	0.151610	0.154722	0.157864
9	0.131446	0.134493	0.137574	0.140690	0.143839
10	0.120241	0.123291	0.126379	0.129505	0.132668
11	0.111092	0.114149	0.117248	0.120389	0.123571
12	0.103484	0.106552	0.109666	0.112825	0.116029
13	0.097062	0.100144	0.103275	0.106456	0.109684
14	0.091571	0.094669	0.097820	0.101024	0.104279
15	0.086825	0.089941	0.093114	0.096342	0.099626
16	0.082685	0.085820	0.089015	0.092270	0.095583
17	0.079043	0.082199	0.085418	0.088699	0.092042
18	0.075817	0.078993	0.082237	0.085546	0.088920
19	0.072940	0.076139	0.079407	0.082745	0.086150
20	0.070361	0.073582	0.076876	0.080243	0.083679
21	0.068037	0.071280	0.074601	0.077996	0.081465
22	0.065932	0.069199	0.072546	0.075971	0.079471
23	0.064019	0.067309	0.070682	0.074137	0.077670
24	0.062273	0.065587	0.068987	0.072471	0.076036
25	0.060674	0.064012	0.067439	0.070952	0.074549
26	0.059205	0.062567	0.066021	0.069564	0.073193
27	0.057852	0.061239	0.064719	0.068292	0.071952
28	0.056603	0.060013	0.063521	0.067123	0.070814
29	0.055445	0.058880	0.062415	0.066046	0.069769
30	0.054371	0.057830	0.061392	0.065051	0.068805
31	0.053372	0.056855	0.060443	0.064132	0.067917
32	0.052442	0.055949	0.059563	0.063280	0.067095
33	0.051572	0.055104	0.058745	0.062490	0.066335
34	0.050760	0.054315	0.057982	0.061755	0.065630
35	0.049998	0.053577	0.057270	0.061072	0.064975
36	0.049284	0.052887	0.056606	0.060434	0.064366
37	0.048613	0.052240	0.055984	0.059840	0.063800
38	0.047982	0.051632	0.055402	0.059284	0.063272
39	0.047388	0.051061	0.054856	0.058765	0.062780
40	0.046827	0.050523	0.054343	0.058278	0.062320
41	0.046298	0.050017	0.053862	0.057822	0.061891
42	0.045798	0.049540	0.053409	0.057395	0.061489
43	0.045325	0.049090	0.052982	0.056993	0.061113
44	0.044878	0.048665	0.052581	0.056616	0.060761
45	0.044453	0.048262	0.052202	0.056262	0.060431
46	0.044051	0.047882	0.051845	0.055928	0.060122
47	0.043669	0.047522	0.051507	0.055614	0.059831
48	0.043306	0.047181	0.051189	0.055318	0.059559
49	0.042962	0.046857	0.050887	0.055040	0.059302
50	0.042634	0.046550	0.050602	0.054777	0.059061
51	0.042322	0.046259	0.050332	0.054529	0.058835
52	0.042024	0.045982	0.050077	0.054294	0.058622
53	0.041741	0.045719	0.049835	0.054073	0.058421
54	0.041471	0.045469	0.049605	0.053864	0.058232
55	0.041213	0.045231	0.049388	0.052667	0.058055
56	0.040967	0.045005	0.049181	0.053480	0.057887
57	0.040732	0.044789	0.048985	0.053303	0.057729
58	0.040508	0.044584	0.048799	0.053136	0.057580
59	0.040294	0.044388	0.048622	0.052978	0.057440
60	0.040089	0.044202	0.048454	0.052828	0.057307

TABLE IV   *Payment Needed Each Period to Amortize a Debt of 1 (continued)*

Values of $\left[\dfrac{i(1 + i)^n}{(1 + i)^n - 1}\right]$

n	$3\frac{1}{2}\%$	4%	$4\frac{1}{2}\%$	5%	$5\frac{1}{2}\%$
61	0.039892	0.044024	0.048295	0.052686	0.057182
62	0.039705	0.043854	0.048143	0.052552	0.057064
63	0.039525	0.043692	0.047998	0.052424	0.056953
64	0.039353	0.043538	0.047861	0.052304	0.056847
65	0.039188	0.043390	0.047730	0.052189	0.056748
66	0.039030	0.043249	0.047606	0.052081	0.056654
67	0.038879	0.043115	0.047488	0.051978	0.056565
68	0.038734	0.042986	0.047375	0.051880	0.056482
69	0.038595	0.042863	0.047267	0.051787	0.056402
70	0.038461	0.042745	0.047165	0.051699	0.056328
71	0.038333	0.042633	0.047068	0.051616	0.056257
72	0.038210	0.042525	0.046975	0.051536	0.056190
73	0.038092	0.042422	0.046886	0.051461	0.056127
74	0.037978	0.042323	0.046802	0.051390	0.056067
75	0.037869	0.042229	0.046721	0.051322	0.056010
76	0.037765	0.042139	0.046644	0.051257	0.055956
77	0.037664	0.042052	0.046571	0.051196	0.055906
78	0.037567	0.041969	0.046501	0.051138	0.055858
79	0.037474	0.041890	0.046434	0.051082	0.055812
80	0.037385	0.041814	0.046371	0.051030	0.055769

n	6%	$6\frac{1}{2}\%$	7%	$7\frac{1}{2}\%$	8%
1	1.060000	1.065000	1.070000	1.075000	1.080000
2	0.545437	0.549262	0.553092	0.556928	0.560769
3	0.374110	0.377576	0.381052	0.384538	0.388034
4	0.288591	0.291903	0.295228	0.298568	0.301921
5	0.237396	0.240635	0.243891	0.247165	0.250456
6	0.203363	0.206568	0.209796	0.213045	0.216315
7	0.179135	0.182331	0.185553	0.188800	0.192072
8	0.161036	0.164237	0.167468	0,170727	0.174015
9	0.147022	0.150238	0.153486	0.156767	0.160080
10	0.135868	0.139105	0.142378	0.145686	0.149029
11	0.126793	0.130055	0.133357	0.136697	0.140076
12	0.119277	0.122568	0.125902	0.129278	0.132695
13	0.112960	0.116283	0.119651	0.123064	0.126522
14	0.107585	0.110940	0.114345	0.117797	0.121297
15	0.102963	0.106353	0.109795	0.113287	0.116830
16	0.098952	0.102378	0.105858	0.109391	0.112977
17	0.095445	0.098906	0.102425	0.106000	0.109629
18	0.092357	0.095855	0.099413	0.103029	0.106702
19	0.089621	0.093256	0.096753	0.100411	0.104128
20	0.087185	0.090756	0.094393	0.098092	0.101852
21	0.085005	0.088613	0.092289	0.096029	0.099832
22	0.083046	0.086691	0.090406	0.094187	0.098032
23	0.081278	0.084961	0.088714	0.092535	0.096422
24	0.079679	0.083398	0.087189	0.091050	0.094978
25	0.078227	0.081981	0.085811	0.089711	0.093679
26	0.076904	0.080695	0.084561	0.088500	0.092507
27	0.075697	0.079523	0.083426	0.087402	0.091448
28	0.074593	0.078453	0.082392	0.086405	0.090489
29	0.073580	0.077474	0.081449	0.085498	0.089619
30	0.072649	0.076577	0.080586	0.084671	0.088827
31	0.071792	0.075754	0.079797	0.083916	0.088107
32	0.071002	0.074997	0.079073	0.083226	0.087451
33	0.070273	0.074299	0.078408	0.082594	0.086852
34	0.069598	0.073656	0.077797	0.082015	0.086304

TABLE IV   **Payment Needed Each Period to Amortize a Debt of 1 (continued)**

$$\text{Values of } \left[\frac{i(1-i)^n}{(1+i)^n - 1} \right]$$

n	6%	$6\frac{1}{2}\%$	7%	$7\frac{1}{2}\%$	8%
35	0.068974	0.073062	0.077234	0.081483	1.085803
36	0.068395	0.072513	0.076715	0.080994	0.085345
37	0.067857	0.072005	0.076237	0.080545	0.084924
38	0.067358	0.071535	0.075795	0.080132	0.084539
39	0.066894	0.071099	0.075387	0.079751	0.084185
40	0.066462	0.070694	0.075009	0.079400	0.083860
41	0.066059	0.070318	0.074660	0.079077	0.083561
42	0.065683	0.069968	0.074336	0.078778	0.083287
43	0.065333	0.069644	0.074036	0.078502	0.083034
44	0.065006	0.069341	0.073758	0.078247	0.082802
45	0.064700	0.069060	0.073500	0.078011	0.082587
46	0.064415	0.068797	0.073260	0.077794	0.082390
47	0.064148	0.068553	0.073037	0.077592	0.082208
48	0.063898	0.068325	0.072831	0.077405	0.082040
49	0.063664	0.068112	0.072639	0.077232	0.081886
50	0.063444	0.067914	0.072460	0.077072	0.081743
51	0.063239	0.067729	0.072294	0.076924	0.081611
52	0.063046	0.067556	0.072139	0.076787	0.081490
53	0.062866	0.067394	0.071995	0.076659	0.081377
54	0.062696	0.067243	0.071861	0.076541	0.081274
55	0.062537	0.067101	0.071736	0.076432	0.081178
56	0.062388	0.066969	0.071620	0.076330	0.081090
57	0.062247	0.066846	0.071512	0.076236	0.081008
58	0.062116	0.066730	0.071411	0.076148	0.080932
59	0.061992	0.066622	0.071317	0.076067	0.080862
60	0.061876	0.066520	0.071229	0.075991	0.080798
61	0.061766	0.066426	0.071147	0.075921	0.080738
62	0.061664	0.066337	0.071071	0.075856	0.080683
63	0.061567	0.066254	0.071000	0.075796	0.080632
64	0.061476	0.066176	0.070934	0.075740	0.080585
65	0.061391	0.066103	0.070872	0.075688	0.080541
66	0.061310	0.066034	0.070814	0.075639	0.080501
67	0.061235	0.065970	0.070760	0.075594	0.080464
68	0.061163	0.065910	0.070710	0.075553	0.080429
69	0.061096	0.065857	0.070663	0.075514	0.080397
70	0.061033	0.065801	0.070620	0.075478	0.080368
71	0.060974	0.065752	0.070579	0.075444	0.080340
72	0.060918	0.065705	0.070541	0.075413	0.080315
73	0.060865	0.065662	0.070505	0.075384	0.080292
74	0.060815	0.065621	0.070472	0.075357	0.080270
75	0.060769	0.065583	0.070441	0.075332	0.080250
76	0.060725	0.065547	0.070412	0.075300	0.080231
77	0.060683	0.065513	0.070385	0.075287	0.080214
78	0.060644	0.065482	0.070359	0.075267	0.080198
79	0.060607	0.065452	0.070336	0.075248	0.080183
80	0.060573	0.065424	0.070314	0.075231	0.080170

From *Finite Mathematics with Applications to Business and the Social Sciences, by* R. E. Wheeler and W. D. Peeples. Copyright © 1981 by Wadsworth, Inc. Reprinted by permission of Brooks/Cole Publishing Company, Monterey, California 93940.

TABLE V

Payment Needed Each Period for a Sinking Fund to Amount to 1

Values of $\left[\dfrac{i}{(1+i)^n - 1}\right]$

n	$\frac{1}{4}\%$	$\frac{1}{2}\%$	$\frac{3}{4}\%$	1%	$1\frac{1}{4}\%$
1	1.000000	1.000000	1.000000	1.000000	1.000000
2	0.499376	0.498753	0.498132	0.497512	0.496894
3	0.332502	0.331672	0.330846	0.330022	0.329201
4	0.249065	0.248133	0.247205	0.246281	0.245361
5	0.199003	0.198010	0.197022	0.196040	0.195062
6	0.165628	0.164595	0.163569	0.162548	0.161534
7	0.141789	0.140729	0.139675	0.138628	0.137589
8	0.123910	0.122829	0.121756	0.120690	0.119633
9	0.110005	0.108907	0.107819	0.106740	0.105671
10	0.098880	0.097771	0.096671	0.095582	0.094503
11	0.089778	0.088659	0.087551	0.086454	0.085368
12	0.082194	0.081066	0.079951	0.078849	0.077758
13	0.075776	0.074642	0.073522	0.072415	0.071321
14	0.070275	0.069136	0.068011	0.066901	0.065805
15	0.065508	0.064364	0.063236	0.062124	0.061026
16	0.061336	0.060189	0.059059	0.057945	0.056847
17	0.057656	0.056506	0.055373	0.054258	0.053160
18	0.054384	0.053232	0.052098	0.050982	0.049885
19	0.051457	0.050303	0.049167	0.048052	0.046955
20	0.048823	0.047666	0.046531	0.045415	0.044320
21	0.046439	0.045282	0.044145	0.043031	0.041937
22	0.044273	0.043114	0.041977	0.040864	0.039772
23	0.042295	0.041135	0.039998	0.038886	0.037797
24	0.040481	0.039321	0.038185	0.037073	0.035987
25	0.038813	0.037652	0.036516	0.035407	0.034322
26	0.037273	0.036112	0.034977	0.033869	0.032787
27	0.035847	0.034686	0.033552	0.032446	0.031367
28	0.034523	0.033362	0.032229	0.031124	0.030049
29	0.033291	0.032129	0.030997	0.029895	0.028822
30	0.032141	0.030979	0.029848	0.028748	0.027679
31	0.031065	0.029903	0.028774	0.027676	0.026609
32	0.030056	0.028895	0.027766	0.026671	0.025608
33	0.029108	0.027947	0.026820	0.025727	0.024668
34	0.028216	0.027056	0.025931	0.024840	0.023784
35	0.027375	0.026215	0.025092	0.024004	0.022951
36	0.026581	0.025422	0.024300	0.023214	0.022165
37	0.025830	0.024671	0.023551	0.022468	0.021423
38	0.025118	0.023960	0.022842	0.021761	0.020720
39	0.024443	0.023286	0.022169	0.021092	0.020054
40	0.023802	0.022646	0.021530	0.020456	0.019421
41	0.023192	0.022036	0.020923	0.019851	0.018821
42	0.022611	0.021456	0.020345	0.019276	0.018249
43	0.022057	0.020903	0.019793	0.018727	0.017705
44	0.021529	0.020375	0.019268	0.018204	0.017186
45	0.021023	0.018971	0.018765	0.017705	0.016690
46	0.020540	0.019389	0.018285	0.017228	0.016217
47	0.020078	0.018927	0.017825	0.016771	0.015764
48	0.019634	0.018485	0.017385	0.016334	0.015331
49	0.019202	0.018061	0.016963	0.015915	0.014916
50	0.018801	0.017654	0.016558	0.015513	0.014518
51	0.018409	0.017263	0.016169	0.015127	0.014136
52	0.018032	0.016887	0.015795	0.014756	0.013769
53	0.017669	0.016525	0.015435	0.014400	0.013417
54	0.017320	0.016177	0.015089	0.014057	0.013078
55	0.016983	0.015841	0.014756	0.013726	0.012751
56	0.016659	0.015518	0.014435	0.013408	0.012437
57	0.016345	0.015206	0.014125	0.013102	0.012135

TABLE V

Payment Needed Each Period for a Sinking Fund to Amount to 1 (continued)

Values of $\left[\dfrac{i}{(1+i)^n - 1}\right]$

n	$\frac{1}{4}\%$	$\frac{1}{2}\%$	$\frac{3}{4}\%$	1%	$1\frac{1}{4}\%$
58	0.016043	0.014905	0.013826	0.012806	0.011843
59	0.015751	0.014614	0.013537	0.012520	0.011562
60	0.015469	0.014333	0.013258	0.012244	0.011290
61	0.015196	0.014061	0.012989	0.011978	0.011028
62	0.014931	0.013798	0.012728	0.011720	0.010774
63	0.014676	0.013543	0.012476	0.011471	0.010529
64	0.014428	0.013297	0.012231	0.011230	0.010292
65	0.014188	0.013058	0.011995	0.010997	0.010063
66	0.013955	0.012826	0.011765	0.010771	0.009841
67	0.013729	0.012602	0.011543	0.010551	0.009626
68	0.013530	0.012384	0.011327	0.010339	0.009417
69	0.013297	0.012172	0.011118	0.010133	0.009215
70	0.013090	0.011967	0.010915	0.009933	0.009019
71	0.012889	0.011767	0.010717	0.009739	0.008829
72	0.012694	0.011573	0.010526	0.009550	0.008645
73	0.012504	0.011384	0.010339	0.009367	0.008466
74	0.012319	0.011201	0.010158	0.009189	0.008292
75	0.012139	0.011022	0.009982	0.009016	0.008123
76	0.011964	0.010848	0.009810	0.008848	0.007959
77	0.011793	0.010679	0.009643	0.008684	0.007800
78	0.011627	0.010514	0.009481	0.008525	0.007644
79	0.011465	0.010354	0.009322	0.008370	0.007493
80	0.011307	0.010197	0.009168	0.008219	0.007347

n	$1\frac{1}{2}\%$	$1\frac{3}{4}\%$	2%	$2\frac{1}{2}\%$	3%
1	1.000000	1.000000	1.000000	1.000000	1.000000
2	0.496278	0.495663	0.495050	0.493827	0.492611
3	0.328383	0.327567	0.326755	0.325137	0.323530
4	0.244445	0.243532	0.242624	0.240818	0.239027
5	0.194089	0.193121	0.192158	0.190247	0.188355
6	0.160525	0.159523	0.158526	0.156550	0.154598
7	0.136556	0.135531	0.134512	0.132495	0.130506
8	0.118584	0.117543	0.116510	0.114467	0.112456
9	0.104610	0.103558	0.102515	0.100457	0.098434
10	0.093434	0.092375	0.091327	0.089259	0.087231
11	0.094294	0.083230	0.082178	0.080106	0.078077
12	0.076680	0.075614	0.074560	0.072487	0.070462
13	0.070240	0.069173	0.068118	0.066048	0.064030
14	0.064723	0.063656	0.062602	0.060537	0.058526
15	0.059944	0.058877	0.057825	0.055766	0.053767
16	0.055765	0.054700	0.053650	0.051599	0.049611
17	0.052080	0.051016	0.049970	0.047928	0.045953
18	0.048806	0.047745	0.046702	0.044770	0.042709
19	0.045878	0.044821	0.043782	0.041761	0.039814
20	0.043246	0.042191	0.041157	0.039147	0.037216
21	0.040865	0.039815	0.038785	0.036787	0.034872
22	0.038703	0.037656	0.036631	0.034647	0.032747
23	0.036731	0.035788	0.034668	0.032696	0.030814
24	0.034924	0.033886	0.032871	0.030913	0.029047
25	0.033263	0.032230	0.031220	0.029276	0.027428
26	0.031732	0.030703	0.029699	0.027769	0.025938
27	0.030315	0.029291	0.028293	0.026377	0.024564
28	0.029001	0.027982	0.026990	0.025088	0.023293
29	0.027719	0.026764	0.025778	0.023891	0.022115
30	0.026639	0.025630	0.024650	0.022778	0.021019

TABLE V   **Payment Needed Each Period for a Sinking Fund to Amount to 1 (continued)**

Values of $\left[\dfrac{i}{(1 + i)^n - 1}\right]$

n	$1\frac{1}{2}\%$	$1\frac{3}{4}\%$	2%	$2\frac{1}{2}\%$	3%
31	0.025574	0.024570	0.023596	0.021739	0.019999
32	0.024577	0.023578	0.022611	0.020768	0.019047
33	0.023641	0.022648	0.021687	0.019859	0.018156
34	0.022762	0.021774	0.020819	0.019007	0.017322
35	0.021934	0.020951	0.020002	0.018206	0.016539
36	0.021152	0.020175	0.019233	0.017452	0.015804
37	0.020414	0.019443	0.018507	0.016741	0.015112
38	0.019716	0.018750	0.017821	0.016070	0.014459
39	0.019055	0.018094	0.017171	0.015436	0.013844
40	0.018427	0.017472	0.016556	0.014836	0.013262
41	0.017831	0.016882	0.015972	0.014268	0.012712
42	0.017264	0.016321	0.015417	0.013729	0.012192
43	0.016725	0.015787	0.014890	0.013217	0.011698
44	0.016210	0.015278	0.014388	0.012730	0.011230
45	0.015720	0.014793	0.013910	0.012268	0.010785
46	0.015251	0.014330	0.013453	0.011827	0.010363
47	0.014803	0.013888	0.013018	0.011407	0.009961
48	0.014375	0.013466	0.012602	0.011006	0.009578
49	0.013965	0.013061	0.012204	0.010623	0.009213
50	0.013572	0.012674	0.011823	0.010258	0.008865
51	0.013195	0.012303	0.011459	0.009909	0.008534
52	0.012833	0.011947	0.011109	0.009574	0.008217
53	0.012485	0.011605	0.010774	0.009254	0.007915
54	0.012151	0.011277	0.010452	0.008948	0.007626
55	0.011830	0.010961	0.010143	0.008654	0.007349
56	0.011521	0.010658	0.009847	0.008372	0.007084
57	0.011223	0.010366	0.009561	0.008102	0.006831
58	0.010937	0.010085	0.009287	0.007842	0.006588
59	0.010660	0.009814	0.009022	0.007593	0.006356
60	0.010393	0.009553	0.008768	0.007353	0.006133
61	0.010136	0.009302	0.008523	0.007123	0.005919
62	0.009888	0.009059	0.008286	0.006901	0.005714
63	0.009647	0.008825	0.009058	0.006688	0.005517
64	0.009415	0.008598	0.007839	0.006482	0.005328
65	0.009191	0.008380	0.007626	0.006285	0.005416
66	0.008974	0.008168	0.007421	0.006094	0.004971
67	0.008764	0.007964	0.007223	0.005910	0.004803
68	0.008560	0.007766	0.007032	0.005733	0.004642
69	0.008363	0.007575	0.006847	0.005562	0.004486
70	0.008172	0.007389	0.006668	0.005397	0.004337
71	0.007987	0.007210	0.006494	0.005238	0.004193
72	0.007808	0.007036	0.006327	0.005084	0.004054
73	0.007634	0.006867	0.006165	0.004936	0.003921
74	0.007465	0.006704	0.006007	0.004792	0.003792
75	0.007301	0.006546	0.005855	0.004654	0.003668
76	0.007141	0.006392	0.005708	0.004520	0.003548
77	0.006987	0.006243	0.005564	0.004390	0.003433
78	0.006836	0.006098	0.005426	0.004265	0.003322
79	0.006690	0.005957	0.005291	0.004143	0.003215
80	0.006548	0.005821	0.005161	0.004026	0.003112

n	$3\frac{1}{2}\%$	4%	$4\frac{1}{2}\%$	5%	$5\frac{1}{2}\%$
1	1.000000	1.000000	1.000000	1.000000	1.000000
2	0.491401	0.490196	0.488998	0.487805	0.486618
3	0.321934	0.320349	0.318773	0.317209	0.315654

TABLE V

Payment Needed Each Period for a Sinking Fund to Amount to 1 (continued)

Values of $\left[\dfrac{i}{(1 + i)^n - 1} \right]$

n	$3\frac{1}{2}$	4%	$4\frac{1}{2}\%$	5%	$5\frac{1}{2}\%$
4	0.237251	0.235490	0.233744	0.232012	0.230294
5	0.186481	0.184627	0.182792	0.180975	0.179176
6	0.152668	0.150762	0.148878	0.147017	0.145179
7	0.128544	0.126610	0.124701	0.122820	0.120964
8	0.110477	0.108528	0.106610	0.104722	0.102864
9	0.096446	0.094493	0.092574	0.090690	0.088839
10	0.085241	0.083291	0.081379	0.079505	0.077668
11	0.076092	0.074149	0.072248	0.070389	0.068571
12	0.068484	0.066552	0.064666	0.062825	0.061029
13	0.062062	0.060144	0.058275	0.056456	0.054684
14	0.056571	0.054669	0.052820	0.051024	0.049279
15	0.051825	0.049941	0.048114	0.046342	0.044626
16	0.047685	0.045820	0.044015	0.042270	0.040583
17	0.044043	0.042199	0.040418	0.038699	0.037042
18	0.040817	0.038993	0.037237	0.035546	0.033920
19	0.037940	0.036139	0.034407	0.032745	0.031150
20	0.035361	0.033582	0.031876	0.030243	0.028679
21	0.033037	0.031280	0.029601	0.027996	0.026465
22	0.030932	0.029199	0.027546	0.025971	0.024471
23	0.029019	0.027309	0.025682	0.024137	0.022670
24	0.027273	0.025587	0.023987	0.022471	0.021036
25	0.025674	0.024012	0.022439	0.020952	0.019549
26	0.024205	0.022567	0.021021	0.019564	0.018193
27	0.022852	0.021239	0.019719	0.018292	0.016952
28	0.021603	0.020013	0.018521	0.017123	0.015814
29	0.020445	0.018880	0.017415	0.016046	0.014769
30	0.019371	0.017830	0.016392	0.015051	0.013805
31	0.018372	0.016855	0.015443	0.014132	0.012917
32	0.017442	0.015949	0.014563	0.013280	0.012095
33	0.016572	0.015104	0.013745	0.012490	0.011335
34	0.015760	0.014315	0.012982	0.011755	0.010630
35	0.014998	0.013577	0.012270	0.011072	0.009975
36	0.014284	0.012887	0.011606	0.010434	0.009366
37	0.013613	0.012240	0.010984	0.009840	0.008800
38	0.012982	0.011632	0.010402	0.009284	0.008272
39	0.012388	0.011061	0.009856	0.008765	0.007780
40	0.011827	0.010523	0.009343	0.008278	0.007320
41	0.011298	0.010017	0.008862	0.007822	0.006891
42	0.010798	0.009540	0.008409	0.007395	0.006489
43	0.010325	0.009090	0.007982	0.006993	0.006113
44	0.009878	0.008665	0.007581	0.006616	0.005761
45	0.009453	0.008262	0.007202	0.006262	0.005431
46	0.009051	0.007882	0.006845	0.005928	0.005122
47	0.008669	0.007522	0.006507	0.005614	0.004831
48	0.008306	0.007181	0.006189	0.005318	0.004559
49	0.007962	0.006857	0.005887	0.005040	0.004302
50	0.007634	0.006550	0.005602	0.004777	0.004061
51	0.007322	0.006259	0.005332	0.004529	0.003835
52	0.007024	0.005982	0.005077	0.004294	0.003622
53	0.006741	0.005719	0.004835	0.004073	0.003421
54	0.006471	0.005469	0.004605	0.003864	0.003232
55	0.006213	0.005231	0.004388	0.003667	0.003055
56	0.005967	0.005005	0.004181	0.003480	0.002887
57	0.005732	0.004789	0.003985	0.003303	0.002729
58	0.005508	0.004584	0.003799	0.003136	0.002580
59	0.005294	0.004388	0.003622	0.002978	0.002440
60	0.005089	0.004202	0.003454	0.002828	0.002307

TABLE V

Payment Needed Each Period for a Sinking Fund to Amount to 1 (*continued*)

Values of $\left[\dfrac{i}{(1+i)^n - 1}\right]$

n	$3\frac{1}{2}\%$	4%	$4\frac{1}{2}\%$	5%	$5\frac{1}{2}\%$
61	0.004892	0.004024	0.003295	0.002686	0.002182
62	0.004705	0.003854	0.003143	0.002552	0.002064
63	0.004525	0.003692	0.002998	0.002424	0.001953
64	0.004353	0.003538	0.002861	0.002304	0.001847
65	0.004188	0.003390	0.002730	0.002189	0.001748
66	0.004030	0.003249	0.002606	0.002081	0.001654
67	0.003879	0.003115	0.002488	0.001978	0.001565
68	0.003734	0.002986	0.002375	0.001880	0.001482
69	0.003595	0.002863	0.002267	0.001787	0.001402
70	0.003461	0.002745	0.002165	0.001699	0.001328
71	0.003333	0.002633	0.002068	0.001516	0.001257
72	0.003210	0.002525	0.001975	0.001536	0.001190
73	0.003092	0.002422	0.001886	0.001461	0.001127
74	0.002978	0.002323	0.001802	0.001390	0.001067
75	0.002869	0.002229	0.001721	0.001322	0.001010
76	0.002765	0.002139	0.001644	0.001257	0.000956
77	0.002664	0.002052	0.001571	0.001196	0.000906
78	0.002567	0.001969	0.001501	0.001138	0.000858
79	0.002474	0.001890	0.001434	0.001082	0.000812
80	0.002385	0.001824	0.001371	0.001030	0.000769

n	6%	$6\frac{1}{2}\%$	7%	$7\frac{1}{2}\%$	8%
1	1.000000	1.000000	1.000000	1.000000	1.000000
2	0.485437	0.484262	0.483092	0.481928	0.480769
3	0.314110	0.312576	0.311052	0.309538	0.308034
4	0.228591	0.226903	0.225228	0.223568	0.221921
5	0.177396	0.175635	0.173891	0.172165	0.170456
6	0.143363	0.141568	0.139796	0.138045	0.136315
7	0.119135	0.117331	0.115553	0.113800	0.112072
8	0.101036	0.099237	0.097468	0.095727	0.094015
9	0.087022	0.085238	0.083486	0.081767	0.080080
10	0.075868	0.074105	0.072378	0.070686	0.069029
11	0.066793	0.065055	0.063357	0.061697	0.060076
12	0.059277	0.057568	0.055902	0.054278	0.052695
13	0.052960	0.051283	0.049651	0.048064	0.046522
14	0.047585	0.045940	0.044345	0.042797	0.041297
15	0.042963	0.041353	0.039795	0.038287	0.036830
16	0.038952	0.037378	0.035858	0.034391	0.032977
17	0.035445	0.033906	0.032425	0.031000	0.029629
18	0.032357	0.030855	0.029413	0.028029	0.026702
19	0.029621	0.028156	0.026753	0.025411	0.024128
20	0.027185	0.025756	0.024393	0.023092	0.021852
21	0.025005	0.023613	0.022289	0.021029	0.019832
22	0.023046	0.021691	0.020406	0.019187	0.018032
23	0.021278	0.019961	0.018714	0.017535	0.016422
24	0.019679	0.018398	0.017189	0.016050	0.014978
25	0.018227	0.016981	0.015811	0.014711	0.013679
26	0.016904	0.015695	0.014561	0.013500	0.012507
27	0.015697	0.014523	0.013426	0.012402	0.011448
28	0.014593	0.013453	0.012392	0.011405	0.010489
29	0.013580	0.012474	0.011449	0.010498	0.009619
30	0.012649	0.011577	0.010586	0.009671	0.008827
31	0.011792	0.010754	0.009797	0.008916	0.008107
32	0.011002	0.009997	0.009073	0.008226	0.007451

TABLE V   **Payment Needed Each Period for a Sinking**
                           Fund to Amount to 1 (continued)

$$\text{Values of } \left[\frac{i}{(1 + i)^n - 1} \right]$$

n	6%	$6\frac{1}{2}$%	7%	$7\frac{1}{2}$%	8%
33	0.010273	0.009299	0.008408	0.007594	0.006852
34	0.009598	0.008656	0.007797	0.007015	0.006304
35	0.008974	0.008062	0.007234	0.006483	0.005803
36	0.008395	0.007513	0.006715	0.005994	0.005345
37	0.007857	0.007005	0.006237	0.005545	0.004924
38	0.007358	0.006535	0.005795	0.005132	0.004539
39	0.007894	0.006099	0.005387	0.004751	0.004185
40	0.006462	0.005694	0.005009	0.004400	0.003860
41	0.006059	0.005318	0.004660	0.004077	0.003561
42	0.005683	0.004968	0.004336	0.003778	0.003287
43	0.005333	0.004644	0.004036	0.003502	0.003034
44	0.005006	0.004341	0.003758	0.003247	0.002802
45	0.004700	0.004060	0.003500	0.003011	0.002587
46	0.004415	0.003797	0.003260	0.002794	0.002390
47	0.004148	0.003553	0.003037	0.002592	0.002208
48	0.003898	0.003325	0.002831	0.002405	0.002040
49	0.003664	0.003112	0.002639	0.002232	0.001886
50	0.003444	0.002914	0.002460	0.002072	0.001743
51	0.003239	0.002729	0.002294	0.001924	0.001611
52	0.003046	0.002556	0.002139	0.001787	0.001490
53	0.002866	0.002394	0.001995	0.001659	0.001377
54	0.002696	0.002243	0.001861	0.001541	0.001274
55	0.002537	0.002101	0.001736	0.001432	0.001178
56	0.002388	0.001969	0.001620	0.001330	0.001090
57	0.002247	0.001846	0.001502	0.001236	0.001008
58	0.002116	0.001730	0.001411	0.001148	0.000932
59	0.001992	0.001622	0.001317	0.001067	0.000862
60	0.001876	0.001520	0.001229	0.000991	0.000798
61	0.001766	0.001426	0.001147	0.000921	0.000738
62	0.001664	0.001337	0.001071	0.000856	0.000688
63	0.001567	0.001254	0.001000	0.000796	0.000632
64	0.001476	0.001176	0.000934	0.000740	0.000585
65	0.001391	0.001103	0.000872	0.000688	0.000541
66	0.001310	0.001034	0.000814	0.000639	0.000501
67	0.001235	0.000970	0.000760	0.000594	0.000464
68	0.001163	0.000910	0.000710	0.000553	0.000429
69	0.001096	0.000854	0.000663	0.000514	0.000397
70	0.001033	0.000801	0.000620	0.000478	0.000368
71	0.000974	0.000752	0.000579	0.000444	0.000340
72	0.000918	0.000705	0.000541	0.000413	0.000315
73	0.000865	0.000662	0.000505	0.000384	0.000292
74	0.000815	0.000621	0.000472	0.000357	0.000270
75	0.000769	0.000583	0.000441	0.000332	0.000250
76	0.000725	0.000547	0.000412	0.000309	0.000231
77	0.000683	0.000513	0.000385	0.000287	0.000214
78	0.000644	0.000482	0.000359	0.000267	0.000198
79	0.000607	0.000452	0.000336	0.000248	0.000183
80	0.000573	0.000424	0.000314	0.000231	0.000170

TABLE VI

Present Value of an Annuity of 1 per Period

$$\text{Values of } \left[\frac{(1+i)^n - 1}{i(1+i)^n} \right]$$

n	$\frac{1}{4}\%$	$\frac{1}{2}\%$	$\frac{3}{4}\%$	1%	$1\frac{1}{4}\%$
1	0.997506	0.995025	0.992556	0.990099	0.987654
2	1.992524	1.985099	1.977723	1.970395	1.963115
3	2.985061	2.970248	2.955556	2.940985	2.926534
4	3.975123	3.950496	3.926110	3.901965	3.878058
5	4.962716	4.925867	4.889439	4.853431	4.817835
6	5.947846	5.896385	5.845597	5.795476	5.746010
7	6.930519	6.862074	6.794637	6.728194	6.662725
8	7.910741	7.822960	7.736613	7.651677	7.568124
9	8.888520	8.779064	8.671576	8.566017	8.462344
10	9.863860	9.730412	9.599579	9.471304	9.345525
11	10.836767	10.677027	10.520674	10.367628	10.217803
12	11.807249	11.618933	11.434912	11.255077	11.079311
13	12.775310	12.556152	12.342345	12.133740	11.930184
14	13.740957	13.488708	13.243022	13.003702	12.770552
15	34.704197	14.416626	14.136994	13.865052	13.600545
16	15.665033	15.339926	15.024312	14.717873	14.420291
17	16.623475	16.258633	15.905024	15.562251	15.229918
18	17.579525	17.172769	16.779180	16.398268	16.029548
19	18.533192	18.082357	17.646829	17.226008	16.819307
20	19.484480	18.987420	18.508019	18.045552	17.599315
21	20.433396	19.887980	19.362798	18.856982	18.369694
22	21.379946	20.784060	20.211214	19.660379	19.130562
23	22.324136	21.675682	21.053314	20.455820	19.882036
24	23.265970	22.562867	21.889145	21.243386	20.624233
25	24.205456	23.445639	22.718754	22.023155	21.357268
26	25.142599	24.324019	23.542188	22.795203	22.081252
27	26.077405	25.198029	24.359492	23.559607	22.796298
28	27.009879	26.067691	25.170711	24.316442	23.502517
29	27.940030	26.933025	25.975892	25.065784	24.200016
30	28.867859	27.794055	26.775079	25.807707	24.888905
31	29.793376	28.650802	27.568317	26.542284	25.569289
32	30.716584	29.503285	28.355649	27.269588	26.241273
33	31.637490	30.351527	29.137121	27.989691	26.904961
34	32.556099	31.195550	29.912775	28.702665	27.560455
35	33.472417	32.035373	30.682655	29.408579	28.207857
36	34.386451	32.871018	31.446804	30.107504	28.847266
37	35.298205	33.702505	32.205264	30.799509	29.478781
38	36.207685	34.529856	32.958079	31.484662	30.102500
39	37.114898	35.353091	33.705289	32.163032	30.718518
40	38.019848	36.172230	34.446937	32.834685	31.326932
41	38.922541	36.987293	35.183064	33.499688	31.927834
42	39.822983	37.798302	35.913711	34.158107	32.521317
43	40.721180	38.605275	36.638919	34.810007	33.107474
44	41.617136	39.408234	37.358729	35.455452	33.686394
45	42.510859	40.207198	38.073180	36.094507	34.258167
46	43.402353	41.002187	38.782312	36.727235	34.822881
47	44.291624	41.793221	39.486166	37.353698	35.380623
48	45.178676	42.580320	40.184780	37.973958	35.931479
49	46.063518	43.363502	40.878194	38.588077	36.475535
50	46.946152	44.142788	41.566445	39.196116	37.012874
51	47.826585	44.918198	42.249573	39.798135	37.543579
52	48.704822	45.689749	42.927616	40.394193	38.067733
53	49.580870	46.457462	43.600612	40.984349	38.585415
54	50.454732	47.221355	44.268597	41.568663	39.096706
55	51.326417	47.981447	44.931610	42.147191	39.601685
56	52.195926	48.737759	45.589687	42.719991	40.100430
57	53.063268	49.490307	46.242866	43.287120	40.593017

TABLE VI   **Present Value of an Annuity of 1 per Period (continued)**

$$\text{Values of} \left[\frac{(1 + i)^n - 1}{i(1 + i)^n} \right]$$

n	$\frac{1}{4}\%$	$\frac{1}{2}\%$	$\frac{3}{4}\%$	1%	$1\frac{1}{4}\%$
58	53.928446	50.239112	46.891182	43.848633	41.079523
59	54.791466	50.984191	47.574672	44.404587	41.560023
60	55.652335	51.725563	48.173372	44.955037	42.034590
61	56.511058	52.463247	48.807317	45.500037	42.503299
62	57.367637	53.197261	49.436542	46.039640	42.966221
63	58.222083	53.927623	50.061085	46.573901	43.423428
64	59.074396	54.654351	50.690977	47.102872	43.874991
65	59.924584	55.377464	51.296255	47.626606	44.320978
66	60.772652	56.096979	51.906953	48.145155	44.761460
67	61.618605	56.812914	52.513105	48.658569	45.196504
68	62.461449	57.525288	53.114744	49.166900	45.626177
69	63.304188	58.234117	53.711905	49.670198	46.050545
70	64.143828	58.939420	54.304620	50.168513	46.469674
71	64.981375	59.641214	54.892923	50.661894	46.883629
72	65.816832	60.339517	55.476847	51.150390	47.292473
73	66.650206	61.034345	56.056424	51.634049	47.696269
74	67.481502	61.725716	56.631686	52.112920	48.095081
75	68.310725	62.413648	57.202666	52.587050	48.488969
76	69.137879	63.098157	57.769395	53.056485	48.877994
77	69.962972	63.779261	58.331906	53.521272	49.262216
78	70.786006	64.456976	58.890229	53.981457	49.641695
79	71.606989	65.131320	59.444396	54.437087	50.016488
80	72.425923	65.802308	59.994438	54.888205	50.386655

n	$1\frac{1}{2}\%$	$1\frac{3}{4}\%$	2%	$2\frac{1}{2}\%$	3%
1	0.985222	0.982801	0.980392	0.975610	0.970874
2	1.955883	1.948699	1.941561	1.927424	1.913470
3	2.812200	2.897984	2.883883	2.856024	2.928611
4	3.854385	3.830942	3.807729	3.761974	3.717098
5	4.782645	4.747855	4.713459	4.645828	4.579707
6	5.697187	5.648997	5.601431	5.508125	5.417191
7	6.598214	6.534641	6.471991	6.349390	6.230283
8	7.485925	7.405053	7.325481	7.170137	7.019692
9	8.360517	8.260494	8.162236	7.970865	7.786109
10	9.222184	9.101223	8.982585	8.752064	8.530203
11	10.071118	9.927492	9.786848	9.514208	9.252624
12	10.907505	10.739549	10.575341	10.257764	9.954004
13	11.731532	11.537641	11.348373	10.983185	10.634955
14	12.543381	12.322005	12.106248	11.690912	11.296073
15	13.343233	13.092880	12.849263	12.381377	11.937935
16	14.131264	13.850496	13.577709	13.055002	12.561102
17	14.907649	14.595082	14.291871	13.712197	13.166118
18	15.672561	15.326862	14.992031	14.353363	13.753513
19	16.426168	16.046056	15.678462	14.978891	14.323799
20	17.168639	16.752881	16.351433	15.589162	14.877475
21	17.900137	17.447549	17.011209	16.184548	15.415024
22	18.620824	18.130269	17.658048	16.765413	15.936916
23	19.330861	18.801247	18.292204	17.332110	16.443608
24	20.030405	19.460685	18.913925	17.884985	16.935542
25	20.719611	20.108781	19.523456	18.424376	17.413147
26	21.398632	20.745731	20.121035	18.950611	17.876842
27	22.067617	21.371726	20.706897	19.464010	18.327031
28	22.726717	21.986954	21.281272	19.964888	18.764108
29	22.376076	22.591601	21.844384	20.453549	19.188454
30	24.015838	23.185849	22.396455	20.930292	19.600441

TABLE VI   Present Value of an Annuity of 1 per Period (continued)

Values of $\left[\dfrac{(1 + i)^n - 1}{i(1 + i)^n}\right]$

n	$1\frac{1}{2}\%$	$1\frac{3}{4}\%$	2%	$2\frac{1}{2}\%$	3%
31	24.646146	23.769876	22.937701	21.395407	20.000428
32	25.267139	24.343858	23.468334	21.849177	20.388765
33	25.878954	24.907969	23.988563	22.291880	20.765792
34	26.481728	25.462377	24.498591	22.723786	21.131836
35	27.075595	26.007250	24.998619	23.145157	21.487220
36	27.660684	26.542752	25.488842	23.556251	21.832252
37	28.237127	27.069044	25.969453	23.957318	22.167235
38	28.805052	27.586284	26.440640	24.348603	22.492461
39	29.364583	28.094628	26.902588	24.730344	22.808215
40	29.915845	28.594229	27.355478	25.102775	23.114772
41	30.458961	29.085237	27.799489	25.466121	23.412400
42	30.994050	29.567801	28.234793	25.820606	23.701359
43	31.521232	30.042064	28.661562	26.166445	23.981902
44	32.040622	30.508171	29.079962	26.503849	24.254274
45	32.552337	30.966262	29.490159	26.833023	24.518712
46	33.056490	31.416473	29.892313	27.154169	24.775449
47	33.553192	31.858942	30.286581	27.467492	25.024708
48	34.042554	32.293800	30.673119	27.773153	25.266706
49	34.524683	32.721180	31.052077	28.071369	25.501657
50	34.999688	33.141209	31.423605	28.362311	25.729764
51	35.467673	33.554013	31.787848	28.646157	25.951227
52	35.928742	33.959718	32.144949	28.923080	26.166240
53	36.382997	34.358445	32.495048	29.193249	26.374990
54	36.830539	34.750315	32.838282	29.456828	26.577660
55	37.271467	35.135445	33.174787	29.713979	26.774427
56	37.705879	35.513950	33.504693	29.964857	26.965464
57	38.133871	35.885946	33.828130	30.209617	27.150935
58	38.555537	36.251544	34.145226	30.448407	27.331005
59	38.970973	36.610854	34.456104	30.681372	27.505830
60	39.380269	36.963985	34.760886	30.908656	27.675564
61	39.783516	37.311041	35.059692	31.130396	27.840353
62	40.180804	37.652129	35.352639	31.346729	28.000343
63	40.572221	37.987351	35.639842	31.557783	28.155672
64	40.957853	38.316806	35.921414	31.763691	28.306478
65	41.337786	38.640596	36.197465	31.964577	28.452891
66	41.712105	38.958817	36.468103	32.160562	28.595040
67	42.080891	39.271564	36.733434	32.351768	28.733049
68	42.444228	39.578933	36.993563	32.538311	28.867038
69	42.802195	39.881015	37.248591	32.720303	28.997124
70	43.154872	40.177902	37.498619	32.897857	29.123421
71	43.502337	40.469682	37.743744	33.071080	29.246040
72	43.844667	40.756445	37.984062	33.240078	29.365987
73	44.181938	41.038275	38.219669	33.404954	29.480667
74	44.514224	41.315258	38.450656	33.565809	29.592881
75	44.841600	41.587477	38.677114	33.722740	29.701826
76	45.164138	41.855014	38.899131	33.875844	29.807598
77	45.481910	42.117950	39.116795	34.025214	29.910290
78	45.794985	42.376364	39.330191	34.170940	30.009990
79	46.103433	42.630333	39.539403	34.313112	30.106786
80	46.407323	42.879934	39.744513	34.451817	30.200763

n	$3\frac{1}{2}$	4%	$4\frac{1}{2}\%$	5%	$5\frac{1}{2}\%$
1	0.966184	0.961538	0.956938	0.952381	0.947867
2	1.899694	1.886095	1.872668	1.859410	1.846320
3	2.801637	2.775091	2.748964	2.723248	2.697933

TABLE VI

Present Value of an Annuity of 1 per Period (continued)

Values of $\left[\dfrac{(1 + i)^n - 1}{i(1 + i)^n}\right]$

n	$3\frac{1}{2}\%$	4%	$4\frac{1}{2}\%$	5%	$5\frac{1}{2}\%$
4	3.673079	3.629895	3.587526	3.545950	3.505150
5	4.515052	4.451822	4.389977	4.329477	4.270284
6	5.328553	5.242137	5.157873	5.075692	4.995530
7	6.114544	6.002055	5.892701	5.786373	5.682967
8	6.873955	6.732745	6.595886	6.463213	6.334566
9	7.607686	7.435331	7.268791	7.107822	6.952195
10	8.316605	8.110896	7.912718	7.721735	7.537626
11	9.001551	8.760477	8.528917	8.306414	8.092536
12	9.663334	9.385074	9.118581	8.863252	8.618518
13	10.302738	9.985648	9.682852	9.393573	9.117078
14	10.920520	10.563123	10.222825	9.898641	9.589648
15	11.517411	11.118387	10.739546	10.379658	10.037581
16	12.094117	11.652295	11.234015	10.837770	10.462162
17	12.651320	12.165669	11.707191	11.274066	10.864608
18	13.189682	12.659197	12.159992	11.689587	11.246074
19	13.709837	13.133939	12.593294	12.085321	11.607653
20	14.212403	13.590326	13.007937	12.462210	11.950382
21	14.697974	14.029160	13.404724	12.821153	12.275244
22	15.167125	14.451115	13.784425	13.163003	12.583170
23	15.620410	14.856841	14.147775	13.488574	12.875042
24	16.058367	15.246963	14.495478	13.798642	13.151699
25	16.481514	15.622080	14.828209	14.093945	13.413933
26	16.890352	15.982769	15.146611	14,375185	13.662495
27	17.285364	16.329585	15.451303	14 643034	13.898100
28	17.667019	16.663063	15.742874	14.898127	14.121422
29	18.035767	16.983714	16.021889	15.141074	14.333101
30	18.392045	17.292033	16.288889	15.372451	14.533745
31	18.736276	17.588493	16.544391	15.592810	14.723929
32	19.068865	17.873551	16.788891	15.802677	14.904198
33	19.390208	18.147645	17.022862	16.002549	15.075069
34	19.700684	18.411197	17.246758	16.192904	15.237033
35	20.000661	18.664613	17.461012	16.374194	15.390552
36	20.290494	18.908282	17.666041	16.546852	15.536068
37	20.570525	19.142579	17.862240	16.711287	15.673998
38	20.841087	19.367864	18.049990	16.867893	15.804738
39	21.102500	19.584485	18.229656	17.017041	15.928662
40	21.355072	19.792774	18.401584	17.159086	16.046125
41	21.599103	19.993052	18.566110	17.294368	16.157464
42	21.834883	20.185627	18.723550	17.423208	16.262999
43	22.062688	20.370795	18.874210	17.545912	16.363032
44	22.282791	20.548841	19.018383	17.662773	16.457851
45	22.495450	20.720040	19.156347	17.774070	16.547726
46	22.700918	20.884653	19.288371	17.880066	16.632915
47	22.899438	21.042936	19.414709	17.981016	16.713664
48	23.091244	21.195131	19.535607	18.077158	16.790203
49	23.276564	21.341472	19.651298	18.168722	16.862751
50	23.455618	21.482184	19.762008	18.255925	16.931518
51	23.628616	21.617495	19.867950	18.338977	16.996699
52	23.795764	21.747582	19.969330	18.418073	17.058483
53	23.957260	21.872675	20.066345	18.493403	17.117045
54	24.113295	21.992956	20.159182	18.565146	17.172555
55	24.264053	22.108612	20.248021	18.633472	17.225170
56	24.409713	22.219819	20.333034	18.698545	17.275043
57	24.550447	22.326749	20.414387	18.760519	17.322316
58	24.686423	22.429567	20.492236	18.819542	17.367124
59	24.817800	22.528429	20.566733	18.875754	17.409596
60	24.944734	22.623490	20.638022	18.929290	17.449854

TABLE VI   **Present Value of an Annuity of 1 per Period (continued)**

Values of $\left[\dfrac{(1 + i)^n - 1}{i(1 + i)^n}\right]$

n	$3\frac{1}{2}\%$	4%	$4\frac{1}{2}\%$	5%	$5\frac{1}{2}\%$
61	25.067376	22.714894	20.706241	18.980276	17.488013
62	25.185870	22.802783	20.771523	19.028834	17.524183
63	25.300358	22.887291	20.833993	19.075080	17.558468
64	25.410974	22.968549	20.893773	19.119124	17.590965
65	25.517849	23.046682	20.950979	19.161070	17.621767
66	25.621110	23.121809	21.005722	19.201019	17.650964
67	25.720879	23.194048	21.058107	19.239066	17.678639
68	25.817275	23.263507	21.108236	19.275301	17.704871
69	25.910410	23.330295	21.156207	19.309810	17.729736
70	26.000397	23.394515	21.202112	19.342677	17.753304
71	26.087340	23.456264	21.246040	19.373978	17.775644
72	26.171343	23.515639	21.288077	19.403788	17.796819
73	26.252505	23.572730	21.328303	19.432179	17.816890
74	26.330923	23.627625	21.366797	19.459218	17.835914
75	26.406689	23.680408	21.403634	19.484970	17.853947
76	26.479892	23.731162	21.438884	19.509495	17.871040
77	26.550621	23.779963	21.472616	19.532853	17.887242
78	26.618957	23.826888	21.504896	19.555098	17.902599
79	26.684983	23.872007	21.535785	19.576283	17.917155
80	26.748776	23.915392	21.565345	19.596460	17.930953

n	6%	$6\frac{1}{2}\%$	7%	$7\frac{1}{2}\%$	8%
1	0.943396	0.938967	0.934579	0.930233	0.925926
2	1.833393	1.820626	1.808018	1.795565	1.783265
3	2.673012	2.648475	2.624316	2.600526	2.577097
4	3.465106	3.425799	3.387211	3.349326	3.312127
5	4.212364	4.155679	4.100197	4.045885	3.992710
6	4.917324	4.841014	4.766540	4.693846	4.622880
7	5.582381	5.484520	5.389289	5.296601	5.206370
8	6.209794	6.088751	5.971298	5.857304	5.746639
9	6.801692	6.656104	6.515232	6.378887	6.246888
10	7.360087	7.188830	7.023581	6.864081	6.710081
11	7.886875	7.689042	7.498674	7.315424	7.138964
12	8.383844	8.158725	7.942686	7.735278	7.536078
13	8.852683	8.599742	8.357651	8.125840	7.903776
14	9.294984	9.013842	8.745468	8.489154	8.244237
15	9.712249	9.402669	9.107914	8.827120	8.559479
16	10.105895	9.767764	9.446649	9.141507	8.851369
17	10.477260	10.110577	9.763223	9.433960	9.121638
18	10.827603	10.432466	10.059087	9.706009	9.371887
19	11.158116	10.734710	10.335595	9.959078	9.603599
20	11.469921	11.018507	10.594014	10.194491	9.818147
21	11.764077	11.284983	10.835527	10.413480	10.016803
22	12.041582	11.535196	11.061240	10.617191	10.200744
23	12.303379	11.770137	11.272187	10.806689	10.371059
24	12.550357	11.990739	11.469334	10.982967	10.528758
25	12.783356	12.197877	11.653583	11.146946	10.674776
26	13.003166	12.392373	11.825779	11.299485	10.809978
27	13.210534	12.574998	11.986709	11.441381	10.935165
28	13.406164	12.746477	12.137111	11.573378	11.051078
29	13.590721	12.907490	12.277674	11.696165	11.158406
30	13.764831	13.058676	12.409041	11.810386	11.257783
31	13.929086	13.200635	12.531814	11.916638	11.349799
32	14.084043	13.333929	12.646555	12.015478	11.434999
33	14.230230	13.459089	12.753790	12.107421	11.513888
34	14.368141	13.576609	12.854009	12.192950	11.586934

TABLE VI   **Present Value of an Annuity of 1 per Period (continued)**

$$\text{Values of } \left[\frac{(1 + i)^n - 1}{i(1 + i)^n} \right]$$

n	6%	$6\frac{1}{2}\%$	7%	$7\frac{1}{2}\%$	8%
35	14.498246	13.686957	12.947672	12.272511	11.654568
36	14.620987	13.790570	13.035208	12.346522	11.717193
37	14.736780	13.887859	13.117017	12.415370	11.775179
38	14.846019	13.979210	13.193473	12.479414	11.828869
39	14.949075	14.064986	13.264928	12.538989	11.878582
40	15.046297	14.145527	13.331709	12.594409	11.924613
41	15.138016	14.221152	13.394120	12.645962	11.967235
42	15.224543	14.292162	13.452449	12.693918	12.006699
43	15.306173	14.358837	13.506962	12.738528	12.043240
44	15.383182	14.421443	13.557908	12.780026	12.077074
45	15.455832	14.480228	13.605522	12.818629	12.108401
46	15.524370	14.535426	13.650020	12.854539	12.137409
47	15.589028	14.587254	13.691608	12.887943	12.164267
48	15.650027	14.635919	13.730474	12.919017	12.189037
49	15.707572	14.681615	13.766799	12.947922	12.212163
50	15.761861	14.724521	13.800746	12.974812	12.233485
51	15.813076	14.764808	13.832473	12.999825	12.253227
52	15.861393	14.802637	13.862124	13.023093	12.271506
53	15.906974	14.838157	13.889836	13.044737	12.288432
54	15.949976	14.871509	13.915735	13.064872	12.304103
55	15.990543	14.902825	13.939939	13.003602	12.318614
56	16.038814	14.932230	13.962560	13.101025	12.332050
57	16.064919	14.959840	13.983701	13.117233	12.344491
58	16.098980	14.985766	14.003459	13.132309	12.356010
59	16.131113	15.010109	14.021924	13.146334	12.366676
60	16.161428	15.032966	14.039181	13.159381	12.376552
61	16.190026	15.054428	14.055309	13.171517	12.385696
62	16.217006	15.074580	14.070383	13.182807	12.394163
63	16.242458	15.093503	14.084470	13.193308	12.402003
64	16.266470	15.111270	14.097635	13.203078	12.409262
65	16.289123	15.127953	14.109940	13.212165	12.415983
66	16.310493	15.143618	14.121439	13.220619	12.422207
67	16.330654	15.128327	14.132186	13.228483	12.427969
68	16.349673	15.172138	14.142230	13.235798	12.433305
69	16.367617	15.185106	14.151617	13.242603	12.438245
70	16.384544	15.197282	14.160389	13.248933	12.442820
71	16.400513	15.208716	14.168588	13.254821	12.447055
72	16.415578	15.219452	14.176251	13.260299	12.450977
73	16.429791	15.229532	14.183412	13.265394	12.454608
74	16.443199	15.238997	14.190105	13.270134	12.457971
75	16.455848	15.247885	14.196359	13.274543	12.461084
76	16.467781	15.256230	14.202205	13.278645	12.463967
77	16.479039	15.264065	14.207668	13.282460	12.466636
78	16.489659	15.271423	14.212774	13.286010	12.469107
79	16.499679	15.278331	14.217546	13.289311	12.471396
80	16.509131	15.284818	14.222005	13.292383	12.473514

TABLE VII

Amount of an Annuity of 1 per Period

Values of $\left[\dfrac{(1 + i)^n - 1}{i} \right]$

n	$\frac{1}{4}\%$	$\frac{1}{2}\%$	$\frac{3}{4}\%$	1%	$1\frac{1}{4}\%$
1	1.000000	1.000000	1.000000	1.000000	1.000000
2	2.002499	2.005000	2.007500	2.010000	2.012500
3	3.007505	3.015025	3.022556	3.030100	3.037656
4	4.015023	4.030100	4.045225	4.060401	4.075627
5	5.025060	5.050251	5.075564	5.101005	5.126572
6	6.037623	6.075502	6.113631	6.152015	6.190654
7	7.052717	7.105880	7.159483	7.213535	7.268037
8	8.070347	8.141409	8.213179	8.285670	8.358888
9	9.090523	9.182116	9.274778	9.368527	9.463374
10	10.113249	10.228017	10.344339	10.462212	10.581666
11	11.138532	11.279167	11.421921	11.566834	11.713936
12	12.166377	12.335563	12.507586	12.682502	12.860361
13	13.196793	13.397241	13.601393	13.809327	14.021115
14	14.229784	14.464227	14.703403	14.947421	15.196379
15	15.265359	15.536549	15.813679	16.096895	16.386334
16	16.303521	16.614231	16.932281	17.257864	17.591163
17	17.344280	17.697302	18.059273	18.430442	18.811502
18	18.387640	18.785789	19.194717	19.614747	20.046190
19	19.433609	19.879818	20.338678	20.810894	21.296767
20	20.482192	20.979116	21.491218	22.019003	22.562977
21	21.533398	22.084012	22.652402	23.239193	23.845014
22	22.587230	23.194432	23.822295	24.471585	25.143077
23	23.643699	24.310404	25.000962	25.716301	26.457365
24	24.702807	25.431957	26.188469	26.973463	27.788082
25	25.764564	26.559116	27.384883	28.243198	29.135433
26	26.828975	27.691912	28.590269	29.525630	30.499626
27	27.896046	28.830372	29.804696	30.820886	31.880871
28	28.965785	29.974524	31.028231	32.129095	33.279382
29	30.038200	31.124396	32.260943	33.450386	34.695374
30	31.113295	32.280018	33.502900	34.784890	36.129066
31	32.191078	33.441419	34.754172	36.132739	37.580679
32	33.271555	34.608626	36.014828	37.494066	39.050438
33	34.354734	35.781669	37.284939	38.869006	40.538568
34	35.440620	36.960577	38.564576	40.257696	42.045300
35	35.529221	38.145380	39.853810	41.660273	43.570866
36	37.620543	39.336107	41.152714	43.076876	45.115502
37	38.714594	40.532788	42.461359	44.507645	46.679446
38	39.811380	41.735452	43.779819	45.952721	48.262939
39	40.910909	42.944129	45.108168	47.412248	49.866225
40	42.013185	44.158850	46.446479	49.886371	51.489553
41	43.118218	45.379644	47.794828	50.375234	53.133172
42	44.226012	46.606543	49.153289	51.878987	54.797337
43	45.336577	47.839575	50.521938	53.397776	56.482304
44	46.449918	49.078773	51.900853	54.931754	58.188332
45	47.566043	50.324167	53.290109	56.481072	59.915686
46	48.684957	51.575788	54.689785	58.045882	61.664632
47	49.806669	52.833667	56.099958	59.626341	63.435440
48	50.931185	54.097835	57.520707	61.222604	65.228383
49	52.058514	55.368324	58.952113	62.834830	67.043738
50	53.188659	56.645166	60.394253	64.463178	68.881784
51	54.321630	57.928392	61.847210	66.107810	70.742806
52	55.457433	59.218034	63.311064	67.768888	72.627092
53	56.596077	60.514125	64.785897	69.446577	74.534930
54	57.737566	61.816695	66.271791	71.141043	76.466616
55	58.881910	63.125778	67.768830	72.852453	78.422449
56	60.029113	64.441408	69.277096	74.580977	80.402730
57	61.179186	65.763614	70.796674	76.326787	82.407764

TABLE VII   **Amount of an Annuity of 1 per Period** (*continued*)

$$\text{Values of} \left[\frac{(1 + i)^n - 1}{i} \right]$$

n	$\frac{1}{4}\%$	$\frac{1}{2}\%$	$\frac{3}{4}\%$	1%	$1\frac{1}{4}\%$
58	62.332134	67.092433	72.327649	78.090055	84.437861
59	63.487963	68.427895	73.870107	79.870956	86.493334
60	64.646682	69.770034	75.424132	81.669665	88.574500
61	65.808299	71.118885	76.989813	83.486361	90.691681
62	66.972818	72.474479	78.567236	85.321225	92.815202
63	68.140251	73.836852	80.156491	87.174437	94.975392
64	69.310600	75.206036	81.757665	89.046181	97.162584
65	70.483877	76.582066	83.370847	90.936643	99.377115
66	71.660086	77.964977	84.996128	92.846010	101.619330
67	72.839236	79.354802	86.633599	94.774470	103.889572
68	74.021333	80.751576	88.283351	96.722214	106.188191
69	75.206386	82.155334	89.945476	98.689436	108.515543
70	76.394402	83.566111	91.620067	100.676330	110.871988
71	77.585387	84.983941	93.307217	102.683094	113.257887
72	78.779350	86.408861	95.007022	104.709924	115.673611
73	79.976298	87.840905	96.719574	106.757024	118.119531
74	81.176238	89.280110	98.444971	108.824594	120.596025
75	82.379178	90.726511	100.183308	110.912840	123.103475
76	83.585124	92.180143	101.934683	113.021968	125.642268
77	84.794088	93.641044	103.699193	115.152188	128.212797
78	86.006071	95.109249	105.476936	117.303709	130.815456
79	87.221088	96.584796	107.268014	119.476747	133.450649
80	88.439139	98.067720	109.072523	121.671514	136.118782

n	$1\frac{1}{2}\%$	$1\frac{3}{4}\%$	2%	$2\frac{1}{2}\%$	3%
1	1.000000	1.000000	1.000000	1.000000	1.000000
2	2.015000	2.017500	2.020000	2.025000	2.030000
3	3.045225	3.052806	3.060400	3.075625	3.090900
4	4.090903	4.106230	4.121608	4.152515	4.183627
5	5.152267	5.178089	5.204040	5.256328	5.309136
6	6.229551	6.268709	6.308121	6.387737	6.468410
7	7.322994	7.378408	7.434283	7.547430	7.662462
8	8.432839	8.507530	8.582969	8.736116	8.892336
9	9.559332	9.656412	9.754628	9.954518	10.159106
10	10.702722	10.825399	10.949720	11.203381	11.463879
11	11.863262	12.014844	12.168715	12.483466	12.807795
12	13.041211	13.225103	13.412089	13.795552	14.192029
13	14.236830	14.456542	14.680331	15.140441	15.617790
14	15.450382	15.709532	15.973937	16.518952	17.086324
15	16.682138	16.984449	17.293416	17.931926	18.598913
16	17.932370	18.281676	18.639284	19.380224	20.156881
17	19.201355	19.601606	20.012070	20.864730	21.761587
18	20.489376	20.944634	21.412311	22.386348	23.414435
19	21.796716	22.311165	22.840558	23.946006	25.116868
20	23.123667	23.701610	24.297369	25.544656	26.870374
21	24.470522	25.116388	25.783316	27.183273	28.676485
22	25.837580	26.555925	27.298982	28.862855	30.536780
23	27.225143	28.020654	28.844962	30.584426	32.452883
24	28.633521	29.511015	30.421861	32.349036	34.426469
25	30.063024	31.027458	32.030298	34.157762	36.459263
26	31.513969	32.570438	33.670904	36.011706	38.553041
27	32.986678	34.140421	35.344322	37.911999	40.709632
28	34.481478	35.737878	37.051208	39.859799	42.930921
29	35.998701	37.363291	38.792232	41.856294	45.218849
30	37.538681	39.017148	40.568077	43.902701	47.575414

TABLE VII

Amount of an Annuity of 1 per Period (*continued*)

Values of $\left[\dfrac{(1 + i)^n - 1}{i}\right]$

n	$1\frac{1}{2}\%$	$1\frac{3}{4}\%$	2%	$2\frac{1}{2}\%$	3%
31	39.101761	40.699948	42.379438	46.000268	50.002677
32	40.688288	42.412197	44.227027	48.150275	52.502757
33	42.298612	44.154411	46.111568	50.354032	55.077840
34	43.933091	45.927113	48.033799	52.612883	57.730175
35	45.592088	47.730837	49.994475	54.928205	60.462080
36	47.275969	49.566127	51.994364	57.301409	63.275942
37	48.985109	51.433534	54.034251	59.733945	66.174221
38	50.719885	53.333621	56.114936	62.227293	69.159447
39	52.480683	55.266959	58.237235	64.782976	72.234231
40	54.267894	57.234131	60.401979	67.402550	75.401258
41	56.081912	59.235728	62.610019	70.087614	78.663295
42	57.923141	61.272353	64.862219	72.839804	82.023194
43	59.791988	63.344619	67.159464	75.660799	85.483890
44	61.688868	65.453150	69.502653	78.552318	89.048408
45	63.614201	67.598580	71.892706	81.516126	92.719858
46	65.568414	69.781555	74.330560	84.554030	96.501454
47	67.551940	72.002732	76.817171	87.667880	100.396498
48	69.565219	74.262780	79.353514	90.859577	104.408392
49	71.608698	76.562378	81.940584	94.131066	108.540644
50	73.682828	78.902220	84.579396	97.484343	112.796863
51	75.788070	81.283009	87.270984	100.921451	117.180769
52	77.924891	83.705461	90.016403	104.444487	121.696192
53	80.093765	86.170307	92.816731	108.055599	126.347078
54	82.295171	88.678287	95.673065	111.756989	131.137490
55	84.529599	91.230157	98.586527	115.550914	136.071615
56	86.797543	93.826684	101.558257	119.439686	141.153763
57	89.099506	96.468651	104.589422	123.425679	146.388376
58	91.435998	99.156852	107.681210	127.511320	151.780027
59	93.807539	101.892097	110.834834	131.699103	157.333428
60	96.214651	104.675209	114.051531	135.991581	163.053431
61	98.657871	107.507025	117.332562	140.391370	168.945034
62	101.137739	110.388398	120.679212	144.901154	175.013384
63	103.654805	113.320195	124.092797	149.523683	181.263786
64	106.209628	116.303298	127.574652	154.261775	187.701699
65	108.802772	119.338605	131.126145	159.118319	194.332750
66	111.434813	122.427031	134.748668	164.096277	201.162733
67	114.106336	125.569504	138.443642	169.198684	208.197614
68	116.817931	128.766970	142.212514	174.428650	215.443543
69	119.570200	132.020392	146.056764	179.789366	222.906849
70	122.363753	135.330748	149.977899	185.284100	230.594054
71	125.199209	138.699030	153.977457	190.916203	238.511875
72	128.077197	142.126269	158.057006	196.689107	246.667232
73	130.998355	145.613479	162.218146	202.606335	255.067249
74	133.963330	149.161715	166.462508	208.671493	263.719266
75	136.972780	152.772045	170.791759	214.888280	272.630844
76	140.027372	156.445555	175.207593	221.260487	281.809769
77	143.127783	160.183352	179.711746	227.791999	291.264062
78	146.274699	163.986561	184.305980	234.486799	301.001983
79	149.468820	167.856326	188.992100	241.348968	311.032043
80	152.710852	171.793811	193.771941	248.382692	321.363004

n	$3\frac{1}{2}\%$	4%	$4\frac{1}{2}\%$	5%	$5\frac{1}{2}\%$
1	1.000000	1.000000	1.000000	1.000000	1.000000
2	2.035000	2.040000	2.045000	2.050000	2.055000
3	3.106225	3.121600	3.137025	3.152500	3.168025

TABLE VII

Amount of an Annuity of 1 per Period (*continued*)

$$\text{Values of } \left[\frac{(1 + i)^n - 1}{i} \right]$$

n	$3\frac{1}{2}\%$	4%	$4\frac{1}{2}\%$	5%	$5\frac{1}{2}\%$
4	4.214943	4.246464	4.278191	4.310125	4.342266
5	5.362466	5.416322	5.470710	5.525631	5.581091
6	6.550152	6.632975	6.716892	6.801913	6.888051
7	7.779407	7.898294	8.019152	8.142008	8.266894
8	9.051687	9.214226	9.380014	9.549109	9.721573
9	10.368496	10.582795	10.802114	11.026564	11.256259
10	11.731393	12.006107	12.288209	12.577892	12.875354
11	13.141992	13.486351	13.841179	14.206787	14.583498
12	14.601961	15.025805	15.464032	15.917126	16.385590
13	16.113030	16.626837	17.159913	17.712983	18.286798
14	17.676986	18.291911	18.932110	19.598632	20.292572
15	19.295680	20.023587	20.784054	21.578563	22.408663
16	20.971029	21.824530	22.719337	23.657492	24.641139
17	22.705015	23.697511	24.741707	25.840366	26.996402
18	24.499691	25.645412	26.855084	28.132384	29.481207
19	26.357180	27.671228	29.063563	30.539004	32.102670
20	28.279681	29.778077	31.371423	33.065954	34.868317
21	30.269470	31.969200	33.783137	35.719251	37.786075
22	32.328901	34.247968	36.303378	38.505214	40.864309
23	34.460413	36.617887	38.937030	41.430475	44.111846
24	36.666527	39.082602	41.689197	44.501998	47.537997
25	38.949855	41.645906	44.565210	47.727098	51.152587
26	41.313100	44.311742	47.570645	51.113453	54.965979
27	43.759059	47.084212	50.711324	54.669126	58.989108
28	46.290626	49.967580	53.993334	58.402582	63.233509
29	48.910798	52.966284	57.423034	62.322711	67.711352
30	51.622675	56.084935	61.007070	66.438846	72.435476
31	54.429469	59.328332	64.752388	70.760789	77.419427
32	57.334500	62.701465	68.666246	75.298828	82.677496
33	60.341208	66.209524	72.756227	80.063770	88.224758
34	63.453150	69.857905	77.030257	85.066958	94.077119
35	66.674010	73.652221	81.496619	90.320306	100.251361
36	70.007600	77.598309	86.163966	95.836321	106.765186
37	73.457866	81.702242	91.041345	101.628137	113.637271
38	77.028891	85.970331	96.138206	107.709544	120.887320
39	80.724903	90.409144	101.464425	114.095021	128.536123
40	84.550274	95.025510	107.030324	120.799772	136.605610
41	88.509534	99.826530	112.846689	127.839761	145.118918
42	92.607367	104.819591	118.924790	135.231749	154.100458
43	96.848625	110.012375	125.276405	142.993336	163.575984
44	101.238326	115.412870	131.913843	151.143003	173.572663
45	105.781668	121.029384	138.849966	159.700153	184.119159
46	110.484026	126.870560	146.098215	168.685160	195.245712
47	115.350967	132.945382	153.672635	178.119419	206.984226
48	120.388251	139.263197	161.587903	188.025389	219.368358
49	125.601839	145.833724	169.859359	198.426659	232.433618
50	130.997904	152.667073	178.503030	209.347992	246.217467
51	136.582830	159.773756	187.535667	220.815391	260.759427
52	142.363229	167.164706	196.974772	232.856160	276.101196
53	148.345942	174.851294	206.838636	245.498969	292.286761
54	154.538050	182.845345	217.146375	258.773917	309.362533
55	160.946882	191.159159	227.917962	272.712612	327.377472
56	167.580022	199.805525	239.174270	287.348243	346.383232
57	174.445322	208.797746	250.937112	302.715655	366.434311
58	181.550909	218.149655	263.229282	318.851437	387.588197
59	188.905191	227.875641	276.074601	335.794010	409.905548
60	196.516872	237.990667	289.497957	353.583710	433.450352

TABLE VII   **Amount of an Annuity of 1 per Period (continued)**

$$\text{Values of } \left[\frac{(1+i)^n - 1}{i} \right]$$

n	$3\frac{1}{2}\%$	4%	$4\frac{1}{2}\%$	5%	$5\frac{1}{2}\%$
61	204.394962	248.510293	303.525365	372.262896	458.290121
62	212.548786	259.450704	318.184007	391.876039	484.496077
63	220.987993	270.828732	333.502287	412.469841	512.143361
64	229.722573	282.661881	349.509890	434.093334	541.311246
65	238.762862	294.968356	366.237835	456.798000	572.083364
66	248.119562	307.767089	383.718538	480.637899	604.547948
67	257.803747	321.077773	401.985872	505.669795	638.798086
68	267.826878	334.920883	421.075236	531.953284	674.931979
69	278.200818	349.317718	441.023622	559.550949	713.053237
70	288.937846	364.290426	461.869685	588.528495	753.271165
71	300.050671	379.862043	483.653821	618.954919	795.701079
72	311.552444	396.056524	506.418243	650.902666	840.464637
73	323.456779	412.898785	530.207064	684.447799	887.690192
74	335.777766	430.414735	555.066382	719.670188	937.513151
75	348.529988	448.631325	581.044370	756.653697	990.076374
76	361.728537	467.576577	608.191366	795.486382	1045.530574
77	375.389035	487.279640	636.559978	836.260701	1104.034753
78	389.527651	507.770825	666.205177	879.073734	1165.756665
79	404.161119	529.081656	697.184410	924.027421	1230.873281
80	419.306757	551.244922	729.557709	971.228793	1299.571310

n	6%	$6\frac{1}{2}\%$	7%	$7\frac{1}{2}\%$	8%
1	1.000000	1.000000	1.000000	1.000000	1.000000
2	2.060000	2.065000	2.070000	2.075000	2.080000
3	3.183600	3.199225	3.214900	3.230625	3.246400
4	4.374616	4.407175	4.439943	4.472922	4.506112
5	5.637093	5.693641	5.750739	5.808391	5.866601
6	6.975318	7.063728	7.153291	7.244020	7.335929
7	8.393838	8.522870	8.654021	8.787322	8.922803
8	9.897468	10.076857	10.259802	10.446371	10.636628
9	11.491316	11.731852	11.977989	12.229849	12.487558
10	13.180795	13.494423	13.816448	14.147087	14.486562
11	14.971642	15.371560	15.783599	16.208119	16.645487
12	16.869941	17.370711	17.888451	18.423728	18.977126
13	18.882137	19.499808	20.140643	20.805507	21.495296
14	21.015066	21.767295	22.550487	23.365920	24.214920
15	23.275970	24.182169	25.129022	26.118364	27.152114
16	25.672528	26.754010	27.888053	29.077242	30.324283
17	28.212879	29.493021	30.840217	32.258035	33.750225
18	30.905652	32.410067	33.999032	35.677387	37.450243
19	33.759991	35.516722	37.378964	39.353191	41.446263
20	36.785591	38.825309	40.995491	43.304681	45.761964
21	39.992726	42.348954	44.865176	47.552532	50.422921
22	43.392289	46.101636	49.005738	52.118972	55.456754
23	46.995827	50.098242	53.436140	57.027894	60.893295
24	50.815576	54.354628	58.176669	62.304987	66.764758
25	54.864511	58.887679	63.249036	67.977861	73.105939
26	59.156381	63.715378	68.676469	74.076200	79.954414
27	63.705764	68.856877	74.483821	80.631915	87.350767
28	68.528110	74.332575	80.697689	87.679309	95.338828
29	73.639797	80.164192	87.346527	95.255257	103.965934
30	79.058184	86.374864	94.460783	103.399401	113.283209
31	84.801676	92.989230	102.073039	112.154356	123.345866
32	90.889776	100.033530	110.218151	121.565933	134.213535
33	97.343163	107.535710	118.933422	131.683377	145.950617
34	104.183752	115.525531	128.258761	142.559631	158.626667

TABLE VII   **Amount of an Annuity of 1 per Period** (*continued*)

$$\text{Values of } \left[\frac{(1 + i)^n - 1}{i} \right]$$

n	6%	$6\frac{1}{2}\%$	7%	$7\frac{1}{2}\%$	8%
35	111.434777	124.034691	138.236874	154.251603	172.316800
36	119.120864	133.096946	148.913455	166.820473	187.102144
37	127.268116	142.748247	160.337397	180.332008	203.070315
38	135.904202	153.026883	172.561014	194.856909	220.315940
39	145.058455	163.973630	185.640285	210.471177	238.941216
40	154.761961	175.631916	199.635105	227.256515	259.056512
41	165.047679	188.047991	214.609562	245.300754	280.781033
42	175.950540	201.271110	230.632231	264.698310	304.243515
43	187.507572	215.353732	247.776488	285.550683	329.582997
44	199.758026	230.351725	266.120841	307.966984	356.949636
45	212.743508	246.324588	285.749300	332.064508	386.505607
46	226.508118	263.335686	306.751749	357.969346	418.426055
47	241.098605	281.452505	329.224373	385.817046	452.900140
48	256.564521	300.746919	353.270078	415.753325	490.132150
49	272.958392	321.295468	378.998984	447.934824	530.342722
50	290.335895	343.179673	406.528912	482.529936	573.770138
51	308.756049	366.486352	435.985936	519.719680	620.671751
52	328.281411	391.307965	467.504951	559.698656	671.325489
53	348.978296	417.742982	501.230297	602.676055	726.031528
54	370.916993	445.896276	537.316416	648.876758	785.114049
55	394.172013	475.879534	575.928566	698.542515	848.923175
56	418.822333	507.811705	617.243564	751.933203	917.837026
57	444.951673	541.819465	661.450614	809.328194	992.263989
58	472.648773	578.037730	708.752155	871.027808	1072.645104
59	502.007700	616.610182	759.364807	937.354893	1159.456715
60	533.128160	657.689845	813.520340	1008.656509	1253.213249
61	566.115851	701.439684	871.466765	1085.305746	1354.470310
62	601.082800	748.033264	933.469437	1167.703677	1463.827931
63	638.147769	797.655426	999.812300	1256.281450	1581.934169
64	677.436635	850.503029	1070.799156	1351.502560	1709.488897
65	719.082832	906.785726	1146.755097	1453.865253	1847.248009
66	763.227802	966.726798	1228.027951	1563.905145	1996.027847
67	810.021470	1030.564038	1314.989908	1682.198029	2156.710075
68	859.622755	1098.550703	1408.039199	1809.362883	2330.246878
69	912.200122	1170.956497	1507.601942	1946.065098	2517.666628
70	967.932127	1248.068670	1614.134075	2093.019979	2720.079956
71	1027.008055	1330.193133	1728.123464	2250.996476	2938.686356
72	1089.628537	1417.655689	1850.092102	2420.821210	3174.781254
73	1156.006250	1510.803308	1980.598549	2603.382801	3429.763757
74	1226.366622	1610.005523	2120.240443	2799.636508	3705.144851
75	1300.948621	1715.655881	2269.657275	3010.609246	4002.556443
76	1380.005534	1828.173516	2429.533280	3237.404937	4323.760948
77	1463.805867	1948.004794	2600.600607	3481.210308	4670.661830
78	1552.634216	2075.625104	2783.642642	3743.301081	5045.314764
79	1646.792271	2211.540734	2979.497633	4025.048657	5449.939954
80	1746.599804	2356.290888	3189.062458	4327.927299	5886.935134

From *Finite Mathematics with Applications to Business and the Social Sciences,* by R. E. Wheeler and W. D. Peeples. Copyright © 1981 by Wadsworth, Inc. Reprinted by permission of Brooks/Cole Publishing Company, Monterey, California 93940.

ANNUAL PERCENTAGE RATE TABLE FOR MONTHLY PAYMENT PLANS
SEE INSTRUCTIONS FOR USE OF TABLES

ANNUAL PERCENTAGE RATE

(FINANCE CHARGE PER $100 OF AMOUNT FINANCED)

NUMBER OF PAYMENTS	10.00%	10.25%	10.50%	10.75%	11.00%	11.25%	11.50%	11.75%	12.00%	12.25%	12.50%	12.75%	13.00%	13.25%	13.50%	13.75%
1	0.83	0.85	0.87	0.90	0.92	0.94	0.96	0.98	1.00	1.02	1.04	1.06	1.08	1.10	1.12	1.15
2	1.25	1.28	1.31	1.35	1.38	1.41	1.44	1.47	1.50	1.53	1.57	1.60	1.63	1.66	1.69	1.72
3	1.67	1.71	1.76	1.80	1.84	1.88	1.92	1.96	2.01	2.05	2.09	2.13	2.17	2.22	2.26	2.30
4	2.09	2.14	2.20	2.25	2.30	2.35	2.41	2.46	2.51	2.57	2.62	2.67	2.72	2.78	2.83	2.88
5	2.51	2.58	2.64	2.70	2.77	2.83	2.89	2.96	3.02	3.08	3.15	3.21	3.27	3.34	3.40	3.46
6	2.94	3.01	3.08	3.16	3.23	3.31	3.38	3.45	3.53	3.60	3.68	3.75	3.83	3.90	3.97	4.05
7	3.36	3.45	3.53	3.62	3.70	3.78	3.87	3.95	4.04	4.12	4.21	4.29	4.38	4.47	4.55	4.64
8	3.79	3.88	3.98	4.07	4.17	4.26	4.36	4.46	4.55	4.65	4.74	4.84	4.94	5.03	5.13	5.22
9	4.21	4.32	4.43	4.53	4.64	4.75	4.85	4.96	5.07	5.17	5.28	5.39	5.49	5.60	5.71	5.82
10	4.64	4.76	4.88	4.99	5.11	5.23	5.35	5.46	5.58	5.70	5.82	5.94	6.05	6.17	6.29	6.41
11	5.07	5.20	5.33	5.45	5.58	5.71	5.84	5.97	6.10	6.23	6.36	6.49	6.62	6.75	6.88	7.01
12	5.50	5.64	5.78	5.92	6.06	6.20	6.34	6.48	6.62	6.76	6.90	7.04	7.18	7.32	7.46	7.60
13	5.93	6.08	6.23	6.38	6.53	6.68	6.84	6.99	7.14	7.29	7.44	7.59	7.75	7.90	8.05	8.20
14	6.36	6.52	6.69	6.85	7.01	7.17	7.34	7.50	7.66	7.82	7.99	8.15	8.31	8.48	8.64	8.81
15	6.80	6.97	7.14	7.32	7.49	7.66	7.84	8.01	8.19	8.36	8.53	8.71	8.88	9.06	9.23	9.41
16	7.23	7.41	7.60	7.78	7.97	8.15	8.34	8.53	8.71	8.90	9.08	9.27	9.46	9.64	9.83	10.02
17	7.67	7.86	8.06	8.25	8.45	8.65	8.84	9.04	9.24	9.44	9.63	9.83	10.03	10.23	10.43	10.63
18	8.10	8.31	8.52	8.73	8.93	9.14	9.35	9.56	9.77	9.98	10.19	10.40	10.61	10.82	11.03	11.24
19	8.54	8.76	8.98	9.20	9.42	9.64	9.86	10.08	10.30	10.52	10.74	10.96	11.18	11.41	11.63	11.65
20	8.98	9.21	9.44	9.67	9.90	10.13	10.37	10.60	10.83	11.06	11.30	11.53	11.76	12.00	12.23	12.46
21	9.42	9.66	9.90	10.15	10.39	10.63	10.88	11.12	11.36	11.61	11.85	12.10	12.34	12.59	12.84	13.08
22	9.86	10.12	10.37	10.62	10.88	11.13	11.39	11.64	11.90	12.16	12.41	12.67	12.93	13.19	13.44	13.70
23	10.30	10.57	10.84	11.10	11.37	11.63	11.90	12.17	12.44	12.71	12.97	13.24	13.51	13.78	14.05	14.32
24	10.75	11.02	11.30	11.58	11.86	12.14	12.42	12.70	12.98	13.26	13.54	13.82	14.10	14.38	14.66	14.95
25	11.19	11.48	11.77	12.06	12.35	12.64	12.93	13.22	13.52	13.81	14.10	14.40	14.69	14.98	15.28	15.57
26	11.64	11.94	12.24	12.54	12.85	13.15	13.45	13.75	14.06	14.36	14.67	14.97	15.28	15.59	15.89	16.20
27	12.09	12.40	12.71	13.03	13.34	13.66	13.97	14.29	14.60	14.92	15.24	15.56	15.87	16.19	16.51	16.83
28	12.53	12.86	13.18	13.51	13.84	14.16	14.49	14.82	15.15	15.48	15.81	16.14	16.47	16.80	17.13	17.46
29	12.98	13.32	13.66	14.00	14.33	14.67	15.01	15.35	15.70	16.04	16.38	16.72	17.07	17.41	17.75	18.10
30	13.43	13.78	14.13	14.48	14.83	15.19	15.54	15.89	16.24	16.60	16.95	17.31	17.66	18.02	18.38	18.74
31	13.89	14.25	14.61	14.97	15.33	15.70	16.06	16.43	16.79	17.16	17.53	17.90	18.27	18.63	19.00	19.38
32	14.34	14.71	15.09	15.46	15.84	16.21	16.59	16.97	17.35	17.73	18.11	18.49	18.87	19.25	19.63	20.02
33	14.79	15.18	15.57	15.95	16.34	16.73	17.12	17.51	17.90	18.29	18.69	19.08	19.47	19.87	20.26	20.66
34	15.25	15.65	16.05	16.44	16.85	17.25	17.65	18.05	18.46	18.86	19.27	19.67	20.08	20.49	20.90	21.31
35	15.70	16.11	16.53	16.94	17.35	17.77	18.18	18.60	19.01	19.43	19.85	20.27	20.69	21.11	21.53	21.95
36	16.16	16.58	17.01	17.43	17.86	18.29	18.71	19.14	19.57	20.00	20.43	20.87	21.30	21.73	22.17	22.60
37	16.62	17.06	17.49	17.93	18.37	18.81	19.25	19.69	20.13	20.58	21.02	21.46	21.91	22.36	22.81	23.25
38	17.08	17.53	17.98	18.43	18.88	19.33	19.78	20.24	20.69	21.15	21.61	22.07	22.52	22.99	23.45	23.91
39	17.54	18.00	18.46	18.93	19.39	19.86	20.32	20.79	21.26	21.73	22.20	22.67	23.14	23.61	24.09	24.56
40	18.00	18.48	18.95	19.43	19.90	20.38	20.86	21.34	21.82	22.30	22.79	23.27	23.76	24.25	24.73	25.22

ANNUAL PERCENTAGE RATE TABLE FOR MONTHLY PAYMENT PLANS
SEE INSTRUCTIONS FOR USE OF TABLES

ANNUAL PERCENTAGE RATE
(FINANCE CHARGE PER $100 OF AMOUNT FINANCED)

NUMBER OF PAYMENTS	14.00%	14.25%	14.50%	14.75%	15.00%	15.25%	15.50%	15.75%	16.00%	16.25%	16.50%	16.75%	17.00%	17.25%	17.50%	17.75%
41	18.47	18.95	19.44	19.93	20.42	20.91	21.40	21.89	22.39	22.88	23.38	23.88	24.38	24.88	25.38	25.88
42	18.93	19.43	19.93	20.43	20.93	21.44	21.94	22.45	22.96	23.47	23.98	24.49	25.00	25.51	26.03	26.55
43	19.40	19.91	20.42	20.94	21.45	21.97	22.49	23.01	23.53	24.05	24.57	25.10	25.62	26.15	26.68	27.21
44	19.86	20.39	20.91	21.44	21.97	22.50	23.03	23.57	24.10	24.64	25.17	25.71	26.25	26.79	27.33	27.88
45	20.33	20.87	21.41	21.95	22.49	23.03	23.58	24.12	24.67	25.22	25.77	26.32	26.88	27.43	27.99	28.55
46	20.80	21.35	21.90	22.46	23.01	23.57	24.13	24.69	25.25	25.81	26.37	26.94	27.51	28.08	28.65	29.22
47	21.27	21.83	22.40	22.97	23.53	24.10	24.68	25.25	25.82	26.40	26.98	27.56	28.14	28.72	29.31	29.89
48	21.74	22.32	22.90	23.48	24.06	24.64	25.23	25.81	26.40	26.99	27.58	28.18	28.77	29.37	29.97	30.57
49	22.21	22.80	23.39	23.99	24.58	25.18	25.78	26.38	26.98	27.59	28.19	28.80	29.41	30.02	30.63	31.24
50	22.69	23.29	23.89	24.50	25.11	25.72	26.33	26.95	27.56	28.18	28.80	29.42	30.04	30.67	31.29	31.92
51	23.16	23.78	24.40	25.02	25.64	26.26	26.89	27.52	28.15	28.78	29.41	30.05	30.68	31.32	31.96	32.60
52	23.64	24.27	24.90	25.53	26.17	26.81	27.45	28.09	28.73	29.38	30.02	30.67	31.32	31.98	32.63	33.29
53	24.11	24.76	25.40	26.05	26.70	27.35	28.00	28.66	29.32	29.98	30.64	31.30	31.97	32.63	33.30	33.97
54	24.59	25.25	25.91	26.57	27.23	27.90	28.56	29.23	29.91	30.58	31.25	31.93	32.61	33.29	33.98	34.66
55	25.07	25.74	26.41	27.09	27.77	28.44	29.13	29.81	30.50	31.18	31.87	32.56	33.26	33.95	34.65	35.35
56	25.55	26.23	26.92	27.61	28.30	28.99	29.69	30.39	31.09	31.79	32.49	33.20	33.91	34.62	35.33	36.04
57	26.03	26.73	27.43	28.13	28.84	29.54	30.25	30.97	31.68	32.39	33.11	33.83	34.56	35.28	36.01	36.74
58	26.51	27.23	27.94	28.66	29.37	30.10	30.82	31.55	32.27	33.00	33.74	34.47	35.21	35.95	36.69	37.43
59	27.00	27.72	28.45	29.18	29.91	30.65	31.39	32.13	32.87	33.61	34.36	35.11	35.86	36.62	37.37	38.13
60	27.48	28.22	28.96	29.71	30.45	31.20	31.96	32.71	33.47	34.23	34.99	35.75	36.52	37.29	38.06	38.83
1	1.17	1.19	1.21	1.23	1.25	1.27	1.29	1.31	1.33	1.35	1.37	1.40	1.42	1.44	1.46	1.48
2	1.75	1.78	1.82	1.85	1.88	1.91	1.94	1.97	2.00	2.04	2.07	2.10	2.13	2.16	2.19	2.22
3	2.34	2.38	2.43	2.47	2.51	2.55	2.59	2.64	2.68	2.72	2.76	2.80	2.85	2.89	2.93	2.97
4	2.93	2.99	3.04	3.09	3.14	3.20	3.25	3.30	3.36	3.41	3.46	3.51	3.57	3.62	3.67	3.73
5	3.53	3.59	3.65	3.72	3.78	3.84	3.91	3.97	4.04	4.10	4.16	4.23	4.29	4.35	4.42	4.48
6	4.12	4.20	4.27	4.35	4.42	4.49	4.57	4.64	4.72	4.79	4.87	4.94	5.02	5.09	5.17	5.24
7	4.72	4.81	4.89	4.98	5.06	5.15	5.23	5.32	5.40	5.49	5.58	5.66	5.75	5.83	5.92	6.00
8	5.32	5.42	5.51	5.61	5.71	5.80	5.90	6.00	6.09	6.19	6.29	6.38	6.48	6.58	6.67	6.77
9	5.92	6.03	6.14	6.25	6.35	6.46	6.57	6.68	6.78	6.89	7.00	7.11	7.22	7.32	7.43	7.54
10	6.53	6.65	6.77	6.88	7.00	7.12	7.24	7.36	7.48	7.60	7.72	7.84	7.96	8.08	8.19	8.31
11	7.14	7.27	7.40	7.53	7.66	7.79	7.92	8.05	8.18	8.31	8.44	8.57	8.70	8.83	8.96	9.09
12	7.74	7.89	8.03	8.17	8.31	8.45	8.59	8.74	8.88	9.02	9.16	9.30	9.45	9.59	9.73	9.87
13	8.36	8.51	8.66	8.81	8.97	9.12	9.27	9.43	9.58	9.73	9.89	10.04	10.20	10.35	10.50	10.66
14	8.97	9.13	9.30	9.46	9.63	9.79	9.96	10.12	10.29	10.45	10.62	10.78	10.95	11.11	11.28	11.45
15	9.59	9.76	9.94	10.11	10.29	10.47	10.64	10.82	11.00	11.17	11.35	11.53	11.71	11.88	12.06	12.24
16	10.20	10.39	10.58	10.77	10.95	11.14	11.33	11.52	11.71	11.90	12.09	12.28	12.46	12.65	12.84	13.03
17	10.82	11.02	11.22	11.42	11.62	11.82	12.02	12.22	12.42	12.62	12.83	13.03	13.23	13.43	13.63	13.83
18	11.45	11.66	11.87	12.08	12.29	12.50	12.72	12.93	13.14	13.35	13.57	13.78	13.99	14.21	14.42	14.64
19	12.07	12.30	12.52	12.74	12.97	13.19	13.41	13.64	13.86	14.09	14.31	14.54	14.76	14.99	15.22	15.44
20	12.70	12.93	13.17	13.41	13.64	13.88	14.11	14.35	14.59	14.82	15.06	15.30	15.54	15.77	16.01	16.25

TABLE VIII   *Board of Governors' APR Tables—Volume I (continued)*

ANNUAL PERCENTAGE RATE

(FINANCE CHARGE PER $100 OF AMOUNT FINANCED)

NUMBER OF PAYMENTS	14.00%	14.25%	14.50%	14.75%	15.00%	15.25%	15.50%	15.75%	16.00%	16.25%	16.50%	16.75%	17.00%	17.25%	17.50%	17.75%
21	13.33	13.58	13.82	14.07	14.32	14.57	14.82	15.06	15.31	15.56	15.81	16.06	16.31	16.56	16.81	17.07
22	13.96	14.22	14.48	14.74	15.00	15.26	15.52	15.78	16.04	16.30	16.57	16.83	17.09	17.36	17.62	17.88
23	14.59	14.87	15.14	15.41	15.68	15.96	16.23	16.50	16.78	17.05	17.32	17.60	17.88	18.15	18.43	18.70
24	15.23	15.51	15.80	16.08	16.37	16.65	16.94	17.22	17.51	17.80	18.09	18.37	18.66	18.95	19.24	19.53
25	15.87	16.17	16.46	16.76	17.06	17.35	17.65	17.95	18.25	18.55	18.85	19.15	19.45	19.75	20.05	20.36
26	16.51	16.82	17.13	17.44	17.75	18.06	18.37	18.68	18.99	19.30	19.62	19.93	20.24	20.56	20.87	21.19
27	17.15	17.47	17.80	18.12	18.44	18.76	19.09	19.41	19.74	20.06	20.39	20.71	21.04	21.37	21.69	22.02
28	17.80	18.13	18.47	18.80	19.14	19.47	19.81	20.15	20.48	20.82	21.16	21.50	21.84	22.18	22.52	22.86
29	18.45	18.79	19.14	19.49	19.83	20.18	20.53	20.88	21.23	21.58	21.94	22.29	22.64	22.99	23.35	23.70
30	19.10	19.45	19.81	20.17	20.54	20.90	21.26	21.62	21.99	22.35	22.72	23.08	23.45	23.81	24.18	24.55
31	19.75	20.12	20.49	20.87	21.24	21.61	21.99	22.37	22.74	23.12	23.50	23.88	24.26	24.64	25.02	25.40
32	20.40	20.79	21.17	21.56	21.95	22.33	22.72	23.11	23.50	23.89	24.28	24.68	25.07	25.46	25.86	26.25
33	21.06	21.46	21.85	22.25	22.65	23.06	23.46	23.86	24.26	24.67	25.07	25.48	25.88	26.29	26.70	27.11
34	21.72	22.13	22.54	22.95	23.37	23.78	24.19	24.61	25.03	25.44	25.86	26.28	26.70	27.12	27.54	27.97
35	22.38	22.80	23.23	23.65	24.08	24.51	24.94	25.36	25.79	26.23	26.66	27.09	27.52	27.96	28.39	28.83
36	23.04	23.48	23.92	24.35	24.80	25.24	25.68	26.12	26.57	27.01	27.46	27.90	28.35	28.80	29.25	29.70
37	23.70	24.16	24.61	25.06	25.51	25.97	26.42	26.88	27.34	27.80	28.26	28.72	29.18	29.64	30.10	30.57
38	24.37	24.84	25.30	25.77	26.24	26.70	27.17	27.64	28.11	28.59	29.06	29.53	30.01	30.49	30.96	31.44
39	25.04	25.52	26.00	26.48	26.96	27.44	27.92	28.41	28.89	29.38	29.87	30.36	30.85	31.34	31.83	32.32
40	25.71	26.20	26.70	27.19	27.69	28.18	28.68	29.18	29.68	30.18	30.68	31.18	31.68	32.19	32.69	33.20
41	26.39	26.89	27.40	27.91	28.41	28.92	29.44	29.95	30.46	30.97	31.49	32.01	32.52	33.04	33.56	34.08
42	27.06	27.58	28.10	28.62	29.15	29.67	30.19	30.72	31.25	31.78	32.31	32.84	33.37	33.90	34.44	34.97
43	27.74	28.27	28.81	29.34	29.88	30.42	30.96	31.50	32.04	32.58	33.13	33.67	34.22	34.76	35.31	35.86
44	28.42	28.97	29.52	30.07	30.62	31.17	31.72	32.28	32.83	33.39	33.95	34.51	35.07	35.63	36.19	36.76
45	29.11	29.67	30.23	30.79	31.36	31.92	32.49	33.06	33.63	34.20	34.77	35.35	35.92	36.50	37.08	37.66
46	29.79	30.36	30.94	31.52	32.10	32.68	33.26	33.84	34.43	35.01	35.60	36.19	36.78	37.37	37.96	38.56
47	30.48	31.07	31.66	32.25	32.84	33.44	34.03	34.63	35.23	35.83	36.43	37.04	37.64	38.25	38.86	39.46
48	31.17	31.77	32.37	32.98	33.59	34.20	34.81	35.42	36.03	36.65	37.27	37.88	38.50	39.13	39.75	40.37
49	31.86	32.48	33.09	33.71	34.34	34.96	35.59	36.21	36.84	37.47	38.10	38.74	39.37	40.01	40.65	41.29
50	32.55	33.18	33.82	34.45	35.09	35.73	36.37	37.01	37.65	38.30	38.94	39.59	40.24	40.89	41.55	42.20
51	33.25	33.89	34.54	35.19	35.84	36.49	37.15	37.81	38.46	39.12	39.79	40.45	41.11	41.78	42.45	43.12
52	33.95	34.61	35.27	35.93	36.60	37.27	37.94	38.61	39.28	39.96	40.63	41.31	41.99	42.67	43.36	44.04
53	34.65	35.32	36.00	36.68	37.36	38.04	38.72	39.41	40.10	40.79	41.48	42.17	42.87	43.57	44.27	44.97
54	35.35	36.04	36.73	37.42	38.12	38.82	39.52	40.22	40.92	41.63	42.33	43.04	43.75	44.47	45.18	45.90
55	36.05	36.76	37.46	38.17	38.88	39.60	40.31	41.03	41.74	42.47	43.19	43.91	44.64	45.37	46.10	46.83
56	36.76	37.48	38.20	38.92	39.65	40.38	41.11	41.84	42.57	43.31	44.05	44.79	45.53	46.27	47.02	47.77
57	37.47	38.20	38.94	39.68	40.42	41.16	41.91	42.65	43.40	44.15	44.91	45.66	46.42	47.18	47.94	48.71
58	38.18	38.93	39.68	40.43	41.19	41.95	42.71	43.47	44.23	45.00	45.77	46.54	47.32	48.09	48.87	49.65
59	38.89	39.66	40.42	41.19	41.96	42.74	43.51	44.29	45.07	45.85	46.64	47.42	48.21	49.01	49.80	50.60
60	39.61	40.39	41.17	41.95	42.74	43.53	44.32	45.11	45.91	46.71	47.51	48.31	49.12	49.92	50.73	51.55

ANNUAL PERCENTAGE RATE TABLE FOR MONTHLY PAYMENT PLANS

SEE INSTRUCTIONS FOR USE OF TABLES

ANNUAL PERCENTAGE RATE

(FINANCE CHARGE PER $100 OF AMOUNT FINANCED)

NUMBER OF PAYMENTS	18.00%	18.25%	18.50%	18.75%	19.00%	19.25%	19.50%	19.75%	20.00%	20.25%	20.50%	20.75%	21.00%	21.25%	21.50%	21.75%
1	1.50	1.52	1.54	1.56	1.58	1.60	1.62	1.65	1.67	1.69	1.71	1.73	1.75	1.77	1.79	1.81
2	2.26	2.29	2.32	2.35	2.38	2.41	2.44	2.48	2.51	2.54	2.57	2.60	2.63	2.66	2.70	2.73
3	3.01	3.06	3.10	3.14	3.18	3.23	3.27	3.31	3.35	3.39	3.44	3.48	3.52	3.56	3.60	3.65
4	3.78	3.83	3.88	3.94	3.99	4.04	4.10	4.15	4.20	4.25	4.31	4.36	4.41	4.47	4.52	4.57
5	4.54	4.61	4.67	4.74	4.80	4.86	4.93	4.99	5.06	5.12	5.18	5.25	5.31	5.37	5.44	5.50
6	5.32	5.39	5.46	5.54	5.61	5.69	5.76	5.84	5.91	5.99	6.06	6.14	6.21	6.29	6.36	6.44
7	6.09	6.18	6.26	6.35	6.43	6.52	6.60	6.69	6.78	6.86	6.95	7.04	7.12	7.21	7.29	7.38
8	6.87	6.96	7.06	7.16	7.26	7.35	7.45	7.55	7.64	7.74	7.84	7.94	8.03	8.13	8.23	8.33
9	7.65	7.76	7.87	7.97	8.08	8.19	8.30	8.41	8.52	8.63	8.73	8.84	8.95	9.06	9.17	9.28
10	8.43	8.55	8.67	8.79	8.91	9.03	9.15	9.27	9.39	9.51	9.63	9.75	9.88	10.00	10.12	10.24
11	9.22	9.35	9.49	9.62	9.75	9.88	10.01	10.14	10.28	10.41	10.54	10.67	10.80	10.94	11.07	11.20
12	10.02	10.16	10.30	10.44	10.59	10.73	10.87	11.02	11.16	11.31	11.45	11.59	11.74	11.88	12.02	12.17
13	10.81	10.97	11.12	11.28	11.43	11.59	11.74	11.90	12.05	12.21	12.36	12.52	12.67	12.83	12.99	13.14
14	11.61	11.78	11.95	12.11	12.28	12.45	12.61	12.78	12.95	13.11	13.28	13.45	13.62	13.79	13.95	14.12
15	12.42	12.59	12.77	12.95	13.13	13.31	13.49	13.67	13.85	14.03	14.21	14.39	14.57	14.75	14.93	15.11
16	13.22	13.41	13.60	13.80	13.99	14.18	14.37	14.56	14.75	14.94	15.13	15.33	15.52	15.71	15.90	16.10
17	14.04	14.24	14.44	14.64	14.85	15.05	15.25	15.46	15.66	15.86	16.07	16.27	16.48	16.68	16.89	17.09
18	14.85	15.07	15.28	15.49	15.71	15.93	16.14	16.36	16.57	16.79	17.01	17.22	17.44	17.66	17.88	18.09
19	15.67	15.90	16.12	16.35	16.58	16.81	17.03	17.26	17.49	17.72	17.95	18.18	18.41	18.64	18.87	19.10
20	16.49	16.73	16.97	17.21	17.45	17.69	17.93	18.17	18.41	18.66	18.90	19.14	19.38	19.63	19.87	20.11
21	17.32	17.57	17.82	18.07	18.33	18.58	18.83	19.09	19.34	19.60	19.85	20.11	20.36	20.62	20.87	21.13
22	18.15	18.41	18.68	18.94	19.21	19.47	19.74	20.01	20.27	20.54	20.81	21.08	21.34	21.61	21.88	22.15
23	18.98	19.26	19.54	19.81	20.09	20.37	20.65	20.93	21.21	21.49	21.77	22.05	22.33	22.61	22.90	23.18
24	19.82	20.11	20.40	20.69	20.98	21.27	21.56	21.86	22.15	22.44	22.74	23.03	23.33	23.62	23.92	24.21
25	20.66	20.96	21.27	21.57	21.87	22.18	22.48	22.79	23.10	23.40	23.71	24.02	24.32	24.63	24.94	25.25
26	21.50	21.82	22.14	22.45	22.77	23.09	23.41	23.73	24.04	24.36	24.68	25.01	25.33	25.65	25.97	26.29
27	22.35	22.68	23.01	23.34	23.67	24.00	24.33	24.67	25.00	25.33	25.67	26.00	26.34	26.67	27.01	27.34
28	23.20	23.55	23.89	24.23	24.58	24.92	25.27	25.61	25.96	26.30	26.65	27.00	27.35	27.70	28.05	28.40
29	24.06	24.41	24.77	25.13	25.49	25.84	26.20	26.56	26.92	27.28	27.64	28.00	28.37	28.73	29.09	29.46
30	24.92	25.29	25.66	26.03	26.40	26.77	27.14	27.52	27.89	28.26	28.64	29.01	29.39	29.77	30.14	30.52
31	25.78	26.16	26.55	26.93	27.32	27.70	28.09	28.47	28.86	29.25	29.64	30.03	30.42	30.81	31.20	31.59
32	26.65	27.04	27.44	27.84	28.24	28.64	29.04	29.44	29.84	30.24	30.64	31.05	31.45	31.85	32.26	32.67
33	27.52	27.93	28.34	28.75	29.16	29.57	29.99	30.40	30.82	31.23	31.65	32.07	32.49	32.91	33.33	33.75
34	28.39	28.81	29.24	29.66	30.09	30.52	30.95	31.37	31.80	32.23	32.67	33.10	33.53	33.96	34.40	34.83
35	29.27	29.71	30.14	30.58	31.02	31.47	31.91	32.35	32.79	33.24	33.68	34.13	34.58	35.03	35.47	35.92
36	30.15	30.60	31.05	31.51	31.96	32.42	32.87	33.33	33.79	34.25	34.71	35.17	35.63	36.09	36.56	37.02
37	31.03	31.50	31.97	32.43	32.90	33.37	33.84	34.32	34.79	35.26	35.74	36.21	36.69	37.16	37.64	38.12
38	31.92	32.40	32.88	33.37	33.85	34.33	34.82	35.30	35.79	36.28	36.77	37.26	37.75	38.24	38.73	39.23
39	32.81	33.31	33.80	34.30	34.80	35.30	35.80	36.30	36.80	37.30	37.81	38.31	38.82	39.32	39.83	40.34
40	33.71	34.22	34.73	35.24	35.75	36.26	36.78	37.29	37.81	38.33	38.85	39.37	39.89	40.41	40.93	41.46

TABLE VIII   Board of Governors' APR Tables—Volume I (continued)

FRB-106-M

ANNUAL PERCENTAGE RATE

NUMBER OF PAYMENTS	18.00%	18.25%	18.50%	18.75%	19.00%	19.25%	19.50%	19.75%	20.00%	20.25%	20.50%	20.75%	21.00%	21.25%	21.50%	21.75%
	(FINANCE CHARGE PER $100 OF AMOUNT FINANCED)															
41	34.61	35.13	35.66	36.18	36.71	37.24	37.77	38.30	38.83	39.36	39.89	40.43	40.96	41.50	42.04	42.58
42	35.51	36.05	36.59	37.13	37.67	38.21	38.76	39.30	39.85	40.40	40.95	41.50	42.05	42.60	43.15	43.71
43	36.42	36.97	37.52	38.08	38.63	39.19	39.75	40.31	40.87	41.44	42.00	42.57	43.13	43.70	44.27	44.84
44	37.33	37.89	38.46	39.03	39.60	40.18	40.75	41.33	41.90	42.48	43.06	43.64	44.22	44.81	45.39	45.98
45	38.24	38.82	39.41	39.99	40.58	41.17	41.75	42.35	42.94	43.53	44.13	44.72	45.32	45.92	46.52	47.12
46	39.16	39.75	40.35	40.95	41.55	42.16	42.76	43.37	43.98	44.58	45.20	45.81	46.42	47.03	47.65	48.27
47	40.08	40.69	41.30	41.92	42.54	43.15	43.77	44.40	45.02	45.64	46.27	46.90	47.53	48.16	48.79	49.42
48	41.00	41.63	42.26	42.89	43.52	44.15	44.79	45.43	46.07	46.71	47.35	47.99	48.64	49.28	49.93	50.58
49	41.93	42.57	43.22	43.86	44.51	45.16	45.81	46.46	47.12	47.77	48.43	49.09	49.75	50.41	51.08	51.74
50	42.86	43.52	44.18	44.84	45.50	46.17	46.83	47.50	48.17	48.84	49.52	50.19	50.87	51.55	52.23	52.91
51	43.79	44.47	45.14	45.82	46.50	47.18	47.86	48.55	49.23	49.92	50.61	51.30	51.99	52.69	53.38	54.08
52	44.73	45.42	46.11	46.80	47.50	48.20	48.89	49.59	50.30	51.00	51.71	52.41	53.12	53.83	54.55	55.26
53	45.67	46.38	47.08	47.79	48.50	49.22	49.93	50.65	51.37	52.09	52.81	53.53	54.26	54.98	55.71	56.44
54	46.62	47.34	48.06	48.79	49.51	50.24	50.97	51.70	52.44	53.17	53.91	54.65	55.39	56.14	56.88	57.63
55	47.57	48.30	49.04	49.78	50.52	51.27	52.02	52.76	53.52	54.27	55.02	55.78	56.54	57.30	58.06	58.82
56	48.52	49.27	50.03	50.78	51.54	52.30	53.06	53.83	54.60	55.37	56.14	56.91	57.68	58.46	59.24	60.02
57	49.47	50.24	51.01	51.79	52.56	53.34	54.12	54.90	55.68	56.47	57.25	58.04	58.84	59.63	60.43	61.22
58	50.43	51.22	52.00	52.79	53.58	54.38	55.17	55.97	56.77	57.57	58.38	59.18	59.99	60.80	61.62	62.43
59	51.39	52.20	53.00	53.80	54.61	55.42	56.23	57.05	57.87	58.68	59.51	60.33	61.15	61.98	62.81	63.64
60	52.76	53.18	54.00	54.82	55.64	56.47	57.30	58.13	58.96	59.80	60.64	61.48	62.32	63.17	64.01	64.86

ANNUAL PERCENTAGE RATE TABLE FOR MONTHLY PAYMENT PLANS
SEE INSTRUCTIONS FOR USE OF TABLES

ANNUAL PERCENTAGE RATE

NUMBER OF PAYMENTS	22.00%	22.25%	22.50%	22.75%	23.00%	23.25%	23.50%	23.75%	24.00%	24.25%	24.50%	24.75%	25.00%	25.25%	25.50%	25.75%
	(FINANCE CHARGE PER $100 OF AMOUNT FINANCED)															
1	1.83	1.85	1.87	1.90	1.92	1.94	1.96	1.98	2.00	2.02	2.04	2.06	2.08	2.10	2.12	2.15
2	2.76	2.79	2.82	2.85	2.88	2.92	2.95	2.98	3.01	3.04	3.07	3.10	3.14	3.17	3.20	3.23
3	3.69	3.73	3.77	3.82	3.86	3.90	3.94	3.98	4.03	4.07	4.11	4.15	4.20	4.24	4.28	4.32
4	4.62	4.68	4.73	4.78	4.84	4.89	4.94	5.00	5.05	5.10	5.16	5.21	5.26	5.32	5.37	5.42
5	5.57	5.63	5.69	5.76	5.82	5.89	5.95	6.02	6.08	6.14	6.21	6.27	6.34	6.40	6.46	6.53
6	6.51	6.59	6.66	6.74	6.81	6.89	6.96	7.04	7.12	7.19	7.27	7.34	7.42	7.49	7.57	7.64
7	7.47	7.55	7.64	7.73	7.81	7.90	7.99	8.07	8.16	8.24	8.33	8.42	8.51	8.59	8.68	8.77
8	8.42	8.52	8.62	8.72	8.82	8.91	9.01	9.11	9.21	9.31	9.40	9.50	9.60	9.70	9.80	9.90
9	9.39	9.50	9.61	9.72	9.83	9.94	10.04	10.15	10.26	10.37	10.48	10.59	10.70	10.81	10.92	11.03
10	10.36	10.48	10.60	10.72	10.84	10.96	11.08	11.21	11.33	11.45	11.57	11.69	11.81	11.93	12.06	12.18
11	11.33	11.47	11.60	11.73	11.86	12.00	12.13	12.26	12.40	12.53	12.66	12.80	12.93	13.06	13.20	13.33
12	12.31	12.46	12.60	12.75	12.89	13.04	13.18	13.33	13.47	13.62	13.76	13.91	14.05	14.20	14.34	14.49
13	13.30	13.46	13.61	13.77	13.93	14.08	14.24	14.40	14.55	14.71	14.87	15.03	15.18	15.34	15.50	15.66
14	14.29	14.46	14.63	14.80	14.97	15.13	15.30	15.47	15.64	15.81	15.98	16.15	16.32	16.49	16.66	16.83

15	15.29	15.47	15.65	15.83	16.01	16.19	16.37	16.56	16.74	16.92	17.10	17.28	17.47	17.65	17.83	18.02
16	16.29	16.48	16.68	16.87	17.06	17.26	17.45	17.65	17.84	18.03	18.23	18.42	18.62	18.81	19.01	19.21
17	17.30	17.50	17.71	17.92	18.12	18.33	18.53	18.74	18.95	19.16	19.36	19.57	19.78	19.99	20.20	20.40
18	18.31	18.53	18.75	18.97	19.19	19.41	19.62	19.84	20.06	20.28	20.50	20.72	20.95	21.17	21.39	21.61
19	19.33	19.56	19.79	20.02	20.26	20.49	20.72	20.95	21.19	21.42	21.65	21.89	22.12	22.35	22.59	22.82
20	20.35	20.60	20.84	21.09	21.33	21.58	21.82	22.07	22.31	22.56	22.81	23.05	23.30	23.55	23.79	24.04
21	21.38	21.64	21.90	22.16	22.41	22.67	22.93	23.19	23.45	23.71	23.97	24.23	24.49	24.75	25.01	25.27
22	22.42	22.69	22.96	23.23	23.50	23.77	24.04	24.32	24.59	24.86	25.13	25.41	25.68	25.96	26.23	26.50
23	23.46	23.74	24.03	24.31	24.60	24.88	25.17	25.45	25.74	26.02	26.31	26.60	26.88	27.17	27.46	27.75
24	24.51	24.80	25.10	25.40	25.70	25.99	26.29	26.59	26.89	27.19	27.49	27.79	28.09	28.39	28.69	29.00
25	25.56	25.87	26.18	26.49	26.80	27.11	27.43	27.74	28.05	28.36	28.68	28.99	29.31	29.62	29.94	30.25
26	26.62	26.94	27.26	27.59	27.91	28.24	28.56	28.89	29.22	29.55	29.87	30.20	30.53	30.86	31.19	31.52
27	27.68	28.02	28.35	28.69	29.03	29.37	29.71	30.05	30.39	30.73	31.07	31.42	31.76	32.10	32.45	32.79
28	28.75	29.10	29.45	29.80	30.15	30.51	30.86	31.22	31.57	31.93	32.28	32.64	33.00	33.35	33.71	34.07
29	29.82	30.19	30.55	30.92	31.28	31.65	32.02	32.39	32.76	33.13	33.50	33.87	34.24	34.61	34.98	35.36
30	30.90	31.28	31.66	32.04	32.42	32.80	33.18	33.57	33.95	34.33	34.72	35.10	35.49	35.88	36.26	36.65
31	31.98	32.38	32.77	33.17	33.56	33.96	34.35	34.75	35.15	35.55	35.95	36.35	36.75	37.15	37.55	37.95
32	33.07	33.48	33.89	34.30	34.71	35.12	35.53	35.94	36.35	36.77	37.18	37.60	38.01	38.43	38.84	39.26
33	34.17	34.59	35.01	35.44	35.86	36.29	36.71	37.14	37.57	37.99	38.42	38.85	39.28	39.71	40.14	40.58
34	35.27	35.71	36.14	36.58	37.02	37.46	37.90	38.34	38.78	39.23	39.67	40.11	40.56	41.01	41.45	41.90
35	36.37	36.83	37.28	37.73	38.18	38.64	39.09	39.55	40.01	40.47	40.92	41.38	41.84	42.31	42.77	43.23
36	37.49	37.95	38.42	38.89	39.35	39.82	40.29	40.77	41.24	41.71	42.19	42.66	43.14	43.61	44.09	44.57
37	38.60	39.08	39.56	40.05	40.53	41.02	41.50	41.99	42.48	42.96	43.45	43.94	44.43	44.93	45.42	45.91
38	39.72	40.22	40.72	41.21	41.71	42.21	42.71	43.22	43.72	44.22	44.73	45.23	45.74	46.25	46.75	47.26
39	40.85	41.36	41.87	42.39	42.90	43.42	43.93	44.45	44.97	45.49	46.01	46.53	47.05	47.57	48.10	48.62
40	41.98	42.51	43.04	43.56	44.09	44.62	45.16	45.69	46.22	46.76	47.29	47.83	48.37	48.91	49.45	49.99
41	43.12	43.66	44.20	44.75	45.29	45.84	46.39	46.94	47.48	48.04	48.59	49.14	49.69	50.25	50.80	51.36
42	44.26	44.82	45.38	45.94	46.50	47.06	47.62	48.19	48.75	49.32	49.89	50.46	51.03	51.60	52.17	52.74
43	45.41	45.98	46.56	47.13	47.71	48.29	48.87	49.45	50.03	50.61	51.19	51.78	52.36	52.95	53.54	54.13
44	46.56	47.15	47.74	48.33	48.93	49.52	50.11	50.71	51.31	51.91	52.51	53.11	53.71	54.31	54.92	55.52
45	47.72	48.33	48.93	49.54	50.15	50.76	51.37	51.98	52.59	53.21	53.82	54.44	55.06	55.68	56.30	56.92
46	48.89	49.51	50.13	50.75	51.37	52.00	52.63	53.26	53.89	54.52	55.15	55.78	56.42	57.05	57.69	58.33
47	50.06	50.69	51.33	51.97	52.61	53.25	53.89	54.54	55.18	55.83	56.48	57.13	57.78	58.44	59.09	59.75
48	51.23	51.88	52.54	53.19	53.85	54.51	55.16	55.83	56.49	57.15	57.82	58.49	59.15	59.82	60.50	61.17
49	52.41	53.08	53.75	54.42	55.09	55.77	56.44	57.12	57.80	58.48	59.16	59.85	60.53	61.22	61.91	62.60
50	53.59	54.28	54.96	55.65	56.34	57.03	57.73	58.42	59.12	59.81	60.51	61.21	61.92	62.62	63.33	64.03
51	54.78	55.48	56.19	56.89	57.60	58.30	59.01	59.73	60.44	61.15	61.87	62.59	63.31	64.03	64.75	65.47
52	55.98	56.69	57.41	58.13	58.86	59.58	60.31	61.04	61.77	62.50	63.23	63.97	64.70	65.44	66.18	66.92
53	57.18	57.91	58.65	59.38	60.12	60.87	61.61	62.35	63.10	63.85	64.60	65.35	66.11	66.86	67.62	68.38
54	58.38	59.13	59.88	60.64	61.40	62.16	62.92	63.68	64.44	65.21	65.98	66.75	67.52	68.29	69.07	69.84
55	59.59	60.36	61.13	61.90	62.67	63.45	64.23	65.01	65.79	66.57	67.36	68.14	68.93	69.72	70.52	71.31
56	60.80	61.59	62.38	63.17	63.96	64.75	65.54	66.34	67.14	67.94	68.74	69.55	70.36	71.16	71.97	72.79
57	62.02	62.83	63.63	64.44	65.25	66.06	66.87	67.68	68.50	69.32	70.14	70.96	71.78	72.61	73.44	74.27
58	63.25	64.07	64.89	65.71	66.54	67.37	68.20	69.03	69.86	70.70	71.54	72.38	73.22	74.06	74.91	75.76
59	64.48	65.32	66.15	67.00	67.84	68.68	69.53	70.38	71.23	72.09	72.94	73.80	74.66	75.52	76.39	77.25
60	65.71	66.57	67.42	68.28	69.14	70.01	70.87	71.74	72.61	73.48	74.35	75.23	76.11	76.99	77.87	78.76

TABLE VIII Board of Governors' APR Tables—Volume I (continued)

ANNUAL PERCENTAGE RATE TABLE FOR MONTHLY PAYMENT PLANS
SEE INSTRUCTIONS FOR USE OF TABLES

FRB-107-M

ANNUAL PERCENTAGE RATE

(FINANCE CHARGE PER $100 OF AMOUNT FINANCED)

NUMBER OF PAYMENTS	26.00%	26.25%	26.50%	26.75%	27.00%	27.25%	27.50%	27.75%	28.00%	28.25%	28.50%	28.75%	29.00%	29.25%	29.50%	29.75%
1	2.17	2.19	2.21	2.23	2.25	2.27	2.29	2.31	2.33	2.35	2.37	2.40	2.42	2.44	2.46	2.48
2	3.26	3.29	3.32	3.36	3.39	3.42	3.45	3.48	3.51	3.54	3.58	3.61	3.64	3.67	3.70	3.73
3	4.36	4.41	4.45	4.49	4.53	4.58	4.62	4.66	4.70	4.74	4.79	4.83	4.87	4.91	4.96	5.00
4	5.47	5.53	5.58	5.63	5.69	5.74	5.79	5.85	5.90	5.95	6.01	6.06	6.11	6.17	6.22	6.27
5	6.59	6.66	6.72	6.79	6.85	6.91	6.98	7.04	7.11	7.17	7.24	7.30	7.37	7.43	7.49	7.56
6	7.72	7.79	7.87	7.95	8.02	8.10	8.17	8.25	8.32	8.40	8.48	8.55	8.63	8.70	8.78	8.85
7	8.85	8.94	9.03	9.11	9.20	9.29	9.37	9.46	9.55	9.64	9.72	9.81	9.90	9.98	10.07	10.16
8	9.99	10.09	10.19	10.29	10.39	10.49	10.58	10.68	10.78	10.88	10.98	11.08	11.18	11.28	11.38	11.47
9	11.14	11.25	11.36	11.47	11.58	11.69	11.80	11.91	12.03	12.14	12.25	12.36	12.47	12.58	12.69	12.80
10	12.30	12.42	12.54	12.67	12.79	12.91	13.03	13.15	13.28	13.40	13.52	13.64	13.77	13.89	14.01	14.14
11	13.46	13.60	13.73	13.87	14.00	14.13	14.27	14.40	14.54	14.67	14.81	14.94	15.08	15.21	15.35	15.48
12	14.64	14.78	14.93	15.07	15.22	15.37	15.51	15.66	15.81	15.95	16.10	16.25	16.40	16.54	16.69	16.84
13	15.82	15.97	16.13	16.29	16.45	16.61	16.77	16.93	17.09	17.24	17.40	17.56	17.72	17.88	18.04	18.20
14	17.00	17.17	17.35	17.52	17.69	17.86	18.03	18.20	18.37	18.54	18.72	18.89	19.06	19.23	19.41	19.58
15	18.20	18.38	18.57	18.75	18.93	19.12	19.30	19.48	19.67	19.85	20.04	20.22	20.41	20.59	20.78	20.96
16	19.40	19.60	19.79	19.99	20.19	20.38	20.58	20.78	20.97	21.17	21.37	21.57	21.76	21.96	22.16	22.36
17	20.61	20.82	21.03	21.24	21.45	21.66	21.87	22.08	22.29	22.50	22.71	22.92	23.13	23.34	23.55	23.77
18	21.83	22.05	22.27	22.50	22.72	22.94	23.16	23.39	23.61	23.83	24.06	24.28	24.51	24.73	24.96	25.18
19	23.06	23.29	23.53	23.76	24.00	24.23	24.47	24.71	24.94	25.18	25.42	25.65	25.89	26.13	26.37	26.61
20	24.29	24.54	24.79	25.04	25.28	25.53	25.78	26.03	26.28	26.53	26.78	27.04	27.29	27.54	27.79	28.04
21	25.53	25.79	26.05	26.32	26.58	26.84	27.11	27.37	27.63	27.90	28.16	28.43	28.69	28.96	29.22	29.49
22	26.78	27.05	27.33	27.61	27.88	28.16	28.44	28.71	28.99	29.27	29.55	29.82	30.10	30.38	30.66	30.94
23	28.04	28.32	28.61	28.90	29.19	29.48	29.77	30.07	30.36	30.65	30.94	31.23	31.53	31.82	32.11	32.41
24	29.30	29.60	29.90	30.21	30.51	30.82	31.12	31.43	31.73	32.04	32.34	32.65	32.96	33.27	33.57	33.88
25	30.57	30.89	31.20	31.52	31.84	32.16	32.48	32.80	33.12	33.44	33.76	34.08	34.40	34.72	35.04	35.37
26	31.85	32.18	32.51	32.84	33.18	33.51	33.84	34.18	34.51	34.84	35.18	35.51	35.85	36.19	36.52	36.86
27	33.14	33.48	33.83	34.17	34.52	34.87	35.21	35.56	35.91	36.26	36.61	36.96	37.31	37.66	38.01	38.36
28	34.43	34.79	35.15	35.51	35.87	36.23	36.59	36.96	37.32	37.68	38.05	38.41	38.78	39.15	39.51	39.88
29	35.73	36.10	36.48	36.85	37.23	37.61	37.98	38.36	38.74	39.12	39.50	39.88	40.26	40.64	41.02	41.40
30	37.04	37.43	37.82	38.21	38.60	38.99	39.38	39.77	40.17	40.56	40.95	41.35	41.75	42.14	42.54	42.94
31	38.35	38.76	39.16	39.57	39.97	40.38	40.79	41.19	41.60	42.01	42.42	42.83	43.24	43.65	44.06	44.48
32	39.68	40.10	40.52	40.94	41.36	41.78	42.20	42.62	43.05	43.47	43.90	44.32	44.75	45.17	45.60	46.03
33	41.01	41.44	41.88	42.31	42.75	43.19	43.62	44.06	44.50	44.94	45.38	45.82	46.26	46.70	47.15	47.59
34	42.35	42.80	43.25	43.70	44.15	44.60	45.05	45.51	45.96	46.42	46.87	47.33	47.79	48.24	48.70	49.16
35	43.69	44.16	44.62	45.09	45.56	46.02	46.49	46.96	47.43	47.90	48.37	48.85	49.32	49.79	50.27	50.74
36	45.05	45.53	46.01	46.49	46.97	47.45	47.94	48.42	48.91	49.40	49.88	50.37	50.86	51.35	51.84	52.33
37	46.41	46.90	47.40	47.90	48.39	48.89	49.39	49.89	50.40	50.90	51.40	51.91	52.41	52.92	53.42	53.93
38	47.77	48.29	48.80	49.31	49.82	50.34	50.86	51.37	51.89	52.41	52.93	53.45	53.97	54.49	55.02	55.54
39	49.15	49.68	50.20	50.73	51.26	51.79	52.23	52.86	53.39	53.93	54.46	55.00	55.54	56.08	56.62	57.16
40	50.53	51.07	51.62	52.16	52.71	53.26	53.81	54.35	54.90	55.46	56.01	56.56	57.12	57.67	58.23	58.79

NUMBER OF PAYMENTS	30.00%	30.25%	30.50%	30.75%	31.00%	31.25%	31.50%	31.75%	32.00%	32.25%	32.50%	32.75%	33.00%	33.25%	33.50%	33.75%
41	51.92	52.48	53.04	53.60	54.16	54.73	55.29	55.86	56.42	56.99	57.56	58.13	58.70	59.28	59.85	60.42
42	53.32	53.89	54.47	55.05	55.63	56.21	56.79	57.37	57.95	58.54	59.12	59.71	60.30	60.89	61.48	62.07
43	54.72	55.31	55.90	56.50	57.09	57.69	58.29	58.89	59.49	60.09	60.69	61.30	61.90	62.51	63.11	63.72
44	56.13	56.74	57.35	57.96	58.57	59.19	59.80	60.42	61.03	61.65	62.27	62.89	63.51	64.14	64.76	65.39
45	57.55	58.17	58.80	59.43	60.06	60.69	61.32	61.95	62.59	63.22	63.86	64.50	65.13	65.77	66.42	67.06
46	58.97	59.61	60.26	60.90	61.55	62.20	62.84	63.49	64.15	64.80	65.45	66.11	66.76	67.42	68.08	68.74
47	60.40	61.06	61.72	62.38	63.05	63.71	64.38	65.05	65.71	66.38	67.06	67.73	68.40	69.08	69.75	70.43
48	61.84	62.52	63.20	63.87	64.56	65.24	65.92	66.60	67.29	67.98	68.67	69.36	70.05	70.74	71.44	72.13
49	63.29	63.98	64.68	65.37	66.07	66.77	67.47	68.17	68.87	69.58	70.29	70.99	71.70	72.41	73.13	73.84
50	64.74	65.45	66.16	66.88	67.59	68.31	69.03	69.75	70.47	71.19	71.91	72.64	73.37	74.10	74.83	75.56
51	66.20	66.93	67.66	68.39	69.12	69.86	70.59	71.33	72.07	72.81	73.55	74.29	75.04	75.78	76.53	77.28
52	67.67	68.41	69.16	69.91	70.66	71.41	72.16	72.92	73.67	74.43	75.19	75.95	76.72	77.48	78.25	79.02
53	69.14	69.90	70.67	71.43	72.20	72.97	73.74	74.52	75.29	76.07	76.85	77.62	78.41	79.19	79.97	80.76
54	70.62	71.40	72.18	72.97	73.75	74.54	75.33	76.12	76.91	77.71	78.50	79.30	80.10	80.90	81.71	82.51
55	72.11	72.91	73.71	74.51	75.31	76.12	76.92	77.73	78.55	79.36	80.17	80.99	81.81	82.63	83.45	84.27
56	73.60	74.42	75.24	76.06	76.88	77.70	78.53	79.35	80.18	81.02	81.85	82.68	83.52	84.36	85.20	86.04
57	75.10	75.94	76.77	77.61	78.45	79.29	80.14	80.98	81.83	82.68	83.53	84.39	85.24	86.10	86.96	87.82
58	76.61	77.46	78.32	79.17	80.03	80.89	81.75	82.62	83.48	84.35	85.22	86.10	86.97	87.85	88.72	89.60
59	78.12	78.99	79.87	80.74	81.62	82.50	83.38	84.26	85.15	86.03	86.92	87.81	88.71	89.60	90.50	91.40
60	79.64	80.53	81.42	82.32	83.21	84.11	85.01	85.91	86.81	87.72	88.63	89.54	90.45	91.37	92.28	93.20

ANNUAL PERCENTAGE RATE TABLE FOR MONTHLY PAYMENT PLANS
SEE INSTRUCTIONS FOR USE OF TABLES

ANNUAL PERCENTAGE RATE

(FINANCE CHARGE PER $100 OF AMOUNT FINANCED)

NUMBER OF PAYMENTS	30.00%	30.25%	30.50%	30.75%	31.00%	31.25%	31.50%	31.75%	32.00%	32.25%	32.50%	32.75%	33.00%	33.25%	33.50%	33.75%
1	2.50	2.52	2.54	2.56	2.58	2.60	2.62	2.65	2.67	2.69	2.71	2.73	2.75	2.77	2.79	2.81
2	3.77	3.80	3.83	3.86	3.89	3.92	3.95	3.99	4.02	4.05	4.08	4.11	4.14	4.18	4.21	4.24
3	5.04	5.08	5.13	5.17	5.21	5.25	5.30	5.34	5.38	5.42	5.46	5.51	5.55	5.59	5.63	5.68
4	6.33	6.38	6.43	6.49	6.54	6.59	6.65	6.70	6.75	6.81	6.86	6.91	6.97	7.02	7.08	7.13
5	7.62	7.69	7.75	7.82	7.88	7.95	8.01	8.08	8.14	8.20	8.27	8.33	8.40	8.46	8.53	8.59
6	8.93	9.01	9.08	9.16	9.23	9.31	9.39	9.46	9.54	9.61	9.69	9.77	9.84	9.92	9.99	10.07
7	10.25	10.33	10.42	10.51	10.60	10.68	10.77	10.86	10.95	11.03	11.12	11.21	11.30	11.39	11.47	11.56
8	11.57	11.67	11.77	11.87	11.97	12.07	12.17	12.27	12.37	12.47	12.57	12.67	12.77	12.87	12.97	13.07
9	12.91	13.02	13.13	13.24	13.36	13.47	13.58	13.69	13.80	13.91	14.02	14.14	14.25	14.36	14.47	14.58
10	14.26	14.38	14.50	14.63	14.75	14.87	15.00	15.12	15.24	15.37	15.49	15.62	15.74	15.86	15.99	16.11
11	15.62	15.75	15.89	16.02	16.16	16.29	16.43	16.56	16.70	16.84	16.97	17.11	17.24	17.38	17.52	17.65
12	16.98	17.13	17.28	17.43	17.58	17.72	17.87	18.02	18.17	18.32	18.47	18.61	18.76	18.91	19.06	19.21
13	18.36	18.52	18.68	18.84	19.00	19.16	19.33	19.49	19.65	19.81	19.97	20.13	20.29	20.45	20.62	20.78
14	19.75	19.92	20.10	20.27	20.44	20.62	20.79	20.96	21.14	21.31	21.49	21.66	21.83	22.01	22.18	22.36
15	21.15	21.34	21.52	21.71	21.89	22.08	22.27	22.45	22.64	22.83	23.01	23.20	23.39	23.58	23.76	23.95
16	22.56	22.76	22.96	23.16	23.35	23.55	23.75	23.95	24.15	24.35	24.55	24.75	24.96	25.16	25.36	25.56
17	23.98	24.19	24.40	24.61	24.83	25.04	25.25	25.47	25.68	25.89	26.11	26.32	26.53	26.75	26.96	27.18
18	25.41	25.63	25.86	26.08	26.31	26.54	26.76	26.99	27.22	27.44	27.67	27.90	28.13	28.35	28.58	28.81
19	26.85	27.08	27.32	27.56	27.80	28.04	28.28	28.52	28.76	29.00	29.25	29.49	29.73	29.97	30.21	30.45
20	28.29	28.55	28.80	29.05	29.31	29.56	29.81	30.07	30.32	30.58	30.83	31.09	31.34	31.60	31.86	32.11

TABLE VIII   Board of Governors' APR Tables—Volume I (continued)

ANNUAL PERCENTAGE RATE

(FINANCE CHARGE PER $100 OF AMOUNT FINANCED)

NUMBER OF PAYMENTS	30.00%	30.25%	30.50%	30.75%	31.00%	31.25%	31.50%	31.75%	32.00%	32.25%	32.50%	32.75%	33.00%	33.25%	33.50%	33.75%
21	29.75	30.02	30.29	30.55	30.82	31.09	31.36	31.62	31.89	32.16	32.43	32.70	32.97	33.24	33.51	33.78
22	31.22	31.50	31.78	32.06	32.35	32.63	32.91	33.19	33.48	33.76	34.04	34.33	34.61	34.89	35.18	35.48
23	32.70	33.00	33.29	33.59	33.88	34.18	34.48	34.77	35.07	35.37	35.66	35.96	36.26	36.56	36.86	37.16
24	34.19	34.50	34.81	35.12	35.43	35.74	36.05	36.36	36.67	36.99	37.30	37.61	37.92	38.24	38.55	38.87
25	35.69	36.01	36.34	36.66	36.99	37.31	37.64	37.96	38.29	38.62	38.94	39.27	39.60	39.93	40.26	40.59
26	37.20	37.54	37.88	38.21	38.55	38.89	39.23	39.58	39.92	40.26	40.60	40.94	41.29	41.63	41.97	42.32
27	38.72	39.07	39.42	39.78	40.13	40.49	40.84	41.20	41.56	41.91	42.27	42.63	42.99	43.34	43.70	44.06
28	40.25	40.61	40.98	41.35	41.72	42.09	42.46	42.83	43.20	43.58	43.95	44.32	44.70	45.07	45.45	45.82
29	41.78	42.17	42.55	42.94	43.32	43.71	44.09	44.48	44.87	45.25	45.64	46.03	46.42	46.81	47.20	47.59
30	43.33	43.73	44.13	44.53	44.93	45.33	45.73	46.13	46.54	46.94	47.34	47.75	48.15	48.56	48.96	49.37
31	44.89	45.30	45.72	46.13	46.55	46.97	47.38	47.80	48.22	48.64	49.06	49.48	49.90	50.32	50.74	51.17
32	46.46	46.89	47.32	47.75	48.18	48.61	49.05	49.48	49.91	50.35	50.78	51.22	51.66	52.09	52.53	52.97
33	48.04	48.48	48.93	49.37	49.82	50.27	50.72	51.17	51.62	52.07	52.52	52.97	53.43	53.88	54.33	54.79
34	49.62	50.08	50.55	51.01	51.47	51.94	52.40	52.87	53.33	53.80	54.27	54.74	55.21	55.68	56.16	56.62
35	51.22	51.70	52.17	52.65	53.13	53.61	54.09	54.58	55.06	55.54	56.03	56.51	57.00	57.48	57.97	58.46
36	52.83	53.32	53.81	54.31	54.80	55.30	55.80	56.30	56.80	57.30	57.80	58.30	58.80	59.30	59.81	60.31
37	54.44	54.95	55.46	55.97	56.49	57.00	57.51	58.03	58.54	59.06	59.58	60.10	60.62	61.14	61.66	62.18
38	56.07	56.59	57.12	57.65	58.18	58.71	59.24	59.77	60.30	60.84	61.37	61.90	62.44	62.98	63.52	64.06
39	57.70	58.24	58.79	59.33	59.88	60.42	60.97	61.52	62.07	62.62	63.17	63.72	64.28	64.83	65.39	65.94
40	59.34	59.90	60.47	61.03	61.59	62.15	62.72	63.28	63.85	64.42	64.99	65.56	66.13	66.70	67.27	67.84
41	61.00	61.57	62.15	62.73	63.31	63.89	64.47	65.06	65.64	66.22	66.81	67.40	67.99	68.57	69.16	69.76
42	62.66	63.25	63.85	64.44	65.04	65.64	66.24	66.84	67.44	68.04	68.65	69.25	69.86	70.46	71.07	71.68
43	64.33	64.94	65.56	66.17	66.78	67.40	68.01	68.63	69.25	69.87	70.49	71.11	71.74	72.36	72.99	73.61
44	66.01	66.64	67.27	67.90	68.53	69.17	69.80	70.43	71.07	71.71	72.35	72.99	73.63	74.27	74.91	75.56
45	67.70	68.35	69.00	69.64	70.29	70.94	71.60	72.25	72.90	73.56	74.21	74.87	75.53	76.19	76.85	77.52
46	69.40	70.07	70.73	71.40	72.06	72.73	73.40	74.07	74.74	75.42	76.09	76.77	77.44	78.12	78.80	79.48
47	71.11	71.79	72.47	73.16	73.84	74.53	75.22	75.90	76.60	77.29	77.98	78.67	79.37	80.07	80.76	81.46
48	72.83	73.53	74.23	74.93	75.63	76.34	77.04	77.75	78.46	79.17	79.88	80.59	81.30	82.02	82.74	83.45
49	74.55	75.27	75.99	76.71	77.43	78.15	78.88	79.60	80.33	81.06	81.79	82.52	83.25	83.98	84.72	85.45
50	76.29	77.02	77.76	78.50	79.24	79.98	80.72	81.46	82.21	82.96	83.70	84.45	85.20	85.96	86.71	87.47
51	78.03	78.79	79.54	80.30	81.06	81.81	82.58	83.34	84.10	84.87	85.63	86.40	87.17	87.94	88.71	89.49
52	79.79	80.56	81.33	82.11	82.88	83.66	84.44	85.22	86.00	86.79	87.57	88.36	89.15	89.94	90.73	91.52
53	81.55	82.34	83.13	83.92	84.72	85.51	86.31	87.11	87.91	88.72	89.52	90.33	91.13	91.94	92.75	93.57
54	83.32	84.13	84.94	85.75	86.56	87.38	88.19	89.01	89.83	90.66	91.48	92.30	93.13	93.96	94.79	95.62
55	85.10	85.93	86.75	87.58	88.42	89.25	90.09	90.92	91.76	92.60	93.45	94.29	95.14	95.99	96.83	97.69
56	86.89	87.73	88.58	89.43	90.28	91.13	91.99	92.84	93.70	94.56	95.43	96.29	97.15	98.02	98.89	99.76
57	88.68	89.55	90.41	91.28	92.15	93.02	93.90	94.77	95.65	96.53	97.41	98.30	99.18	100.07	100.96	101.85
58	90.49	91.37	92.26	93.14	94.03	94.92	95.82	96.71	97.61	98.51	99.41	100.31	101.22	102.12	103.03	103.94
59	92.30	93.20	94.11	95.01	95.92	96.83	97.75	98.66	99.58	100.50	101.42	102.34	103.26	104.19	105.12	106.05
60	94.12	95.04	95.97	96.89	97.82	98.75	99.68	100.62	101.56	102.49	103.43	104.38	105.32	106.27	107.21	108.16

ANNUAL PERCENTAGE RATE TABLE FOR MONTHLY PAYMENT PLANS
SEE INSTRUCTIONS FOR USE OF TABLES

ANNUAL PERCENTAGE RATE

(FINANCE CHARGE PER $100 OF AMOUNT FINANCED)

NUMBER OF PAYMENTS	34.00%	34.25%	34.50%	34.75%	35.00%	35.25%	35.50%	35.75%	36.00%	36.25%	36.50%	36.75%	37.00%	37.25%	37.50%	37.75%
1	2.83	2.85	2.87	2.90	2.92	2.94	2.96	2.98	3.00	3.02	3.04	3.06	3.08	3.10	3.12	3.15
2	4.27	4.30	4.33	4.36	4.40	4.43	4.46	4.49	4.52	4.55	4.59	4.62	4.65	4.68	4.71	4.74
3	5.72	5.76	5.80	5.85	5.89	5.93	5.97	6.02	6.06	6.10	6.14	6.19	6.23	6.27	6.31	6.36
4	7.18	7.24	7.29	7.34	7.40	7.45	7.50	7.56	7.61	7.66	7.72	7.77	7.83	7.88	7.93	7.99
5	8.66	8.72	8.79	8.85	8.92	8.98	9.05	9.11	9.18	9.24	9.31	9.37	9.44	9.50	9.57	9.63
6	10.15	10.22	10.30	10.38	10.45	10.53	10.61	10.68	10.76	10.83	10.91	10.99	11.06	11.14	11.22	11.29
7	11.65	11.74	11.83	11.91	12.00	12.09	12.18	12.27	12.35	12.44	12.53	12.62	12.71	12.80	12.88	12.97
8	13.17	13.27	13.36	13.46	13.56	13.66	13.76	13.86	13.97	14.07	14.17	14.27	14.37	14.47	14.57	14.67
9	14.69	14.81	14.92	15.03	15.14	15.25	15.37	15.48	15.59	15.70	15.82	15.93	16.04	16.15	16.27	16.38
10	16.24	16.36	16.48	16.61	16.73	16.86	16.98	17.11	17.23	17.36	17.48	17.60	17.73	17.85	17.98	18.10
11	17.79	17.93	18.06	18.20	18.34	18.47	18.61	18.75	18.89	19.02	19.16	19.30	19.43	19.57	19.71	19.85
12	19.36	19.51	19.66	19.81	19.96	20.11	20.25	20.40	20.55	20.70	20.85	21.00	21.15	21.31	21.46	21.61
13	20.94	21.10	21.26	21.43	21.59	21.75	21.91	22.08	22.24	22.40	22.56	22.73	22.89	23.05	23.22	23.38
14	22.53	22.71	22.88	23.06	23.23	23.41	23.59	23.76	23.94	24.11	24.29	24.47	24.64	24.82	25.00	25.17
15	24.14	24.33	24.52	24.71	24.89	25.08	25.27	25.46	25.65	25.84	26.03	26.22	26.41	26.60	26.79	26.98
16	25.76	25.96	26.16	26.37	26.57	26.77	26.97	27.17	27.38	27.58	27.78	27.99	28.19	28.39	28.60	28.80
17	27.39	27.67	27.82	28.04	28.25	28.47	28.69	28.90	29.12	29.34	29.55	29.77	29.99	30.20	30.42	30.64
18	29.04	29.27	29.50	29.73	29.96	30.19	30.42	30.65	30.88	31.11	31.34	31.57	31.80	32.03	32.26	32.49
19	30.70	30.94	31.18	31.43	31.67	31.91	32.16	32.40	32.65	32.89	33.14	33.38	33.63	33.87	34.12	34.36
20	32.37	32.63	32.88	33.14	33.40	33.66	33.91	34.17	34.43	34.69	34.95	35.21	35.47	35.73	35.99	36.25
21	34.05	34.32	34.60	34.87	35.14	35.41	35.68	35.96	36.23	36.50	36.78	37.05	37.33	37.60	37.88	38.15
22	35.75	36.04	36.32	36.61	36.89	37.18	37.47	37.76	38.04	38.33	38.62	38.91	39.20	39.49	39.78	40.07
23	37.46	37.76	38.06	38.36	38.66	38.96	39.27	39.57	39.87	40.18	40.48	40.78	41.09	41.39	41.70	42.00
24	39.18	39.50	39.81	40.13	40.44	40.76	41.08	41.40	41.71	42.03	42.35	42.67	42.99	43.31	43.63	43.95
25	40.92	41.25	41.58	41.91	42.24	42.57	42.90	43.24	43.57	43.90	44.24	44.57	44.91	45.24	45.58	45.91
26	42.66	43.01	43.36	43.70	44.05	44.40	44.74	45.09	45.44	45.79	46.14	46.49	46.84	47.19	47.54	47.89
27	44.42	44.78	45.15	45.51	45.87	46.23	46.60	46.96	47.32	47.69	48.05	48.42	48.78	49.15	49.52	49.88
28	46.20	46.57	46.95	47.33	47.70	48.08	48.46	48.84	49.22	49.60	49.98	50.36	50.75	51.13	51.51	51.89
29	47.98	48.37	48.77	49.16	49.55	49.95	50.34	50.74	51.13	51.53	51.93	52.32	52.72	53.12	53.52	53.92
30	49.78	50.19	50.60	51.00	51.41	51.82	52.23	52.65	53.06	53.47	53.88	54.30	54.71	55.13	55.54	55.96
31	51.59	52.01	52.44	52.86	53.29	53.71	54.14	54.57	55.00	55.43	55.85	56.28	56.72	57.15	57.58	58.01
32	53.41	53.85	54.29	54.73	55.17	55.62	56.06	56.50	56.95	57.39	57.84	58.29	58.73	59.18	59.63	60.08
33	55.24	55.70	56.16	56.62	57.07	57.53	57.99	58.45	58.92	59.38	59.84	60.30	60.77	61.23	61.70	62.16
34	57.09	57.56	58.04	58.51	58.99	59.46	59.94	60.42	60.89	61.37	61.85	62.33	62.81	63.30	63.78	64.26
35	58.95	59.44	59.93	60.42	60.91	61.40	61.90	62.39	62.89	63.38	63.88	64.38	64.88	65.37	65.87	66.37
36	60.82	61.33	61.83	62.34	62.85	63.36	63.87	64.38	64.89	65.41	65.92	66.43	66.95	67.47	67.98	68.50
37	62.70	63.22	63.75	64.27	64.80	65.33	65.85	66.38	66.91	67.44	67.97	68.51	69.04	69.57	70.11	70.64
38	64.59	65.14	65.68	66.22	66.76	67.31	67.85	68.40	68.95	69.49	70.04	70.59	71.14	71.69	72.25	72.80
39	66.50	67.06	67.62	68.18	68.74	69.30	69.86	70.43	70.99	71.56	72.12	72.69	73.26	73.83	74.40	74.97
40	68.42	68.99	69.57	70.15	70.73	71.31	71.89	72.47	73.05	73.63	74.22	74.80	75.39	75.98	76.56	77.15

TABLE VIII   Board of Governors' APR Tables—Volume I (continued)

ANNUAL PERCENTAGE RATE

(FINANCE CHARGE PER $100 OF AMOUNT FINANCED)

NUMBER OF PAYMENTS	34.00%	34.25%	34.50%	34.75%	35.00%	35.25%	35.50%	35.75%	36.00%	36.25%	36.50%	36.75%	37.00%	37.25%	37.50%	37.75%
41	70.35	70.94	71.53	72.13	72.73	73.32	73.92	74.52	75.12	75.72	76.32	76.93	77.53	78.14	78.74	79.35
42	72.29	72.90	73.51	74.12	74.74	75.35	75.97	76.59	77.20	77.82	78.44	79.07	79.69	80.31	80.94	81.56
43	74.24	74.87	75.50	76.13	76.76	77.40	78.03	78.67	79.30	79.94	80.58	81.22	81.86	82.50	83.14	83.79
44	76.20	76.85	77.50	78.15	78.80	79.45	80.10	80.76	81.41	82.07	82.72	83.38	84.04	84.70	85.36	86.03
45	78.18	78.84	79.51	80.18	80.85	81.52	82.19	82.86	83.53	84.21	84.88	85.56	86.24	86.92	87.60	88.28
46	80.17	80.85	81.53	82.22	82.91	83.60	84.28	84.98	85.67	86.36	87.06	87.75	88.45	89.15	89.85	90.55
47	82.16	82.87	83.57	84.27	84.98	85.69	86.39	87.10	87.81	88.53	89.24	89.95	90.67	91.39	92.11	92.83
48	84.17	84.89	85.61	86.34	87.06	87.79	88.52	89.24	89.97	90.70	91.44	92.17	92.91	93.64	94.38	95.12
49	86.19	86.93	87.67	88.41	89.16	89.90	90.65	91.40	92.14	92.89	93.65	94.40	95.15	95.91	96.67	97.42
50	88.22	88.98	89.74	90.50	91.26	92.03	92.79	93.56	94.33	95.10	95.87	96.54	97.41	98.19	98.96	99.74
51	90.26	91.04	91.82	92.60	93.38	94.16	94.95	95.74	96.52	97.31	98.10	98.89	99.69	100.48	101.28	102.07
52	92.32	93.11	93.91	94.71	95.51	96.31	97.12	97.92	98.73	99.54	100.35	101.16	101.97	102.79	103.60	104.42
53	94.38	95.20	96.01	96.83	97.65	98.47	99.30	100.12	100.95	101.78	102.61	103.44	104.27	105.10	105.94	106.78
54	96.45	97.29	98.13	98.96	99.80	100.64	101.49	102.33	103.18	104.03	104.87	105.73	106.58	107.43	108.29	109.14
55	98.54	99.39	100.25	101.11	101.97	102.83	103.69	104.55	105.42	106.29	107.16	108.03	108.90	109.77	110.65	111.53
56	100.63	101.51	102.38	103.26	104.14	105.02	105.90	106.79	107.67	108.56	109.45	110.34	111.23	112.13	113.02	113.92
57	102.74	103.63	104.53	105.43	106.32	107.22	108.13	109.03	109.94	110.85	111.75	112.67	113.58	114.49	115.41	116.33
58	104.85	105.77	106.68	107.60	108.52	109.44	110.36	111.29	112.21	113.14	114.07	115.00	115.93	116.87	117.81	118.74
59	106.98	107.91	108.85	109.79	110.73	111.67	112.61	113.55	114.50	115.45	116.40	117.35	118.30	119.26	120.22	121.17
60	109.12	110.07	111.02	111.98	112.94	113.90	114.87	115.83	116.80	117.77	118.74	119.71	120.68	121.66	122.64	123.62

TABLE IX *Exact-Day Calendar (Excluding Leap Year)*

Day of Month	Jan.	Feb.	Mar.	Apr.	May	June	July	Aug.	Sept.	Oct.	Nov.	Dec.
1	1	32	60	91	121	152	182	213	244	274	305	335
2	2	33	61	92	122	153	183	214	245	275	306	336
3	3	34	62	93	123	154	184	215	246	276	307	337
4	4	35	63	94	124	155	185	216	247	277	308	338
5	5	36	64	95	125	156	186	217	248	278	309	339
6	6	37	65	96	126	157	187	218	249	279	310	340
7	7	38	66	97	127	158	188	219	250	280	311	341
8	8	39	67	98	128	159	189	220	251	281	312	342
9	9	40	68	99	129	160	190	221	252	282	313	343
10	10	41	69	100	130	161	191	222	253	283	314	344
11	11	42	70	101	131	162	192	223	254	284	315	345
12	12	43	71	102	132	163	193	224	255	285	316	346
13	13	44	72	103	133	164	194	225	256	286	317	347
14	14	45	73	104	134	165	195	226	257	287	318	348
15	15	46	74	105	135	166	196	227	258	288	319	349
16	16	47	75	106	136	167	197	228	259	289	320	350
17	17	48	76	107	137	168	198	229	260	290	321	351
18	18	49	77	108	138	169	199	230	261	291	322	352
19	19	50	78	109	139	170	200	231	262	292	323	353
20	20	51	79	110	140	171	201	232	263	293	324	354
21	21	52	80	111	141	172	202	233	264	294	325	355
22	22	53	81	112	142	173	203	234	265	295	326	356
23	23	54	82	113	143	174	204	235	266	296	327	357
24	24	55	83	114	144	175	205	236	267	297	328	358
25	25	56	84	115	145	176	206	237	268	298	329	359
26	26	57	85	116	146	177	207	238	269	299	330	360
27	27	58	86	117	147	178	208	239	270	300	331	361
28	28	59	87	118	148	179	209	240	271	301	332	362
29	29	—	88	119	149	180	210	241	272	302	333	363
30	30	—	89	120	150	181	211	242	273	303	334	364
31	31	—	90	—	151	—	212	243	—	304	—	365

TABLE X   Federal Income Tax Withholding Table

SINGLE Persons — WEEKLY Payroll Period

And the wages are—		And the number of withholding allowances claimed is—										
At least	But less than	0	1	2	3	4	5	6	7	8	9	10 or more
		The amount of income tax to be withheld shall be—										
$170	$180	$26.00	$22.80	$19.70	$17.00	$14.40	$11.80	$9.20	$6.60	$4.30	$2.00	$0
180	190	28.30	25.00	21.90	18.80	16.20	13.60	11.00	8.40	5.90	3.60	1.30
190	200	30.70	27.20	24.10	20.90	18.00	15.40	12.80	10.20	7.60	5.20	2.90
200	210	33.10	29.60	26.30	23.10	19.90	17.20	14.60	12.00	9.40	6.80	4.50
210	220	35.50	32.00	28.60	25.30	22.10	19.00	16.40	13.80	11.20	8.60	6.10
220	230	38.10	34.40	31.00	27.50	24.30	21.20	18.20	15.60	13.00	10.40	7.80
230	240	40.90	36.80	33.40	29.90	26.50	23.40	20.20	17.40	14.80	12.20	9.60
240	250	43.70	39.60	35.80	32.30	28.80	25.60	22.40	19.20	16.60	14.00	11.40
250	260	46.50	42.40	38.40	34.70	31.20	27.80	24.60	21.40	18.40	15.80	13.20
260	270	49.30	45.20	41.20	37.20	33.60	30.20	26.80	23.60	20.40	17.60	15.00
270	280	52.10	48.00	44.00	40.00	36.00	32.60	29.10	25.80	22.60	19.50	16.80
280	290	54.90	50.80	46.80	42.80	38.70	35.00	31.50	28.10	24.80	21.70	18.60
290	300	57.70	53.60	49.60	45.60	41.50	37.50	33.90	30.50	27.00	23.90	20.70
300	310	60.80	56.40	52.40	48.40	44.30	40.30	36.30	32.90	29.40	26.10	22.90
310	320	64.00	59.40	55.20	51.20	47.10	43.10	39.00	35.30	31.80	28.30	25.10
320	330	67.20	62.60	58.00	54.00	49.90	45.90	41.80	37.80	34.20	30.70	27.30
330	340	70.40	65.80	61.20	56.80	52.70	48.70	44.60	40.60	36.60	33.10	29.70
340	350	73.60	69.00	64.40	59.70	55.50	51.50	47.40	43.40	39.40	35.50	32.10
350	360	76.80	72.20	67.60	62.90	58.30	54.30	50.20	46.20	42.20	38.10	34.50
360	370	80.40	75.40	70.80	66.10	61.50	57.10	53.00	49.00	45.00	40.90	36.90
370	380	84.00	78.80	74.00	69.30	64.70	60.10	55.80	51.80	47.80	43.70	39.70
380	390	87.60	82.40	77.20	72.50	67.90	63.30	58.70	54.60	50.60	46.50	42.50
390	400	91.20	86.00	80.80	75.70	71.10	66.50	61.90	57.40	53.40	49.30	45.30
400	410	94.80	89.60	84.40	79.20	74.30	69.70	65.10	60.50	56.20	52.10	48.10
410	420	98.40	93.20	88.00	82.80	77.60	72.90	68.30	63.70	59.10	54.90	50.90
420	430	102.00	96.80	91.60	86.40	81.20	76.10	71.50	66.90	62.30	57.70	53.70
430	440	105.60	100.40	95.20	90.00	84.80	79.60	74.70	70.10	65.50	60.90	56.50
440	450	109.20	104.00	98.80	93.60	88.40	83.20	78.00	73.30	68.70	64.10	59.40
450	460	112.80	107.60	102.40	97.20	92.00	86.80	81.60	76.50	71.90	67.30	62.60
460	470	116.40	111.20	106.00	100.80	95.60	90.40	85.20	80.10	75.10	70.50	65.80
470	480	120.00	114.80	109.60	104.40	99.20	94.00	88.80	83.70	78.50	73.70	69.00
480	490	123.60	118.40	113.20	108.00	102.80	97.60	92.40	87.30	82.10	76.90	72.20
490	500	127.20	122.00	116.80	111.60	106.40	101.20	96.00	90.90	85.70	80.50	75.40
500	510	130.80	125.60	120.40	115.20	110.00	104.80	99.60	94.50	89.30	84.10	78.90
510	520	134.40	129.20	124.00	118.80	113.60	108.40	103.20	98.10	92.90	87.70	82.50
520	530	138.00	132.80	127.60	122.40	117.20	112.00	106.80	101.70	96.50	91.30	86.10
530	540	141.60	136.40	131.20	126.00	120.80	115.60	110.40	105.30	100.10	94.90	89.70
540	550	145.20	140.00	134.80	129.60	124.40	119.20	114.00	108.90	103.70	98.50	93.30
550	560	148.80	143.60	138.40	133.20	128.00	122.80	117.60	112.50	107.30	102.10	96.90
560	570	152.40	147.20	142.00	136.80	131.60	126.40	121.20	116.10	110.90	105.70	100.50
570	580	156.00	150.80	145.60	140.40	135.20	130.00	124.80	119.70	114.50	109.30	104.10
580	590	159.60	154.40	149.20	144.00	138.80	133.60	128.40	123.30	118.10	112.90	107.70
590	600	163.20	158.00	152.80	147.60	142.40	137.20	132.00	126.90	121.70	116.50	111.30
600	610	166.80	161.60	156.40	151.20	146.00	140.80	135.60	130.50	125.30	120.10	114.90
610	620	170.40	165.20	160.00	154.80	149.60	144.40	139.20	134.10	128.90	123.70	118.50
620	630	174.00	168.80	163.60	158.40	153.20	148.00	142.80	137.70	132.50	127.30	122.10
630	640	177.60	172.40	167.20	162.00	156.80	151.60	146.40	141.30	136.10	130.90	125.70
640	650	181.20	176.00	170.80	165.60	160.40	155.20	150.00	144.90	139.70	134.50	129.30
650	660	184.80	179.60	174.40	169.20	164.00	158.80	153.60	148.50	143.30	138.10	132.90
660	670	188.40	183.20	178.00	172.80	167.60	162.40	157.20	152.10	146.90	141.70	136.50
670	680	192.00	186.80	181.60	176.40	171.20	166.00	160.80	155.70	150.50	145.30	140.10
680	690	195.60	190.40	185.20	180.00	174.80	169.60	164.40	159.30	154.10	148.90	143.70
690	700	199.20	194.00	188.80	183.60	178.40	173.20	168.00	162.90	157.70	152.50	147.30
700	710	202.80	197.60	192.40	187.20	182.00	176.80	171.60	166.50	161.30	156.10	150.90
710	720	206.40	201.20	196.00	190.80	185.60	180.40	175.20	170.10	164.90	159.70	154.50
		36 percent of the excess over $720 plus—										
$720 and over		208.20	203.00	197.80	192.60	187.40	182.20	177.00	171.90	166.70	161.50	156.30

TABLE X   *Federal Income Tax Withholding Table (continued)*

MARRIED Persons — **WEEKLY** Payroll Period

And the wages are—		And the number of withholding allowances claimed is—										
At least	But less than	0	1	2	3	4	5	6	7	8	9	10 or more
		The amount of income tax to be withheld shall be—										
$0	$60	$0	$0	$0	$0	$0	$0	$0	$0	$0	$0	$0
60	62	.10	0	0	0	0	0	0	0	0	0	0
62	64	.40	0	0	0	0	0	0	0	0	0	0
64	66	.70	0	0	0	0	0	0	0	0	0	0
66	68	1.00	0	0	0	0	0	0	0	0	0	0
68	70	1.30	0	0	0	0	0	0	0	0	0	0
70	72	1.60	0	0	0	0	0	0	0	0	0	0
72	74	1.90	0	0	0	0	0	0	0	0	0	0
74	76	2.20	0	0	0	0	0	0	0	0	0	0
76	78	2.50	.30	0	0	0	0	0	0	0	0	0
78	80	2.80	.60	0	0	0	0	0	0	0	0	0
80	82	3.10	.90	0	0	0	0	0	0	0	0	0
82	84	3.40	1.20	0	0	0	0	0	0	0	0	0
84	86	3.70	1.50	0	0	0	0	0	0	0	0	0
86	88	4.00	1.80	0	0	0	0	0	0	0	0	0
88	90	4.30	2.10	0	0	0	0	0	0	0	0	0
90	92	4.60	2.40	.20	0	0	0	0	0	0	0	0
92	94	4.90	2.70	.50	0	0	0	0	0	0	0	0
94	96	5.20	3.00	.80	0	0	0	0	0	0	0	0
96	98	5.50	3.30	1.10	0	0	0	0	0	0	0	0
98	100	5.80	3.60	1.40	0	0	0	0	0	0	0	0
100	105	6.30	4.10	2.00	0	0	0	0	0	0	0	0
105	110	7.10	4.90	2.70	.50	0	0	0	0	0	0	0
110	115	8.00	5.60	3.50	1.30	0	0	0	0	0	0	0
115	120	8.90	6.40	4.20	2.00	0	0	0	0	0	0	0
120	125	9.80	7.20	5.00	2.80	.60	0	0	0	0	0	0
125	130	10.70	8.10	5.70	3.50	1.40	0	0	0	0	0	0
130	135	11.60	9.00	6.50	4.30	2.10	0	0	0	0	0	0
135	140	12.50	9.90	7.30	5.00	2.90	.70	0	0	0	0	0
140	145	13.40	10.80	8.20	5.80	3.60	1.50	0	0	0	0	0
145	150	14.30	11.70	9.10	6.50	4.40	2.20	.10	0	0	0	0
150	160	15.70	13.10	10.50	7.90	5.50	3.30	1.20	0	0	0	0
160	170	17.50	14.90	12.30	9.70	7.10	4.80	2.70	.50	0	0	0
170	180	19.30	16.70	14.10	11.50	8.90	6.30	4.20	2.00	0	0	0
180	190	21.10	18.50	15.90	13.30	10.70	8.10	5.70	3.50	1.40	0	0
190	200	22.90	20.30	17.70	15.10	12.50	9.90	7.30	5.00	2.90	.70	0
200	210	24.70	22.10	19.50	16.90	14.30	11.70	9.10	6.50	4.40	2.20	0
210	220	26.50	23.90	21.30	18.70	16.10	13.50	10.90	8.30	5.90	3.70	1.50
220	230	28.40	25.70	23.10	20.50	17.90	15.30	12.70	10.10	7.50	5.20	3.00
230	240	30.60	27.50	24.90	22.30	19.70	17.10	14.50	11.90	9.30	6.70	4.50
240	250	32.80	29.60	26.70	24.10	21.50	18.90	16.30	13.70	11.10	8.50	6.00
250	260	35.00	31.80	28.60	25.90	23.30	20.70	18.10	15.50	12.90	10.30	7.70
260	270	37.20	34.00	30.80	27.70	25.10	22.50	19.90	17.30	14.70	12.10	9.50
270	280	39.40	36.20	33.00	29.80	26.90	24.30	21.70	19.10	16.50	13.90	11.30
280	290	41.80	38.40	35.20	32.00	28.90	26.10	23.50	20.90	18.30	15.70	13.10
290	300	44.30	40.70	37.40	34.20	31.10	27.90	25.30	22.70	20.10	17.50	14.90
300	310	46.80	43.20	39.60	36.40	33.30	30.10	27.10	24.50	21.90	19.30	16.70
310	320	49.30	45.70	42.10	38.60	35.50	32.30	29.10	26.30	23.70	21.10	18.50
320	330	51.80	48.20	44.60	41.00	37.70	34.50	31.30	28.20	25.50	22.90	20.30
330	340	54.30	50.70	47.10	43.50	39.90	36.70	33.50	30.40	27.30	24.70	22.10
340	350	56.80	53.20	49.60	46.00	42.40	38.90	35.70	32.60	29.40	26.50	23.90
350	360	59.30	55.70	52.10	48.50	44.90	41.30	37.90	34.80	31.60	28.40	25.70
360	370	62.10	58.20	54.60	51.00	47.40	43.80	40.10	37.00	33.80	30.60	27.50
370	380	64.90	60.80	57.10	53.50	49.90	46.30	42.60	39.20	36.00	32.80	29.60
380	390	67.70	63.60	59.60	56.00	52.40	48.80	45.10	41.50	38.20	35.00	31.80
390	400	70.50	66.40	62.40	58.50	54.90	51.30	47.60	44.00	40.40	37.20	34.00
400	410	73.30	69.20	65.20	61.20	57.40	53.80	50.10	46.50	42.90	39.40	36.20
410	420	76.10	72.00	68.00	64.00	59.90	56.30	52.60	49.00	45.40	41.80	38.40
420	430	78.90	74.80	70.80	66.80	62.70	58.80	55.10	51.50	47.90	44.30	40.70
430	440	81.80	77.60	73.60	69.60	65.50	61.50	57.60	54.00	50.40	46.80	43.20

TABLE X   *Federal Income Tax Withholding Table (continued)*

SINGLE Persons — BIWEEKLY Payroll Period

And the wages are—		And the number of withholding allowances claimed is—										
At least	But less than	0	1	2	3	4	5	6	7	8	9	10 or more
		The amount of income tax to be withheld shall be—										
$340	$360	$52.00	$45.70	$39.30	$33.90	$28.70	$23.50	$18.30	$13.20	$8.60	$4.00	$0
360	380	56.60	50.10	43.70	37.50	32.30	27.10	21.90	16.80	11.80	7.20	2.60
380	400	61.40	54.50	48.10	41.80	35.90	30.70	25.50	20.40	15.20	10.40	5.80
400	420	66.20	59.20	52.50	46.20	39.90	34.30	29.10	24.00	18.80	13.60	9.00
420	440	71.00	64.00	57.10	50.60	44.30	37.90	32.70	27.60	22.40	17.20	12.20
440	460	76.20	68.80	61.90	55.00	48.70	42.30	36.30	31.20	26.00	20.80	15.60
460	480	81.80	73.70	66.70	59.80	53.10	46.70	40.40	34.80	29.60	24.40	19.20
480	500	87.40	79.30	71.50	64.60	57.70	51.10	44.80	38.40	33.20	28.00	22.80
500	520	93.00	84.90	76.80	69.40	62.50	55.60	49.20	42.80	36.80	31.60	26.40
520	540	98.60	90.50	82.40	74.30	67.30	60.40	53.60	47.20	40.90	35.20	30.00
540	560	104.20	96.10	88.00	79.90	72.10	65.20	58.20	51.60	45.30	38.90	33.60
560	580	109.80	101.70	93.60	85.50	77.40	70.00	63.00	56.10	49.70	43.30	37.20
580	600	115.40	107.30	99.20	91.10	83.00	75.00	67.80	60.90	54.10	47.70	41.40
600	620	121.60	112.90	104.80	96.70	88.60	80.60	72.60	65.70	58.80	52.10	45.80
620	640	128.00	118.80	110.40	102.30	94.20	86.20	78.10	70.50	63.60	56.70	50.20
640	660	134.40	125.20	116.00	107.90	99.80	91.80	83.70	75.60	68.40	61.50	54.60
660	680	140.80	131.60	122.30	113.50	105.40	97.40	89.30	81.20	73.20	66.30	59.30
680	700	147.20	138.00	128.70	119.50	111.00	103.00	94.90	86.80	78.70	71.10	64.10
700	720	153.60	144.40	135.10	125.90	116.70	108.60	100.50	92.40	84.30	76.30	68.90
720	740	160.80	150.80	141.50	132.30	123.10	114.20	106.10	98.00	89.90	81.90	73.80
740	760	168.00	157.60	147.90	138.70	129.50	120.20	111.70	103.60	95.50	87.50	79.40
760	780	175.20	164.80	154.40	145.10	135.90	126.60	117.40	109.20	101.10	93.10	85.00
780	800	182.40	172.00	161.60	151.50	142.30	133.00	123.80	114.80	106.70	98.70	90.60
800	820	189.60	179.20	168.80	158.40	148.70	139.40	130.20	121.00	112.30	104.30	96.20
820	840	196.80	186.40	176.00	165.60	155.30	145.80	136.60	127.40	118.10	109.90	101.80
840	860	204.00	193.60	183.20	172.80	162.50	152.20	143.00	133.80	124.50	115.50	107.40
860	880	211.20	200.80	190.40	180.00	169.70	159.30	149.40	140.20	130.90	121.70	113.00
880	900	218.40	208.00	197.60	187.20	176.90	166.50	156.10	146.60	137.30	128.10	118.90
900	920	225.60	215.20	204.80	194.40	184.10	173.70	163.30	153.00	143.70	134.50	125.30
920	940	232.80	222.40	212.00	201.60	191.30	180.90	170.50	160.10	150.10	140.90	131.70
940	960	240.00	229.60	219.20	208.80	198.50	188.10	177.70	167.30	156.90	147.30	138.10
960	980	247.20	236.80	226.40	216.00	205.70	195.30	184.90	174.50	164.10	153.70	144.50
980	1,000	254.40	244.00	233.60	223.20	212.90	202.50	192.10	181.70	171.30	160.90	150.90
1,000	1,020	261.60	251.20	240.80	230.40	220.10	209.70	199.30	188.90	178.50	168.10	157.80
1,020	1,040	268.80	258.40	248.00	237.60	227.30	216.90	206.50	196.10	185.70	175.30	165.00
1,040	1,060	276.00	265.60	255.20	244.80	234.50	224.10	213.70	203.30	192.90	182.50	172.20
1,060	1,080	283.20	272.80	262.40	252.00	241.70	231.30	220.90	210.50	200.10	189.70	179.40
1,080	1,100	290.40	280.00	269.60	259.20	248.90	238.50	228.10	217.70	207.30	196.90	186.60
1,100	1,120	297.60	287.20	276.80	266.40	256.10	245.70	235.30	224.90	214.50	204.10	193.80
1,120	1,140	304.80	294.40	284.00	273.60	263.30	252.90	242.50	232.10	221.70	211.30	201.00
1,140	1,160	312.00	301.60	291.20	280.80	270.50	260.10	249.70	239.30	228.90	218.50	208.20
1,160	1,180	319.20	308.80	298.40	288.00	277.70	267.30	256.90	246.50	236.10	225.70	215.40
1,180	1,200	326.40	316.00	305.60	295.20	284.90	274.50	264.10	253.70	243.30	232.90	222.60
1,200	1,220	333.60	323.20	312.80	302.40	292.10	281.70	271.30	260.90	250.50	240.10	229.80
1,220	1,240	340.80	330.40	320.00	309.60	299.30	288.90	278.50	268.10	257.70	247.30	237.00
1,240	1,260	348.00	337.60	327.20	316.80	306.50	296.10	285.70	275.30	264.90	254.50	244.20
1,260	1,280	355.20	344.80	334.40	324.00	313.70	303.30	292.90	282.50	272.10	261.70	251.40
1,280	1,300	362.40	352.00	341.60	331.20	320.90	310.50	300.10	289.70	279.30	268.90	258.60
1,300	1,320	369.60	359.20	348.80	338.40	328.10	317.70	307.30	296.90	286.50	276.10	265.80
1,320	1,340	376.80	366.40	356.00	345.60	335.30	324.90	314.50	304.10	293.70	283.30	273.00
1,340	1,360	384.00	373.60	363.20	352.80	342.50	332.10	321.70	311.30	300.90	290.50	280.20
1,360	1,380	391.20	380.80	370.40	360.00	349.70	339.30	328.90	318.50	308.10	297.70	287.40
1,380	1,400	398.40	388.00	377.60	367.20	356.90	346.50	336.10	325.70	315.30	304.90	294.60
1,400	1,420	405.60	395.20	384.80	374.40	364.10	353.70	343.30	332.90	322.50	312.10	301.80
1,420	1,440	412.80	402.40	392.00	381.60	371.30	360.90	350.50	340.10	329.70	319.30	309.00
		36 percent of the excess over $1,440 plus—										
$1,440 and over		416.40	406.00	395.60	385.20	374.90	364.50	354.10	343.70	333.30	322.90	312.60

TABLE X Federal Income Tax Withholding Table (continued)

MARRIED Persons — BIWEEKLY Payroll Period

And the wages are—		And the number of withholding allowances claimed is—										
At least	But less than	0	1	2	3	4	5	6	7	8	9	10 or more
		The amount of income tax to be withheld shall be—										
$0	$120	$0	$0	$0	$0	$0	$0	$0	$0	$0	$0	$0
120	124	.10	0	0	0	0	0	0	0	0	0	0
124	128	.70	0	0	0	0	0	0	0	0	0	0
128	132	1.30	0	0	0	0	0	0	0	0	0	0
132	136	1.90	0	0	0	0	0	0	0	0	0	0
136	140	2.50	0	0	0	0	0	0	0	0	0	0
140	144	3.10	0	0	0	0	0	0	0	0	0	0
144	148	3.70	0	0	0	0	0	0	0	0	0	0
148	152	4.30	0	0	0	0	0	0	0	0	0	0
152	156	4.90	.60	0	0	0	0	0	0	0	0	0
156	160	5.50	1.20	0	0	0	0	0	0	0	0	0
160	164	6.10	1.80	0	0	0	0	0	0	0	0	0
164	168	6.70	2.40	0	0	0	0	0	0	0	0	0
168	172	7.30	3.00	0	0	0	0	0	0	0	0	0
172	176	7.90	3.60	0	0	0	0	0	0	0	0	0
176	180	8.50	4.20	0	0	0	0	0	0	0	0	0
180	184	9.10	4.80	.50	0	0	0	0	0	0	0	0
184	188	9.70	5.40	1.10	0	0	0	0	0	0	0	0
188	192	10.30	6.00	1.70	0	0	0	0	0	0	0	0
192	196	10.90	6.60	2.30	0	0	0	0	0	0	0	0
196	200	11.50	7.20	2.90	0	0	0	0	0	0	0	0
200	210	12.60	8.30	3.90	0	0	0	0	0	0	0	0
210	220	14.20	9.80	5.40	1.10	0	0	0	0	0	0	0
220	230	16.00	11.30	6.90	2.60	0	0	0	0	0	0	0
230	240	17.80	12.80	8.40	4.10	0	0	0	0	0	0	0
240	250	19.60	14.40	9.90	5.60	1.30	0	0	0	0	0	0
250	260	21.40	16.20	11.40	7.10	2.80	0	0	0	0	0	0
260	270	23.20	18.00	12.90	8.60	4.30	0	0	0	0	0	0
270	280	25.00	19.80	14.70	10.10	5.80	1.40	0	0	0	0	0
280	290	26.80	21.60	16.50	11.60	7.30	2.90	0	0	0	0	0
290	300	28.60	23.40	18.30	13.10	8.80	4.40	.10	0	0	0	0
300	320	31.30	26.10	21.00	15.80	11.00	6.70	2.40	0	0	0	0
320	340	34.90	29.70	24.60	19.40	14.20	9.70	5.40	1.00	0	0	0
340	360	38.50	33.30	28.20	23.00	17.80	12.70	8.40	4.00	0	0	0
360	380	42.10	36.90	31.80	26.60	21.40	16.20	11.40	7.00	2.70	0	0
380	400	45.70	40.50	35.40	30.20	25.00	19.80	14.60	10.00	5.70	1.40	0
400	420	49.30	44.10	39.00	33.80	28.60	23.40	18.20	13.00	8.70	4.40	.10
420	440	52.90	47.70	42.60	37.40	32.20	27.00	21.80	16.60	11.70	7.40	3.10
440	460	56.70	51.30	46.20	41.00	35.80	30.60	25.40	20.20	15.00	10.40	6.10
460	480	61.10	54.90	49.80	44.60	39.40	34.20	29.00	23.80	18.60	13.40	9.10
480	500	65.50	59.20	53.40	48.20	43.00	37.80	32.60	27.40	22.20	17.00	12.10
500	520	69.90	63.60	57.20	51.80	46.60	41.40	36.20	31.00	25.80	20.60	15.40
520	540	74.30	68.00	61.60	55.40	50.20	45.00	39.80	34.60	29.40	24.20	19.00
540	560	78.70	72.40	66.00	59.70	53.80	48.60	43.40	38.20	33.00	27.80	22.60
560	580	83.60	76.80	70.40	64.10	57.70	52.20	47.00	41.80	36.60	31.40	26.20
580	600	88.60	81.30	74.80	68.50	62.10	55.80	50.60	45.40	40.20	35.00	29.80
600	620	93.60	86.30	79.20	72.90	66.50	60.20	54.20	49.00	43.80	38.60	33.40
620	640	98.60	91.30	84.10	77.30	70.90	64.60	58.30	52.60	47.40	42.20	37.00
640	660	103.60	96.30	89.10	81.90	75.30	69.00	62.70	56.30	51.00	45.80	40.60
660	680	108.60	101.30	94.10	86.90	79.70	73.40	67.10	60.70	54.60	49.40	44.20
680	700	113.60	106.30	99.10	91.90	84.70	77.80	71.50	65.10	58.80	53.00	47.80
700	720	118.60	111.30	104.10	96.90	89.70	82.50	75.90	69.50	63.20	56.80	51.40
720	740	124.20	116.30	109.10	101.90	94.70	87.50	80.30	73.90	67.60	61.20	55.00
740	760	129.80	121.70	114.10	106.90	99.70	92.50	85.30	78.30	72.00	65.60	59.30
760	780	135.40	127.30	119.20	111.90	104.70	97.50	90.30	83.10	76.40	70.00	63.70
780	800	141.00	132.90	124.80	116.90	109.70	102.50	95.30	88.10	80.90	74.40	68.10
800	820	146.60	138.50	130.40	122.30	114.70	107.50	100.30	93.10	85.90	78.80	72.50
820	840	152.20	144.10	136.00	127.90	119.90	112.50	105.30	98.10	90.90	83.70	76.90
840	860	157.80	149.70	141.60	133.50	125.50	117.50	110.30	103.10	95.90	88.70	81.40
860	880	163.60	155.30	147.20	139.10	131.10	123.00	115.30	108.10	100.90	93.70	86.40

TABLE X   *Federal Income Tax Withholding Table (continued)*

MARRIED Persons — BIWEEKLY Payroll Period

And the wages are—		And the number of withholding allowances claimed is—										
At least	But less than	0	1	2	3	4	5	6	7	8	9	10 or more
		The amount of income tax to be withheld shall be—										
$880	$900	$170.00	$160.90	$152.80	$144.70	$136.70	$128.60	$120.50	$113.10	$105.90	$98.70	$91.40
900	920	176.40	167.20	158.40	150.30	142.30	134.20	126.10	118.10	110.90	103.70	96.40
920	940	182.80	173.60	164.40	155.90	147.90	139.80	131.70	123.60	115.90	108.70	101.40
940	960	189.20	180.00	170.80	161.50	153.50	145.40	137.30	129.20	121.20	113.70	106.40
960	980	195.60	186.40	177.20	167.90	159.10	151.00	142.90	134.80	126.80	118.70	111.40
980	1,000	202.00	192.80	183.60	174.30	165.10	156.60	148.50	140.40	132.40	124.30	116.40
1,000	1,020	208.40	199.20	190.00	180.70	171.50	162.30	154.10	146.00	138.00	129.90	121.80
1,020	1,040	215.30	205.60	196.40	187.10	177.90	168.70	159.70	151.60	143.60	135.50	127.40
1,040	1,060	222.50	212.20	202.80	193.50	184.30	175.10	165.80	157.20	149.20	141.10	133.00
1,060	1,080	229.70	219.40	209.20	199.90	190.70	181.50	172.20	163.00	154.80	146.70	138.60
1,080	1,100	236.90	226.60	216.20	206.30	197.10	187.90	178.60	169.40	160.40	152.30	144.20
1,100	1,120	244.10	233.80	223.40	213.00	203.50	194.30	185.00	175.80	166.60	157.90	149.80
1,120	1,140	251.30	241.00	230.60	220.20	209.90	200.70	191.40	182.20	173.00	163.80	155.40
1,140	1,160	258.50	248.20	237.80	227.40	217.00	207.10	197.80	188.60	179.40	170.20	161.00
1,160	1,180	265.70	255.40	245.00	234.60	224.20	213.80	204.20	195.00	185.80	176.60	167.30
1,180	1,200	272.90	262.60	252.20	241.80	231.40	221.00	210.60	201.40	192.20	183.00	173.70
1,200	1,220	280.10	269.80	259.40	249.00	238.60	228.20	217.80	207.80	198.60	189.40	180.10
1,220	1,240	287.30	277.00	266.60	256.20	245.80	235.40	225.00	214.60	205.00	195.80	186.50
1,240	1,260	294.50	284.20	273.80	263.40	253.00	242.60	232.20	221.80	211.50	202.20	192.90
1,260	1,280	301.70	291.40	281.00	270.60	260.20	249.80	239.40	229.00	218.70	208.60	199.30
1,280	1,300	308.90	298.60	288.20	277.80	267.40	257.00	246.60	236.20	225.90	215.50	205.70
1,300	1,320	316.10	305.80	295.40	285.00	274.60	264.20	253.80	243.40	233.10	222.70	212.30
1,320	1,340	323.30	313.00	302.60	292.20	281.80	271.40	261.00	250.60	240.30	229.90	219.50
1,340	1,360	330.50	320.20	309.80	299.40	289.00	278.60	268.20	257.80	247.50	237.10	226.70
1,360	1,380	337.70	327.40	317.00	306.60	296.20	285.80	275.40	265.00	254.70	244.30	233.90
1,380	1,400	344.90	334.60	324.20	313.80	303.40	293.00	282.60	272.20	261.90	251.50	241.10
1,400	1,420	352.10	341.80	331.40	321.00	310.60	300.20	289.80	279.40	269.10	258.70	248.30
1,420	1,440	359.30	349.00	338.60	328.20	317.80	307.40	297.00	286.60	276.30	265.90	255.50
1,440	1,460	366.50	356.20	345.80	335.40	325.00	314.60	304.20	293.80	283.50	273.10	262.70
1,460	1,480	373.70	363.40	353.00	342.60	332.20	321.80	311.40	301.00	290.70	280.30	269.90
1,480	1,500	380.90	370.60	360.20	349.80	339.40	329.00	318.60	308.20	297.90	287.50	277.10
1,500	1,520	388.10	377.80	367.40	357.00	346.60	336.20	325.80	315.40	305.10	294.70	284.30
1,520	1,540	395.30	385.00	374.60	364.20	353.80	343.40	333.00	322.60	312.30	301.90	291.50
1,540	1,560	402.50	392.20	381.80	371.40	361.00	350.60	340.20	329.80	319.50	309.10	298.70
1,560	1,580	409.70	399.40	389.00	378.60	368.20	357.80	347.40	337.00	326.70	316.30	305.90
1,580	1,600	416.90	406.60	396.20	385.80	375.40	365.00	354.60	344.20	333.90	323.50	313.10
1,600	1,620	424.10	413.80	403.40	393.00	382.60	372.20	361.80	351.40	341.10	330.70	320.30
1,620	1,640	431.30	421.00	410.60	400.20	389.80	379.40	369.00	358.60	348.30	337.90	327.50
1,640	1,660	438.50	428.20	417.80	407.40	397.00	386.60	376.20	365.80	355.50	345.10	334.70
1,660	1,680	445.70	435.40	425.00	414.60	404.20	393.80	383.40	373.00	362.70	352.30	341.90
1,680	1,700	452.90	442.60	432.20	421.80	411.40	401.00	390.60	380.20	369.90	359.50	349.10
1,700	1,720	460.10	449.80	439.40	429.00	418.60	408.20	397.80	387.40	377.10	366.70	356.30
1,720	1,740	467.30	457.00	446.60	436.20	425.80	415.40	405.00	394.60	384.30	373.90	363.50
1,740	1,760	474.50	464.20	453.80	443.40	433.00	422.60	412.20	401.80	391.50	381.10	370.70
1,760	1,780	481.70	471.40	461.00	450.60	440.20	429.80	419.40	409.00	398.70	388.30	377.90
1,780	1,800	488.90	478.60	468.20	457.80	447.40	437.00	426.60	416.20	405.90	395.50	385.10
1,800	1,820	496.10	485.80	475.40	465.00	454.60	444.20	433.80	423.40	413.10	402.70	392.30
1,820	1,840	503.30	493.00	482.60	472.20	461.80	451.40	441.00	430.60	420.30	409.90	399.50
1,840	1,860	510.50	500.20	489.80	479.40	469.00	458.60	448.20	437.80	427.50	417.10	406.70
1,860	1,880	517.70	507.40	497.00	486.60	476.20	465.80	455.40	445.00	434.70	424.30	413.90
1,880	1,900	524.90	514.60	504.20	493.80	483.40	473.00	462.60	452.20	441.90	431.50	421.10
1,900	1,920	532.10	521.80	511.40	501.00	490.60	480.20	469.80	459.40	449.10	438.70	428.30
1,920	1,940	539.30	529.00	518.60	508.20	497.80	487.40	477.00	466.60	456.30	445.90	435.50
1,940	1,960	546.50	536.20	525.80	515.40	505.00	494.60	484.20	473.80	463.50	453.10	442.70
1,960	1,980	553.70	543.40	533.00	522.60	512.20	501.80	491.40	481.00	470.70	460.30	449.90
		36 percent of the excess over $1,980 plus—										
$1,980 and over		557.30	547.00	536.60	526.20	515.80	505.40	495.00	484.60	474.30	463.90	453.50

TABLE X *Federal Income Tax Withholding Table (continued)*

SINGLE Persons — SEMIMONTHLY Payroll Period

And the wages are—		And the number of withholding allowances claimed is—										
At least	But less than	0	1	2	3	4	5	6	7	8	9	10 or more
		The amount of income tax to be withheld shall be—										
$400	$420	$63.50	$56.30	$49.40	$42.50	$36.70	$31.10	$25.40	$19.80	$14.30	$9.30	$4.30
420	440	68.30	60.80	53.80	46.90	40.30	34.70	29.00	23.40	17.80	12.50	7.50
440	460	73.10	65.60	58.20	51.30	44.50	38.30	32.60	27.00	21.40	15.80	10.70
460	480	77.90	70.40	62.90	55.70	48.90	42.00	36.20	30.60	25.00	19.40	13.90
480	500	83.20	75.20	67.70	60.20	53.30	46.40	39.80	34.20	28.60	23.00	17.30
500	520	88.80	80.10	72.50	65.00	57.70	50.80	43.90	37.80	32.20	26.60	20.90
520	540	94.40	85.70	77.30	69.80	62.30	55.20	48.30	41.40	35.80	30.20	24.50
540	560	100.00	91.30	82.50	74.60	67.10	59.60	52.70	45.80	39.40	33.80	28.10
560	580	105.60	96.90	88.10	79.40	71.90	64.40	57.10	50.20	43.40	37.40	31.70
580	600	111.20	102.50	93.70	85.00	76.70	69.20	61.70	54.60	47.80	41.00	35.30
600	620	116.80	108.10	99.30	90.60	81.80	74.00	66.50	59.00	52.20	45.30	38.90
620	640	122.40	113.70	104.90	96.20	87.40	78.80	71.30	63.80	56.60	49.70	42.80
640	660	128.30	119.30	110.50	101.80	93.00	84.30	76.10	68.60	61.10	54.10	47.20
660	680	134.70	124.90	116.10	107.40	98.60	89.90	81.10	73.40	65.90	58.50	51.60
680	700	141.10	131.10	121.70	113.00	104.20	95.50	86.70	78.20	70.70	63.20	56.00
700	720	147.50	137.50	127.50	118.60	109.80	101.10	92.30	83.60	75.50	68.00	60.50
720	740	153.90	143.90	133.90	124.20	115.40	106.70	97.90	89.20	80.40	72.80	65.30
740	760	160.30	150.30	140.30	130.30	121.00	112.30	103.50	94.80	86.00	77.60	70.10
760	780	166.70	156.70	146.70	136.70	126.70	117.90	109.10	100.40	91.60	82.90	74.90
780	800	173.90	163.10	153.10	143.10	133.10	123.50	114.70	106.00	97.20	88.50	79.70
800	820	181.10	169.90	159.50	149.50	139.50	129.50	120.30	111.60	102.80	94.10	85.30
820	840	188.30	177.10	165.90	155.90	145.90	135.90	125.90	117.20	108.40	99.70	90.90
840	860	195.50	184.30	173.00	162.30	152.30	142.30	132.30	122.80	114.00	105.30	96.50
860	880	202.70	191.50	180.20	169.00	158.70	148.70	138.70	128.70	119.60	110.90	102.10
880	900	209.90	198.70	187.40	176.20	165.10	155.10	145.10	135.10	125.20	116.50	107.70
900	920	217.10	205.90	194.60	183.40	172.10	161.50	151.50	141.50	131.50	122.10	113.30
920	940	224.30	213.10	201.80	190.60	179.30	168.10	157.90	147.90	137.90	127.90	118.90
940	960	231.50	220.30	209.00	197.80	186.50	175.30	164.30	154.30	144.30	134.30	124.50
960	980	238.70	227.50	216.20	205.00	193.70	182.50	171.20	160.70	150.70	140.70	130.70
980	1,000	245.90	234.70	223.40	212.20	200.90	189.70	178.40	167.20	157.10	147.10	137.10
1,000	1,020	253.10	241.90	230.60	219.40	208.10	196.90	185.60	174.40	163.50	153.50	143.50
1,020	1,040	260.30	249.10	237.80	226.60	215.30	204.10	192.80	181.60	170.30	159.90	149.90
1,040	1,060	267.50	256.30	245.00	233.80	222.50	211.30	200.00	188.80	177.50	166.30	156.30
1,060	1,080	274.70	263.50	252.20	241.00	229.70	218.50	207.20	196.00	184.70	173.50	162.70
1,080	1,100	281.90	270.70	259.40	248.20	236.90	225.70	214.40	203.20	191.90	180.70	169.40
1,100	1,120	289.10	277.90	266.60	255.40	244.10	232.90	221.60	210.40	199.10	187.90	176.60
1,120	1,140	296.30	285.10	273.80	262.60	251.30	240.10	228.80	217.60	206.30	195.10	183.80
1,140	1,160	303.50	292.30	281.00	269.80	258.50	247.30	236.00	224.80	213.50	202.30	191.00
1,160	1,180	310.70	299.50	288.20	277.00	265.70	254.50	243.20	232.00	220.70	209.50	198.20
1,180	1,200	317.90	306.70	295.40	284.20	272.90	261.70	250.40	239.20	227.90	216.70	205.40
1,200	1,220	325.10	313.90	302.60	291.40	280.10	268.90	257.60	246.40	235.10	223.90	212.60
1,220	1,240	332.30	321.10	309.80	298.60	287.30	276.10	264.80	253.60	242.30	231.10	219.80
1,240	1,260	339.50	328.30	317.00	305.80	294.50	283.30	272.00	260.80	249.50	238.30	227.00
1,260	1,280	346.70	335.50	324.20	313.00	301.70	290.50	279.20	268.00	256.70	245.50	234.20
1,280	1,300	353.90	342.70	331.40	320.20	308.90	297.70	286.40	275.20	263.90	252.70	241.40
1,300	1,320	361.10	349.90	338.60	327.40	316.10	304.90	293.60	282.40	271.10	259.90	248.60
1,320	1,340	368.30	357.10	345.80	334.60	323.30	312.10	300.80	289.60	278.30	267.10	255.80
1,340	1,360	375.50	364.30	353.00	341.80	330.50	319.30	308.00	296.80	285.50	274.30	263.00
1,360	1,380	382.70	371.50	360.20	349.00	337.70	326.50	315.20	304.00	292.70	281.50	270.20
1,380	1,400	389.90	378.70	367.40	356.20	344.90	333.70	322.40	311.20	299.90	288.70	277.40
1,400	1,420	397.10	385.90	374.60	363.40	352.10	340.90	329.60	318.40	307.10	295.90	284.60
1,420	1,440	404.30	393.10	381.80	370.60	359.30	348.10	336.80	325.60	314.30	303.10	291.80
1,440	1,460	411.50	400.30	389.00	377.80	366.50	355.30	344.00	332.80	321.50	310.30	299.00
1,460	1,480	418.70	407.50	396.20	385.00	373.70	362.50	351.20	340.00	328.70	317.50	306.20
1,480	1,500	425.90	414.70	403.40	392.20	380.90	369.70	358.40	347.20	335.90	324.70	313.40
		36 percent of the excess over $1,500 plus—										
$1,500 and over		429.50	418.30	407.00	395.80	384.50	373.30	362.00	350.80	339.50	328.30	317.00

TABLE X   Federal Income Tax Withholding Table (continued)

MARRIED Persons — SEMIMONTHLY Payroll Period

And the wages are—		And the number of withholding allowances claimed is—										
At least	But less than	0	1	2	3	4	5	6	7	8	9	10 or more
		The amount of income tax to be withheld shall be—										
$940	$960	$179.70	$170.30	$161.60	$152.80	$144.10	$135.30	$126.80	$119.00	$111.10	$103.30	$95.50
960	980	186.10	176.10	167.20	158.40	149.70	140.90	132.20	124.00	116.10	108.30	100.50
980	1,000	192.50	182.50	172.80	164.00	155.30	146.50	137.80	129.00	121.10	113.30	105.50
1,000	1,020	198.90	188.90	178.90	169.60	160.90	152.10	143.40	134.60	126.10	118.30	110.50
1,020	1,040	205.30	195.30	185.30	175.30	166.50	157.70	149.00	140.20	131.50	123.30	115.50
1,040	1,060	211.70	201.70	191.70	181.70	172.10	163.30	154.60	145.80	137.10	128.30	120.50
1,060	1,080	218.10	208.10	198.10	188.10	178.10	168.90	160.20	151.40	142.70	133.90	125.50
1,080	1,100	224.50	214.50	204.50	194.50	184.50	174.50	165.80	157.00	148.30	139.50	130.80
1,100	1,120	231.20	220.90	210.90	200.90	190.90	180.90	171.40	162.60	153.90	145.10	136.40
1,120	1,140	238.40	227.30	217.30	207.30	197.30	187.30	177.30	168.20	159.50	150.70	142.00
1,140	1,160	245.60	234.30	223.70	213.70	203.70	193.70	183.70	173.80	165.10	156.30	147.60
1,160	1,180	252.80	241.50	230.30	220.10	210.10	200.10	190.10	180.10	170.70	161.90	153.20
1,180	1,200	260.00	248.70	237.50	226.50	216.50	206.50	196.50	186.50	176.50	167.50	158.80
1,200	1,220	267.20	255.90	244.70	233.40	222.90	212.90	202.90	192.90	182.90	173.10	164.40
1,220	1,240	274.40	263.10	251.90	240.60	229.40	219.30	209.30	199.30	189.30	179.30	170.00
1,240	1,260	281.60	270.30	259.10	247.80	236.60	225.70	215.70	205.70	195.70	185.70	175.70
1,260	1,280	288.80	277.50	266.30	255.00	243.80	232.50	222.10	212.10	202.10	192.10	182.10
1,280	1,300	296.00	284.70	273.50	262.20	251.00	239.70	228.50	218.50	208.50	198.50	188.50
1,300	1,320	303.20	291.90	280.70	269.40	258.20	246.90	235.70	224.90	214.90	204.90	194.90
1,320	1,340	310.40	299.10	287.90	276.60	265.40	254.10	242.90	231.60	221.30	211.30	201.30
1,340	1,360	317.60	306.30	295.10	283.80	272.60	261.30	250.10	238.80	227.70	217.70	207.70
1,360	1,380	324.80	313.50	302.30	291.00	279.80	268.50	257.30	246.00	234.80	224.10	214.10
1,380	1,400	332.00	320.70	309.50	298.20	287.00	275.70	264.50	253.20	242.00	230.70	220.50
1,400	1,420	339.20	327.90	316.70	305.40	294.20	282.90	271.70	260.40	249.20	237.90	226.90
1,420	1,440	346.40	335.10	323.90	312.60	301.40	290.10	278.90	267.60	256.40	245.10	233.90
1,440	1,460	353.60	342.30	331.10	319.80	308.60	297.30	286.10	274.80	263.60	252.30	241.10
1,460	1,480	360.80	349.50	338.30	327.00	315.80	304.50	293.30	282.00	270.80	259.50	248.30
1,480	1,500	368.00	356.70	345.50	334.20	323.00	311.70	300.50	289.20	278.00	266.70	255.50
1,500	1,520	375.20	363.90	352.70	341.40	330.20	318.90	307.70	296.40	285.20	273.90	262.70
1,520	1,540	382.40	371.10	359.90	348.60	337.40	326.10	314.90	303.60	292.40	281.10	269.90
1,540	1,560	389.60	378.30	367.10	355.80	344.60	333.30	322.10	310.80	299.60	288.30	277.10
1,560	1,580	396.80	385.50	374.30	363.00	351.80	340.50	329.30	318.00	306.80	295.50	284.30
1,580	1,600	404.00	392.70	381.50	370.20	359.00	347.70	336.50	325.20	314.00	302.70	291.50
1,600	1,620	411.20	399.90	388.70	377.40	366.20	354.90	343.70	332.40	321.20	309.90	298.70
1,620	1,640	418.40	407.10	395.90	384.60	373.40	362.10	350.90	339.60	328.40	317.10	305.90
1,640	1,660	425.60	414.30	403.10	391.80	380.60	369.30	358.10	346.80	335.60	324.30	313.10
1,660	1,680	432.80	421.50	410.30	399.00	387.80	376.50	365.30	354.00	342.80	331.50	320.30
1,680	1,700	440.00	428.70	417.50	406.20	395.00	383.70	372.50	361.20	350.00	338.70	327.50
1,700	1,720	447.20	435.90	424.70	413.40	402.20	390.90	379.70	368.40	357.20	345.90	334.70
1,720	1,740	454.40	443.10	431.90	420.60	409.40	398.10	386.90	375.60	364.40	353.10	341.90
1,740	1,760	461.60	450.30	439.10	427.80	416.60	405.30	394.10	382.80	371.60	360.30	349.10
1,760	1,780	468.80	457.50	446.30	435.00	423.80	412.50	401.30	390.00	378.80	367.50	356.30
1,780	1,800	476.00	464.70	453.50	442.20	431.00	419.70	408.50	397.20	386.00	374.70	363.50
1,800	1,820	483.20	471.90	460.70	449.40	438.20	426.90	415.70	404.40	393.20	381.90	370.70
1,820	1,840	490.40	479.10	467.90	456.60	445.40	434.10	422.90	411.60	400.40	389.10	377.90
1,840	1,860	497.60	486.30	475.10	463.80	452.60	441.30	430.10	418.80	407.60	396.30	385.10
1,860	1,880	504.80	493.50	482.30	471.00	459.80	448.50	437.30	426.00	414.80	403.50	392.30
1,880	1,900	512.00	500.70	489.50	478.20	467.00	455.70	444.50	433.20	422.00	410.70	399.50
1,900	1,920	519.20	507.90	496.70	485.40	474.20	462.90	451.70	440.40	429.20	417.90	406.70
1,920	1,940	526.40	515.10	503.90	492.60	481.40	470.10	458.90	447.60	436.40	425.10	413.90
1,940	1,960	533.60	522.30	511.10	499.80	488.60	477.30	466.10	454.80	443.60	432.30	421.10
1,960	1,980	540.80	529.50	518.30	507.00	495.80	484.50	473.30	462.00	450.80	439.50	428.30
1,980	2,000	548.00	536.70	525.50	514.20	503.00	491.70	480.50	469.20	458.00	446.70	435.50
2,000	2,020	555.20	543.90	532.70	521.40	510.20	498.90	487.70	476.40	465.20	453.90	442.70
2,020	2,040	562.40	551.10	539.90	528.60	517.40	506.10	494.90	483.60	472.40	461.10	449.90
		36 percent of the excess over $2,040 plus—										
$2,040 and over		566.00	554.70	543.50	532.20	521.00	509.70	498.50	487.20	476.00	464.70	453.50

TABLE X Federal Income Tax Withholding Table (continued)

SINGLE Persons — MONTHLY Payroll Period

And the wages are—		And the number of withholding allowances claimed is—										
At least	But less than	0	1	2	3	4	5	6	7	8	9	10 or more
		The amount of income tax to be withheld shall be—										
$760	$800	$117.50	$103.80	$90.00	$77.40	$66.20	$54.90	$43.70	$32.40	$22.10	$12.10	$2.10
800	840	127.00	112.60	98.80	85.10	73.40	62.10	50.90	39.60	28.50	18.50	8.50
840	880	136.60	121.60	107.60	93.90	80.60	69.30	58.10	46.80	35.60	24.90	14.90
880	920	146.20	131.20	116.40	102.70	88.90	76.50	65.30	54.00	42.80	31.50	21.30
920	960	155.80	140.80	125.80	111.50	97.70	84.00	72.50	61.20	50.00	38.70	27.70
960	1,000	166.40	150.40	135.40	120.40	106.50	92.80	79.70	68.40	57.20	45.90	34.70
1,000	1,040	177.60	160.10	145.00	130.00	115.30	101.60	87.80	75.60	64.40	53.10	41.90
1,040	1,080	188.80	171.30	154.60	139.60	124.60	110.40	96.60	82.90	71.60	60.30	49.10
1,080	1,120	200.00	182.50	165.00	149.20	134.20	119.20	105.40	91.70	78.80	67.50	56.30
1,120	1,160	211.20	193.70	176.20	158.80	143.80	128.80	114.20	100.50	86.70	74.70	63.50
1,160	1,200	222.40	204.90	187.40	169.90	153.40	138.40	123.40	109.30	95.50	81.90	70.70
1,200	1,240	233.60	216.10	198.60	181.10	163.60	148.00	133.00	118.10	104.30	90.60	77.90
1,240	1,280	244.80	227.30	209.80	192.30	174.80	157.60	142.60	127.60	113.10	99.40	85.60
1,280	1,320	256.50	238.50	221.00	203.50	186.00	168.50	152.20	137.20	122.20	108.20	94.40
1,320	1,360	269.30	249.70	232.20	214.70	197.20	179.70	162.20	146.80	131.80	117.00	103.20
1,360	1,400	282.10	262.10	243.40	225.90	208.40	190.90	173.40	156.40	141.40	126.40	112.00
1,400	1,440	294.90	274.90	254.90	237.10	219.60	202.10	184.60	167.10	151.00	136.00	121.00
1,440	1,480	307.70	287.70	267.70	248.30	230.80	213.30	195.80	178.30	160.80	145.60	130.60
1,480	1,520	320.50	300.50	280.50	260.50	242.00	224.50	207.00	189.50	172.00	155.20	140.20
1,520	1,560	333.40	313.30	293.30	273.30	253.30	235.70	218.20	200.70	183.20	165.70	149.80
1,560	1,600	347.80	326.10	306.10	286.10	266.10	246.90	229.40	211.90	194.40	176.90	159.40
1,600	1,640	362.20	339.70	318.90	298.90	278.90	258.90	240.60	223.10	205.60	188.10	170.60
1,640	1,680	376.60	354.10	331.70	311.70	291.70	271.70	251.80	234.30	216.80	199.30	181.80
1,680	1,720	391.00	368.50	346.00	324.50	304.50	284.50	264.50	245.50	228.00	210.50	193.00
1,720	1,760	405.40	382.90	360.40	337.90	317.30	297.30	277.30	257.30	239.20	221.70	204.20
1,760	1,800	419.80	397.30	374.80	352.30	330.10	310.10	290.10	270.10	250.40	232.90	215.40
1,800	1,840	434.20	411.70	389.20	366.70	344.20	322.90	302.90	282.90	262.90	244.10	226.60
1,840	1,880	448.60	426.10	403.60	381.10	358.60	336.10	315.70	295.70	275.70	255.70	237.80
1,880	1,920	463.00	440.50	418.00	395.50	373.00	350.50	328.50	308.50	288.50	268.50	249.00
1,920	1,960	477.40	454.90	432.40	409.90	387.40	364.90	342.40	321.30	301.30	281.30	261.30
1,960	2,000	491.80	469.30	446.80	424.30	401.80	379.30	356.80	334.30	314.10	294.10	274.10
2,000	2,040	506.20	483.70	461.20	438.70	416.20	393.70	371.20	348.70	326.90	306.90	286.90
2,040	2,080	520.60	498.10	475.60	453.10	430.60	408.10	385.60	363.10	340.60	319.70	299.70
2,080	2,120	535.00	512.50	490.00	467.50	445.00	422.50	400.00	377.50	355.00	332.50	312.50
2,120	2,160	549.40	526.90	504.40	481.90	459.40	436.90	414.40	391.90	369.40	346.90	325.30
2,160	2,200	563.80	541.30	518.80	496.30	473.80	451.30	428.80	406.30	383.80	361.30	338.80
2,200	2,240	578.20	555.70	533.20	510.70	488.20	465.70	443.20	420.70	398.20	375.70	353.20
2,240	2,280	592.60	570.10	547.60	525.10	502.60	480.10	457.60	435.10	412.60	390.10	367.60
2,280	2,320	607.00	584.50	562.00	539.50	517.00	494.50	472.00	449.50	427.00	404.50	382.00
2,320	2,360	621.40	598.90	576.40	553.90	531.40	508.90	486.40	463.90	441.40	418.90	396.40
2,360	2,400	635.80	613.30	590.80	568.30	545.80	523.30	500.80	478.30	455.80	433.30	410.80
2,400	2,440	650.20	627.70	605.20	582.70	560.20	537.70	515.20	492.70	470.20	447.70	425.20
2,440	2,480	664.60	642.10	619.60	597.10	574.60	552.10	529.60	507.10	484.60	462.10	439.60
2,480	2,520	679.00	656.50	634.00	611.50	589.00	566.50	544.00	521.50	499.00	476.50	454.00
2,520	2,560	693.40	670.90	648.40	625.90	603.40	580.90	558.40	535.90	513.40	490.90	468.40
2,560	2,600	707.80	685.30	662.80	640.30	617.80	595.30	572.80	550.30	527.80	505.30	482.80
2,600	2,640	722.20	699.70	677.20	654.70	632.20	609.70	587.20	564.70	542.20	519.70	497.20
2,640	2,680	736.60	714.10	691.60	669.10	646.60	624.10	601.60	579.10	556.60	534.10	511.60
2,680	2,720	751.00	728.50	706.00	683.50	661.00	638.50	616.00	593.50	571.00	548.50	526.00
2,720	2,760	765.40	742.90	720.40	697.90	675.40	652.90	630.40	607.90	585.40	562.90	540.40
2,760	2,800	779.80	757.30	734.80	712.30	689.80	667.30	644.80	622.30	599.80	577.30	554.80
2,800	2,840	794.20	771.70	749.20	726.70	704.20	681.70	659.20	636.70	614.20	591.70	569.20
2,840	2,880	808.60	786.10	763.60	741.10	718.60	696.10	673.60	651.10	628.60	606.10	583.60
2,880	2,920	823.00	800.50	778.00	755.50	733.00	710.50	688.00	665.50	643.00	620.50	598.00
2,920	2,960	837.40	814.90	792.40	769.90	747.40	724.90	702.40	679.90	657.40	634.90	612.40
		36 percent of the excess over $2,960 plus—										
$2,960 and over		844.60	822.10	799.60	777.10	754.60	732.10	709.60	687.10	664.60	642.10	619.60

TABLE X   Federal Income Tax Withholding Table (continued)

MARRIED Persons — MONTHLY Payroll Period

And the wages are—		And the number of withholding allowances claimed is—										
At least	But less than	0	1	2	3	4	5	6	7	8	9	10 or more
		The amount of income tax to be withheld shall be—										
$1,880	$1,920	$359.30	$340.70	$323.20	$305.70	$288.20	$270.70	$253.50	$237.90	$222.30	$206.70	$191.00
1,920	1,960	372.10	352.10	334.40	316.90	299.40	281.90	264.40	247.90	232.30	216.70	201.00
1,960	2,000	384.90	364.90	345.60	328.10	310.60	293.10	275.60	258.10	242.30	226.70	211.00
2,000	2,040	397.70	377.70	357.70	339.30	321.80	304.30	286.80	269.30	252.30	236.70	221.00
2,040	2,080	410.50	390.50	370.50	350.50	333.00	315.50	298.00	280.50	263.00	246.70	231.00
2,080	2,120	423.30	403.30	383.30	363.30	344.20	326.70	309.20	291.70	274.20	256.70	241.00
2,120	2,160	436.10	416.10	396.10	376.10	356.10	337.90	320.40	302.90	285.40	267.90	251.00
2,160	2,200	448.90	428.90	408.90	388.90	368.90	349.10	331.60	314.10	296.60	279.10	261.60
2,200	2,240	462.40	441.70	421.70	401.70	381.70	361.70	342.80	325.30	307.80	290.30	272.80
2,240	2,280	476.80	454.50	434.50	414.50	394.50	374.50	354.50	336.50	319.00	301.50	284.00
2,280	2,320	491.20	468.70	447.30	427.30	407.30	387.30	367.30	347.70	330.20	312.70	295.20
2,320	2,360	505.60	483.10	460.60	440.10	420.10	400.10	380.10	360.10	341.40	323.90	306.40
2,360	2,400	520.00	497.50	475.00	452.90	432.90	412.90	392.90	372.90	352.90	335.10	317.60
2,400	2,440	534.40	511.90	489.40	466.90	445.70	425.70	405.70	385.70	365.70	346.30	328.80
2,440	2,480	548.80	526.30	503.80	481.30	458.80	438.50	418.50	398.50	378.50	358.50	340.00
2,480	2,520	563.20	540.70	518.20	495.70	473.20	451.30	431.30	411.30	391.30	371.30	351.30
2,520	2,560	577.60	555.10	532.60	510.10	487.60	465.10	444.10	424.10	404.10	384.10	364.10
2,560	2,600	592.00	569.50	547.00	524.50	502.00	479.50	457.00	436.90	416.90	396.90	376.90
2,600	2,640	606.40	583.90	561.40	538.90	516.40	493.90	471.40	449.70	429.70	409.70	389.70
2,640	2,680	620.80	598.30	575.80	553.30	530.80	508.30	485.80	463.30	442.50	422.50	402.50
2,680	2,720	635.20	612.70	590.20	567.70	545.20	522.70	500.20	477.70	455.30	435.30	415.30
2,720	2,760	649.60	627.10	604.60	582.10	559.60	537.10	514.60	492.10	469.60	448.10	428.10
2,760	2,800	664.00	641.50	619.00	596.50	574.00	551.50	529.00	506.50	484.00	461.50	440.90
2,800	2,840	678.40	655.90	633.40	610.90	588.40	565.90	543.40	520.90	498.40	475.90	453.70
2,840	2,880	692.80	670.30	647.80	625.30	602.80	580.30	557.80	535.30	512.80	490.30	467.80
2,880	2,920	707.20	684.70	662.20	639.70	617.20	594.70	572.20	549.70	527.20	504.70	482.20
2,920	2,960	721.60	699.10	676.60	654.10	631.60	609.10	586.60	564.10	541.60	519.10	496.60
2,960	3,000	736.00	713.50	691.00	668.50	646.00	623.50	601.00	578.50	556.00	533.50	511.00
3,000	3,040	750.40	727.90	705.40	682.90	660.40	637.90	615.40	592.90	570.40	547.90	525.40
3,040	3,080	764.80	742.30	719.80	697.30	674.80	652.30	629.80	607.30	584.80	562.30	539.80
3,080	3,120	779.20	756.70	734.20	711.70	689.20	666.70	644.20	621.70	599.20	576.70	554.20
3,120	3,160	793.60	771.10	748.60	726.10	703.60	681.10	658.60	636.10	613.60	591.10	568.60
3,160	3,200	808.00	785.50	763.00	740.50	718.00	695.50	673.00	650.50	628.00	605.50	583.00
3,200	3,240	822.40	799.90	777.40	754.90	732.40	709.90	687.40	664.90	642.40	619.90	597.40
3,240	3,280	836.80	814.30	791.80	769.30	746.80	724.30	701.80	679.30	656.80	634.30	611.80
3,280	3,320	851.20	828.70	806.20	783.70	761.20	738.70	716.20	693.70	671.20	648.70	626.20
3,320	3,360	865.60	843.10	820.60	798.10	775.60	753.10	730.60	708.10	685.60	663.10	640.60
3,360	3,400	880.00	857.50	835.00	812.50	790.00	767.50	745.00	722.50	700.00	677.50	655.00
3,400	3,440	894.40	871.90	849.40	826.90	804.40	781.90	759.40	736.90	714.40	691.90	669.40
3,440	3,480	908.80	886.30	863.80	841.30	818.80	796.30	773.80	751.30	728.80	706.30	683.80
3,480	3,520	923.20	900.70	878.20	855.70	833.20	810.70	788.20	765.70	743.20	720.70	698.20
3,520	3,560	937.60	915.10	892.60	870.10	847.60	825.10	802.60	780.10	757.60	735.10	712.60
3,560	3,600	952.00	929.50	907.00	884.50	862.00	839.50	817.00	794.50	772.00	749.50	727.00
3,600	3,640	966.40	943.90	921.40	898.90	876.40	853.90	831.40	808.90	786.40	763.90	741.40
3,640	3,680	980.80	958.30	935.80	913.30	890.80	868.30	845.80	823.30	800.80	778.30	755.80
3,680	3,720	995.20	972.70	950.20	927.70	905.20	882.70	860.20	837.70	815.20	792.70	770.20
3,720	3,760	1,009.60	987.10	964.60	942.10	919.60	897.10	874.60	852.10	829.60	807.10	784.60
3,760	3,800	1,024.00	1,001.50	979.00	956.50	934.00	911.50	889.00	866.50	844.00	821.50	799.00
3,800	3,840	1,038.40	1,015.90	993.40	970.90	948.40	925.90	903.40	880.90	858.40	835.90	813.40
3,840	3,880	1,052.80	1,030.30	1,007.80	985.30	962.80	940.30	917.80	895.30	872.80	850.30	827.80
3,880	3,920	1,067.20	1,044.70	1,022.20	999.70	977.20	954.70	932.20	909.70	887.20	864.70	842.20
3,920	3,960	1,081.60	1,059.10	1,036.60	1,014.10	991.60	969.10	946.60	924.10	901.60	879.10	856.60
3,960	4,000	1,096.00	1,073.50	1,051.00	1,028.50	1,006.00	983.50	961.00	938.50	916.00	893.50	871.00
4,000	4,040	1,110.40	1,087.90	1,065.40	1,042.90	1,020.40	997.90	975.40	952.90	930.40	907.90	885.40
4,040	4,080	1,124.80	1,102.30	1,079.80	1,057.30	1,034.80	1,012.30	989.80	967.30	944.80	922.30	899.80
		36 percent of the excess over $4,080 plus—										
$4,080 and over		1,132.00	1,109.50	1,087.00	1,064.50	1,042.00	1,019.50	997.00	974.50	952.00	929.50	907.00

TABLE XI Federal Income Tax Table

Tax Table
Based on Taxable Income
For persons with taxable incomes of less than $50,000.

Example: Mr. and Mrs. Brown are filing a joint return. Their taxable income on line 34 is $23,270. First, they find the $23,250-23,300 income line. Next, they find the column for married filing jointly and read down the column. The amount shown where the income line and filing status column meet is $4,082. This is the tax amount they must write on line 35 of their return.

At least	But less than	Single	Married filing jointly *	Married filing separately	Head of a household
			Your tax is—		
23,200	23,250	5,208	4,069	6,438	4,805
23,250	23,300	5,224	(4,082)	6,462	4,820
23,300	23,350	5,241	4,096	6,486	4,836

First column group

If line 34 (taxable income) is— At least	But less than	Single	Married filing jointly *	Married filing separately	Head of a household
			Your tax is—		
0	1,700	0	0	0	0
1,700	1,725	0	0	a2	0
1,725	1,750	0	0	5	0
1,750	1,775	0	0	9	0
1,775	1,800	0	0	12	0
1,800	1,825	0	0	16	0
1,825	1,850	0	0	19	0
1,850	1,875	0	0	22	0
1,875	1,900	0	0	26	0
1,900	1,925	0	0	29	0
1,925	1,950	0	0	33	0
1,950	1,975	0	0	36	0
1,975	2,000	0	0	40	0
2,000					
2,000	2,025	0	0	43	0
2,025	2,050	0	0	47	0
2,050	2,075	0	0	50	0
2,075	2,100	0	0	54	0
2,100	2,125	0	0	57	0
2,125	2,150	0	0	60	0
2,150	2,175	0	0	64	0
2,175	2,200	0	0	67	0
2,200	2,225	0	0	71	0
2,225	2,250	0	0	74	0
2,250	2,275	0	0	78	0
2,275	2,300	0	0	81	0
2,300	2,325	b2	0	85	b2
2,325	2,350	5	0	88	5
2,350	2,375	9	0	92	9
2,375	2,400	12	0	95	12
2,400	2,425	16	0	99	16
2,425	2,450	19	0	102	19
2,450	2,475	22	0	105	22
2,475	2,500	26	0	109	26
2,500	2,525	29	0	112	29
2,525	2,550	33	0	116	33
2,550	2,575	36	0	119	36
2,575	2,600	40	0	123	40
2,600	2,625	43	0	126	43
2,625	2,650	47	0	130	47
2,650	2,675	50	0	133	50
2,675	2,700	54	0	137	54
2,700	2,725	57	0	140	57
2,725	2,750	60	0	143	60
2,750	2,775	64	0	147	64
2,775	2,800	67	0	151	67
2,800	2,825	71	0	155	71
2,825	2,850	74	0	159	74
2,850	2,875	78	0	163	78
2,875	2,900	81	0	167	81
2,900	2,925	85	0	171	85
2,925	2,950	88	0	175	88
2,950	2,975	92	0	179	92
2,975	3,000	95	0	183	95

Second column group

If line 34 (taxable income) is— At least	But less than	Single	Married filing jointly *	Married filing separately	Head of a household
			Your tax is—		
3,000					
3,000	3,050	100	0	189	100
3,050	3,100	107	0	197	107
3,100	3,150	114	0	204	114
3,150	3,200	121	0	212	121
3,200	3,250	128	0	220	128
3,250	3,300	135	0	228	135
3,300	3,350	142	0	236	142
3,350	3,400	149	0	244	149
3,400	3,450	156	c3	252	156
3,450	3,500	164	10	260	162
3,500	3,550	172	17	268	169
3,550	3,600	180	24	276	176
3,600	3,650	188	31	283	183
3,650	3,700	196	38	291	190
3,700	3,750	203	45	299	197
3,750	3,800	211	52	307	204
3,800	3,850	219	59	316	211
3,850	3,900	227	66	324	218
3,900	3,950	235	73	333	225
3,950	4,000	243	79	342	232
4,000					
4,000	4,050	251	86	351	238
4,050	4,100	259	93	360	245
4,100	4,150	267	100	369	252
4,150	4,200	275	107	378	259
4,200	4,250	282	114	387	266
4,250	4,300	290	121	395	273
4,300	4,350	298	128	404	280
4,350	4,400	306	135	413	287
4,400	4,450	315	142	422	294
4,450	4,500	323	149	431	302
4,500	4,550	332	156	440	310
4,550	4,600	341	162	449	318
4,600	4,650	350	169	458	326
4,650	4,700	359	176	467	334
4,700	4,750	368	183	475	342
4,750	4,800	377	190	484	350
4,800	4,850	386	197	493	357
4,850	4,900	395	204	502	365
4,900	4,950	403	211	511	373
4,950	5,000	412	218	520	381
5,000					
5,000	5,050	421	225	529	389
5,050	5,100	430	232	538	397
5,100	5,150	439	238	547	405
5,150	5,200	448	245	555	413
5,200	5,250	457	252	564	421
5,250	5,300	466	259	573	429
5,300	5,350	474	266	582	436
5,350	5,400	483	273	591	444
5,400	5,450	492	280	600	452
5,450	5,500	501	287	609	460

Third column group

If line 34 (taxable income) is— At least	But less than	Single	Married filing jointly *	Married filing separately	Head of a household
			Your tax is—		
5,500	5,550	510	294	618	468
5,550	5,600	519	302	627	476
5,600	5,650	528	310	635	484
5,650	5,700	537	318	644	492
5,700	5,750	546	326	653	500
5,750	5,800	554	334	662	508
5,800	5,850	563	342	671	515
5,850	5,900	572	350	680	523
5,900	5,950	581	357	689	531
5,950	6,000	590	365	698	539
6,000					
6,000	6,050	599	373	709	547
6,050	6,100	608	381	719	555
6,100	6,150	617	389	730	563
6,150	6,200	626	397	740	571
6,200	6,250	634	405	750	579
6,250	6,300	643	413	761	587
6,300	6,350	652	421	771	594
6,350	6,400	661	429	781	602
6,400	6,450	670	436	792	610
6,450	6,500	679	444	802	618
6,500	6,550	688	452	812	627
6,550	6,600	697	460	823	635
6,600	6,650	707	468	833	644
6,650	6,700	716	476	844	653
6,700	6,750	726	484	854	662
6,750	6,800	735	492	864	671
6,800	6,850	744	500	875	680
6,850	6,900	754	508	885	689
6,900	6,950	763	515	895	698
6,950	7,000	772	523	906	707
7,000					
7,000	7,050	782	531	916	715
7,050	7,100	791	539	927	724
7,100	7,150	801	547	937	733
7,150	7,200	810	555	947	742
7,200	7,250	819	563	958	751
7,250	7,300	829	571	968	760
7,300	7,350	838	579	978	769
7,350	7,400	848	587	989	778
7,400	7,450	857	594	999	787
7,450	7,500	866	602	1,009	795
7,500	7,550	876	610	1,020	804
7,550	7,600	885	618	1,030	813
7,600	7,650	894	627	1,041	822
7,650	7,700	904	635	1,051	831
7,700	7,750	913	644	1,061	840
7,750	7,800	923	653	1,072	849
7,800	7,850	932	662	1,082	858
7,850	7,900	941	671	1,092	867
7,900	7,950	951	680	1,103	875
7,950	8,000	960	689	1,113	884

Continued on next page

*This column must also be used by a qualifying widow(er).

a If your taxable income is exactly $1,700, your tax is zero.
b If your taxable income is exactly $2,300, your tax is zero.
c If your taxable income is exactly $3,400, your tax is zero.

TABLE XI   Federal Income Tax Table (continued)

Tax Table (Continued)

If line 34 (taxable income) is— At least	But less than	Single	Married filing jointly *	Married filing separately *	Head of a household
8,000					
8,000	8,050	969	698	1,124	893
8,050	8,100	979	707	1,136	902
8,100	8,150	988	715	1,148	911
8,150	8,200	998	724	1,160	920
8,200	8,250	1,007	733	1,172	929
8,250	8,300	1,016	742	1,184	938
8,300	8,350	1,026	751	1,195	947
8,350	8,400	1,035	760	1,207	955
8,400	8,450	1,045	769	1,219	964
8,450	8,500	1,054	778	1,231	973
8,500	8,550	1,064	787	1,243	982
8,550	8,600	1,074	795	1,255	991
8,600	8,650	1,085	804	1,266	1,000
8,650	8,700	1,095	813	1,278	1,009
8,700	8,750	1,105	822	1,290	1,019
8,750	8,800	1,116	831	1,302	1,029
8,800	8,850	1,126	840	1,314	1,040
8,850	8,900	1,136	849	1,326	1,051
8,900	8,950	1,147	858	1,338	1,062
8,950	9,000	1,157	867	1,349	1,073
9,000					
9,000	9,050	1,167	875	1,361	1,084
9,050	9,100	1,178	884	1,373	1,095
9,100	9,150	1,188	893	1,385	1,106
9,150	9,200	1,199	902	1,397	1,116
9,200	9,250	1,209	911	1,409	1,127
9,250	9,300	1,219	920	1,421	1,138
9,300	9,350	1,230	929	1,432	1,149
9,350	9,400	1,240	938	1,444	1,160
9,400	9,450	1,250	947	1,456	1,171
9,450	9,500	1,261	955	1,468	1,182
9,500	9,550	1,271	964	1,480	1,192
9,550	9,600	1,282	973	1,492	1,203
9,600	9,650	1,292	982	1,503	1,214
9,650	9,700	1,302	991	1,515	1,225
9,700	9,750	1,313	1,000	1,527	1,236
9,750	9,800	1,323	1,009	1,539	1,247
9,800	9,850	1,333	1,018	1,551	1,258
9,850	9,900	1,344	1,027	1,563	1,268
9,900	9,950	1,354	1,035	1,575	1,279
9,950	10,000	1,364	1,044	1,586	1,290
10,000					
10,000	10,050	1,375	1,053	1,598	1,301
10,050	10,100	1,385	1,062	1,610	1,312
10,100	10,150	1,396	1,071	1,623	1,323
10,150	10,200	1,406	1,080	1,637	1,334
10,200	10,250	1,416	1,089	1,651	1,344
10,250	10,300	1,427	1,098	1,664	1,355
10,300	10,350	1,437	1,106	1,678	1,366
10,350	10,400	1,447	1,115	1,692	1,377
10,400	10,450	1,458	1,124	1,706	1,388
10,450	10,500	1,468	1,133	1,720	1,399
10,500	10,550	1,479	1,142	1,734	1,410
10,550	10,600	1,489	1,151	1,747	1,421
10,600	10,650	1,499	1,160	1,761	1,431
10,650	10,700	1,510	1,169	1,775	1,442
10,700	10,750	1,520	1,178	1,789	1,453

If line 34 (taxable income) is— At least	But less than	Single	Married filing jointly *	Married filing separately *	Head of a household
10,750	10,800	1,530	1,186	1,803	1,464
10,800	10,850	1,541	1,195	1,817	1,475
10,850	10,900	1,553	1,204	1,830	1,486
10,900	10,950	1,565	1,213	1,844	1,497
10,950	11,000	1,577	1,222	1,858	1,507
11,000					
11,000	11,050	1,589	1,231	1,872	1,518
11,050	11,100	1,601	1,240	1,886	1,529
11,100	11,150	1,613	1,249	1,899	1,540
11,150	11,200	1,624	1,258	1,913	1,551
11,200	11,250	1,636	1,266	1,927	1,562
11,250	11,300	1,648	1,275	1,941	1,573
11,300	11,350	1,660	1,284	1,955	1,583
11,350	11,400	1,672	1,293	1,969	1,594
11,400	11,450	1,684	1,302	1,982	1,605
11,450	11,500	1,696	1,311	1,996	1,616
11,500	11,550	1,707	1,320	2,010	1,627
11,550	11,600	1,719	1,329	2,024	1,638
11,600	11,650	1,731	1,338	2,038	1,649
11,650	11,700	1,743	1,346	2,052	1,659
11,700	11,750	1,755	1,355	2,065	1,670
11,750	11,800	1,767	1,364	2,079	1,681
11,800	11,850	1,778	1,373	2,093	1,693
11,850	11,900	1,790	1,382	2,107	1,704
11,900	11,950	1,802	1,392	2,121	1,716
11,950	12,000	1,814	1,402	2,134	1,728
12,000					
12,000	12,050	1,826	1,412	2,148	1,740
12,050	12,100	1,838	1,423	2,162	1,752
12,100	12,150	1,850	1,433	2,176	1,764
12,150	12,200	1,861	1,443	2,190	1,776
12,200	12,250	1,873	1,454	2,204	1,787
12,250	12,300	1,885	1,464	2,217	1,799
12,300	12,350	1,897	1,475	2,232	1,811
12,350	12,400	1,909	1,485	2,248	1,823
12,400	12,450	1,921	1,495	2,264	1,835
12,450	12,500	1,933	1,506	2,280	1,847
12,500	12,550	1,944	1,516	2,295	1,858
12,550	12,600	1,956	1,526	2,311	1,870
12,600	12,650	1,968	1,537	2,327	1,882
12,650	12,700	1,980	1,547	2,343	1,894
12,700	12,750	1,992	1,558	2,359	1,906
12,750	12,800	2,004	1,568	2,374	1,918
12,800	12,850	2,015	1,578	2,390	1,930
12,850	12,900	2,027	1,589	2,406	1,941
12,900	12,950	2,040	1,599	2,422	1,953
12,950	13,000	2,053	1,609	2,438	1,965
13,000					
13,000	13,050	2,065	1,620	2,453	1,977
13,050	13,100	2,078	1,630	2,469	1,989
13,100	13,150	2,091	1,640	2,485	2,001
13,150	13,200	2,104	1,651	2,501	2,013
13,200	13,250	2,117	1,661	2,517	2,024
13,250	13,300	2,130	1,672	2,532	2,036
13,300	13,350	2,142	1,682	2,548	2,048
13,350	13,400	2,155	1,692	2,564	2,060
13,400	13,450	2,168	1,703	2,580	2,072
13,450	13,500	2,181	1,713	2,596	2,084

If line 34 (taxable income) is— At least	But less than	Single	Married filing jointly *	Married filing separately *	Head of a household
13,500	13,550	2,194	1,723	2,611	2,095
13,550	13,600	2,207	1,734	2,627	2,107
13,600	13,650	2,219	1,744	2,643	2,119
13,650	13,700	2,232	1,755	2,659	2,131
13,700	13,750	2,245	1,765	2,675	2,143
13,750	13,800	2,258	1,775	2,690	2,155
13,800	13,850	2,271	1,786	2,706	2,167
13,850	13,900	2,284	1,796	2,722	2,178
13,900	13,950	2,296	1,806	2,738	2,190
13,950	14,000	2,309	1,817	2,754	2,202
14,000					
14,000	14,050	2,322	1,827	2,769	2,214
14,050	14,100	2,335	1,837	2,785	2,226
14,100	14,150	2,348	1,848	2,801	2,238
14,150	14,200	2,361	1,858	2,817	2,250
14,200	14,250	2,373	1,869	2,833	2,261
14,250	14,300	2,386	1,879	2,848	2,273
14,300	14,350	2,399	1,889	2,864	2,285
14,350	14,400	2,412	1,900	2,880	2,297
14,400	14,450	2,425	1,910	2,896	2,309
14,450	14,500	2,438	1,920	2,912	2,321
14,500	14,550	2,450	1,931	2,927	2,332
14,550	14,600	2,463	1,941	2,943	2,344
14,600	14,650	2,476	1,952	2,959	2,356
14,650	14,700	2,489	1,962	2,975	2,368
14,700	14,750	2,502	1,972	2,991	2,380
14,750	14,800	2,515	1,983	3,006	2,392
14,800	14,850	2,528	1,993	3,022	2,404
14,850	14,900	2,540	2,003	3,038	2,415
14,900	14,950	2,553	2,014	3,054	2,427
14,950	15,000	2,566	2,024	3,071	2,439
15,000					
15,000	15,050	2,580	2,034	3,089	2,451
15,050	15,100	2,595	2,045	3,107	2,464
15,100	15,150	2,609	2,055	3,126	2,477
15,150	15,200	2,624	2,066	3,144	2,490
15,200	15,250	2,639	2,076	3,162	2,503
15,250	15,300	2,654	2,086	3,180	2,516
15,300	15,350	2,669	2,097	3,199	2,528
15,350	15,400	2,684	2,107	3,217	2,541
15,400	15,450	2,698	2,117	3,235	2,554
15,450	15,500	2,713	2,128	3,254	2,567
15,500	15,550	2,728	2,138	3,272	2,580
15,550	15,600	2,743	2,149	3,290	2,593
15,600	15,650	2,758	2,159	3,308	2,606
15,650	15,700	2,772	2,169	3,327	2,618
15,700	15,750	2,787	2,180	3,345	2,631
15,750	15,800	2,802	2,190	3,363	2,644
15,800	15,850	2,817	2,200	3,381	2,657
15,850	15,900	2,832	2,211	3,400	2,670
15,900	15,950	2,846	2,221	3,418	2,683
15,950	16,000	2,861	2,232	3,436	2,695
16,000					
16,000	16,050	2,876	2,243	3,455	2,708
16,050	16,100	2,891	2,254	3,473	2,721
16,100	16,150	2,906	2,266	3,491	2,734
16,150	16,200	2,921	2,278	3,509	2,747
16,200	16,250	2,935	2,290	3,528	2,760

*This column must also be used by a qualifying widow(er).

Continued on next page

TABLE XI Federal Income Tax Table (continued)

Tax Table (Continued)

If line 34 (taxable income) is— At least	But less than	Single	Married filing jointly *	Married filing separately *	Head of a house-hold
16,250	16,300	2,950	2,302	3,546	2,772
16,300	16,350	2,965	2,314	3,564	2,785
16,350	16,400	2,980	2,326	3,582	2,798
16,400	16,450	2,995	2,337	3,601	2,811
16,450	16,500	3,009	2,349	3,619	2,824
16,500	16,550	3,024	2,361	3,637	2,837
16,550	16,600	3,039	2,373	3,655	2,849
16,600	16,650	3,054	2,385	3,674	2,862
16,650	16,700	3,069	2,397	3,692	2,875
16,700	16,750	3,083	2,409	3,710	2,888
16,750	16,800	3,098	2,420	3,729	2,901
16,800	16,850	3,113	2,432	3,747	2,914
16,850	16,900	3,128	2,444	3,765	2,926
16,900	16,950	3,143	2,456	3,783	2,939
16,950	17,000	3,158	2,468	3,802	2,952
17,000					
17,000	17,050	3,172	2,480	3,820	2,965
17,050	17,100	3,187	2,491	3,838	2,978
17,100	17,150	3,202	2,503	3,856	2,991
17,150	17,200	3,217	2,515	3,875	3,003
17,200	17,250	3,232	2,527	3,893	3,016
17,250	17,300	3,246	2,539	3,911	3,029
17,300	17,350	3,261	2,551	3,930	3,042
17,350	17,400	3,276	2,563	3,948	3,055
17,400	17,450	3,291	2,574	3,966	3,068
17,450	17,500	3,306	2,586	3,984	3,081
17,500	17,550	3,320	2,598	4,003	3,093
17,550	17,600	3,335	2,610	4,021	3,106
17,600	17,650	3,350	2,622	4,041	3,119
17,650	17,700	3,365	2,634	4,062	3,132
17,700	17,750	3,380	2,646	4,083	3,145
17,750	17,800	3,395	2,657	4,104	3,158
17,800	17,850	3,409	2,669	4,126	3,170
17,850	17,900	3,424	2,681	4,147	3,183
17,900	17,950	3,439	2,693	4,168	3,196
17,950	18,000	3,454	2,705	4,189	3,209
18,000					
18,000	18,050	3,469	2,717	4,210	3,222
18,050	18,100	3,483	2,728	4,232	3,235
18,100	18,150	3,498	2,740	4,253	3,247
18,150	18,200	3,513	2,752	4,274	3,260
18,200	18,250	3,529	2,764	4,295	3,274
18,250	18,300	3,546	2,776	4,317	3,290
18,300	18,350	3,562	2,788	4,338	3,305
18,350	18,400	3,579	2,800	4,359	3,320
18,400	18,450	3,596	2,811	4,380	3,336
18,450	18,500	3,613	2,823	4,402	3,351
18,500	18,550	3,630	2,835	4,423	3,366
18,550	18,600	3,646	2,847	4,444	3,381
18,600	18,650	3,663	2,859	4,465	3,397
18,650	18,700	3,680	2,871	4,486	3,412
18,700	18,750	3,697	2,883	4,508	3,427
18,750	18,800	3,713	2,894	4,529	3,443
18,800	18,850	3,730	2,906	4,550	3,458
18,850	18,900	3,747	2,918	4,571	3,473
18,900	18,950	3,764	2,930	4,593	3,489
18,950	19,000	3,781	2,942	4,614	3,504

If line 34 (taxable income) is— At least	But less than	Single	Married filing jointly *	Married filing separately *	Head of a house-hold
19,000					
19,000	19,050	3,797	2,954	4,635	3,519
19,050	19,100	3,814	2,965	4,656	3,535
19,100	19,150	3,831	2,977	4,678	3,550
19,150	19,200	3,848	2,989	4,699	3,565
19,200	19,250	3,865	3,001	4,720	3,580
19,250	19,300	3,881	3,013	4,741	3,596
19,300	19,350	3,898	3,025	4,762	3,611
19,350	19,400	3,915	3,037	4,784	3,626
19,400	19,450	3,932	3,048	4,805	3,642
19,450	19,500	3,949	3,060	4,826	3,657
19,500	19,550	3,965	3,072	4,847	3,672
19,550	19,600	3,982	3,084	4,869	3,688
19,600	19,650	3,999	3,096	4,890	3,703
19,650	19,700	4,016	3,108	4,911	3,718
19,700	19,750	4,032	3,120	4,932	3,733
19,750	19,800	4,049	3,131	4,954	3,749
19,800	19,850	4,066	3,143	4,975	3,764
19,850	19,900	4,083	3,155	4,996	3,779
19,900	19,950	4,100	3,167	5,017	3,795
19,950	20,000	4,116	3,179	5,038	3,810
20,000					
20,000	20,050	4,133	3,191	5,060	3,825
20,050	20,100	4,150	3,202	5,081	3,841
20,100	20,150	4,167	3,214	5,102	3,856
20,150	20,200	4,184	3,226	5,123	3,871
20,200	20,250	4,200	3,239	5,145	3,887
20,250	20,300	4,217	3,253	5,166	3,902
20,300	20,350	4,234	3,267	5,187	3,917
20,350	20,400	4,251	3,280	5,208	3,932
20,400	20,450	4,267	3,294	5,230	3,948
20,450	20,500	4,284	3,308	5,251	3,963
20,500	20,550	4,301	3,322	5,272	3,978
20,550	20,600	4,318	3,336	5,293	3,994
20,600	20,650	4,335	3,350	5,314	4,009
20,650	20,700	4,351	3,363	5,336	4,024
20,700	20,750	4,368	3,377	5,357	4,040
20,750	20,800	4,385	3,391	5,378	4,055
20,800	20,850	4,402	3,405	5,399	4,070
20,850	20,900	4,419	3,419	5,421	4,086
20,900	20,950	4,435	3,433	5,442	4,101
20,950	21,000	4,452	3,446	5,463	4,116
21,000					
21,000	21,050	4,469	3,460	5,484	4,131
21,050	21,100	4,486	3,474	5,506	4,147
21,100	21,150	4,503	3,488	5,527	4,162
21,150	21,200	4,519	3,502	5,548	4,177
21,200	21,250	4,536	3,516	5,569	4,193
21,250	21,300	4,553	3,529	5,590	4,208
21,300	21,350	4,570	3,543	5,612	4,223
21,350	21,400	4,586	3,557	5,633	4,239
21,400	21,450	4,603	3,571	5,654	4,254
21,450	21,500	4,620	3,585	5,675	4,269
21,500	21,550	4,637	3,598	5,697	4,285
21,550	21,600	4,654	3,612	5,718	4,300
21,600	21,650	4,670	3,626	5,739	4,315
21,650	21,700	4,687	3,640	5,760	4,330
21,700	21,750	4,704	3,654	5,782	4,346

If line 34 (taxable income) is— At least	But less than	Single	Married filing jointly *	Married filing separately *	Head of a house-hold
21,750	21,800	4,721	3,668	5,803	4,361
21,800	21,850	4,738	3,681	5,824	4,376
21,850	21,900	4,754	3,695	5,845	4,392
21,900	21,950	4,771	3,709	5,866	4,407
21,950	22,000	4,788	3,723	5,888	4,422
22,000					
22,000	22,050	4,805	3,737	5,909	4,438
22,050	22,100	4,821	3,751	5,930	4,453
22,100	22,150	4,838	3,764	5,951	4,468
22,150	22,200	4,855	3,778	5,973	4,483
22,200	22,250	4,872	3,792	5,994	4,499
22,250	22,300	4,889	3,806	6,015	4,514
22,300	22,350	4,905	3,820	6,036	4,529
22,350	22,400	4,922	3,833	6,058	4,545
22,400	22,450	4,939	3,847	6,079	4,560
22,450	22,500	4,956	3,861	6,100	4,575
22,500	22,550	4,973	3,875	6,121	4,591
22,550	22,600	4,989	3,889	6,142	4,606
22,600	22,650	5,006	3,903	6,164	4,621
22,650	22,700	5,023	3,916	6,185	4,637
22,700	22,750	5,040	3,930	6,206	4,652
22,750	22,800	5,056	3,944	6,227	4,667
22,800	22,850	5,073	3,958	6,249	4,682
22,850	22,900	5,090	3,972	6,270	4,698
22,900	22,950	5,107	3,986	6,293	4,713
22,950	23,000	5,124	3,999	6,317	4,728
23,000					
23,000	23,050	5,140	4,013	6,341	4,744
23,050	23,100	5,157	4,027	6,365	4,759
23,100	23,150	5,174	4,041	6,389	4,774
23,150	23,200	5,191	4,055	6,414	4,790
23,200	23,250	5,208	4,069	6,438	4,805
23,250	23,300	5,224	4,082	6,462	4,820
23,300	23,350	5,241	4,096	6,486	4,836
23,350	23,400	5,258	4,110	6,510	4,851
23,400	23,450	5,275	4,124	6,535	4,866
23,450	23,500	5,292	4,138	6,559	4,881
23,500	23,550	5,310	4,151	6,583	4,898
23,550	23,600	5,329	4,165	6,607	4,916
23,600	23,650	5,348	4,179	6,631	4,934
23,650	23,700	5,367	4,193	6,656	4,951
23,700	23,750	5,387	4,207	6,680	4,969
23,750	23,800	5,406	4,221	6,704	4,987
23,800	23,850	5,425	4,234	6,728	5,005
23,850	23,900	5,444	4,248	6,752	5,022
23,900	23,950	5,464	4,262	6,776	5,040
23,950	24,000	5,483	4,276	6,801	5,058
24,000					
24,000	24,050	5,502	4,290	6,825	5,076
24,050	24,100	5,521	4,304	6,849	5,094
24,100	24,150	5,541	4,317	6,873	5,111
24,150	24,200	5,560	4,331	6,897	5,129
24,200	24,250	5,579	4,345	6,922	5,147
24,250	24,300	5,598	4,359	6,946	5,165
24,300	24,350	5,618	4,373	6,970	5,182
24,350	24,400	5,637	4,386	6,994	5,200
24,400	24,450	5,656	4,400	7,018	5,218
24,450	24,500	5,675	4,414	7,043	5,236

*This column must also be used by a qualifying widow(er).

Continued on next page

TABLE XI   *Federal Income Tax Table (continued)*

Tax Table (Continued)

If line 34 (taxable income) is—		And you are—			
At least	But less than	Single	Married filing jointly *	Married filing separately	Head of a household
		Your tax is—			
24,500	24,550	5,695	4,428	7,067	5,254
24,550	24,600	5,714	4,442	7,091	5,271
24,600	24,650	5,733	4,457	7,115	5,289
24,650	24,700	5,752	4,472	7,139	5,307
24,700	24,750	5,772	4,488	7,164	5,325
24,750	24,800	5,791	4,504	7,188	5,342
24,800	24,850	5,810	4,520	7,212	5,360
24,850	24,900	5,829	4,536	7,236	5,378
24,900	24,950	5,849	4,551	7,260	5,396
24,950	25,000	5,868	4,567	7,285	5,413
25,000					
25,000	25,050	5,887	4,583	7,309	5,431
25,050	25,100	5,906	4,599	7,333	5,449
25,100	25,150	5,926	4,615	7,357	5,467
25,150	25,200	5,945	4,630	7,381	5,485
25,200	25,250	5,964	4,646	7,406	5,502
25,250	25,300	5,984	4,662	7,430	5,520
25,300	25,350	6,003	4,678	7,454	5,538
25,350	25,400	6,022	4,694	7,478	5,556
25,400	25,450	6,041	4,709	7,502	5,573
25,450	25,500	6,061	4,725	7,526	5,591
25,500	25,550	6,080	4,741	7,551	5,609
25,550	25,600	6,099	4,757	7,575	5,627
25,600	25,650	6,118	4,773	7,599	5,645
25,650	25,700	6,138	4,788	7,623	5,662
25,700	25,750	6,157	4,804	7,647	5,680
25,750	25,800	6,176	4,820	7,672	5,698
25,800	25,850	6,195	4,836	7,696	5,716
25,850	25,900	6,215	4,852	7,720	5,733
25,900	25,950	6,234	4,867	7,744	5,751
25,950	26,000	6,253	4,883	7,768	5,769
26,000					
26,000	26,050	6,272	4,899	7,793	5,787
26,050	26,100	6,292	4,915	7,817	5,805
26,100	26,150	6,311	4,931	7,841	5,822
26,150	26,200	6,330	4,946	7,865	5,840
26,200	26,250	6,349	4,962	7,889	5,858
26,250	26,300	6,369	4,978	7,914	5,876
26,300	26,350	6,388	4,994	7,938	5,893
26,350	26,400	6,407	5,010	7,962	5,911
26,400	26,450	6,426	5,025	7,986	5,929
26,450	26,500	6,446	5,041	8,010	5,947
26,500	26,550	6,465	5,057	8,035	5,965
26,550	26,600	6,484	5,073	8,059	5,982
26,600	26,650	6,503	5,089	8,083	6,000
26,650	26,700	6,523	5,104	8,107	6,018
26,700	26,750	6,542	5,120	8,131	6,036
26,750	26,800	6,561	5,136	8,156	6,053
26,800	26,850	6,580	5,152	8,180	6,071
26,850	26,900	6,600	5,168	8,204	6,089
26,900	26,950	6,619	5,183	8,228	6,107
26,950	27,000	6,638	5,199	8,252	6,124
27,000					
27,000	27,050	6,657	5,215	8,276	6,142
27,050	27,100	6,677	5,231	8,301	6,160
27,100	27,150	6,696	5,247	8,325	6,178
27,150	27,200	6,715	5,262	8,349	6,196
27,200	27,250	6,735	5,278	8,373	6,213

If line 34 (taxable income) is—		And you are—			
At least	But less than	Single	Married filing jointly *	Married filing separately	Head of a household
		Your tax is—			
27,250	27,300	6,754	5,294	8,397	6,231
27,300	27,350	6,773	5,310	8,422	6,249
27,350	27,400	6,792	5,326	8,446	6,267
27,400	27,450	6,812	5,341	8,470	6,284
27,450	27,500	6,831	5,357	8,494	6,302
27,500	27,550	6,850	5,373	8,518	6,320
27,550	27,600	6,869	5,389	8,543	6,338
27,600	27,650	6,889	5,405	8,567	6,356
27,650	27,700	6,908	5,420	8,591	6,373
27,700	27,750	6,927	5,436	8,615	6,391
27,750	27,800	6,946	5,452	8,639	6,409
27,800	27,850	6,966	5,468	8,664	6,427
27,850	27,900	6,985	5,484	8,688	6,444
27,900	27,950	7,004	5,499	8,712	6,462
27,950	28,000	7,023	5,515	8,736	6,480
28,000					
28,000	28,050	7,043	5,531	8,760	6,498
28,050	28,100	7,062	5,547	8,785	6,516
28,100	28,150	7,081	5,563	8,809	6,533
28,150	28,200	7,100	5,578	8,833	6,551
28,200	28,250	7,120	5,594	8,857	6,569
28,250	28,300	7,139	5,610	8,881	6,587
28,300	28,350	7,158	5,626	8,906	6,604
28,350	28,400	7,177	5,642	8,930	6,622
28,400	28,450	7,197	5,657	8,954	6,640
28,450	28,500	7,216	5,673	8,978	6,658
28,500	28,550	7,235	5,689	9,002	6,676
28,550	28,600	7,254	5,705	9,026	6,693
28,600	28,650	7,274	5,721	9,051	6,711
28,650	28,700	7,293	5,736	9,075	6,729
28,700	28,750	7,312	5,752	9,099	6,747
28,750	28,800	7,331	5,768	9,123	6,764
28,800	28,850	7,352	5,784	9,147	6,784
28,850	28,900	7,374	5,800	9,172	6,804
28,900	28,950	7,395	5,815	9,196	6,825
28,950	29,000	7,417	5,831	9,220	6,846
29,000					
29,000	29,050	7,439	5,847	9,244	6,867
29,050	29,100	7,461	5,863	9,268	6,887
29,100	29,150	7,482	5,879	9,293	6,908
29,150	29,200	7,504	5,894	9,317	6,929
29,200	29,250	7,526	5,910	9,341	6,950
29,250	29,300	7,547	5,926	9,365	6,970
29,300	29,350	7,569	5,942	9,389	6,991
29,350	29,400	7,591	5,958	9,414	7,012
29,400	29,450	7,613	5,973	9,438	7,032
29,450	29,500	7,634	5,989	9,462	7,053
29,500	29,550	7,656	6,005	9,486	7,074
29,550	29,600	7,678	6,021	9,510	7,095
29,600	29,650	7,700	6,037	9,535	7,115
29,650	29,700	7,721	6,052	9,559	7,136
29,700	29,750	7,743	6,068	9,583	7,157
29,750	29,800	7,765	6,084	9,607	7,178
29,800	29,850	7,786	6,100	9,631	7,198
29,850	29,900	7,808	6,116	9,656	7,219
29,900	29,950	7,830	6,133	9,680	7,240
29,950	30,000	7,852	6,151	9,704	7,261

If line 34 (taxable income) is—		And you are—			
At least	But less than	Single	Married filing jointly *	Married filing separately	Head of a household
		Your tax is—			
30,000					
30,000	30,050	7,873	6,169	9,729	7,281
30,050	30,100	7,895	6,187	9,756	7,302
30,100	30,150	7,917	6,206	9,783	7,323
30,150	30,200	7,939	6,224	9,809	7,344
30,200	30,250	7,960	6,242	9,836	7,364
30,250	30,300	7,982	6,261	9,863	7,385
30,300	30,350	8,004	6,279	9,889	7,406
30,350	30,400	8,025	6,297	9,916	7,426
30,400	30,450	8,047	6,315	9,943	7,447
30,450	30,500	8,069	6,334	9,969	7,468
30,500	30,550	8,091	6,352	9,996	7,489
30,550	30,600	8,112	6,370	10,023	7,509
30,600	30,650	8,134	6,388	10,049	7,530
30,650	30,700	8,156	6,407	10,076	7,551
30,700	30,750	8,177	6,425	10,103	7,572
30,750	30,800	8,199	6,443	10,129	7,592
30,800	30,850	8,221	6,461	10,156	7,613
30,850	30,900	8,243	6,480	10,183	7,634
30,900	30,950	8,264	6,498	10,209	7,655
30,950	31,000	8,286	6,516	10,236	7,675
31,000					
31,000	31,050	8,308	6,535	10,263	7,696
31,050	31,100	8,330	6,553	10,289	7,717
31,100	31,150	8,351	6,571	10,316	7,738
31,150	31,200	8,373	6,589	10,343	7,758
31,200	31,250	8,395	6,608	10,369	7,779
31,250	31,300	8,416	6,626	10,396	7,800
31,300	31,350	8,438	6,644	10,423	7,821
31,350	31,400	8,460	6,662	10,449	7,841
31,400	31,450	8,482	6,681	10,476	7,862
31,450	31,500	8,503	6,699	10,503	7,883
31,500	31,550	8,525	6,717	10,529	7,903
31,550	31,600	8,547	6,735	10,556	7,924
31,600	31,650	8,569	6,754	10,583	7,945
31,650	31,700	8,590	6,772	10,609	7,966
31,700	31,750	8,612	6,790	10,636	7,986
31,750	31,800	8,634	6,809	10,663	8,007
31,800	31,850	8,655	6,827	10,689	8,028
31,850	31,900	8,677	6,845	10,716	8,049
31,900	31,950	8,699	6,863	10,743	8,069
31,950	32,000	8,721	6,882	10,769	8,090
32,000					
32,000	32,050	8,742	6,900	10,796	8,111
32,050	32,100	8,764	6,918	10,823	8,132
32,100	32,150	8,786	6,936	10,849	8,152
32,150	32,200	8,808	6,955	10,876	8,173
32,200	32,250	8,829	6,973	10,902	8,194
32,250	32,300	8,851	6,991	10,929	8,215
32,300	32,350	8,873	7,010	10,956	8,235
32,350	32,400	8,894	7,028	10,982	8,256
32,400	32,450	8,916	7,046	11,009	8,277
32,450	32,500	8,938	7,064	11,036	8,297
32,500	32,550	8,960	7,083	11,062	8,318
32,550	32,600	8,981	7,101	11,089	8,339
32,600	32,650	9,003	7,119	11,116	8,360
32,650	32,700	9,025	7,137	11,142	8,380
32,700	32,750	9,046	7,156	11,169	8,401

*This column must also be used by a qualifying widow(er).

Continued on next page

TABLE XI Federal Income Tax Table (continued)

Tax Table (Continued)

If line 34 (taxable income) is— At least	But less than	Single	Married filing jointly*	Married filing separately	Head of a household
32,750	32,800	9,068	7,174	11,196	8,422
32,800	32,850	9,090	7,192	11,222	8,443
32,850	32,900	9,112	7,210	11,249	8,463
32,900	32,950	9,133	7,229	11,276	8,484
32,950	33,000	9,155	7,247	11,302	8,505
33,000					
33,000	33,050	9,177	7,265	11,329	8,526
33,050	33,100	9,199	7,284	11,356	8,546
33,100	33,150	9,220	7,302	11,382	8,567
33,150	33,200	9,242	7,320	11,409	8,588
33,200	33,250	9,264	7,338	11,436	8,609
33,250	33,300	9,285	7,357	11,462	8,629
33,300	33,350	9,307	7,375	11,489	8,650
33,350	33,400	9,329	7,393	11,516	8,671
33,400	33,450	9,351	7,411	11,542	8,691
33,450	33,500	9,372	7,430	11,569	8,712
33,500	33,550	9,394	7,448	11,596	8,733
33,550	33,600	9,416	7,466	11,622	8,754
33,600	33,650	9,438	7,485	11,649	8,774
33,650	33,700	9,459	7,503	11,676	8,795
33,700	33,750	9,481	7,521	11,702	8,816
33,750	33,800	9,503	7,539	11,729	8,837
33,800	33,850	9,524	7,558	11,756	8,857
33,850	33,900	9,546	7,576	11,782	8,878
33,900	33,950	9,568	7,594	11,809	8,899
33,950	34,000	9,590	7,612	11,836	8,920
34,000					
34,000	34,050	9,611	7,631	11,862	8,940
34,050	34,100	9,633	7,649	11,889	8,961
34,100	34,150	9,656	7,667	11,916	8,983
34,150	34,200	9,680	7,685	11,942	9,006
34,200	34,250	9,704	7,704	11,969	9,028
34,250	34,300	9,729	7,722	11,996	9,051
34,300	34,350	9,753	7,740	12,022	9,074
34,350	34,400	9,777	7,759	12,049	9,096
34,400	34,450	9,801	7,777	12,076	9,119
34,450	34,500	9,825	7,795	12,102	9,142
34,500	34,550	9,850	7,813	12,129	9,164
34,550	34,600	9,874	7,832	12,156	9,187
34,600	34,650	9,898	7,850	12,182	9,210
34,650	34,700	9,922	7,868	12,209	9,233
34,700	34,750	9,946	7,886	12,236	9,255
34,750	34,800	9,971	7,905	12,262	9,278
34,800	34,850	9,995	7,923	12,289	9,301
34,850	34,900	10,019	7,941	12,316	9,323
34,900	34,950	10,043	7,959	12,342	9,346
34,950	35,000	10,067	7,978	12,369	9,369
35,000					
35,000	35,050	10,092	7,996	12,396	9,392
35,050	35,100	10,116	8,014	12,422	9,414
35,100	35,150	10,140	8,033	12,449	9,437
35,150	35,200	10,164	8,051	12,476	9,460
35,200	35,250	10,188	8,071	12,502	9,482
35,250	35,300	10,212	8,092	12,529	9,505
35,300	35,350	10,237	8,113	12,556	9,528
35,350	35,400	10,261	8,134	12,582	9,551
35,400	35,450	10,285	8,156	12,609	9,573
35,450	35,500	10,309	8,177	12,636	9,596
35,500	35,550	10,333	8,198	12,662	9,619
35,550	35,600	10,358	8,219	12,689	9,641
35,600	35,650	10,382	8,240	12,716	9,664
35,650	35,700	10,406	8,262	12,742	9,687
35,700	35,750	10,430	8,283	12,769	9,710
35,750	35,800	10,454	8,304	12,796	9,732
35,800	35,850	10,479	8,325	12,822	9,755
35,850	35,900	10,503	8,347	12,849	9,778
35,900	35,950	10,527	8,368	12,876	9,800
35,950	36,000	10,551	8,389	12,902	9,823
36,000					
36,000	36,050	10,575	8,410	12,929	9,846
36,050	36,100	10,600	8,432	12,956	9,869
36,100	36,150	10,624	8,453	12,982	9,891
36,150	36,200	10,648	8,474	13,009	9,914
36,200	36,250	10,672	8,495	13,035	9,937
36,250	36,300	10,696	8,516	13,062	9,959
36,300	36,350	10,721	8,538	13,089	9,982
36,350	36,400	10,745	8,559	13,115	10,005
36,400	36,450	10,769	8,580	13,142	10,028
36,450	36,500	10,793	8,601	13,169	10,050
36,500	36,550	10,817	8,623	13,195	10,073
36,550	36,600	10,842	8,644	13,222	10,096
36,600	36,650	10,866	8,665	13,249	10,118
36,650	36,700	10,890	8,686	13,275	10,141
36,700	36,750	10,914	8,708	13,302	10,164
36,750	36,800	10,938	8,729	13,329	10,187
36,800	36,850	10,962	8,750	13,355	10,209
36,850	36,900	10,987	8,771	13,382	10,232
36,900	36,950	11,011	8,792	13,409	10,255
36,950	37,000	11,035	8,814	13,435	10,277
37,000					
37,000	37,050	11,059	8,835	13,462	10,300
37,050	37,100	11,083	8,856	13,489	10,323
37,100	37,150	11,108	8,877	13,515	10,346
37,150	37,200	11,132	8,899	13,542	10,368
37,200	37,250	11,156	8,920	13,569	10,391
37,250	37,300	11,180	8,941	13,595	10,414
37,300	37,350	11,204	8,962	13,622	10,436
37,350	37,400	11,229	8,984	13,649	10,459
37,400	37,450	11,253	9,005	13,675	10,482
37,450	37,500	11,277	9,026	13,702	10,505
37,500	37,550	11,301	9,047	13,729	10,527
37,550	37,600	11,325	9,068	13,755	10,550
37,600	37,650	11,350	9,090	13,782	10,573
37,650	37,700	11,374	9,111	13,809	10,595
37,700	37,750	11,398	9,132	13,835	10,618
37,750	37,800	11,422	9,153	13,862	10,641
37,800	37,850	11,446	9,175	13,889	10,664
37,850	37,900	11,471	9,196	13,915	10,686
37,900	37,950	11,495	9,217	13,942	10,709
37,950	38,000	11,519	9,238	13,969	10,732
38,000					
38,000	38,050	11,543	9,260	13,995	10,754
38,050	38,100	11,567	9,281	14,022	10,777
38,100	38,150	11,592	9,302	14,049	10,800
38,150	38,200	11,616	9,323	14,075	10,823
38,200	38,250	11,640	9,344	14,102	10,845
38,250	38,300	11,664	9,366	14,129	10,868
38,300	38,350	11,688	9,387	14,155	10,891
38,350	38,400	11,712	9,408	14,182	10,913
38,400	38,450	11,737	9,429	14,209	10,936
38,450	38,500	11,761	9,451	14,235	10,959
38,500	38,550	11,785	9,472	14,262	10,981
38,550	38,600	11,809	9,493	14,289	11,004
38,600	38,650	11,833	9,514	14,315	11,027
38,650	38,700	11,858	9,536	14,342	11,050
38,700	38,750	11,882	9,557	14,369	11,072
38,750	38,800	11,906	9,578	14,395	11,095
38,800	38,850	11,930	9,599	14,422	11,118
38,850	38,900	11,954	9,62?	14,449	11,140
38,900	38,950	11,979	9,642	14,475	11,163
38,950	39,000	12,003	9,663	14,502	11,186
39,000					
39,000	39,050	12,027	9,684	14,529	11,209
39,050	39,100	12,051	9,705	14,555	11,231
39,100	39,150	12,075	9,727	14,582	11,254
39,150	39,200	12,100	9,748	14,609	11,277
39,200	39,250	12,124	9,769	14,635	11,299
39,250	39,300	12,148	9,790	14,662	11,322
39,300	39,350	12,172	9,812	14,689	11,345
39,350	39,400	12,196	9,833	14,715	11,368
39,400	39,450	12,221	9,854	14,742	11,390
39,450	39,500	12,245	9,875	14,769	11,413
39,500	39,550	12,269	9,896	14,795	11,436
39,550	39,600	12,293	9,918	14,822	11,458
39,600	39,650	12,317	9,939	14,849	11,481
39,650	39,700	12,342	9,960	14,875	11,504
39,700	39,750	12,366	9,981	14,902	11,527
39,750	39,800	12,390	10,003	14,929	11,549
39,800	39,850	12,414	10,024	14,955	11,572
39,850	39,900	12,438	10,045	14,982	11,595
39,900	39,950	12,462	10,066	15,009	11,617
39,950	40,000	12,487	10,088	15,035	11,640
40,000					
40,000	40,050	12,511	10,109	15,062	11,663
40,050	40,100	12,535	10,130	15,089	11,686
40,100	40,150	12,559	10,151	15,115	11,708
40,150	40,200	12,583	10,172	15,142	11,731
40,200	40,250	12,608	10,194	15,168	11,754
40,250	40,300	12,632	10,215	15,195	11,776
40,300	40,350	12,656	10,236	15,222	11,799
40,350	40,400	12,680	10,257	15,248	11,822
40,400	40,450	12,704	10,279	15,275	11,845
40,450	40,500	12,729	10,300	15,302	11,867
40,500	40,550	12,753	10,321	15,328	11,890
40,550	40,600	12,777	10,342	15,355	11,913
40,600	40,650	12,801	10,364	15,382	11,935
40,650	40,700	12,825	10,385	15,408	11,958
40,700	40,750	12,850	10,406	15,435	11,981
40,750	40,800	12,874	10,427	15,462	12,004
40,800	40,850	12,898	10,448	15,488	12,026
40,850	40,900	12,922	10,470	15,515	12,049
40,900	40,950	12,946	10,491	15,542	12,072
40,950	41,000	12,971	10,512	15,568	12,094

*This column must also be used by a qualifying widow(er).

Continued on next page

TABLE XI   *Federal Income Tax Table (continued)*

Tax Table (Continued)

If line 34 (taxable income) is— At least	But less than	Single	Married filing jointly *	Married filing separately	Head of a household
41,000					
41,000	41,050	12,995	10,533	15,595	12,117
41,050	41,100	13,019	10,555	15,622	12,140
41,100	41,150	13,043	10,576	15,648	12,163
41,150	41,200	13,067	10,597	15,675	12,185
41,200	41,250	13,092	10,618	15,702	12,208
41,250	41,300	13,116	10,640	15,728	12,231
41,300	41,350	13,140	10,661	15,755	12,253
41,350	41,400	13,164	10,682	15,782	12,276
41,400	41,450	13,188	10,703	15,808	12,299
41,450	41,500	13,213	10,724	15,835	12,322
41,500	41,550	13,238	10,746	15,862	12,344
41,550	41,600	13,265	10,767	15,888	12,367
41,600	41,650	13,292	10,788	15,915	12,390
41,650	41,700	13,320	10,809	15,942	12,412
41,700	41,750	13,347	10,831	15,968	12,435
41,750	41,800	13,374	10,852	15,995	12,458
41,800	41,850	13,401	10,873	16,022	12,481
41,850	41,900	13,428	10,894	16,048	12,503
41,900	41,950	13,455	10,916	16,075	12,526
41,950	42,000	13,483	10,937	16,102	12,549
42,000					
42,000	42,050	13,510	10,958	16,128	12,571
42,050	42,100	13,537	10,979	16,155	12,594
42,100	42,150	13,564	11,001	16,182	12,617
42,150	42,200	13,591	11,022	16,208	12,640
42,200	42,250	13,618	11,043	16,235	12,662
42,250	42,300	13,646	11,064	16,262	12,685
42,300	42,350	13,673	11,085	16,288	12,708
42,350	42,400	13,700	11,107	16,315	12,730
42,400	42,450	13,727	11,128	16,342	12,753
42,450	42,500	13,754	11,149	16,368	12,776
42,500	42,550	13,781	11,170	16,395	12,798
42,550	42,600	13,808	11,192	16,422	12,821
42,600	42,650	13,836	11,213	16,448	12,844
42,650	42,700	13,863	11,234	16,475	12,867
42,700	42,750	13,890	11,255	16,502	12,889
42,750	42,800	13,917	11,277	16,528	12,912
42,800	42,850	13,944	11,298	16,556	12,935
42,850	42,900	13,971	11,319	16,585	12,957
42,900	42,950	13,999	11,340	16,614	12,980
42,950	43,000	14,026	11,361	16,644	13,003
43,000					
43,000	43,050	14,053	11,383	16,673	13,026
43,050	43,100	14,080	11,404	16,702	13,048
43,100	43,150	14,107	11,425	16,731	13,071
43,150	43,200	14,134	11,446	16,760	13,094
43,200	43,250	14,161	11,468	16,789	13,116
43,250	43,300	14,189	11,489	16,818	13,139
43,300	43,350	14,216	11,510	16,847	13,162
43,350	43,400	14,243	11,531	16,877	13,185
43,400	43,450	14,270	11,553	16,906	13,207
43,450	43,500	14,297	11,574	16,935	13,230
43,500	43,550	14,324	11,595	16,964	13,253
43,550	43,600	14,352	11,616	16,993	13,275
43,600	43,650	14,379	11,637	17,022	13,298
43,650	43,700	14,406	11,659	17,051	13,321
43,700	43,750	14,433	11,680	17,081	13,344
43,750	43,800	14,460	11,701	17,110	13,366
43,800	43,850	14,487	11,722	17,139	13,389
43,850	43,900	14,515	11,744	17,168	13,412
43,900	43,950	14,542	11,765	17,197	13,434
43,950	44,000	14,569	11,786	17,226	13,457

If line 34 (taxable income) is— At least	But less than	Single	Married filing jointly *	Married filing separately	Head of a household
44,000					
44,000	44,050	14,596	11,807	17,255	13,480
44,050	44,100	14,623	11,829	17,284	13,503
44,100	44,150	14,650	11,850	17,314	13,525
44,150	44,200	14,677	11,871	17,343	13,548
44,200	44,250	14,705	11,892	17,372	13,571
44,250	44,300	14,732	11,913	17,401	13,593
44,300	44,350	14,759	11,935	17,430	13,616
44,350	44,400	14,786	11,956	17,459	13,639
44,400	44,450	14,813	11,977	17,488	13,662
44,450	44,500	14,840	11,998	17,518	13,684
44,500	44,550	14,868	12,020	17,547	13,707
44,550	44,600	14,895	12,041	17,576	13,730
44,600	44,650	14,922	12,062	17,605	13,752
44,650	44,700	14,949	12,083	17,634	13,775
44,700	44,750	14,976	12,105	17,663	13,800
44,750	44,800	15,003	12,126	17,692	13,826
44,800	44,850	15,030	12,147	17,721	13,853
44,850	44,900	15,058	12,168	17,751	13,880
44,900	44,950	15,085	12,189	17,780	13,906
44,950	45,000	15,112	12,211	17,809	13,933
45,000					
45,000	45,050	15,139	12,232	17,838	13,960
45,050	45,100	15,166	12,253	17,867	13,986
45,100	45,150	15,193	12,274	17,896	14,013
45,150	45,200	15,221	12,296	17,925	14,040
45,200	45,250	15,248	12,317	17,954	14,066
45,250	45,300	15,275	12,338	17,984	14,093
45,300	45,350	15,302	12,359	18,013	14,120
45,350	45,400	15,329	12,381	18,042	14,146
45,400	45,450	15,356	12,402	18,071	14,173
45,450	45,500	15,384	12,423	18,100	14,200
45,500	45,550	15,411	12,444	18,129	14,226
45,550	45,600	15,438	12,465	18,158	14,253
45,600	45,650	15,465	12,487	18,188	14,280
45,650	45,700	15,492	12,508	18,217	14,306
45,700	45,750	15,519	12,529	18,246	14,333
45,750	45,800	15,546	12,550	18,275	14,360
45,800	45,850	15,574	12,573	18,304	14,386
45,850	45,900	15,601	12,597	18,333	14,413
45,900	45,950	15,628	12,621	18,362	14,440
45,950	46,000	15,655	12,646	18,391	14,466
46,000					
46,000	46,050	15,682	12,670	18,421	14,493
46,050	46,100	15,709	12,694	18,450	14,520
46,100	46,150	15,737	12,718	18,479	14,546
46,150	46,200	15,764	12,742	18,508	14,573
46,200	46,250	15,791	12,767	18,537	14,600
46,250	46,300	15,818	12,791	18,566	14,626
46,300	46,350	15,845	12,815	18,595	14,653
46,350	46,400	15,872	12,839	18,624	14,680
46,400	46,450	15,899	12,863	18,654	14,706
46,450	46,500	15,927	12,888	18,683	14,733
46,500	46,550	15,954	12,912	18,712	14,760
46,550	46,600	15,981	12,936	18,741	14,786
46,600	46,650	16,008	12,960	18,770	14,813
46,650	46,700	16,035	12,984	18,799	14,840
46,700	46,750	16,062	13,009	18,828	14,866
46,750	46,800	16,090	13,033	18,858	14,893
46,800	46,850	16,117	13,057	18,887	14,920
46,850	46,900	16,144	13,081	18,916	14,946
46,900	46,950	16,171	13,105	18,945	14,973
46,950	47,000	16,198	13,130	18,974	15,000

If line 34 (taxable income) is— At least	But less than	Single	Married filing jointly *	Married filing separately	Head of a household
47,000					
47,000	47,050	16,225	13,154	19,003	15,026
47,050	47,100	16,253	13,178	19,032	15,053
47,100	47,150	16,280	13,202	19,061	15,080
47,150	47,200	16,307	13,226	19,091	15,106
47,200	47,250	16,334	13,251	19,120	15,133
47,250	47,300	16,361	13,275	19,149	15,160
47,300	47,350	16,388	13,299	19,178	15,186
47,350	47,400	16,415	13,323	19,207	15,213
47,400	47,450	16,443	13,347	19,236	15,240
47,450	47,500	16,470	13,371	19,265	15,266
47,500	47,550	16,497	13,396	19,295	15,293
47,550	47,600	16,524	13,420	19,324	15,320
47,600	47,650	16,551	13,444	19,353	15,346
47,650	47,700	16,578	13,468	19,382	15,373
47,700	47,750	16,606	13,492	19,411	15,400
47,750	47,800	16,633	13,517	19,440	15,426
47,800	47,850	16,660	13,541	19,469	15,453
47,850	47,900	16,687	13,565	19,498	15,480
47,900	47,950	16,714	13,589	19,528	15,506
47,950	48,000	16,741	13,613	19,557	15,533
48,000					
48,000	48,050	16,768	13,638	19,586	15,560
48,050	48,100	16,796	13,662	19,615	15,586
48,100	48,150	16,823	13,686	19,644	15,613
48,150	48,200	16,850	13,710	19,673	15,640
48,200	48,250	16,877	13,734	19,702	15,666
48,250	48,300	16,904	13,759	19,731	15,693
48,300	48,350	16,931	13,783	19,761	15,720
48,350	48,400	16,959	13,807	19,790	15,746
48,400	48,450	16,986	13,831	19,819	15,773
48,450	48,500	17,013	13,855	19,848	15,800
48,500	48,550	17,040	13,880	19,877	15,826
48,550	48,600	17,067	13,904	19,906	15,853
48,600	48,650	17,094	13,928	19,935	15,879
48,650	48,700	17,122	13,952	19,965	15,906
48,700	48,750	17,149	13,976	19,994	15,933
48,750	48,800	17,176	14,001	20,023	15,959
48,800	48,850	17,203	14,025	20,052	15,986
48,850	48,900	17,230	14,049	20,081	16,013
48,900	48,950	17,257	14,073	20,110	16,039
48,950	49,000	17,284	14,097	20,139	16,066
49,000					
49,000	49,050	17,312	14,121	20,168	16,093
49,050	49,100	17,339	14,146	20,198	16,119
49,100	49,150	17,366	14,170	20,227	16,146
49,150	49,200	17,393	14,194	20,256	16,173
49,200	49,250	17,420	14,218	20,285	16,199
49,250	49,300	17,447	14,242	20,314	16,226
49,300	49,350	17,475	14,267	20,343	16,253
49,350	49,400	17,502	14,291	20,372	16,279
49,400	49,450	17,529	14,315	20,402	16,306
49,450	49,500	17,556	14,339	20,431	16,333
49,500	49,550	17,583	14,363	20,460	16,359
49,550	49,600	17,610	14,388	20,489	16,386
49,600	49,650	17,637	14,412	20,518	16,413
49,650	49,700	17,665	14,436	20,547	16,439
49,700	49,750	17,692	14,460	20,576	16,466
49,750	49,800	17,719	14,484	20,605	16,493
49,800	49,850	17,746	14,509	20,635	16,519
49,850	49,900	17,773	14,533	20,664	16,546
49,900	49,950	17,800	14,557	20,693	16,573
49,950	50,000	17,828	14,581	20,722	16,599

*This column must also be used by a qualifying widow(er).

50,000 or over — use tax rate schedules

TABLE XII   **Single Equivalent Discount Rates**

Series of Discounts (%)	Single Equivalent Cost Rate	Single Equivalent Discount Rate
50/50	0.25000	0.75000
50/40	0.30000	0.70000
50/35	0.32500	0.67500
50/33⅓	0.33333	0.66667
50/30	0.35000	0.65000
50/25	0.37500	0.62500
50/20	0.40000	0.60000
50/15	0.42500	0.57500
50/10	0.45000	0.55000
50/5	0.47500	0.52500
50/40/40	0.18000	0.82000
50/40/35	0.19500	0.80500
50/40/33⅓	0.20000	0.80000
50/40/30	0.21000	0.79000
50/40/25	0.22500	0.77500
50/40/20	0.24000	0.76000
50/40/15	0.25500	0.74500
50/40/10	0.27000	0.73000
50/40/5	0.28500	0.71500
50/35/35	0.21125	0.78875
50/35/33⅓	0.21667	0.78333
50/35/30	0.22750	0.77250
50/35/25	0.24375	0.75625
50/35/20	0.26000	0.74000
50/35/15	0.27625	0.72375
50/35/10	0.29250	0.70750
50/35/5	0.30875	0.69125
50/33⅓/33⅓	0.22222	0.77778
50/33⅓/30	0.23333	0.76667
50/33⅓/25	0.25000	0.75000
50/33⅓/20	0.26667	0.73333
50/33⅓/15	0.28333	0.71667
50/33⅓/10	0.30000	0.70000
50/33⅓/5	0.31667	0.68333
50/30/30	0.24500	0.75500
50/30/25	0.26250	0.73750
50/30/20	0.28000	0.72000
50/30/15	0.29750	0.70250
50/30/10	0.31500	0.68500
50/30/5	0.33250	0.66750
50/25/25	0.28125	0.71875
50/25/20	0.30000	0.70000
50/25/15	0.31875	0.68125
50/25/10	0.33750	0.66250
50/25/5	0.35625	0.64375
50/20/20	0.32000	0.68000
50/20/15	0.34000	0.66000
50/20/10	0.36000	0.64000
50/20/5	0.38000	0.62000
50/15/15	0.36125	0.63875
50/15/10	0.38250	0.61750
50/15/5	0.40375	0.59625
50/10/10	0.40500	0.59500
50/10/5	0.42750	0.57250
50/5/5	0.45125	0.54875
45/45	0.30250	0.69750
45/40	0.33000	0.67000
45/35	0.35750	0.64250
45/33⅓	0.36667	0.63333
45/30	0.38500	0.61500
45/25	0.41250	0.58750
45/20	0.44000	0.56000
45/15	0.38250	0.61750

TABLE XII   **Single Equivalent Discount Rates (continued)**

Series of Discounts (%)	Single Equivalent Cost Rate	Single Equivalent Discount Rate
45/10	0.49500	0.50500
45/5	0.52250	0.47750
45/45/40	0.18150	0.81850
45/45/35	0.19663	0.80337
45/45/33⅓	0.20167	0.79833
45/45/30	0.21175	0.78825
45/45/25	0.22688	0.77312
45/45/20	0.24200	0.75800
45/45/15	0.25713	0.74287
45/45/10	0.27225	0.72775
45/45/5	0.28738	0.71262
45/40/40	0.19800	0.80200
45/40/35	0.21450	0.78550
45/40/33⅓	0.22011	0.77989
45/40/30	0.23100	0.76900
45/40/25	0.24750	0.75250
45/40/20	0.26400	0.73600
45/40/15	0.28050	0.71950
45/40/10	0.29700	0.70300
45/40/5	0.31350	0.68650
45/35/35	0.23238	0.76762
45/35/33⅓	0.23833	0.76167
45/35/30	0.25025	0.74975
45/35/25	0.26813	0.73187
45/35/20	0.28600	0.71400
45/35/15	0.30388	0.69612
45/35/10	0.32175	0.67825
45/35/5	0.33963	0.66037
45/33⅓/33⅓	0.24444	0.75556
45/33⅓/30	0.25667	0.74333
45/33⅓/25	0.27500	0.72500
45/33⅓/20	0.29333	0.70667
45/33⅓/15	0.31167	0.68833
45/33⅓/10	0.33000	0.67000
45/33⅓/5	0.34833	0.65167
45/30/30	0.26950	0.73050
45/30/25	0.28875	0.71125
45/30/20	0.30800	0.69200
45/30/15	0.32725	0.67275
45/30/10	0.34650	0.65350
45/30/5	0.36575	0.63425
45/25/25	0.30940	0.69060
45/25/20	0.33000	0.67000
45/25/15	0.35063	0.64937
45/25/10	0.37125	0.62875
45/25/5	0.39188	0.60812
45/20/20	0.35200	0.64800
45/20/15	0.37400	0.62600
45/20/10	0.39600	0.60400
45/20/5	0.41800	0.58200
45/15/15	0.39738	0.60262
45/15/10	0.42075	0.57925
45/15/5	0.44413	0.55587
45/10/10	0.44550	0.55450
45/10/5	0.47025	0.52975
45/5/5	0.49638	0.50362
40/40	0.36000	0.67000
40/35	0.39000	0.61000
40/33⅓	0.40000	0.60000
40/30	0.42000	0.58000
40/25	0.45000	0.55000
40/20	0.48000	0.52000
40/15	0.51000	0.49000

TABLE XII   **Single Equivalent Discount Rates (continued)**

Series of Discounts (%)	Single Equivalent Cost Rate	Single Equivalent Discount Rate
40/10	0.54000	0.46000
40/5	0.57000	0.43000
40/40/40	0.21600	0.78400
40/40/35	0.23400	0.76600
40/40/33$\frac{1}{3}$	0.24000	0.76000
40/40/30	0.25200	0.74800
40/40/25	0.27000	0.73000
40/40/20	0.28800	0.71200
40/40/15	0.30600	0.69400
40/40/10	0.32400	0.67600
40/40/5	0.34200	0.65800
40/35/35	0.25350	0.74650
40/35/33$\frac{1}{3}$	0.26000	0.74000
40/35/30	0.27300	0.72700
40/35/25	0.29250	0.70750
40/35/20	0.31200	0.68800
40/35/15	0.33150	0.66850
40/35/10	0.35100	0.64900
40/35/5	0.37050	0.62950
40/33$\frac{1}{3}$/33$\frac{1}{3}$	0.26667	0.73333
40/33$\frac{1}{3}$/30	0.28000	0.72000
40/33$\frac{1}{3}$/25	0.30000	0.70000
40/33$\frac{1}{3}$/20	0.32000	0.68000
40/33$\frac{1}{3}$/15	0.34000	0.66000
40/33$\frac{1}{3}$/10	0.36000	0.64000
40/33$\frac{1}{3}$/5	0.38000	0.62000
40/30/30	0.29400	0.70600
40/30/25	0.31500	0.68500
40/30/20	0.33600	0.66400
40/30/15	0.35700	0.64300
40/30/10	0.37800	0.62200
40/30/5	0.39900	0.60100
40/25/25	0.33750	0.66250
40/25/20	0.36000	0.64000
40/25/15	0.38250	0.61750
40/25/10	0.40500	0.59500
40/25/5	0.42750	0.57250
40/20/20	0.38400	0.61600
40/20/15	0.40800	0.59200
40/20/10	0.43200	0.56800
40/20/5	0.45600	0.54400
40/15/15	0.43350	0.56650
40/15/10	0.45900	0.54100
40/15/5	0.48450	0.51550
40/10/10	0.48600	0.51400
40/10/5	0.51300	0.48700
40/5/5	0.54150	0.45850
35/35	0.42250	0.57750
35/33$\frac{1}{3}$	0.43333	0.56667
35/30	0.45500	0.54500
35/25	0.48750	0.51250
35/20	0.52000	0.48000
35/15	0.55250	0.44750
35/10	0.58500	0.41500
35/5	0.61750	0.38250
35/35/35	0.27463	0.72537
35/35/33$\frac{1}{3}$	0.28167	0.71833
35/35/30	0.29575	0.70425
35/35/25	0.31688	0.68312
35/35/20	0.33800	0.66200
35/35/15	0.35913	0.64087
35/35/10	0.38025	0.61975
35/35/5	0.40138	0.59862

TABLE XII   **Single Equivalent Discount Rates (continued)**

Series of Discounts (%)	*Single Equivalent Cost Rate*	*Single Equivalent Discount Rate*
$35/33\frac{1}{3}/33\frac{1}{3}$	0.28888	0.71112
$35/33\frac{1}{3}/30$	0.30333	0.69667
$35/33\frac{1}{3}/25$	0.32500	0.67500
$35/33\frac{1}{3}/20$	0.34667	0.65333
$35/33\frac{1}{3}/15$	0.36833	0.63167
$35/33\frac{1}{3}/10$	0.39000	0.61000
$35/33\frac{1}{3}/5$	0.41167	0.58833
35/30/30	0.31850	0.68150
35/30/25	0.34125	0.65875
35/30/20	0.36400	0.63600
35/30/15	0.38675	0.61325
35/30/10	0.40950	0.59050
35/30/5	0.43225	0.56775
$33\frac{1}{3}/33\frac{1}{3}/33\frac{1}{3}$	0.29630	0.70370
$33\frac{1}{3}/33\frac{1}{3}/30$	0.31111	0.68889
$33\frac{1}{3}/33\frac{1}{3}/25$	0.33333	0.66667
$33\frac{1}{3}/33\frac{1}{3}/20$	0.35555	0.64445
$33\frac{1}{3}/33\frac{1}{3}/15$	0.37778	0.62222
$33\frac{1}{3}/33\frac{1}{3}/10$	0.40000	0.60000
$33\frac{1}{3}/33\frac{1}{3}/5$	0.42222	0.57778
$33\frac{1}{3}/30/30$	0.32667	0.67333
$33\frac{1}{3}/30/25$	0.35000	0.65000
$33\frac{1}{3}/30/20$	0.37333	0.62667
$33\frac{1}{3}/30/15$	0.39667	0.60333
$33\frac{1}{3}/30/10$	0.42000	0.58000
$33\frac{1}{3}/30/5$	0.44333	0.55667
$33\frac{1}{3}/25/25$	0.37500	0.62500
$33\frac{1}{3}/25/20$	0.40000	0.60000
$33\frac{1}{3}/25/15$	0.42500	0.57500
$33\frac{1}{3}/25/10$	0.45000	0.55000
$33\frac{1}{3}/25/5$	0.47500	0.52500
$33\frac{1}{3}/20/20$	0.42667	0.57333
$33\frac{1}{3}/20/15$	0.45333	0.54667
$33\frac{1}{3}/20/10$	0.48000	0.52000
$33\frac{1}{3}/20/5$	0.50667	0.49333
$33\frac{1}{3}/15/15$	0.48167	0.51833
$33\frac{1}{3}/15/10$	0.51000	0.49000
$33\frac{1}{3}/15/5$	0.53833	0.46167
$33\frac{1}{3}/10/10$	0.54000	0.46000
$33\frac{1}{3}/10/5$	0.57000	0.43000
$33\frac{1}{3}/5/5$	0.60167	0.39833
30/30/30	0.34300	0.65700
30/30/25	0.36750	0.63250
30/30/20	0.39200	0.60800
30/30/15	0.41650	0.58350
30/30/10	0.44100	0.55900
30/30/5	0.46550	0.53450
30/25/25	0.39375	0.60625
30/25/20	0.42000	0.58000
30/25/15	0.44625	0.55375
30/25/10	0.47250	0.52750
30/25/5	0.49875	0.50125
30/20/20	0.44800	0.55200
30/20/15	0.47600	0.52400
30/20/10	0.50400	0.49600
30/20/5	0.53200	0.46800
30/15/15	0.50575	0.49425
30/15/10	0.53550	0.46450
30/15/5	0.56525	0.43475
30/10/10	0.56700	0.43300
30/10/5	0.59850	0.40150
30/5/5	0.63175	0.36825
25/25	0.56250	0.43750

TABLE XII   *Single Equivalent Discount Rates (continued)*

Series of Discounts (%)	Single Equivalent Cost Rate	Single Equivalent Discount Rate
25/20	0.60000	0.40000
25/15	0.63750	0.36250
25/10	0.67500	0.32500
25/5	0.71250	0.28750
25/25/25	0.42188	0.57812
25/25/20	0.45000	0.55000
25/25/15	0.47813	0.52187
25/25/10	0.50625	0.49375
25/25/5	0.53438	0.46562
25/20/20	0.48000	0.52000
25/20/15	0.51000	0.49000
25/20/10	0.54000	0.46000
25/20/5	0.57000	0.43000
25/15/15	0.54188	0.45812
25/15/10	0.57375	0.42625
25/15/5	0.60563	0.39437
25/10/10	0.60750	0.39250
25/10/5	0.64125	0.35875
25/5/5	0.67688	0.32312
20/20	0.64000	0.36000
20/15	0.68000	0.32000
20/10	0.72000	0.28000
20/5	0.76000	0.24000
20/20/20	0.51200	0.48800
20/20/15	0.54400	0.45600
20/20/10	0.57600	0.42400
20/20/5	0.60800	0.39200
20/15/15	0.57800	0.42200
20/15/10	0.61200	0.38800
20/15/5	0.64600	0.35400
20/10/10	0.64800	0.35200
20/10/5	0.68400	0.31600
20/5/5	0.72200	0.27800
15/15	0.72250	0.27750
15/10	0.76500	0.23500
15/5	0.80750	0.19250
15/15/15	0.61413	0.38587
15/15/10	0.65025	0.34975
15/15/5	0.68638	0.31362
15/10/10	0.68850	0.31150
15/10/5	0.72675	0.27325
15/5/5	0.76713	0.23287
10/10	0.81000	0.19000
10/5	0.85500	0.14500
10/10/10	0.72900	0.27100
10/10/5	0.76950	0.23050
10/5/5	0.81225	0.18775
5/5	0.90250	0.09750
5/5/5	0.85738	0.14262

Solutions to Odd-Numbered Exercises

Exercises 1.1

1. $\dfrac{1 \times 6}{2 \times 6} = \dfrac{6}{12}$

3. $\dfrac{8 \times 5}{10 \times 5} = \dfrac{40}{50}$

5. $\dfrac{9 \times 10}{10 \times 10} = \dfrac{90}{100}$

7. $\dfrac{8 \div 2}{10 \div 2} = \dfrac{4}{5}$

9. $\dfrac{75 \div 5}{100 \div 5} = \dfrac{15}{20}$

11. $\dfrac{10 \div 2}{12 \div 2} = \dfrac{5}{6}$

13. $\dfrac{20 \div 5}{35 \div 5} = \dfrac{4}{7}$

15. $50 \times 1 = 5 \times 10$; yes.

17. 9×9 does not equal 10×8; no.

19. Yes

21. Either; they are equivalent.

Exercises 1.2

1. $\dfrac{1 + 4}{8} = \dfrac{5}{8}$

3. $\dfrac{1 + 4 + 1}{12} = \dfrac{6}{12} = \dfrac{1}{2}$

5. $\dfrac{7 - 3}{8} = \dfrac{4}{8} = \dfrac{1}{2}$

7. $\dfrac{5 - 4}{13} = \dfrac{1}{13}$

9. $\dfrac{4 \times 1 + 3 \times 1}{3 \times 4} = \dfrac{7}{12}$

11. $\dfrac{3 \times 2 + 11 \times 1}{2 \times 11} = \dfrac{17}{22}$

13. $\dfrac{9 \times 2 - 1 \times 10}{2 \times 10} = \dfrac{8}{20} = \dfrac{2}{5}$

15. $\dfrac{6 \times 2 - 3 \times 1}{6 \times 3} = \dfrac{9}{18} = \dfrac{1}{2}$

17. $\dfrac{1}{2} + \dfrac{2}{5} = \dfrac{5 \times 1 + 2 \times 2}{5 \times 2} = \dfrac{9}{10}$ of the job

19. $\dfrac{2}{100} + \dfrac{1}{25} = \dfrac{2}{100} + \dfrac{4}{100} = \dfrac{6}{100} = \dfrac{3}{50}$

Exercises 1.3

1. $\dfrac{2 \times 5}{3 \times 4} = \dfrac{10}{12} = \dfrac{5}{6}$

3. $\dfrac{1 \times 1}{2 \times 2} = \dfrac{1}{4}$

5. $\dfrac{2 \times 5}{5 \times 2} = \dfrac{10}{10} = 1$

7. $\dfrac{5 \times 2}{9 \times 10} = \dfrac{10}{90} = \dfrac{1}{9}$

9. $\dfrac{60 \times 2}{1 \times 3} = \dfrac{120}{3} = 40$

11. $6 \times \dfrac{2}{1} = 12$

13. $\dfrac{5}{8} \times \dfrac{3}{2} = \dfrac{15}{16}$

15. $\dfrac{3}{5} \times \dfrac{5}{3} = 1$

17. $\dfrac{5}{8} \times \dfrac{5}{8} = \dfrac{25}{64}$

19. $\dfrac{1}{4} \times \$240 = \$60$

21. $\$375\left(\dfrac{4}{5}\right) = \$300$

23. $\$837\left(\dfrac{1}{3}\right) = \$279$

25. $\dfrac{1}{3} \div 4 = \dfrac{1}{3} \times \dfrac{1}{4} = \dfrac{1}{12}$

27. $\dfrac{3}{5} \times \$4000 = \$2400$

Exercises 1.4

1. $1\frac{2}{10}$ or $1\frac{1}{5}$

3. $6\frac{1}{2}$

5. $4\frac{4}{6}$ or $4\frac{2}{3}$

7. $\dfrac{2 \times 1 + 1}{2} = \dfrac{3}{2}$

9. $\dfrac{5 \times 2 + 1}{5} = \dfrac{11}{5}$

11. $\dfrac{3 \times 5 + 2}{3} = \dfrac{17}{3}$

13. $\frac{1}{2} + \frac{1}{3} - \frac{2}{4} + \frac{1}{6} = \frac{6+4-6+2}{12} = \frac{6}{12} = \frac{1}{2}$ **15.** $\frac{2}{3} + \frac{5}{6} - \frac{1}{2} = \frac{4+5-3}{6} = \frac{6}{6} = 1$

17. $\frac{4}{7} \times \frac{2}{3} + \frac{24}{21} = \frac{8}{21} + \frac{24}{21} = \frac{32}{21} = 1\frac{11}{21}$ **19.** $5\frac{1}{4} + 1\frac{2}{3} + 10\frac{1}{5} = \frac{21}{4} + \frac{5}{3} + \frac{51}{5} = \frac{315 + 100 + 612}{60} = \frac{1027}{60} = 17\frac{7}{60}$ yd

21. $\frac{51}{8} - \frac{7}{8} \cdot \frac{44}{8} = 5\frac{1}{2}$ **23.** $\frac{39}{4} + \frac{2}{4} = \frac{41}{4} = 10\frac{1}{4}\%$

Review Exercises/Chapter 1

1. $\frac{8}{52}$ **3.** Yes   **5.** 1   **7.** $\frac{3}{2}$ **9.** $\frac{13}{10}$ **11.** $\frac{3}{2}$

13. $6\frac{5}{6}$ **15.** $\frac{7}{8}$ **17.** \$2500   **19.** $\frac{1}{6}$ **21.** $\frac{3}{8}$ **23.** $2\frac{1}{4}$ hr overtime

25. \$66   **27.** \$105

Exercises 2.1

1. 14.2   **3.** 27.1   **5.** 42.1   **7.**   98.6   **9.**   275.4   **11.**   2.649
     13.7   18.62   30.01 -42.3 $-\ 74.5$ -0.723
     21.8   9.0   6.029   ——   ——   ——
     ——   ——   341.2   56.3   200.9   1.926
     49.7   54.72   ——
                       419.339

13.   600   **15.**   \$5.38   **17.**   \$399   **19.** \$144.97   **21.** \$42.38
     -234.1 $-\$4.72$ $-\$\ 82.67$
     ——   ——   ——
     365.9   \$0.66   \$316.33

Exercises 2.2

1.   6.3 8   **3.**   1 3 2.7   **5.**   7 2 1   **7.** 0.001   **9.** \$ 2.25
     1.2 2   2.6 4   3.3 1   0.1   6
     ——   ——   ——   ——   ——
     1 2 7 6   5 3 0 8   7 2 1   0.0001   \$13.50
     1 2 7 6   7 9 6 2   2 1 6 3
     6 3 8   2 6 5 4   2 1 6 3
     ——   ——   ——
     7.7 8 3 6   3 5 0.3 2 8   2 3 8 6.5 1

11. Plywood   Nails   *Total*   **13.** $120 \times \$0.18 = \$21.60$ **15.** 0.0687115
      \$9.98 $+$ \$0.49 $=$ \$43.11
        4   6.5   (rounded)
      ——   ——
      39.92   245
                294
                ——
                \$3.185

17. $\$10.56 + \$0.52 = \$11.08$ **19.** $2.403 \times \$6999.95 = \$16,820.88$ (rounded)

Exercises 2.3

    5 quotient   11 quotient   5.5   2.976
1. $5\overline{)28}$ **3.** $121\overline{)1382}$ **5.** $31\overline{)171.6}$ or $5.5\frac{11}{31}$ **7.** $125\overline{)372.000}$
  -25 -121 -155 -250
  ——   ——   ——   ——
   3 remainder   172   166   1220
                       -121 -155 -1125
                       ——   ——   ——
                        51 remainder   11   950
                                                            -875
                                                            ——
                                                             750
                                                           -750
                                                           ——
                                                             0

9.
$$\begin{array}{r} .375 \\ 8\overline{)3.00} \\ -24 \\ \hline 60 \\ -56 \\ \hline 40 \\ -40 \\ \hline 0 \end{array}$$

11.
$$\begin{array}{r} .12 \\ 50\overline{)6.00} \\ -50 \\ \hline 100 \\ -100 \\ \hline 0 \end{array}$$

13. 1.78

15. 1.79

17. $2408.54

19. 17.93 mpg

21. **a.** $\frac{7}{25}$ **b.** $\frac{3}{50}$ **c.** $\frac{3}{125}$ **d.** $\frac{6}{5}$

Review Exercises/Chapter 2

1. $267.26 **3.** 0.07475 **5.** 4, $R = 1$ **7.** $238.46 **9.** 0.517 **11.** $327.60
13. $177.51 **15.** $37.88

Exercises 3.1

	Check No.	Date	Check Issued To	Amount of Check	√	Date of Dep.	Amount of Dep.	Balance
Example	3226	6/27	Jones Co.	227 32				2897 42
1.	3227	6/29	Ace Cleaning Supply	384 29				2513 13
3.						7/3	127 42	2547 66
5.	3230	7/7	VOID		√			2312 66
5.	3231	7/7	Reliable Util. Co.	138 62				2174 04

Exercises 3.3

		Check Register	*Bank Statement*
1.	Balance	$ 527.32	$686.54
	Outstanding Checks		− 384.22
	Deposit		+ 225.00
		$527.32	$527.32
3.	Balance	$204.76	$483.65
	Automatic Deposit	200.00	
	Outstanding Checks		− 409.88
	Deposits		+ 330.99
		$404.76	$404.76
5.	Balance	$848.05	$987.80
	Automatic Deposit	+ 235.00	
	Automatic Draft	− 185.00	
	Outstanding Checks		− 89.75
		$898.05	$898.05

Check Register

7.

Check No.	Date	Check Issued to	Amount of Check	√	Date Dep.	Amount of Deposit	Balance
							1388 90
1042	6/12	Hanover Co.	42 60	√			1346 30
1043	6/13	Wessl Adv.	21 88	√			1324 42
				√	6/14	375 00	1699 42
1044	6/16	Morris Supply	44 11	√			1655 31
1045	6/18	Ace Chemical	73 42	√			1581 89
				√	6/20	1037 64	2619 53
1046	6/21	Tebco Inc.	200 00	√			2419 53
1047	6/21	National Sales	63 75	√			2355 78
1048	6/22	Hart Insurance	247 12	√			2108 66
1049	6/23	Mercantile Nat'l	245 72	√			1862 94
1050	6/24	Mitchell & Garcia	64 94	√			1798 00
1051	6/25	Nat'l Mortgage	365 50	√			1432 50
1052	6/28	Star Leasing	380 27	√			1052 23
1053	6/29	Liberty Gazette	22 00	√			1030 23
				√	6/30	1000 01	2030 24
1054	7/2	Mitcher Co.	18 38	√			2011 86
1055	7/5	Allen & Allen	67 53	√			1944 33
1056	7/6	Reliable Elec. Co.	77 45	√			1866 88
1057	7/9	L. K. Adams	38 00	√			1828 88
1058	7/10	Norton & Evans	46 60	√			1782 48
				√	7/11	125 00	1907 48
1059	7/12	Consumer Gas Co.	34 94	√			1872 54
1060	7/16	Armstrong Elem. Sch.	15 00	√			1857 54
1061	7/17	Pearce Tire Co.	227 00				1630 54
1062	7/19	Anderson Plumbers	103 20				1527 34
				√	7/20	250 00	1777 34
1063	7/22	Bug Away Exterminator	47 50				1729 84
1064	7/22	AAA Service	103 27				1626 57

Bank Statement

Checks and Debits			Deposits and Credits	Date	Balance
				6/16	1346 30
21 88			375 00	6/19	1699 42
44 11	73 42		1037 64	6/21	2619 53
63 75	200 00			6/23	2355 78
64 94	245 72			6/26	2045 12
380 27	365 50		1000 01	7/1	2299 36
22 00	247 12			7/5	2030 24
18 38				7/8	2011 86
67 53	77 45			7/9	1866 38
			125 00	7/12	1991 88
38 00	34 94			7/14	1918 94
46 40				7/16	1872 54
15 00				7/17	1857 54

Using the completed statements above:

		Check Register	*Bank Statement*
	Balance	$1626.57	$1857.54
	Unrecorded Deposits		+ 250.00
	Outstanding Checks		− 480.97
		$1626.57	$1626.57
9.	Statement Balance	$136.22	
	Add: Deposits since statement	+ 327.65	
	Subtract: Outstanding Checks	− 354.28	
		$109.59	
11.	Check register balance	$513.82	
	less service charge	− 3.25	
	less check returned	− 125.00	
	less deposit correction	− 10.00	
	Balance	$375.57	
	Bank statement	$401.76	
	less outstanding checks	− 336.94	
	plus deposits of	+ 310.75	
	Balance	$375.57	

Exercises 3.4

		Order Register	Account Statement
1.	Balance	$202.29	$412.36
	Service charge	− 4.00	
	Interest	+ 1.09	
	Orders Outstanding		− 212.98
	Account Balance	$199.38	$199.38
3.	Balance	?	$2204.36
	Order Processing Fee (21 @ 10¢ ea)	−2.10	
	Interest Earned	+8.28	
	Orders Outstanding		− 843.76
	Deposit		+ 500.00
		?	$1860.60

a. The true account balance is $1860.60

b. Therefore, the order register should show $1860.60 − $8.28 + $2.10 = $1854.42

		Order Register	Account Statement
5.	Balance	$1686.74	$1134.34
	Interest Earned	+ 3.95	
	Rent	− 225.00	
	Car Payment	− 178.44	
	Outstanding Orders		− 493.27
	Deposits		+ 645.28
	Recording Error	− (39.85 − 38.95)	
	Account Balance	$1286.35	$1286.35
7.	Balance	$1371.49	$1395.34
	Interest	+ 4.81	
	Outstanding Orders		− 219.04
	Deposit		+ 200.00
	Account Balance	$1376.30	$1376.30
9.	Balance	$1307.90	$1104.36
	Interest	+ 2.96	
	Service Charge	− 3.00	
	Telephone Payment	− 96.38	
	Deposits		+ 311.00
			+ 196.04
	Outstanding Orders		− 11.37
			− 146.33
			− 99.06
			− 143.16
	Account Balance	$1211.48	$1211.48

Review Exercises / Chapter 3

Answer: $302.15.

Exercises 4.1

1. $\dfrac{7}{100} = 7\%$

3. $\dfrac{14}{100} = 14\%$

5. $\dfrac{3}{50} = \dfrac{6}{100} = 6\%$

7. $\dfrac{3}{2} = \dfrac{150}{100} = 150\%$

9. $\dfrac{1}{4} = \dfrac{25}{100} = 25\%$

11. $\dfrac{12}{100} = \dfrac{3}{25}$

13. $\dfrac{32}{100} = \dfrac{8}{25}$

15. $\dfrac{5.5}{100} = \dfrac{55}{1000} = \dfrac{11}{200}$

17. $5\frac{1}{4}\% = 5.25\% = \dfrac{5.25}{100} = \dfrac{525}{10{,}000} = \dfrac{21}{400}$

19. $\dfrac{1000}{5000} = \dfrac{1}{5} = 20\%$

21. 80%

Exercises 4.2

1. $0.25 = 25\%$ **3.** $4.81 = 481\%$ **5.** $0.023 = 2.3\%$ **7.** $50\% = 0.5$ **9.** $6\% = 0.06$ **11.** $0.3\% = 0.003$

13. $\frac{1}{8} = 0.125 = 12.5\%$ **15.** $\frac{1}{3} = 0.33\frac{1}{3} = 33\frac{1}{3}\%$ **17.** $\frac{1}{40} = 0.025 = 2.5\%$ **19.** $\frac{40}{100} = \frac{2}{5}$

Exercises 4.3

1. $0.5 + 0.33 + 0.02 = 0.85$ **3.** $0.05 + 0.68 + 0.25 = 0.98$ **5.** $0.6 + 0.02 - 0.03 = 0.59$ **7.** $\frac{1}{3} + \frac{1}{2} = \frac{5}{6}$

9. $\frac{1}{12} + \frac{1}{6} = \frac{3}{12} = \frac{1}{4}$ **11.** $\frac{4}{10} + 5 = 5\frac{4}{10}$ or $5\frac{2}{5}$ **13.** $\frac{1}{9} \times 198 = 22$ **15.** $(0.04)(250) = 10$

17. $\frac{1}{6} \times 600 = 100$ **19.** $\frac{1}{15} = 0.06\frac{2}{3} = 6\frac{2}{3}\%$ **21.** $\frac{1}{40} = 0.025 = 2.5\%$ **23.** $\frac{1}{6} \times \$600{,}000 = \$100{,}000$

25. $\frac{1}{12} \times \$600 = \$50$

Exercises 4.4

1. $(0.07)(170) = 11.9$ **3.** $\frac{1}{12} \times 1200 = 100$ **5.** $\frac{110}{0.05} = 2200$ **7.** $100 \div \frac{1}{7} = 700$ **9.** $\frac{60}{15} = 4$ or 400%

11. $\frac{60}{180} = \frac{1}{3}$ or $33\frac{1}{3}\%$ **13.** $(0.5)(\$160) = \$80$ **15.** $(28)(\frac{1}{7}) = 4$ **17.** $\frac{20}{500} = \frac{4}{100} = 4\%$

19. $\frac{20}{0.10} = 200$ members **21.** $\frac{\$15}{0.05} = \$300$ **23.** $\frac{\$10}{\$100} = 0.10$ or 10% **25.** $15\frac{5}{13}\%$

27. $22\frac{1}{2}\%$

Review Exercises / Chapter 4

1. 14% **3.** 200% **5.** $\frac{17}{200}$ **7.** 0.09 **9.** 6% **11.** $\$33.96$

13. $\$1.38$ **15.** 360 **17.** Yes

Exercises 5.1

1. $x + 5 = 9$, $4 + 5 = 9$, $9 = 9$. Yes, both sides equal. **3.** $2x + 1 = 10$, $2(3) + 1 = 10$, $6 + 1 = 10$, $7 = 10$. No, not equal.
5. $\frac{1}{2}x - 7 = 0$, $\frac{1}{2}(14) - 7 = 0$, $7 - 7 = 0$, $0 = 0$. True. **7.** $I = (100)(0.05)(2)$, $10 = 10$. True.
9. $\frac{2}{3}y + \frac{1}{2} = 1\frac{1}{2}$, $\frac{2}{3}(\frac{3}{2}) + \frac{1}{2} = 1\frac{1}{2}$, $1 + \frac{1}{2} = 1\frac{1}{2}$. True. **11.** $7x = 21$, $7(3) = 21$, $21 = 21$. True.
13. $2x + 3y = 13$, $2(2) + 3(3) = 13$, $4 + 9 = 13$. True. **15.** (c) $2x - 8 = 4$, $2(6) - 8 = 4$, $12 - 8 = 4$, $4 = 4$.

Exercises 5.2

1. $\frac{5x}{5} = \frac{20}{5}$
$x = 4$

3. $\begin{aligned} 2x - 3 &= 5 \\ +3 & +3 \\ \hline 2x &= 8 \\ x &= 4 \end{aligned}$

5. $\begin{aligned} 5x + 7 &= 17 \\ -7 & -7 \\ \hline 5x &= 10 \\ x &= 2 \end{aligned}$

7. $\begin{aligned} \tfrac{1}{2}x &= 8 \\ 2(\tfrac{1}{2})x &= 2(8) \\ x &= 16 \end{aligned}$

9. $\begin{aligned} \tfrac{1}{2}x + 4 &= 5 \\ -4 & -4 \\ \hline \tfrac{1}{2}x &= 1 \\ 2(\tfrac{1}{2})x &= 2(1) \\ x &= 2 \end{aligned}$

11. $\begin{aligned} \tfrac{4}{5}w + 1 &= 2 \\ -1 & -1 \\ \hline \tfrac{4}{5}w &= 1 \\ \tfrac{5}{4}(\tfrac{4}{5})w &= \tfrac{5}{4}(1) \\ w &= \tfrac{5}{4} \end{aligned}$

13. $\begin{aligned} 4x &= 28 \\ x &= 7 \end{aligned}$

15. $\begin{aligned} 3x &= 18 \\ x &= 6 \end{aligned}$

17. $\begin{aligned} 2x &= 40 \\ x &= 20 \end{aligned}$

19. $\begin{aligned} 5x &= 90 \\ x &= 18 \end{aligned}$

21. $x = \frac{2}{3}$

23. $\begin{aligned} 2x &= 7 \\ x &= \frac{7}{2} \end{aligned}$

25. $-2x = 10 - 3x$
$ +3x +3x$
$ x = 10$

27. $\dfrac{S}{2} = \dfrac{\cancel{2}C}{\cancel{2}}$

$C = \dfrac{S}{2}$

29. $P = 2l + 2w$
$P - 2l = 2w$

$\dfrac{P - 2l}{2} = w$

31. $ S = C + M$
$ S - C = M$

33. $\dfrac{A}{Pt} = \dfrac{\cancel{P}d\cancel{t}}{\cancel{P}\cancel{t}}$

$d = \dfrac{A}{Pt}$

35. $D = \dfrac{C - S}{L}$

$L(D) = \cancel{L}\left(\dfrac{C - S}{\cancel{L}}\right)$

$\dfrac{L\cancel{D}}{\cancel{D}} = \dfrac{C - S}{D}$

$L = \dfrac{C - S}{D}$

37. $D = \dfrac{C - S}{L}$

$DL = C - S$
$DL + S = C$

39. $\dfrac{p}{r} = \dfrac{\cancel{r}b}{\cancel{r}}$

$b = \dfrac{p}{r}$

Exercises 5.3

1. S = selling price
C = cost
M = markup
$S = C + M$

3. I = interest
P = principal
R = rate
T = time
$I = PRT$

5. A = average cost
C = cost
U = unit
$A = C \div U$

7. Let x = a number
$3x = 18$
$x = 6$

9. $3x - 4 = 2$
$3x = 6$
$x = 2$

11. $4x + 2 = 18$
$x = 4$

13. $x + 2x = 24$
$3x = 24$
$x = 8$

15. $100 = P + 10$
$P = 90$

17. $R - \$3 = \$12$
$R = \$15$

19. $P + 2P = 300{,}000$
$3P = 300{,}000$
$P = 100{,}000$

Review Exercises/Chapter 5

1. Yes

3. No

5. $x = 7$

7. $x = 9$

9. $x = 21$

11. $x = a + b$

13. $t = \dfrac{A - P}{Pr}$

15. $20

17. $F = P + I$

19. $x - x = 0$

21. $2000

23. $x = 36$

Part One

Cumulative Review Exercises

1. $\dfrac{13}{15}$

3. $\dfrac{1}{2}$

5. 38.368

7. 25.155

9. 16

11. 12.5

13. 12

15. 15

17. $\dfrac{c - b}{a}$

19. 20

21. $F = P + I$

23. $440

25. No

27. $\frac{12}{28}$

29. $\frac{1}{6}$

31. 5.6%

Exercises 6.1

1. 12 doz. × \$4.00/doz. = \$48.00

3. 4560 × \$0.75 = \$3420.00

5. (24 doz. × 12) × \$0.50 = \$144.00

7. (2600 ÷ 100) × \$38.00 = \$988.00

9. (1500/100) × \$12.00 = \$180.00
 (144/12) × \$22.00 = 264.00
 11,000 × \$0.09 = 990.00
 \$1434.00

11. (200 × 15) × \$3.75 = \$11,250
 [(20 × 144) ÷ .12] × \$1.50 = 360
 920 × \$2.00 = 1,840
 \$13,450

13. Wholesaler A
$130,000 \times \$0.35 = \$45,500$

Wholesaler B
$35,000 \times \$0.55 = \$19,250$
$35,000 \times \$0.30 = \$10,500$
$60,000 \times \$0.25 = \$15,000$
_____
$\$44,750$

Choose B; $750 savings

15. $[10 \text{ doz} \times 12 = 120 \text{ boxes}] \times \$0.22 = \$26.40$
  $4 \text{ cases} \times \$2.60 \qquad = 10.40$
  $6 \text{ doz.} \times \$0.32 \qquad = \underline{\ \ 1.92}$
        $\$38.72$

17. $\$51.80 \div 4 = \$12.95$ on subsequent orders.
 $\$12.95 - \$12.64 = \$0.31$ savings per unit on first order.

Exercises 6.2

1. $\$25.00 \times 10\% = \$2.50$

3. $\$295 \times 18\% = \$53.10$

5. $\$1080 \times 36\% = \$388.80$

7. $\$47.50 \times 10\% = \$4.75; \$47.50 - \$4.75 = \$42.75$

9. $\$3800 \times 30\% = \$1140; \$3800 - \$1140 = \$2660$

11. $\$130 \times 15\% = \$19.50; \$130 - \$19.50 = \$110.50$

13. $\$140 \times (100\% - 15\%) = \$119$

15. $\$25,000 \times (100\% - 12\%) = \$22,000$

17. $1.0 - 0.10 = 0.9; 1.0 - 0.05 = 0.95$
$(0.9)(0.95) = 0.855$
$1.0 - 0.855 = 14.5\%$ discount rate
Net price $\$750 \times 0.855 = \$641.25$

19. $1 - 0.2 = 0.8; 1 - 0.15 = 0.85$
$(0.8)(0.85) = 0.68$
$1 - 0.68 = 32\%$ discount rate
Net price $\$900 \times 0.68 = \$612$

21. $1 - 0.3 = 0.7; 1 - 0.2 = 0.8; 1 - 0.05 = 0.95$
$(0.7)(0.8)(0.95) = 0.532$
$1 - 0.532 = 46.8\%$ discount rate
Net price $\$1500 \times 0.532 = \$798$

23. $1 - 0.15 = 0.85; 1 - 0.1 = 0.9; 1 - 0.05 = 0.95$
$(0.85)(0.9)(0.95) = 0.72675$
$1 - 0.72675 = 27.325\%$ discount rate
Net price $\$2000 \times 0.72675 = \$1453.50$

25. Jayco, $[1 - (0.80)(0.90)(0.95)] = 31.6\%$ discount rate
Jeffco, $[1 - (0.8)(0.85)] = 32\%$ discount rate

27. The net price = list price $\times [(0.9)(0.9)(0.95)]$, or
list price $= \$76.95 \div 0.7695 = \$100.00$

29. Single equivalent discount rate = $[\$247 \div 400 = 0.6175; 1 - 0.6175 = 38.25\%]$. Additional discount required = $[0.6175 \div 0.65 = 0.95$, which is $1 -$ the new discount rate; hence the additional discount rate is 5%].

Exercises 6.3

1. Aug. 4 **3.** Apr. 4 **5.** Oct. 10

	Discount		Amount Due
7.	$\$1800 \times 1\frac{1}{2}\% = \$27$		$\$1800 - \$27 = \$1773$
9.	$\$1100 \times 3\% = \$33$		$\$1100 - \$33 = \$1067$
11.	0		$\$2000$
13.	$\$2000 \times 5\% = \$100$		$\$2000 - \$100 = \$1900$

15.
$\$525$ Invoice total
$\underline{-\ \ 25}$ Freight
$\$500$
$\underline{\times\ \ \ \ 2\%}$
$\$\ 10$ Discount

$\$500$
$\underline{-\ \ 10}$ Discount
$\$490$
$\underline{+\ \ 25}$ Freight
$\$515$ Due

17.
$\$900$
$\underline{-\ \ 40}$ Freight
$\$860$
$\underline{-\ \ 60}$ Return
$\$800$
$\underline{\times\ \ 1\frac{1}{2}\%}$
$\$\ 12$ Discount

$\$800$
$\underline{-\ \ 12}$ Discount
$\$788$
$\underline{+\ \ 40}$ Freight
$\$828$ Amount due

19. The discount is lost since payment was not made within the discount period. The amount due is

$$
\begin{array}{ll}
\$1800 & \\
-\ \ \ 200 & \text{Returns} \\
\hline
\$1600 & \text{Amount due}
\end{array}
$$

21. Jacks   Re-Tred

$$
\begin{array}{ll}
\$500 & \$500 \\
\times\ \ \ 2\% & -\ \ \ 10 \\
\hline
\$\ 10 \ \ \text{Discount} & \$490 \ \ \text{Due}
\end{array}
$$

$$
\begin{array}{ll}
\$650 & \$500.00 \\
-\ \ 40 \ \ \text{Freight} & -\ \ \ 7.50 \\
\hline
\$610 & \$492.50 \\
-\ 110 \ \ \text{Returns} & +\ \ 40.00 \ \ \text{Freight} \\
\hline
\$500 & \$532.50 \\
\times\ \ \ 1\frac{1}{2}\% & \\
\hline
\$\ \ 7.50 \ \ \text{Discount} &
\end{array}
$$

Pay Jacks. A \$10 discount from Jacks is \$2.50 more than the discount from Re-Tred.

23.
$$
\begin{array}{ll}
\$450.00 & \\
-\ \ \ 35.00 \ \ \text{Shipping} & \\
\hline
415.00 & \\
-\ \ \ 75.00 \ \ \text{Returned merchandise} & \\
\hline
\$340.00 &
\end{array}
$$

$$
\begin{array}{l}
\$340.00 \\
\times\ \ \ \ \ \ 2\% \ \ \text{Discount available} \\
\hline
\$\ \ 6.80
\end{array}
$$

Amount due $= \$340.00 - \$6.80 + \$35.00 = \$368.20$; no further amount due.

Review Exercises/Chapter 6

1. \$2961.53   **3. a.** 0.472   **b.** 0.5395   **5. a.** \$3.21   **b.** None

7. Discount—\$16.69; discount rate—30.0%.

9. Single equivalence discount rate—27.325%; net price—\$137.72.

11. \$148.28.

Exercises 7.1

1. $S = C + M = \$14.60 + \$2.10 = \$16.70$ **3.** $M = S - C = \$11.65 - \$9.49 = \$2.16$

5. $S = C + M = \$0.96 + \$0.19 = \$1.15$ **7.** $S = \$0.59 + \$0.30 = \$0.89$

9. $C = \$0.19 - \$0.08 = \$0.11$

11. $M = \$100 - \$80 = \$20$ **13.** $C = \$300 - \$50 = \$250$ **15.** $C = \$1500 - \$250 = \$1250$

$$M_s\% = \frac{\$20}{\$100} = 20\% \qquad M_s\% = \frac{\$50}{\$300} = 16.67\% \qquad M_s\% = \frac{\$250}{\$1500} = 16.67\%$$

$$M_c\% = \frac{\$20}{\$80} = 25\% \qquad M_c\% = \frac{\$50}{\$250} = 20\% \qquad M_c\% = \frac{\$250}{\$1250} = 20\%$$

17. $M = \$0.60 - \$0.35 = \$0.25$ **19.** $M_c\% = \dfrac{M}{C}$ $S = C + M$

$$M_s\% = \frac{\$0.25}{\$0.60} = 41.67\% \qquad\qquad 30\% = \frac{M}{\$15.00} \qquad\qquad = \$15.00 + \$4.50$$

$$\qquad\qquad\qquad\qquad\qquad\qquad\qquad\qquad\qquad = \$19.50$$

$$M_c\% = \frac{\$0.25}{\$0.35} = 71.43\% \qquad\qquad M = (30\%)(\$15.00)$$

$$\qquad\qquad\qquad\qquad\qquad\qquad\qquad\qquad = \$4.50$$

21. a. Cost to Hard Ware $= \$25 \times 60\% = \$15.00$; selling price $= \$25.00 \times 85\% = \$21.25$.

    b. Markup $= \$21.25 - \$15.00 = \$6.25$; $M_c = \dfrac{\$6.25}{\$15.00} = 41.7\%$; $M_s = \dfrac{\$6.25}{\$21.25} = 29.4\%$.

23. Cost $= \$40.00 \times [(0.8)(0.9)] = \$28.80$. $M_c = $ Markup $\div$ cost; $20\% = $ markup $\div \$28.80$, so markup $= \$5.76$. Selling price $= \$5.76 + \$28.80 = \$34.56$.

Exercises 7.2

1. $\$90 \times 112.5\% = \$101.25$ **3.** $\$800 \times 118\% = \$944$ **5.** $\$7.60 \times 120\% = \$9.12$

7. $\$630 \times 125\% = \$787.50$ **9.** $\$210 \div 70\% = \$300$ **11.** $\$1800 \div 90\% = \$2000$

13. $\$37,500 \div 75\% = \$50,000$ **15.** $\$2870 \div 82\% = \$3500$ **17.** $M_c = \dfrac{10\%}{100\% - 10\%} = 11.1\%$

19. $M_c = \dfrac{30\%}{100\% - 30\%} = 42.9\%$ **21.** $M_c = \dfrac{40\%}{100\% - 40\%} = 66.7\%$

23. Selling price $= \$3.25 \times 140\% = \$4.55$ **25.** Selling price $= \$2700 \div 90\% = \$3000$
 Markup $= \$4.55 - \$3.25 = \$1.30$

27. Selling price $= \$8.00 \div 75\% = \$10.67$. Yes, you can charge a price that will cover your normal markup rate.

29. Cost $= 5 \times \$20 = \$100$ for 5 tires   Blemish sells for $20
 Total selling price $= \$100 \times 140\%$ (4 tires)(selling price) $= \$120$
          $= \$140$ selling price $= \$30.00$

31. $M_c = \dfrac{28\%}{100\% - 28\%} = 38.9\%$ old supplier; no.

Exercises 7.3

1. $\$350 - \$75 = \$275$ **3.** $\$592.50 - \$97.50 = \$495.00$ **5.** $\$420 - \$48 = \$372$

7. $\$1250 - \$250 = \$1000$ **9.** $\$800 - \$200 = \$600$ **11.** $\$9.95 - \$2.45 = \$7.50$

 Markdown rate $= \dfrac{\$250}{\$1250} = 20\%$ Markdown rate $= \dfrac{\$200}{\$800} = 25\%$ Markdown rate $= \dfrac{\$2.45}{\$9.95} = 24.6\%$

13. Markdown rate $= 50\%$, so new selling price is 50% of original price. New selling price $= (\$1800)(50\%) = \$900$. Markdown then equals $1800 original price $-$ $900 new price $= \$900$.

15. The lamps are selling for 40% of the original price (i.e., $100\% - 60\%$ reduction). So (original price) $\times (40\%) = \$30.00$.
 Original price $= \dfrac{\$30.00}{40\%} = \$75.00$

17. No. A 35% reduction is $\$200 \times 35\% = \$70$. The actual reduction is only $60 or 30%.

19. M_s = markup $\div$ selling price; 20% = markup $\div \$35.00$. Markup $= \$35.00 \times 20\% = \$7.00$. Cost was $\$35 - \$7.00 = \$28.00$. Hence, the lamps sold for $3.00 below cost. The lamps sold at $\$10 \div \$35.00 = 28.6\%$ markdown.

Review Exercises/Chapter 7

1. Markup $11.45; $M_c = 29.7\%$; $M_s = 22.9\%$ **3.** $11.05   **5. a.** $26.92   **b.** $26.25

7. Go Gettum: comparing markup on cost, they are $3\frac{1}{3}\%$ higher.

9. 35 shirts; $7.65 in change

11. a. $14.25   **b.** 29.4% **c.** 22.7%

Exercises 8.1

1. Vehicle   6302 $ 5,890   **3.** No. Pickups currently are 32.4% of the inventory.
          6318 $ 5,135
          6335 $ 4,860
          6356 $ 5,125
          6383 $ 4,695
          6388 $ 3,795
              $29,500   Total inventory

5. 10,000 units at $0.68 = $ 6,800   **7.** June 20   10,000 units at $0.65 = $ 6,500
  8,000 units at $0.70 = $ 5,600   July 1   15,000 units at $0.70 = $10,500
 10,000 units at $0.72 = $ 7,200   July 12   10,000 units at $0.68 = $ 6,800
 28,000 units $19,600   35,000 units $23,800   Avg. cost = $0.68

 Avg. cost $= \$19,600 \div 28,000$ units $= \$0.70$ Avg. cost inv. value = 11,000 units at $0.68 = $7480
 Avg. cost inventory $= 4500 \times \$0.70 = \$3150$

 FIFO $= 4500$ units $\times \$0.72 = \$3240$ FIFO = 10,000 units at $0.68 = $6800
 LIFO $= 4500$ units $\times \$0.68 = \$3060$ 1,000 units at $0.70 = $ 700
                                    11,000 $7500

                    LIFO = 10,000 units at $0.65 = $6500
                         1,000 units at $0.70 = $ 700
                        11,000 units $7200

9. Aug. 1   1000 units at $2.35 = $2350.00
Aug. 12   1200 units at $2.10 = $2520.00
Aug. 30   1400 units at $2.00 = $2800.00
Sept. 15   900 units at $1.90 = $1710.00
4500 units $9380.00   Avg. cost = $2.084

Avg. cost inv. value = 1100 units at $2.084 = $2292.40

FIFO =   900 units at $1.90 = $1710
200 units at $2.00 = $ 400
1100 units $2110
LIFO = 1000 units at $2.35 = $2350
100 units at $2.10 = $ 210
1100 units $2560

11. a. March 3,000 units at $0.65 = $1950
June   4,000 units at $0.70 = $2800
Nov.   6,000 units at $0.75 = $4500
13,000 units $9250
Average cost = $9250 ÷ 13,000 units = $0.7115 per unit
Avg. cost inventory value = 3800 units × $0.7115 = $2703.70

b. FIFO = 3800 units at $0.75 = $2850
c. LIFO = 3000 units at $0.65 =   1950
800 units at $0.70 =   560
3800 units $2510

13. a. Beginning inventory   300 units at $12.00 = $ 3,600
March   1200 units at $14.00 = $16,800
June   600 units at $13.00 = $ 7,800
Nov.   500 units at $13.50 = $ 6,750
2600 units $34,950 Avg. cost = $13.442.
Avg. cost inventory value = 400 units at $13.442 = $5376.80

b. LIFO = 300 units at $12.00 = $3600
100 units at $14.00 = $1400
400 units $5000
c. FIFO = 400 units at $13.50 = $5400

15. a. Beginning inventory 9,000 units at $0.30   = $ 2,700
10,000 units at $0.35   = $ 3,500
14,000 units at $0.37   = $ 5,180
11,000 units at $0.365 = $ 4,015
44,000 units $15,395 Avg. cost = $0.3499
Avg. cost inventory value = 12,000 units at $0.3499 = $4198.80

b. LIFO =   9,000 units at $0.30   = $2700
3,000 units at $0.35   = $1050
12,000 units $3750
c. FIFO = 11,000 units at $0.365 = $4015
1,000 units at $0.37   = $ 370
12,000 units $4385

Exercises 8.2

1. $6800 + $1800 − $2750 = $5850

3. $12,000 + $21,000 − $19,200 = $13,800

5. COGS = $65,000 × 70% = $45,500
End. inv. = $15,000 + $35,000 − $45,500 = $4500

7. COGS = $37,900 × 80% = $30,320
End. inv. = $13,450 + $29,600 − $30,320 = $12,730

9. Cost of goods sold = $109,200 ÷ 140% = $78,000
Ending inventory = $22,000 + $96,400 − $78,000 = $40,400

11. Cost of goods sold = $233,220 ÷ 138% = $169,000
Ending inventory = $89,650 + $172,400 − $169,000 = $93,050

13. **a.** Cost of goods sold = $56,000 × 60% = $33,600
Ending inventory = $18,200 + $32,000 − $33,600 = $16,600
b. Cost of goods sold = $56,000 ÷ 145% = $38,620.69
Ending inventory = $18,200 + $32,000 − $38,620.69 = $11,579.31

15. Ending inventory (retail) = $19,400 + $47,600 − $58,000 = $9000
Ending inventory (cost) = $9000 × 70% = $6300

17. Ending inventory (retail) = $212,400 + $1,417,200 − $1,516, 200 = $113,400
Ending inventory (cost) = $113,400 ÷ 140% = $81,000

19. Ending inventory (retail) = $22,500 + $56,800 − $64,200 = $15,100
a. Ending inventory (cost) = $15,100 × 75% = $11,325
b. Ending inventory (cost) = $15,100 ÷ 130% = $11,615.38

21. Markup rate = $\dfrac{\text{cost}}{\text{retail}} = \dfrac{\$27,200}{\$34,000} = 80\%$

Inventory = ($10,000 + $24,000 − $28,000) × 80% = $4800

23. Markup rate = $\dfrac{\text{cost}}{\text{retail}} = \dfrac{\$33,320}{\$47,600} = 70\%$

Beginning inventory	$ 9,200
+ Purchases	$38,400
+ Markups	$ 800
− Markdowns	$ 1,100
− Sales	$36,200
= Ending inventory (at retail)	$11,100

Ending inventory at cost = $11,100 × 70% = $7770

Exercises 8.3

1. $13,500 ÷ $2250 = 6 times

3. $2780 × 5.5 times = $15,290

5. $14,950 × 8.6 times = $128,570

7. $46,875 ÷ $6250 = 7.5 times

9. $8100 × 7.8 = $63,180

11. $14,280 × 10.3 = $147,084

13. Avg. inv. = ($17,860 + $21,350 + $21,800 + $18,990) ÷ 4 = $20,000

Begin. inv.	$ 19,250
+ Purchases	$179,740
− Ending inv.	$ 18,990
= COGS	$180,000

Inv. turnover = $\dfrac{\text{COGS}}{\text{avg. inv. (at cost)}} = \dfrac{\$180,000}{\$20,000} = 9$ times

15. Avg. inv. = ($34,900 + $38,700 + $40,600 + $36,800) ÷ 4 = $37,750

Inv. turnover = $\dfrac{\text{sales}}{\text{avg. inv. (at retail)}} = \dfrac{\$169,875}{\$37,750} = 4.5$ times

17.

Est. sales	$96,000		$93,300 planned purchases
+ End inv.	$26,000		− $75,900 ordered
− Beg. inv.	$28,700		$17,400 open-to-buy (at retail)
Planned purchase	$93,300 (at retail)		× 70%
	× 70%		$12,180 (at cost)
	$65,310 (at cost)		

19.

Est. sales	$147,000		$149,400 planned purchases
+ End. inv.	$ 21,000		− $ 39,000 ordered and received
− Beg. inv.	$ 18,600		− $ 68,000 ordered and not received
Planned purchases	$149,400 (at retail)		= $ 42,400 open-to-buy
	× 65%		× 65%
	$ 97,110 (at cost)		$ 27,560 at cost

Exercises 8.4

	Department	Ratio		Total Overhead		Department Overhead
1.	Plant	$\dfrac{40,000}{60,000} = \dfrac{2}{3}$	$\times$	$60,000	$=$	$40,000
	Sales	$\dfrac{10,000}{60,000} = \dfrac{1}{6}$	$\times$	$60,000	$=$	$10,000
	Accounting	$\dfrac{10,000}{60,000} = \dfrac{1}{6}$	$\times$	$60,000	$=$	$10,000
		$\dfrac{6}{6} = 100\%$				$60,000
3.	A	$\dfrac{750}{2500} = 30\%$	$\times$	$5000	$=$	$1500
	B	$\dfrac{1250}{2500} = 50\%$	$\times$	$5000	$=$	$2500
	C	$\dfrac{500}{2500} = 20\%$	$\times$	$5000	$=$	$1000
		100%				$5000
5.	Admin.	$\dfrac{2500}{10,000} = 25\%$	$\times$	$46,000	$=$	$11,500
	Design	$\dfrac{1500}{10,000} = 15\%$	$\times$	$46,000	$=$	$6,900
	Production	$\dfrac{6000}{10,000} = 60\%$	$\times$	$46,000	$=$	$27,600
		100%				$46,000

	Product	Units Produced		Selling Price		Sales Value	Ratio		Total Overhead	Allocated Overhead
7.	1	60,000	$\times$	$2.50	$=$	$150,000	$\dfrac{\$150,000}{\$300,000} = 50\%$		$22,000	$11,000
	2	30,000	$\times$	$5.00	$=$	$150,000	$\dfrac{\$150,000}{\$300,000} = 50\%$			$11,000
							100%			$22,000
9.	Good	20,000	$\times$	$3.00	$=$	$60,000	$\dfrac{\$60,000}{\$180,000} = \dfrac{1}{3}$		$45,000	$15,000
	Better	15,000	$\times$	$4.00	$=$	$60,000	$\dfrac{\$60,000}{\$180,000} = \dfrac{1}{3}$			$15,000
	Best	10,000	$\times$	$6.00	$=$	$60,000	$\dfrac{\$60,000}{\$180,000} = \dfrac{1}{3}$			$15,000
							$\dfrac{3}{3}$ or 100%			$45,000
11.	Solids	50,000	$\times$	$0.70	$=$	$35,000	$\dfrac{\$35,000}{\$50,000} = 70\%$		$2200	$ 1540
	Stripes	50,000	$\times$	$0.30	$=$	$15,000	$\dfrac{\$15,000}{\$50,000} = 30\%$			$ 660
							100%			$ 2200

13. Line 1: $\dfrac{3 \text{ machines}}{18 \text{ machines}} = \dfrac{1}{6} \times \$30{,}000 = \$\ 5{,}000$

Line 2: $\dfrac{6 \text{ machines}}{18 \text{ machines}} = \dfrac{1}{3} \times \$30{,}000 = \$10{,}000$

Line 3: $\dfrac{9 \text{ machines}}{18 \text{ machines}} = \dfrac{1}{2} \times \$30{,}000 = \$15{,}000$

$\dfrac{6}{6}$ or 100% $\quad \$30{,}000$

Review Exercises Chapter 8

1. a. $5577.94   **b.** $5875.00   **c.** $5294.50   **d.** Yes; $30 for lower of cost or market   **3.** $130,341

5. a. $62,230   **b.** No; $1230 before offer.

7. a. $1917.60
   b. $1913.00
   c. $1895.50

9. a. $26,525.93
   b. $26,857.50

Exercises 9.1

1. ($900 − $100 = $800) ÷ 4 years = $200/year depreciation. Depreciation rate $= \frac{1}{4} = 25\%$

3. ($2500 − $100 = $2400) ÷ 12 years = $200/year depreciation. Depreciation rate $= \frac{1}{12} = 8\frac{1}{3}\%$

5. ($4850 − $350 = $4500) ÷ 9 years = $500/year depreciation. Depreciation rate $= \frac{1}{9} = 11.1\%$

7. ($4500 − $500 = $4000) ÷ 4 years = $1000/year depreciation

9. $150,000 ÷ $15,000 annual depreciation = 10 years of life. Depreciation rate $= \frac{1}{10} = 10\%$

11. Year 1—accumulated depreciation = $4000
   Year 2—annual depreciation = $4000
   Year 3—book value = $10,000
   Year 4—accumulated depreciation = $16,000
   Year 5—salvage value = $2000

13. ($500 annual depreciation × 6-year life = $3000) + $750 salvage = $3750 original cost

15. ($17,500 cost − $2500 = $15,000 depreciation base) ÷ 5 years = $3000 annual depreciation. 3 years × $3000 = $9000 accumulated depreciation. Book value = $17,500 − $9000 = $8500

17. $\left(\dfrac{\$69{,}500 \text{ cost } - \$9500 \text{ salvage}}{12 \text{ years}} \right) \times \dfrac{6}{12}$ years of use $= \$2500$

19. $\left(\dfrac{\$105{,}000 - \$5000}{10} \right) \times \dfrac{9}{12} = \$7500$

21. $\left(\dfrac{\$127{,}500 - \$7500}{20} \right) \times \dfrac{6}{12} = \$3000$

23.

Year	Annual Depreciation	Accumulated Depreciation	Book Value
1	$300	$ 300	$950
2	$400	$ 700	$550
3	$400	$1100	$150
4	$100	$1200	$ 50(salvage)

25. $4000 ÷ 10 years = $400/year

Exercises 9.2

1. ($50,000 − $5000 = $45,000) ÷ 90,000 units = $0.50/unit

3. ($42,500 − $500 = $42,000) ÷ 70,000 units = $0.60/unit

5. ($11,000 − $1000 = $10,000) ÷ 10,000 units = $1.00/unit

7. 100,000 units × $0.15/unit = $15,000 annual depreciation

9. 185,000 units × $0.125/unit = $23,125 annual depreciation

11. 196,000 units × $0.30/unit = $58,800 annual depreciation

13. [($48,000 − $4000 = $44,000) ÷ 200,000 hr] × 80,000 hr = $17,600

15. [($9500 − $1000 = $8500) ÷ 100,000 miles] × 50,000 miles = $4250

17. 100,000 units × $0.02 = $2000

19. 98,700 units × $0.10 = $9870

21. $\left(\dfrac{\$9635\ \text{cost} - \$635\ \text{salvage}}{30,000\ \text{units}}\right) \times 4850\ \text{units} = \$1455$

23. $\left(\dfrac{\$10,000,000}{500,000\ \text{tons}}\right) 75,000\ \text{tons} = \$1,500,000$

25. $\left(\dfrac{\$450,000}{10,000\ \text{tons}}\right) 2750\ \text{tons} = \$123,750$

Exercises 9.3

		Year	Digit	Depreciation Rate
1.	3 years	1	3	$\frac{3}{6}$
		2	2	$\frac{2}{6}$
		3	1	$\frac{1}{6}$
			6	$\frac{6}{6} = 1$
3.	5 years	1	5	$\frac{5}{15}$
		2	4	$\frac{4}{15}$
		3	3	$\frac{3}{15}$
		4	2	$\frac{2}{15}$
		5	1	$\frac{1}{15}$
			15	$\frac{15}{15} = 1$

5. Year 1 $(\frac{4}{10})(\$10,000) = \$4000$
      Year 2 $(\frac{3}{10})(\$10,000) = \$3000$
      Year 3 $(\frac{2}{10})(\$10,000) = \$2000$
      Year 4 $(\frac{1}{10})(\$10,000) = \$1000$

7.

Year	Annual Depreciation	Accumulated Depreciation	Book Value
1	$6000	$ 6,000	$19,000
2	$5000	$11,000	$14,000
3	$4000	$15,000	$10,000
4	$3000	$18,000	$ 7,000
5	$2000	$20,000	$ 5,000
6	$1000	$21,000	$ 4,000
			(salvage value)

9. Depr. fraction $= \frac{3}{36}$, or $\frac{1}{12}$
     Depreciation $= (\frac{1}{12})(\$40,000 - \$4000) = \$3000$

11. Depr. fraction $= \frac{3}{45}$
      Depreciation $= (\frac{3}{45})(\$155,000 - \$20,000) = \$9000$

13. Depreciation $= (\frac{3}{55})(\$123,000 - \$13,000) = \$6000$

15. Depreciation $= (\frac{4}{21})(\$72,500 - \$9500) = \$12,000$

17.

Year	Annual Depreciation	Accumulated Depreciation	Book Value
1	$150	$150	$700
2	$250	$400	$450
3	$150	$550	$300
4	$50	$600	$250 (salvage)

19.

Year	Annual Depreciation	Accumulated Depreciation	Book Value
1	$750	$750	$9250
2	$2850	$3600	$6400
3	$2250	$5850	$4150
4	$1650	$7500	$2500
5	$1050	$8550	$1450
6	$450	$9000	$1000 (salvage)

Exercises 9.4

	Straight Line	Double Declining Balance
1.	$\frac{1}{3}$, or $0.33\frac{1}{3}$, or $33\frac{1}{3}\%$	$0.66\frac{2}{3}$, or $66\frac{2}{3}\%$
3.	$\frac{1}{6}$, or $0.16\frac{2}{3}$, or $16\frac{2}{3}\%$	$0.33\frac{1}{3}$, or $33\frac{1}{3}\%$
5.	$\frac{1}{25}$, or 0.04, or 4%	0.08, or 8%

	Current-Year Depreciation	Book Value (End of Year)
7.	$4000 \times 75\% = \$3000$	$4000 - \$3000 = \$1000$
9.	$15,000 \times 33\frac{1}{3}\% = \$5000$	$15,000 - \$5000 = \$10,000$
11.	$12,500 \times 50\% = \$6250$	$12,500 - \$6250 = \$6250$

	Depreciation Rate	Current-Year Depreciation	Accumulated Depreciation	Book Value (End of Year)
13.	$\frac{2}{3}$ or $66\frac{2}{3}\%$ ($\frac{1}{3} \times 200\%$)	$4000 ($6000 \times \frac{2}{3}$)	$4000	$2000 ($6000 - \$4000$)
15.	$\frac{1}{3}$ or $33\frac{1}{3}\%$ ($\frac{1}{6} \times 200\%$)	$6000 ($\frac{1}{3} \times \$18,000$)	$6000	$12,000 ($18,000 - \$6000$)

	Year	Book Value (Beginning of Year)	Depreciation Rate	Current-Year Depreciation	Accumulated Depreciation	Book Value (End of Year)
17.	1	$8000	50%	$4000	$4000	$4000
	2	$4000	50%	$2000	$6000	$2000
	3	$2000	50%	$2000	$8000	0
19.	1	$30,000	30%	$9000	$ 9,000	$21,000
	2	$21,000	30%	$6300	$15,300	$14,700
	3	$14,700	30%	$4410	$19,710	$10,290
	4	$10,290	30%	$3087	$22,797	$ 7,203
	5	$ 7,203	30%	$2203	$25,000	$ 5,000
21.	1	$80,000	25%	$20,000	$20,000	$60,000
	2	$60,000	25%	$15,000	$35,000	$45,000
	3	$45,000	25%	$11,250	$46,250	$33,750
	4	$33,750	25%	$ 8,437.50	$54,687.50	$25,312.50
	5	$25,312.50	25%	$ 6,328.13	$61,015.63	$18,984.37
	6	$18,984.37	25%	$ 3,984.37	$65,000	$15,000

23. ($9000 × $33\frac{1}{3}$%) × $\frac{4}{12}$ = $1000 current-year depreciation. Book value = $9000 − $1000 = $8000

25. ($18,000 × $66\frac{2}{3}$%) × $\frac{8}{12}$ = $8000 current-year depreciation. Book value = $18,000 − $8000 = $10,000

27.

Year	Annual Depreciation	Accumulated Depreciation	Book Value
1	$6000	$ 6,000	$24,000
2	$9600	$15,600	$14,400
3	$5760	$21,360	$ 8,640
4	$3456	$24,816	$ 5,184
5	$2073.60	$26,889.60	$ 3,110.40
6	$3110.40	$30,000	0

Exercises 9.5

	Type of Asset	Life Class	Year of Life	Recovery Percent
1.	Research equipment	3	3	37
3.	Production-line equipment	5	1	15
5.	"Over-the-road" truck	5	3	21
7.	Railroad tank car	10	8	9
9.	Business computer system	5	3	21

11. $12,000 × 37% = $4440

13. a. $135,400 × 8% = $10,832
b. $135,400 × 10% = $13,540
c. $135,400 × 9% = $12,186

15.

Year	Annual Cost Recovered	Accumulated Cost Recovered	Book Value
1	$2055	$ 2,055	$11,645
2	$3014	$ 5,069	$ 8,631
3	$2877	$ 7,946	$ 5,754
4	$2877	$10,823	$ 2,877
5	$2877	$13,700	$ 0

17. a. $2,300,000 × 9% = $207,000
b. $2,300,000 × 7% = $161,000
c. $2,300,000 × 6% = $138,000

19. a. Car 1 $\dfrac{\$7250 - \$250}{4} = \$1750$
Car 2 $7875 × 25% = $1968.75
Total $3718.75

b. Car 1 $\dfrac{\$7250 - \$250}{4} = \$1750$
Car 2 $7875 × 38% = $2992.50
Total $4742.50

c. Car 1 $\dfrac{\$7250 - \$250}{4} = \$1750$
Car 2 $7875 × 37% = $2913.75
Total $4663.75

d. Car 1 $\dfrac{1}{4}\left(\dfrac{\$7250 - \$250}{4}\right) = \$437.50$
Car 2 $= \dfrac{0}{\$437.50}$
Total

21. Cost Recovered
a.
b.
c.
Book Value
a. $176,500 − $ 5295 = $171,205
b. $171,205 − $19,415 = $151,790
c. $151,790 − $17,650 = $134,140

23.

Year	Annual Cost Recovered	Accumulated Cost Recovered	Book Value
1984	$14,000	$ 14,000	$336,000
1985	$38,500	$ 52,500	$297,500
1986	$35,000	$ 87,500	$262,500
1987	$31,500	$119,000	$231,000
1988	$28,000	$147,000	$203,000

Review Exercises/Chapter 9

1. a. Depreciation—$5000   **b.** Accumulated depreciation—$10,000   **c.** Life—6 years

3. $3125 annual depreciation; accumulated depreciation = $11,250

5.

Year	Annual Depreciation	Accumulated Depreciation	Book Value
1	$1000	$ 1,000	$11,500
2	$3750	$ 4,750	$ 7,750
3	$2750	$ 7,500	$ 5,000
4	$1750	$ 9,250	$ 3,250
5	$ 750	$10,000	$ 2,500 (salvage)

7. a. $2825   **9. a.** $4535
b. $4294   **b.** $5718
c. $4181   **c.** $5549
d. $0   **d.** $1500

Exercises 10.1

1. $1,487,000 − $446,100 = $1,040,900

3. $22,987,000 − $17,106,000 = $5,881,000

5. $876,400 − $535,400 = $341,000

7. Inventory = $137,500 − $109,500 = $28,000
Owner's equity = $137,500 − $92,000 = $45,500

9. Complete the vertical analysis and missing information on the following balance sheet. Round percents to the nearest tenth.

		Percent
Current assets		
Cash	$ 38,000	8.0
Accounts receivable	88,000	18.5
Inventory	106,000	22.3
Total current assets	$232,000	48.8
Land	64,000	13.5
Building (net)	147,600	31.1
Equipment (net)	31,400	6.6
Total noncurrent assets	243,000	51.2
Total assets	$475,000	100
Current liabilities		
Accounts payable	$ 84,000	17.7
Notes payable	14,800	3.1
Total current liabilities	98,800	20.8
Noncurrent liabilities		
Mortgage	$128,500	27.1
Bonds payable	167,700	35.3
Total noncurrent liabilities	$296,200	62.4
Total liabilities	$395,000	83.2
Owner's equity	$ 80,000	16.8
Total liabilities and owner's equity	$475,000	100

11. Complete the missing information and perform a horizontal analysis on the following balance sheet.

	Current Year	Previous Year	Increase (Decrease) Amount	Increase (Decrease) Percent	Percent Current Year	Percent Previous Year
Current assets						
Cash	$ 68,500	$ 72,900	($ 4,400)	(6.0)	7.2	8.6
Marketable securities	48,900	36,400	12,500	34.3	5.1	4.3
Accounts receivable	153,000	127,600	25,400	19.9	16.1	15.0
Inventory	193,600	182,100	11,500	6.3	20.4	21.4
Total current assets	$464,000	$419,000	$45,000	10.7	48.8	49.3
Noncurrent assets						
Land	$ 78,000	$ 78,000	$0	0	8.2	9.2
Buildings (net)	226,900	205,900	21,000	10.2	23.9	24.2
Equipment (net)	181,100	147,300	33,800	22.9	19.1	17.3
Total noncurrent assets	$486,000	$431,200	$54,800	12.7	51.2	50.7
Total assets	$950,000	$850,200	$99,800	11.7	100	100
Current liabilities						
Accounts payable	$126,400	$118,800	$ 7,600	6.4	13.3	14.0
Notes payable	32,200	40,200	(8,000)	(19.9)	3.4	4.7
Taxes	58,500	47,600	10,900	22.9	6.2	5.6
Total current liabilities	$217,100	$206,600	$10,500	5.1	22.9	24.3
Noncurrent liabilities						
Mortgage	$242,400	$249,300	($ 6,900)	(2.8)	25.5	29.3
Bonds payable	$289,000	292,700	($ 3,700)	(1.3)	30.4	34.4
Total noncurrent liabilities	$531,400	$542,000	($10,600)	(2.0)	55.9	63.7
Total liabilities	$748,500	$748,600	($ 100)	(0.01)	78.8	88.0
Owners' equity	$201,500	$101,600	$99,900	98.3	21.2	12.0
Total liabilities and owners' equity	$950,000	$850,200	$99,800	11.7	100	100

Exercises 10.2

1. Complete the following income statement including vertical analysis. Round answers to the nearest tenth.

Sales revenue			Percent
Gross sales		$982,000	103.0
Less: sales returns and allowances		(28,400)	3.0
Net sales		$953,600	100.0
Cost of goods sold			
Beginning inventory	$ 89,400		
Purchases	691,500		
Less: returns and allowances	(14,900)		
Goods available for sale	766,000		
Less: ending inventory	(97,400)		
Cost of goods sold		$668,600	70.1
Gross profit on sales		$285,000	29.9

Operating expenses		
Salaries	$ 76,000	8.0
Rent	18,000	1.9
Utilities	12,200	1.3
Supplies	8,700	0.9
Advertising	22,300	2.3
Depreciation	45,800	4.8
Administrative	12,100	1.3
Total operating expenses	$195,100	20.5
Operating income	$ 89,900	9.4
Taxes	39,900	4.2
Net income	$ 50,000	5.2

---

3. Complete the following income statements including horizontal analysis. Round answers to the nearest tenth.

	Current Year	Previous Year	Increase (Decrease) Amount	Increase (Decrease) Percent	Percent Current Year	Percent Previous Year
Sales revenue						
Gross sales	$878,400	$859,800	$18,600	2.2	101.5	101.8
Less: sales returns and allowances	(13,400)	(14,800)	(1,400)	(9.5)	1.5	1.8
Net sales	$865,000	$845,000	$20,000	2.4	100.0	100.0
Cost of goods sold						
Beginning inventory	$ 78,400	$ 86,800	($8,400)	(9.7)		
Purchases	630,400	639,750	(9,350)	(1.5)		
Less: returns and allowances	(18,800)	(14,400)	4,400	30.6		
Goods available for sale	690,000	$712,150	(22,150)	(3.1)		
Less: ending inventory	(84,500)	(78,400)	6,100	7.8		
Cost of goods sold	$605,500	$633,750	($28,250)	(4.5)	70.0	75.0
Gross profit on sales	$259,500	$211,250	$48,250	22.8	30.0	25.0
Operating expenses						
Salaries	$ 47,300	$ 54,600	$(7,300)	(13.4)	5.5	6.5
Rent	8,200	8,200	$ 0	0	0.9	1.0
Utilities	6,900	7,100	$ (200)	(2.8)	0.8	0.8
Supplies	8,400	8,900	$ (500)	(5.6)	1.0	1.1
Advertising	11,900	13,400	$(1,500)	(11.2)	1.4	1.6
Depreciation	12,200	12,800	$ (600)	(4.7)	1.4	1.5
Administrative	8,900	9,600	$ (700)	(7.3)	1.0	1.1
Total operating expense	$103,800	$114,600	($10,800)	(9.4)	12.0	13.6
Operating income	$155,700	$ 96,650	$59,050	61.1	18.0	11.4
Taxes	69,200	$ 38,950	$30,250	77.7	8.0	4.6
Net income	$ 86,500	$ 57,700	$28,800	49.9	10.0	6.8

Exercises 10.3

	Ratio or Comparison	*Calculation*	*Financial Statements*
1.	Return on average total assets =	$\dfrac{\text{net income}}{\text{average total assets}}$	income statement balance sheet
3.	Operating ratio =	$\dfrac{\text{cost of goods sold} + \text{operating expenses}}{\text{net sales}}$	income statement income statement

5. Accounts receivable turnover $= \dfrac{\text{net sales}}{\text{average accounts receivable}}$ $\dfrac{\text{income statement}}{\text{balance sheet}}$

7. Debt ratio $= \dfrac{\text{total debt}}{\text{total assets}}$ $\dfrac{\text{balance sheet}}{\text{balance sheet}}$

9. Debt-to-equity ratio $= \dfrac{\text{total debt}}{\text{total owners' equity}}$ $\dfrac{\text{balance sheet}}{\text{balance sheet}}$

11. Times interest earned $= \$194{,}500 \div \$22{,}400 = 8.7$ times **13.** Current ratio $= \$382{,}900 \div \$187{,}600 = 2.0$

15. Average Age of accounts receivable $= 365 \div 8.3 = 44.0$ days **17.** Equity ratio $= \$417{,}900 \div \$796{,}800 = 52.4\%$

19. Quick ratio $= \$194{,}300 \div \$187{,}600 = 1.04$

Exercises 10.4

1. Each partner receives $\frac{1}{2} \times \$18{,}000 = \$9000$ **3.** Petrich—$70\% \times \$8000 = \$5600$; Quince—$30\% \times \$8000 = \$2400$

5. South—$(\$20{,}000 \times 9\%) + 20\%(\$4800 - \$1800) = \$2400$. Other partners—$40\% \times (\$4800 - \$1800) = \$1200$ each

7. Without a formal partnership agreement all profits are divided equally, so each gets $\frac{1}{3} \times \$12{,}000 = \$6000$.

9. Andrews $= (\$8000 \times 8\%) + \frac{1}{2}[\$12{,}000 - (\$7000 + (\$8000 \times 8\%) + (\$10{,}000 \times 8\%))] = \$2420$
   Bostich $= \$7000$ salary $+ (\$10{,}000 \times 8\%) + [\$12{,}000 - (\$7000 + (\$8000 \times 8\%) + (\$10{,}000 \times 8\%))]\frac{1}{2} = \$9580$

Review Exercises/Chapter 10

1. Refer to text. **3.** Owners' equity—$\$472{,}700$; inventory—$\$137{,}400$; total assets—$\$1{,}188{,}600$.

5. a. 0.92 **b.** 1.09 **c.** 3.83 **d.** 4.36.

Part Two

Cumulative Review Exercises

1. $18.50/case—save $0.02/can **3.** Discount $= 0.496$; price $= \$1134.00$

5. $30.53 **7.** $M = \$5.99$; $C = \$13.97$

9. $1452 to supplier; chair $= \$181.50$ **11.** $4.50 loss

13. $29,080 **15.** 3.05

17. Dartan—$2116.31; Arty—$1075.69; Ports—$608.00 **19.** $9200

21. $1800 **23.** A $= \$1830$; B $= \$780$; C $= \$8390$

25. Goldman $= \$16{,}531$
   Silverman $= \$16{,}154$

27. Charge $86.13
   Below cost $4.31

29. $13,400

31. a. $14,100
   b. $19,740
   c. $19,740
   d. 0

Exercises 11.2

1. $\begin{aligned} I &= \$100 \times 6\% \times 2 \\ &= \$100 \times 0.12 \\ &= \$12 \end{aligned}$

3. $\begin{aligned} I &= \$100(6\%)\left(\dfrac{60}{360}\right) \\ &= \$100(0.01) \\ &= \$1.00 \end{aligned}$

5. $\begin{aligned} I &= \$800(0.08)(2) \\ &= \$800(0.16) \\ &= \$128 \end{aligned}$

7. $\begin{aligned} I &= \$1000(0.01)(4) \\ &= \$40 \end{aligned}$

9. $\begin{aligned} I &= \$1000(6\%)(2) \\ &= \$1000(0.12) \\ &= \$120 \end{aligned}$

11. $\begin{aligned} I &= \$5000(9\%)(1) \\ &= \$5000(0.09) \\ &= \$450 \end{aligned}$

13. $I = \$1000(6.39\%)(5)$
$= \$319.50$

15. $I = \$1000(12\%)\left(\dfrac{146}{365}\right)$
$= \$48$

17. $I = \$10,000(7.3\%)\left(\dfrac{15}{365}\right)$
$\doteq \$30$

19. $I = \$1000(8.5\%)(4)$
$= \$340$

21. $I = \$100(18\%)\left(\dfrac{60}{360}\right) = \$3$

23. $\$4.80 = \$80(r)(1)$
$\dfrac{\$4.80}{\$80} = r$
$0.06 = r$, or $r = 6\%$

25. $I = \$600(5\frac{1}{4}\%)(4)$
$= \$126$

27. $\$80 = \$200(5\%)(t)$
$\$80 = \$10t$
$8 = t\text{(years)}$

Exercises 11.3

1. $A = \$100\left(1 + 10\% \times \dfrac{1}{2}\right)$
$= \$100(1.05)$
$= \$105$

3. $A = \$100\left(1 + 10\% \times \dfrac{90}{360}\right)$
$= \$100(1 + 0.025)$
$= \$102.50$

5. $A = \$300\left(1 + 8\% \times \dfrac{9}{4}\right)$
$= \$300(1 + 0.18)$
$= \$354$

7. $P = \dfrac{\$1000}{1 + 9\% \times 2}$
$= \dfrac{\$1000}{1 + 0.18}$
$= \dfrac{\$1000}{1.18}$
$= \$847.46$

9. $P = \dfrac{\$1000}{1 + 9\% \times \frac{1}{4}}$
$= \dfrac{\$1000}{1 + 0.0225}$
$= \$978$

11. $P = \dfrac{\$1600}{1 + 6\% \times 1\frac{1}{2}}$
$= \dfrac{\$1000}{1 + 0.09}$
$= \dfrac{\$1600}{1.09}$
$= \$1467.89$

13. $A = \$700(1 + 9\% \times 2)$
$= \$700(1.18)$
$= \$826$

15. $A = \$1000(1 + 12.6\% \times \frac{1}{2})$
$= \$1000(1 + 0.063)$
$= \$1063$

17. $A = \$1800(1 + 8\% \times \frac{3}{4})$
$= \$1800(1 + 0.06)$
$= \$1908$

19. $A = 850\left(1 + 12\% \times \dfrac{5}{12}\right)$
$= \$850(1.05)$
$= \$892.50$

21. $A = \$2000(1 + 8\% \times 3)$
$= \$2000(1 + 0.24)$
$= \$2480$

23. $A = \$1800\left(1 + 9\% \times \dfrac{6}{12}\right)$
$= \$1800(1 + 0.045)$
$= \$1881$

25. $P = \dfrac{\$2000}{1 + 10\% \times 10}$
$= \dfrac{\$2000}{1 + 1}$
$= \$1000$

27. $\$300 = \$200(1 + r \times 5)$
$\$300 = \$200 + \$1000r$
$\$100 = \$1000r$
$\dfrac{\$100}{\$1000} = r$
$0.10 = r$
$r = 10\%$

29. $P = \dfrac{\$1120}{1 + 6\% \times 2}$
$= \dfrac{\$1120}{1.12}$
$= \$1000$

Exercises 11.4

1. Apr. $11 \rightarrow$ 101
Feb. $3 \rightarrow -34$
Term $\quad$ 67 days

3. May $15 \rightarrow$ 135
Jan. $10 \rightarrow -10$
Term $\quad$ 125 days

5. Oct. $10 \rightarrow$ 283
Apr. $10 \rightarrow -100$
Term $\quad$ 183 days

7. May $31 \rightarrow$ 151
Mar. $10 \rightarrow -69$
Term $\quad$ 82 days

9. Nov. $12 \rightarrow$ 316
Aug. $10 \rightarrow -222$
Term $\quad$ 94 days

11. May 5 is day 125 of 1982. (240 days remain in 1982.) August 31 is day 243 of 1983. The term is $240 + 243 = 483$ days.

13. Mar. 12 → 71
$$\frac{+60}{131}$$
May 11 is the maturity date.

17. Nov. 6 → 310
$$\frac{+29}{\text{Dec. } 5 \leftarrow 339}$$

15

Loan Date	Elapsed Months
Aug. 10	0
Sept. 10	1
Oct. 10	2
Nov. 10	3
Dec. 10	4

Maturity date is Dec. 10.

19. $I = \$1000(9\%)\left(\dfrac{60}{360}\right) = \$15,\ A = \$1000 + \$15 = \$1015$

21. $I = \$200(12\%)\left(\dfrac{60}{360}\right) = \$4,\ A = \$204$ **23.** $I = \$500(10\%)\left(\dfrac{36}{360}\right) = \$5,\ A = \$505$

25. Apr. 1 → 91
$$\frac{+180}{271}$$
Due Sept. 28
Robert owes \$525 on Sept. 28.

$A = \$500\left(1 + 10\% \times \dfrac{180}{360}\right)$
$= \$500(1 + 0.05)$
$= \$525$

27. May 2 → 122
$$\frac{+45}{167}$$
Due June 16

$A = \$5000\left(1 + 8\% \times \dfrac{45}{360}\right)$
$= \$5000(1 + 0.01)$
$= 5050$

Review Exercises/Chapter 11

1. $I = \$750 \times 0.01 = \$7.50$

5. $A = \$5000(1 + 0.09 \times 3) = \$5000(1.27) = \$6350$

9. Exact year, it will give a smaller amount of interest.

3. $P = \dfrac{\$1000}{1 + (0.10)(2)} = \dfrac{\$1000}{1.2} = \$833.33$

7. $\$20 = \$500(0.08)t$
$= \$40t$
$\frac{1}{2} = t(\text{year})$

11. $744 = 600(1 + 0.12t)$
$= 600 + 72t$
$144 = 72t$
$2 = t(\text{years})$

Exercises 12.1

1. $B = \$1000(8\%)(1) = \$80;\ D = \$1000 - \$80 = \$920$

3. $B = \$1000(8\%)(5) = \$400;\ D = \$1000 - \$400 = \$600$

5. $B = \$500(10\%)(\frac{1}{2}) = \$25;\ D = \$500 - \$25 = \$475$

7. $B = \$600(5\%)(1.5) = \$45;\ D = \$600 - \$45 = \$555$

9. $D = \$600(1 - 5\% \times \frac{6}{12}) = 600(0.975) = \$585$

11. $D = \$500(1 - 7\% \times \frac{13}{52}) = \$500(0.9825) = \$491.25$

13. $D = \$1175(1 - 0.14) = \$1175(0.86) = \$1010.50$

15. $A = \dfrac{\$6000}{1 - 10\% \times \frac{90}{360}} = \dfrac{\$6000}{0.975} = \$6153.85$

17. $A = \dfrac{\$1200}{1 - 13\% \times \frac{6}{52}} = \dfrac{\$1200}{0.985} = \$1218.27$

19. $D = \$800(1 - 9\% \times \frac{30}{360}) = \$800(0.9925) = \$794;\ \$800$

21. $D = 10,000(1 - 6.5\% \times \frac{2}{52}) = \$10,000(0.9975) = \$9975$

23. $D = \$500(1 - 10\% \times 2) = \$500(0.8) = \$400$

25. Interest $(B) = \$30;\ 30 = 1000(d)(\frac{1}{2})$
$30 = 500d$
$d = 0.06,\ \text{or } 6\%$

27. Interest $(B) = \$60;\ 60 = 500(d)(2)$
$60 = 1000d$
$d = 0.06,\ \text{or } 6\%$

29. $D = \$5000(1 - 9\% \times \frac{1}{12})$
$= \$5000(0.9925)$
$= \$4962.50$

Exercises 12.2

1. $A = \$1000(1 + 0.08 \times 1) = \$1080;\ D = \$1080(1 - 0.10 \times \frac{1}{2}) = \$1026$

3. $A = \$5000(1 + 0.06 \times \frac{1}{2}) = \$5150;\ D = \$5150(1 - 0.09 \times \frac{1}{9}) = \$5098.50$

5. **a.** $A = \$1000(1 + 9\% \times \frac{4}{12}) = \$1000(1.03) = \$1030$

  b. The remaining time is 1 month. $D = \$1030(1 - 12\% \times \frac{1}{12}) = \$1030(0.99) = \$1019.70$

7. a. $A = \$800(1 + 9\% \times \frac{90}{360}) = \$800(1.0225) = \$818$

  b. The remaining time is 30 days. $D = \$818(1 - 12 \times \frac{30}{360}) = \$818(0.99) = \$809.82$

  c. The note was \$800 and the Misc. Co. received \$809.82. Hence, they earned \$9.82.

  d. The total amount of interest is \$18 of which \$9.82 was earned by Misc. Co. Hence, the bank received \$18 − \$9.82 = \$8.18.

  e. Since the note was sold *with recourse*, Misc. Co. must pay the bank and attempt to collect.

9. a. $A = \$2000(1 + 9\% \times \frac{90}{360}) = \$2000(1.0225) = \$2045$

  b. March 1 → day 60 + 90 days = day 150 → May 30. May 30 is the due date.

  c. May 30 (due date)   → day 150

   Apr. 24 (discount date) → day 114

      discount term → $\overline{ 36 \text{ days}}$

   $D = \$2045(1 - 0.10 \times \frac{36}{360}) = \$2045(0.99) = \$2024.55$

  d. Smith Supply would have gotten \$2045 at maturity but accepted \$2024.55. They lost \$20.45.

Exercises 12.3

1. $r = \dfrac{0.01}{1 - 0.01} = \dfrac{0.01}{0.99} = 1.0101\%$

3. $r = \dfrac{0.03}{1 - 0.03} = \dfrac{0.03}{0.97} = 3.09278\%$

5. $r = \dfrac{0.045}{0.955} = 4.71204\%$

7. $r = \dfrac{\$10}{\$100 \times 1} = \dfrac{10}{100} = 0.10, \text{ or } 10\%$

9. $r = \dfrac{\$20}{\$1000 \times \frac{90}{360}} = \dfrac{\$20}{\$250} = 0.08, \text{ or } 8\%$

11. $r = \dfrac{\$7.50}{\$600 \times \frac{45}{360}} = \dfrac{\$7.50}{\$75} = 0.10, \text{ or } 10\%$

13. $r = \dfrac{0.20}{1 - 0.20} = 0.25 \text{ or } 25\%, \text{ yes.}$

15. $r = \dfrac{\$20}{\$1000 \times \frac{20}{360}} = \dfrac{\$20}{55.555} = 0.36, \text{ or } 36\%$

17. $r = \dfrac{\$60}{\$500} = 12\%$

Review Exercises / Chapter 12

1. $B = \$10,000(0.08)(5) = \$4000$

3. $A = \dfrac{\$850}{1 - 0.09 \times \frac{1}{3}} = \dfrac{\$850}{0.97} = \$876.29$

5. Amount of interest = \$60. $\$60 = \$2000(d)(\frac{1}{2})$, $d = 6\%$. Effective rate $r = \dfrac{\$60}{\$1940 \times \frac{1}{2}} = \dfrac{\$60}{\$970} = 6.19\%$ (rounded)

7. $A = \$600(1 + 0.10 \times \frac{1}{8}) = \$607.50$; $D = \$607.50(1 - 0.14 \times \frac{15}{360}) = \$603.96$

9. $r = \dfrac{0.08}{1 - 0.08} = 8.70\%$ rounded

Exercises 13.1

1. 1.47746

3. 2.41171

5. $A = \$1000(1 + \frac{3}{4}\%)^{24} = \$1000(1.19641) = \$1196.41$

7. $A = \$100(1 + 6\%)^2 = \$100(1.12360) = \$112.36$

9. $A = \$100(1 + 1\frac{1}{2}\%)^8 = \$100(1.12649) = \$112.65$

11. $A = \$1000(1 + 5\frac{1}{4}\%)^{20} = \$1000(2.78254) = \$2782.54$

13. $A = \$10,000(1 + \frac{3}{4}\%)^{36} = \$10,000(1.30864) = \$13,086.40$

15. $A = \$2000(1 + 9\% \times 2) = \$2000(1.18) = \$2360$ at simple interest

   $A = \$2000(1 + 2\frac{1}{4}\%)^8 = \$2000(1.19483) = \$2389.66$ at compound interest

17. $A = \$10,000(1 + 2\%)^6 = \$10,000(1.12616) = \$11,261.60$

19. $A = \$2(1 + 5\%)^{40} = \$2(7.03999) = \$14.08$. He lost \$12.08.

21. The future value of \$2000 is $A = \$2000(1 + \frac{1}{2}\%)^{12} = \$2123.36$.

   You would have \$23.36 more by accepting it now and earning interest rather than taking \$2100 a year from now.

23. $A = \$1000(1.013028415) = \$1013.03$.

25. From March 3 to September 1 = 182 days. $A = \$500(1.026521806) = \$513.26$.

27. $e^{0.27} = 1.30996$

29. $e^{(7\%)(2)} = e^{0.14} = 1.15027$

31. $A = \$1000e^{(6\%)(3)} = \$1000e^{0.18} = \$1000(1.19722) = \$1197.22$

33. $A = \$800e^{(4\%)(\frac{1}{2})} = \$800e^{0.02} = \$800(1.02020) = \$816.16$

35. $A = \$200e^{(4\%)(3)} = \$200e^{0.12} = \$200(1.12750) = \$225.50$

37. $A = \$100e^{(5\frac{1}{4}\%)(4)} = \$100e^{0.21} = \$100(1.23368) = \$123.67$ $A = \$6000\,(1.0003219)\,280 = \$6565.82$

39. $A = \$1000e^{(5\%)(3)} = \$1000e^{0.15} = \$1000(1.16183) = \$1161.83$

41. $A = \$6000\,(1.0003219)^{280} = \$6565.82$ **43. a.** 6   **b.** 4.

Exercises 13.2

1. By Table I, $\dfrac{1}{(1 + 3\%)^5} = \dfrac{1}{1.15927} = 0.8626118$

3. By Table III, $\dfrac{1}{e^{(3\%)(10)}} = \dfrac{1}{e^{0.3}} = \dfrac{1}{1.34986} = 0.74082$

5. $P = \dfrac{\$100}{(1 + 3\frac{1}{2}\%)^6} = \dfrac{\$100}{1.22926} = \$81.35$

7. $P = \dfrac{\$100}{e^{(7\%)(3)}} = \dfrac{\$100}{e^{0.21}} = \dfrac{\$100}{1.23368} = \$81.06$

9. $P = \dfrac{\$500}{(1 + 2\%)^8} = \dfrac{\$500}{1.17166} = \$426.74$

11. a. $P = \dfrac{\$2000}{(1 + 9\%)^2} = \dfrac{\$2000}{(1.09)^2} = \dfrac{\$2000}{1.1881} = \$1683.36$ Long computation required because 9% not in Table I.

    b. $P = \dfrac{\$2000}{(1 + 2\frac{1}{4}\%)^8} = \dfrac{\$2000}{1.19483} = \$1673.88$ **c.** $P = \dfrac{\$2000}{e^{(9\%)(2)}} = \dfrac{\$2000}{e^{0.18}} = \dfrac{\$2000}{1.19722} = \$1670.54$

13. $P = \dfrac{\$10,000}{e^{(5\%)(20)}} = \dfrac{\$10,000}{e^1} = \dfrac{\$10,000}{2.71828} = \$3678.80$

15. \$300; the present value of \$330 is only \$292.95.

Exercises 13.3

1. $r = (1 + 3\%)^2 - 1 = 1.06090 - 1 = 0.06090$, or 6.09%

3. $r = (1 + \frac{1}{2}\%)^{12} - 1 = 1.06168 - 1 = 0.06168$, or 6.168%

5. $r = \dfrac{6\%}{100\% - 6\%} = \dfrac{0.06}{0.94} = 0.0638297$, or 6.38297%

7. $r = (1 + 2\frac{1}{4}\%)^4 - 1 = 1.09308 - 1 = 0.09308$, or 9.308%

9. $r = e^{9\%} - 1 = e^{0.09} - 1 = 1.09417 - 1 = 0.09417$, or 9.417%

11. $r = (1 + 5\frac{1}{4}\%/365)^{365} - 1 = 1.053898584 - 1 = 0.053898584$, or 5.39%

13. 10.669%

Review Exercises/Chapter 13

1. 2.66584   **3.** 1.37713   **5.** $\dfrac{1}{1.70814} = 0.5854321$

7. $A = \$500(1 + 6\%)^{12} = \$500(2.01220) = \$1006.10$ **9.** $A = \$500e^{0.72} = \$500(2.05443) = \$1027.22$

11. $P = \dfrac{\$600}{(1 + 1\%)^{48}} = \dfrac{\$600}{1.61222} = \$372.16$ **13.** $r = (1 + 5\%)^2 - 1 = 0.1025 = 10.25\%$

15. $A = \$900(1 + 2\%)^{12} = \$900(1.26824) = \$1141.42$ **17.** Accept \$1700; the present value of \$2000 is only \$1576.99.

19. $A = \$750(1 + 4\%)^{32} = \$750(3.50806) = \$2631.05$ **21.** 10.516 daily; 10.517% continuous

---

Exercises 14.1

1. a. The rate fraction in the level method is one over the number of payments for each payment. It is $\frac{1}{5}$ for each.

    b. Rule of 78's.

3. a. $R = \dfrac{\$300 + \$21}{6} = \$53.50$

    b. $\frac{1}{6} \times \$21 = \$3.50$ for each of the 6 payments

    c. Rule of 78's

Payment Number	Fraction
1	$\frac{5}{15}$
2	$\frac{4}{15}$
3	$\frac{3}{15}$
4	$\frac{2}{15}$
5	$\frac{1}{15}$
Sum = 15 (denominator)	

Payment Number	Fraction	Interest per Payment
1	$\frac{6}{21}$	$(\frac{6}{21} \times \$21) = \$6.00$
2	$\frac{5}{21}$	\$5.00
3	$\frac{4}{21}$	\$4.00
4	$\frac{3}{21}$	\$3.00
5	$\frac{2}{21}$	\$2.00
6	$\frac{1}{21}$	\$1.00
Sum = 21		Total $I = \$21.00$

    d. Effective rate = 24%, Table 23.75%

    e. Level = \$10.50, rule of 78's = \$15

5. $P = \$450 - \$50 = \$400$

a. $R = \dfrac{\$400 + \$96}{12} = \$41.33$

b. Rule of 78's

Payment No.	Fraction	Interest per Period	
1	$\frac{12}{78}$	$14.77	⎫
2	$\frac{11}{78}$	$13.54	⎪
3	$\frac{10}{78}$	$12.31	⎬ Total for first 6 payments = $70.17
4	$\frac{9}{78}$	$11.08	⎪
5	$\frac{8}{78}$	$ 9.85	⎪
6	$\frac{7}{78}$	$ 8.62	⎭
⋮	⋮	Paid off	
12	$\frac{1}{78}$		
Sum = 78			

c. $r = \dfrac{(2)(12)(\$96)}{(\$400)(12 + 1)} = \dfrac{2304}{5200} = 44.31\%$

7. a. Installment cost $= \$119.92 \times 48 = \$5756.16$ **b.** Interest $= \$5756.16 - \$4427.47 = \$1328.69$

c. $r = \dfrac{(2)(12)(\$1328.69)}{(\$4427.47)(48 + 1)} = \dfrac{31888.56}{216946.03} = 14.7\%$, Table 13.75%

9. The return would be the same, because the loan was not repaid early. The two methods apportion the interest differently; they do not determine how much it is.

Exercises 14.2

1. $R = \dfrac{\$1000 + \$80}{12} = \$90$

3. $R = \dfrac{\$5000 + \$500}{24} = \$229.17$

5. $R = \dfrac{\$1000 + \$270}{6} = \$211.67$

7. $I = (\$800)(6\%)(2) = \$96$

$R = \dfrac{\$896}{24} = \$37.33$

$r = \dfrac{(2)(12)(\$96)}{\$800(24 + 1)} = \dfrac{2304}{20{,}000} = 11.52\%$

9. $I = (\$3000)(5\%)(1.5) = \$225$

$R = \dfrac{\$3225}{18} = \$179.17$

11. $I = (\$1000)(9\%)(\frac{1}{3}) = \$30$

$R = \$257.50$

13. $I = (\$100)(8\%)(\frac{1}{4}) = \$2$; $R = \dfrac{\$102}{3} = \$34$ per month

Rule of 78's

Payment Number	Fraction	Interest per Payment
1	$\frac{3}{6}$	$1.00
2	$\frac{2}{6}$	$0.67
3	$\frac{1}{6}$	$0.33
Sum = 6		Total I = $2.00

Exercises 14.3

1. a. $R = \$1000 \left[\dfrac{\frac{3}{4}\%(1 + \frac{3}{4}\%)^6}{(1 + \frac{3}{4}\%)^6 - 1} \right] = \$1000 \left[\dfrac{(0.0075)(1.04585)}{(1.04585) - 1} \right] = \$171.08$

b. $(171.08 \times 6) - 1000 = \$26.48$

c. $r = 9\%$

3. a. $R = \$2000 \left[\dfrac{1\%(1 + 1\%)^3}{(1 + 1\%)^3 - 1} \right] = \$2000 \left[\dfrac{(0.01)(1.03030)}{(1.03030) - 1} \right] = \$680.07$

b. Amortization Schedule

Payment Number	Principal Remaining	Amount R	Amount of Interest	Amount Paid on Principal
1	$2000	$680.07	$20	$660.07
2	$1339.93	$680.07	$13.40	$666.67
3	$ 673.26	$679.99	$ 6.73	$673.26
Total		$2040.13	$40.13	$2000

The last payment should be adjusted to $679.99.

c. The interest paid was $40.13. Yes, they saved $200 − $40.13 = $159.87 by borrowing the money.

5. $I = \$40.13$

Rule of 78's (Problem 3)

Payment Number	Fraction	Interest per Payment
1	$\frac{3}{6}$	$20.07
2	$\frac{2}{6}$	$13.37
3	$\frac{1}{6}$	$ 6.69
Sum = 6		$I = \$40.13$

They are slightly different.

7. There is relatively little difference (no preference). However, as the number of payments and principal increases the rule of 78's takes out significantly more at the beginning.

9. 12% add-on, $120 versus $66.19 as shown in Example 4, p. 328

11. $R = \$200 \left[\dfrac{1\frac{1}{2}\% (1 + 1\frac{1}{2}\%)^4}{(1 + 1\frac{1}{2}\%)^4 - 1} \right]$

   $= \$200 [0.259445] = \$51.89$

13. a. $25.48

   b. $200

15. a. $16,400   **b.** $R = \$65,600 [0.01457641] = \$956.21$

17. a. $0   **b.** $R = \$82,000 [0.01457641] = \$1195.27$

19. $956.21. Same as 15 except balance due at the end of 5 years.

21. a. $R = \$100,000 [0.0151743] = \$1517.43$ **b.** $455,229.00

23. a. $R = \$100,000 [0.00644301] = \$644.30$ **b.** $193,290.43

Exercises 14.4

1. $R = \$1000 \left[\dfrac{1\%}{(1 + 1\%)^{24} - 1} \right] = \$1000 \left[\dfrac{0.01}{1.26973 - 1} \right] = \$37.07$

3. $R = \$10,000 \left[\dfrac{2\%}{(1 + 2\%)^{20} - 1} \right] = \$10,000 \left[\dfrac{0.02}{1.48595 - 1} \right] = \$411.56$

5. $R = \$5000 \left[\dfrac{\frac{1}{2}\%}{(1 + \frac{1}{2}\%)^{18} - 1} \right] = \$5000 \left[\dfrac{0.005}{1.09393 - 1} \right] = \$266.16$

7. $A = \$5000(1 + 3\%)^8 = \$5000(1.26677) = \$6333.85$

   $R = \$6333.85 \left[\dfrac{1\%}{(1 + 1\%)^8 - 1} \right] = \$6333.85 \left[\dfrac{0.01}{1.08286 - 1} \right] = \$764.40$

9. $R = \$500,000 \left[\dfrac{5\%}{(1 + 5\%)^{20} - 1} \right] = \$500,000 \left[\dfrac{0.05}{2.65330 - 1} \right] = \$15,121.27$

11. $R = \$10,000 [0.011290]$

   $= \$112.90$ per month

Exercises 14.5

1. $P = \$600\,(7.360087) = \$4416.05$

3. $P = \$10,000\,(8.110896) = \$81108.96$

5. $F = \$800\,(15.464032) = \$12371.23$

7. **a.** $P = \$100\,(37.973958) = \$3797.40$

   b. $A = \$3797.40\,(1 + 1\%)^{48} = \$3797.40\,(1.61222) = \$6122.24$

   c. $F. = \$100\,(61.222604) = \$6122.26$

9. $P = \$200\,(12.770552) = \$2554.11$

11. $P = \$500\,(21.889145) = \$10,944.57$

   $P = \$4000/(1 + \frac{3}{4}\%)^{36} = \$3,056.61$

   Present value is $\$14,001.18$

13. $F = \$500\,(29.778077) = \$14,889.04$

15. $F = \$300\,(44.501998) = \$13,350.60$

Review Exercises Chapter 14

1. **a.** $213   **b.** $13 per month   **c.** $19.50, $13, $6.50   **d.** 39%   **e.** $26   **f.** $32.50

3. **a.** $171.69   **c.** $15.07   **d.** 18.08%

5. **a.** $750   **b.** $5750   **c.** $159.72   **d.** 9.73%

7. $266.71

Exercises 15.1

1. $\$1000 \times 0.085 = \$85.00$

3. $\$1000 \times 0.0475 = \$47.50$

5. $\$1000 \times 0.09 = \$90.00$

7. $\$1000 \times 0.0625 = \$62.50$

9. $\$10,000 \times 0.04 = \$400.00$

11. $(\$1000 \times 0.044) \div 2 = \$22.00$

13. $(\$1000 \times 0.0585) = \$58.50$

15. $(\$1000 \times 0.06) \div 4 = \$15.00$

17. $(\$100 \times 0.0275) = \$2.75$

19. $(\$1000 \times 0.05) \div 2 = \$25.00$

21. $\$10,000,000 \times 0.0525 = \$525,000.00$

Exercises 15.2

1. $\$1030 - \$1000 = \$30$ premium

3. $\$1000 - \$995 = (\$5)$ discount

5. $\$1000 - \$1000 = 0$ (i.e., no premium or discount)

7. $\$85 \div \$1030 = 8.25\%$

9. $\$75 \div \$500 = 15\%$

11. $(\$1000 \times 0.1075) \div 0.095 = \$1131.58$

13. $(\$1000 \times 0.0875) \div 0.095 = \$921.05$

15. $(\$1000 \times 0.12) \div 0.095 = \$1263.16$

17. $1000 face value - $985 quoted price = ($15) discount

$(\$1000 \times 0.08) \div \$985 = 8.1\%$ current yield

19. $460 quoted price + $40 discount = $500 face value

$(\$500 \times 0.065) \div \$460 = 7.07\%$ current yield

21. $675 quoted price + $325 discount = $1000 face value

$(\$1000 \times 0.055) \div \$675 = 8.1\%$ current yield

23. $(\$1000 \times 0.105) \div 0.095 = \$1105.26$ current price

$\$1105.26 - \$1000$ face value $= \$105.26$ premium

25. Current yield $= \dfrac{\text{interest}}{\text{current price}}$

$9\% = \dfrac{(\$1000 \times \text{coupon rate})}{\$1050}$, or $\dfrac{(0.09)(\$1050)}{\$1000} = $ coupon rate   Coupon rate $= 9.45\%$.

27. $1060 purchase price - $1000 face value = $60 premium

Avg. annual return $= (\$1000 \times 0.125) - (\$60 \text{ premium} \div 5 \text{ years}) = \$113$

29. $1000 face value - $960 purchase price = ($40) discount

Avg. return $= (\$1000 \times 0.075) + (\$40 \text{ discount} \div 10 \text{ years}) = \$79.00$

31. $1000 face value - $988 purchase price = ($12) discount

Avg. return $= (\$1000 \times 0.085) + (\$12 \text{ discount} \div 4 \text{ years}) = \$88.00$

33. $\dfrac{\$1000 + \$990}{2} = \$995$

35. $\dfrac{\$500 + \$520}{2} = \$510$

37. $\dfrac{\$1000 + \$984}{2} = \$992$

39. $\dfrac{(\$1000 \text{ face value} \times 0.085 \text{ coupon rate}) + (\$20 \text{ discount} \div 4 \text{ years})}{(\$1000 + \$980) \div 2} = \dfrac{\$85.00 + \$5}{\$990} = 9.09\%$

41. $\dfrac{(\$500 \times 0.045) + (\$100 \div 4)}{(\$500 + \$400) \div 2} = 10.56\%$

43. $\dfrac{(\$1000 \times 0.099) - (\$6 \div 6)}{(\$1000 + \$1006) \div 2} = 9.77\%$

45. $\dfrac{(\$1000 \times 0.079) + (\$80 \div 4)}{(\$1000 + \$920) \div 2} = 10.31\%$

47. Bond A $\dfrac{(\$1000 \times 0.0925) + (\$30 \div 6 \text{ years})}{(\$1000 + \$970) \div 2} = 9.90\%$ Bond B $\dfrac{(\$1000 \times 0.105) - (\$40 \div 4 \text{ years})}{(\$1000 + \$1040) \div 2} = 9.31\%$

Buy Bond A. better return.

49. ($1000 × 0.072) × 2/12 = $12.00 accrued interest
Selling price = $960 + $12 = $972

51. ($1000 × 0.144) × 1/12 = $12.00 accrued interest
Selling price = $1060 + $12 = $1072

53. ($1000 × 0.084) × 1/12 = $7.00 accrued interest
Selling price = $990 + $7.00 = $997

55. ($1000 × 0.132) × 1/12 = $11.00 accrued interest
Selling price = $1000 + $11 = $1011

57. ($1000 × 0.06) × 5/12 = $25.00 accrued interest
Selling price = $980 + $25.00 = $1005

59. ($1000 × 0.055) = $55.00 for 1 year

Exercises 15.3

Baker Manufacturing Company

1. $\dfrac{\$3,000,000 \text{ earnings}}{500,000 \text{ shares}} = \$6.00$ per share of common stock

3. $3,000,000 earnings

−$2,000,000	reinvested
$1,000,000	available for dividends
−$ 120,000	preferred dividends
$ 880,000	available for common stock dividends

5. $6.00 per share. i.e., 6% × $100 par value.

Anders Company

7. $100,000 earnings − ($75,000 reinvested + $7000 pfd. div.) = $18,000.
$18,000 ÷ 25,000 shares = $0.72 per share.

9. $100,000 total earnings × 75% = $75,000 reinvested.

Exercises 15.4

1. $76 − $38 = ($38) loss
$38 ÷ $76 = (50%) loss

3. $22 − $22 = 0, or no gain or loss ; 0% gain or loss

5. $75 − $50 = ($25) loss
$25 ÷ $75 = ($33\frac{1}{3}$%) loss

7. $38.00 loss + $3.80 dividend (gain) = $34.20 loss
$34.20 ÷ $75 = (45.6%) loss

9. Purchase price = $12.00 + $\dfrac{\$35}{100 \text{ shares}}$ = $12.35 per share

Selling price = $16.00 − $\dfrac{\$42}{100 \text{ shares}}$ = $15.58

Gain = $15.58 − $12.35 = $3.23 per share; $\dfrac{\$3.23}{\$12.35} = 26.2\%$

11. Cost = $78.50 + $\dfrac{\$85}{100 \text{ shares}}$ = $79.35

Sold = $84.75 − $\dfrac{\$95}{100 \text{ shares}}$ = $83.80

Gain = ($83.80 − $79.35 = $4.45) + $0.25 dividend = $4.70; or $4.70 ÷ $79.35 = 5.9%

13. $1.80 ÷ $18 = 10%   **15.** $4.35 ÷ $87 = 5%   **17.** $4.20 ÷ $56 = 7.5%   **19.** $2.64 ÷ $33 = 8%

21. Stock A   Stock B   Stock C

$\dfrac{\$7.80}{\$192} = 4.1\%$ $\dfrac{\$2.10}{\$36.00} = 5.8\%$ $\boxed{\dfrac{\$1.80}{\$19.75} = 9.1\%}$

23. $\dfrac{\$0.25}{\$19.25} = 1.3\%$ $\dfrac{\$1.00}{\$28.25} = 3.5\%$ $\boxed{\dfrac{\$3.60}{\$47.00} = 7.7\%}$

Review Exercises/Chapter 15

1. $27   **3.** $10,900   **5.** Stock C

7. Pay $596.49; discount = $403.51

9. $932.92   **11.** $6.42 per share or $642.00

Part Three

Cumulative Review Exercises

1. $1000 now   **3. a.** $126   **b.** $10, 8, 6, 4, 2   **c.** 20%   **5.** Stick's, lower effective rate

7. 5%   **9.** Yes: $2.41   **11.** 9 years   **13.** 9.553%

15. $2153.84   **17.** 157 days   **19.** $290.61 per month   **21.** 16.183%

23. 16.422%   **25.** 10.6%   **27.** $22.15 per share; 34.37%

Exercises 16.1

	Yearly	Monthly	Semimonthly	Biweekly	Weekly
1.	—	$1,500	$ 750	$ 692.31	$346.15
3.	$ 7,200	$ 600	—	$ 276.92	$138.46
5.	$11,700	$ 975	$ 487.50	$ 450	—
7.	—	$2,500	$1.250	$1,153.85	$576.92
9.	$15,600	$1,300	$ 650	—	$300.00

11. $22,000 ÷ 12 = $1833.33   **13.** $525 × 26 = $13,650; yes.   **15.** [($575 × 26) ÷ 12] × 10% = $124.58

17. $26,000 ÷ 52 = $500 month   **19.** $750 × 52 = $39,000; yes.

Exercises 16.2

1. 39 hr × $5.75 = $224.25   **3.** 40 hr × $4.30 = $172.00   **5.** 38.25 hr × $3.80 = $145.35

	Mon.	Tues.	Wed.	Thurs.	Fri.	Total
7.	$4\frac{1}{4} + 4\frac{1}{4}$	$4\frac{1}{2} + 4$	$4 + 4$	$4 + 3\frac{3}{4}$	$4 + 4\frac{3}{4}$	$41\frac{1}{2}$
9.	$3\frac{3}{4} + 4\frac{1}{4}$	$3\frac{1}{2} + 4\frac{1}{4}$	$3\frac{1}{4} + 4\frac{3}{4}$	$4 + 4$	$3\frac{1}{2} + 4\frac{1}{4}$	$39\frac{1}{2}$

11. 36 hr × $5.70 = $205.20   **13.** (40 hr × $8.40) + [$1\frac{3}{4}$ hr × ($8.40 + $4.20)] = $345.45

15. (40 hr × $4.50) + [4 hr × ($4.50 + $2.25)] = $207

17. Dale—(40 hr × $4.60) + [$1\frac{3}{4}$ hr × ($4.60 + $2.30)] = $196.08
Mumfry—(40 hr × $8.20) + [$4\frac{1}{2}$ hr × ($8.20 + $4.10)] = $383.35
Starr—(40 hr × $6.20) + [10 hr × ($6.20 + $3.10)] = $341.00

19. $247.00 ÷ 38 hr = $6.50/hr; (38 hr × $6.50) + [2 hr × ($6.50 + $3.25)] = $266.50.

21. Thomas—45 hours, of which 6 are at double time and 5 are at $1\frac{1}{2}$ time, or
(6 hr × $9.20) + (34 hr × $4.60) + [5 hr × ($4.60 + $2.30)] = $246.10.
Doutery—41 hr. of which $7\frac{1}{2}$ is paid at holiday rate of $1\frac{1}{2}$ time, and 1 hr at $1\frac{1}{2}$ for overtime, or
(32.5 hr × $5.80) + [8.5 hr × ($5.80 + $2.90)] = $262.45.
Charms (32 hrs × $6.20) + [8 hrs × ($6.20 + $3.10)] = $272.80

Exercises 16.3

1. 17 × $0.55 = $9.35   **3.** 35 × $0.16 = $5.60   **5.** 23 × $0.20 = $4.60   **7.** 680 × $0.05 = $34.00

9. Hr 1 = 22 × $0.08 = $1.76, or minimum of $3.60
Hr 2 = 32 × $0.08 = $2.56, or minimum of $3.60
Hr 3 = 45 × $0.08 = $3.60, or minimum of $3.60
Hr 4 = 48 × $0.08 = $3.84 $3.84   Total = $14.64

11. Hr 1 = 14 × $0.40 = $5.60
Hr 2 = 15 × $0.40 = $6.00 plus 1 unit × $0.50 = $0.50, or total of $6.50
Hr 3 = 12 × $0.40 = $4.80
Hr 4 = 15 × $0.40 = $6.00 plus 3 units × $0.50 = $1.50, total $7.50
Pay for the morning = $5.60 + $6.50 + $4.80 + $7.50 = $24.40.

13. (3950 × $0.02) + (? × $0.03) = $100; (? × $0.03) = $100 − $79; ? = 700 units. Total units required = 3950 + 700 = 4650.

15. Allen: total of 885 units; (800 × $0.25) + (85 × $0.30) = $225.50
Camp: total of 1092 units; (800 × $0.25) + (292 × $0.30) = $287.60
Erwin: total of 679 units; (679 × $0.25) = $169.75; pay $200.00
Flores: total of 1198 units; (800 × $0.25) + (300 × $0.30) + (98 × $0.35) = $324.30

Exercises 16.4

1. $1800 × 15% = $270
3. $3650 × 9% = $328.50
5. $820 × 35% = $287
7. (4 weeks × $100) + ($12,000 × 12%) = $1840
9. ($2500 × 12%) + ($2500 × 14%) + ($1000 × 16%) = $810
11. $500 + [($10,000 − $5000) × ?] = $1000; ? = 10%
13. ($20,000 × 3%) + ($41,000 × 4%) + $500 bonus = $2740
15. $400 + [($28,000 − $10,000 − $3000) × 3%] = $850
17. $300 + (2% × $16,380) + 0.003($97,640 − $16,380) = $871.38

Exercises 16.5

	F.I.C.A.	Withholding
1.	$1800 × 6.7% = $120.60	$434.20
3.	$1150 × 7.15% = $82.23	$237.80
5.	$2325 × 6.7% = $155.78	$553.90
7.	$1120 × 6.7% = $75.04	$197.30
9.	$ 750 × 7.15% = $53.63	$208.20 + [36% × ($750 − $720)] = $219.00

11. Week 1 = (40 hr × $6.80) + [3 hr × ($6.80 + $3.40)] = $302.60. Week 2 = (40 hr × $6.80) + [4½ hr × ($6.80 + $3.40)] = $317.90. F.I.C.A. = [($302.60 + $317.90) × 6.70%] = $41.57. Withholding = $77.30; net pay = $302.60 + $317.90 − $41.57 − $77.30 − $18.75 = $482.88.

13. Gross pay = $33,650 × 10% = $3365.00. F.I.C.A. = ($39,600 − $38,000) × 7.15% = $114.40. Withholding = [($3365.00 − $2960) × 36%] + $822.10 = $967.90. Net pay = $3365 − $114.40 − $967.90 = $2282.70.

15. Gross pay = (1000 × $0.30) + (150 × $0.35) = $352.50. F.I.C.A. = none; over the limit. Withholding = $48.50. Net pay = $352.50 − $48.50 − $30 − $20 = $254.00.

Review Exercises/Chapter 16

1. $740 biweekly
3. $335
5. $915.95
7. $559.69
9. $444.66
11. $603.63
13. $1468.45

Exercises 17.1

1. $2.16 × 3½% = $0.08
3. $18.29 into Fig. 17.1 = $0.91
5. $189.95 × 4½% = $8.55
7. **a.** $29.95 × 3½% state tax = $1.05 **b.** $29.95 × ½% city tax = $0.15 **c.** $29.95 + $1.05 + $0.15 = $31.15
9. $175 × 5% = $8.75
11. Price = $1.18 ÷ 3% = $39.33
13. Price = $1.00 ÷ 5% = $20.00
15. Mary Jo's share = $11.25 + ($11.25 × 3%) = $11.59   Friend = $19.89 − $11.59 = $8.30
17. Parts price = $124.80 ÷ 1.04 = $120
19. Price = $5.00 ÷ 5% = $100. Total = $100 + $5 = $105
21. Tax rate = $2.70 ÷ $90.00 = 3%

Exercises 17.2

	Percent	$/$100	$/$1000	Mills
1.	3.85	$3.85	$38.50	39
3.	3.95	$3.95	$39.50	40
5.	5.22	$5.22	$52.20	53

7. $72,500 × 45% = $32,625
9. $36,200 × 55% = $19,910
11. $104,000 × 35% = $36,400

13. $500,000 \div $12,500,000 = 0.04, or 4%; $4.00 per $100; $40 per $1000, 40 mills

15. $100,000 \div ($40,000,000 × 50%) = 0.005, or 0.5%   **17.** ($28,000 \div $100) × $4.25 = $1190

19. ($95,000 × 35%) × 5.6% = $1862   **21.** (Fair value × 55%) × 0.025 = $1787.50. Fair value = $130,000

23. ($80,000 × tax rate) = $3200. Tax rate = 0.04, or 4%

25. (Assessed value × 3.75%) = $2250. Assessed value = $60,000. Fair value = $60,000 \div 60% = $100,000

Exercises 17.3

1. Adjusted gross income = $27,000 + 0 = $27,000
Taxable income = $27,000 − 0 − (4 × $1000) = $23,000

3. Adjusted gross income = $35,940 − $1800 = $34,140
Taxable income = $34,140 − $2246 − (4 × $1000) = $27,894

5. Adjusted gross income = $38,942 − $2682 = $36,260
Taxable income = $36,260 − $3412 − (3 × $1000) = $29,848

7. Gross income   **9.** Gross income
11. Deduction   **13.** Gross income
15. Adjustment to income   **17.** $12,767
19. $8906   **21.** $6991

23. Taxable income = ($32,400 + 3600 = $36,000) − (4 × $1000) = $32,000
Tax = $6900

25. Taxable income = ($29,150 − $2000 = $27,150) − (2 × $1000) = $25,150
Tax = $5485

27. Taxable income = ($9800 − $5800 = $4000) − (2 × $1000) = $2000
Tax = 0

29. Taxable income = ($28,400 + $350 + $3940 − $4200 − $1916 − $2000 = $24,574) − (1 × $1000) = $23,574
Tax = $5329

31. Taxable income = ($18,000 + $22,000 − $3200 = $36,800) − (3 × $1000) = $33,800
Tax due = $7558; refund of $8540 − $7558 = $982

Review Exercises Chapter 17

1. Selling price = $468.50; tax = $28.11   **3.** Total paid = $127.20; price = $120.00
5. 4.25%   **7.** New rate = $130 per $1000, or an increase of $10 per $1000.
9. $6973   **11.** $6589

Exercises 18.1

1. ($0.46)($15,000 \div 100) = $69.00   **3.** ($0.26)($112,000 \div 100) = $291.20
5. ($0.33)($58,600 \div 100) = $193.38   **7.** (0.467)($38,400 \div 100) = $179.33
9. [(0.102)($28,000 \div 100)] × 60% = $17.14   **11.** (0.182)[($42,500 + $22,500) \div 100] = $118.30

13. Insurance required = $45,000 × 80% = $36,000. Insurance carried \div insurance required = $30,000 \div $36,000 = 83.33%. Insurance company will pay 83.33% × $15,000 loss = $12,500.

15. Since the face amount of the policy ($60,000) exceeds the coinsurance requirement ($70,000 × 80% = $56,000), the insurance company will pay all $40,000 of the loss.

17. Metropolis Co. share = ($80,000 \div $240,000) × $180,000 loss = $60,000
Northern Co. share = ($160,000 \div $240,000) × $180,000 loss = $120,000

19. Mutual of Teneha share = ($80,000 \div $200,000) × $80,000 = $32,000
Rock of Ages share = ($120,000 \div $200,000) × $80,000 = $48,000

Exercises 18.2

1. $60.26 + $64.05 = $124.31   **3.** $19.94 + $18.36 = $38.30   **5.** $58.50 + $69.12 = $127.62

7. $60.26 + $64.05 = $124.31 semiannually or $248.62 annually.

9. Territory 28 = $58.50 + $67.20 = $125.70 semiannually × 2 = $251.40
Territory 29 = $60.26 + $64.05 = $124.31 semiannually × 2 = $248.62
Change of $2.78, decrease.

11. Driver $8000 and $5000 aid by insurance. Additional $1000 property not covered. Passenger injury·= $10,000 maximum paid by insurance. Additional $3500 paid by Pettit. (*Note:* Order of payment to passenger or driver is irrelevant.)

13. Collision = $217.45   Comprehensive = $21.00   **15.** Collision = $160.14   Comprehensive = $13.00

17. $44.71 + $11.00 = $55.71   **19.** Premium = $46.71 + $17.00 = $63.71; $483.72 − $50 = $433.72

21. Liability = $19.94 + $19.74   = $ 39.68
Collision and comp. = $52.72 + $15.00 = $ 67.72
Total $107.40

23. Current year = [($58.50 + $67.20) + $106.76 + $12.00] × 2 = $488.92
Next year = [($58.50 + $67.20) + $101.27 + $11.00] × 2 = $475.94
The $12.98 change is due to the aging of car on coll. and comp.

Exercises 18.3

1. $15.55 × 5 = $77.75   **3.** $27.15 × 20 = $543.00   **5.** $18.04 × 50 = $902.00

7. $12.44 − $10.57 = $1.87   **9.** Term $4.84 × 50 = $242.00
$1.87 × 20 = $37.40 annual savings

11. ($11.56 × 20) × 30 years = $6936.00 paid in.   **13.** Paid in—[($14.62 per $1000 premium × 25) × 10 years] =
Cash value = $600.02 × 20 = $12,000.40. $3655. Term insurance coverage for 29 years and 92 days
(Fig. 18.7). Term coverage—$25,000 for the 29 years and 92
days.

15. a. [($9.59 × 25) × 45] − [$573.71 × 25] = −$3554   **b.** [($9.59 × 25) × 45] − [($573.71 × 25) + $2378] = −$5932

17. Per Fig. 18.9(a)—$500 per month for 114 months. Per Fig. 18.9(b)—($6.87 × 50) = $343.50 per month for 15 years.

19. Yes. Lifetime annuity is $3.60 × 30 = $108.00/month.

21. Guaranteed 15 years—($81.33 × 10 = $813.30) for 15 years = $12,199.50. Annuity for life—$5.15 × 10 = $51.50/month,
or $618.00/year. $618.00/year for 20 years = $12,360. Yes.

Review Exercises/Chapter 18

1. $28,125   **3.** $396.41; property damage = $5000 insurance; $3000 Douglas to driver/owner of the other car. Bodily
injury = $10,000 insurance; $2000 Douglas to driver of other car. Property damage = $1800 to Douglas
for his car.

5. a. $199,999.99   **b.** $347,826.08   **7.** $500.78   **9.** $450.80

Part Four

Cumulative Review Exercises

1. $323   **3.** 6800 units   **5.** Marked price $67.50; total $71.55   **7.** $39,500

9. $86,538 divided as follows: A—$34,615.20; B—$30,288.30; C—$21,634.50.   **11.** $291.29; decrease $214.83

13. $346.44   **15.** Purchase price = $172.83; total = $180.61

17. $81,486   **19.** $1526.31   **21.** $755.53

23. $2140.32   **25.** Taxable refund of $136

27. Company A—$66,500
Company B—$47,500
Company C—$76,000

Exercises 19.1

1.

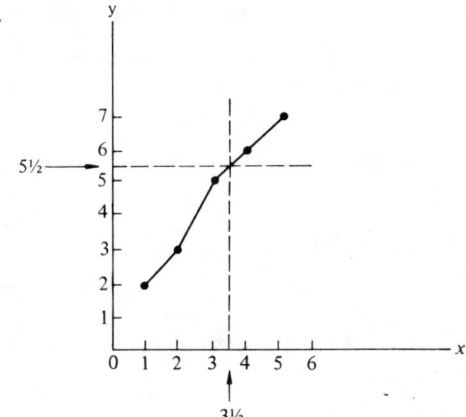

At $x = 3\frac{1}{2}$, $y = 5\frac{1}{2}$.

7.

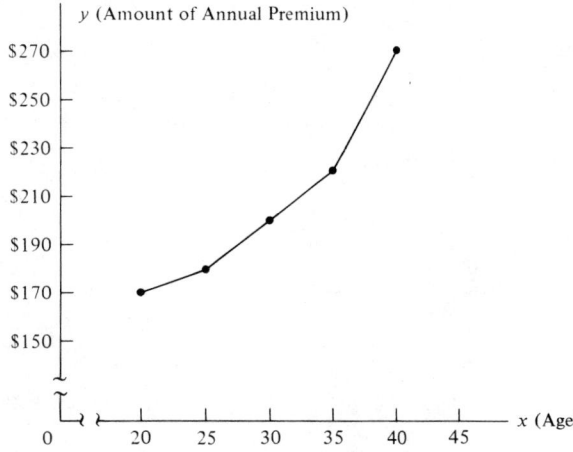

3.

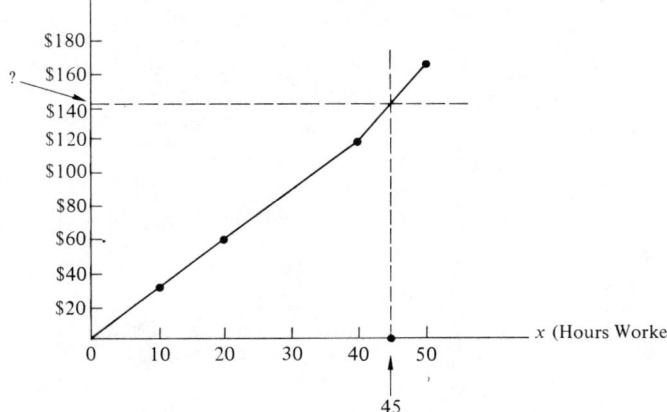

The amount is $142.50.

5.

y (Production Cost)

$3500
$3000
$2500
$2000
$1500
$1000
$500

0   1000   2000   3000   4000   5000   x (Units Produced)

2500

The estimated cost of 2500 units is $1500.

9. a.   *y* (Items Remaining)   **b.** 265

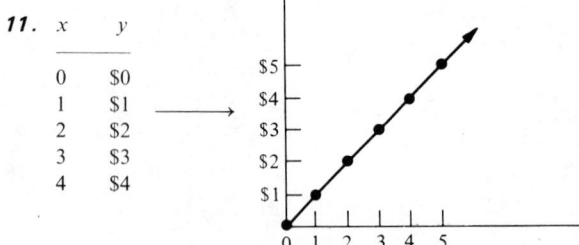

Note: The initial value of 300 units corresponds to day zero.

11.

x	*y*
0	$0
1	$1
2	$2
3	$3
4	$4

$\longrightarrow$

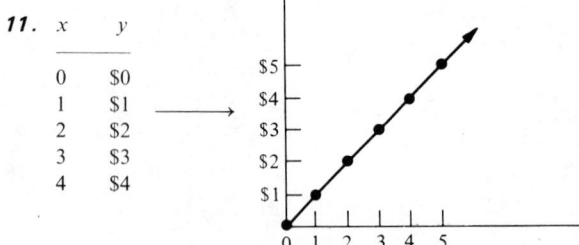

13.

x	*y*
0	$0
1	$1
2	$2
3	$3
4	$4

$\longrightarrow$

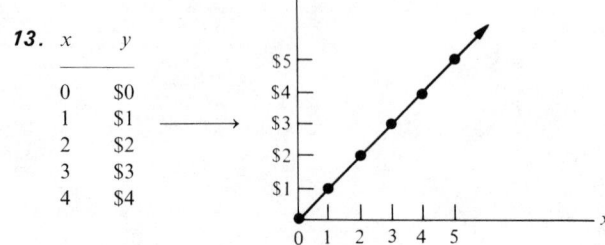

15.

x	*y*
0	1
1	3
2	5
3	7
4	9

$\longrightarrow$

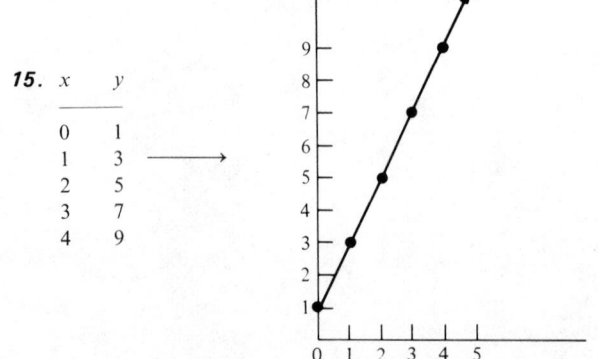

17.

x	y
0	$0
1	$5
2	$10
3	$15
4	$20
5	$25

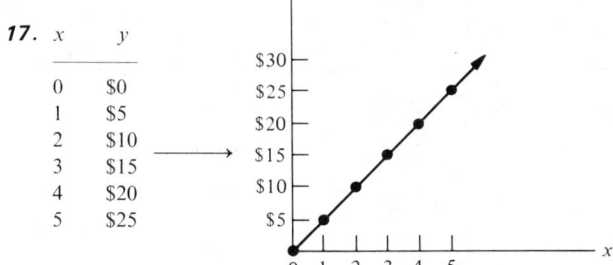

Exercises 19.2

1. a.

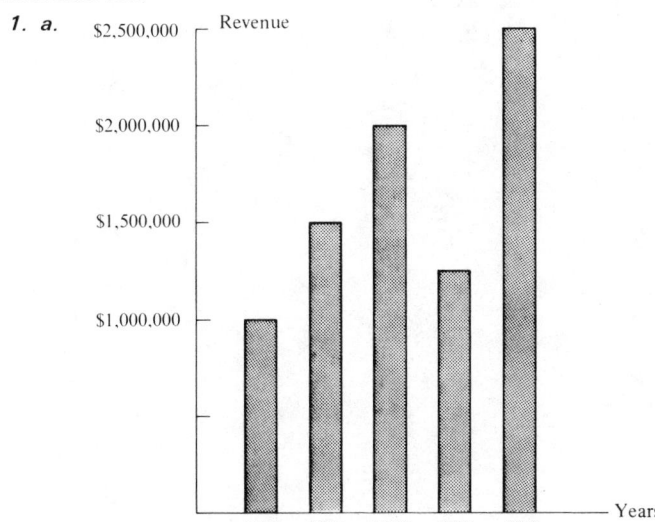

b.

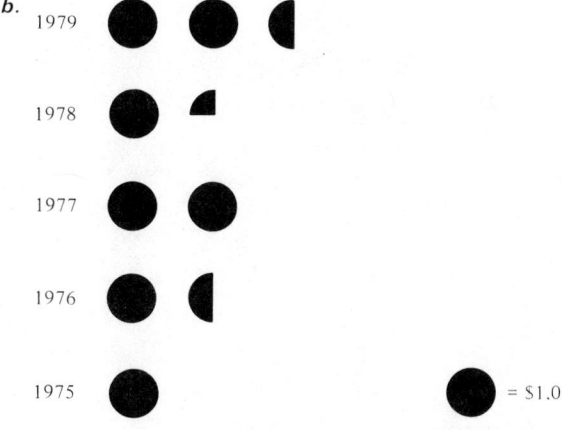

3. a.   Employee

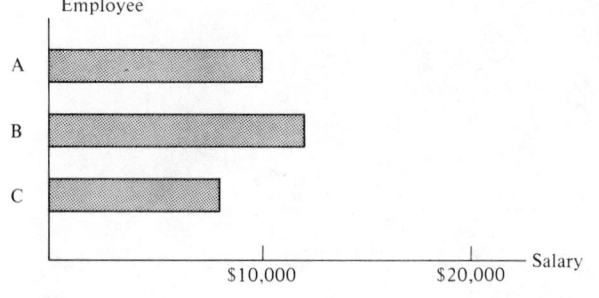

b. Employee

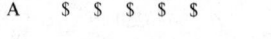

A $ $ $ $ $

B $ $ $ $ $ $ $ = $2000

C $ $ $ $

5. a.   Weekly Sales

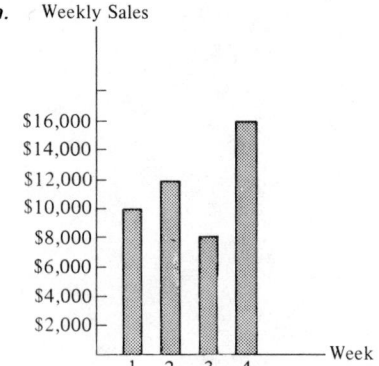

b.   Week

▲ = $4000

Exercises 19.3

1. Labor $3.6 \times 40 = 144°$
Material $3.6 \times 20 = 72°$
Taxes $3.6 \times 10 = 36°$
Other $3.6 \times 30 = 108°$

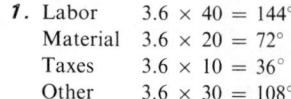

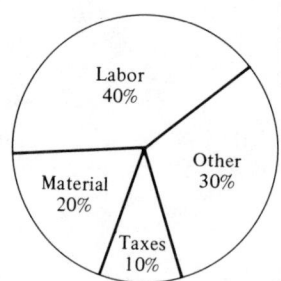

3. Sleeping $144°$
Eating $36°$
Class $72°$
Studying $36°$
Free time $72°$

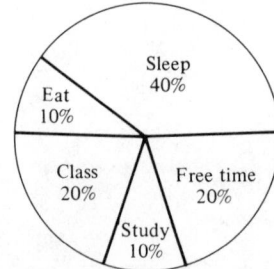

5. TVs $\qquad \dfrac{300}{1000} = 30\%$ or $108°$

Refrigerators $\qquad \dfrac{250}{1000} = 25\%$ or $90°$

Ranges $\qquad \dfrac{100}{1000} = 10\%$ or $36°$

Vacuum cleaners $\qquad \dfrac{200}{1000} = 20\%$ or $72°$

Others $\qquad \dfrac{150}{1000} = 15\%$ or $54°$

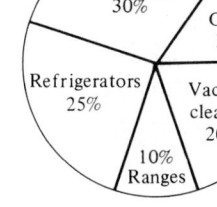

Review Exercises/Chapter 19

1.

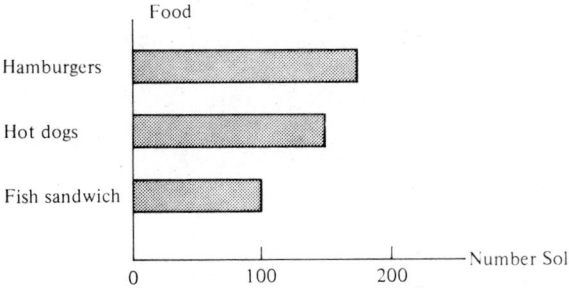

3.

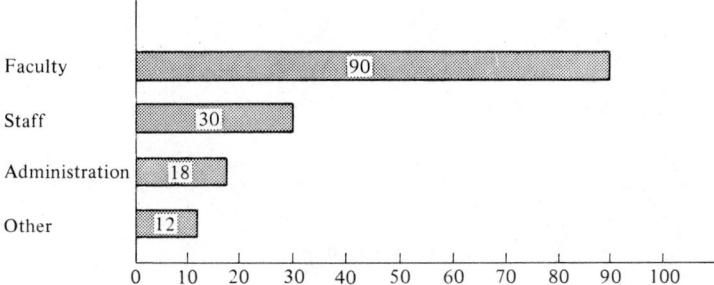

Exercises 20.1

1. Data Array—Domestic Tractor

0	1	2	2	3	4	5
0	1	2	3	3	4	6
0	2	2	3	3	5	6
1	2	2	3	4	5	7

3. Grouped Frequency Distribution

Group	Frequency
Low (0–2)	13
Average (3–5)	12
High (6–more)	3
	Total = 28

5. **a.** Numerical or quantitative
  b. Nominal or categorical or qualitative

9. No, not mutually exclusive. 3 is passing and failing.

11. Low—12; average—6; excessive—2

7. **Scores on 5-Point Quiz**

Score	Frequency
0	4
1	3
2	5
3	5
4	4
5	4
	Total = 25

Exercises 20.2

1. Mean $= \dfrac{1 + 2 + 4 + 6 + 7}{5} = 4$

3. Mean $= \dfrac{1(0) + 2(1) + 3(3) + 2(4) + 2(5) + 1(6) + 3(2)}{14} = \dfrac{41}{14} = 2.93$

5. Mean $= \dfrac{20(\$3) + 8(\$4) + 12(\$6)}{40} = \$4.10$

7. Mean $= \dfrac{93 + 16 + 94 + 89 + 100}{5} = \dfrac{392}{5} = 78.4$; no.

9. Mean $= \dfrac{0.25 + 0.30 + 0.15 + 0 + 0.40}{5} = \dfrac{1.10}{5} = \$0.22$

11. Mean $= \dfrac{100(0.80) + 200(0.70) + 300(0.85)}{600} = \dfrac{475}{600} = \$0.79$

13. No; the data are not quantitative.

Exercises 20.3

1. Middle number (median) is 11.

3. Since there is an even number of values, the median is $\dfrac{3 + 9}{2} = 6$.

5. In order: 1, 3, 7, 9, 15; median $= 7$.

7. In order: 2, 10, 15, 23; median $= \dfrac{10 + 15}{2} = 12.5$.

9. In order: 76, 82, 85, 90, 100; median $= 85$; mean $= 86.6$

11. In order: 0.32, 0.39, 0.50, 0.64; median $= \dfrac{0.39 + 0.50}{2} = \$0.445$; mean $= \$0.4625$.

13. The median rating is "better."

15. Median $= 3$, mean $= 3.75$ days.

Exercises 20.4

1. Mode is 1; it occurs most often.

5. Multimodal 1, 2.

3. No mode; each value occurs equally often.

7. Mode $= 78$, median $= 78$, mean $= 80.4$.

9.

	Frequency
1	4
2	3
3	4
4	2
5	2

The modes are 1 and 3 (multimodal).

11. Mode $= \$14,000$; median $= \$14,000$; mean $= \dfrac{\$81,500}{6} = \$13,583.33$.

13. No, there is no "middle" appliance; nominal data cannot be ordered.

15. Mode $= 0$ days.

Exercises 20.5

1. $S = \sqrt{26/5} = 2.8.$ $R = 6$
3. $S = \sqrt{26/5} = 2.8,$ $R = 6$
5. $S = \sqrt{424/5} = 9.21,$ $R = 26$
7. all equal 60
9. 16%
11. $2/5 = 40\%$
13. Doubles

Review Exercises / Chapter 20

1. a. 74   **b.** 79   **c.** 98, 92, 86, 67, 49   **d.**   **e.** 19 passed   **3.** $2.48

Grade	f
A	6
B	6
C	3
D	4
F	6

g. 18.44   **h.** 64%
i. 96% **j.** 14   **k.** 11
l. Not symmetric

Exercises 21.1

1. $2.5 \text{ m} \times 100 = 250 \text{ cm}$ **3.** $1532 \text{ m} \times \dfrac{1}{1000} = 1.532 \text{ km}$ **5.** $280 \text{ cm} \times \dfrac{1}{100} = 2.8 \text{ m}$

7. $10 \text{ in} \times 25.4 = 254 \text{ mm}$ **9.** $6 \text{ ft} \times 0.3048 = 1.8288 \text{ m}$ **11.** $20 \text{ mi} \times 1.60934 = 32.1868 \text{ km}$
13. $5 \text{ m} \times 3.28084 = 16.4042 \text{ ft}$ **15.** $80 \text{ km} \times 0.621371 = 49.70968 \text{ mi}$ **17.** $14 \text{ mi} \times 1.60934 = 22.5 \text{ km}$ (rounded)
19. $6.5 \text{ ft} \times 0.3048 = 1.9812 \text{ m}.$ $1.9812 \text{ m} \times 100 = 198.12 \text{ cm}$

Exercises 21.2

1. $2.8 \text{ kg} \times 1000 = 2800 \text{ g}$ **3.** $1250 \text{ g} \times \dfrac{1}{1000} = 1.25 \text{ kg}$ **5.** $20 \text{ g} \times 0.035274 = 0.70548 \text{ oz}$

7. $50 \text{ kg} \times 2.20462 = 110.231 \text{ lb}$ **9.** $16 \text{ oz} \times 28.3495 = 453.592 \text{ g}$ **11.** $7.75 \text{ lb} \times 0.453592 = 3.52 \text{ kg}$ (rounded)
13. $1 \text{ lb} = 0.453592 \text{ kg};$ $0.453592 \text{ kg} \times 1000 = 453.592 \text{ g}$ **15.** $1.5 \text{ gr} \times 0.0648 = 0.0972 \text{ g};$ $0.0972 \text{ g} \times 1000 = 97.2 \text{ mg}$

Exercises 21.3

1. $3 \text{ l} \times 1000 = 3000 \text{ ml}$ **3.** $835 \text{ ml} \times \dfrac{1}{1000} = 0.835 \text{ l}$ **5.** $5 \text{ qt} \times 0.946353 = 4.73 \text{ l}$ (rounded)

7. $1 \text{ l} \times 1.05669 = 1.05669 \text{ qt};$ $1.05669 \text{ qt} \times 4 = 4.22676 \text{ pt}$ **9.** $\frac{1}{2} \text{ pt} = 0.25 \text{ qt};$ $0.25 \text{ qt} \times 0.946353 = 0.237 \text{ l}$ (rounded)
11. $12 \text{ oz} \div 32 = 0.375 \text{ qt};$ $0.375 \text{ qt} \times 0.946353 = 0.3548823;$ $0.3548823 \text{ l} \times 1000 = 354.8823 \text{ ml}.$ Such cans are usually labeled 355 ml.
13. 237 ml (see problem 9)   **15.** $C = \dfrac{5(72) - 160}{9} = 22.2°$ **17.** $F = \dfrac{9(100) + 160}{5} = 212°$

Review Exercises / Chapter 21

1. 101.6 cm   **3.** 304.8 m   **5.** 2.27 kg   **7.** 1.05669 qt   **9.** $-40°$

Part Five

Cumulative Review Exercises

5. Mean = 14.667, median = 14.5, no mode.   **7.** 64-oz bottle by 7 cents.   **9.** No; 295.4 lb.
11. Mean = 1.088, median = 1.005, mode = 0.99   **13.** 6213.71 miles
15. 11.9°C

Index

Accelerated Cost Recovery System (ACRS), 173, 174, 194
Account number, bank, 45
Accounts payable, 208
Accounts receivable, 208, 227
  average age of, 228
  factoring, 271
Accounts receivable turnover, 228
Accrued interest, 351
Acid test ratio, 227
ACRS (see Accelerated Cost Recovery System)
Addition
  of decimals, 29
  of fractions, 11, 13
  of mixed numbers, 22
Additional first-year depreciation, 195
Add-on interest, 317–318
Adjusted gross income, 407
Aliquot parts, 79
Amortization,
  of debt, 308
  premium, of a bond, 350
Amortization schedule, 324
Analysis
  horizontal, 207, 211
  techniques of financial (see Ratios)
  vertical, 207, 208
Annual percentage rate, 280, 302, 313
Annuities
  amortization of, 320
  effective rate of, 313–314
  formulas for, 309, 318, 321
  from life insurance, 437–438
  ordinary, 320
  present value, 335
  regular payment for, 320
  sinking funds, 330
Arithmetic (see specific topics, e.g., Addition)
Arithmetic mean, 484
Array, 480
Assessed value (property), 402
Assets
  current, 208
  definition of, 208
  life of, 174
  noncurrent, 208
  quick (liquid), 227
Automatic deposits, 50
Automatic drafts (withdrawals), 50
Automobile insurance (see Motor vehicle insurance)

Average, mean as arithmetic, 484
  (see also Median; Mode)
Average age of accounts receivable, 228
Average amount invested, in a bond, 350
Average annual return, of a bond, 349
Average inventory cost, 146
Axes, 454

Balance, checking account, 46, 50–51
Balance forward, 46
Balance sheet, 207
Bank discount, 267–268
Bank draft, 49
Bank number, 45
Bank statement, 48–49
  reconciliation of, 50–51
Bar graph, 464
Base
  for depreciation, 174
  for percent, 82
Base 10 system, 28
Beneficiary, 417
Bodily injury liability insurance, 424–425
Bond
  adjusted selling price of, 351
  and average amount invested, 350
  average annual return of, 349
  corporate, 342
  coupon rate, 343
  definition of, 342
  discount accumulation of, 350
  discounting of, 347
  interest on, 343
  municipal, 342–343
  premium amortization of, 350
  premium for, 348
  price of, 349
  yield-current, 346
  yield-to maturity, 349
Bonus plan, of compensation, 383
Book value, 174
Brokers, stock, 359
Business insurance (see specific type)
Business ratios 222–230 (see also Ratios)

Calculator, 2, 331
Cancellation, of insurance policies, 419
Carrying charge, 316

Cash discounts, 117
Cash value, of life insurance, 434
Catalog (list) price, 108, 112
Celsius temperature scale, 511
Central tendency, measure of, 484–494
Chain of discounts, 114
Check, 45
Checking account, 44–47
Check register, 46
Class, of grouped data, 481
Coinsurance, 420
Collateral, 249
Collision insurance, 423, 425
Commission
    definition of, 385
    graduated, 386
    stock brokerage, 360
    straight, 386
Common fractions (see Fractions)
Common stock, 357
Company (corporate) financing, 342
Comparative balance sheet, 211
Comparative income statement, 218
Compensation (see Salary; Wages)
Compounding period, 287
Compound interest, 285
    continuously, 293
    daily, 292
    effective rate of, 302
    future value at, 289
    periodic, 287
    present value at, 297
Comprehensive insurance, 423, 425
Computation, 1
Consumer, 107, 125
Conversion period, 287
Convertible stock, 357
Coordinate system, 454
Corporation, 233, 237
    financing for, 342
Cost, 125
    of goods sold, 144, 152
    markup based on, 130–131
    recovery, 173
    recovery table, 196, 199
    single equivalent rate, 114
Coupon rate, of bonds, 343
Creative financing, 327
Cross products, 9
Current assets, 208
Current liabilities, 208
Current ratio, 226

Daily interest, 292
Data
    array of, 480
    categorical, 483
    grouping of, 481
    numerical, 482
    qualitative, 483

quantitative, 482
raw, 480
Data set, 480
Debt
    financing of (see Bond)
    ratio of, to equity, 230
Debt ratio, 229
Decimals
    addition of, 28
    conversion of, to percent, 75
    definition of, 27
    division of, 35
    multiplication of, 33
    place value of, 28
    repeating, 36
    rounding of, 39
    subtraction of, 30
Declining-balance method, of depreciation, 190
Deductible, in auto insurance, 425
Deductions, from income, 407
Deductions, from pay
    social security, 388
    voluntary, 391
    withholding tax, 390
Denomination, of bonds, 343
Denominator
    of a fraction, 4
    least common, 14
Depletion, 182
Deposit, 44
Deposit slip, 45
Depreciation
    accelerated, 185
    accumulated, 174
    additional first-year, 195
    base, 174
    declining-balance method of, 190
    definition of, 173
    other terms for, 173, 178, 182
    partial-year, 178, 182, 187, 192, 195
    rate of, 176
    schedule of, 176–177
    straight-line method of, 175
    sum-of-the-years-digits method of, 185
    units-of-production method of, 181
Depreciation base, 174
Difference, 30
Digits, 28
Discount accumulation, 350
Discounts
    bank, 267
    bond, 347
    cash, 117
    chain of, 114
    markdown as, 138, 158
    on notes, 273
    series of, 114
    single equivalent rate of, 114

trade, 112
Distribution of profits, 233–236, 357
Dividend
  cumulative, from stock, 357
  in division, 35
  from insurance, 433, 435
Division
  as a check, 37
  of decimals, 35
  of equations, 92
  of fractions, 19
  by zero, 18
Divisor, 35
Double time, 378
Down payment, 326
Driver classification, 423, 424
Due date
  for cash discounts, 117
  for notes, 262

Earning performance, 222–226
Earnings
  of business operations, 356
  distribution of, 233–236, 357
  individual (*see* Salary; Wages)
  per share of stock, 226, 358
Effective rate
  of continuous compounding, 304
  of discount, 278, 280
  of installments, 313, 314
  of interest, 278
  of periodic compounding, 302
End-of-month sales terms, 120
Endowment life insurance, 429
Equations
  conditional, 89
  definition of, 89
  literal, 93
  operations on, 92
  solving, 90, 91
  with word problems, 95–98
Equity, owners', 206, 208, 356
Equity financing (*see* Financing)
Equity ratio, 229
Equivalent fractions, 6
Exact-day calendar, 119, 260
Exact interest, 250
Exact time period, 250
Exemptions, 407
Expenses, 125, 166, 206
Extended fire insurance coverage,
  417
Extended price, 108
Extended term life insurance,
  435

Face amount, of insurance, 417
Face value
  of bonds, 343
  of notes, 248
Factor, 34

Factoring, of accounts receivable,
  271
Fahrenheit temperature scale, 511
Fair Labor Standards Act, 380
Fair market value, of property, 402
Federal Income tax, 406–411
  withholding, 390
Federal Insurance Contributions Act,
  388
Federal Reserve System, 44
F.I.C.A., 388
Finance charge (*see* Interest)
Financial condition, corporate, 222,
  226–230
Financial statements
  analysis techniques for (*see* Ratios)
  balance sheet, 207–212
  income statement, 216–219
Financing
  debt, 342 (*see also* Bond)
  equity, 342
Fire insurance
  and coinsurance, 420
  compensation for loss through, 420
  with extended coverage, 417
  with multiple coverage, 421
  premiums for, 417
  short-rate cancellation of, 419
First-in-first-out method, of inventory
  valuation, 147
Fractions
  addition of, 11
  conversion of, to decimals, 38
  conversion of, to percents, 76
  definition of, 3
  division of, 19
  equivalent, 6, 9
  improper, 5, 22
  least common denominator of, 14
  in mixed numbers, 22
  multiplication of, 17
  proper, 5
  reduced, 7
  subtraction of, 12
  terms of, 5
Freight, 118
Frequency distribution, 481
Future value
  at compound interest, 289
  at simple interest, 254

Gain on stock, 360
Graduated commission, 386
Gram, 506
Graphs
  bar, 464
  circle, 472
  distortion of, 459,469
  line, 454
  pictogram as, 469
Gross income, 406

Gross pay, 373, 374, 377, 385
Gross profit, 126, 216
Gross profit method of inventory
    estimation, 152
Grouped data, 481

Half year convention (ACRS), 195
Higher terms, 6
Horizontal analysis, 207, 211
Hourly wage, 377

Improper fraction, 5
Incentive plans, 383
Income
    adjusted gross, 407
    gross, 406
    taxable, 407
Income statements
    multiple-step, 216–217
    single-step, 216–217
Income tax (see Tax)
Installment costs, 309
Installment loans, 308–341
Installment plans, 308
    effective rate of, 313, 314
Insurance
    annuities from, 437–438
    beneficiary of, 417
    cash value of, 434
    co-, 420
    collision, 423, 425
    comprehensive, 423, 425
    definition of, 416
    dividends from, 433, 435
    with double indemnity, 433
    endowment, 429
    with extended coverage, 417
    extended term, 435
    face amount of, 417
    fire, 417–421
    level payment rates of, 432
    liability, 423, 424
    life, 428–442
    limited payment, 429
    limited payment rates of, 432
    mortality table for, 428, 431
    motor vehicle, 423–426
    with multiple coverage, 421
    net cost of, 435
    nonforfeiture options with, 433–
      435
    ordinary life, 429
    paid up, 435
    participating, 433
    policy for, 416
    premium for, 417
    property, 417, 423
    settlement options with, 437–438
    short-rate cancellation of, 419
    term, 429
    unemployment, 392

    universal, 429
    waiver of premium in, 433
Insured, 416
Insurer, 416
Interest
    accrued, on bonds, 351
    add-on, 318
    bond, coupon rate and, 343
    compound, 285
    compounded continuously, 293
    compounded daily, 292
    effective rate of, 302
    nominal rate of, 278, 302
    ordinary, 250
    simple, 249
    six-percent, sixty-day method of,
      251
    stated rate of, 278
Interest-bearing note, 255
Interpolation, 456
Inventory
    average cost of, 146
    definition of, 143
    first-in-first-out method of valuing,
      147
    gross profit method of estimating,
      152
    last-in-first-out method of valuing,
      148
    periodic, 144
    perpetual, 143
    retail method of estimating, 154
    specific identification method of
      valuing, 145
    turnover ratio of, 160, 227
    valuation of, 144, 145
Invoice, 108

Last-in-first-out method, of inventory
    valuation, 148
Least common denominator, 14
Level method, of apportioning in-
    terest, 310
Liabilities, 206, 208
    current, 208
    noncurrent, 208
Life, of an asset, 174
Life class (ACRS), 195
Life insurance
    annuity from, 437–438
    beneficiary of, 417
    cash value of, 434
    Commissioners' 1958 Standard
      Ordinary Mortality Table for,
      428, 431
    dividends from, 433, 435
    with double indemnity, 433
    endowment, 429
    extended term, 435
    level premium, 429
    limited payment, 429

and mutual companies, 433
net cost of, 435
nonforfeiture options with, 433–435
nonparticipating, 433
ordinary, 429
paid-up, 435
participating, 433
premiums for, 417
proceeds from, 437
purpose of, 428
settlement options with, 437–438
term, 429
and waiver of premium, 433
whole, 429
Limited payment life insurance, 429
Line graph, 454
List price, 108
Liter, 509
Literal number, 3, 89
Loan date, 249
Loss, 361, 206, 216
Lowest terms, 7

Markdown, 138, 158
Markup, 126, 158
allowing for spoilage, 134
change of base for, 133
cost-based, 130–131
definition of, 126
rate of, 127
selling-price-based, 131–132
Mass, metric measures of, 506
Maturity date
of bonds, 343
of loans, 249
Maturity value, 289 (see also Future value)
Mean, 484
Median, 488
Meter, 502
Metric system, 501
measures of length in, 502
measures of temperature in, 511
measures of volume in, 509
measures of weight in, 506
Mills, 402
Minimum wage, 380, 382
Minuend, 30
Mixed number, 22
Mode, 491
Mortality table, 428, 431
Mortgage, 326
Motor vehicle insurance
and bodily injury liability, 424
collision, 423, 425
comprehensive, 423, 425
deductible with, 425
driver classification for, 423–424
liability, 423, 424
Multiple coverage, 421

Multiplication
of decimals, 33
of fractions, 17
Multiplicative inverse, 18
Mutual insurance companies, 433
Mutually exclusive classes, 482

Negotiable Order of Withdrawals (NOW), 60–62
Net cost (see also Net price)
of insurance, 435
Net income, 216
Net pay, 373, 388
Net price, 113
Net profit, 216
Nominal interest rate, 278
Nonforfeiture options, 433–435
Normal distribution, 496
Notes, 248
discounted, 273
interest-bearing, 255
non-interest-bearing, 268
promissory, 248
as quick assets, 227
secured, 249
short-term, 249
unsecured, 248
Numerator, 4

Open to buy, 163
Operating expenses, 125, 166 (see also Overhead)
Operating ratio, 225
Operations, arithmetic (see specific operation, e.g., Addition)
Order of operations, 22
Ordinary annuity, 320
Ordinary dating method, 119, 250
Ordinary interest, 250
Ordinary life insurance, 429
Origin, on graph, 454
Outstanding checks, 50
Over the counter (stock market), 359
Overhead, 125, 166
allocation of, 166
Overtime, 378
Owners' equity, 206, 208, 356

Paid-up insurance, 435
Partnerships, 233–234
Par value, 356
Pay (see Salary; Wages)
Pay period, 374
Percent, 72
conversion of, to decimal, 76
conversion of, to fraction, 72
decimals changed to, 75
decrease, 85
definition of, 72
equation containing, 82
equivalent forms of, 79

fractions changed to, 76
increase, 85
word problems with, 81
Percentage, 82
Pictogram, 469
Piece rate, 382
Place value, 28
Planning purchases, 162
Plotting points, 455
Policy, insurance, 416
Preferred stock, 357
Premium
  amortization of, 350
  bond, 348
  insurance, 417
Present value
  at compound interest, 297
  at simple interest, 254
Price
  extended, 108
  list, 108
  net, 113
  selling, 126, 130–132
  total, 108
  unit, 108
Price-earnings ratio, 226
Prime number, 8
Principal
  bond, 343
  invested (borrowed), 249
Problem solving, word, 95
Proceeds
  of a discounted note, 367
  of life insurance, 437
Product, in multiplication, 16
Profits, 125, 206, 216
  distribution of corporate, 357
  distribution of partnership's, 233–236
Promissory note, 248
Proper fraction, 5
Property
  personal, 402
  real, 402, 199
  tax, 402
Property damage, liability insurance for, 423–424
Property tax, 402–404
Proprietorship, 233

Quick ratio, 227
Quotient, 35

Rate
  annual percentage, 278
  bank discount, 278
  compound interest, 302
  effective bank discount, 278, 280
  effective continuous compounding, 304
  effective installment, 313, 314

effective periodic compounding, 302
  nominal, 278
  as percent saved, 81
  property tax, 402
  of return (stock), 362
  short, for cancellation, 419
  simple interest, 249
Ratios
  accounts receivable turnover, 228
  acid test (quick), 227
  average age of accounts receivable, 228
  current (working capital), 226
  debt, 229
  debt to equity, 230
  equity, 229
  inventory turnover, 160, 227
  operating, 225
  quick, 227
  return on average total assets, 222
  times interest earned, 225
Receipt of goods sales terms, 120
Reciprocal, 18
Reconciliation, of bank statement, 50–51
Reduced price, 138, 158
Remainder, 36
Repeating decimals, 36
Retailer, 107–108
Retail method, 154
Retail sales, 107, 125
Retained (reinvested) earnings, 342, 357
Returned check, for insufficient funds, 52
Return
  (on) average total assets, 222
  (on) stock, 362
Returns and allowances, 118
Revenue, 206
Rounding off, 39
Rule of 72, 295
Rule of 78's, 311

Salary, 373
Sales
  retail, 107, 125
  tax on, 398
  terms used in, 109
  trade, 107
Salvage (scrap) value, 174
Sector, 473
Selling price
  allowing for spoilage, 134
  of bonds, 351–352
  and formula for markup, 126, 130–132
  reductions in, 138
Series discount, 114
Share (see Stock)

Short-term insurance rate, 419
Signature card, 45
Simple interest, 249
   present value at, 256
   six-percent, sixty-day method of, 251
Single equivalent cost rate, 114
Single equivalent discount rate, 114
Sinking fund, 330
Six-percent, sixty-day method, 251
Slide, 55
Social security, 388
Sole proprietorship, 233
Stated interest rate, 278
Statement
   bank, 48–49
   financial (*see* Financial statements)
Statistics, 479
Stock
   brokers, 359
   common, 357
   convertible, 357
   cumulative preferred, 357
   dividends from, 356
   exchange, 359
   gain on, 360
   loss on, 361
   par value of, 356
   preferred, 357
   share of, 356
   yield on, 359
Stock market, 359
Straight-line method, of depreciation, 175
Subtraction
   of decimals, 30
   of fractions, 11
Subtrahend, 30
Sum, in addition, 11
Sum-of-the-years-digits method, of depreciation, 185

Tables
   amount of an annuity of 1, 556
   Board of Governor's APR, 562
   exact day, 573
   federal income tax, 583
   federal income tax withholding, 574
   payment to amortize a debt of 1, 538
   payment to a sinking fund of 1, 544
   present value of an annuity, 550
   single equivalent discount rates, 589
   values of $(1 + i)^n$, 528
   values of $(1 + i)^n$ for 5¼% compounded daily, 535
   values of e^{st}, 537

Tax
   income, 406–411
   property, 402
   rate of, (property), 402
   refund, 410
   sales, 398–400
   social security, 388
   unemployement, 392
   withholding, 390
Taxable income, 407
Term life insurance, 429
Terms
   of a fraction, 5
   of a cash discount, 117, 119
   of a loan, 249
Time and a half, 378
Times interest earned, 225
Trade discounts, 112
Trade sales, 107, 112
Transposition, 55
Turnover
   accounts receivable, 228
   inventory, 160, 227

Underwriter, 416
Unemployment insurance, 392
Unknown, in equation 89
Useful life, 174

Valuation of inventory, 144
Value, assessed, 402
Variable, 89
   nominal, 483
   numerical, 482
Vertical analysis, 207, 208

Wages
   commission as, 385
   gross, 373, 374, 377
   hourly, 377
   net, 373
   overtime, 378
   piece-rate, 382
Weight, metric measures of, 506
Whole life insurance, 429
Whole number, 3
Wholesaler, 107–108
Withholding tax, 390
Word problems, 95
Working capital ratio, 226

Year
   exact, 250
   ordinary interest, 250
Yield
   average annual, to maturity, of bonds, 349
   current, of bonds, 346
   on stocks, 362

To the
Student

To Assist You

Solutions: The *solutions* (not just the answers) to all odd-numbered problems are presented in the answer section.

Workbook: The accompanying workbook, *A Study Guide for Operational Mathematics for Business* by Bruce Judkins, provides additional exercises and practical applications of text material.

To Assist Us

Your Comments: We have attempted to provide material that will teach you now and serve as a valuable reference for years to come. We would like your comments on our success. What items were not clearly presented? What additional material would be beneficial? Most especially, what errors did you find in the text? Please let us have your comments and criticisms in care of:

Wadsworth Publishing Company
10 Davis Drive
Belmont, California 96002

Thank You,

R. C. Pierce, Jr.
W. J. Tebeaux